A History of the Canadian Army Veterinary Corps in the Great World War 1914 - 1919

A History of the Canadian Army Veterinary Corps in the Great World War 1914-1919

Cecil French

Edited by
C.A.V. Barker
and
Ian K. Barker

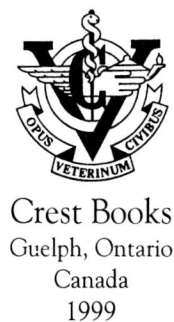

Crest Books
Guelph, Ontario
Canada
1999

Crest Books
Published by
C.A.V. Barker Museum
of
Canadian Veterinary History
Ontario Veterinary College
University of Guelph
Guelph, Ontario
Canada N1G 2W1

ISBN 0-88955-472-2

Canadian Cataloguing in Publication Data

French, Cecil, b. 1871-1951
A history of the Canadian Army Veterinary Corps in the Great World War, 1914-1919

Includes bibliographical references and index.
ISBN 0-88955-472-2

1. Canada. Canadian Army Veterinary Corps – History – World War, 1914-1918. 2. World War, 1914-1918 – Veterinary service – Canada. 3. Veterinary service, Military – Canada – History. I. Barker, C. A. V. (Clifford Albert Victor), 1919- . II. Barker, Ian K., 1945- . III. Title.

D629.C2F73 1999 940.4'75 C99-931894-2

Printed by
Greenmor Printing
Guelph, Ontario, Canada

Canadian Army Veterinary Corps cap badge, c.1912[1]
worn by Permanent Active Militia 1912-1922
Non-Permanent Active Militia 1912-1936
(*from NAC PA 5830*)

Catalogue of an exhibition in which 'A Mobile Veterinary Unit in France' was displayed

Front Cover

'A Mobile Veterinary Unit in France'
Oil on canvas, painted in 1919 by Algernon M. Talmage.[2]
It illustrates the evacuation to the rear of wounded and sick horses by men of a Mobile Veterinary Section of the Canadian Army Veterinary Corps, probably on the road to Hénin-Beaumont, near Cambrai, France, September/October, 1918.
German shells are bursting on the horizon in the right background.
The painting is displayed in the Red Chamber (Senate) on Parliament Hill, Ottawa.
© Canadian War Museum - *CN 8735*

Back Cover

'The Canadian Mounted Veterinary Corps at Work with the Field Artillery, 1916'
R. Caton Woodville[3]
It depicts men of a Mobile Veterinary Section, C.A.V.C., loading a wounded horse into an ambulance, with incoming artillery fire in the vicinity. The horse is supported by a sling between pairs of men on either side, and the left forelimb also is in a sling.
© Canadian War Museum - *CN 75100*

'Dumb Heroes'
Published in 'The Salient and other Poems', by Captain T.A. Girling,[4] C.A.V.C.
1918.

TABLE OF CONTENTS

List of Figures

Sources of illustrations are attributed in the caption. In the main these are the Photographic Holdings of The National Archives of Canada (*NAC*); the French Papers in the National Archives of Canada (*French Papers, NAC*); and The C.A.V. Barker Museum of Canadian Veterinary History, Ontario Veterinary College, University of Guelph (*C.A.V. Barker Museum*); with contributions from the Manitoba Provincial Archives, The Royal Canadian Artillery Museum, The Royal Canadian Dragoons Archives, Lord Strathcona's Horse (Royal Canadians) Museum and Archives, and the Stubbs Collection. Donors of material in the C.A.V. Barker Museum are indicated in the notes to the List of Figures. Several illustrations, taken from publications, we were unable to attribute to a source. In these cases, the original publication is cited; the full bibliographic reference is found in the Sources.

Canadian Army Veterinary Corps cap badge c.1916-1917
Canadian Expeditionary Force[16]
(*from NAC PA 5830*)

ARMY VETERINARY SERVICE[17]

Circular Letter to Officers, Warrant Officers, Non-Commissioned Officers and Men of the Canadian Army Veterinary Corps, serving with the British Expeditionary Force, France.

On Demobilization of the Expeditionary Force in France, I desire to express my appreciation of the good Services which have been rendered by the Officers, Warrant officers, Non-Commissioned Officers and Men of the Canadian Army Veterinary Corps, and to tender to one and all my grateful and sincerest thanks for all that has been achieved by them during the past four and a half years.

Side by side with the Royal Army Veterinary Corps, Canadian Veterinary Service under a good organization and tempered by experience has grown in power and efficiency to a degree that at the end left very little to be desired. Circumstances have been difficult and trying but it has consistently proved its mettle. Contagious animal disease, our bugbear of war, has on the whole been satisfactorily kept in subjection, and the care and treatment of animals well carried out. I should like all ranks to feel that such efficiency is not due to any one individual, but is the result of the combined efforts of all. I am glad that Canadian Veterinary Organization in France included a Veterinary Hospital on Lines of Communication, and my appreciation of the valuable Services rendered by the C.A.V.C. as a whole is not complete without a large amount of praise to the well-ordered Veterinary Hospital at HAVRE, the up-to-date treatment which has been carried out there, and the labour of love on the part of the personnel to make their Hospital a Show Place as well as a successful institution for the care and treatment of sick animals.

J. MOORE
Major-General,
DIRECTOR OF VETERINARY SERVICES

Headquarters D.V.S.
25th February, 1919.

Headquarters, Overseas Military Forces of Canada,
Argyll House, 246, Regent Street, W.1.
10th February, 1919.

To: The Officers of the Canadian Army Veterinary Corps.[18]

Now that our enemies have seen fit to sign an Armistice, bringing to a close over four years of the most terrible war the world has ever experienced, let me convey to you my wholehearted appreciation of your splendid efforts.

You unselfishly sacrificed your civilian practices, abandoned your ambitious plans with their possibilities for the future - gave up home and loved ones and all that man holds dear, to serve your King and Country. This initial step meant much to you, as it did to every virile man.

During these strenuous years of War, you have well measured up and met every requirement of your varied duties as real men.

By the continued deep personal interest in your work, you have materially assisted in the splendid record attained by the Army Veterinary Services in the B.E.F., in confining contagious diseases to the smallest possible limits; in relieving the suffering of the sick and wounded animals, and in aiding their speedy recovery to health and strength. In these you have rendered valuable service in the mobility of the Forces in the Field.

Having been in close personal contact with you these years, and seen and known the value of your earnest endeavours, I look forward to the splendid assistance you are bound to render to Canada, as a result of your invaluable experiences in the Field, not only in the betterment of the Live Stock conditions, but in Public Health and Sanitary questions generally. Furthermore you will be worthy assets to her higher citizenship, by carrying back with you into civilian life that bigger and broader principle of self-sacrifice, which you have so magnificently shown, to the benefit of your fellow men.

Your horizon is large, and opportunities now lie before you which to many professions must seem enviable, and in developing these you will, I know, continue so to conduct yourselves as to redound to the honour and glory of the profession in years to come; and when the record of your services is read in after years, you will have so left your foot-print in the sands of time that it will be a stimulus to the younger generations in striving for the higher and nobler things of life and be the means of developing a deeper national spirit.

I trust that circumstances may soon permit of your return to home and loved ones, where you will receive the welcome you so justly deserve.

I am indeed proud to have had the honour and the privilege of acting as your Director for the last seven months and I assure you it has been a great pleasure to assist in developing that helping spirit which has tended so much to the efficiency of the C.A.V.C. and the satisfactory completion of a great work.

Yours sincerely,

C.E. Edgett

Colonel
Director of Veterinary Services.

CEE/EE

FOREWORD

Their Last Trip
Ammunition Team Killed by Shell Fire in the Forward Area
(*Tamblyn, The Horse in War, p. 69*)

Despite the advent of motor transport, horses and mules carried the supplies to the soldiers of the Canadian Expeditionary Force manning the trenches in the mud of the European Western Front. The forward lines of communication were always within artillery range, and the devastation wrought by shell-fire is evident above. The matter-of-fact need to carry on with the job in the face of this hazard is reflected in the string of pack mules stoically bypassing the unburied debris, sharing with their handlers the risk of another incoming round.

Members of the Canadian Army Veterinary Corps attached to forward units experienced the same dangers. A British veterinary officer recalled: "We were sheltering from aeroplane vision by the side of a wood when a German shrapnel shell burst upon percussion among the trees, killing four horses outright (all thoracic wounds) and wounding ten others, two of these so severely that I shot them immediately...".[1] C.A.V.C. officers and men had to deal with horses injured by shellbursts and some themselves fell victim to artillery fire.

But as the reader will discover, the main rôle of the C.A.V.C. was more mundane preventive medicine - promoting the best animal husbandry possible under very difficult circumstances, 'picking up nails' before horses did, and averting epidemics of disease. It also required timely intervention to evacuate injured, sick and debilitated animals rapidly, promoting humane conditions and minimizing animal wastage. It incorporated medical and surgical therapy to salvage animals for further use. And always, it involved reams of paperwork, accounting for the cost of care, and for the movement of horses between active army units and veterinary units, among veterinary and remount units, between the Canadian and British governments, and out of military service.

The Canadian Army Veterinary Corps, despite its non-combatant nature and small size, in many ways reflected in microcosm the C.E.F. at large. Embedded in its history are political patronage and merit rewarded; shell-shock and bravery; mismanagement and efficiency; incompetence and professionalism; dissipation and devotion to duty in most trying circumstances; self-service and self-sacrifice; lack of imagination and resourcefulness; jealousy and generosity; and, explicitly or implicitly, men being boys and boys being men. We see an unquestioning response to the call to serve king and country. In the C.E.F. and C.A.V.C., as institutions, separate from, but part of, a British force defending the pride of the Empire, we see reflected the curious concept of nationalist imperialism. And we sense growth of the Canadian self-image and nationalism, often expressed by somewhat anti-British British-born Canadians, such as the author himself. We see Anglo-Canadian racism and cultural bias, personal and systemic; French-Canadian cultural compromise; socio-economic class and place emphasized. We feel the fatalism of men who were tiny cogs on small wheels of a huge, senseless war machine fueled by animal and human flesh. Men who, even if they survived the mental and physical trauma of war, might die from the rigors of 'Spanish flu'. And along the way we even encounter 'Winnie-the-Pooh', before he was!

None of the reasons that the author invoked in his Preface (following) can justify publication of this history now. The last C.A.V.C. officer died in 1985, so none are left to cherish memories that might be stirred. Nor is there any longer a Canadian Army Veterinary Corps to apply the lessons recorded in these pages regarding care of the horse in war. The army veterinary service passed from the Canadian scene with the last cavalry charger and artillery gun horse, early in World War II. But Canadian veterinarians and the public deserve to learn, in the words of the time, the part their professional forebears played in a defining national experience, and the essential service rendered to their country by application of their skills in the theatre of war. They wanted their story told, and it now can be, the politics, personalities and perceptions that caused its apparent suppression having faded.

Based on the attention that it received in official and unofficial histories of The Great War, the C.A.V.C. might have been the Secret Service. Even its former Commanding Officer, recounting in a newspaper interview his background and war service, did not mention the C.A.V.C.,[2] and it was the only Corps not named on the National War Memorial in Ottawa.[3] In the first volume of a series '*The Official History of the Canadian Forces in the Great War 1914-1919*',[4] covering the period from the outbreak of hostilities until September 1915, Colonel A. Fortescue Duguid adequately reflected the activities of the C.A.V.C. in the larger context, from mobilization at Camp Valcartier to activity at Shorncliffe and in France. However, subsequent volumes were not forthcoming, and it was not until 1962 and Nicholson's '*Official History of the Canadian Army in the First World War. Canadian Expeditionary Force 1914-1919*'[5] that the entire Canadian effort in the First World War was summarized, necessarily in an abridged form to fit into one volume. But, presumably in the cause of brevity, Nicholson never mentioned the C.A.V.C. by name; the four indirect references probably were taken from Duguid. The only other 'official' Canadian World War I history published was Macphail's '*The Medical Services*', in 1925,[6] where, obviously, there is no reference to veterinary care. Histories of the artillery and Permanent Force cavalry regiments[7] also pay little or no attention to the Veterinary Service that kept them mobile.

The history of the Royal Army Veterinary Corps to 1919 by Smith,[8] and the reports on the Veterinary Service of the British Army in World War I by Blenkinsop and Rainey[9] and by Moore,[10] refer to the 'colonial' army veterinary corps that fell under British command, including the C.A.V.C., the South African Veterinary Corps, the New Zealand Veterinary Corps, and the Australian Army Veterinary Corps.[11] Taken together with the work on the United States Army Veterinary Corps by Merillat and Campbell[12] and information on the French Army Veterinary Corps,[13] these sources provide a comprehensive picture of the issues faced by army veterinary services on the allied side, and how they were dealt with. But they throw little light on matters specifically Canadian.

Following the war, short contributions on the C.A.V.C. were published by Donnell in 1920 as an appendix to a six volume popular history of The Great World War;[14] in 1920 by Lieut.-Col. David Tamblyn as an article in an American veterinary journal;[15] in 1921 in the Canadian veterinary periodical of the time as a commentary under the pseudonym 'Biscum';[16] and in 1922-23 by Cecil French, in a series of articles extracted from several chapters in this manuscript.[17] Tamblyn subsequently published a small book in 1932,[18] which reflected his hippophilia, but offered few insights on the C.A.V.C. Gattinger inserted anecdotes, sometimes embellished, on the C.A.V.C., and several of the same photographs published here, as context for parts of his 1962 history of the Ontario Veterinary College,[19] while in 1993, Dukes published a short historical summary of the Canadian Army Veterinary Service.[20]

This book ultimately owes its existence to Sir Max Aitken, Lord Beaverbrook, the New Brunswick-born financier, newspaperman, lobbyist, politician, socialite and Canadian patriot, who orbited in the galaxy of the Canadian War Establishment in London, in its several guises.[21] Sir Sam Hughes, Minister of Militia, in 1915 appointed Aitken as 'Canadian Eye Witness' in Flanders, and he became an unofficial adviser and informant in England. But with the ouster of Hughes in fall 1916, and the inception of the Overseas War Ministry of Canada in London, Aitken's role in the Canadian war effort became less overtly political, and he channeled his energies into the Canadian War Records Office and the Canadian War Memorials Fund, which he had established.

The Canadian War Records Office was to document and publicize Canadian involvement in The Great War in all its forms. It recognized the limitations of the official war diaries maintained by military units to record actions and activities, so it attempted to obtain information of a broader and more personal type to include in eventual histories of each unit;[22] as early as 1917 it tried to stimulate the production of such histories. It also sponsored photographers and correspondents who documented the Canadian war effort and produced patriotic propaganda.

The history of the C.A.V.C. was conceived several times, had a prolonged gestation, and appeared to have been stillborn, only to be resurrected belatedly here. In January 1917, Capt. C.H. Higgins C.A.V.C., through the offices of the Department of Militia and Defence, Ottawa, suggested that a Veterinary History of the C.E.F. be written, and supplied a draft outline. "It will...record...posterity...the part Canadians have played... It is a good business proposition. It is an economic necessity. Furthermore, without such a history the experiences gained will be almost valueless." In April 1917, Brig.-Gen. William Neill, Director of Veterinary Services, responded that while Higgins might be the person to compile the history, he was short of officers, and he would rather Higgins came over in a professional capacity, with the possibility of writing the history as work permitted. Higgins did not go overseas, and nothing more was found in the record on his initiative.[23]

Meanwhile, during 1916-1918 the C.W.R.O. was collecting war diaries and statistics, and circulating questionnaires to officers commanding small units, in order to collect more detailed information.[24] In May 1917, a letter to the Director of Veterinary Services required submission of a "general narrative on broad lines of the Establishment and Organization of the Veterinary and Remount Services...more interesting" than war diaries.[25] About this time, Neill went to Canada on a tour regarding availability of remounts, and Lieut.-Col. H.D. Smith, acting in his stead, over the next 4 months fielded a number of increasingly testy memos from O.M.F.C. Headquarters seeking a copy of this historical narrative.[26] Sgt. A. Kelly, training at Witley, England, had been tasked with preparation of this submission. His qualifications are uncertain, but apparently he had little opportunity to concentrate on the project. On 13 September 1917, the narrative finally was forwarded to Headquarters by Neill, just returned from Canada. This document[27] is melodramatic and obsequiously laudatory of Neill and his headquarters staff, but in its layout and content one can detect patterns and material adapted by French. In the War Records Office, collation of material relating to the C.A.V.C. rested with Sgt. C. Stirling Moyse, who had been charged by Beaverbrook with producing a history of the auxilliary units of the C.E.F., of which the C.A.V.C. was but one.[28]

In early November 1917, while stationed at No. 2 Canadian Veterinary Hospital, Shorncliffe, England, Cecil French wrote , "...the job of compiling the History of the Canadian Army Veterinary Corps has been assigned to me, and I have begun work on same." How or why French was selected is unknown, but it must be assumed that Sgt. Kelly was found wanting. French had deposited a copy of his text on canine surgery with C.A.V.C. Headquarters when he enlisted in April 1917,[29] so perhaps his ability to publish a book had been noted in high places. It was planned to seek private support to publish the history "...to avoid the delay and trouble incident to the unraveling of red tape..." involved in government sponsorship, and it seems that there was a plan to sell subscriptions in advance. Any profits accruing from its sale likely would be directed to the Canadian Branch of the Purple Cross, "....but all such details will rest...with our General". Neill seems to have planned in October 1917 to fund the publication of the history using donations from the Montreal Purple Cross Fund, an animal welfare charity.[30] However, he explicitly forbad French spending any money on preparations for the book without "further instructions", though French was "willing to take a chance" on using his own resources, and being reimbursed when the financial arrangements had been firmed up.[31]

During the first two weeks of November, French corresponded actively with the War Records Office in London, establishing relationships, and sorting out access to statistical, narrative and illustrative material. A photographer was sent from the C.W.R.O. to Shorncliffe to take pictures, and Lord Beaverbrook authorized access to photographic sources and informed Moyse of French's status as official C.A.V.C. historian, presumably opening access to War Records Office resources. However, by early December, it was apparent to French that his tenure at Shorncliffe was limited, and he expressed reservations about his capacity to carry on if sent to France. In response, Lieut. C.H. Hastings of the Historical Section, C.W.R.O. indicated that other units had historians attached to his section, and that perhaps that might be an option for French.[32]

In early January 1918, French was assigned to the 5th Canadian Division, training at Witley, England, which presumably allowed him to continue some work on the history. But in early March, after the 5th Division was broken up, he was transferred to No. 1 Canadian Veterinary Hospital in Le Havre France. He recognized that this was the prelude to a posting at the front, and in April he wrote to Hastings that due to being "...under Imperial control, and Canadian in name only..." it was impossible for him to get recognition from British authorities that time must be made for work on the history. The only recourse he saw was to get a secondment to the C.W.R.O., which he asked Hastings to attempt to arrange. This was taken up with Lord Beaverbrook, who was favourably disposed, but sought to evaluate a sample of French's work. The 20 page draft that was forwarded was but an edited version of that prepared by Sgt. Kelly in summer 1917, and it only superficially resembles the final work.[33] We do not know Beaverbrook's reaction to the document, but French was sent to the front with the artillery.

He undoubtedly was unable to work on the project during the summer of 1918, while at the front, or in the early fall, while recovering from an injury in hospital in England, but he retained his commission to do so from the new Director of Veterinary Services, Colonel C.E. Edgett, who took over after Neill and his assistant, Capt. E.A. Frape, resigned in March 1918. Prior to his departure, Frape had sent a Confidential Circular Memorandum to all veterinary officers requesting "cordial co-operation" in providing access to personal diaries etc., and with a list of questions, the replies to which seem to have provided much of the information found in Appendix A.[34]

After his hospitalization, French was attached first to C.A.V.C. Headquarters, then to the Canadian War Records Office. At the time that he began work full-time on the history in October 1918, French had little to show. Capt. Alfred Savage, who visited Moyse and French right after the Armistice, commented bluntly that he found the manuscript "fairly rotten".[35] But French energetically set about soliciting written contributions from the officers and some of the men in France, via the Deputy Assistant Directors of Veterinary Services for each Division, to supplement the C.W.R.O. material and war diaries. As might be expected, the response varied, some officers replying enthusiastically with detailed accounts, others contributing little or nothing.[36] But with the help of information provided by his colleagues, and as the result of original research in the C.W.R.O., presumably assisted by Sgt. Moyse, Cecil French assembled a body of data on the C.A.V.C., and began to craft his narrative.

In May 1919, French moved to the Historical Section, Department of Militia and Defence in Ottawa to complete his work. Here he came into dispute with an unnamed superior officer over the quality of his work, or over his interpretation of events. This may have been the director of the Historical Section at the time, Brigadier-General Ernest A. Cruickshank. Cruickshank, an amateur military historian, was retired in 1920 as a result of the incompetence evident in his initial history of Canadian participation in W.W. I up to April 1915, which was printed but not issued.[37] At any rate, French separated from the Army in August 1919, apparently completing his manuscript unofficially. French, in his Author's Preface, which follows, implies that the manuscript was suppressed, since it did not receive the "official sanction" that would permit publication. Such sanction must have been withheld by Col. A.F. Duguid, who succeeded Cruickshank in 1921.

The reasons for this are uncertain. French suggests in his Preface that some might find him too critical. Knowing what we know of the quality of the leadership of the C.A.V.C., and the opinion of it held by many veterinary officers, it easily can be argued that French was not critical enough. The major area of obvious controversy or scandal is the disposition of charitable donations made to several animal welfare agencies, discussed in Chapter 15, but by today's standards, the problems revealed are of minor import. None-the-less, in 1933, Duguid asked Lieut.-Col. David Tamblyn, Officer Administering Canadian Army Veterinary Services, to comment on the manuscript "with a view to removing injustice done to those involved, and with the object of eventually achieving a fair and balanced result..."[38] This implies some of the motives for withholding the manuscript from publication, but perusal of Tamblyn's peevish, weak, and in some cases openly self-serving comments suggests that there was little substantive criticism that even a contemporary 'insider' to the organization could offer.[39] To our knowledge, Duguid did not remark on the fact that the French manuscript was undocumented, and to that extent unprofessional. Our research suggests that the content should not be highly suspect on that account.

French obviously retained a copy of his work, which to our knowledge has not been preserved, from which he published the excerpts noted earlier. Why he did not proceed with the original plans to publish the book privately, or at least outside official government channels, is not clear. But the fact that he did not, and that his series of articles in *The Canadian Veterinary Record* was incomplete, suggests outside intervention, possibly the Crown exercising its copyright.

Two copies of the manuscript, and supporting documentary and photographic material, are found in the National Archives of Canada as The French Papers.[40] The provenance of these documents is uncertain, since the Manuscript Group number suggests that they are not of official Department of Militia and Defence origin. They probably were not deposited by French, despite the name. That the file contains a letter from Col. Duguid, dated 25 April 1933, and Tamblyn's annotations, and that the manuscripts have been heavily edited, suggests that they were in the Historical Section, retained as a potential contribution to the projected but largely unpublished series of 'official' histories of Canadian units in World War I.

Knowledge of the existence at one time of the French manuscript, based on the excerpts in *The Canadian Veterinary Record*,[41] served as the impetus for this book. Awareness of the C.A.V.C. was heightened by the fact that the R.C.A.V.C. was disbanded in the fall of 1940, while the senior editor was in final year at the Ontario Veterinary College, and while members of his class were contemplating their futures under the cloud of the Second World War. Disbandment of the R.C.A.V.C. denied veterinarians the opportunity of a commission in the armed forces where their professional education would be recognized and put to good use (see Chapter 17).

Research for other publications on the history of the veterinary profession in Canada[42] had highlighted the importance of the C.A.V.C./R.C.A.V.C. and their militia antecedents in professional life of the times, and revealed how often veterinarians prominent in other aspects of the profession had belonged to the militia. Collection of material relevant to Canadian military veterinary medicine has been an ongoing research activity, highlighted by museum displays which stimulated accession of artefacts and documents.

With the recognition that French's manuscript '*History of the Canadian Army Veterinary Corps in the Great World War*' was intact in the National Archives of Canada, a plan was activated to bring it to print. Financial sponsorship was established through the generosity of benefactors listed in the Acknowledgments. Supplementary research was undertaken in the National Archives, the C.A.V. Barker Museum of Canadian Veterinary History, and elsewhere, seeking ancillary information and illustrations. The archive copy of the manuscript was transcribed and edited to a publishable form, and illustrations were selected.

In order to provide context for the material in French's manuscript, and since there is unlikely to be another major publication on the C.A.V.C., further research was undertaken to provide background on the origins and development of military veterinary medicine in Canada; to place the activities of the C.A.V.C. in the wartime military setting on the Western Front, and, to a minor extent, in the military, socio-political and veterinary professional setting in Canada, North America and England; and to trace the fate of the organization from the end of the First World War to its disbandment early in the Second World War. To avoid adulterating markedly the original manuscript,[43] this ancillary material is segregated in the Foreword, the Epilogue, captions to Figures, and some of the Appendices, and is embedded in the Notes to the manuscript, with all of the compromises relating to completeness and level of detail, coherence and continuity that such an arrangement implies. Authorities for information cited are found in Sources.

Acknowledgments

The editors note with admiration the skill and energy that the author, Capt. Cecil French C.A.V.C., invested in the manuscript that it has been our pleasure finally to bring to print.

The very generous financial assistance of the Ontario Veterinary College Class of 1950; The Ontario Veterinary Medical Association; The Ontario Veterinary College Alumni Association; The College of Veterinarians of Ontario; Parke-Davis Pharmaceutical Company; E.E. (Gus) Lagerquist, Central Sales Ltd.; the Bull Fellowship; and supporters of the C.A.V. Barker Museum of Canadian Veterinary History made this project possible.

We owe special thanks to our researchers, Alan Cameron and Arnold Kay (R.C.M.P. retired), and to the staff of the National Archives of Canada, especially Barbara Wilson and Timothy Dubé, who tracked down information and illustrations. Staff of the former Directorate of History, now Directorate of History and Heritage, Department of National Defence, Ottawa also assisted. They include W.A.B. Douglas, W.A. MacIntosh, B. Greenhous, and latterly Steve Harris and Jennie Marvin. Laura Brandon, Margo Weiss, and C. Clement, Canadian War Museum, Ottawa, also responded to our queries and assisted with illustrations.

David Mattison, British Columbia Archives and Reference Service, provided valuable information on Cecil French and others who lived in British Columbia. David Hull, Bernard Katz, Maxine Crispin, Romie Smith, Jim Brett, Carol Perry, Jeanette Davidson and other staff of the University of Guelph Library have been most helpful. Military Museums, Archives and Libraries that have contributed include: Royal Canadian Dragoons, C.F.B. Petawawa Ont., M.Cpl. George Wallace; Lord Strathcona's Horse (Royal Canadians), Calgary Alta., W.O. Darryl H. Crowell, Sgt. Rick D. Dennis and Cpl. Lee J. Ramsden; Royal Canadian Artillery, C.F.B. Shilo Manitoba, Jodi Ann Eskritt; Royal Canadian Military Institute, Toronto Ont., Arthur Manvell and Gregory Laughton; First Hussars, London Ont., Alastair Neely and Jennifer Mousseau. We also have been aided by the following: Sue M. Baptie, City of Vancouver Archives; Mme Barot, Ville du Havre Archives; John Bevan, National Museum of Wales; Phebe Chartrand, McGill University Archives; Rev. J.K. Davies, Dyfed, Wales; Mary Davies, National Library of Wales; Glen Gordon, Royal Canadian Mounted Police, Ottawa; Benita Horder, Royal College of Veterinary Surgeons, London; Philip M. Teigen, National Library of Medicine, Washington; Linda Wills, Greater Vernon Museum and Archives, Vernon, B.C.; and Guelph Museums.

The following individuals kindly responded to queries, provided personal or family information or artefacts, or otherwise assisted research: Jack Arundel, Tanguy Barker, Don Barnum, S.H. Bramley, Brig. J. Clabby, Phillipe David, Larry Donovan, J.D. Dugmore, Tom W. Dukes, George Fisher, Fred Forrest, E.M. Fox, Joe H. Harper, James A. Henderson, Neill Henderson, Wilson Henderson, David Howes, Keith Hughes, Jack Hyatt, Ross Irwin, Jay Isa, Trevor Lloyd Jones, Morgan Knight, Clive M. Law, Robbin Lindsay, Sam Luker, Don M. McLellan, Fred Milton, Desmond Morton, C. Nichols, Linda Pallett, Eric Pallister, Michel Pepin, June Raeburn, Brian Reid, Mark J. Relf, Leon Z. Saunders, Mary and Gary Savage, Jim Schroder, Rosalie B. Woodland.

This work has been informed by personal reminiscences of the following now-deceased former officers of the C.A.V.C. or the A.V.C. (Imperial), contributed in interviews with C.A.V. Barker: David J. McLellan, M.I. Neely, William A. Robertson, Gordon A. Rose, M. Sparrow and A.R. Younie.

The editors have benefited from the opinions, suggestions and encouragement of L.G. Coleman, Terry Crowley, Brian Derbyshire, A. Margaret Evans, Bernard McSherry and Zbigniew Wojcinski.

Betty Henry transcribed the manuscript, and Ruthie Tucker and Lyn Rumig did further stenographic work, while Norm Rogers provided scanning and computer assistance.

Other staff of the Dean's Office, Ontario Veterinary College who have been of great assistance over the years include: Lily Arpa, Fernanda Clark, Judy Fletcher, Willa Hopkinson, Martha Leibbrandt and Máire Pratschke.

The encouragement and space provided by Deans of the Ontario Veterinary College, particularly N. Ole Neilsen and the current Dean, Alan Meek, have facilitated the activities of the C.A.V. Barker Museum of Canadian Veterinary History.

Dave Traves, of Greenmor Printing, has been most professional, patient and accommodating.

We also owe a large debt to Dr. Charles A. Mitchell, the dean of Canadian veterinary history, and champion of a national Canadian veterinary organization, for foundations laid, the example set, and encouragement offered.

We wish to express here our special thanks to Jean Barker and Susy Carman, 'war widows' during the final preparation of this book, for their tolerance and support.

ABOUT THE AUTHOR

Captain Cecil French C.A.V.C.
(*NAC PA 7220*)

Big game hunter, soldier, veterinarian, professor and manufacturer, as he was depicted in his obituaries,[1] Cecil French was a multifaceted man. He was born November 9, 1871 in London, England, and was educated at Hastings in England and at Bingen-am-Rhine, near Mainz, Germany.[2] He landed in Halifax, Nova Scotia on April 20, 1889, only 17 years old;[3] his motivation to immigrate is unknown. A brilliant student at the Faculty of Comparative Medicine and Veterinary Science at McGill University in Montreal, French won two scholarships and the medal for General Proficiency. He obtained a Doctor of Veterinary Science (D.V.S.) degree in 1894, and subsequently attended the Royal Veterinary College, Munich, Germany as a Special Student,[4] likely in 1894-95.

While a veterinary student, French enlisted (1892-94) as a Private in the 3rd Battalion Victoria Rifles, a Montreal militia unit.[5] Probably about the time that he graduated from McGill, French married Florence Slocum of Montreal;[6] their son, Cecil Ernest French, was born there on November 1, 1897.[7]

Upon his return from Munich, French moved to Washington D.C., where he was a pioneer small animal veterinarian. By 1896 he had established the Washington Canine Infirmary at 714 Twelfth St.,[8] where he practiced until 1917, and he claimed to have called at the White House to treat President Teddy Roosevelt's dog.[9] French published reports in *The Journal of Comparative Medicine and Veterinary Archives*, and in 1906, he wrote and published *Surgical Diseases and Surgery of the Dog*.[10] He also lectured on a part-time basis at the United States College of Veterinary Surgeons.[11] His reputation as a big game hunter seems to arise from expeditions that he made to Africa, capturing live animals for zoos.[12]

After his son completed school in Switzerland in 1915, French went with him to Canada, and attempted to enlist. Refused on the basis of his age (45), he returned to Washington, while Ernest became a bank clerk and joined the McGill C.O.T.C. In 1916, at age 18, Ernest was commissioned Lieutenant in the 91st Infantry Battalion, Canadian Expeditionary Force, and he sailed for England in June. Transferring to the Royal Flying Corps, he became a Flying Officer in 56 Squadron on March 14, 1917. Flying an SE.5 fighter on operations on May 20, 1917, 33 days into active duty, he was shot down by anti-aircraft fire behind German lines, becoming a prisoner-of-war. He was repatriated to England in mid-December 1918, and was Mentioned in Despatches for escapes as a P.O.W.[13]

Early in 1917, Cecil French proceeded independently to England, possibly to be near his son. The Canadian

Army Veterinary Corps, desperate for veterinarians, commissioned him a Temporary Captain effective 17 April, 1917. He was assigned to No. 2 Canadian Veterinary Hospital, Shorncliffe where he became an instructor at the Veterinary Training School. In January 1918, he joined the 15th Canadian Infantry Brigade, 5th Canadian Division, training at Witley, England. He took charge of 'A' Squadron, No. 1 Canadian Veterinary Hospital, Le Havre, France, on 23 March, 1918. In late April he became V.O. to the 6th Brigade, Canadian Field Artillery, at the front, where his proximal left fibula was fractured when his horse fell on him in late June. He served through the build-up to the second Battle of Cambrai, but in September problems with his knee forced him to hospital in England.[14]

He had begun work on the history of the C.A.V.C. in England in late fall 1917. In mid-October 1918, after his release from hospital, he was attached to C.A.V.C. Headquarters in London to work full-time on the history, and on 10 January, 1919, was assigned to the Canadian War Records Office, London. It was closed at general demobilization, and from late May to mid August 1919, Captain French was in the Historical Section, Militia Headquarters, Ottawa. Subsequent to his disagreement with superiors unknown regarding the tone and content of the history, discussed in the Foreword, and alluded to in the Author's Preface, French left the army. Where he lived while he completed the manuscript unofficially is not known, but he was in Montreal later in 1919.[15]

In 1920, French and his wife moved to Victoria, British Columbia, where they resided in the Empress Hotel for the rest of their lives. He now re-embarked on a business career. In 1920, he was an "agent for motor boats". By 1921 he is listed as "of the ffrench Motor Boat Co. and manager ffrench Remedy Co." Although the motor boat business seems to have been discontinued, French's proprietary medicine manufacturing company thrived. He is reputed to have invented, in 1895, the use of the gelatine capsule to contain the noxious compounds then used as vermifuges or vermicides to treat parasitic worms in dogs, cats and fur farm foxes. The ffrench Remedy Company almost annually produced a substantial booklet entitled *For Your Dog*, which had run to 40 editions by 1948, suggesting that the business was begun in Washington prior to World War I. French's apparent relative prosperity and freedom of movement during the war probably were the product of wealth generated in part by that means. Certainly, manufacture of proprietary veterinary medicines sustained him comfortably throughout the remainder of his life.

On October 20, 1927, the 'ffrench Remedy Company Ltd.' was incorporated in British Columbia. Manufacturing was carried on at Courtney and Gordon streets in Victoria. The trademark, 'ff' in white letters on a black circle surrounded by a border of double lines, was on animal medicines reported to have been shipped "from Victoria to almost every country in the world". The 'ff' trademark and company name was based on the archaic original spelling of the family name. In its last Annual Report, October 1950, Cecil French was listed as the Managing Director, with his wife Florence Slocum French and his son C. Ernest French, of Toronto, as Directors.[16]

French was a cultured and literate man. Though frustrated in his goal to publish officially the History of the Canadian Army Veterinary Corps, French succeeded in publishing one chapter and part of a second in instalments in *The Canadian Veterinary Record* during 1922-23 (see Foreword)[17]. He also used his knowledge of German culture and language to seek out, translate into English, and publish in 1930, the 1781 report by Henry Zimmerman of his experiences as a member of Captain Cook's scientific party on his third voyage around the world, which explored the Pacific Northwest. In his later years, French assisted invalid veterans in Victoria in raising silkworms as a hobby, and he published a short illustrated treatise on the topic in 1942. He also was interested in the history of Victoria and Vancouver Island, and left notes and typescripts on several such topics.[18]

Cecil French died in St. Joseph's Hospital, Victoria, on September 6, 1951, at the age of 80,[19] having lived a full, varied, creative and prosperous life. His son Ernest after 1920 lived in Toronto, and, thwarted in his attempts to join the fledgling Canadian Air Force or to become a commercial pilot, he worked for his uncle's company, Howard Smith Paper Mills, for the rest of his life. During the Second World War he became president of the Toronto Flying Club and was Major and O.C. 2nd Reserve Armoured Division Ordnance Field Park, Royal Canadian Ordnance Corps, Toronto. He died at age 64 in 1961, apparently survived only by his wife.[20] Florence Slocum French lived on in the Empress Hotel until she died on September 25, 1962, aged 91. Described as tall and gracious, kind and considerate, though quiet and retiring, she was renowned for having driven an antique electric brougham automobile, with a top speed of 6 miles per hour, around Victoria until the 1940's. Her ashes were scattered at sea, and she left the bulk of her estate of over $245,000 to the Salvation Army.[21]

AUTHOR'S PREFACE[1]

Cecil French

This volume contains a narrative of the part played by the overseas organization of the Canadian Army Veterinary Corps in the Great War. The object in producing it has been twofold - firstly, that the men of Canada who participated in the corps in the stirring times of 1914-1918, shall have, as their own, a permanent record of the events and scenes with which they were intimately concerned, in order that it may serve as an example of patriotism to their children, and that in their declining years they may, by turning to its pages, again live through those never-to-be forgotten days. Secondly, in years to come, when the Great War is but a memory of the past, there may be afforded to posterity, by an orderly disposal of its parts, a clear and concise story of the wartime organization, its origin and the many vicissitudes and evolutionary processes by which it passed in its development from one stage to another, as well as of the true causes of those changes and the events that led to them.

An effort has been made to give the reader an easy view of the things only that counted and without any attempt at glossing over the inevitable mistakes that were made, but it has nevertheless been the constant endeavour of the writer, as a non-professional soldier, to approach the subject from a wholly unbiased point of view in a spirit which aimed only at recording the truth and to relate impartially what was both good and bad without the injection of undeserved flattery or malice.

It may be objected by some that at times a too critical attitude has been adopted, but a fearless portrayal of the truth cannot be deemed an error, and after all, it is what really happened, and not what some might prefer had happened, that deserves to find room in these pages. Romance has not been allowed to intrude itself at any stage of the story, everything stated having been gathered from the war diaries of veterinary units and other official documents on file at Argyll House and from copious contemporary notes on observations made by the writer on the spot.

Of the glamour and heroic side of warfare, the reader will find in the succeeding pages scarcely a trace, for it did not lie within the province of the veterinary corps to distinguish itself in this respect; its duty, by virtue of its noncombatant character, having been to remain in the rear where it could best perform its appointed function of constantly helping to maintain the mobility of the combatant units and to repair some of the ravages of the battlefield.

Its activities found scope in three main directions, to wit: at the front in association with the combatant troops; at isolated points with other noncombatant units away from the fighting zone; and at the veterinary hospitals at the bases far removed from the scene of conflict. Consequently, its lot was to endure the everlasting drudgery inherent to that situation without the soul stirring excitement experienced by the combatant solder in going 'over the top'. Yet at all times it had patiently to bear its full share of the risks and sacrifices incident to modern long range warfare, and there were one or two incidences where its members were called upon to participate in actual fighting. It is not too much to state that the achievements of the corps have been neither fully understood nor recognized, nor has the corps received due credit for the part it played in the war. This part, though not spectacular, was none the less of incalculable worth, for, expressed in material terms, the value of Canadian property watched over by the corps was upwards of ten million dollars.[2]

Amidst all the changing conditions and varying circumstances, one undeniable fact stood out prominently, namely the indispensability of the horse. The mobility of an army depends ultimately on its transport, whether that transport be by mechanical propulsion or by equine motive power. For several years prior to the war it was freely predicted that the horse in warfare was a thing of the past and that with the perfection of the motor, the armies of the future would be served by nothing but mechanical means. But this, like so many other preconceived notions, was proven to have been erroneous, for the mud of Flanders had not been thought of. Perhaps it was mud more than anything else that brought the horse back into its own, mud that impeded and finally completely tied up the motor transport so that the front lines were forced to depend on the horse, employed as an animal, for bringing up the supplies and ammunition. The army, both men and guns, would have starved at Passchendaele for want of food and ammunition, had it not been for the devotion of the animals. The horse thus became the final line in the Lines of Communication, and to the veterinary corps fell the duty of maintaining its effectiveness for performing this absolutely essential task.

This book has been written under difficulty. No official historian was granted the Canadian Army Veterinary Corps as was the case with the Medical Corps, where the officer allotted to the task held the appointment of Assistant Director of Medical Services with the rank of colonel, and was assisted by a staff consisting of a major, a captain, and two civilian stenographers. The work was inaugurated at the behest of Brigadier-General W.J. Neill, Director of Veterinary Services and Remounts, by the individual effort of one of its officers, Captain C. French, who at first was obligated to find opportunity for the necessary researches in the intervals of his regular duties. It was continued under direction of Brigadier-General Neill's successor, Colonel C.E. Edgett, who realized the importance of carrying out the undertaking whilst events were fresh in mind, and afforded every possible assistance. Later, Canadian War Records Office came to the rescue and made application that the work be completed under its auspices. Accordingly, Captain French was attached to the latter organization for this particular duty from the 10th of January, 1919, onward.

The removal of the War Records Office to Canada the following spring (1919) necessitated the continuation of the narrative under new authority, namely the Historical section of the Militia Department. This change disclosed a fundamental difference of opinion as to the true mission of the historian, and the writer being unwilling to conform to the viewpoint of a superior officer who lacked experience of the veterinary service in the field, it became necessary to complete the work without official recognition at Ottawa. Consequently, the book occupies a unique position, official sanction for its compilation having been provided by General Headquarters of Canada's overseas war forces, but denied by the responsible home authority appointed by the Militia Department. It is left to the reader to form his own judgment as to its merits.

Throughout the narrative, the reader will notice frequent employment of the term 'Imperial'. This is a purely arbitrary use of a very convenient and appropriate appellation, which, however, had no official standing. For instance, the correct designation of the unit in the British army having the function corresponding to that of the Canadian Army Veterinary Corps was 'The Army Veterinary Corps', or, as it became entitled to call itself towards the close of the War, 'The Royal Army Veterinary Corps'. But to the Canadian, soldiers of the British army were always known as 'Imperials'[3]. It was a good name for distinctive purposes and it stuck, and it has been thought best to retain it and to use it where it is desired to distinguish between the two services.

To all individuals is ascribed the rank they were holding at the time of the incidents referred to. Thus it comes about that in a single chapter an officer may be successively mentioned as a captain, a major and a lieutenant-colonel.

For the splendid collection of photographs from which most of the illustrations have been reproduced[4] the corps acknowledge its indebtedness to the Canadian War Records Office (official); to the British Ministry of Information (official); to the Associated Illustration Agencies, Limited, of London; to the Topical Press Agency of London; and to the Central Press Photos, Limited, of London.

It is hoped that the members of the corps whose information as to what was transpiring in other portions of their branch of the service was greatly restricted during their sojourn at the front, will appreciate the opportunity for enlightenment and it is confidently believed that those who succeed the present generation and those whose mission it will be to carry on the work and traditions of the corps will be enabled to profit by the experiences of their predecessors recorded in these pages.

Cecil French

REGULATIONS

FOR THE

CANADIAN ARMY VETERINARY SERVICE

1912

Published under the authority of the Militia Council.

OTTAWA
GOVERNMENT PRINTING BUREAU
1912

H. Q.—621-3-7.
500-4-12.

Title Page
Regulations for the Canadian Army Veterinary Service, 1912
(*C.A.V. Barker Museum*)

CHAPTER 1

ORIGIN - PREWAR DAYS[1]

REGIMENTAL SYSTEM Prior to 1910, the veterinary interests of the military forces of Canada were cared for by the old regimental system. This system was entirely lacking in any sort of centralized direction or control, and depended for efficiency on the patriotic efforts of individual practitioners in civil life who held commissions in the active militia with appointment to the regimental staffs of the various mounted corps. Each year the officer holding such appointment left his private practice and turned out with his unit for a period of from 10 to 15 days to undergo his annual training under service conditions and to supervise the welfare of the horses that were hired to meet the requirements of the occasion (Figure 1.1). Only one or two permanent mounted corps had carried on their strength a permanently employed regimental veterinary officer.[3] This was the extent to which veterinary services were utilized in the Canadian forces at the end of the Boer War.[4]

Figure 1.1. Third 'Montreal' Field Battery of Artillery at militia camp, 1890. Veterinary Surgeon Charles McEachran on the far right.[2]
(*Royal Canadian Artillery Museum Collection, CFB Shilo*)

INCEPTION OF CORPS SYSTEM

In the year 1910 it was decided to do away gradually with the old order of things by ceasing to appoint new officers and to establish in its place an organization of a more centralized and permanent character. According to Lieutenant-Colonel J.H. Wilson, Lieutenant-Colonel W.B. Hall,[5] veterinary officer of the Royal Canadian Dragoons (Figure 1.2), was the first officer of the Canadian militia to broach the subject of organizing the veterinary corps. Hence arose the Canadian Army Veterinary Service with ultimate responsibility vested in the Quartermaster-General of the Canadian Militia and consisting of three branches, namely:

(a) The Canadian Permanent Army Veterinary Corps
(b) The Canadian Army Veterinary Corps
(c) The Regimental Veterinary Service (in process of dissolution)

By 1914, at the outbreak of the late war, the old regimental service had practically ceased to exist.[7]

The number of the personnel of both the Canadian Permanent Army Veterinary Corps and the Canadian Army Veterinary Corps was to be as laid down in the establishment annually approved by the government.[8]

Figure 1.2. Officers of the Royal Canadian Dragoons, Permanent Force, Toronto, 1903. Vet.-Maj. Wm. B. Hall, centre, back row.[6]
(*Royal Canadian Dragoons Archives, CFB Petawawa*)

LIEUTENANT R. DUHAULT.
Canadian Permanent Army Veterinary Corps, Commanding No. 5 Detachment, C. P. A. V. C., and Veterinary Officer to Lord Strathcona's Horse (Royal Canadians).

Figure 1.3. Lieut. R. Duhault
C.P.A.V.C.[10]
No. 5 Detachment, Winnipeg Manitoba
(*Steele, 1914, p. 163*)

CAPTAIN ANGUS W. TRACEY.
Commanding No. 4 Section Canadian Army Veterinary Corps.

Figure 1.4. Capt. Angus Tracy C.A.V.C.[12]
O.C. No. 4 Section, Sherbrooke P.Q.
(*Steele, 1914, p. 162*)

C.P.A.V.C. It was provided that the Canadian Permanent Army Veterinary Corps should consist of veterinary officers gazetted to the corps (Figure 1.3) and of non-commissioned officers and privates enlisted therein, but as a matter of fact, at the outbreak of the war, the process of organization was still incomplete, having only reached the stage of appointment of five officers, and some three non-commissioned officers, engaged in performing necessary clerical work.[9]

C.A.V.C. The Canadian Army Veterinary Corps consisted of veterinary graduates in civil life gazetted as officers of that corps (Figure 1.4), and of non-commissioned officers and privates enlisted therein, and detailed for duty with the mounted corps of the active militia as required, for a period not exceeding four years, but subject to an extension of such period when deemed advisable.[11]

SECTIONS In the militia service, nine Sections were provided for in the corps establishment in the following divisional areas and districts, numbered according to the number of the area or district in which they were situated.

1. London, Ontario	6. Halifax, Nova Scotia
2. Toronto, Ontario	10. Winnipeg, Manitoba
3. Kingston, Ontario	13. Calgary, Alberta
5. Quebec, Quebec	

It will be noted that no provision was made for veterinary Sections in certain areas.[13]

S.V.O. The Senior Veterinary Officer,[14] with headquarters at Kingston, was charged with the administration of the service, the recommendations for appointments and promotions, the supervision of veterinary duties, the supply of veterinary stores, and the preparation of statistical returns and estimates for these services.

P.V.O. To each enumerated divisional area and district, appointed from either corps, there was allocated a Principal Veterinary Officer, who was made responsible for the administration of the Army Veterinary Service, the veterinary stores, and the command of the Canadian Permanent Army Veterinary Corps and Canadian Army Veterinary Corps within his division or district.[15]

SCHOOLS Provision was also made for the establishment, staffing and maintenance of the Canadian Army Veterinary School, for instructional courses in farriery, and for veterinary hospitals.[16]

Thus, it will be seen that there existed a framework or nucleus, capable of expansion, and around which an extensive organization could be built up as occasion might demand.

CHAPTER 2

OTHER RANKS - WAR DAYS

TYPE AND SOURCE OF SUPPLY Whilst the officers, by virtue of their special knowledge, may be said to have formed the backbone of the corps, the non-commissioned officers and men (Appendix D), also trained along special lines, formed indispensable support. Recruited in the first instance like all other units of the expeditionary force,[1] they came in the prime of manhood, of blameless physique and expert in horsemanship, from all parts of Canada.

COMB-OUT They were all selected with regard to the special work in view. For the first two years, reinforcements were secured from the same sort of material, but there came a time, towards 1917, when the insistent call from the fighting units for every able-bodied man to fill their depleted ranks forced the corps not only to renounce seeking the type of man compatible with the object of its existence, but to render up for combatant purposes many of its own personnel who were deemed by the higher military authorities to be of the calibre urgently needed by the infantry battalions, and to accept in their stead men who could, after a course of training, perform the duties but with less efficiency, and who were quite unable to withstand the hardships and rigorous existence of trench warfare. It was an undesirable but unavoidable state of affairs due to the inexorable demands of the war.

In commenting on this fact, no reflection is intended on the late comers into the ranks of the corps; indeed the corps was immensely proud to welcome to itself the many heroes who had suffered in the first line of defence and been partly broken in answering the first great call to duty. The fact is merely recorded to indicate that the efficiency of the corps was necessarily impaired by the withdrawal of men trained in its special line of work and the substitution of less vigorous and withal untrained novices.

OPPORTUNITIES In some respects, service in the ranks of the veterinary corps offered opportunities to progressive individuals which the latter might never have met with in other units. It has been shown elsewhere that promotion to the acting rank of sergeant, with equivalent emoluments, was attainable by considerable numbers of those who qualified themselves as efficient to render first aid treatment in the field. In the case of those who served in France, this rank was made substantive after a successful probationary period of one month, so if the individual made good in the special capacity, he ran no risk of losing the job and having to revert to his original rank. In the case of those created first aid sergeants in England for duty in the British Isles, the rank was not confirmed, except that under the general ruling made at the time of the armistice, all those who were then acting were allowed to return home with the rank.

Moreover the job was interesting and entirely free from any irksomeness that surrounded the life of a private or non-commissioned officer in the combatant units, for it carried with it practical immunity from drills and similar regimental duties. The first aid sergeant, like his chief, the veterinary officer, was attached to a unit to perform a special function and was not expected to do anything else than assist the veterinary officer and to act as his representative during his absence.

This particular post owed its incidence to the shortage of veterinary officers in the Imperial Army Veterinary Corps in the early stages of the war, when in a measure to meet the void, the Imperial authorities set about creating a number of first aid assistants from the ranks, and the Canadian service, being a component element of the Imperial army, automatically followed suit.

TOTAL OTHER RANKS OF C.A.V.C. The total number of other ranks in the Canadian Army Veterinary Corps in July, 1918, was as follows: in England - 64; in France - 715; Total: 779.[2]

PAY The scale of pay per day was the same as that in other units, viz:

	Pay	Field Allowance		Pay	Field Allowance
Trooper	$1.00	.10	Staff Sergeant	$1.60	.20
Corporal	$1.10	.10	Warrant Officer		
Sergeant	$1.35	.15	(First Class)	$2.00	.30

CHAPTER 3

EARLY DAYS AT VALCARTIER AND VOYAGE TO ENGLAND

Sections Ready It has been stated that an expansible framework or nucleus for a comprehensive veterinary service had been created, but it must not be understood from this that the general scheme had been put into an actual state of operation, for such was not the case. Indeed, the whole project existed largely on paper and at the outbreak of the war, but two of the Sections, namely those of Winnipeg and Montreal, were in a state approaching anything like organization.[1]

These two Sections had brought themselves to a degree of readiness that fitted them to attend training camps but it can scarcely be said that they were in a condition enabling them to take the field in a campaign of the sort that was now looming up. They were not even equipped for overseas service, and excepting those of the two Sections mentioned, the majority of the officers of the corps lacked military experience, which naturally increased the difficulties to be contended with in order to maintain the standard of efficiency absolutely necessary for the proper conduct of veterinary duties during a campaign.

Winnipeg Section On the call to arms, the Section of Winnipeg left home on August 23rd, 1914, and proceeded to Valcartier Camp, concentrating with a nominal roll of 3 officers and 23 other ranks, composed as follows:

Officers Captain H.J. Elliott, Lieutenants H. Colebourn and C.E. Edgett

Non-commissioned officers Staff Sergeant F. Johnson, Sergeants T.H. Southern, W. Denton, J. Cameron and J. Burton, Corporals J.A. Court, G.L. Brodie and J. Farr.

Troopers Troopers G. Chase, A. Henderson, W. Miller, J. McKay, H. Oliver, A.G. Evans, N. Buckboro, J.A. Mullen, S. Richards, J. Walmsley, J. Skinner, J. Salmon, F.A. McCourt and J. Hembroff.

Valcartier[2] On arrival at Valcartier, both officers and other ranks at once proceeded to pitch their tents and of their own initiative to establish sick lines for the area, though no instructions had been issued as to their line of action. The work was facilitated by the readiness with which the ordnance and engineer services supplied every need. By this prompt action, the Section made its presence known, the other units thereby becoming aware that the Canadian Army Veterinary Corps was on the spot and ready to lend its assistance in its own special capacity.

Figure 3.1. Section 10, C.A.V.C., Winnipeg, at Valcartier, bell tents behind.[3] Identifiable are Lieut. C.E. Edgett, middle row, second from right, and Lieut. Harry Colebourn, middle row, second from left. Officer seated middle row with Stetson hat is probably H.J. Elliott. On ground front fourth from left is Cpl. G.I. Brodie. Bear cub 'Winnie' is in lap of man to right of Brodie. (*NAC PA 203595*)

EARLY ACTIVITIES It was well that these preparations had been made as the need immediately became apparent, for influenza broke out amongst the horses of the various units and the sick lines had soon to be enlarged until they occupied the entire area allotted to the Section. Two incidents soon occurred which added a little variety to the work. A stampede took place at midnight in the remount depot at the far end of the camp. Details were at once despatched to render first aid and escort injured animals to the lines, where other details awaited their arrival. Another stampede occurred at the same place a few days later. A feature which made both of these stampedes of more than usual interest was the fact that the remount depot was not sufficiently enclosed to prevent the horses getting into the adjacent river with the result that some were drowned. Soon after this episode, comfortable stables were erected for the use of the Section.

A.D.V.S. APPOINTED Meanwhile, Lieutenant-Colonel W.J. Neill had been appointed Assistant Director of Veterinary Services of the first contingent,[4] and with other officers of the corps together with individual officers who were arriving independently and with the assembling regimental units, there came into being the nucleus of the overseas veterinary services which it was necessary to organize forthwith for the Canadian Expeditionary Force (Appendix E).

FIELD VETERINARY HOSPITAL ESTABLISHED As there were over 9,000 horses in Valcartier Camp it was decided to establish a field veterinary hospital, the personnel of which was furnished by the Winnipeg Section with five officers of the Canadian Army Veterinary Corps attached. By these means, hundreds of serious cases of disease and injury were successfully treated and returned to their respective units, debilitated animals being passed through the convalescent lines of the remount depot. Veterinary equipment and supplies were purchased at Ottawa and Quebec and to each veterinary officer were issued quantities sufficient to carry him overseas, all contingencies being considered and provided for.

Despite the inevitable difficulties encountered through congestion of traffic and bad roads, the issue of forage provided by the Canadian Army Service Corps was all that could be desired, the quantity of hay, oats, etc., being ample and the quality generally first-class. The lack of a convenient water supply was a source of considerable trouble at first, there being no water mains. During the period the camp was being piped, the horses had to be taken to the river at a point some distance below the intake for the supply of the troops, and the time consumed by this operation naturally interfered very much with the feeding and training hours.

C.A.V.C. MASCOT Like most of the other units, the veterinary corps had its mascot in the form of a bear cub, which Lieutenant Colebourn had bought on his way down to camp (Figure 3.2). The cub accompanied the first contingent overseas but had to be left behind in England when the First Division went to France. It, however, found a permanent place of abode at the Zoological Gardens in London.[5]

Figure 3.2. 'Winnie', mascot of the C.A.V.C. Winnipeg contingent, with Lieut. Harry Colebourn at Salisbury Plain, late 1914. (*Manitoba Provincial Archives Colebourn Coll. 8, N10466*)

EMBARKATION Embarkation began at Quebec on September 23rd, 1914, and continued until September 30th, 1914, when the last ship containing horses moved out from the quay to its rendezvous in Gaspé Basin, where the convoy was organized for the voyage to England. Owing to the very incomplete state of stalling on shipboard, due to the limited time at the disposal of the working parties, the work of loading was much hindered. However, all horses were embarked without casualty and much credit was due to all who performed that arduous duty. There had been a serious outbreak of strangles (Appendix F) prior to embarkation and which persisted during the trip but the attention bestowed on the infected horses by the veterinary officers reduced the losses therefrom to a minimum.

SHIPS Following is a list of the ships containing horses, the numbers in each and the number of losses sustained en route:

Ship	No. of horses	Losses en route
S/S Athenia	331	7
S/S Montezuma	973	6
S/S Manitoba	592	9
S/S Corinthian	298	4
S/S Ivernian	634	7
S/S Sicilian	518	11
S/S Montreal	819	6
S/S Alaunia	19	-
S/S Royal George	11	-
S/S Lakonia	631	12
S/S Grampion	660	8
S/S Monmouth	605	5
S/S Manhattan	863	11
S/S Iona	682	-
Total	**7,636**	**86**

VOYAGE BEGUN It was a great relief to all concerned when orders were issued on the morning of October 3rd, 1914, to move out, for until that time the horses on the lower decks had suffered intensely from lack of ventilation due to the ships being stationary, some of them having been at the rendezvous for seven days. A large number of animals developed sickness but a marked improvement became evident a few days after the ships were in motion and the vitiated atmosphere of the lower decks cleared. After an uneventful voyage of 12 days, the transports arrived at Plymouth, where disembarkation took place. The horses, on the whole, stood the trip remarkably well, the losses en route being notably small as the preceding table shows, a tribute to the skill and devotion of the veterinary officers in charge.[6]

Figure 3.3. Officers, C.A.V.C., 1914.[7] L-r. Lieut. J.J. McCarrey, Capt. T.C. Evans, Lieut. E. Strathy, Lieut.-Col. M.A. Piché, P.V.O. Division 4, Capt. F.A. Daigneault, and Lieut. Louis Grignon. (*Merillat & Campbell, p. 346*)

CHAPTER 4

ARRIVAL IN ENGLAND - SALISBURY PLAIN

DISEMBARKATION[1] On arrival at Devonport, the horses were kept on board an unnecessary length of time, in some cases four or five days, and owing to the vessels not being in motion, the ventilation on the lower deck became very bad, which caused a great deal of catarrhal signs and a number of cases of pneumonia. Of the sick, 40 had to be detained at Devonport, of which 11 died or were destroyed.

When landing was finally accomplished, it was found there was a shortage of head gear and picketing ropes, so that the animals had to be tied to vehicles by whatever loose straps and ropes were at hand.

DIFFICULTIES For leading the horses from the ships to the entraining point, Imperial Territorial troops were employed and since these men were unaccustomed to handling horses, a number of the latter broke away and much valuable time was lost in trying to recover them. This difficulty was taken advantage of by some unprincipled men amongst the Canadian troops disposing of horses to citizens of Plymouth and a good deal of trouble was experienced in recovering the same, the assistance of the police having to be invoked. The missing animals were eventually identified, thanks to the Canadian army brand.

In the meantime, Lieutenant-Colonel Neill, having landed on October 16th, proceeded to Salisbury Plain, where he inspected the Lines and completed arrangements for the reception of the horses.

TRANSPORTATION TO SALISBURY PLAIN The transportation of the horses from Plymouth to Salisbury Plain was carried out without casualty, the railway officials rendering every assistance that lay in their power. The time occupied in this task was about seven days.

TRIALS AND TRIBULATIONS Upon arrival at Salisbury Plain, the veterinary corps was assigned to a place known as West Down South,[2] where again, owing to lack of head ropes, halters and picketing gear, the animals had to be tied up to trees and vehicles by any odd piece of rope or strap that could be found. Then began a series of trials that would have disheartened any but the most resolute. Complete absence of shelter, almost continuous rain and a biting wind that swept down from the neighboring hills, all conduced to bring about a most deplorable situation. The animals were soon standing in a veritable sea of mud and every time one raised its foot it sank deeper and deeper into the mire, a condition that led to the development of a large number of cases of gangrenous dermatitis for which in several instances there was no remedy but the destruction of the afflicted. The few blankets that were obtained scarcely improved matters for they soon became soaked and plastered with mud and even the hay was blown away from in front of the horses by the force of the wind.

OUTBREAK OF DISEASE As might be expected, this state of affairs was responsible for the death of a number of horses not fully recovered from the effects of the sea voyage[3] and for an outbreak of influenza and pneumonia that supervened. There was also an outbreak of ringworm which spread very rapidly, due in large measure to the impossibility of carrying out proper grooming, but this disease was soon stamped out by isolation and proper treatment. In the course of a few weeks, an improvement was effected by partial removal to Keeper's Farm,[2] where cow barns were made use of for shelter.

FIELD HOSPITAL At West Down South it had been necessary to set up a field hospital, where all serious cases were sent for treatment. Owing to the entire absence of shelter for the patients, this work was carried out under extremely adverse conditions, but the results achieved were satisfactory. The hospital was taken in charge by the original No. 10 Section from Winnipeg, with Lieutenant M.G. O'Gogarty in command, but with the arrival of Nos. 3 and 4 Veterinary Sections from Canada[4] at the end of November, 1914, the duties were taken over by the latter. These two units had, in the meantime, been organized and fully equipped with remarkable celerity in Montreal, each with a personnel 115 strong, by Lieutenant-Colonel M.A. Piché,[5] Principal Veterinary Officer of the Fourth Divisional Area, the first under Captain T.C. Evans, and the second under Captain F.A. Daigneault, getting away two weeks later (Figures 3.2, 3.3 and 4.1).

SECTIONS REORGANIZED No. 10 Section was then reorganized into Nos. 1 and 2 Veterinary Mobile Sections and Base Depot of Veterinary Supplies, under Lieutenants O'Gogarty, Edwards and Frape, respectively. No. 3 Veterinary Section and the two new mobile Sections moved to the cavalry barracks at Netheravon,[2] No. 4 Veterinary Section remaining in charge of the hospital at Keeper's Farm with Major J.H. Wilson in command. No. 2 Mobile Section was later disbanded, part of the personnel going to strengthen No. 1 Mobile Section and the remainder being transferred to No. 3 Veterinary Section and to the Base Depot.

No. 1 Mobile Section proceeded as such to France with the First Division, whilst the reinforced No. 3 Veterinary Section became No. 1 Veterinary Hospital, and after it had brought up the strength of its personnel to nearly double the original figure by transfer of suitable men from practically every unit on the Plains, proceeded, about two months later, to take up its permanent location at Havre, France. No. 4 Veterinary Section remained in England, going towards the summer of 1915, to Shorncliffe to become No. 2 Canadian Veterinary Hospital and where it also increased its strength in a manner similar to No. 1 and carried on its functions not only as a hospital, but as the regimental depot of the corps till the end of 1917, when it was disbanded, the personnel being mainly transferred to No. 1 Veterinary Hospital at Havre.

INSPECTION BY IMPERIAL AUTHORITIES In a report of an inspection made by Major-General F. Smith,[6] Deputy Director of Veterinary Services (Imperial), in January, 1915, he remarked that he had found Lieutenant-Colonel Neill to be a capable officer with a good grip of service requirements, that he had closely supervised the organization and training of his branch and was well supported by his officers.[7] Though he did not regard horsemastership as a strong point in the force yet, veterinary advice was followed and encouraged and officers of the unit were receiving practical training which reflected itself in the condition of the animals. He drew especial attention to a certain group of horses stating that it was doubtful whether a civilian horsemaster would credit the fact that those particular horses had been in the open for weeks during the weather experienced that winter on Salisbury Plains, so excellent was their condition, which proved conclusively that it was the horsemastership and not the weather which had to be taken into account, and that the whole question hinged on the supervision by the officers and that nothing could take its place.

Figure 4.1. Postcard of the Canadian Contingent, Veterinary Corps.
No. 4 Section C.A.V.C. from Montreal.[8] The Veterinary Officers are Capt. F.A. Daigneault (front, 4th from right) and Lieut. L. Grignon (front, 3rd from right). (*C.A.V. Barker Museum*)

CHAPTER 5

SHORNCLIFFE AND OTHER AREAS

SHORNCLIFFE AREA.
(a) The Shorncliffe area
(b) No. 2 Canadian Veterinary Hospital
(c) The Canadian Veterinary Training School
(d) The Instructional School for Farriers

OTHER AREAS
The Shoreham and Seaford areas
The Crowborough area
The Bramshott area
The Witley area
The Borden area
The Canadian Railway Troops Depot
The Canadian Forestry Corps Depot

THE SHORNCLIFFE AREA
At the beginning of 1915 the location for the training of Canadian troops was transferred from Salisbury Plain to the important military encampment of Shorncliffe, which place for several decades had served as a training station for the British army and where commodious barracks existed.

ORIGIN OF SHORNCLIFFE CAMP It was in 1794, when England was menaced with invasion on the part of the French, that an encampment was first established at Shorncliffe and it was through the establishment of this encampment that the neighboring town of Sandgate came into existence. It was at Shorncliffe that Sir John Moore, the hero of Coruna and subject of the famous poem, directed the training of many of those regiments which afterwards proved themselves invincible during the Peninsular War. On the resumption of peace in 1815, the encampment was gradually abandoned until the outbreak of the Crimean War in 1854, when it was once more utilized and since then it has continued in active existence. It is worthy of note that the German contingent of the Foreign Legion, some 3000 strong, raised for participation in the Crimean conflict, was accommodated in wooden huts at the encampment.

CANADA AT SHORNCLIFFE IN 1858 The arrival of the Canadian contingent in 1915 was not the first appearance of troops of Canadian origin at this historic spot, for in 1858 there marched into the encampment, direct from Canada, the newly-formed Prince of Wales's Royal Canadian or 100th Regiment of Infantry, raised by the people of Canada as a spontaneous offering to the Imperial army. This body of men, recruited largely from amongst lumbermen and hardy pioneers of those days, was remarkable for the physical development of its members, over 400 of whom were of herculean strength and stature. It remained some time at Shorncliffe, went later to Gibraltar and Malta, and returned to Canada at the time of the Fenian troubles in 1866. Eventually it was merged with another battalion and is now represented by the Prince of Wales's Leinster Regiment.

BEAUTIFUL SURROUNDINGS All who had the good fortune to pass some summer months at Shorncliffe will recall with feelings of admiration the lovely prospect that is offered to view from the camp. The scenery, viewed from any point, but particularly westward from the vicinity of the garrison church over the valley towards Hythe and the country beyond, is exceedingly picturesque. To the north the landscape is set off by the range of hills known as the Downs, giving prominence to the eminence called Caesar's Camp, where to this day may be seen the entrenchments thrown up by the Romans; to the south is the sea affording in the distance on a clear day a view of the coast of France; whilst to the east, intersected by a pretty valley, appear the habitations of modern Folkestone framed in the distance by the chalk hills of Dover.

FOLKESTONE Two miles from Shorncliffe Camp lies Folkestone, easily reached by footpath or road or by the more expeditious method of motorbus, whilst six miles beyond is the great naval base of Dover. With the exception of certain defined areas, Folkestone was at all time 'in bounds' to the troops, and when off duty the latter were privileged to wend their way thither to make their purchases at the well-stocked shops or to wile away their leisure hours in the enjoyment of the numerous attractions, namely, sea bathing, roller-skating, high-class theatrical performances, vaudeville and moving picture shows, or to stroll on the famous cliff promenade known as the Leas, whence they could gaze out on the blue of the Channel or watch the passage to and fro of the military transports. Beyond question, considering the health giving climate of that part of Britain's coast, it would be difficult to conceive of a more delightful environment in which to pursue one's daily vocation.

TRAINING CENTRE At the Shorncliffe Camp, the Second Division and units of the Third were prepared for their part in the conflict and after the departure of the latter the area was still maintained for the training of reserve units of all arms, excepting the Siege Artillery, for supplying reinforcing drafts to the troops at the front. There being of necessity a large number of horses (6000 during the winter of 1915-1916) to serve such a considerable body of men, the area logically presented itself as a centre for training operations of the Canadian Army Veterinary Corps in England and made necessary the establishment of a hospital which became known as No. 2 Canadian Veterinary Hospital.

SCOPE OF WORK The scope of the veterinary work in this area being very extensive, it was administered by an Assistant Director of Veterinary Services, whose duties were:

Inspection of all horses and mules allocated to the units within the area
Posting of veterinary officers and personnel to units within the area and supervision of their work
Supervision of No. 2 Canadian Veterinary Hospital
Supervision of Canadian Veterinary Training School
Supervision of the temporary Canadian Remount Depot

A.D.V.S. The officers who served in this capacity were:

Lieutenant-Colonel (at first Major) J.H. Wilson, from April, 1915 to July, 1916
Lieutenant-Colonel H.D. Smith, from July, 1916 to November, 1916
Acting Lieutenant-Colonel (at first Acting Major) F. Walsh from November, 1916 to February, 1918

These officers conducted their duties with a small clerical staff varying from 2 to 5 in number.

DECLINE At the beginning of 1918, because of the dwindling in importance of the veterinary interests in the area and the disbandment of No. 2 Canadian Veterinary Hospital as a depot for the corps, there was no longer any need for the rank and station of an Assistant Director of Veterinary Services and thereafter the area was administered by a Senior Veterinary Officer of the rank of captain. Lieutenant-Colonel Walsh continued till September, 1918, in the new capacity but had to relinquish both his higher acting ranks and revert to captaincy. On his case being reviewed and when his return to Canada as a surplus officer was imminent, he was given the substantive rank of major.

ADMINISTRATIVE METHODS The units within the area possessed of a large number of horses, such as the Reserve Regiment of Cavalry and Field Artillery had each a veterinary officer and an assisting sergeant of the corps exclusively attached to them, whilst units disposing of but few mounts, such as the infantry battalions, were grouped and depended for veterinary care on an attached sergeant of the corps quartered with the unit most conveniently situated and a veterinary officer doing duty at No. 2 Canadian Veterinary Hospital, who made daily rounds of inspection. Thus, the outlying units in East and West Sandling, Westenhanger and Etching Hill formed one allocation, whilst the nearby units at St. Martin's Plain, Caesar's Camp, Dibgate and Shorncliffe, Divisional Headquarters and the Canadian Mounted Police, formed another.

The aforesaid cavalry and artillery units maintained each its own sick lines where horses suffering from trouble of a transitory or non-contagious nature were treated instead of evacuating them to the main hospital, in a manner similar to that followed in the field in France. When the contingency for evacuation arose, it entailed striking the animal permanently off the strength of its unit and transferring it to that of the hospital whereby the unit was rendered short of a mount until replacement could be effected from the hospital remount lines which, in turn, depended on the availability at the time of the type of horse required. Naturally, the officers commanding such units were loath to see their animals evacuated since it involved temporarily incapacitating an equivalent number of troopers or artillerymen from active training; they, therefore, encouraged local treatment though at all times deferring to the discretionary opinion of the veterinary officer. In none of the other units was any attempt made at carrying out treatment excepting of troubles of a minor nature, any animal requiring actual hospital attention being evacuated to the main hospital.

REMOUNTS When a remount was required to replace an animal that had been evacuated to the hospital or otherwise to bring up to full strength the authorized establishment of any particular unit, an indent had to be made by the commanding officer of the unit on the temporary remount depot conducted since August, 1915, in connection with the main hospital, which indent had first to be approved by the Assistant Director of Veterinary Services of the area, who was thus enabled to keep a check on the whereabouts of each individual animal. A unit that had been obliged to evacuate one of its animals to the hospital could never be certain of getting back that particular animal, since all animals were supposed to be impartially issued from remounts after they had passed into the same from the hospital lines; nevertheless, an effort was always made to reassign a horse to the unit from which it had originally come, because of the particular training such animal had undergone.

At one time, the practice arose of chargers being brought in by officers from outside sources, of indiscriminate transferring from one unit to another or of making exchanges at the remount depot without the knowledge or sanction of the competent authority, action that caused considerable interference with the keeping of accurate records and anxiety over the risk of introduction of contagious maladies from without. In consequence, it became necessary to issue positive orders forbidding the irregular introduction, transfer or exchange of horses within the area.

NO. 2 CANADIAN VETERINARY HOSPITAL

LOCATION As already stated, it was at the beginning of April, 1915, that the Section, originally organized in Montreal as No. 4, took up its quarters at Shorncliffe, as No. 2 Canadian Veterinary Hospital, occupying a portion of the stables of Ross Barracks. For the first three months, the members of the personnel were quartered in the barracks, but they then moved to an adjoining tract of open land overlooking the pretty valley of the Enbrook Estate where they were sheltered under canvas for the remainder of the summer, going to nearby billets or other barracks in winter. It cannot be said that the men were comfortably accommodated every winter. The first part of the winter of 1916-1917 sufficient huts were at their disposal at St. Martin's Plain, but the number allotted to them was very soon reduced on account of the arrival of other troops in the area and a certain proportion was obliged to take up quarters under canvas in the open for the remainder of the winter. The tents were old and leaky and in consequence, the sick list became heavy which greatly impeded the work of the hospital. Even the cooking had to be done in a tent which had been condemned as unfit and the messing arrangements had to be made in a marquee which was entirely unsatisfactory.

DEVELOPMENT In September, 1915, the hospital was transferred to the rows of loose boxes to the north of Ross Barracks till then occupied by the Imperial Veterinary Corps. In pace with the development of requirements, it became necessary to increase the extent of the hospital confines by the erection of several additional rows of open structures of galvanized iron, which came to be familiarly known as 'the tin stables' (Figure 5.1).

FUNCTIONS The hospital not only fulfilled the function which its name indicates but it became in addition the regimental depot and training and reinforcing base of the corps, a temporary Remount Department, the home of the Canadian Veterinary Training School and the Base Depot of Veterinary Supplies after the latter had been broken up at Salisbury Plain.

Figure 5.1. No. 2 Canadian Veterinary Hospital, Shorncliffe, England, the 'tin stables'. Entrance in 1917. (*NAC PA 5005*)

PERSONNEL The strength of its personnel was kept going by influx of new officers and a few recruits direct from Canada, by casualties from the front and by transfers from other branches of the service; and it supplied trained reinforcements direct to No. 1 Canadian Veterinary Hospital at Havre for reposting to the divisions at the front as well as to detached units in both France and England from amongst its most physically fit, its men of low categories being retained to form the permanent hospital staff. It was a completely self-contained unit. It had at all times a complement of veterinary officers, sergeants trained to assist the latter and to act as dressers, quartermaster, warrant officers and a number of regimental sergeants, corporals, troopers and grooms, sufficient to take care of all contingencies excepting those of a very extraordinary nature.

TRAINING OF MOBILE SECTIONS We have seen in the preceding chapter that two of the mobile veterinary sections, which during the entire period of the war performed such valuable service, were formed at Salisbury Plain, that one of these proceeded to France with the First Division and that the other was disbanded. With the exception of the initial permanent one referred to, all the mobile sections that were subsequently prepared for service with the succeeding divisions and with the Cavalry Brigade were organized at Shorncliffe. We shall read of their good work in a separate chapter.

ADMINISTRATION The hospital was divided into four departments known respectively as A, B, C, and D Lines, besides the remount depot alluded to above. The first named was devoted to the isolation and eradication of parasitic skin diseases, the second was used for the treatment of all kinds of lameness, the third for medical and surgical cases, whilst the fourth served as a convalescent quarter for the reconditioning of debilitated animals after the discharge of the latter from the other departments, each department being looked after by one of the four troops composing the personnel.

The strength of the four troops was varied by interchange from day to day, to meet the needs of the respective departments, but it was occasionally necessary to draw fatigue parties from other units in the area to supplement the hospital staff when the latter was insufficient to properly care for any unusual increase in the number of inmates. It is laid down in the regulations governing the Imperial Army Veterinary Services that orderlies in the proportion of one to three (or less) horses should be detailed to afford the attention required by sick animals but the numbers of both personnel and patients being at all times inconstant, owing to continuous comings and goings, there was never a fixed relationship between the attendants and their charges. When the four troops were up to full strength and patients not plentiful, the latter received ample care and attention and it was, moreover, possible to detail fatigue parties to undertake the innumerable jobs that arise round a military camp, but when the conditions were reversed, all hands were hard pressed to cope with the work which it was not permissible under any circumstances to leave undone.

NUMBER OF HORSES UNDER TREATMENT The greatest number of animals taken on the strength of the hospital proper at any one time was in the spring of 1916 when 370 were under treatment, whilst the greatest number of animals cared for at any one time, including both sick ones and healthy remounts was in the neighborhood of 800 in January, 1916, when artillery detachments departing for France left a large number of horses behind. Shortly after this, there was a total of 2686 horses in the Shorncliffe area. In the fall of 1916, when there was a serious outbreak of mange (Appendix F), there were over 250 cases of that disease under treatment at one time.

There was no dipping tank at Shorncliffe, though plans were prepared by Captain E.A. Watson, for the construction of one at an estimated cost of from £130 to £150 ($650 to $750). But, difficulty being experienced in obtaining the necessary authority for its construction in the Shorncliffe area, the project was abandoned and instead a sulphur fume sweat box was erected by the artificers of the unit. This did not prove satisfactory and the most effective treatment was by means of a spray of calcium sulphide (see Fig. 16.1), prepared as follows: sulphur - 11 ounces; quicklime - 5 ounces; water - 1 gallon; boiled for 4 hours, water being added to maintain the original level.

The animal being clipped, it was dressed with a dilution of 1 part of the solution to 3 of water, and left untouched for 3 days. At the end of this period, it was groomed and again dressed with the solution in increased strength. Afterwards, the treatment was repeated every 4 days with undiluted solution till a cure was effected.

In November, 1917, glanders (Appendix F) was discovered in the lines, nine animals that reacted to the mallein test (Figures 5.2, 5.3) having to be destroyed.[1] With relation to the total number of horses in the area, it was generally reckoned that an average of 10%, including both sick and healthy remounts, would be within the hospital lines at a time.

The Imperial Military Police at Folkestone disposed of about 20 horses for their own use and it was arranged as an act of courtesy that an officer from the hospital should undertake veterinary service for the same and make an inspection twice weekly. No charge was made for this service, but whenever it became necessary to bring any of these animals into the lines for treatment, a charge of 2s.6d. (60 cents) per day was made to cover cost of forage and medicines. A similar charge was made by the Imperial authorities for the care of horses of Canadian units that had to be taken to Imperial hospitals at other points in England. Shoeing of the police horses was also done at the School of Farriery at 4s.6d. ($1.10) per set, 147 sets being supplied between April and December, 1917, at a total charge of £33.1s.6d. ($160).

COMMANDING OFFICERS The commanding officers covering the entire period of the hospital's existence were as follows:

Lieutenant-Colonel (at first Major) J.H. Wilson[2] from April, 1915, till September, 1915
Captain R. Waddy, from September, 1915 till January, 1916
Captain E.A. Watson, from January, 1916 till March, 1916
Captain J.F. Wood, from March, 1916 till February, 1917
Captain V.C. Best, from February, 1917 till October, 1917
Captain M.G. O'Gogarty, from November, 1917 till disbandment

Major Wilson, during the period of his incumbency was also charged with the responsibility of administering the veterinary affairs of the entire area, in consequence of which it was found necessary to relieve him of active duty at the hospital and to appoint in his place, consecutively, in acting capacity, Captains H.J. Elliot and W.T. Rogers.

Directions for using the Special Mallein for the Intradermopalpebral Test.

1. While under the test animals should be left at rest and in an atmosphere which is as far as possible free from dust.

2. The dose of the special mallein is one-tenth cc., or roughly 2 drops.

It is injected into the thickness of the lower eyelid by means of a small hypodermic syringe of 1cc. capacity fitted with adjustable piston and a special needle having a short shank. Both syringe and needle should be sterilised by boiling in water for five minutes before use.

3. In making the injection one may adopt one of two procedures. One may either pinch up a fold of skin close to the edge of the eyelid or one may introduce the forefinger into the conjunctival sac and grasp the lid between this finger and the thumb.

As a rule no restraint beyond a headrope or a halter is necessary.

4. While it is of little importance if the dose specified be slightly exceeded, great care should be taken to see that a smaller quantity be not introduced.

5. A typical reaction in a glandered animal is shown by :—

(i) Swelling of the eyelid injected.

(ii) Inflammatory changes in the conjunctival sac

Wt.1983/R1671. 60M. 6/17. B.&F.,Ltd. EB61. G17/360 (3):

(i) In most non-glandered animals a slight swelling of the eyelid injected is shown within the first 24 hours, but this does not persist and is of no significance.

If the animal be glandered, the swelling which is at all times extremely painful continues to increase in size during the second 24 hours and does not completely disappear for several days. Though there are varying degrees of reaction, the swelling is often so considerable as to almost close the eye.

(ii) Inflammatory changes in the conjunctival sac are shown by more or less marked congestion of the conjunctival vessels and increased lachrymation accompanied by the accumulation of mucopus at the inner canthus.

In all cases comparison should be made with the opposite eye which is left as a control.

If one eye shews any deviation from the normal, such as increased lachrymation, etc., the sound eye should be chosen for the test.

6. If the animal gives a doubtful reaction he should be isolated (together with his stable kit) and retested in the other eye after the lapse of a week, or one may apply the ordinary subcutaneous test after a similar lapse of time.

7. A record of the test should be kept in A.F. C331.

8. The mallein should be kept in a cool place and protected from light. Should it lose its transparency or become cloudy it must not be used

ARMY VETERINARY SCHOOL,
ALDERSHOT.

Figure 5.2. Intrapalpebral skin test for glanders using special mallein. See also Figure 5.3. (*French Papers, NAC*)

In the summer of 1917, Captain Best fell ill[3] and was not again able to perform his duties and during that period and until just previous to disbandment, Captains C.T. Beaven, J.R.J. Duhault, J.T.M. Hughes and Lieutenant W.J. Prinn carried on in acting capacity.

DISCIPLINE Discipline at the hospital, though of the nature with which every soldier from the Dominions was familiar, was well and impartially maintained without the necessity of having frequent recourse to the corrective influences of the orderly room, a fact attributable in no small degree to the admirable tact and good example shown by both officers and non-commissioned officers, particularly to the efforts of the four warrant officers who administered the disciplinary duties that fell to their lot. The warrant officers were:

WARRANT OFFICERS Acting Sergeant-Major (then Staff Sergeant) H. Foster, from April, 1915 till October, 1915
Sergeant-Major J. Cotton (1st class) from October, 1915 till April, 1916
Sergeant-Major A. Newell (1st class) from April, 1916 till December, 1916
Sergeant-Major J. Cotton, from December,1916 till September,1917
Sergeant-Major T.A. Moore (2nd class) from September, 1917 till November, 1917
Sergeant-Major J. Cotton, from November, 1917 till disbandment

Figure 5.3. Minimum response to intrapalpebral mallein justifying destruction of a horse as a reactor. Eyelid swollen and conjunctivitis (pus in conjunctival space). (*Merillat & Campbell, p. 830*)

DAILY ROUTINE The working hours of the morning and afternoon were devoted to the general care of the horses in the hospital, to instructional courses and to fatigue work. The daily routine varied slightly according to the season of the year and the needs of the hospital work, but that in force during the fall of 1917, when the personnel were under canvas, may be taken as an example:

5:30 a. m.	Reveille	11:50	Delivery of mail
5:45	Sick parade	12:00 p. m.	Dismiss
6:00	Fall in and stables	12:15	Dinner
6:30	Water	1:30	Fall in and stables
6:45	Feed	4:30	Water
7:00	Dismiss	4:45	Feed
7:15	Breakfast		Fall in picket for night
8:30	General parade	4:50	Delivery of mail
8:35	Stables	5:00	Dismiss
10:00	Disposal of disciplinary cases within the jurisdiction of the commanding officer	5:15	Supper
		9:00	Roll call by orderly sergeant from tent to tent
11:30	Water	10:15	Lights out
11:45	Feed		

The routine of the attached class of farriers was similar except that it was carried out one-half hour earlier.

ADORNMENT OF SURROUNDINGS When the corps took over the structures and surroundings that ultimately became the hospital, the approaches and open ground were in a deplorable condition, becoming in bad weather little better than a quagmire. In fact, so bad were the conditions after a heavy rain up till the summer of 1916 that it was impossible at times to exercise the horses for fear of their becoming mired. Eventually, this state of affairs was righted, and there being no lack amongst the men of a due proportion with individual taste for pretty surroundings, that which in 1915 had been a desolate waste became, by the summer of 1916, under the painstaking and fostering care of Sergeants A. Winwood and F. Davey, one of the most attractive little spots in the area, adorned with lawns, rustic fences and charming floral effects; nor were utilitarian considerations neglected, for several bushels of choice potatoes were raised in out-of-the-way corners and served to supplement the army rations.

OFFICERS BILLETED During the greater part of the nearly three years' occupancy of the camp, the officers for the most part lived out in billets in either Cheriton or Folkestone, or partook of their meals in the messes of the officers of other units, as there were never enough of them continuously on hand to enable them to maintain a mess of their own, nor, excepting for a period of three or four months during 1915, were quarters allotted for that purpose.

RATIONS The non-commissioned officers and men were provided for in camp, at first by the Imperial system known as 'short rationing and commuted allowances' through which the army authorities supplied seven staple articles, viz. fresh meat or fish, bacon, bread, tea, sugar, salt and pepper, and supplemented the same with a cash allowance of 5 1/2d. (11 cents) per day per man, to enable the soldiers to furnish themselves with additional foodstuffs of their own choice, which they did of the following articles: rolled oats, condensed milk, butter, potatoes, green vegetables, materials for making puddings and sometimes extra meat.

Later, when the prices of all foodstuffs had risen greatly, this system was substituted by that known as 'long varied rationing' in which a full and complete dietary of a caloric value of 3,200 was provided in lieu of part rations and part cash, and it was the consensus of opinion that the change proved more than satisfactory. The cooking, under the skillful direction of Sergeant J. Richardson, left nothing to be desired and there was rarely any complaint concerning the food served to the unit. Though there was invariably sufficient food to satisfy the demands of a healthy appetite, rigid economy at all times prevailed; nothing was wasted, even left-over bread scraps being subsequently made over into appetizing puddings.

RECOVERY OF FATS In line with the demand for nation-wide conservation of all resources, it was required by War Office order that kitchen refuse be submitted to a process for the recovery of fats. Accordingly, a series of trap-tanks was constructed in the ground outside the cookhouse into which dish-water was conducted and allowed to settle; the grease rising to the surface was skimmed and collected and turned over to agents of the munition factories to be reduced into glycerin and finally to appear as explosives.

N.C.O.'S MESS The non-commissioned officers conducted a mess of their own to which a subscription fee of 2s.6d. (60 cents) was charged, and after the first year they instituted a bar in connection with the same, at which, besides tobacco and cigarettes, whiskey, brandy, gin, rum and port wine would be obtained, but at which the bulk of the liquor consumed consisted of mild ale and non-alcoholic gingerbeer. The prices charged fluctuated between 4d. (8 cents) and 6d. (12 cents) per drink of spirituous liquors, 5d. (10 cents) and 7d. (14 cents) per pint of ale and 4d. (8 cents) per pint of gingerbeer. It was an army regulation that a profit of 33 1/3% must be made on the sale of all drinks. Tobacco was sold at 5d. (10 cents) to 8d. (16 cents) per ounce and cigarettes at 4d. (8 cents) to 5d. (10 cents) per package of ten.

MEN'S CANTEEN In the men's canteen, on the other hand, the only liquor sold consisted of very mild ale, on which a profit of 25% had to be made, and the price charged varied from 4d. (8 cents) to 5d. (10 cents) per pint. To the credit of the corps, it should be added that moderation prevailed at all times, there were no instances of abuse of canteen privileges and it was never necessary to inflict punishment for drunkenness arising from the same. Out of the profits so obtained arose two funds which were always maintained in a healthy state, and which, under the supervision of the officers, served to provide the means for the extension of hospitality and the performance of acts of charity. In 1917, the non-commissioned officers who had hitherto made use of a marquee, were enabled to expend a sum of £100 (nearly $500) on the purchase of material for the erection of a comfortable frame mess building in which a rented piano was subsequently installed.

ENTERTAINMENT In a truly noteworthy spirit of generosity, on one occasion the sum of £50 (nearly $250) was appropriated for the purchase of tickets for an entertainment given at Folkestone by the blind musicians of St. Dunstan's Hostel of London in aid of blinded heroes of the war. Other appropriations were made from time to time for the purchase of baseball outfits and for prizes for competition at the corps sports. As an indication of the kindly fraternal spirit existing in the ranks, it may be added that it was the custom of the men to expend from their fund various sums in the purchase of cigars and cigarettes and other comforts for distribution amongst those of their comrades who were leaving for the front. Towards the end of 1917, the disbandment of the hospital becoming imminent and the men's canteen having a balance to its credit of close on £140 (nearly $700), a sum of nearly £100 (nearly $500) was disposed of in giving a dinner and smoking concert at the Pavilion Hotel in Folkestone.

The members of the veterinary corps were never backward at lending their assistance to the furtherance of legitimate projects on the part of the civil population for the raising of funds for charitable purposes. At Folkestone, one of the foremost women in getting up entertainments for the benefit of local hospitals was Miss Bridget Keir. In July 1917, she organized a grand fête which was held in the cricket grounds on the Shorncliffe road and to which the men of No. 2 Canadian Veterinary Hospital contributed a fake side show on the Barnum order and incidentally had lots of fun. A marquee was erected and decorated on the outside with a most startling painting of a horse with its head growing out of its rump and its tail out of its neck, and bearing the extraordinary announcement as to its origin depicted in the handbill illustrated (Figure 5.4). Showmen and barkers, all clad in fantastic costumes, invited the public, in approved circus style, to part with its pennies for the privilege of viewing the greatest curiosity of the German army, and the proceedings were further enlivened by discordant music, rendered by an improvised band consisting of cornet, trombone and bass drum. In the interior of the marquee, the great curiosity proved to be a horse, tied up in a roughly constructed stall with its tail towards the manger and its head in the other direction.

AT THE FETE ON SATURDAY
DON'T FAIL TO SEE
"VON LUDENDORFF"
THE
Marvellous Boche Horse
With it's head where its tail ought to be

HISTORY.

This remarkable animal was discovered by Hagenbeck in the wilds of Silesia, and by him presented to the Kaiser. The latter handed it over to Marshal von Hindenburg so that the Marshal could at any time go backwards at a moment's notice. At the Battle of Vimy Ridge the Marshal got the horse so excited that it went the wrong way and was captured by the Canadians who sent it to No. 2 C.V.H. at Shorncliffe to be fixed up right end to.

DON'T MISS THIS!
IT'S SOME HORSE!
ADMISSION - 1D.

AT FOLKESTONE CRICKET GROUND,
Saturday, July 21st, Afternoon & Evening

Figure 5.4. Handbill advertising 'The Marvellous Boche Horse' (*French Papers, NAC*)

SPORTS Sports played no small part in the recreation of the men at Shorncliffe, though it was not until the incumbency of Captains Wood and Best as commanding officers that this form of diversion was fostered to any extent. Football teams were organized and pitted their skill against that of other units, sustaining defeat only in the spring of 1917 at the hands of the 11th Reserve Battalion of Infantry, the champions of the area. In September, 1916, an afternoon was devoted to corps sports, a large concourse of visitors being present, and the events including foot-racing, wrestling on horseback, etc.; on this occasion, amongst many other prizes, a silver cup was offered for competition by Lieutenant-Colonel H.D. Smith (Figure 5.5) and awarded to Sergeant F. Goffin as the best all-round athlete of the hospital.

But, it was in that peculiarly military attainment of tent-pegging that the personnel excelled; not without reason, for who could be expected to be better judges of horseflesh than the members of the veterinary corps? Tent-pegging sections were sent to compete at the sports held by the cavalry in May and September, 1917, and with a single exception, won everything in sight. One section composed of Staff-Sergeant J.A. Reeves, Sergeant A. Leviston, Corporal A. Patriquin and Trooper J. Clake acquired a reputation for invincibility.

ZEPPELIN RAID The Shorncliffe area, at all times within hearing of the gun-fire on the Flanders front, from time to time experienced a full measure of the realities of war through the visitation of enemy aircraft. The first Zeppelin raid over a military encampment took place at Otterpool, at one extremity of the area, at 9 p.m. on October 13th, 1915, when bombs were dropped on the tents and horse lines of the soldiers quartered there and took toll of the lives of a few of the artillerymen. On this occasion some 30 horses were killed and 45 others sustained varying degrees of injury, severe enough to render necessary the removal of all but three to the hospital by ambulance. A considerable distance having to be traversed, since Otterpool lay at one extremity of the area and the hospital at the other, it took two ambulances, each carrying two horses at a trip, the best part of two days to complete the undertaking. Of the injured, one died the day following and four had to be destroyed (Appendix G), the remainder being returned to duty after they had completely recovered.

AEROPLANE RAID Towards evening of May 25th, 1917, occurred the memorable German aeroplane raid on Folkestone and vicinity.[4] Sixteen bombing machines, flying at a great height, passed overhead, eleven of which attacked the numerous camps of the area extending from West Sandling to Shorncliffe, terminating their career of death and destruction by murderous bombing of the inoffensive populace of Folkestone, where a total of 249 casualties occurred, 79 of which ended fatally. Very little harm was done to the camps, but amongst the troops 116 casualties were sustained, including 18 deaths.

No less than six bombs fell within the precincts of the camp of No. 2 Canadian Veterinary Hospital, an area of some four acres in extent, and that no serious harm befell the members of the corps stationed there was little short of marvelous. About 300 personnel in all were in camp, engaged at that hour, namely 6:15 p.m., in recreation after the evening meal. Some 30 were in individual tents and 35 non-commissioned officers were in a marquee holding a meeting. Hearing the noise of repeated explosions drawing nearer and nearer, everybody went outside and on looking upward and observing the unusual flight of machines, instinctively grasped the situation and ran for shelter behind a convenient bank, scarcely reaching the same before the explosions began.

CASUALTIES The only grievous wounding sustained by any member of the corps was suffered by Trooper J. Preston who received in his body 23 splinters from an exploding bomb, from which, however, he ultimately recovered. Trooper J.C. Cuddy was slightly wounded on the left ear whilst Captain N. McCarthy was struck on the side of the head by a clod of earth thrown up by the force of one of the explosions. There were some noteworthy escapes; the non-commissioned officers who were holding the aforesaid meeting had that very morning moved their marquee from a spot upon which a bomb fell, after it had been in position 18 months, and Lieutenant Prinn had just emerged from his tent when another bomb fell immediately outside, riddling that tent and a dozen others, whilst one of the farriers at the time was sitting in a bathtub which was pierced by a fragment of bomb that did not touch him.

SHELTER TRENCHES Soon after the above mentioned raid, it was decided that the soldiers throughout the area must provide themselves with adequate means of protection against the recurrence of the menace which seemed likely to threaten them, so it was required that shelter trenches be constructed. At the veterinary hospital a series of trenches was speedily dug at points easy of access from quarters, and some of the men improved the occasion by tunneling into the banks which bordered the enclosure.

AIR RAID WARNING Many were the occasions, thereafter, on the receipt of the 'take air raid action' warning having been given, and every man, save three or four that it was necessary to post in charge of the animals, being lined up, there was unfolded to full view the stirring spectacle of an enemy aeroplane attack on Dover, some five miles away. It was customary to await the receipt of official warning from headquarters before proceeding to the trenches, but the public warning provided by the town of Folkestone usually anticipated the official one by a few minutes, the latter having to be relayed through official channels. This public warning was given by means of a very powerful siren which could be heard fully ten miles away.

Whilst there were many alarms subsequently to the great May raid, they were mostly incident to the passage over nearby territory of machines on their way to or from an attack on London, though sometimes a stray machine or two, having been prevented by the shell barrage from getting far inland, wandered aimlessly about in the dark over the area, apparently at a loss as to its whereabouts, and dropped a bomb here and there without hitting anybody or anything of importance. The reader must bear in mind that in an air raid, there was just as great, if not greater, danger from our own projectiles as from those of the raiders. Every shell that was sent up into the sky to explode in the hope of striking an aeroplane, had to come again to earth in a thousand fragments, which in descending were scattered over a wide area, so that he was a wise man who sought shelter instead of letting his curiosity get the better of him.

DECLINE By the fall of 1917, the number of horses in the area having undergone a considerable diminution through the gradual departure of units (the total then being approximately 700) and there being no enzootics to contend with as there had been in the two previous years amongst the newly-arrived and unacclimatized animals, and moreover, a policy of retrenchment having been decided on, it became apparent that local conditions no longer justified the perpetuation of No. 2 Canadian Veterinary Hospital. The upkeep of the place was costing in the neighborhood of £60 (nearly $300) per day and the number of horses under treatment had dwindled to less than 50, a state of affairs which regarded as a purely business proposition, could not be entertained, and it was evident that the needs for hospital treatment of such horses as remained in the area could be met by conducting simple sick lines.

The Instructional School for Farriers was still in full blast, but that undertaking was deemed to have served its purpose and it was believed, though wrongly, that the corps could get along with a depot and that the question of reinforcements for the field could be handled entirely from the hospital at Havre.

DISBANDMENT So disbandment was decided on and was put into effect on February 1st, 1918, and in addition to the hospital and its adjuncts the corps depot for a time ceased to exist. When the breakup occurred, the non-commissioned officers and men of lower medical categories, not being suited to any other occupation and being needed to reinforce the personnel of No. 1 Canadian Veterinary Hospital in France, in order to release therefrom men fit to withstand the hardships of the front lines, were sent over to Havre, but those of higher categories, amongst whom were many expert horsemen, of high value to the corps, were drafted into infantry battalions. However, several of these men were later returned to the corps when it was discovered that their services were indispensable.

RESUSCITATION The above-mentioned changes took place by direction of the High Command towards the close of Brigadier-General Neill's incumbency and for a time the affairs of the corps were adrift and in a state bordering on disorganization. The need for maintaining the corps in a high state of efficiency, coupled with the continued demand for trained reinforcements, and particularly for keeping up the flow of veterinary officers from Canada, had not been taken into account, and those questions soon thrust themselves to the fore. It was then realized that a serious mistake had been made in abolishing the corps depot in England. Soon reinforcements were urgently called for from France and there was no direct source of supply excepting the general depot at Shorncliffe. Many men belonging to the corps and of high value because of their special training, were coming back from France as casualties and were being sent to the general depot thence to be re-allocated to other units and thereby lost to the corps.

Early in 1918, a re-categorization of all ranks occurred throughout the army. Many men of higher category were taken from the hospital at Havre to be sent to fighting units, whereby the hospital was rendered short of trained men. Several appeals were made to headquarters in England for reinforcements which could not be complied with, except with a quite insufficient number of untrained men from the general depot. At this stage, Colonel Edgett assumed direction of affairs at the corps headquarters and he, with a clear conception of the requirements that the situation called for, succeeded in convincing the higher authorities that a mistake had been made and that it was essential to resuscitate the corps depot, which action was duly authorized and put into effect in June, 1918. The Senior Veterinary Officer of the area, in addition to his executive duties, was placed in command with a small staff consisting of a staff sergeant and a sergeant-clerk as a permanent cadre. It was further authorized that the reinforcements carried at any one time should not exceed a quartermaster, 5 veterinary officers, and 40 other ranks.

SUBSEQUENT TRAINING There remained the need for continuing to provide adequate training facilities for both officers and men. The depot of the Imperial Army Veterinary Corps at Woolwich offered itself as an available place and an arrangement was entered into whereby Canadian Army Veterinary Corps personnel, both officers and men, were sent there in groups at convenient intervals to undergo a course of elementary training lasting from four to seven weeks, whenever there were vacancies for their reception. This course, from its curriculum, promised a greater attempt at systematic instruction than did that which the junior veterinary officers, newly-arrived from Canada, had previously been able to obtain at Shorncliffe. The instruction was supposed to cover the following subjects: organization and administration of the veterinary services, military law, military veterinary hygiene, map reading, foot drill and equitation, and practical instruction at the local Imperial hospital.

But when the first lot of newly-arrived officers returned from the prescribed sojourn, it was found that the time spent at Woolwich had been practically wasted for the instruction had been quite deficient in essentials and had the war continued some other arrangement would have been necessary.

REMOVAL OF BASE At the end of November, 1918, the base was moved to Witley.

Let us now direct our attention to an important adjunct of the hospital, namely the Canadian Veterinary Training School and its subsidiary Instructional School for Farriers.

THE CANADIAN VETERINARY TRAINING SCHOOL

IMPERIAL ARMY VETERINARY SCHOOL The Imperial army maintained at Aldershot an army veterinary school, where all officers of the mounted branches of the service, excepting the cavalry, were compelled to attend a course of a duration of one month for the purpose of receiving training in horsemastership.

FIRST AID FARRIERS Of no less importance was the course, lasting six weeks, for the training of the army shoeing smiths and farrier sergeants in first aid principles of veterinary science, the object having been to make these men proficient as assistants to the officers of the army veterinary corps. Attendance at these classes was on the part of recruits who on entering the army were already practical shoeing smiths or by men who after recruitment had undergone a regimental two years' training in farriery. Despite some drawbacks, the system, on the whole, worked well, and much of the efficiency of the army veterinary service was due to the skill and adaptiveness of the farrier sergeants, though the latter were not members of the army veterinary corps.

The old idea was that there existed no necessity for retaining a trained body of hospital orderlies or experts to watch over and care for sick horses in the same manner that sisters and orderlies in the military hospitals minister to the needs of sick soldiers, but that the trooper or driver to whom an animal had been allotted should accompany it to the sick lines to look after its needs under the direction and orders of the veterinary officer, supplemented by the assistance of the aforesaid farrier sergeants. At all centres where the number of horses warranted it, veterinary hospitals were maintained with an authorized establishment of personnel for the conduct of the interior economy and to act as dressers.

PROJECTED CANADIAN ARMY VETERINARY SCHOOL Having briefly reviewed the system of specialized training in vogue in the Imperial army, let us see how far Canada has progressed along similar lines. For at least fifteen years prior to the war the importance of the subject was recognized, lectures on horsemastership having been part of the curriculum of the officers, non-commissioned officers and men at the School of Artillery at Kingston, Ontario. And when the establishment of the Canadian Army Veterinary Services was laid down in 1910, provision was made for an army veterinary school, where particular instruction might be systematically carried out. But the project never materialized and with the advent of the war, lapsed into a state of quiescence. The formation of the expeditionary force brought the subject once more to the fore and the necessity for giving the members of the mounted branches some sort of instruction in animal management and conservation early became apparent.

LECTURES DURING VOYAGE Already on the voyage over, lectures were given on the different ships by the veterinary officers to the officers and men of the mounted units on horsemastership and the results were shown till the end of the war in the number of horses that remained in active service in France.

LECTURES AT SALISBURY PLAIN On January 1st, 1915, a corps order was issued at Bustad Camp, Salisbury Plain, that veterinary officers attached to units must give lectures, at least twice a week, to all transport officers and non-commissioned officers and farriers of the units to which they were attached on the following subjects: management of animals on the march, in camp and on shipboard, feeding, watering, grooming, proper methods of securing animals in stables and in camp, especially with regard to picketing, selection of ground for picketing lines, fitting of saddlery and harness, shoeing and care of feet, and first aid to sick and injured animals.

ESTABLISHMENT OF SCHOOL AT SHORNCLIFFE As time progressed and it became evident that the war would be of longer duration than had originally been expected and that reinforcements in vast numbers would be required, the commanding officer of the corps decided to resuscitate the project of the school and to put it into actual operation at the training base at Shorncliffe. At first the course of instruction was confined to the training of

Figure 5.5. Canadian Farriers' Instructional Class, No. 2 Canadian Veterinary Hospital, Ross Barracks, Shorncliffe, 1916. Centre front, Lieut.-Col. H.D. Smith, Assistant Director Veterinary Services C.A.V.C.; left of Smith, with dog, Capt. J.F. Wood, O. C. No. 2 C.V. H.; right of Smith, Sgt.-Major W.J. Prinn, Warrant Officer Instructor of farriery. (*C.A.V. Barker Museum*)

shoeing smiths and farrier sergeants (Figure 5.5) to meet the urgent and ever increasing demand for experts in that line of work, these men receiving not only lectures on their own particular subject of shoeing but also in elementary veterinary science somewhat after the manner adopted in the case of their comrades of the Imperial service. But this is an age of specialization and the views formerly held with respect to the utilization of first aid services underwent a change. We have seen that in the Imperial service, reliance had hitherto been placed on specially trained farrier sergeants to supply a body of assistants to the veterinary officers.

FIRST AID N.C.O'S With the development of the war and the needs to which it gave rise, the subject began to be regarded in the light of greater importance, for it was deemed that the duties of the farriers would keep them fully occupied in their particular line of work and that an experiment should be made of training a special body of men in first aid work from amongst the personnel of the veterinary corps only, conferring upon them the rank, upon qualification, of acting sergeant with equivalent pay and allowances, whose duty it would be to relieve, second the efforts of, and in certain instances take the place of, the veterinary officers.

For instance, in the field one veterinary officer had charge of the veterinary interests of the four separate batteries composing a brigade of artillery. These batteries might be stationed at widely separated points and the officer, not being able to be present at all points at once, it was very necessary that somebody with a certain amount of first aid experience should be on hand at all times to act in case of emergency. Again, in the Shorncliffe area, were many outlying infantry camps, several miles apart, at which a few horses were stationed. Obviously, it would have been a great tax on the time and energies of the veterinary officer in charge of the area to personally, on his rounds, make a daily inspection of every horse under his supervision, particularly, be it remembered, that at the time of his visit some of the animals might be doing duty away from their quarters. Here again, it was necessary to depend on the sergeants, one of whom was attached to the units of a definite territory. Thus it came about that, in due course, the component elements of the several divisions, as well as units working outside the scope of the latter, were supplied with a complement of first aid sergeants.

INSTRUCTION TO FIRST AID N.C.O.S The instruction given the sergeants was directed towards enabling them to acquire as much fundamental and common sense knowledge of veterinary work as the period embraced by the course permitted. It consisted of lectures and clinics comprising: elementary anatomy, physiology and pathology; therapeutics; methods of diagnosis; the study of infectious, contagious and parasitic diseases; lameness, shoeing; surgery, first aid treatment; nursing and stable management; and was scheduled to last over a period of two months. Colonel Neill thought to dignify the position by awarding successful aspirants with certificates of proficiency signed by himself as Director of Veterinary Services and Remounts (Figures 5.6, 5.8).

These certificates of which 731 were issued, recognized the holders by the designation 'veterinary sergeant' (Figure 5.6), a term which, though a very convenient one, did not prove to be a happy one any more than would have been the case had the orderlies of the medical corps been termed 'medical sergeants', for it led a few of the holders to an exaggerated idea of its importance which reached a climax when in the summer of 1918, one or two made so bold as to apply for commissions as veterinary officers, on the basis of their possession of these certificates. Moreover, some apprehension was felt that in civil life after the war the public might fail to discriminate between the terms 'veterinary surgeon' and 'veterinary sergeant'. Hence, in the summer of 1918, shortly after he had taken over the direction of affairs, Colonel Edgett suppressed this presumptive title and substituted therefor the more simple one of 'sergeant, C.A.V.C.'.

The experiment turned out to be a success in some instances and a failure in others where the wrong men had been allowed to qualify or the course of training had been curtailed, for not only did the sergeants who made good ably fulfil their particular duties, but by example and precept were the means of disseminating amongst the troopers, drivers and grooms who had immediate management of the horses, the knowledge and correct principles they had absorbed during the period of their training. Under the stress of urgent demand some instances must be noted of candidates being hurried through an abbreviated course or of not being possessed of the natural bent or inclination for the work, with consequent falling short in the standard of efficiency requisite to meet the exigencies of service in the field, and it was subsequently found necessary to relieve of their appointments men who failed to make good. But the majority of the sergeants underwent adequate training and became proficient, the introduction of the new scheme being amply justified by results.

It will be seen in the chapter devoted to No. 1 Canadian Veterinary Hospital at Havre that similar training was carried out there.

INSTRUCTION TO OTHER UNITS In addition to the course outlined above, other and less pretentious classes were inaugurated for the special benefit of officers, cadets and other ranks of any unit in which horses were employed.

NEED FOR INSTRUCTION The necessity for giving instruction to infantry officers who may be entitled to have a mount and yet be woefully ignorant of the proper care of a horse was exemplified by an incident that formed the subject of a court of enquiry at Shorncliffe. A major of an infantry battalion, accompanied by his commanding

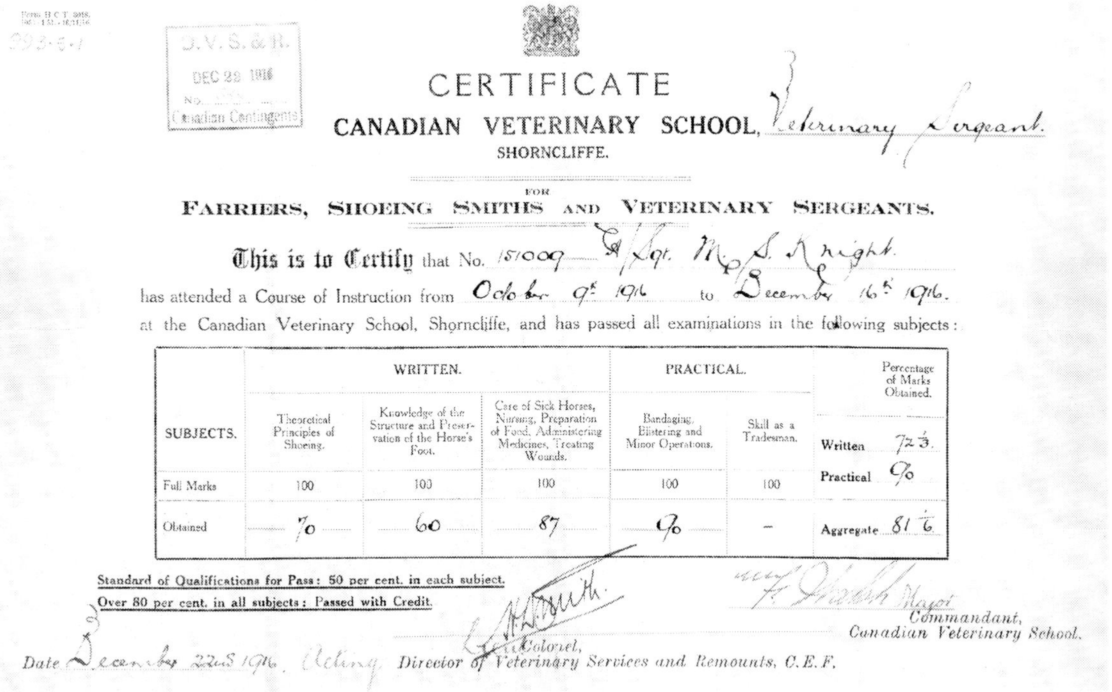

D.V.S. & R.
DEC 28 1916
Canadian Contingents

CERTIFICATE

CANADIAN VETERINARY SCHOOL, Veterinary Sergeant.

SHORNCLIFFE.

FOR

FARRIERS, SHOEING SMITHS AND VETERINARY SERGEANTS.

This is to Certify that No. 151009 A/Sgt. M. S. Knight.
has attended a Course of Instruction from October 9th 1916 to December 16th 1916.
at the Canadian Veterinary School, Shorncliffe, and has passed all examinations in the following subjects:

SUBJECTS.	WRITTEN.			PRACTICAL.		Percentage of Marks Obtained.
	Theoretical Principles of Shoeing.	Knowledge of the Structure and Preservation of the Horse's Foot.	Care of Sick Horses, Nursing, Preparation of Food, Administering Medicines, Treating Wounds.	Bandaging, Blistering and Minor Operations.	Skill as a Tradesman.	Written 72⅓.
Full Marks	100	100	100	100	100	Practical 90
Obtained	70	60	87	90	–	Aggregate 81⅙

Standard of Qualifications for Pass: 50 per cent. in each subject.
Over 80 per cent. in all subjects: Passed with Credit.

F. Walsh Major
Commandant,
Canadian Veterinary School.

A. Smith
Colonel,
Date December 22nd 1916. Acting Director of Veterinary Services and Remounts, C.E.F.

Figure 5.6. Veterinary Sergeant Certificate, Canadian Veterinary School, Shorncliffe, December, 1916. (*C.A.V. Barker Museum*)

officer, went for a long ride and on the way back, whilst still four miles from camp, his horse cast a shoe from a hind foot. It never occurred to either of these officers that a horse's foot was anything else than a block of wood and they continued the ride at a rapid pace over the hard roads. After arrival at camp the animal was so lame that it could scarcely put the foot to the ground and the veterinary officer under whose care the case subsequently came found that the sole of the hoof had been so worn by friction that it could be indented by pressure exerted with the thumb. As a result of this neglectful treatment, the horse was incapacitated for nearly a month.

Captain Best tested a new draft from Canada as to knowledge of horsemanship. Amongst 142 men he found three good horsemen, 40 who had handled horses but whose knowledge was superficial, and that the remainder had never had anything to do with horses.

In the early days at Shorncliffe, there was a good deal of complaint on account of officers and other ranks of the cavalry, artillery and infantry making improper use of government horses in that they indulged in hunting, joy riding with lady friends, and attendance at social functions at night, often leaving the animals standing around for hours at a time in the care of a groom or tied to a post. In addition to this, fast trotting and even galloping over the hard roads were quite prevalent and Colonel Neill felt impelled to write to headquarters to request that these conditions be rectified. Colonel A.D. McCrae, Director of Supplies and Transport, also wrote in a similar strain, stating that it was not an uncommon sight to see officers and grooms proceeding at full gallop on the Sandgate road with the result that lame horses were becoming numerous and that in the fall of 1915 nearly half the horses had been lame. He added that the majority of Canadians were but poor horsemen and knew little about handling of a horse and hoped that in the interest of the horses binding regulations might be made. The result was a War Office order prohibiting chargers and troop horses being hunted during the war and the Assistant Provost Marshal stopped all fast riding.

The subjects taught the officers and cadets comprised: the conformation and conservation of the energy of the horse; forage; saddlery and harness; shoeing; physical examination for soundness; detection of the seat and cause of lameness; care of the horse on the march; prevention of infectious, contagious and parasitic diseases; and first aid treatment and stable management. The instruction given the non-commissioned officers and privates was along similar lines but more confined to demonstrations than to lectures, the idea having been that the sphere handled by these men was less extensive and essentially practical and not to the same degree theoretical.

Lectures Appreciated The ultimate benefits resulting from these instructional courses were far reaching and will yet make their influence felt throughout the length and breadth of our land. Much of the good accomplished was due to the ability and energy displayed by Captains J.F. Wood (Figure 5.5) and V.C. Best, the officers commanding the hospital during the greater part of the period referred to, and to the officers working under them. A tribute to the interest evoked by Captain Best was shown by the voluntary attendance at one lecture of 679 men, from practically every unit in the area, including the engineers, artillery, Army Service Corps and infantry battalions.

The lectures were begun in a marquee tent, but as the number of attending students increased it became necessary to secure more commodious quarters, the recreation hut, recreation hall and Young Men's Christian Association building being successively occupied. But the methods of instruction in horsemastership did not stop short at the course system; they extended to the individual trooper working in the lines. Here the troop sergeants directed the men towards acquiring a knowledge of the correct principles of stable management, emphasis being laid on the importance of proper grooming as a factor in the prevention of disease and on special feeding for reconditioning debilitated animals.

The Instructional School of Farriery In the introduction of this work it has been shown that despite the degree of perfection to which military motor transport had been developed, the horse was proven to be still indispensable as a final means of locomotion. It is almost unnecessary to add that any shortcoming or defect in the equipment of this animal would have been like an unseen weakness in a piece of metal which might give way at the first strain placed upon it. Not the least important part of equipment were the everyday means adopted for the protection of the animal's foot against the wear incident to the service it was called upon to perform.

This is a truth that has ever had to be taken into account in all great military undertakings. We learn from ancient history that before the invention of horseshoeing the advance of armies was impeded and often considerably delayed by the wear to which the feet of the accompanying horses were subjected. It is recorded that the horses of Alexander's army suffered severely during their marches through Asia owing to the wearing of the feet, and that vast numbers, becoming lame, had to be abandoned until their feet grew strong enough to make them again available, whilst Mithridates, King of Pontus in the first century, B.C., while laying siege to Cyzicus, was obliged to send his entire cavalry to Bithynia for treatment because of the manner in which the horses' feet had suffered from prolonged marching. The Romans are known to have adopted all sorts of devices for the protection of their horses' hoofs including the smearing of fluid pitch on the same, and the standing of the animals on stone or oaken floors to render the hoof hard and resistant. They also employed protecting soles of woven broom or reeds, devices used to this day in the remote districts of Japan, as well as sandals of metal, the so-called ‘hippo-sandals’, all of which were fastened to the hoof by straps. The Celts are credited, especially by the French, with having been the first to employ nail-on shoes and William the Conqueror is said to have introduced the prototype of the modern shoe into Great Britain for it is known that he commissioned one of his noblemen to superintend and encourage the art of farriery.

What was true of the conditions surrounding the mobility of the horses of the armies of the ancients was equally true of the mobility of the horses of the armies employed in the recent war, but with this difference: that in the late conflict the opportunity offered of taking full advantage of the modern science of horseshoeing, as has indeed been more or less done since the early Christian era.

Need for Farriers and Shoeing Smiths It had early been realized by Colonel Neill that the mobility of the horse transport service must not be jeopardized by entrusting the care of the horses' feet to incompetent workmen and that provision must be made for systematic training of a body of men to replace casualties that might occur amongst the shoeing smiths already employed in the mounted units; a body of men who could be depended on to apply the correct principles of farriery. The regimental shoeing smiths already employed consisted of men enlisted from civil occupation of horseshoeing on the strength of regiments and it was found that amongst them were many who, when tested, proved to be incompetent from the habit of practising faulty methods of technique handed down to them by their predecessors. These faulty methods were mainly rasping of the wall and too free use of the hoof knife on the sole and frog, practices which from having become a fixed habit, were very difficult to overcome and which required constant vigilance on the part of the veterinary officers to correct.

Nature has endowed the horse with an organ of locomotion, namely the foot, which will not withstand wear and tear under conventional conditions of usage unless provided with a protective covering in the shape of a shoe, and the first great principle of correct shoeing is that the shoe must be made to fit the foot, and not the foot to fit the shoe. So prevalent in civil life is the error of fitting the foot to the shoe with the consequent cutting and mutilation of the hoof leading to ultimate injury to the delicate structures within, that a strict regulation exists in the army prohibiting interference with the organ, excepting under the direction of a veterinary officer.

NUMBER OF HORSES USED BY CANADIANS The greatest number of horses and mules employed by the British forces on the western front at any one time was in the neighborhood of half a million, of which, on an average, some 23,500 were used by the Canadians, besides some 2,500 horses and mules in the service of the Canadian forces in the British Isles.

NUMBER OF FARRIERS AND SHOEING SMITHS To serve this large number of animals used by the Canadians alone, there were employed by July, 1918, 315 farriers and shoeing smiths in France and 56 in the British Isles. But as there was a constant wastage from sickness, leave and casualties, a very much larger number had to be provided for. It was estimated by Brigadier-General Neill that the number required by formations in France to be trained every 2 months would be: for 4 divisions (22 men each) - 88; Canadian corps troops - 10; Mounted Brigade - 10; Fifth Divisional Artillery Brigade - 8: Total - 116

Where could such a body of men properly trained to carry on this indispensable work be procured? Those already enlisted in the mounted units formed the total of available members of the craft in Canada.

SCHOOL ESTABLISHED So the establishment of training quarters was decided on, to be modelled after their counterpart in the Imperial army which had already been long in existence. It is worthy of note that our late enemies were the first to recognise the importance of correct shoeing for military forces, for it was at Gottesane, near Karlsruhe, that the first military school of farriery was inaugurated in 1847, since which date numerous similar places of instruction have sprung into existence in the various provinces of the German empire.

INSTRUCTOR As the instruction was to be mainly confined to farriery, an expert in the latter line of work was sought, and in July, 1915, the services of Farrier Quartermaster Sergeant W. J. Prinn (Figure 5.7) were requisitioned as chief instructor. As a reward for his highly efficient services, Mr. Prinn was commissioned lieutenant and under his able direction and instruction this department gradually grew from being a small detail with a single forge under canvas at its inauguration in July, 1915, to one of the most important branches of the mounted and transport services in 1917, with no less than 26 forges in roomy quarters in a state of instructional activity, though its importance was perhaps never fully appreciated.

Figure 5.7. Sgt.-Maj. W.J. Prinn Warrant Officer Instructor, Farriery[5] (*Detail, Figure 5.5*)

TEMPORARY DIFFICULTIES It is not too much to venture the assertion that had it not been for the existence of these training quarters, the Canadian forces would have found themselves in a very serious predicament in January, 1916, when it was decided to abolish the working pay of artificers and clerks of all units. Working pay was an extra emolument in 3 grades of 50 cents, 75 cents and 1 dollar, respectively, over and above the ordinary pay of a soldier, offered as an inducement to attract men skilled in special lines of work and needed to fill out and complete an army establishment.

As the government had made a solemn covenant with these men when securing their services for the army, the only thing that could be done under the circumstances was to let all who claimed it have their discharge. An attempt was made to retain them by an offer of 3 months' furlough, but unhappily, a large proportion, thinking they had been shabbily treated and letting mercenary considerations outweigh their sense of patriotism, threw up their jobs and returned home. Those who preferred to stand by their comrades in the hour of need not only preserved their self-respect but later had good reason to congratulate themselves, when, on the approach of the elections at home at the end of 1917, the working pay was restored to them, including arrears covering the period from the date of the suspension.

It will be appreciated that the situation was perplexing to a degree, but thanks to the foresight of Colonel Neill, the machinery for bringing order out of chaos had already been created and it only remained to send out a call for volunteers from amongst the numerous units of all branches of the service and to pass the word along to Lieutenant Prinn for a speeding up of action. At once there was a notable influx from all quarters and within two months the deficiency had been made good.

Later, in March, 1917, a larger measure of recognition was accorded this establishment by a corps order, making it a branch of the Canadian Veterinary Training School, but it was never placed on the basis of an authorized military school by the General Staff but treated as an adjunct to the veterinary hospital.

SOURCES OF SUPPLY Students were procured by voluntary attendance of non-commissioned officers and men from any of the numerous Canadian units in the British Isles, as allotted by the General Staff, and were attached to the veterinary hospital during their stay. The first class started with an attendance of 33 candidates and eventually over 1000 men passed through the school, an exceptionally small percentage failing to make good. This was largely due to the fact that, apart from the intelligence generally displayed by the candidates, they were complete novices at the craft, were taught correctly from the start, and had no bad lessons to unlearn. At first autographic certificates signed by the officer commanding the hospital were handed to those who had completed the course and desired some sort of credential, and it was not until the course had been established some time that there were issued printed certificates of proficiency bearing the signature of the Director of Veterinary Services, and of these some 632 were issued (Figure 5.8).

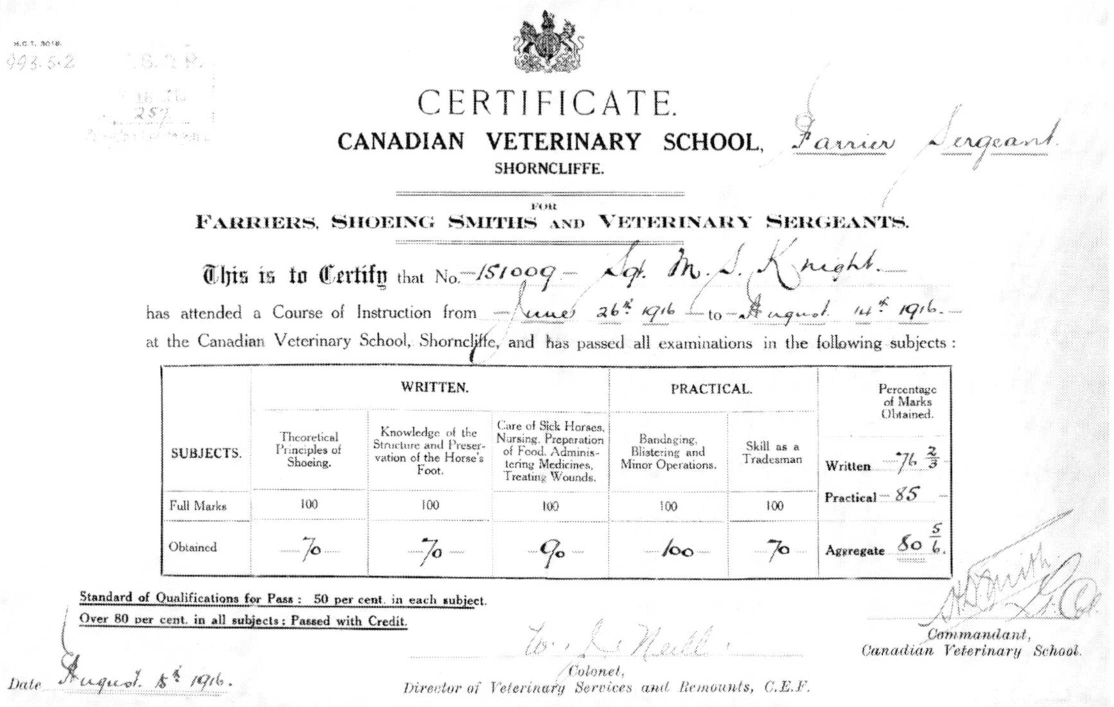
CERTIFICATE.
CANADIAN VETERINARY SCHOOL, Farrier Sergeant.
SHORNCLIFFE.
FOR
FARRIERS, SHOEING SMITHS AND VETERINARY SERGEANTS.

This is to Certify that No. 151009 Sgt. M. J. Knight
has attended a Course of Instruction from June 26th 1916 to August 14th 1916.
at the Canadian Veterinary School, Shorncliffe, and has passed all examinations in the following subjects :

SUBJECTS.	WRITTEN. Theoretical Principles of Shoeing.	Knowledge of the Structure and Preservation of the Horse's Foot.	Care of Sick Horses, Nursing, Preparation of Food, Administering Medicines, Treating Wounds.	PRACTICAL. Bandaging, Blistering and Minor Operations.	Skill as a Tradesman	Percentage of Marks Obtained.
Full Marks	100	100	100	100	100	Written 76 2/3 / Practical 85
Obtained	70	70	90	100	70	Aggregate 80 5/6

Standard of Qualifications for Pass: 50 per cent. in each subject.
Over 80 per cent. in all subjects: Passed with Credit.

Date August 15th 1916.

Colonel,
Director of Veterinary Services and Remounts, C.E.F.

Commandant,
Canadian Veterinary School.

Figure 5.8. Farrier Sergeant Certificate, Canadian Veterinary School, Shorncliffe, August, 1916.
(*C.A.V. Barker Museum*)

NATURE OF INSTRUCTION The course of instruction was very thorough; it lasted two months and embraced both theoretical and practical teaching. On the theoretical side, lectures were given by the chief instructor on the anatomy of the horse from the knee to the foot, and history of shoeing and the methods of making differentiated shoes to meet the requirements of each of the many diseases and injuries to which the foot is subject. These lectures were rendered particularly attractive by the exhibition from the school collection of a great variety of the different types of shoes in use at the present day, as well as those of historical interest, including the ancient 'hippo-sandal' employed by the Romans; the first shoe in Great Britain known to have been attached by means of nails, introduced by William the Conqueror; down to the modern plain-fullered shoe used in the service today. The practical side comprised instruction at the forges by the assistant instructors under the direction of the chief instructor, all of whom had been trained by the latter. These assistant instructors were picked men having a thorough knowledge of their work; they demonstrated to their classes: the correct methods of handling and securing horses whilst the latter were being shod, particularly those of nervous, fidgety, stubborn or vicious temperament; the removal of worn shoes; the preparation of the foot; the forging of new shoes and the fitting and application of the latter.

Following is a nominal roll of the instructors just before the break-up:

Farrier Quartermaster Sergeant W. Foy	Medicine Hat, Alta.
Farrier Staff Sergeant W.A. Findlay	Saskatoon, Sask.
Farrier Staff Sergeant R.T. Glew	Toronto, Ont.
Farrier Staff Sergeant J. A. Reeves	Vegreville, Alta.
Farrier Staff Sergeant A.C. Woodd	Taber, Alta.
Farrier Sergeant A. Gough	Quebec, P.Q.
Farrier Sergeant W.B. Halliday	Virden, Man.
Farrier Sergeant J. Neil	Victoria, B.C.
Farrier Sergeant W.J. Newman	Victoria, B.C.
Farrier Sergeant F. Russ	Devizes, Wilts, England
Farrier Sergeant W. Young	Valcartier, P.Q.
Acting-Farrier Sergeant R. Glanville	New Westminster, B.C.
Acting-Farrier Sergeant J. McKinnon	Medicine Hat, Alta.
Sergeant Clerk R.A. Robison	Winnipeg, Man.

COLD SHOEING VERSUS HOT SHOEING At first the system known as 'cold shoeing' was taught as opposed to that of 'hot shoeing', but it was followed with so many evil results and consequent interference with the mobility of the horse transport service that it was entirely discarded in favor of the latter. For the information of those who do not know the difference between the two systems, it may be mentioned that the former term is applied, as the name indicates, to a method of shoeing by means of ready-forged shoes of mild steel, standardized to one pattern but in different weights and of some ten different sizes. The employment of this type of shoe obviates the necessity of carrying a forge in the field, but there is a distinct objection to it inasmuch as it necessitates more or less cutting and mutilation of the foot in order to make the latter fit the shoe, to the ultimate permanent injury of the organ. On the other hand, the employment of 'hot shoeing' enables the farrier to fit the shoe to the foot.

Moreover, the modern type of compact, lightly constructed portable forge, weighing about 150 pounds (Figure 5.9), does not offer much impediment to the mobility of an army, such as there is being quite offset by the advantages gained, so that all things considered, of the two systems that of 'hot shoeing' is generally conceded to be the preferable, though if a greater range of sizes and patterns of 'cold shoes' could be carried, there would be little choice in the matter.

FIELD FORGES It is true that at first field forges were not provided by the army authorities, but that fact did not hinder the farriers from procuring what they needed, either by gift on the part of societies that exist for improving the lot of the horse, or by the soldier's own way of 'salvaging'. Later, 'Champion' field forges, at a cost of £5.5.0 (approximately $25) each, were provided by the Canadian military authorities to some of the newly-organized units.

Figure 5.9. Farriers of the 12th Battalion at work, Salisbury Plain, England. (*NAC PA 4920*)

TRAINING ELSEWHERE Though in November, 1917, there were complaints of a shortage of competent shoeing smiths in the Canadian divisions, Canadian headquarters did not consider it necessary to transfer the disbanded school to No. 1 Canadian Veterinary Hospital at Havre, it being estimated that any personnel in France could receive training in farriery through the same medium as Imperial units, thus doing away with the necessity of maintaining a Canadian school. Accordingly, farriers for the Canadian forces in France were then trained at the temporary Imperial School of Farriery at Abbeville until the time of the German advance in the spring of 1918, when this school was transferred to Woolwich, at which place the training was continued.

OTHER AREAS Besides the Shorncliffe area, there were, from 1916 onwards, other areas occupied for longer or shorter periods by Canadian troops in training with varying numbers of horses necessitating representation on the part of the veterinary corps.

THE SHOREHAM AND SEAFORD AREAS The interests of these areas were supervised in the first instance by Captain J. Biron, stationed at the former place and assisted by two first aid sergeants. This officer was succeeded at the end of March, 1917, by Captain E. Bowler, who received the appointment of Senior Veterinary Officer, with residence at Seaford, and duties embracing not only the Shoreham area but the outlying districts of Hastings, Bexhill and Brighton. In the whole of this consolidated area there were, at the period of greatest activity, some 800 horses. The sickness was confined mostly to mange, ringworm and pneumonia, the latter due to the open, unprotected stabling, a condition of affairs which was remedied during Captain Bowler's tenure of office.

THE CROWBOROUGH AREA In this area there were approximately 300 horses. Captain T.R.R. Hoggan was first placed in charge and later Captain H.J. Elliott. A first aid sergeant was also stationed there.

THE BRAMSHOTT AREA In view of the fact that part of the Third Division and the whole of the Fourth were organized in this area, veterinary interests assumed some importance, there being, in May, 1916, 3092 horses employed. Lieutenant-Colonel T.J. de M. Taschereau was the first officer to be appointed Assistant Director of Veterinary Services of this area. Upon the organization of the Fourth Division, he was succeeded by Captain C.E. Edgett, promoted to major, who assumed the administrative veterinary duties of both the area and the Fourth Division. After the departure of the Fourth Division for France, the area was still continued as a training centre with Captain H.J. Elliott, Major E.C. Thurston and Captains H. Colebourn and A. Cowan successively in charge of veterinary interests.

THE WITLEY AREA
Veterinary interests were of considerable importance at Witley, there being 4,936 horses there in the Canadian service in January, 1917. Lieutenant-Colonel H.D. Smith was first to be appointed Administrative Veterinary Officer of the troops in training there, and in the same capacity to the nucleus of the Fifth Division (Figure 5.10). He was succeeded by Captain W.G. Stedman when he was transferred to headquarters in London to assume the duties of Acting Director of Veterinary Services and Remounts upon Brigadier-General Neill's departure for Canada on behalf of the British Remount Commission. Captain Stedman soon received the acting rank of major and the appointment as Administrative Veterinary Officer of the Fifth Division. After the break up of the latter division, Major Thurston officiated as Senior Veterinary Officer and he was followed successively by Captains A.H. Hunter, H. Sproston and T.R.R. Hoggan.

Figure 5.10. Captain D.J. McLellan C.A.V.C., Veterinary First Aid Sergeants and Farrier Sergeants (horseshoe on shoulder) attached to the 5th Canadian Division, training at Witley, England, 1917.[6] *(C.A.V. Barker Museum)*

THE BORDEN AREA This area had only existed for a short period when the armistice went into effect. There were approximately 800 horses there. Major Thurston held the appointment of Senior Veterinary Officer.

THE CANADIAN RAILWAY TROOPS DEPOT This being an organizing depot for the railway troops at Purfleet, a veterinary officer and first aid sergeant were posted there for duty and proceeded to France as soon as the unit then in process of organization was completed. This arrangement was continued until the requisite number of battalions had been formed.

THE CANADIAN FORESTRY CORPS DEPOT The regimental depot of this unit was stationed at Sunningdale, whence all veterinary personnel required to care for the horses was despatched for posting to the various districts and companies. At first an officer of the corps, Captain W.E. Gough, was stationed at Sunningdale to exercise the necessary veterinary supervision, but later the Imperials took over control in so far as supplying veterinary officers was concerned, and thereafter, only Canadian first aid sergeants continued to be posted as per the establishment, namely one per company, which at the time of the armistice amounted to 38 in all.

CHAPTER 6

HAVRE
NO. 1 CANADIAN VETERINARY HOSPITAL

Reason For Existence To judge by its designation, one might infer that the function of No. 1 Canadian Veterinary Hospital at Havre was to deal with sickness and injury arising amongst Canadian horses or the horses of the Canadian forces in France. Originally, that had been the intention, but, as a matter of fact, though the hospital was the outgrowth of a unit organized for that purpose in Montreal under Canadian auspices and was continuously thereafter officered and served by Canadian Army Veterinary Corps personnel, no horse of actual Canadian ownership entered its portals.

At the outset, Canada had undertaken to pay all the expenses of her own forces, including the provision of a veterinary hospital of a capacity adequate for the requirements of the 5000 and odd horses then in the field, and Lieutenant-Colonel Neill arranged that the Montreal unit should be held together as a hospital organization at Netheravon under the command of Captain T.C. Evans, until arrangements could be perfected for its transfer to France. In the meantime, such horses of the First Division as required hospital treatment were being cared for by the Imperial veterinary service at the same charge as had been arranged in England, namely 2s.6d. (60 cents) per diem per animal, wherever similar conditions prevailed.

At this stage, it was realized by Lieutenant-Colonel Neill that any attempt to conduct a purely Canadian institution of such a nature with its activities limited to the handling of animals emanating solely from Canadian units, could, under the conditions that were looming up and likely to prevail during the war, result in nothing but chaos. So, he proposed that there should be a fusion of resources, the veterinary hospital interests to be pooled, so to speak, and that Canada should contribute her share in the general scheme, not by conducting an enterprise of this nature on her own account, but by providing and paying the personnel for the maintenance of a fully equipped and extensive veterinary hospital at Havre under Imperial control.

The only features about it that were really Canadian were its name, its up-to-date Canadian methods and its personnel, the whole body of officers and men being provided and paid by the Canadian government and loaned, as it were, to the Imperial authorities and coming entirely under the jurisdiction of the latter. All lands, buildings and equipment were supposed to be furnished, free of cost to Canada by the Imperial government. It is important to bear this point in mind to visualize and properly understand the role which the hospital played in the scheme and the relationship it bore to the rest of the Canadian forces operating on the continent.

The theory on which this arrangement was based was that the number of horses in the Canadian forces on the continent would entail the maintenance of a hospital of a certain capacity, it being estimated that the ratio of sick animals under treatment all the time would approximate 8% of the number in the field. This figure was afterwards found to be rather too high, something slightly less than 7% being more near the truth. So it came about that the hospital acted as an Imperial veterinary hospital, dealing with any and all animals, irrespective of the source from which they came.

Every horse of the Canadian forces in France and Flanders, suffering from more than a transitory trouble that could not be expeditiously treated in the local sick lines in the field and whereby it became necessary to evacuate it to hospital, was turned over to the Imperial authorities, full credit being allowed for such animal to the Canadian government, no matter what the degree of disability, on the basis of a value mutually agreed upon and which is referred to in the chapter on Remounts. The horse straightway became Imperial property and was sent to one of the hospitals, of which there were 18 on the Lines of Communication besides the four convalescent depots. When cured, it entered an Imperial remount depot, whence it was ultimately issued with impartiality to any unit, Canadian or otherwise.

Having learned the raison d'être for its existence, let us proceed to consider its origin, organization or otherwise.

Location Occupying an elevated position in the suburb of Graville at the edge of the heights overlooking the seaport of Havre (Figure 6.1), the hospital lay about equidistant from the Havre seafront and the adjacent town of Harfleur. Commanding as it did an extensive view of the manufacturing district of the city, the broad valley of the

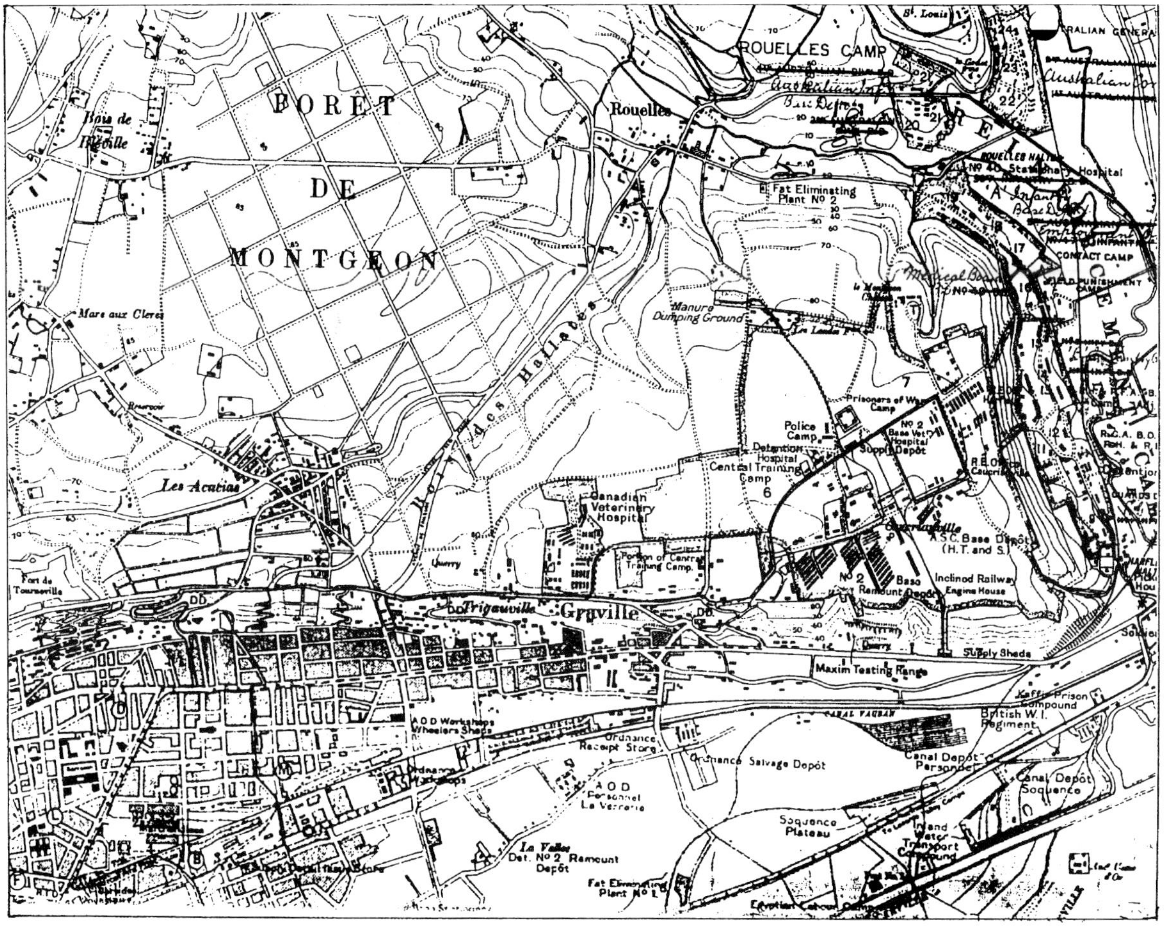

Figure 6.1. Site of the No. 1 Canadian Veterinary Hospital, Le Havre, France, in the suburb of Graville (centre) overlooking the port. To the east (right) of No. 1 C.V.H. lie the Imperial Army Veterinary Corps No. 2 Base Veterinary Hospital, from which mange cases were received, and the British Army No. 2 Base Remount Depot, to which recovered horses were sent. (*French Papers, NAC*)

Seine and the hills beyond, the outlook reminded one somewhat of the view to be got from the top of Mount Royal.[1] It is worth recalling that Harfleur was the scene of an exploit made famous for all time by Shakespeare when in 1415 King Henry V, having landed at Kaux on the site of which Havre was founded a century later, performed his prodigy of valor.

The site comprised some 26 acres and on it, at the beginning of the war, stood the old disused Molon's brick-field, a filthy quagmire, consisting of a brick kiln and some dilapidated open sheds, a number of exhausted clay pits filled with stagnated water and heaps of brick rubble and manure (Figure 6.2). This ugly and unpromising spot became transformed by Canadian enterprise in the course of a few months into a well-ordered and attractive scene of activities (Figures 6.3, 6.4), the wonderment and admiration of all who visited it.[2] Indeed, eventually it enjoyed the reputation of being the best appointed of all the similar wartime institutions in France.[3]

INCEPTION The place, when the Canadians arrived, already existed in a very dilapidated and primitive condition since shortly after the beginning of the war as a sort of receiving station for sick and wounded horses from the front, some 8 non-commissioned officers and 14 men of the Imperial Army Veterinary Corps being found looking after 529 animals. Minor cases were being kept and treated, the severe ones being sent to No. 2 Veterinary Hospital, an Imperial institution also located at Havre, not to be confused with No. 2 Canadian Veterinary Hospital at Shorncliffe.

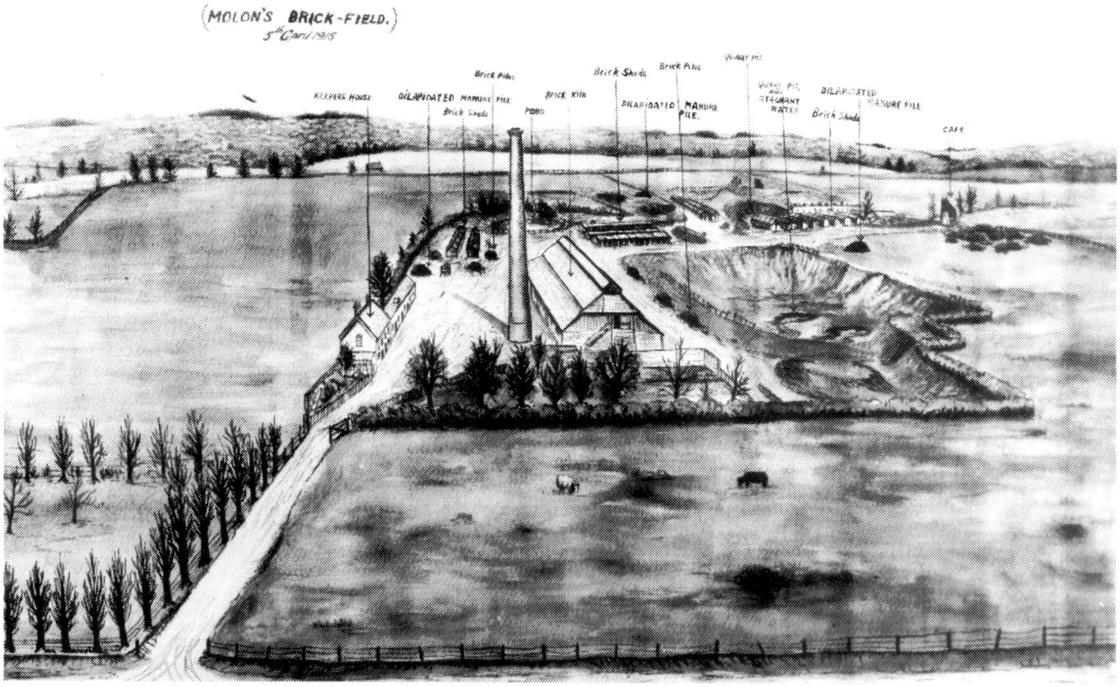

Figure 6.2. Molon's brick-field, April 5, 1915, at the time that it was taken over as the site for No. 1 Canadian Veterinary Hospital, Le Havre, France. (*NAC PA 5855*)

SCOPE OF WORK The Canadian unit, having equipped itself at Netheravon, entrained at Amesbury on the 2nd of April, 1915, and proceeding via Southampton, landed at Havre two days later with 6 officers and 196 other ranks, 14 horses and 5 Bain wagons. At first it went to the Imperial Veterinary Hospital and seven days later started

Figure 6.3. No. 1 Canadian Veterinary Hospital, Le Havre, France, 1918. (*NAC PA 5569*)

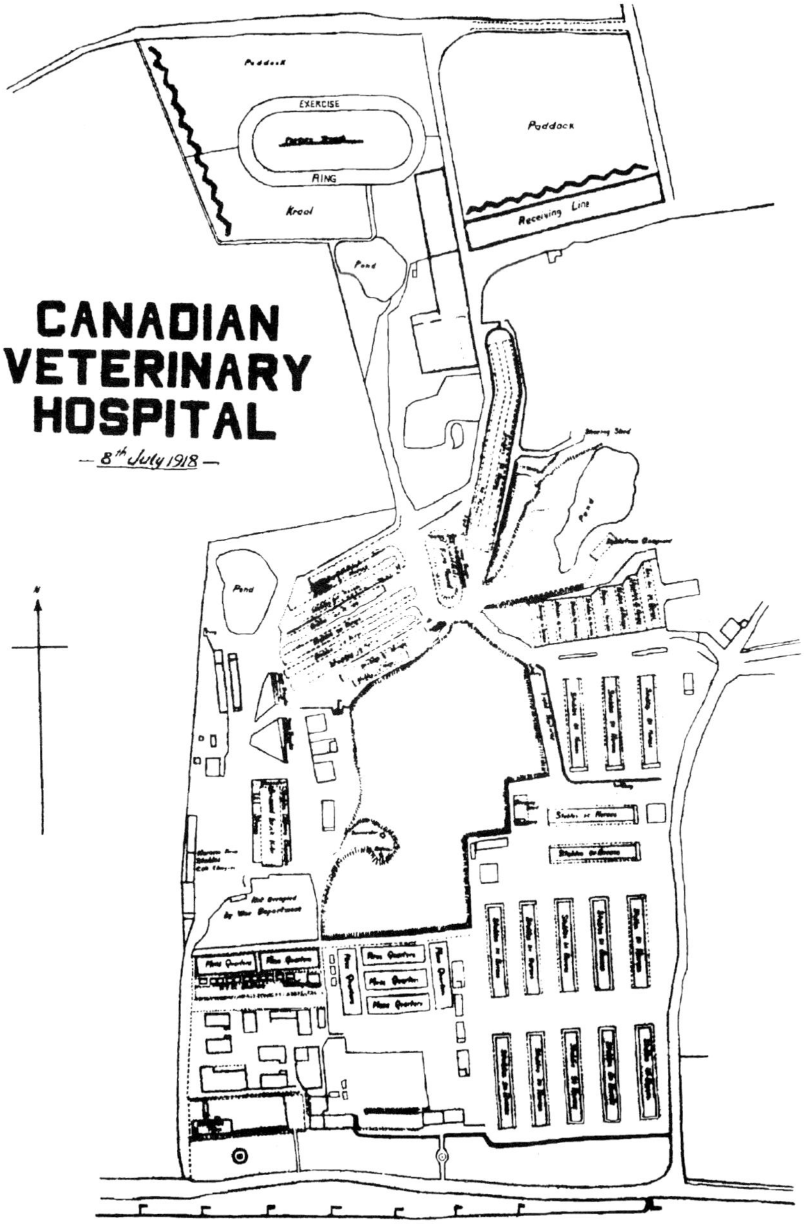

Figure 6.4. Plan of No. 1 Canadian Veterinary Hospital, Le Havre, 8 July, 1918.[4] The 15 galvanized iron stables arranged in rows occupy the east side of the main southern part of the grounds. In the centre is the large irregularly-shaped abandoned clay pit. The brick-yard kiln (see Fig. 6.2) is the large elongate north-south structure to the west of the pit. Men's quarters, messes, service and administration buildings are in the southwest corner. Rows of brick sheds converted to stables lie northwest and northeast of the clay pit; adjacent to the latter is the long narrow mange plunge dip. In the northern extension of the grounds are the oval exercise ring and paddocks, corrals or kraals with zig-zag shelter belts. In the southeast part of that area is the Receiving Line, where horses newly arrived from the front were isolated until tested for glanders and triaged to the Treatment Lines in the stables on the southern part of the grounds. Several shallow ponds in which horses with laminitis waded are present northeast and northwest of the clay pit, and in the neck of land to the north. Figure 6.3 looks over the fountain ("bull's-eye" in the very southwest corner of the grounds), in a slightly northeasterly direction along the front paddocks beside the road, toward the rows of stables.
(French Papers, NAC)

operations by taking over the station with the animals it found on hand, just as everything stood. At first all cases were kept but later infectious ones were transferred to No. 2. On the other hand, cases involving the skin, including mange, were sent by No. 2 to No. 1, and throughout its existence the hospital was considered as one mainly devoted to the handling of skin cases with or without medical or surgical complications.

Prior to the fall of 1917, it received cases emanating from any source, but after that date it was not allowed, for reasons best known to the Imperial authorities, to receive from anywhere excepting from No. 2 and other hospitals and the Havre Remount Depot and in trainloads of straight skin cases from up the line. Consequently, it lay within the power of the other hospitals to make of the Canadian hospital a sort of dumping ground for their own surgical failures and cases of chronic and obscure lameness, not to speak of 'bad actors' that could only be shod with a maximum of difficulty, a situation of which they did not hesitate to take advantage, but which the Canadians were shrewd enough to accept as an implied tribute to superior professional attainments. So flagrant did this practice become that on one occasion the commanding officer of No. 1 felt impelled to offer a remonstrance.

Up till the fall of 1916, the average number of cases under treatment was in the neighborhood of 700 and

YEAR.	Number Admitted.		PASSED THROUGH HOSPITAL.				
Beginning April 1915.		Discharged fit to Remounts.	Sold to Butchers.	Died or Destroyed.	Sold under Demobilization Scheme.	Discharged to Convalescent Depôts and to other Hospitals	TOTAL
	3308	2652	111	53			2816
1916	7921	6402	378	186			6966
1917	10423	8322	513	740			9575
1918	11754	10427	566	151			11144
1919 till March	515	522	167	106	655		1550
Period 1915-1919						1870	1870
TOTAL	33921	28125	1735	1236	655	1870	33921

Figure 6.5. Disposition of animals entering No. 1 Canadian Veterinary Hospital, April 1915 - March 1919. (*French Papers, NAC*)

about 250 animals were cured monthly. After the extension of facilities, which occurred at that time, the number of discharges rose to 600, an average of 1,480 being under treatment at all times. No case was supposed to be held under treatment longer than three months, at the end of which time, if there was no prospect of an early cure, it was deemed unprofitable and was disposed of. Above is a table (Figure 6.5) showing the number of animals received and passed through the hospital during the whole period of its existence.

In June, 1915, the personnel numbered 196, but being found insufficient to properly discharge the duties, a reinforcing draft of 25 non-commissioned officers and men was brought over from No. 2 Canadian Veterinary Hospital.

DEVELOPMENT It has been stated that the capacity of the hospital that Canada had undertaken to look after had been estimated on a basis of 8% of the number of horses in the field. Upon the formation of the Third Division and the consequent increase in the number of animals, the General Officer Commanding-in-Chief announced on February 1st, 1916, that it had been found necessary to consider provision of additional veterinary hospital accommodation and personnel.

That the Imperial authorities apparently underestimated rather than overestimated the degree of Canada's responsibility would seem to have been the case from the fact that after all four Canadian divisions had come into being, the latter, together with the Brigade of Cavalry, disposed, on an average, of 24,000 horses of Canadian ownership, which at an 8% calculation would have entailed the maintenance of a hospital of a capacity of 1920 animals. But this liberality in treatment was more apparent than real, since the number actually cared for fell not far short of the last named figure.

On the 10th of April, 1916, the unit was augmented by the arrival of 200 non-commissioned officers and men, drafted from the disbanded Canadian Remount Depot in France, and was permanently placed on the establishment of a hospital for 1,250 animals, calling for a total permanent personnel of 6 officers and 419 non-commissioned officers and men, with an additional 34 to be kept on hand as reinforcements for the front. In the course of time, the stabling accommodation was extended to provide normally for 1,364 animals, but this figure was more often exceeded than not, and at one time of exceptional activity passed the 2,000 mark.

COMMANDING OFFICERS The following were the commanding officers in order of succession:
Captain T.C. Evans, from date of organization till June, 1915

6. HAVRE

Captain V.G. Leckie (Imperial Army) from June, 1915 till August, 1915
Captain T.C. Evans, from August, 1915, till December, 1915
Acting Major C.G. Saunders, from December, 1915 till August, 1917
Acting Major S.C. Richards, from August, 1917 till disbandment.
Captain W.G. Stedman filled the post of acting adjutant during Major Saunders' time and Captain F.T. Sear, the quartermaster, during the rest of the time.

CAPTAIN V.G. LECKIE Captain Leckie, an officer of the Imperial Army Veterinary Corps, who was thoroughly familiar with the routine work of a hospital, temporarily filled the position in order that Captain Evans, who up till that time had not been able to acquire an adequate knowledge of army methods of administration, might in the intervening period, gain some experience at the Imperial establishment at Abbeville. Captain Leckie was possessed of a well-poised mentality and an all-round proficiency and of the four officers who occupied the post of responsibility, none endeared himself to the personnel so much as he, and none more fully exemplified in himself the ideal of 'an officer and a gentleman'. He went to Rouen to command the Indian veterinary hospital at that point.

CAPTAIN T.C. EVANS[5] Captain Evans (Figure 6.6), who afterwards made a success in an administrative capacity as Deputy Assistant Director of Veterinary Services with the Second Division, held the position of pathologist in the Department of Agriculture at the outbreak of war. With the very best intentions, he worked hard, but like most of the veterinary officers at the beginning of the war, was handicapped by being insufficiently experienced in military matters to do justice to a command of this nature. It must be remembered that he had to bear the burden of making the initial venture at Havre, under circumstances of exceptional difficulty, which was no small responsibility to shoulder. At his own request, prompted by a laudable desire to take advantage of every opportunity for perfecting himself in the work that lay before him, he was allowed to go to one of the important Imperial veterinary hospitals at Abbeville, where his time was largely spent in observation of military procedure and routine work, Captain Leckie, in the meanwhile, carrying on in his absence and getting things into smooth running order for his return.

Figure 6.6. Lieut.-Colonel T.C. Evans (*NAC PA 7089*)

Some two or three months after his return, the Imperial authorities intimated to Colonel Neill that they would like to show their appreciation of Canadian veterinary endeavor by bestowing a decoration, and in recognition of Captain Evans's strenuous efforts at launching the hospital on its career, selected him as a fit recipient. He was Mentioned in Despatches and given the Military Cross.

After his second period of command had lasted about four months, it was decided to give him the opportunity of acquiring some experience in the actual war zone. About that time, the Fifth Brigade, C.F.A., was in England preparing for service in France. It was composed of units with which Captain Evans had previously done duty in Canada and the commanding officer specially requested his services as veterinary officer. Accordingly, he was recalled to England to prepare himself for this duty which ultimately led to his appointment as Administrative Veterinary Officer of the Second Division. Later, when Colonel Neill considered he had spent sufficient time at the front, an effort was made to have him returned to the hospital, Colonel Neill writing to Brigadier-General Moore, Director of Veterinary Services (Imperial), that he had promised Captain Evans at the time of exchange of duties that in due time he would ask that he be reinstated as commanding officer, as he had every confidence in him that he would administer the command to the entire satisfaction of the Imperial authorities. The latter, however, did not concur.

The improvements about the hospital were due to his initiative and were carried out in his time. That he gave the best that was in him to bring the hospital up to a high standard may be gauged by a quaint and forceful remark in a letter he wrote to Captain Frape, dated January 12th, 1918: *Did Stedman show the pictures of the hospital? He and I worked like hell to make it a credit to the Canadian service.*

Brigadier-General Moore looked upon his work as of a high order and when, in April, 1916, Colonel Neill wanted Captain Evans reinstated as commanding officer and Major Saunders sent to take the former's place as veterinary officer of the Fifth Brigade, C.F.A., Brigadier-General Moore replied that he thought it would be most unwise to make a further change in the command at that time.

MAJOR C.G. SAUNDERS Judged by the standard of his accomplishments at the hospital, his tenure of command must be pronounced to have been a success, but unfortunately, as time went on, cordial cooperation on the part of the personnel in the maintenance of discipline was not forthcoming and it was deemed best by the authorities to make a change in the command.[6] He was, accordingly, moved to another sphere of work, being appointed Deputy Assistant Director of Veterinary Services of the First Division. He was Mentioned in Despatches in June, 1916.

Upon Major Saunders' departure, Brigadier-General Moore expressed to Brigadier-General Neill his opinion that a strong disciplinarian was necessary and suggested Lieutenant-Colonel Tamblyn as most likely. General Lipsett, G.O.C., 3 Division, refused to permit Tamblyn to leave the division.

Failing Lieutenant-Colonel Tamblyn, Brigadier-General Moore wanted to reappoint Major Leckie. At that time, Brigadier-General Neill was in Canada and Lieutenant-Colonel Smith, who was acting in the latter's place, suggested that Major Leckie should only assume temporary command pending Brigadier-General Neill's return, this permitting of the expression of the latter's personal views in the matter. However, nothing was done in that direction and Captain Richards carried on in acting capacity. On returning to Europe, Brigadier-General Neill recommended the appointment of Captain Richards, though there were 22 C.A.V.C. officers senior at the time. Commenting on the need of a strict disciplinarian, Brigadier-General Neill wrote: *...In addition to Captain Richards' capabilities and long standing with the Unit, he fulfils this requirement and is recommended for the appointment.*

MAJOR S.C. RICHARDS[7] Major Richards (Figure 6.7), prior to the war, had acted as a Dominion Veterinary Inspector in Alberta and British Columbia and had also served in the North West Mounted Police. He was identified with the hospital practically all through its existence as he served but two short terms at the front. He possessed average technical ability, was an excellent horseman and polo enthusiast, and being good-natured and displaying at all times a sympathetic regard for the welfare of his men, he secured both harmony and smooth-running during his period of command. He was awarded the Order of the British Empire for his services, besides being Mentioned in Despatches.

At one time there was some talk of appointing Lieutenant-Colonel Wilson to fill the position, but Brigadier-General Moore opposed this proposal on the ground that:
(l) The commanding officer of the Canadian veterinary hospital, according to war establishment, must be a major or captain.
(2) The commanding officer of No. 2 Veterinary Hospital (Imperial) at Havre, Major McKenzie was virtually the local representative of the veterinary directorate and to put a more senior officer there would have complicated matters.

CAPTAIN F.T. SEAR Honorary Captain Sear (Figure 6.7), the acting adjutant to Major Richards, had soldiered in the Imperial army for many years and consequently was well able to assist his chief to steer the hospital along its course. He had been appointed honorary lieutenant and quartermaster during the period in which Captain Leckie was in command. He carried out his duties in an earnest and highly efficient manner and was painstaking to a degree to see that the most minute details were carried out.

WARRANT OFFICERS The warrant officer who served with the hospital throughout the whole period of its existence was Regimental Sergeant-Major (W.O. 1st Class) A.J. Shirt (Figure 6.7). He was a soldier of over 22 years' experience in the Imperial Army, 14 of which had been spent in India, an advantage which he was able to put to good use in the fulfilment of the difficult and onerous duties that came within the scope of his office. He was

Figure 6.7. C.A.V.C. Officers and N.C.O.'s of No. 1 Canadian Veterinary Hospital, Le Havre, France, March, 1919, on the occasion of the inspection of the 4th Canadian Division by King Albert of Belgium. Front row, l-r: S.Sgt. J. Smith, R.S.M. A.J. Shirt, Capt. F.T. Sear, Maj.(A) S.C. Richards, Capt. A.H Hunter, possibly Capt. H.S. Clapp, S.Sgt. W.J. Buttling. (*NAC PA 4252*)

originally attested in August, 1914, as a driver in the Canadian Army Service Corps, where he was quickly promoted to staff sergeant. But, in order that he might go overseas, he reverted and transferred as a trooper to No. 3 Section, the precursor of the hospital, where he was again quickly promoted to staff sergeant and on January 1st, 1915, to warrant officer (first class). He was awarded the Meritorious Service Medal in recognition of his valuable services.

Squadron Sergeant-Major A. Bethell, (W.O. 2nd class) joined the unit on April 11th, 1916, from the Canadian Remount Depot and served with it until invalided to England on September 22nd, 1916. He did good work in the earlier part of the construction work in the extension of the hospital.

STAFF SERGEANTS AND SERGEANTS So many of the non-commissioned officers worked so ably and conscientiously in special lines of duty that it would almost seem invidious to give particular mention to one more than the others, but recognition may well be accorded to the senior staff sergeant, William J. Buttling (Figure 6.7), who always seconded the efforts of R.S.M. Shirt and carried on with outstanding efficiency in the absence of the latter. Staff Sergeant J. Smith (Figure 6.7), as regimental quartermaster-sergeant, performed his duties very efficiently; Sergeant A. Woodley, Staff Sergeant P.J. Lee and Sergeant G. Cunningham, in subdivisional work, acquitted themselves in a highly satisfactory manner; Sergeant F.G. Ashton, as orderly room sergeant and pay sergeant, gave exemplary service which earned for him the Meritorious Service Medal; whilst Sergeant J.F. Bell, in construction work, Sergeant A.C.D. Larivière, as transport sergeant, Sergeant R.C. Wilson, in charge of the receiving corrals, Sergeant J.H. Rogers, who regularly accompanied the animals to the remount depot, and Sergeant H.G. Buchanan in orderly room work, one and all rendered particularly good service.

FIRST AID TRAINING Provision was made for the constant training of non-commissioned officers and men as first aid dressers with acting rank of sergeant to function as assistants to the veterinary officers doing duty with combatant units at the front and with non combatant units in outlying areas, but nothing of the nature of a certificate was given as at Shorncliffe. The candidates passed 3 or 4 weeks in the surgical dressing sheds and attended a course of lectures given by the resident officers, lasting over a period of 2 months. There being far more extensive practical work at Havre than at Shorncliffe, the experience gained at the former place was superior in every respect and practically every candidate made good, only one being returned from up the line for inefficiency.

PRIVILEGES OF PERSONNEL[8] The sergeants did not lack privileges. They had permanent passes for Havre, good between the hours of 5 p.m. and 10 p.m. and on Sundays between 2 p.m. and 10 p.m., and each had a horse, not only for duty, but which he could ride for recreation on Sunday afternoons and holidays.

The corporals and men had monthly passes entitling them to go at leisure between 5 p.m. and 9 p.m. to the nearby suburban village of Rouelles, where there were a few shops and cafés. Passes for Havre, good between 5p.m. and 9 p.m. were also issued in rotation and were supposed to be limited to 5% of the strength of the personnel, but this figure was not strictly adhered to, as many as 15% sometimes being away. Men who had done picket duty during the night before could go to Havre between 2 p.m. and 9 p.m.

CATEGORIES OF PERSONNEL Until April, 1917, when the first 'comb-out' occurred, the men were mostly of high medical category but the need about that time of every able-bodied individual to keep up the strength of the fighting units caused a change in policy and thereafter the personnel was made up of lower categories, many who formed the personnel of No. 2 Canadian Veterinary Hospital at Shorncliffe being brought over when the latter institution was in process of disbandment and others being procured from amongst men of fighting units who had been invalided to the general base at Etaples as unfit for further service at the front. New hands obtained from the latter source were kept on probation for one month and permanently if found suitable, whilst those found to be unfit for the work were returned to Etaples to be placed elsewhere.

From 30 to 40 thoroughly fit men were retained at all times to form reinforcements for the mobile veterinary sections at the front and for doing certain very hard work at the hospital, such as was demanded at the dip, but if at any time a larger number of fit men accumulated, through raising of their medical categories, the surplus was sent to Etaples for distribution to infantry or other first line units.

MEDICAL ATTENTION Any man requiring medical or surgical attention was promptly conveyed to the Imperial Detention Hospital about a mile away, where he was given rest for a day or two or detained for treatment, as was considered necessary by the medical officer in charge. In case of accident or other emergency the patient was taken to the hospital in an ambulance.

GERMAN PRISONERS OF WAR About a mile from the hospital was a large camp containing several thousand German prisoners. The latter were employed more or less continuously by Imperial units but the hospital made no use of them until just before the armistice, when, upon need being felt for additional help, from 50 to 100 of those who had been in captivity the longest and who it was presumed by that time had become fairly well civilized, were brought over daily under guard and set to tasks of grooming and cleaning up. They entered into the work with a zest and did very well, but there was no fraternization with them on the part of our men.

They did not seem capable of ingratiating themselves in the favor of the mules. The latter would have none of them and one particularly discerning specimen of the race put two of them to sleep so that they had to be carried away on an ambulance, and did his best to lay out a third.

DISCIPLINE Discipline varied considerably according to circumstances. Until the great demand in the fighting ranks for all high category individuals, there remained in the ranks of the corps at Havre many men of a pugnacious type. So strong was the combatant spirit amongst them that at the first Christmas, some of them fought amongst themselves all day for amusement. These men, yearning to be in the thick of the fighting and seeing little prospect of their wish being gratified as long as they remained at Havre, believed that by agitating and acting generally in a refractory manner the authorities might be glad to get rid of them by sending them up the line, and when a call was made for volunteers for the combatant units, 75% of their total offered to go.

Consequently, discipline, during the period referred to, was not of the best, but later, when the fire-eaters had been transferred to their proper environment, things quieted down and ran along smoothly, the late comers, for the most part recently from service in the fighting line, recognizing the hospital as a haven of refuge after their hard experiences in the trenches.

DAILY ROUTINE For the summer of 1918, was as follows:

5:00 a.m.	Reveille	12:15 p.m.	Feed
5:30	Fall in and stables	12:30	Dismiss
5:50	Water	12:45	Dinner
6:20	Sick parade	2:00	Stables
7:00	Hay	4:00	Water
7:20	Feed	4:30	Feed
7:30	Dismiss	4:45	Dismiss
7:45	Breakfast	5:00	Supper
9:00	General parade	5:45	Fall in picket for night
9:05	Stables	7:00	Hay
11:30	Water	9:45	Roll call
12:00 p.m.	Disposal of disciplinary cases within the jurisdiction of the commanding officer.	10:00	Lights out

Reveille in winter was 3/4 hour later.

SPORTS Corps sports were indulged in during the summer months, field days being held May 25th, 1916, July 2nd, 1917, and August 21st, 1918. There were the usual events of running, jumping, tent-pegging, and tug of war competitions, 3 or 4 of the events being open to garrison troops. On one occasion, many French residents were present and were particularly impressed by a typical 'wildwest' display at which a dozen or so of the men, including two full-blooded Indians belonging to the corps, attired in Indian war costume and riding a number of piebalds that had been retained at the hospital for the occasion, whooped and halloaed to the amazement of the juveniles present.

The Y.M.C.A. presented sporting outfits for tennis, baseball and football, and in the spring of 1918, a Havre baseball league was organized amongst the Canadian and American troops with the assistance of the Y.M.C.A., one of the teams being formed from amongst men of No. 1.

ACCOMMODATION FOR PERSONNEL For about a month after the unit's arrival, the only accommodation available for the men was the brick kiln in which they lived and slept until tents and Aylwyn huts were procured. Work was soon begun on permanent buildings and when a dining hut and cookhouse for the men, huts for offices and stores, bath house and quarters for the officers had been constructed, a reasonable standard of comfort was secured.

OFFICERS' QUARTERS The officers' quarters, enlarged from time to time eventually contained a number of individual sleeping rooms, a large comfortably furnished lounge with piano and a dining room with kitchen and pantry attached.

SERGEANTS' QUARTERS The sergeants at first found quarters in a room of a farmhouse on the brickyard property and after a while in a small hut which was later enlarged and a dining room and kitchen added by means of funds kindly donated by friends and in the course of time it boasted of comfortable sitting, writing and smoking rooms. The sergeants slept in individual Aylwyn huts.

In November, 1915, two dining huts, each capable of seating 100 men were constructed by the Royal Engineers.

MEN'S QUARTERS In the early part of 1917, the men were provided with sleeping quarters in seven huts, each accommodating 20 persons, which were erected with material obtained from the Royal Engineers. They had four dining rooms, each capable of accommodating 120 persons seated six to a table. Each table had its own meat and vegetable dishes and each room its own machine for slicing bread and meat. Cooking accommodation for 750 persons was provided in the regimental kitchen, in charge of a sergeant cook and four certified cooks. Sufficient men were sent as necessary to an army school of cookery in order to have at least four substitute cooks in case they were required to replace the regular ones, the substitutes being kept in training by doing a week's duty in the cookhouse alternately.

A recreation room for the men was found in the expeditionary force canteen, one of several similar institutions conducted by the War Office throughout the army zones. Opened on June 15th, 1915, it was first conducted in a marquee tent, but later occupied a building 80 feet long by 35 feet wide, having at one end a small stage and beer counter and at the other a grocery counter and pantry, at which staples such as canned goods, candies, chewing gum, tobacco, cigarettes, toilet articles and sundries could be purchased at moderate prices, the profits passing to the War Office to be devoted to the benefit of the army at large and its dependents, which was the case with all the canteens in the army zones. It had a piano and tables and afforded a convenient place for the holding during the winter months of weekly entertainments presented by the talent of nearby units. There was a small separate contiguous room for the exclusive use of the corporals. Doors were opened only at the hours of recreation and none but soldiers might be served.

Besides the canteen, the men could resort to another room for reading and writing, which, however, was rather small having a seating capacity for but 42. Here were to be found books lent by the Y.M.C.A. as well as a free supply of all letter paper that was needed.

RATIONS The food supplied to all ranks, though of excellent quality and plentiful at first, was quite insufficient towards the latter part of the war, when general scarcity prevailed, to satisfy the appetite of a healthy man doing the hard work that pertained to the duties of the hospital. The scale of rations was that supplied to 'lines of communications', quite a bit less than the troops at the front received, and consisted of the ordinary staple articles which one and all had to supplement with viands purchased from outside sources, a state of affairs that led to considerable discontent on the part of the men, using up, as it did, no small part of their semimonthly allowance of pay. Following is the scale of daily rations for the years 1914-1915 and after it, for comparison, for the years 1917-1918:

1914-1915

Meat, fresh	1 lb.	Milk, condensed	1 oz.
Bread	1 1/4 lbs.	Salt	1/2 oz.
Bacon	4 ozs.	Pepper	1/36 oz.
Butter	2 ozs.	Mustard	1/50 oz.
Cheese	4 ozs.		
Vegetables, fresh	8 oz.	Tobacco or Cigarettes	2 ozs. weekly
Jam	4 ozs.	Matches	1 box weekly
Tea	5/8 oz.		
Sugar	3 ozs.		

1917-1918

Meat, fresh	7 1/5 oz.	Butter	1 oz.
Meat, preserved	1 11/16 ozs.	Cheese	2 oz.
Meat & vegetables, canned	1 4/5 oz. (3 days in week)	Vegetables, fresh	8 oz.
Pork & beans, canned	1/4 tin (4 days in week)	Jam	3 oz.
		Tea	1/2 oz.
Bread	8 1/4 oz.	Sugar	1/2 oz.
Biscuits	3 3/30 oz.	Milk, condensed	2/29 tin
Bacon	3 oz.	Salt	1/4 oz.

Pepper	1/100 oz.	Lime juice	1/10 gill
Mustard	1/100 oz.	(if recommended by M.O.)	
Pickles	1 oz.		

EQUIVALENTS

4 oz. Rice	equalled	4 oz. Biscuits	10 oz. Flour	"	1 lb. Bread
4 oz. Fruit	"	4 oz. Jam	10 oz. Oatmeal	"	1 lb. Bread
2 oz. Honey	"	4 oz. Jam	1 oz. Dried veg.	"	4 oz. Fresh veg.
4 oz. Bacon	"	1/4 tin M. & V. ration	1 oz. Sauce	"	3 oz. Pickles

NOTES
Fresh vegetables were not issued with M. & V. ration, one tin of the latter equalling one meat ration plus a vegetable. Nine ozs. preserved meat equalled 1 lb. fresh meat. Chestnuts, when available, were issued in lieu of potatoes, 2 oz. of the former equalling 4 ozs. of the latter. Oranges, when available, were issued twice weekly, 1 orange in lieu of 1 oz. onions plus 1/2 oz. potatoes.

OFFICERS' MESS The officers' mess was conducted as follows: An officer, on joining, was assessed a contribution equivalent to 4 days' pay, of which the sum of Frcs. 25 ($5.00; Fr. 1=20 cents) was collected at once and a like amount in 3 months' time if he was still at the hospital, besides a monthly subscription of the equivalent of one day's pay, all of which went to support the general account. In addition were the messing expenses, the total of which worked out on the average at Frcs. 2.25 (45 cents) per day. Transient officers were accommodated at a flat rate of Frcs. 5 ($1) per day.

Four separate accounts were kept, namely: general, messing, wine and entertainment. The general account covered the furnishings, table-ware, curtains, rent of piano, magazines, etc. The messing account was to meet the actual cost of foodstuffs, over and above the regular army rations drawn by all alike and was devoted to the purchase of such articles as eggs, milk, biscuits, fresh vegetables and delicacies. The wine account was an individual transaction all drinks being sold with a moderate margin of profit. The price of a whisky and soda or glass of wine or liqueur was usually 50 centimes (10 cents) though sometimes it had to be higher.[9] The entertainment account was charged pro rata amongst all members.

SERGEANTS' MESS The sergeants' mess charged an entrance fee of Frcs. 15 ($3) and a weekly subscription of Frcs.3 (60 cents). There were between 30 and 40 members from amongst whom at monthly meetings were chosen three, for carrying on all business matters pertaining to the mess, whilst the actual conduct of affairs was placed in the hands of a sergeant caterer, responsible to the mess committee, who made purchases of canned goods, fresh vegetables, fish and meat. The only liquor sold consisted of beer at 50 to 70 centimes (10 to 14 cents) per quart, port wine at 20 to 30 centimes (4 to 6 cents) per glass, and non-alcoholic ginger-beer at 20 centimes (4 cents) per glass.

The profits arising from the bar account were transferred to the general account, of which the sergeants were allowed to keep on hand a balance not exceeding Frcs. 125 ($25), anything over and above that being devoted to whist drives, concert parties and the entertainment of their comrades when on the point of leaving. The mess possessed a piano and gramophone, the former being rented at Frcs. 20 ($4) per month, the latter being a gift and the records for which were at first donated and then continuously exchanged at the Canadian Y.M.C.A. in Havre.

MEN'S MESS The men's mess depended for extra foodstuffs solely on the refuse fund through which were purchased at the discretion of the officer in charge to a value of some Frcs. 70 ($14) per week extra potatoes, fresh vegetables, raisins for puddings, custard powders, sage and parsley for stews and occasionally fish and eggs, but as the latter cost from Frcs. 2.50 to Frcs. 7 (50 cents to $1.40) per dozen, the men seldom got them.

The refuse fund had its origin in a regimental fund started at Salisbury Plain, to which a firm of military contractors having the canteen privileges in those days, paid the sum of 2s. (50 cents) per man per month, and which

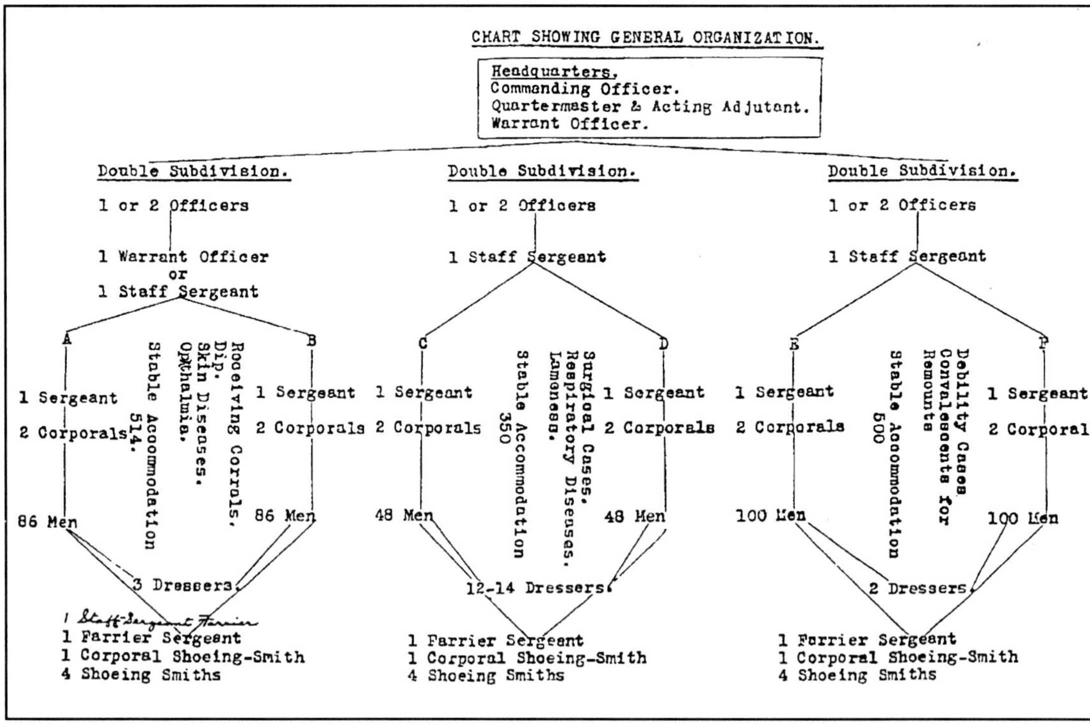

Figure 6.8. Organization of No. 1 Canadian Veterinary Hospital, Le Havre. (*French Papers, NAC*)

remained quiescent until it was transferred to France with the unit. The refuse fund was kept going by the profits derived from the sale of the grease, kitchen refuse, etc., of the camp. The refuse from all cookhouses and mess rooms was collected, the fat sorted out and taken to the hospital fat-reducing plant where it was boiled for two or three days. The liquid was then strained into pans, clarified with salt (a handful to a pint of water) and when set, was cut into blocks and turned into the quartermaster's stores, whence it was disposed of once every two weeks to a local munition plant for rendition into glycerin and ultimately to appear as explosives. The average monthly amount of fat saved for this purpose was 816 pounds, and realized Frcs. 341 ($68). The fund was further augmented by the sale at Fr. 1 (20 cents) per day to a civilian contractor of all the swill apart from the fats.

Anything else that the men wished, they had to buy themselves and this they did by patronizing the expeditionary force canteen, or when they had leave to proceed to Havre, by having a good feed in a restaurant. The breakfast and dinner served to the men were good and sufficient but the evening meal, consisting as it did of but a slice of bread with a little jam or cheese on alternate days and a mug of tea, left a void that could not be satisfied with less than a daily expenditure of from 50 centimes to Fr. 1 (10 to 20 cents) for which latter sum 5 thin sandwiches of canned salmon represented about all that could be purchased.

A fairly good meal downtown cost not less than Fr. 1.50 (30 cents). Beer at from 70 to 90 centimes (14 to 16 cents) per quart could be obtained at the canteen. Some individuals found horse and mule meat so palatable that they lost no opportunity to obtain choice cuts from the flesh of animals that were destroyed on the place on account of broken legs.

GROWING VEGETABLES During the years 1917-1918 the unit materially assisted the provisioning of the troops by raising in the small area of ground available for the purpose, 30,000 pounds of vegetables, of which 26,000 pounds were used in lieu of vegetable rations issuable by the government, thereby relieving the food shortage to that extent. The remainder, 4,000 pounds was used in the form of salads for the benefit of the personnel. This equalled the vegetable ration for 500 men for 120 days.

At the vegetable and flower show held at Havre in August, 1918, for the whole of the allied troops stationed in the area, the hospital was awarded third prize.

Figure 6.9. Capt. Alfred Savage with Subdivision "D", No. 1 Canadian Veterinary Hospital, Le Havre, France. Capt. Savage is seated centre, middle row, with light tie. The large abandoned clay pit that lay in the centre of the hospital precinct is in the background. (*NAC PA 203438*)

FUNCTIONS OF HOSPITAL The hospital acted as: a reinforcement base for the corps, most of the members destined for the front passing a certain length of time there before proceeding up the line; as a training base for first aid sergeants similar to the institution at Shorncliffe; as a hospital proper. During the period of its existence, some 70 officers and nearly 700 other ranks proceeded as reinforcements to the front.

ORGANIZATION The organization (Figure 6.8) consisted of subdivisions, each being in charge of an officer (Figure 6.9) and handling a particular group of diseases, and each being, as far as possible, regarded as a separate self-contained unit, particularly in matters pertaining to hospital work and interior economy. This principle was carried out even to the messing arrangements, a complete chain of authority being thereby established and responsibility fixed. The underlying idea was that the men, finding themselves continuously under the same officers and non-commissioned officers, would feel a better esprit de corps than if they were detailed to do duty under different authority daily.[10]

ACCOMMODATION FOR HORSES

WOODEN STABLES Accommodation for the horses was at first provided by transforming the original wooden bricksheds into fairly comfortable stables arranged as loose boxes and convertible stalls, with flooring of brick and stones, in addition to forage and harness rooms, but they did not permit of convenient adaptation as to capacity and situation.

IRON STABLES During the summer of 1916 the Royal Society for the Prevention of Cruelty to Animals presented the hospital with material for the construction of 15 galvanized iron stables, together with forges and dressing sheds for 750 horses. All the labor of leveling the ground and erection of the structures was performed by the men of the unit under the supervision of Sergeant-Majors A. Bethel and A. Moore, and Sergeant J.F. Bell. Each stable was of uniform size and held 50 horses in rows of 25, head to head and separated by partitions, and each had its own forage and saddle rooms at one end and its own watering trough immediately outside. The stalls were 9 feet long by 6 feet wide, divided by swinging bails and open to the rear with overhanging roof, the whole supplied with electric lighting. Between each stable was a grass plot 15 feet wide and at the back of the stalls a walkway 9 feet wide. The flooring was formed of 2 inch beech planks laid lengthwise on 3 inches of well packed ashes. This proved to be very serviceable material as it required no repairing but had the disadvantage of becoming slippery when wet, a condition that led to one or two accidents of animals falling and breaking their legs.

RENOVATION SUGGESTED Apropos the subject of standings, the reproduction of a circular letter which emanated from Imperial veterinary headquarters and which caused no small amount of amusement in hospital circles, will no doubt strike a responsive chord at home: ... *To avoid so much fouling of standings, would it be possible to induce animals to urinate in a common place outside their stables? For instance, in ordinary times many horses only urinate when they return to their stables and have a little straw of their bedding in their stall on which to do it. Perhaps, therefore, if a convenient place was selected outside their stables, a little straw put down, an inducement to urinate on it might be created if animals were led to it. Once the practice was known to them, it is likely that they might continue it. In any case, it is worth a trial, and would save many a dirty wet standing. It is frequently done by syces in India, and animals at liberty in corrals often urinate in one particular spot.*

The metal partitions separating the two rows of stalls were not altogether satisfactory, sustaining damage from the pawing of the animals and necessitating replacement up to 3 feet, by wood. The entire area of stabling was served by a light railway for the delivery of forage and removal of manure.

WIND SCREENS The open stables having a very exposed situation and in consequence a very large number of debilitated animals having died from cold during the severe winter of 1916-1917, it was decided by Major Richards to have canvas wind screens 10 feet in height made and erected behind the standings (Figure 6.10) so as to form a complete enclosure. Condemned canvas and baled hay wire were utilized for this purpose, and as a result not a single death occurred thereafter from exposure. The canvas was sewn together and mounted on strands of twisted wire, 12 inches apart; the posts supporting the same stood at intervals of 15 feet, were planted 4 feet in the ground and braced on the one side to the roof of the stable and on the other, by means of a further employment of the twisted wire, to stakes driven into the ground. Finally, the canvas was treated with a mixture of whale oil and tar (3:1). In all, many thousands of square yards of this screening were put up.

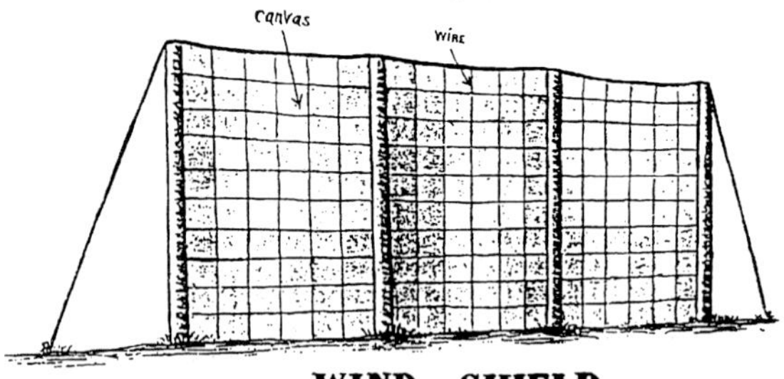

Figure 6.10. Wind shield or screen used to protect horses. (*French Papers, NAC*)[11]

CORRALS Besides the two kinds of stables, a number of acres of waste ground were enclosed with mud walls 8 feet high, sufficient for the accommodation of hundreds of animals.

ROADS, ETC. An idea of the immense amount of labor expended in making improvements may be gathered from the fact that all the yards, stable floors, roads, etc., had to be made on a clay foundation with material hauled from a distance of 4 miles for which purpose thousands of loads of stones were brought from the beach and cinders from factories by the hospital's own transport service, 4 wagons being employed on this duty daily.

DRESSING SHEDS In the vicinity of the stables and conveniently arranged were the dressing sheds, floored with concrete or brick, each having a Soyer stove for heating water, and some of them provided with stocks and squeezes for purposes of restraint (Figure 6.11).[12]

OPERATING ROOM The operating room formed a separate building, 28 feet square, well lighted on all sides, floored with concrete and supplied with hot and cold water and electricity. Its principal feature was a mat, 20 feet square, formed of a double layer of canvas stuffed with sawdust and built onto the floor, on which, in the absence of an operating table, all cases requiring radical operative measures had to be thrown and anaesthetised. There was

Figure 6.11. At the Dressing Shed, adjacent to the stables, where bandages were applied to wounds and dressings changed. Capt. W. F. R. Stubbs (far right) stands with a Staff Sergeant, probably P.J. Lee; the other men are unidentified. c. November 1918. (*Stubbs Collection*)

an ample supply of hobbles, restraining ropes, rubber sheets, sterilizing utensils, instruments and all the usual accessory paraphernalia. This room was characterized by the employment at all times of the most modern methods of technique and at least one operation was originated there which will receive consideration in another chapter. Up till December, 1917, there were performed under chloroform 4,487 major operations of which 3,940 animals were cured and returned to the front - a high percentage. Most of the operating was done by Captains Evans, Leckie, Saunders, Richards, Sproston and Savage.

PHARMACY In a well-equipped pharmacy were to be found stocks of all the drugs used in the hospital, Sergeants J.W. Clisdell and T. Sutherland, pharmacists in civil life, doing the dispensing, though as the war went on, a certain shortage of preparations made itself felt.

LABORATORY Quarters for bacteriological and research work were improvised in the beginning with small equipment donated by the Royal Society for the Prevention of Cruelty to Animals and by the personal expenditure on the part of Captain Hunter of some $65 for which sum he was afterwards reimbursed by the Blue Cross Fund. From this modest beginning, there developed a fairly well equipped laboratory, sufficient to meet all needs of the hospital. It was much resorted to for confirmation of diagnosis of certain contagious diseases, such as mange, ulcerative cellulitis, epizootic lymphangitis and glanders by examination of skin scrapings, wound discharges, blood tests and experimental inoculations. Swabs were made of all wounds every two weeks and examination made for pathogenic microorganisms. Bacterins, both autogenous and polyvalent, were also manufactured for treatment of suppurating wounds.

The following shows the work that was accomplished during the course of some 14 months:

Examination of wound discharges	998

Examination of mange scrapings	954
Examination of blood samples	354
Amount of autogenous bacterin administered (litres)	24
Amount of polyvalent bacterin administered (litres)	41

Previous to May 15th, 1917, several hundred microscopical examinations for mange were made, but no record was maintained. After the date mentioned and until January 23rd, 1919, a total of 1101 examinations were made, the results being as follows:

Symbiotic	Psoroptic	Sarcoptic	Eggs	Negative	Total
9	235	212	5	640	1101

It should be remarked that negative results were often obtained two or three times before the parasite was found in animals which showed the clinical signs of the disease. Many scrapings were examined macroscopically by heating but the usual method was microscopical examination of centrifuged precipitate, potassium hydrate being employed.

Amongst those who, possessing the necessary technical knowledge, carried on this particular work may be mentioned: Captain A. Savage (Figure 6.9), Captain A.H. Hunter (Figure 6.7), Sergeant R.J. Hamilton (B.S.A. McGill), Corporal J.S. Glover[13] (undergraduate of Ontario Veterinary College), Trooper E. Bird.

CLIPPING Until the summer of 1918, the clipping was done altogether by means of Stewart hand power clippers, five of which were in constant operation with two or three extra ones in times of great activity. Each machine needed two men to run it and with each seven horses were clipped daily. In 1918, some kind friend presented three electric clipping machines which were installed in a vacant building and were driven by means of an old dynamo obtained from ordnance, power for the dynamo being derived from the same engine that drove the hay chopping and oat grinding machines. These machines greatly facilitated the work of clipping which was always in demand, every horse having to be clipped on admission to the hospital, summer or winter. With each electric machine, an average of one horse per hour could be clipped, with one man in attendance.

FUMIGATOR There was a steam fumigator in which 20 horse blankets would be disinfested at a time, disinfestation being carried out every time an animal went through the dip if the latter was in the mange lines, and monthly in all other cases.

NAIL BOXES So carefully was everything thought out that could inure to the benefit of the animals that 'offertory' boxes were posted about the grounds for the deposit of picked up nails and other foreign bodies that might be a menace to the feet.

FORAGE Foraging facilities were conveniently arranged, there being individual feed rooms to each row of stables with two men in each kept constantly engaged in mixing and in filling hay nets. There was a main storage barn where reserve forage was held and a mixing shed in which a 9 horse power gasoline engine motor-driven chaff cutter and oat crusher, the gift of the Royal Society for the Prevention of Cruelty to Animals, were installed. The boiler at the dip was also used to furnish steam to a tank in which the oats were boiled - the tank, of a 400 gallon capacity, holding 40 half-sacks or 2,000 pounds; this afforded a nightly feed of boiled oats, mixed with chaff, to each animal in the hospital. The animals were dieted according to their different ailments, being fed from three to five times daily. The feed consisted of hay, oats, bran, linseed, roots, locust beans and green fodder, when available.

STRUCTURAL ACHIEVEMENTS All that the corps achieved at Havre in a structural sense was effected by the skill and inventive genius of its own members, amongst whom were many prominent in civil life in the building and allied trades in Canada. Practically all the roads were made from rock quarried on the spot, the hutments and stables erected, drains installed and ornamental cement foundation and steps built by the men under the superintendence of Sergeant John Frederick Bell, a well-known contractor of Grand View, Vancouver, whilst the installation of the electric lighting of the entire camp, some 450 lamps in all, with overhead connecting wires, was carried out by Lance Corporal G.S. Whelpton, an electrical contractor of Wilkie, Saskatchewan. Both these non-commissioned officers so demonstrated their ability to prosecute this work that the Royal Engineers, officially in charge of the same, were glad to step aside and leave them to their own devices.

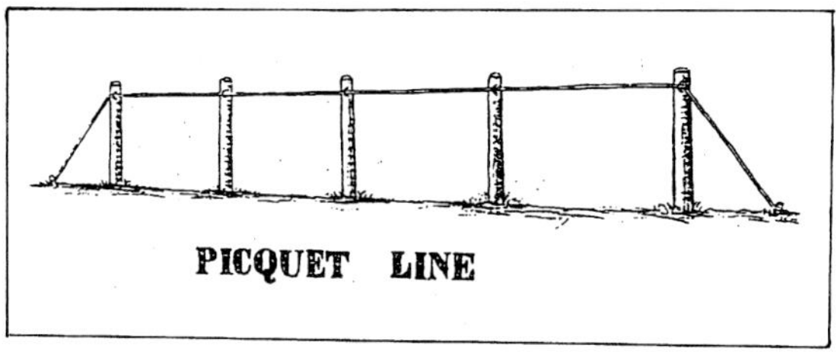

Figure 6.12. Picket line to which horses were tethered. (*French Papers, NAC*)

ORIGINAL DEVICES Corporal Whelpton was also the producer of several articles which with remarkable dexterity and by means of a special apparatus he fashioned out of wire obtained from baled hay. Amongst these articles were: nearly all the fencing on the place, the framework of the wind screens, cables of 35 strands used in place of rope for picketing lines (Figure 6.12), netting of 5-inch mesh between the heads of horses to prevent them biting one another, baskets for holding grooming kits, and hay cages (Figure 6.13) to take the place of the ordinary hay nets made of twine which were found to be too costly owing to rapid wastage from the horses getting them beneath their feet and stamping on them.

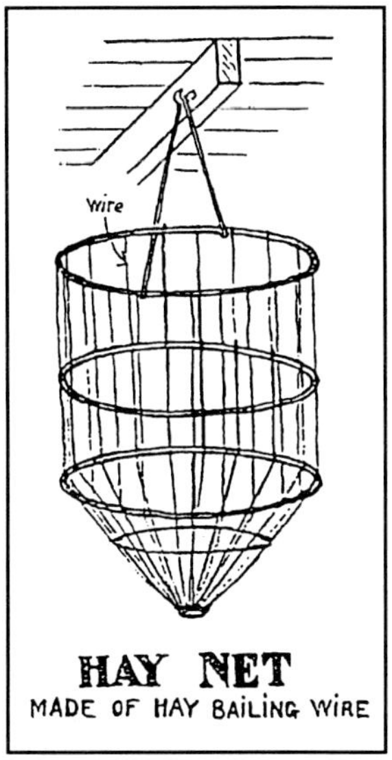

Figure 6.13. Hay net made from baling wire. (*French Papers, NAC*)

Another very useful article invented by Farrier Staff Sergeant T. McLaren, and turned out in numbers which undoubtedly conduced to prevent many an accident, was a quick release hook for holding up the chains by which the swinging bails employed to separate the horses in the stables were suspended. If a horse got its leg over a bail, which not infrequently happened as a result of kicking, the weight of the animal caused the device which was hooked on to a ring on the rear stanchions, to assume a position from which it could, with a slight tap, be made to release itself.

Two or three other original devices were used in a practical manner about the place. One of these was an anti-spilling attachment for nosebags suggested by Captain Hunter, another was a manger which was fashioned in numbers out of discarded oil drums (Figure 6.14), still another the meat and vegetable dishes used in the men's mess, whilst many of the stoves used for heating were constructed by Farrier Sergeant Tappan.

To take care of the large amount of conveyancing called for by the many activities of the place, the hospital maintained its own transport service in charge of Sergeant A.C.D. Larivière. The unit, on coming from England, brought with it 10 draft horses and 5 Bain wagons and by the end of 1918 was employing for its own transport no less than 38 animals and 12 wagons, 12 2-wheeled carts and one motor lorry, all of which were constantly employed fetching rations, forage, fuel, clothing, equipment and material for construction and repairs and carrying away manure and unserviceable stores. Manure was moved daily to a distance of from one to four miles to be distributed to farm lands.

ADORNMENT OF SURROUNDINGS Full advantage was taken of the aesthetic qualities found existing in no small degree in such a considerable body of men to encourage the adornment of the place by floriculture. In fact, the summer visitor was at once struck with the charming effect produced by the multitude of shrubs, plants and flowers that

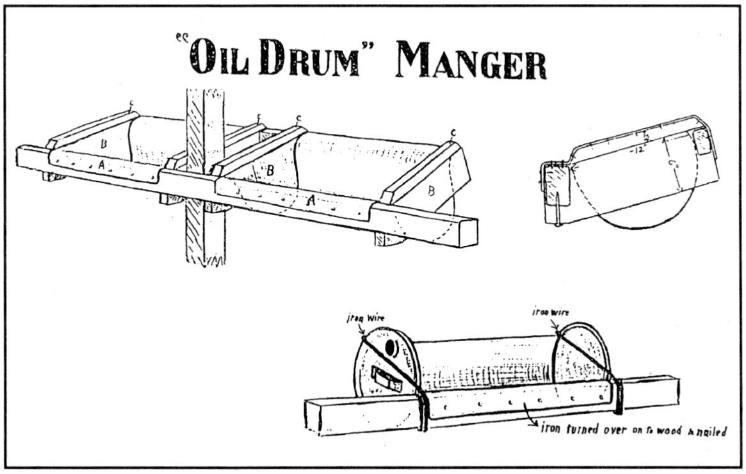

Figure 6.14. Oil drum manger improvised at No. 1 Canadian Veterinary Hospital, Le Havre. (*French Papers, NAC*)

Figure 6.15. Mange treatment in the horse dip at No. 1 Canadian Veterinary Hospital, Le Havre, France, September, 1918. A horse is leaving the race (top centre), while a second is emerging up the steps from the plunge, with a halter lead to a man on each side (centre). (*NAC PA 1928*)

greeted the eye on all sides, even in out of the way places amongst the stables. Many of the plants were obtained from local florists without cost by the exchange, surreptitiously, of a load or two of manure. This statement may sound surprising, but it was only till February, 1917, that the hospital had the disposal of its own manure, at which period the base commandant at Havre claimed the right, and thereafter, if the hospital wanted to favor any individual farmer or florist on its own account, it had to pay from Fr. 1 to Frcs. 5 (20 cents to $1) per load according to the distance of the haul, besides supplying its own teams for the work. But whilst the privilege lasted, the unit effected many a beneficial deal, amongst which may be recalled the bountiful supply of turkeys and chickens obtained for the Christmas dinner of 1916.

DISPOSAL OF ANIMALS ON ARRIVAL The arrival of every animal was attended with certain formalities, a part of the entire system by which the health of the army horses was guarded. First, the animal was isolated at the receiving corral and kept there till inspected. Next, it was clipped and passed through the dip on the presumption that it was a mange contact case, and then sorted and transferred to one of the subsections the same afternoon. As many as 40 could be dealt with in this manner in a day. It was further branded on the near fore hoof with an R to indicate subsequently that it had been an inmate of this particular hospital, whilst for purpose of identification, tags of tin, bearing serial numbers stamped thereon, were affixed to both the halter and tail.

With each animal coming from another hospital came a medical history card on which were detailed particulars as to identity, unit of origin, disease, treatment hitherto given, date of last malleining and shoeing, etc., but the particulars which were supposed to have been accurately stated by the preceding hospital were often incomplete and in some cases had been so carelessly made out that they were quite unintelligible, a fact that gave considerable trouble in making identification. All animals were supposed to have been malleined on arrival, coming as they did from other hospitals, but the test was applied 15 days later and then again in 60 days at the discretion of the officer in charge of the case.

DIPPING TANK As already stated, the hospital having to deal largely with skin diseases, it became necessary to provide facilities for expeditious treatment in that direction, so in November, 1915, the construction of a horse dip or plunge bath for the treatment of mange and dermatitis was begun. It was first put into operation on May 12th, 1916 and through it every horse on entering the hospital had to pass as a precautionary measure against lurking parasites. It became the main feature of the place (Figure 6.15).

It was planned on the same model as similar structures already long in use in western Canada and the United States for the control of mange in range cattle and the destruction of the Texas fever tick, and was the first of its kind to be built in France.[14] Constructed of concrete, lined with 2-inch planking, and holding solution to a depth of 7 1/2 feet, it had a capacity of 3,000 gallons. The total length of the actual plunge was 30 feet, the width 4 feet, and the approaches were lined on either side with a fence converging to the same width, thereby admitting horses in single file only. Each animal, in making the passage, was led in turn to the brink, whereupon, after a momentary hovering, it usually plunged forthwith into the liquid, or, if it showed hesitancy, it was goaded and pushed from behind, the man who had led it in the meanwhile having to get clear by climbing the fence with utmost dexterity. Whilst horses on going in usually plunged, thereby wetting their heads, mules tended to slide in on their haunches in a somewhat frog-like fashion.

Originally, the dip was built with a gradual decline extending to the bottom, down which the animals slid into the solution, but this resulted in so many broken legs, grazed hocks and tearing off of shoes, that it was deemed advisable to make an alteration in the manner of approach. The decline was then shortened and gave place to a sudden drop at the edge of the solution. Thereafter, accidents were few and where formerly 50 or 60 cast shoes might be found after the passage of 1,000 animals, but two or three were to be seen.

The animal, on plunging into the solution, immediately made for the opposite end, but as it reached half way, it was held up by being caught round the lower part of the neck by means of a quick-release belt made of 2-ply leather, 5 inches wide and 4 feet long, slung across the passage and operated by one man through an opening in the fence. Another man then seized its halter with a hooked iron rod 3/8 inch in diameter and 9 feet long, in order to steady and hold up its head and prevent struggling. A pad on either side of the dip at this level acted as a further protection against injury arising from the animal throwing its head about. It being hard for one man to hold up a heavy horse with the rod, the latter had a ring at its free extremity to which was fastened a 1/2 inch rope, 10 feet long, which rope was passed back through another ring fixed in the fence and forward again to the rod, making a sort of block and tackle to relieve the strain. Whilst the animal was held in this manner, a third man on the opposite side proceeded to scoop up some of the solution in a large dipper fastened to the end of a broomstick and to pour it over the head and also to scrub the withers by means of an implement made of a broomstick having a V-shaped iron extension to which 2 dandy brushes were bolted side by side.

This procedure was necessary whenever actual cases of mange were being dealt with and the treatment was meant to be thorough, but some risk was involved in thus holding an animal for not only might the halter break but by struggling, it might slip its head free and, throwing itself over backwards, turn upside down, when, if it were not immediately righted and pulled out it would quickly drown. In such an event, an effort was made to save it by lassoing it and forcibly pulling it over and out. On one occasion, a refractory mule turned upside down and made a very ludicrous spectacle by swimming in that position the length of the dip and back again before succumbing, its feet moving so rapidly that it could not possibly be roped.

About 25 horses could pass through the dip in one hour when each was held for two minutes, 40 could make the passage in the same length of time when allowed to swim straight through, whilst on extraordinary occasions as many as 280 were hustled through in one hour and a half.

On emerging from the dip, the animal was held up for a few minutes in a small dripping off enclosure that drained back to the dip, being given a quick scraping if time permitted, and was then led back to its stall. In cold weather, it was turned into the exercising ring and chased round for half an hour or so till dry and was then blanketed.

Every animal had to make the passage at least once in 10 days as long as it remained in the hospital and no grooming was allowed for 4 days afterwards.

The solution in the dip was heated to a temperature of from 95° to 110°F, the latter being the highest temperature it was safe to reach without fear of blistering the skin, by live steam generated in a boiler in a hut in the immediate vicinity and conducted thence by a pipe leading to the bottom. The solution generally used was of sulphide of lime, which proved to be quite satisfactory for both the sarcoptic and psoroptic forms of mange. It required 224 lbs. of sulphur and 100 lbs. of unslaked lime, boiled by steam heat for four hours in 2 tanks, each holding 400 gallons of water, to make, with water added, 5,600 gallons of solution. Another mange preparation sometimes used was the proprietary one known as 'Cooper's' of which it took 12 gallons to make the full amount of solution. A third mixture introduced by Major Richards, which proved very effectual for cleansing scaly skins, was made with 20 lbs. of washing soda to 3,600 gallons of water.

The mange solutions, having disinfectant properties, were allowed to remain in use for about 10 days when an average of 250 horses was passing through daily, the length of time depending on the amount of mud deposited from the feet and coats of the new arrivals, but the soda solution, containing no disinfectant, rapidly became foul if left longer than a day, and had to be frequently renewed.

It took 4 or 5 hours to heat the solution to the proper temperature and in the process 400 gallons of water were used to form steam, whilst the fuel consumed daily amounted to 448 lbs. of coal, mixed with 4 or 5 bags of sawdust, the furnace being lit at 5 a. m. and going continuously till 4 p.m.

As an indication of the arduous nature of the labor performed at the dip, entailing as it did a great deal of running over the hard flint approachway, it may be mentioned that a pair of boots rarely lasted a man longer than a week and one man wore out 3 pairs in 10 days.

On account of the rapid accumulation of large quantities of sediment in the bottom of the dip, someone conceived the idea of subjecting the animals to a preliminary foot cleansing before they entered the plunge. So a foot bath, something like the dip on a small scale and containing water knee-high in depth, was constructed at a point immediately in front of the approachway, the animals passing from one directly into the other.

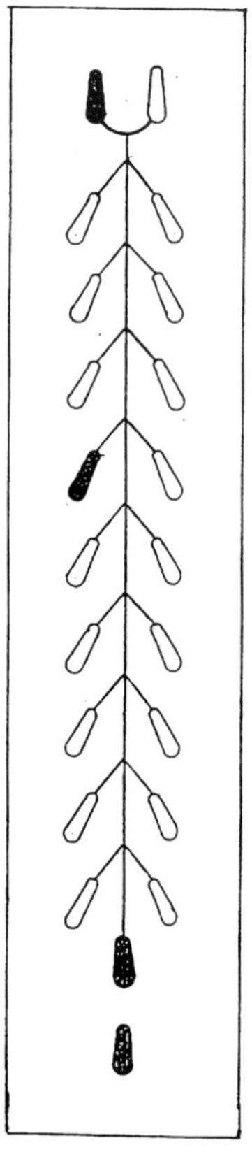

Figure 6.16. Exercising 21 horses. (*French Papers, NAC*)

EXERCISING METHODS To properly exercise such a large number of animals was not the least of the many problems that confronted the staff. Horses arriving from hard labor at the front and kept long in hospital tended rapidly to soften in condition and the units that afterwards received them in such shape were very much hampered for a time. In recognition of this fact, an effort was always made at this hospital to keep the animals hard in muscle and it is worthy of note that Lieutenant-Colonel Edgett, in his war diary under date of November 7, 1917, at the front mentions that he "distributed 80 remounts from Havre Remount Depot which were an exceptionally good lot."

In the early days, the horses were taken on to the highway, one groom, mounted, leading two other horses, but later, more comprehensive methods calculated to conserve labor were put into operation.

An exercising ring, 20 feet wide and having a circumference of 700 feet was constructed. Into this enclosure, 50 animals were turned at a time, divided into two lots, each herded by a mounted groom. The latter, by keeping behind and cracking his whip, kept the animals continually on the move in one direction for a period of from one to two hours.

Another unique method, practised since early in 1917, was carried out by means of 3/4 inch cable, 117 feet long, to which, in all, 21 horses were attached and which required the presence of but three attendants (Figure 6.16). Two leading horses were attached by breast collars to the front extremity of the cable, the near one being ridden by one of the grooms. At the rear extremity, also ridden by a groom, was a single animal, usually a very heavy one and harnessed with a breeching, to act as an anchor or rudder. All along the rope, at intervals of 10 feet, the rest of the animals were tethered on either side, one on the near side at the level of the middle being also ridden by a groom to act as a control of the others. A non-commissioned officer, mounted, rode apart in charge of the line, and the distance covered was about 4 miles. There was sometimes a little trouble in getting the line away due to restiveness on the part of some of the horses, but when it once got started, it went very well, and when 3 or 4 such lines went out in charge of a staff sergeant, the spectacle presented was quite an imposing one.[15]

DISCHARGE TO REMOUNTS Twice or thrice weekly, according to demand, all animals deemed past the convalescent stage and fit for work were sorted out and sent to the Imperial Remount Depot, about a mile away. The number of horses accepted by the depot was limited to its conveniences and once, for a period of three weeks, none was allowed to be discharged, the remount stable accommodation being filled. At the depot, they were passed in review, one after the other, before the commanding officer who exercised his discretion at accepting or rejecting. If an animal was accepted, it then had to undergo a brief examination, principally for incompletely cured or lurking mange and lameness, at the hands of an Imperial veterinary officer attached to the depot, and having been found fit in a veterinary sense, it straightway passed on to the strength of the remounts to be issued once more for duty. All rejected animals were brought back to the hospital for further treatment.

This entire procedure, though part of the regular system of the British army, was regarded by the Canadian veterinary officers as somewhat of a farce and smacking of superfluous red tape, for it was felt by them that they, who but recently had the animals under their care and observation, were better judges as to their fitness to return to work than a remount officer and they naturally did not like to see the latter reject selections they themselves had made.

Consequently, they could not resist the temptation, when opportunity offered, to essay a little practical joking in order to prove that the judgment of the remount officers was subject to caprice and not always consistent. Noticing it to be a frequent occurrence for animals to be turned down one day and accepted a day or two later, they more than once picked out such as had been sent in as hospital cases from the remount depot in the morning and which, upon examination, in their judgment were not found to be affected with any trouble that justified laying them up in hospital, and sent them back mixed in with the regular consignment a couple of hours later, only to see them accepted by the reviewing remount officers who failed to recognize their own rejections of a few hours previously. On another occasion, there were sent over some 30 odd animals which had been doing duty for several weeks in the hospital's own transport service and by which they had been rendered somewhat reduced in weight, yet withal hard and eminently fit for service, and of these, at least three-fourths were turned down whilst others from amongst the hospital cases, hog fat and correspondingly soft, were accepted.

CONVALESCENT DEPOTS At one time, horses that were not fit to be passed to remounts were sent in trainloads of about 280 head to a convalescent depot at Gournay-en-Bras where there was ample pasturage to enable them to recuperate. But in the summer of 1917 this arrangement was discontinued and it was not till the early summer of 1918 that a new convalescent farm near Rouen began receiving debility cases. For this purpose, Sergeant E. Bird, with a detail of three or four men, was permanently employed accompanying from 25 to 40 animals weekly, which were conveyed up the river by boat, hospital cases being brought down on the return journey.

DISPOSAL OF UNFIT ANIMALS[16] At one time, animals which were of no further use to the army were sent downtown and sold to dealers at prices varying from Frcs. 300 to Frcs. 600 ($60 to $120), but the local humane society agitating against this method of getting rid of creatures that had 'done their bit' and there being a great demand in France for horsemeat, all cast animals were thereafter disposed of at the abattoir, excepting such as were unfit for food, which were sent to the carcass economiser plant maintained by the army authorities for recovery of the fat, hoofs and hides.

At first, the best price obtained at the abattoir was Frcs. 200 ($40) per horse and Frcs. 140 ($28) per mule, but by the beginning of 1918 this figure was offered for thin animals fit only for sausage meat and for animals in prime condition had risen to Frcs. 400 ($80) for those weighing less than 1100 lbs. and to Frcs. 500 ($100) for those exceeding that weight, while by the end of the year, the prices had gradually risen to Frcs. 550 ($110) and Frcs. 700 ($140) respectively and finally to Fr. 1.50 per kilo (equivalent to about 15 cents per lb.) live weight for all kinds.

DISTINGUISHED VISITORS From beginning to end, the hospital had many distinguished visitors. In October, 1917, H.R.H. the Duke of Connaught honored the place with his presence. Officers of the French army and mayors of neighboring communes came to gratify their curiosity.

During 1916, Captain W.P. Hill, veterinary attaché of the American Embassies in Europe, inspected the hospital on behalf of his government, whilst two officers of the American Expeditionary Force, Major Gibbs of the engineers and Captain Bell of the Remount Department, visited the camp on May 28th, 1918, for the purpose of getting information and ideas to which end they were offered every facility.[17]

HUMANE SOCIETY OF HAVRE The local humane society made formal recognition of its admiration of the capable and humane treatment of the animals at the hospital, by presenting Major Richards and Captain Savage each with a medal and diploma, whilst three of the best dressers were selected to receive each a bronze medal (Figures 6.17, 6.18).[18] This was the only hospital in France that was so honored.

Figure 6.17. Obverse of bronze medal awarded by the Humane Society of Le Havre to W.H. Dugmore. Inscribed 'VILLE DU HAVRE' above shield, 'NUTRISCO ET EXTINGUO' below.[19] (*C.A.V. Barker Museum*)

Figure 6.18. Reverse of bronze medal awarded by the Humane Societry of Le Havre to W.H. Dugmore. Inscribed 'SOCIETE HAVRAISE DE PROTECTION DES ANIMAUX' around periphery. (*C.A.V. Barker Museum*)

FINIS The career of Canada's veterinary hospital was brought to a close on April 2nd, 1919, when the last of the personnel bade farewell to the scene of their labors, thus rounding out exactly four years from the date the original section left Salisbury Plain. A short time prior to closing, 655 animals were disposed of by sale under the Imperial demobilization scheme, the remainder being discharged to remounts or sold to local butchers.

COLONEL A. C. NEWSOM This chapter must not close without cordial recognition of the unvarying interest and courtesy at all times shown by the Imperial officer who had immediate supervision of activities of the hospital, namely, Colonel A.C. Newsom, C.M.G., Deputy Director of Veterinary Services (Imperial).

AIR RAIDS In respect to annoyance from enemy aircraft, Havre was singularly free, owing to its distance from the actual war zone, and at no time were the men of No. 1 exposed like their comrades at Shorncliffe. Alarms were sounded once in a while when an aeroplane had been seen flying past the battle lines in a westerly direction, but only on one occasion, in the summer of 1918, did a solitary German machine appear and drop one or two bombs on the city without effecting much damage. Nevertheless, as a precautionary measure, the men were ordered to construct shelter trenches.

CHAPTER 7

THE ADMINISTRATIVE VETERINARY OFFICER IN THE FIELD

CHAIN OF RESPONSIBILITY In a preceding chapter it has been pointed out that the Canadian Veterinary Service in the United Kingdom worked under the control and direction of its own director at Canadian headquarters, always subject, of course, to the supreme military control of the War Office. In other words, it enjoyed a full measure of 'home rule' and was not interfered with in any manner by the Imperial authorities. It carried on just as if it were at home in Canada. But the moment it crossed the English Channel and became part of the British Expeditionary Force, it, together with the veterinary services of the other self-governing dependencies, came automatically under the jurisdiction of the Imperial Veterinary Service. Indeed, matters could not have been otherwise.

It is true that in a measure it conducted its own affairs within the range of the Canadian corps in so far as its executive officers in the field were responsible to its own administrative officers, but at the latter point a break occurred in the continuity of responsibility to Canadian officialdom, for the administrative officers were responsible, in their turn, not to the Director of Canadian Veterinary Services in Great Britain, but to the next higher administrative officers of the Imperial Veterinary Services and through them to the Director of Imperial Veterinary Services at General Headquarters in France. The latter official had under his immediate direction a number of deputy directors (Imperial), one of whom was attached to the headquarters of each of the five separate armies eventually composing the British Expeditionary Force operating in the field as well as to each of two groups of Lines of Communication known respectively as the Northern and Southern Commands. It was to these deputy directors (Imperial) that the Canadian Service was responsible.

At first, and until the late summer of 1917, each of the Canadian Divisions had as its chief administrative officer a Canadian Assistant Director of Veterinary Services and each made returns independently of the others to the Deputy Director (Imperial) of the army of which it happened to form a part. But, at the period mentioned, a reorganization took place by which the chain of responsibility passed from a deputy assistant director appointed for each division to and through a single assistant director, representing the entire Canadian corps.

The remarks in the foregoing apply to the four divisions of the Canadian forces which formed the Canadian corps proper, the only portion of the British Expeditionary Force in which officers of the Canadian Army Veterinary Corps held administrative positions. Outside the scope of the Canadian corps was also the Canadian Cavalry Brigade, which, though preserving its identity as such, at all times worked as a component element of one of the Imperial cavalry divisions. In this unit, which had its full complement of Canadian veterinary officers, responsibility lay to the Assistant Director (Imperial) of the cavalry division of which it formed an element. Then there were the noncombatant units, such as the Forestry Corps and Railway Troops, which though in reality organized as Imperial troops were manned by Canadian personnel and carried a complement of Canadian veterinary officers.

The former, with the exception of the companies of two districts which moved about wherever their services were required, operated under the Southern Command of the Lines of Communication, its veterinary officers making their returns to that command, whilst the latter moved about a great deal and were employed now with one of the armies, now with another, so that their veterinary officers, together with the veterinary officers of the two mobile districts of the Forestry Corps, became responsible to the assistant director of the corps (Imperial) with which they might happen to be working at the time. Finally, there was the Canadian veterinary hospital at Havre, which came directly under the control of the deputy director of the Southern Command.

A.D.V.S. The Assistant Director at corps headquarters was the responsible officer of administration of the veterinary services of the four divisions through the deputy assistant directors. He also had immediate supervision of the veterinary officers attached to the units forming corps troops as well as of the officer commanding the corps evacuating station.

DUTIES His function, in addition to general supervision, was to form a channel of communication in veterinary matters between the veterinary service of the Canadian Army Corps, on the one hand, and the Imperial Veterinary Service on the other.

D.A.D.V.S. The Deputy Assistant Director with each division had under his direction the efforts of the veterinary officers working in the divisional area.

DUTIES He had constantly to initiate the methods of precaution against the outbreak, spread and recurrence of disease, and generally speaking, he supervised the treatment of illness and injury within his territory. He was the final authority on all questions concerning evacuation of hospital cases from the division to which he was attached, and it was his business periodically to compile a divisional census of animals according to the shortage revealed by the returns made by the individual veterinary officers to indent for remounts as needed. By means of these same returns, he prepared a consolidated return showing the disposition of all animals left with inhabitants by individual veterinary officers and collected by mobile sections. He also had to be observant of the general conditions of the animals with a view to determining any cause of wastage and to devise methods for correcting the same, whilst he was also responsible for seeing that shoeing, grooming, feeding, watering and sanitation of transport and wagon lines were not neglected.

LECTURING Most of the officers who filled this important position devoted a certain amount of their time to lecturing the personnel of different divisional units on horsemastership when opportunity occurred. Large audiences were by no means rare.

FIELD DIPPING TANKS One of the most important functions of this office was to superintend the construction and operation of field dipping tanks, several of which were brought into existence to combat the mange menace.

DIFFICULTY IN GETTING ABOUT Though, according to establishment, each deputy assistant director was entitled to the use of a car for the more expeditious carrying on of his duties, not one was kept regularly supplied with this means of getting about. Consequently, one and all found considerable difficulty, particularly during active operations, in keeping in touch with their units, some of which were at times distant a day's ride by horseback.[1]

Figure 7.1. Lieut.-Col. C.G. Saunders. *(NAC PA 203431)*

IMPERIAL SUPERVISING OFFICER It is a pleasure to record that Colonel Martin, Deputy Director of Veterinary Services (Imperial) of the First Army, under whom the veterinary service of the Canadian Army Corps most often operated, was always at pains to see that as much consideration was received by the Canadians as by any of the British units.

Let us now consider the administrative veterinary activities, first of each individual division and then of the Canadian corps as a whole.

WITH THE FIRST DIVISION

LIEUTENANT-COLONEL W.J. NEILL

MOVEMENTS Lieutenant-Colonel Neill, chief veterinary officer of the Canadian Expeditionary Force, entrained at Salisbury Plain on the 9th of February 1915, for Avonmouth, when sailing at midnight, he arrived at St. Nazaire at 11 p. m. two days later. Disembarking on the 12th, he left at once by train for Hazebrouck where he arrived at 8:30 p. m. on the 14th. At that point he detrained and moved on to Prudelles, where he established his headquarters. Three days later, he proceeded to Abbeville, there to interview General Moore, the director of Imperial Veterinary Services, for there were many questions concerning the organization and adjustment of the Canadian Veterinary Service to be discussed.

NEW APPOINTMENT On the 11th of March, 1915, he received notification that he had been appointed Director of Veterinary Services for all Canadian contingents arriving in England, and on the 14th of the same month, he handed over the duties of Assistant Director of the First Division to Captain A.B. Cutcliffe and returned to England.

CAPTAIN A.B. CUTCLIFFE

Captain Cutcliffe remained as administrative officer of the First Division until August, 1917, meanwhile receiving special mention and successively attaining the rank of major and lieutenant-colonel, when he was promoted to assume the supervision of the entire Veterinary Service of the Canadian Army Corps. He was succeeded in the First Division by Major C.G. Saunders who held the position till the end of the war. Captain A.E. Coulombe officiated in an acting capacity during the absence of the assistant director.

Lieutenant-Colonel Cutcliffe was a very good administrator of the slow, plodding type, methodical and interested in his work. He was over conscientious, but by his fair-mindedness won the respect of all with whom he came in contact.

ACTIVITIES He made many observations and practical suggestions, amongst which was one that the skins of horses dying should be saved and utilized for making leather, a procedure which was afterwards ordered to be put into effect by the Imperial authorities. In July, 1916, at Hooggraaf, he had to deal with a serious outbreak of mange when, upon a reorganization of the artillery and free intertransfer of the animals belonging to the howitzer brigade, the infestation spread to all units of his division. Mange again broke out in January and February, 1917, but the employment of the dipping tank soon had a beneficial effect. Eventually, by virtue of seniority, he attained to the highest position open to the officers of the veterinary corps in the field, and was awarded the D.S.O.

MAJOR C.G. SAUNDERS

Major Saunders (Figure 7.1), whose activities at Havre had raised the Canadian veterinary hospital to a high standard of efficiency, found an even better sphere in administrative work with the First Division. He made good in this position and was rewarded with the Distinguished Service Order, besides being Mentioned in Despatches a second time.

LOCATION Amongst the places at which headquarters were located from time to time were the following: Prudelles, Bailly sur la Lys, Estraires, Oxelaire, Breilen, Nieppe, Hinges, Verdin les Béthune, Hooggraaf, Tilques, Canaples, Rubempre, Albert, Camblain l'Abbé, Bruay, Barlin, Ecoivres, Château d'Acq, Bracquemont, Château de la Haie, Eecke, Villers Chatel, Etrun, St. Fuscien, Arras, Warlus, Masny, Jemappes, Nivelles, Gembloux, Ahin, Ochain, Grand Halleux, Bruhl, Cologne, Marienburg and Huy.

WITH THE SECOND DIVISION

LIEUTENANT-COLONEL H.D. SMITH

With the Second Division went Lieutenant-Colonel H.D. Smith. His party left Shorncliffe on September 13th, 1915, arrived the following day at Havre and entraining the same evening, reached St. Omer on the 15th.

MOVEMENTS Thence it proceeded by road to Caestre. In July, 1916, Lieutenant-Colonel Smith, who was then well over 50 years of age, felt the strain of active service and it was arranged that he should exchange duties for a period of three months with Lieutenant-Colonel J.H. Wilson, who at that time was administering the veterinary work in the Shorncliffe area. But he never sufficiently regained his health to permit of his retaking the field.[2] He was one of the better class of officers and by his never failing courtesy and regard for social amenities elicited the favorable regard of both his superiors and inferiors in rank.

LIEUTENANT-COLONEL J.H. WILSON

Lieutenant-Colonel Wilson (Figure 7.2), due to his rank, twice was accorded the honor of temporarily carrying on the duties of the Deputy Director (Imperial) at army headquarters. He was instrumental in securing the erection of the first dipping tank at the front on the suggestion of Captain A.E. Cameron, who had experience in that line of work in western Canada. He was twice Mentioned in Despatches. He returned to Canada in April, 1917, the position being filled by Captain T.C. Evans, M.C.

Figure 7.2. Lieut.-Col. J.H. Wilson. (*NAC PA 203435*)

Figure 7.3. Veterinary Officers and N.C.O.s, 2nd Canadian Division, Buzet, Belgium, March 1919.[3] Front row, l-r: Lieut. J.W. Heppleston, Capt. W.E.R. Stubbs, Capt. M.P. Kennedy, Capt. A.E. Cameron,[4] Capt. W.G. Walks, Capt. J.G. Harvey, and Capt. R.J. Vickers. (*NAC PA 4226*)

CAPTAIN T.C. EVANS

Captain T.C. Evans (Figure 6.6), who had been serving as veterinary officer to the ammunition column of the Second Division, and who successively attained the rank of major and lieut.-colonel, was far above the average of his rank. We have seen in a former chapter that Captain Evans, during the earlier stages of his career, at Havre, had his troubles. But they were the troubles of a novitiate and we need think none the less of him on that account. He was endowed with many gifts and by example and precept ever strove to elevate the veterinary service to a higher plane. The Acting Director of Canadian Veterinary Services in a letter to the Quartermaster-General, dated June 26th, 1917, wrote that he was a very capable and reliable officer and he was a second time Mentioned in Despatches. And, the Secretary of War, under date of April 22nd, 1918, paid him a high and gratifying compliment when he addressed the Canadian Military Secretary that he had been commanded by the Army Council to inform the latter that it was desired to employ his services as a pathologist in the army veterinary school at Aldershot because his previous training rendered him eminently suitable for the position and because there was no officer in the Imperial Service qualified to take up the work.

NEW APPOINTMENT He relinquished his appointment the following June and repaired to Aldershot, but not finding the work as congenial, or the emoluments as remunerative, as he had anticipated, and furthermore, discovering that his martial ardor was still burning strongly, he was permitted in September to return to his old position where he remained until the end of the war, when he was a third time Mentioned in Despatches.

When still an executive officer, he produced a helpful little brochure entitled : 'Notes on Care of the Light Draft Horse for Officers and N.C.Os.' which was much appreciated by all ranks.

Officers of the corps (Figure 7.3) who filled the administrative position at different times in acting capacity were: Captain W.G. Church; Captain A.E. Cameron;[4] Captain H. Colebourn; Captain M.P. Kennedy; Captain R. Vickers; Captain E.M. Dixon; Captain A.E. Coulombe.

DISEASES ENCOUNTERED Mange was encountered soon after the arrival of the division and in September, 1916, there were some cases of forage poisoning in one of the artillery brigades, 24 animals being stricken of which 10 died. Contagious stomatitis (Appendix F) occurred at Mont St. Eloi in February, 1917.

LOCATION Places at which headquarters were established were as follows: Caestre, Westoutre, Reninghelst, Tilques, Albert, Canaples, Bruay, Barlin, Mont St. Eloi, Estrée Cauchie, Gauchin Legal, Château d'Acq, Aux Rietz,

Sains-en-Gechelle, Camblain l'Abbé, Brandhook, Norrent-Fontes, Château de la Haie, Auchel, Basseux, Le Caurey, Warlus, Cagny, Caix, Agnez-les-Duisans, Warlus, Cherisy, Sains-lez-Marquion, Sailly, Aniche, La Fosse Farm, Lens, Dury, Masny, Aniche, St. Saulve, Quievrechain, Petit Wasmes, Frameries, Village d'Haire, Mons, Gossellies, Namur, Libois, Durbuy, St. Vith, Rheinbach, and Bonn.

On the homeward march, Bonn was left on January 25th, 1919, for Liege, Profondville and thence to England.

WITH THE THIRD DIVISION

CAPTAIN F. WALSH

As is well known, the Third Division was made up in the field and its administrative veterinary service began at Fletre on February 1st, 1916, Captain F. Walsh, veterinary officer of the First Infantry Brigade, receiving the appointment which led to his elevation to the rank of major. Major Walsh met with an accident the following September,[5] which obliged him to give up active service and return to England. The duties were thereupon taken over by Captain D.S. Tamblyn, who shortly afterwards received the appointment and held the same till the close of the war, attaining the rank of major and lieutenant-colonel.

Officers who carried on at different times in temporary acting capacity were: Captain H.R. Cleveland; Captain T.A. Girling; Captain R.G. Matthew.

CAPTAIN D.S. TAMBLYN[6]

On Major Walsh's return to England and whilst the question of his successor was pending, Brigadier-General A.C. Macdonnell wrote to Colonel Neill under date of September 28th, 1916, that they had no one superior to Captain D.S. Tamblyn for the position of Assistant Director of Veterinary Services of the division, that he did not want to lose him, but that he was such a good officer that he simply had to recommend him strongly for advancement, that he had earned it all the way and would never let anybody down, that he was invaluable and was a keen, capable, efficient man.

Lieutenant-Colonel Tamblyn (Figure 7.4), who had previously risen to the rank of captain in the Imperial Veterinary Service during the Boer War, turned out to be one of the two 'discoveries' of the Canadian Army Veterinary Corps in the Great War.[7] It only needed the opportunity to show the mettle of which he was made. Possessed of a tireless energy, an unflagging interest in, and extraordinary capacity for his work, with a positive genius for developing fertile ideas, he soon proved himself more than capable of holding his position. It is a pleasure to read his war diary, replete as it is with interesting matter even to appended duplicates of his reports and sketches of suggested devices.[8] His splendid work won for him the first Distinguished Service Order awarded to the veterinary corps. He was also thrice Mentioned in Despatches and subsequently received the Order of the British Empire and the Belgian Order of Leopold.

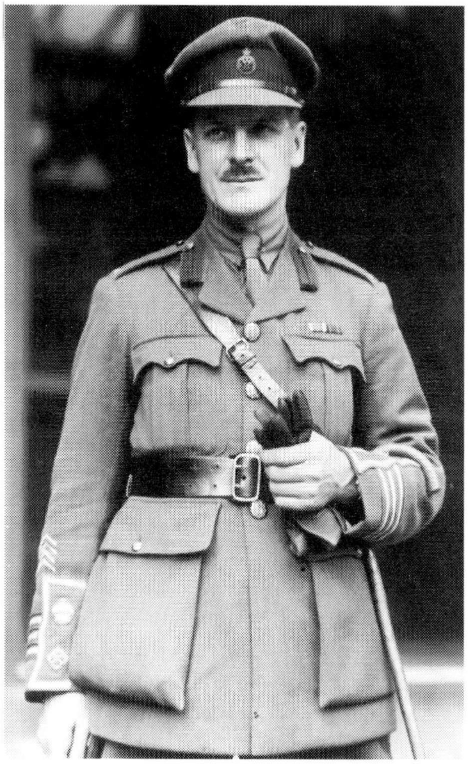

Figure 7.4. Lieut.-Col. D.S. Tamblyn[9] (*NAC PA 7884*)

ACTIVITIES

SAVING MIRED HORSES He came across several mired horses which were about to be abandoned by their not overenthusiastic drivers and insisted upon having them dug out (Figure 7.5). At that time, the condition of the roads travelled by the horses was well nigh indescribable, consisting as these did of ill-defined narrow paths, bordering the edges of water-filled shell craters, along which the men and animals had to grope their way in the dark and where a misstep would cause the animals, and sometimes the men, to meet a watery

Figure 7.5. Horse and water cart mired in mud after straying off a fascine road. The fascines, or bundles of sticks, which form the road bed, as logs do in a corduroy road, are exposed beneath the man carrying cans on the left. The horse was rescued, but the water cart sank from sight.
(*Tamblyn, The Horse in War, p. 62*)

grave.[10] With characteristic promptitude, he inaugurated a patrol of first aid sergeants to traverse the roads nightly and kept this going six weeks till the conditions moderated.

PROGRESSIVE METHODS He was always alive to the needs of the veterinary service and for the promotion of animal comfort and economy. He planned an improved field dipping tank and the overhead hay net system of feeding, and asked that this system be enforced to do away with a good deal of waste in forage. He also urged the introduction of portable chaff cutting and oat crushing plants. He advocated the employment of the 'watch case atomizer', a very useful article for the convenient carrying of iodine and by which a saving of at least 75% of the drug can be effected in application to wounds.

Conscious of the great amount of preventable injury done to the horses' feet by picked-up nails carelessly littered about, he would send out patrols to cover the roads and trails in the forward area frequented by the divisional transports and to pick up nails, spikes, wire, etc., action that resulted in the gathering up of large quantities of these foreign bodies. This action led to the general adoption of the 'gather up the nails' idea by the Imperial authorities; the fact is that subsequently, throughout the army zone, were to be seen little 'offertory' boxes affixed to telegraph posts and other prominent positions at the approaches to all camps, depots and dumps, labeled 'Nails'. As a further means of reducing the number of picked-up nail cases, he devised a metal plate for use on horses that had to visit ammunition dumps where there was always a large number of nails lying about. The employment of this plate met with a good measure of success.[11]

Another brilliant idea was the Tamblyn equine dugout, the squaring of shell holes as a quick means of finding cover for animals from bomb and shell fragments.[12]

CENTRAL CLIPPING STATIONS It was this officer who introduced the system of maintaining central clipping stations conducted by experienced hands instead of leaving the clipping to be done indiscriminately by units. Three such stations were established in his division, each with seven clipping machines and a sharpening machine, whereby 180 animals could be clipped in a day.

EVACUATION OF CIVILIAN ANIMALS In April, 1918, it devolved on Lieutenant-Colonel Tamblyn to make arrangements for the evacuation of civilian animals from the threatened forward areas. He established concentration camps at Masingarbe, Boyeffles, Bully Grenay and Bouvigny Boyeffles and detailed a first áid sergeant to visit these localities and render any veterinary assistance necessary.

DISEASES ENCOUNTERED Mange threatened trouble in July, 1916, at Reninghelst, but prompt isolation and scrubbing with sulphide of lime of all suspected cases and contacts speedily resulted in eradication of the disease. Mange again broke out in December of the same year at Aubigny, but was under control again by the following month.

SIGNING THE GOLDEN BOOK OF MONS In company with many distinguished officers, Lieutenant-Colonel Tamblyn had the honor of signing the city's 'Golden Book' at the Hotel de Ville, as representative of the Canadian Army Veterinary Corps upon the occasion of the formal entry of the Third Division into Mons.[13]

HOMEWARD BOUND When Lieutenant-Colonel Tamblyn was transferred to the staff of the Canadian Section at General Headquarters, Captain R.G. Matthew took his place in acting capacity for the final events. Captain Matthew left Tournai on February 23rd, 1919, with the office records and staff and proceeded via Calais to Bramshott Camp where he arrived two days later. On the 17th of March, he delivered the records to the Director of Veterinary Services (Canadian) in London, and on the 19th, left for Canada.

LOCATION Various places at which headquarters were situated were as follows: Fletre, Reninghelst, Steenvoorde, Albert, Warley, Villers Chatel, Aubigny, Hermaville, Mont St. Eloi, Bruay, Villers-au-Bois, Barlin, Château d'Acq, Mingoval, Mersey Camp, Watou, Norrent-Fontes, Braquemont, Auchel, Château de la Haie, Château-Bryas, Basseux, Horney, Arras, Warlus, Bourlon, Somain, Wallers, Valenciennes, Jemappes, Mons, Nivelles, La Hulpe, Tournai, Renaix, and finally at Tournai, this division not having participated in the march into Germany.

WITH THE FOURTH DIVISION

MAJOR C. E. EDGETT

Major C.E. Edgett (Figure 7.6), in charge of the veterinary interests of this division, left Bramshott on August 11th, 1916, and entraining at Liphook for Southampton, reached Havre the following day.

MOVEMENTS Two days later, he arrived at Hooggraaf and there opened his first office. He remained in charge with this division, meanwhile being promoted to lieutenant-colonel, until June, 1917, when he took up the duties of the new appointment of Assistant Director of Veterinary Services at Canadian Army Corps Headquarters, but returned to his division six weeks later.[14] On April 13th, 1918, he received orders to proceed to London, there to take over the direction of Canadian veterinary affairs in the United Kingdom, shortly before relinquished by Brigadier-General Neill. During his two periods of absence, the acting duties were performed by Captain W.A. Robertson, until May, 1918, when Major W.G. Stedman, late of the Fifth Division disbanded at Witley, arrived to take over the appointment.

It has been stated that Lieutenant-Colonel Tamblyn was one of the two 'discoveries' of the veterinary corps in the war. Lieutenant-Colonel Edgett was the other. Energetic and resourceful, he was at all times keenly interested in his work, and amidst the multitudinous duties of a utilitarian character that fell to his lot, he never forgot the humane side of his calling. He possessed that indefinable quality that inspires the confidence of others and thereby gained and retained the respect of all with whom he had dealings, whether officers or men. He received the award of the Distinguished Service Order, besides being twice Mentioned in Despatches.

Figure 7.6. Colonel C.E. Edgett, Director of Veterinary Services O.M.F.C., formerly D.A.D.V.S., 4th Division. (*NAC PA 7127*)

DISEASES ENCOUNTERED On his arrival, he found mange prevalent in the area, which kept him busy. At Albert, in the following October, he had to deal with some cases of forage poisoning, whilst in December some cases of contagious stomatitis were brought to his notice by Captain W.M. Parsons, one of his divisional veterinary officers. The origin of the outbreak of this latter trouble, which involved 75 animals, though in no instance fatally, was traced to an animal that had recently arrived from a base remount depot. Prompt steps were taken to stamp out the disorder by emptying and disinfecting all the watering troughs in the area and by placing a veterinary officer in charge of each group of troughs to closely watch all the animals and prevent from drinking any that showed the slightest sign of being infected.

SAVING HORSE POWER Ever mindful of the welfare of the horses, he was able at one time to check a lot of unnecessary doubling of work which was going on at Camblain l'Abbé in March, 1917. Teams were being ordered to report to battalion orderly rooms, two or three miles in advance of the transport lines, then given orders to go to towns four or five miles in rear of the latter, to return to battalion headquarters and then back again to the lines. Many trips were being made, whereby the exercise of a little judgment a single trip would have sufficed. Furthermore, long trips were thoughtlessly being made to towns in the rear every few days for supplies for the officers' messes. It was eternal vigilance of this nature that alone justified the existence of the veterinary corps and saved an immense amount of horse power to the army.

He also recommended and arranged with camp commandants and town majors to have men specially detailed in each area to patrol roads and dumps for the purpose of picking up nails with the idea of reducing casualties from nail pricks.

ACTIVITIES COMMENDED From the General Officer Commanding, the following letter of appreciation, dated November 10th, 1917, was received by the veterinary service of this division:

I am directed by the General Officer Commanding to inform you of the appreciation he feels for the work done by yourself, the veterinary officers and mobile veterinary section, during the period leading up to and through the sixth phase of the Third Battle of Ypres.

The results, from a veterinary standpoint, reflect credit on the organization and display the fact that yourself, the other officers, N.C.O.s, and men concerned, handled the situation to the credit of this division.

MAJOR W.G. STEDMAN

Major Stedman developed into a very efficient administrative officer. He had made his mark with the Fifth Division at Witley, and it was on this account that he was given the appointment to the Fourth Division upon the transfer of Lieutenant-Colonel Edgett. Aside from his well-proven efficiency, one of his strong points was his pleasing personality, through which he might always be counted on making a favorable impression upon unit commanders, a very important feature of a staff officer's qualifications. At all times, he gave his wholehearted support to his executive officers, never attempting to meddle with them in the conduct of their duties and consequently securing from them their unswerving co-operation and loyalty.

LOCATION Following are some of the places at which headquarters were established from time to time: Hooggraaf, Reninghelst, Westoutre, Tilques, Warley, Albert, Bruay, Camblain l'Abbé, Hersin, Château d'Acq, Villers-au-Bois, Villers Chatel, Brias, Pernes, Sachin, Sins-en-Amieneis, Beaucourt Wood, Hermaville, Bernaville, Arras, Agny, Inchy-en-Artois, Etrun, Escaudin, Denain, Valenciennes, Mons, Gossellies, Jodoigne, and La Hulpe.

WITH THE CANADIAN ARMY CORPS

LIEUTENANT-COLONEL C.E. EDGETT

Under authority of a War Office letter, Lieutenant-Colonel Edgett assumed the duties of Assistant Director of Veterinary Services for the entire Corps on June 24th, 1917, and opened an office at Camblain l'Abbé. Colonel Neill had written to the Adjutant General, under date of April 30th, 1917 submitting "the name of Lieutenant-Colonel C.E. Edgett as the most eligible and available for the position" and at the same time he had written Lieutenant-Colonel Edgett informing him of that fact and that it was expected he would in a short time be given the appointment.

PROGRESSIVE METHODS The new arrangement promised well for it enabled Lieutenant-Colonel Edgett immediately to put into effect a long-planned centralized system of accounting and handling of the horse returns of the entire corps, the want of which had long made itself felt. It was not until this action was taken that Canadian veterinary headquarters in London began regularly to receive the statistical returns that had hitherto come to hand in but a fragmentary manner. For once, the corps was congratulating itself that a promotion had been made on the ground of merit.

LIEUTENANT-COLONEL A.B. CUTCLIFFE[15]

But at that period, the policy of promotion by seniority generally prevailed, and in the meantime, Lieutenant-Colonel Cutcliffe (Figure 7.7), who was senior to Lieutenant-Colonel Edgett in point of service, laid claim to the appointment, and as there was nothing against the record of the former, the latter was ordered to relinquish the position, which he did on August 7th, 1917. This was in accordance with a wish expressed by Lieutenant-General Sir Arthur Currie, K.C.B., K.C.M.G., who wrote to the Military Secretary (Canadian) under date of July 19th, 1917, to the effect that he did not recommend Lieutenant-Colonel Edgett for appointment as Assistant Director of Veterinary Services of the Canadian Army Corps but that he recommended that Lieutenant-Colonel Cutcliffe be appointed for the reason that the latter was then senior veterinary officer in the Canadian corps and had performed his duties satisfactorily, a recommendation in which Lieutenant-Colonel Smith, then acting as Director of Veterinary Services (Canadian) during the absence of Brigadier-General Neill in Canada, had no choice but to concur.

Figure 7.7. Lieut.-Col. A.B. Cutcliffe,[16] Assistant Director of Veterinary Services, Canadian Army Corps. (*NAC P983.14.10a, Mrs. R.B. Woodland*)

But eight months later, compensation came to Lieutenant-Colonel Edgett in the form of an appointment to London that led to the supreme position of Director of Veterinary Services, Overseas Military Forces of Canada. And before going away, there was received at headquarters of the Canadian Army Corps the following communication from the Deputy Director of Veterinary Services (Imperial) of the First Army:

I should like to bring to your notice the very excellent work Lieutenant-Colonel C. E. Edgett, C.A.V.C., has done in starting the office of the A.D.V.S., Canadian Corps.

I consider he has organized the work on very sound lines and have seldom had an officer who has given me more satisfaction.

I should be very glad if this could be notified officially to the 4th Canadian Division to which Lieutenant-Colonel C. E. Edgett is returning.

Lieutenant-Colonel Cutcliffe carried on the corps work in as efficient a manner as he had previously done with the First Division. In due course, his services were recognized by the award of the Distinguished Service Order, and a second Mention in Despatches.

LOCATION Localities at which administrative headquarters operated were as follows: Ecoivres, Achiecourt, Denain, Valenciennes, Mons, Gossellies, Huy, Vielsalm, Schleiden, and Bonn. The homeward move was made on January 26th, 1919, to Liége and next day to Andenne and then to Jodoigne.

CORPS HORSEMASTER In connection with administrative matters of a veterinary nature, it should be mentioned that there was provided for the Canadian Corps an official horsemaster, who, however, was not a veterinarian or connected with the veterinary corps. This position was filled by Major Critchley of Calgary, who with three sons had gone to the front with the Strathcona Horse, accompanying the machine gun section rather than be left behind. It was his duty to visit all units having horses and render advice on proper care of the same.

Opinion differed amongst the veterinary officers as to the necessity of having such an official, some regarding the appointment as superfluous and an encroachment on their prerogative, but the majority welcomed his advent and recognized that any appointment made in the interests of the horses at the front, especially when filled by a person of Major Critchley's qualifications and attainments, could not but result in increased efficiency of horse-line management. There is no doubt that the supervision exercised by the corps horsemaster militated greatly to the advantage of the horses.

RESPONSIBILITY The extent of responsibility attached to this position will be appreciated when it is mentioned that the general average strength of animals in the Canadian Army Corps was approximately 21,000 of a total value of not less than 7 million dollars and that apart from this number of Canadian owned animals, brigades attached to the Canadian Army Corps for veterinary administration, when the total number of animals under supervision might be double the number mentioned, and in one instance reached the high figure of 50,000 in one week.

REPRESENTATION AT GENERAL HEADQUARTERS

Save for a single official with staff until the summer of 1918, Canada had no adequate representation at Imperial Headquarters in France. At the period mentioned was formed the Canadian Section to act as an intermediary for all matters affecting the Canadian services in France. But the Canadian Veterinary Service was still without direct technical representation, though the Australians had all along maintained there a Deputy Director of Veterinary Services, until the beginning of 1919, when Colonel Edgett arranged for the appointment of Lieutenant-Colonel Tamblyn, who actually assumed the appointment on the staff of the Section with the duty of acting as the representative in the field of the Director of Veterinary Services (Canadian) in London. Had the war continued, there is no doubt that the new arrangement would have met a long-felt want and eliminated many difficulties that had hitherto existed.

WITH THE NORTH RUSSIAN EXPEDITIONARY FORCE[17]

With the Sixteenth Brigade, Canadian Field Artillery, which accompanied the forces sent to the Murmansk coast the latter part of 1918, went an officer and two first aid sergeants of the Canadian Army Veterinary Corps, under an administrative veterinary officer of the Royal Army Veterinary Corps. The officer was Lieutenant T.H. Hungerford, recently commissioned from the rank of sergeant in the Second Canadian Machine Gun Battalion, in which capacity he had seen service in France. The sergeants were F.J. Frape and F.L. Lawson.

On arrival at Archangel the first duty was to procure native horses for the forces. The method followed was by enforced purchase from the villagers under protection of an armed party. The head man of each village would be called on to produce all the animals in the place for inspection, whereupon the largest and best conditioned were selected, very little notice being taken of age. The animals were of the pony type, weighing from 500 to 600 pounds. They were very hardy, were picketed in the open and though they received no oats and but little hay, stood up very well until the spring by which time they were in poor shape. It required eight of them to make up a gun team. The chief trouble experienced was from hvorst poisoning. Hvorst is a weed occurring plentifully in hay in North Russia and is similar to what was known as 'mare's tail' in Canada. Its toxic effect is exhibited only when hay is fed alone, a mixed ration of oats acting as a preventive.

In recognition of his work, Captain Hungerford was decorated by the Archangel government with the Russian Order of St. Anne. It fell to Sergeant Frape to distinguish himself in actual fighting in a most conspicuous manner. His conduct called forth the following citation[18] in the London Gazette of May 23, 1919:

For conspicuous gallantry in action. He played a decisive part in the first phase of the attack. Gathering together a number of drivers, he took charge and fought stubbornly, falling back slowly in face of superior numbers. He himself accounted for several of the enemy, this work contributing largely to the saving of the situation. By this check on the enemy, time was given for preparation of the defence of the guns.

These three members of the corps returned with the brigade in midsummer of 1919.

WITH THE SIBERIAN EXPEDITIONARY FORCE[19]

LIEUTENANT-COLONEL T.J. DE M. TASCHEREAU

The veterinary services for the Siberian Expeditionary Force were organized at Petawawa, Canada in September, 1918, Lieutenant-Colonel T.J. de M. Taschereau being appointed Assistant Director of Veterinary Services.

Lieutenant-Col. Taschereau, who had had a long and distinguished career in the Canadian Militia, had held a similar appointment at Valcartier Camp in the early days of the war and went to Europe as veterinary officer of the Royal Canadian Dragoons. In England he was detailed for several months with the Imperial army and later held the administrative appointment of the Bramshott area. In September, 1916, he returned to Canada for personal reasons and on account of his rank and attainments was selected for the administrative position with the Siberian force.

Canadian Daily Record, 4/7/18.

DOMINION AROUSED BY SINKING OF CANADIAN HOSPITAL SHIP.

CANADIAN DAILY RECORD

ISSUED BY THE CANADIAN WAR RECORDS OFFICE TO ALL UNITS OF THE OVERSEAS MILITARY FORCES OF CANADA.

No. 456. THURSDAY, JULY 4, 1918.

THE KING HANDS V.C. TO MOTHER OF DEAD CAVALRY OFFICER.

Brig.-Gen. Odlum, C.B., C.M.G., D.S.O.

Lt.-Col. C. R. Hill, D.S.O.

Lt.-Col. C. E. Edgett, D.S.O.

Mrs. Flowerdew with her dead son's V.C.

Lt.-Col. Tamblyn, D.S.O.

At the last Investiture, the King presented the V.C. won by the late Lieut. Flowerdew to the deceased officer's mother, and also decorated other Canadians. Lieut. Flowerdew, of the Canadian Cavalry, headed a brilliant charge through the enemy lines.

Figure 7.8. Canadian Daily Record, 4 July 1918, issued by the Canadian War Records Office. Lieut.-Col. C.E. Edgett (bottom left) and Lieut.-Col. D.S. Tamblyn (bottom right) receive DSOs. At the same ceremony the Victoria Cross was presented to the mother of Lieut. Gordon Muriel Flowerdew, Lord Strathcona's Horse, who died after leading a cavalry charge into murderous machine-gun fire at Moreuil Wood, 30 March 1918.[20] (*National Archives of Canada*)

CHAPTER 8

THE EXECUTIVE VETERINARY OFFICER IN THE FIELD

The executive veterinary officer, together with his assistant first aid sergeants, represented the ultimate ramifications of the veterinary service in the field. He formed the eyes of that service, ever watchful of the health and well-being of the animal strength of the army. His duties, in whatever fighting branch of the forces he might be attached, were practically the same, being of a mobile character. Such slight differences of procedure as were necessitated by circumstances will be noted as we go along. The differences were more pronounced in the case of a stationary branch such as the Forestry Corps.

Complement of Veterinary Officers In the early days of the war, each Canadian division, by establishment, was allowed a complement of 11 veterinary officers, whilst in each of the British and Australian divisions there were but 7. In October, 1916, the General Officer Commanding-in-Chief recommended that a reduction be made in the strength of the Canadian veterinary officers to conform to that of the other forces. At that time, the number and distribution of Canadian veterinary officers was as follows:

With the First Division	12
With the Second Division	11
With the Third Division	11
With the Fourth Division	6

Eventually, when the system had been shaken down into good working order, with a good supply of first aid sergeants coming along, and the difficulty presented through a scarcity of fresh officers necessitated an economical posting of the same, these numbers were cut down to seven, exclusive of the administrative officer and the officer in command of the mobile section.

Besides the officers with each division there were others with the headquarters or corps troops, with the Cavalry Brigade and with the noncombatant units. The total complement of executive veterinary officers, with the Canadian Army Corps, the Canadian Cavalry Brigade, the Canadian Forestry Corps and the lesser units, but exclusive of No. 1 Canadian Veterinary Hospital, during the period 1917-1918, was 52, whilst the total complement of Canadian Army Veterinary Corps sergeants assisting the same was 169, allocated as follows:

	Officers	Sergeants
With Headquarters & Army Corps troops		
Corps miscellaneous troops	1	1
Corps field artillery	1	4
Fifth Divisional artillery (2 brigades, 1 ammunition column)	3	11
Garrison artillery	-	2
Total	**5**	**18**
With each Division (4):		
3 infantry brigades	3	3
2 artillery brigades	2	8
Ammunition column	1	3
Train (C.A.S.C.)	1	-
Engineer brigade	-	3
Machine gun battalion	-	1
Total	**7 X 4 = 28**	**18 X 4 = 72**
With the Cavalry Brigade:		
3 cavalry regiments	3	-
Horse artillery	1	-
Total	**4**	**-**
With the Forestry Corps		
13 Battalions	**6**	**65**

With the Railway Troops		
9 districts	**9**	**12**
With the Auxiliary Horse Transport	**-**	**2**
Grand Total:	**52**	**169**

TOTAL NUMBER OF ANIMALS IN SERVICE OF CANADIANS IN FRANCE

The total number of animals in the service of the Canadian forces in the month of January, 1918, over which this small force of veterinary personnel was required to exercise supervision, but not including additional animals belonging to Imperial units, which also had to be taken care of, was distributed as follows:

First Canadian Infantry Division	3974
Second Canadian Infantry Division	4057
Third Canadian Infantry Division	4032
Fourth Canadian Infantry Division	4038
Total	**16,101**
Canadian Cavalry Brigade	
Royal Canadian Horse Artillery	536
Royal Canadian Dragoons	552
Lord Strathcona Horse	558
Fort Garry Horse	575
Machine Gun Squadron	281
Signal Troop	16
'A' Canadian Mobile Veterinary Section	26
Field Ambulance	56
Brigade Headquarters	34
Total	**2,634**
Independent Units	
Canadian Corps Headquarters	44
Canadian Light Horse	525
Canadian Corps Cyclists	16
Canadian Corps Signals	146
1st Army Troop Company Engineers	27
2nd Army Troop Company Engineers	27
3rd Army Troop Company Engineers	27
4th Army Troop Company Engineers	28
1st Canadian Labor Battalion	26
2nd Canadian Labor Battalion	26
3rd Canadian Labor Battalion	26
4th Canadian Labor Battalion	26
13th Brigade Canadian Field Artillery	681
14th Brigade Canadian Field Artillery	655
5th Canadian Divisional Ammunition Column	723
8th Army Brigade Canadian Field Artillery	917
1st Canadian Tunnelling Company	10
2nd Canadian Tunnelling Company	10
3rd Canadian Tunnelling Company	10
5th Canadian Divisional Train (Detached)	83
1st Canadian Reserve Park	358
2nd Canadian Reserve Park	358
Total	**4,749**
Grand Total of horses:	**23,484**

WITH THE FIGHTING BRANCHES

DUTIES It should be borne in mind that a veterinary officer attached to any of the divisional units was not there to treat cases of sickness and injury, other than those of a minor or transitory nature. It is scarcely necessary to point out that the mobility of a combatant unit would have been seriously interfered with had the latter been encumbered with a lot of animals incapacitated and fit only for hospital. On the other hand, he was not expected to remain in a state of passivity till sickness was brought to his notice, but rather to be ever on the alert to discover all latent and incipient troubles and prevent them, when possible, from developing into hospital cases; in other words, to practise preventive rather than curative methods.

Figure 8.1. Capt. A.B. Cutcliffe (left), Veterinary Officer attached 1st Canadian Division Engineers early 1915, and Medical Corps Captain. (*NAC P983.14.9a, Mrs. R.B. Woodland*)

He, therefore, held a position of considerable responsibility and to enable him to properly discharge his duties, he was delegated with considerable authority. Being charged with the important duty of maintaining the effectiveness of the animals to the end that his unit might at all times be capable of mobility, it was essential that he should have the decision as to the fitness of an animal for its work. Moreover, it fell to him to decide whether an injured animal would be likely to recover or not and to cause its destruction in the event of a negative decision.

DAILY ROUTINE His daily routine was somewhat as follows: his living quarters were supposed to be at the headquarters of the brigade or unit to which he was attached, where he invariably formed one of the mess, but more often than not he slept at some nearby billet or in a dugout when it was prudent to do so.

RESPONSIBILITY He was under the command of the brigade or unit commander for discipline but was under the orders of the administrative veterinary officer of the division in regard to all veterinary matters. It will be seen that he thus owed fealty to a sort of dual allegiance and it might be questioned how it was possible for him to serve two masters. But, as a matter of fact, he had little to do with brigade or unit commanders who left him to his own devices as long as he conducted himself in a manner befitting his position and abided by the regulations in force in the brigade.

He was not called upon to perform any regimental duties and he came and went and conducted his veterinary responsibilities in the manner that his administrative veterinary officer directed and that circumstances permitted. He was usually up betimes and, mounted on his charger, made the round of the various horse lines which came under his supervision.

FIRST AID SERGEANT On arrival at the lines, he usually called for his first aid sergeant, who was at all times quartered in the vicinity of the lines where he would be immediately available in cases of sudden sickness or injury, and received from him a report of the happenings of the period since his previous visit. Then, in company with the sergeant, he proceeded to inspect the lines and their occupants, previously, as a matter of courtesy, speaking with the transport or wagon lines officer if the latter happened to be present. He noted the general management of the lines, the sanitation of the standings, the quality of the forage, the conduct of the watering parades, the extent of the grooming, the condition of the thin and debilitated animals and a hundred and one little things that immediately arrested the trained eye.

SICK LINES Having completed the inspection of the lines and the work of the shoeing smiths, he and the sergeant repaired to the unit sick lines. This was a sort of makeshift field hospital, in the open, adjacent to the unit lines, organized by the veterinary officer in each unit as a simple but effective system of controlling and caring for the sick. All sick and injured animals had in the first instance to be sent into these sick lines, which were made the particular care of the sergeant and for which the veterinary officer was responsible.

The sergeant was usually made aware of sickness by the non-commissioned officers or men of the unit, whereupon any animal so reported to him came under his charge and remained in his charge whether in camp or on the line of march, until discharged to duty by the veterinary officer or until it was destroyed, died, or was evacuated to the mobile section. The sergeant, like the officer, was attached to the unit for the performance of veterinary duties only. He was the resident representative of the officer, placed there to afford first aid in all cases of sickness and injury until the officer could take over the direction of the same.

Occasionally, unit officers endeavoured to detail him to irrelevant duties, to which it was incumbent on the veterinary officer to take exception. On one occasion, the veterinary officer, noticing the protracted absence of his sergeant, found, upon enquiry, that the latter had been appointed to the droll function of 'O.C. Beer' by the officer in charge of the wagon lines, and was at that moment scouring the country in an effort to assuage the cravings of a thirsty community!

The sergeant went freely about the lines but unit officers generally preferred that he should not put in an appearance whilst grooming was in progress in order not to divert the attention of the men from the latter important operation.

Figure 8.2. No. 2 Canadian Mobile Veterinary Section. "Nanny", the Section mascot, welcomes sick animals arriving from the front on the celebrated Belgian horse ambulance, August, 1917.
(*NAC PA 1708*)

In the sick lines, the veterinary officer examined all the ineffectives, undertook minor operations and outlined to his sergeant the course of treatment it was desirable to pursue with respect to such cases as it was not necessary to evacuate. In the early days of the war, veterinary officers were instructed to evacuate more freely than at the later stages, when a serious shortage of remounts began to make itself felt. The policy was then to a certain extent reversed and it was urged that every possible effort be made to retain an animal on the strength of the unit, particularly when a stay of some duration was taking place in any particular locality, but, of course, when movements and battles were in progress, it became necessary to resort to evacuations more freely.

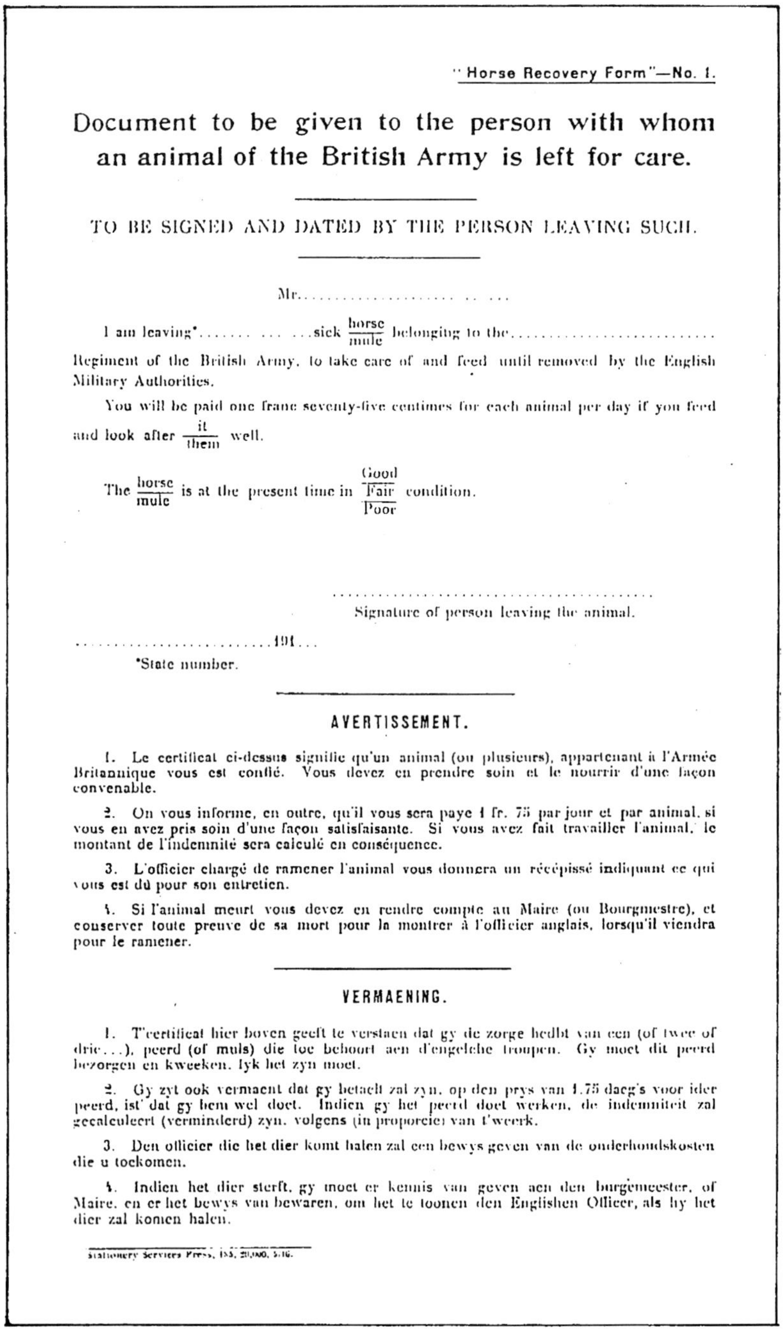
"Horse Recovery Form"—No. 1.

Document to be given to the person with whom an animal of the British Army is left for care.

TO BE SIGNED AND DATED BY THE PERSON LEAVING SUCH.

Mr.............................

I am leaving*..................sick horse/mule belonging to the........................ Regiment of the British Army, to take care of and feed until removed by the English Military Authorities.

You will be paid one franc seventy-five centimes for each animal per day if you feed and look after it/them well.

The horse/mule is at the present time in Good/Fair/Poor condition.

....
Signature of person leaving the animal.

..............................191...

*State number.

AVERTISSEMENT.

1. Le certificat ci-dessus signifie qu'un animal (ou plusieurs), appartenant à l'Armée Britannique vous est confié. Vous devez en prendre soin et le nourrir d'une façon convenable.

2. On vous informe, en outre, qu'il vous sera payé 1 fr. 75 par jour et par animal, si vous en avez pris soin d'une façon satisfaisante. Si vous avez fait travailler l'animal, le montant de l'indemnité sera calculé en conséquence.

3. L'officier chargé de ramener l'animal vous donnera un récépissé indiquant ce qui vous est dû pour son entretien.

4. Si l'animal meurt vous devez en rendre compte au Maire (ou Bourgmestre), et conserver toute preuve de sa mort pour la montrer à l'officier anglais, lorsqu'il viendra pour le ramener.

VERMAENING.

1. T'certificat hier boven geeft te verstaen dat gy de zorge hedbt van een (of twee of drie...), peerd (of muls) die toe behoort aen d'engelche troupen. Gy moet dit peerd bezorgen en kweeken, lyk het zyn moet.

2. Gy zyt ook vermaent dat gy betaelt zal zyn, op den prys van 1.75 daeg's voor ider peerd, ist' dat gy hem wel doet. Indien gy het peerd doet werken, de indemniteit zal gecalculeert (verminderd) zyn, volgens (in proporcie) van t'weerk.

3. Den officier die het dier komt halen zal een bewys geven van de onderhoudskosten die u toekomen.

4. Indien het dier sterft, gy moet er kennis van geven aen den burgemeester, of Maire, en er het bewys van bewaren, om het te toonen den Englishen Officer, als hy het dier zal komen halen.

Stationery Services Press, 153, 20,000, 5.16.

Figure 8.3. Horse Recovery Form No. 1, which accompanied horses abandoned to the care of a local farmer. (*French Papers, NAC*)

EVACUATIONS When, in the opinion of the veterinary officer, it was necessary to evacuate an animal, he ordered its removal to the nearest mobile veterinary section. If a walking case, the animal went over the road in charge of a man from the unit to which it belonged; if it was unable to walk, it made the journey in one of the ambulances belonging to the mobile section, which came for the purpose upon notification (Figure 8.2). With the animal was sent an army form, known as W3752, with full particulars inscribed thereon, and the officer commanding the mobile section gave his receipt on another form, 4V1, which served as a voucher to the officer commanding the unit on whose charge it had lately been. In cases where an animal was turned over to an Imperial or Australian mobile section, the receipt was forwarded to the administrative veterinary officer of the division to which the animal had belonged to serve as a voucher in the final accounting between the different services concerned. At the same time, the veterinary officer notified the transport or wagon lines officer in writing of his action in the matter.

ABANDONED ANIMALS So far we have assumed that everything was in smooth running order as was contemplated, with a mobile section available to take over all immobile cases. But what of those instances where conditions were otherwise and an animal was totally incapacitated from moving? In such an event, the officer commanding the unit, or more often the veterinary officer, proceeded to 'abandon' the animal, whenever opportunity offered, leaving it in charge of a local peasant and delivering with it an official document, known as No. 1 Horse Recovery Form, printed in English, French and Flemish (Figure 8.3), or in the absence of such a document, a certificate similarly worded. The officer then notified the local mayor and reported the full particulars by wire to the administrative veterinary officer of the division. The latter passed on the information to the Deputy Director of Veterinary Services (Imperial) who at once notified the nearest mobile section, which proceeded as soon as possible to collect the animal in the manner described in the chapter on the mobile section.

REMOUNTS When remounts were needed, the unit commander, or in some divisions the executive veterinary officer acting for him, sent an indent twice monthly to the administrative veterinary officer of the division, who prepared a consolidated demand, covering the needs of all the units, and forwarded the same to the administrative veterinary officer of the corps, who in turn transmitted the demand through the proper channels to the Remount Department.

On receipt of the remounts, the unit commander notified the administrative veterinary officer of the division of the number received and their distribution. Only in this manner could a check be kept on the current animal strength. It may be pointed out here that the preparation of indents for remounts as well as the making of returns of the animal strength was not a strictly veterinary one, and constituted an extra obligation cheerfully assumed by the veterinary officers, the like of which was not required of the officers of the medical corps, who did not have to turn in a count of the man strength of the units over which they had medical supervision.

EXTRA WORK It will thus be seen that the time and energies of the veterinary officers were very fully occupied in attending to their multifarious duties, a fact which will become more apparent when one considers the rather lengthy list of reports and returns that they were required to render at regular intervals. Furthermore, the work at times was very much increased owing to the presence of numerous attached units, and it became laborious when one veterinary officer had to take over the work of another who had become a casualty, and continue the supervision of practically double the number of animals ordinarily assigned to him until a reinforcement arrived, which sometimes took a month or six weeks or even longer. Then there was a steady call for attendance on the sick animals of the local inhabitants to which our veterinary officers were ever ready to respond.

What has been stated above with regard to first aid sergeants did not apply to the cavalry, where the establishment did not provide for the same. Likewise, no sick lines were maintained, excepting when the brigade was quartered long in one area, and then, at the discretion of the commanding officer, all sick and wounded animals as a rule being immediately sent to the mobile section where they were cared for until fit to return to duty or whence they were evacuated to hospital. The nearest approach to sick lines was the debility or 'thin' line, where animals down in condition were picketed apart and fed extra rations.

Figure 8.4. Veterinary Officer's Field Chest, with contained top tray, dressings, saline infusion apparatus and instrument tray. Contents were listed on a sheet affixed inside the lid. (*C.A.V. Barker Museum*)

INSTRUMENTS AND DRUGS Each veterinary officer was supplied with a Field Veterinary Chest (Figures 8.1, 8.4), containing a few

Figure 8.5. Canadian Army Veterinary Corps Officer's Wallet. (*NAC PA 4971*)

drugs and instruments, sufficient to meet current demands, and in addition, with a leather wallet for attachment to his saddle, containing a pocketcase of instruments and a hypodermic outfit (Figure 8.5). The first contingent carried over some chests of Canadian design (Figures 8.1, 8.6) which, however, proved to be too cumbersome and were replaced by the more compact and easily handled chests of the Imperial Veterinary Service (Figure 8.4).

The first aid sergeants were supplied with a leather wallet containing a few appliances for their immediate needs.

The Officer returning this Chest will account for deficiencies.

CHEST No. 6.

TRAY.

1 Microscope in Leather Case, containing 3 Objectives, 2 Needle Holders, Needles, Oil Cedar, Stains, Slides, Cover Glasses, Mechanical Stage and Double Nose Piece.

2 Case Books, 3 Note Books, 6 Pencils (indelible), 20 Army Forms A. 2000, 1 book Indent Forms (Army Form G. 994), 25 Envelopes, 3 tins Plaster Adhesive, 5 yards Jaconet, 3 lbs. Tow (compressed), 3½ lbs. Absorbent Wool, 10 yards Linen.

BOTTOM OF CHEST.

64 packets Gauze, each 2½ yards, 4 lbs. 14 ozs. Lint in 1 oz. packets, 9 lbs. 8 ozs. Medicated Tow in 2 oz. packets.

4824--2108 500 6/15 H W V(P 882)

Figure 8.6. Contents of Canadian design C.A.V.C. Officer's Chest. (*C.A.V. Barker Museum*)

There was also a Unit Chest, containing drugs and bandages, for use in cases of emergency, which was supplied to units.

All these chests and wallets were refilled from time to time as needed from the base on indent approved by the administrative veterinary officer.

REPORTS AND RETURNS On Friday of each week, before 3 p. m., the veterinary officer was required to render a report, in person, to his administrative superior, the Deputy Assistant Director of Veterinary Services, at Divisional Headquarters. He had to bring with him a previously prepared army field form, known as A2000 (Figure 8.7), on which were shown all cases of disease and injury sustained by the animals under his supervision during the week immediately passed, as well as a statement of the present strength of such animals after allowing for deaths, evacuation and admissions.

Army form A2000 was the *poena assinorum* of the newly joined veterinary officer, to whom it was a veritable stumbling block to understanding, but when once mastered, proved to be a very comprehensible document. If the uninitiated reader will but glance at the accompanying example of the form, he will probably acknowledge himself somewhat bewildered, until closer study with the aid of the explanatory remarks will enable him to grasp the method by which the authorities in the rear were kept informed as to what was transpiring in the matter of horse strength at the front.

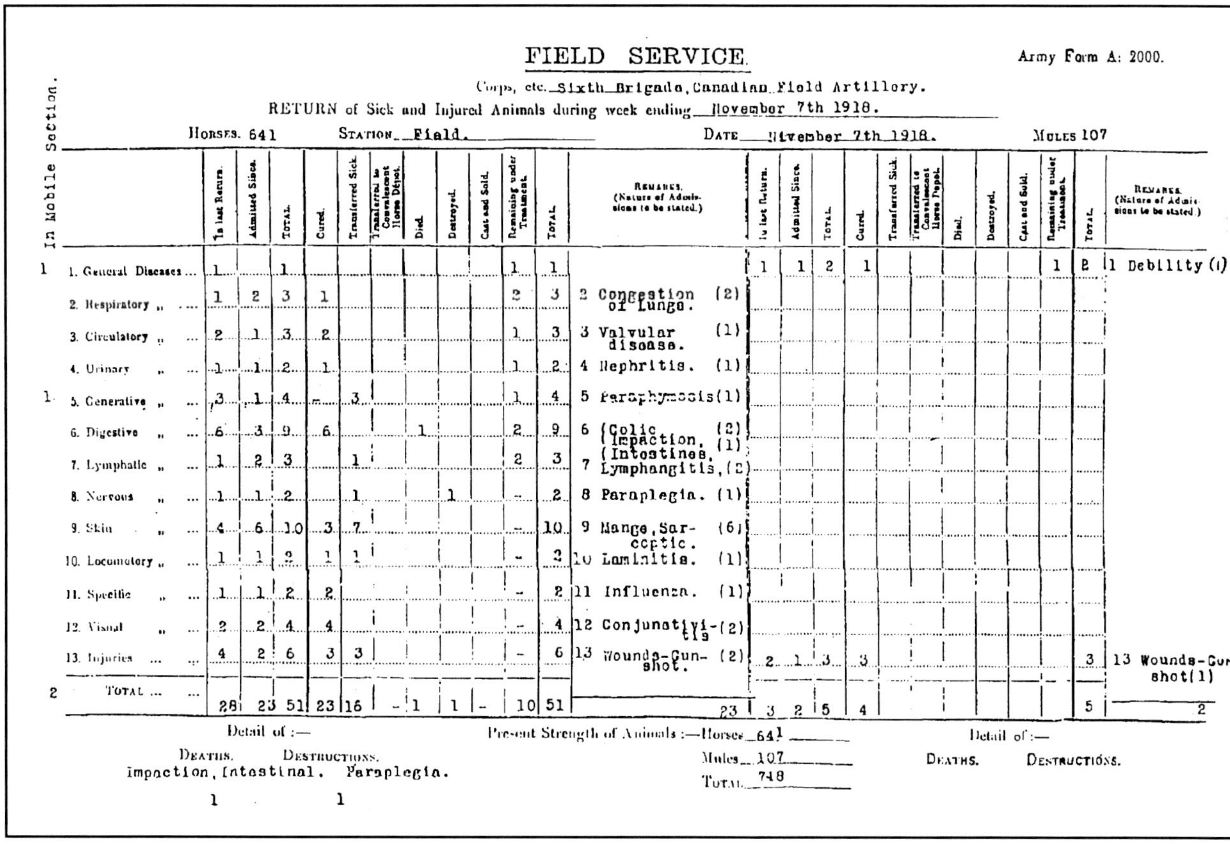

FIELD SERVICE. Army Form A: 2000.

Corps, etc. Sixth Brigade, Canadian Field Artillery.

RETURN of Sick and Injured Animals during week ending November 7th 1918.

HORSES. 641 STATION Field. DATE Nivember 7th 1918. MULES 107

In Mobile Section.

In Mobile Section		Horses: In last Return.	Admitted Since.	Total.	Cured.	Transferred Sick.	Transferred to Convalescent Horse Depot.	Died.	Destroyed.	Cast and Sold.	Remaining under Treatment.	Total.	Remarks. (Nature of Admissions to be stated.)	Mules: In last Return.	Admitted Since.	Total.	Cured.	Transferred Sick.	Transferred to Convalescent Horse Depot.	Died.	Destroyed.	Cast and Sold.	Remaining under Treatment.	Total.	Remarks. (Nature of Admissions to be stated.)
1	1. General Diseases	1		1							1	1		1	1	2	1						1	2	1 Debility (1)
	2. Respiratory "	1	2	3	1						2	3	2 Congestion of Lungs. (2)												
	3. Circulatory "	2	1	3	2						1	3	3 Valvular disease. (1)												
	4. Urinary "	1	1	2	1						1	2	4 Nephritis. (1)												
1	5. Generative "	3	1	4	–	3					1	4	5 Paraphymosis (1)												
	6. Digestive "	6	3	9	6			1			2	9	6 (Colic (2) (Impaction, (Intestines. (1)												
	7. Lymphatic "	1	2	3		1					2	3	7 Lymphangitis, (2)												
	8. Nervous "	1	1	2		1			1		–	2	8 Paraplegia. (1)												
	9. Skin "	4	6	10	3	7					–	10	9 Mange, Sarcoptic. (6)												
	10. Locomotory "	1	1	2	1	1					–	2	10 Laminitis. (1)												
	11. Specific "	1	1	2	2						–	2	11 Influenza. (1)												
	12. Visual "	2	2	4	4						–	4	12 Conjunctivitis- (2)												
	13. Injuries	4	2	6	3	3					–	6	13 Wounds-Gun-shot. (2)	2	1	3	3							3	13 Wounds-Gun shot (1)
2	TOTAL	28	23	51	23	16	–	1	1	–	10	51	23	3	2	5	4							5	2

Detail of:—

DEATHS. Impaction, Intestinal. 1

DESTRUCTIONS. Paraplegia. 1

Present Strength of Animals:—Horses 641

Mules 107

TOTAL 748

Detail of:—

DEATHS.

DESTRUCTIONS.

Figure 8.7. Army Field Service Form A2000. (*French Papers, NAC*)

In addition to the A2000, he had to bring also a statement showing the number of cases of mange under treatment in the sick lines of each unit.

Then, as if the abovc-mentioned returns were not sufficient to satisfy the most exacting requirements, he was further ordered to render to the staff at brigade headquarters a separate weekly return, showing:

a) Number of animals available for work
b) Number of animals on the sick lines
c) Number of animals evacuated since previous return
d) Number of animals died or killed since previous return
e) Number of remounts received since previous return

Besides the weekly returns to the veterinary service, it was required that a monthly 'increase and decrease return' (Figures 8.8, 8.9) be rendered to reach the office of the Deputy Assistant Director by the 28th day. This was to afford the latter an opportunity to check up the weekly returns of the animal strength. It embodied the following particulars:

a) Establishment (horses and mules by classes)
b) Actual strength (horses and mules by classes)
c) Surplus and deficiencies (horses and mules by classes)

Note: Animals attached to a unit for service from some other unit were shown on the strength of the unit from which detached.

A special Monthly Report of Animal Management was demanded by some of the administrative officers. Lieutenant-Colonel Edgett's requirements in this respect, from the veterinary officers of the Fourth Division, were quite voluminous, as will be seen by the following items:

Form Q.M.G. 4021

Monthly Strength "Increase and Decrease" Return

Tenth Infantry Brigade.
Fourth Canadian Division

Month of February 1918

UNIT	STRENGTH LAST RETURN	STRENGTH STRUCK OFF							TAKEN ON				PRESENT STRENGTH	REMARKS
		Died	Destroyed	Missing	Evacuated to Hospital	Date	Transferred to	Date	Transferred from	Date	Remounts	Date		
Brigade Headquarters	20												20	
44th Battalion.	53	1 LD 2nd.			1 LD	12th					2 LD	15th.	53	
46th Battalion.	55		1 HD 4th.										54	
47th Battalion.	51						1 R 10th. Bde. H.Q.	9th.			2 R 3 LD	15th.	55	Transfer to Brigade Major.
50th Battalion.	52								1 LD 4th. D.A.C.	17th.	3 LD	15th.	56	
12th Field Ambulance.	48		2 HD 4th.		2 HD	17th.					4 LD	15th.	48	
	279												286	

This Report rendered to A.D.V.S. of Division by Veterinary Officers.

Captain. Veterinary Officer.

10th. C.I. Bde Unit.

NOTE.—When Horses are transferred it must be fully stated as to what Unit they are transferred to or from.

Figure 8.8. Form QMG 4021, Monthly Strength 'Decrease and Increase' Return.
(French Papers, NAC)

General Report on Animal Management in the Fourth Division to be rendered by Veterinary Officers Monthly

1) Watering
2) Feeding
3) Grooming
4) Condition of lines
5) Mange
6) Casualties
7) Picked-up nails
8) Gas attacks
9) Ophthalmia
10) Preventable injuries
11) Contagious diseases other than mange
12) Remounts
13) Shoeing, farrier shops, efficiency of smiths (where and when trained in cases of inefficiency)
14) Conduct, efficiency or inefficiency of first aid sergeants
15) Medicines and instruments
16) Condition and health of animals
17) Interest taken in animals, or support given veterinary service by officers commanding units
18) Suggestions

Immediately after each move from one locality to another, a special report had to be sent in, giving the location of the veterinary officer's quarters, the location of the horse lines, the condition of the latter, the watering

COPY

FORM Q.M.C. 4916.
2M. 10409 10-8-17.

SECOND CANADIAN DIVISION. MONTHLY RETURN OF HORSES AND MULES. MONTH OF FEBRUARY, 1919

UNIT	Strength Last Return.	STRENGTH TAKEN ON: REMOUNTS. NO.	DATE	TRANSFERS. NO.	FROM	DATE	STRENGTH STRUCK OFF: EVACUATED NO.	DATE	DIED NO.	DESTROY'D NO.	MISSING NO.	TRANSFERRED NO.	TO.	DATE	PRESENT STRENGTH	RE-MARKS.
2nd C.D. H.Q.	76						1	11							74	
4th Cdn.Inf.Bde.	239			6	Surplus	18									245	
5th " " "	239			11	Surplus	11									250	
6th " " "	237			11 16	Surplus	16) 2)	1	1							247	
2nd C.M.G. Bn.	354						2	12	1 17	2 16					349	
2nd P.B&T. UNIT.	71														71	
2nd C.D.A. H.Q.,	11														11	
5th Bde. C.F.A.	831	19	3"				14	1 2 12	2 11 12	4 16 28	1				829	S.off S.by C.of E.(Auth.P.36-4/422, (Q.M.C.14012/195, Q.D.2.)
6th " "	590	22	3"				33	7 24	2 1 20	1 7					584	
2nd C.D. A.C.	676						11	2 11							665	
2nd C.E. Bde. H.Q.,	8														8	
4th C.E. Bn.	145														145	
5th " "	130						7	1		1 23		1	6th Bn.CE	18	129	
6th " "	149			1	5th Bn. C.E.	18									150	
2nd C.D. Signal .	115														115	
2nd C.D. Train.	389						2	9	2 9 13						385	
2nd C.D.Fld.Amb.	131						1	11							130	(D.A.D.V.S.) 2nd CANADIAN DIVISION
2nd C.M.V.S.	16														16	No.-----------
2nd C.D.Salvage Coy.	9														9	DATE-----------
2nd C.D.Sanitary Sect.	1														1	
	4,232	41		29			72		7	8	1	1			4215	

NOTE:- This Return to be rendered in duplicate.
One to D.V.S. & R., O.M.F. of Canada, Monthly.
One to be kept by Officer making Return.

(Signed.) John Doe. Lieut-Col.
D.A.D.V.S., 2nd Cdn.Division.

Classification of Evacuations.

R.	LD.	HD.	Pk.	LCM.	PM.	TOTAL.
7	49	1	2	12	1	72.

Figure 8.9. Form QMG 4916, 'Monthly Return of Horses and Mules'.
(*French Papers, NAC*)

facilities (distance from horse lines, source of supply, etc.). Immediate reports, to be sent by wire, were required in the following cases:

a) Casualties - deaths and animals destroyed, with classification, unit and cause
b) Animals left behind, with statement of place and map location, date, classification, unit and disease
c) Contagious diseases. Any outbreak of contagious disease or suspected contagious disease, with full particulars, particularly as to unit involved

Besides the above mentioned reports, the veterinary officer was charged to maintain a Field Case Book in which a complete record of each sick animal had to be entered (Figure 8.10).

DIFFICULTIES Some of the difficulties that now and then confronted the veterinary officer in the discharge of his duties may be mentioned at this juncture. They demanded the display of infinite tact and patience in order to avoid misunderstandings which might have resulted inimically to the interests of the service. At the same time, the necessity sometimes arose for an insistence, in as firm but obliging a manner as possible, on the recognition of certain prerogatives, without which it would have been impossible to carry on expeditiously.

LIMITATIONS TO AUTHORITY The theoretical limitations to the authority of a veterinary officer have been dealt with in the chapter on The Veterinary Officer. There it has been pointed out that, strictly speaking, the position of the veterinary officer in the army was one of a purely advisory capacity and that he had no real authority over army animals until the same had been regularly transferred to a veterinary hospital. Things could hardly have been

(B/10975)-Wt.W745/780-5000 Bks.-
6/15 S. & S. ,Ltd.

VETERINARY FIELD CASE BOOK

REGIMENT,etc. Fifth Brigade,C.F.A.

No. of Case Progressively.	Color	Sex.	Class	DISEASE	Date of Admission	Date of Discharge	Result	To Mobile Section.	REMARKS	ACTION.
18	B	G	LD	Lacerated Wound (Gunshot)	12-2-18.	28-2-18,	Cured	------	Night Bombing.	Reported to C.O. V/12. 13-2-18.
19.	G	M	HD	Gastritis	12-2-18	24-2-18	Cured	----	Mouldy Hay.	
20	Brl.	Jk	Mule	Punctured Wound (P.U.N.)	13-2-18	21-2-18	Evacuated	15-2-18	Picked up near Ammn/ Dump.	Reported to D.A.D V.S., V/13 14-2-18.
21	B	M	R.	Tetanus.	13-2-18	19-2-18	Died	---	Nail Wound inner Buttock.	Reported to C.O. V/14. 15-2-18.
22	Bl.	G	R	Fracture (O.Tibia)	15-2-18	15-2-18	Destroyed	----	Runaway Accident.	

Figure 8.10. Extract from Veterinary Field Case Book. (*French Papers, NAC*)

otherwise for one has only to imagine a military emergency when, to save a situation, it would be unavoidable for a commanding officer to throw all veterinary necessities aside. And, to pursue the argument to its logical conclusion, ultimate authority over even the animals in veterinary hospitals would rest in the supreme command.

But, granted always that purely military necessity did not have to be considered, such limitations were intended to be complied with in times of peace, before this unparalleled war had been thought of and when there was ample time and opportunity for the observance of the niceties of formality. The duties of the veterinary officer are governed by paragraph 5, Regulations for Army Veterinary Services:

> **REGULATIONS** *The Officers of the Army Veterinary Service are charged with the care of sick animals, the administration of Veterinary Hospitals, the duty of reporting to General or other Officers Commanding, verbally or in writing, on all matters relating to animals, stables, camps, transport, stable management, forges and shoeing, and of recommending any measures which may in their opinion conduce to the health and efficiency of the animals of the Army and to mitigate or prevent disease among them.*
>
> *The function of Officers of the Veterinary Services are, therefore, executive as regards veterinary services and sick horses under veterinary treatment and advisory to Unit Commanders as regards condition of animals and matters affecting their efficiency.*

ASSUMPTION OF AUTHORITY In actual practice, under the exigencies of service in the field, it became necessary for the veterinary officer to assume and exert greater authority than was perhaps ever contemplated by the army regulations as originally laid down. This was a state of affairs that was the outgrowth of the circumstance of this extraordinary war and could not be avoided, and it was tacitly recognized by the higher authorities and all unit commanders whose actions were governed by the dictates of prudence.

One may go further and aver that in view of the standing orders and official directions for the guidance of veterinary officers that emanated from time to time from the War Office and the Commander-in-Chief, full authority was granted by implication for the absolute and unrestricted control of all matters of a veterinary nature. Nevertheless, because of a certain ambiguity that resulted from apparently conflicting authority, the subject from time to time formed a bone of contention between the veterinary officers and the junior officers representing the officers commanding the units to which they were attached.

RESPONSIBILITY FOR ANIMALS All animals issued to a unit were on the charge of the officer in command of that unit and in the last analysis he was the individual responsible not only for their custody but for the maintenance of their health, condition and mobility. To enable him to protect his interests in the latter respect, he was provided with his veterinary officer, on whose advice it was imposed on him to act. If he failed to heed such advice, he did so at his own risk.

This was the theory of the arrangement, but in actual practice, the commanding officer, as a rule, left all such matters entirely at the discretion of the veterinary officer, who went ahead in the discharge of these duties on his own assumed responsibility, relegating mildly indisposed animals to the unit sick lines and evacuating the more serious cases to the mobile section, and only making his actions known after they had become a *fait accompli.* With a conscientious and efficient veterinary officer carrying on in this virtually independent manner, commanding officers who realized the importance of wholehearted cooperation, never had cause to complain. Most of them were only too thankful to be blest with the assistance of such a useful individual, on whom they might place their reliance to relieve them of responsibility, not only for the maintenance of the health of thc animals but in looking after the matter of remounts.

Mutual confidence begat that highly desirable understanding so well expressed by Brigadier-General Macdonnell, when recommending the advancement of Captain Tamblyn to the appointment of an administrative position, in the words: "He will never let you down".

CLASH OF AUTHORITY Owing to the arduous duties of commanding officers in other directions, provision was made for the delegation of their authority over the animals through their junior officers, of whom one was known as the transport officer or wagon lines officer. It was with this latter that divergence of view, if any, usually arose.

In the cavalry, the officers all being expert horsemen, with a consequent understanding of the issues involved, invariably worked in harmony with the veterinary officers; likewise, in the infantry, the officers being for the most part but indifferent horsemen, were only too glad to leave all veterinary matters in the hands of those who were there for that purpose. On the other hand, in the artillery, the officers, taken as a whole, were neither one thing nor the other, their chief interest naturally lying with their guns. But, there were certain amongst them who believed themselves fully competent to handle veterinary problems. With these, it was particularly difficult to deal on account of their propensity to interfere in affairs with which they were not properly concerned. Matters were made worse by the practice of permitting unit officers to go for short periods to a school of instruction at the Imperial veterinary establishment at Abbeville, a privilege designed to give them an opportunity to brush up on their knowledge of horsemastership, but which more often than not resulted instead in their returning with an inflated idea of their knowledge of veterinary science.

Lieutenant-Colonel Tamblyn pointed out that the system of providing unit officers in charge of wagon lines was susceptible of improvement. Many of these were sent there primarily for a ‘rest’ from their arduous duties at the guns, and having little knowledge of horses proved themselves incompetent to take charge, whereas several non-commissioned officers who were good horsemen with practical experience before the war would have made ideal officers for this duty.

At times, the artillery officers came dangerously near to imperiling the smooth working and efficiency of the veterinary service and many instances of ‘bucking’ might be related but of which one or two will suffice.

One which occurred in an Imperial unit, temporarily attached to the Canadians, and where the unit officers pursued a line of conduct counter to their own interests without realizing it, had to be settled by an appeal to Lieutenant-Colonel Edgett, at that time administrative veterinary officer of the division concerned. In the temporary absence of the executive veterinary officer, the unit officers segregated an animal they suspected of mange. The veterinary officer, on his return, examined the animal and pronounced against the suspicion. In the face of this authoritative opinion, the unit officers persisted in segregating the animal until Lieutenant-Colonel Edgett had concurred in the diagnosis of the veterinary officer and endorsed the latter's direction that it should be returned to duty. In this particular battery, the veterinary officer had an uphill fight for a period of two months in getting his advice heeded generally, the wholehearted cooperation of the unit officers being lacking.

In another instance, an artillery officer endeavored to dissuade a newly joined veterinary officer from maintaining unit sick lines and to persuade him to discharge to duty animals which were not yet fit. In still another instance, a wagon lines officer attempted to evacuate a segregated animal in the temporary absence of the veterinary officer, the latter alone having the right to decide on such a step. This particular wagon lines officer even objected to the veterinary officer passing through his lines for the purpose of inspecting the animals unless he had previously made known his wish, a formality which, needless to say, was quite superfluous, and had it been required, would have reacted to the detriment of the service, for the veterinary officer was expected to circulate freely at any time or place amongst the animals over which he had supervision.

In these and similar cases, the veterinary officers were invariably upheld by the authorities when it became necessary to make an appeal higher up.

The regulations provided that for every three horses standing in the sick lines, the unit should provide an attendant, whose full time was supposed to be occupied in undertaking this work. Few of the artillery officers wanted to abide by this provision. They preferred to send along the particular driver of each isolated animal to do the grooming and cleaning, claiming that such an individual would take more interest in bringing his own animal back to condition than any other, a claim that had more than a shadow of truth in it. The result, however, would be the coming and going of several men into and from the sick lines, which was a highly undesirable state of affairs from the veterinary officer's point of view, particularly when he might have an animal segregated for suspected contagious disease. Even in Siberia, similar experiences were encountered and it became necessary, in the interests of harmony, to transfer the veterinary officer from the 85th Battery, in which unit no co-operation was forthcoming.

Then, in France, there was the question of bedding. As the war progressed and it became necessary to conserve all material that could serve as forage, straw was banned for littering purposes, and veterinary officers were instructed to report all cases of its unauthorized use. Some unit officers, and particularly commanding officers, otherwise patriotic to a degree, were frequent offenders in this respect. What was a veterinary officer to do? Had he reported such cases to the higher authorities, he would speedily have rendered himself *persona non grata* in the unit, which would have had a tendency to handicap him in the discharge of his ordinary veterinary duties.

LIMITATIONS TO UNIT OFFICERS' AUTHORITY It has been stated that the officer commanding a unit was the individual really responsible for the animals on the strength of the same. Nevertheless, his authority was hedged by certain limitations. For instance, once an animal had been issued to his unit, he had no authority to evacuate it, excepting on the advice of his veterinary officer and subject to the approval of the administrative veterinary officer of the division. Neither might he make an exchange with any other unit excepting as between sub-units under his immediate command.

TRANSFERS AND EXCHANGES All transfers or exchanges between units of a division could be made on the authority of divisional headquarters only, whilst all transfers or exchanges between divisions or between units comprising corps troops could be made on the authority of corps headquarters only, and then only provided the executive veterinary officer certified freedom from contagious disease. Transfers between Canadian and Imperial units could take place on the authority of corps headquarters only, and in each case an army form known as 0.1640 (Figure 8.11) had to be signed in duplicate by an officer of both units concerned, as well as by a veterinary officer, and returned to divisional headquarters for accounting purposes.

All deaths had to be certified by the administrative veterinary officer of the division. Destruction on account of grievous wounding might only be carried out on the order of the executive veterinary officer excepting where an animal was obviously incurably injured and suffering great pain, when any officer might assume this authority subject to his reporting his action to the veterinary officer. In the case of an animal missing, a board of inquiry had to be held by the unit to which it belonged and the particulars forwarded to the administrative veterinary officer of the corps, by whose authority alone it might be struck off the strength.

The commanding officer of a unit could not even get rid of a bad actor or outlaw, where no reason of a veterinary nature could be advanced, but had to await the intervention of the Remount Department for that purpose. It need hardly be added that veterinary officers generally obligingly contrived to find a veterinary reason for ridding the unit of such an animal, though such action might result in some other unit eventually being saddled with it.

STORK VISITS LINES On one or two rare occasions, a stork visited the lines and left behind an unsolicited reinforcement. 'Vimy', the mascot of the Sixth Brigade, C.F.A., first saw the light of day and the Canadians on an auspicious occasion, April 9th, 1917, just as the Vimy operations were being ushered in, and whilst snow lay on the ground. The mother had newly arrived from England with a reinforcing battery and was assigned to the 22nd Battery. Everybody took a great interest in 'Vimy', who wandered round at will in the lines of Sixth Brigade Headquarters, until just prior to the march into Germany in November, 1918, when it became necessary to part with her and she was accordingly sent down to the base.

EVASION OF REGULATIONS The above-mentioned regulations, like regulations in general, were surreptitiously evaded at times. This remark applies more particularly to the matter of exchanges.

Now for the facts, for we are recording not only what ought to have taken place, but what actually did take place. Human nature is the same all the world over when it comes to a question of 'swapping' horses and Canadian soldiers were no exception to the rule. As long as a unit lay in a quiet sector of the line or at rest in the rear the regulations were generally observed and a stray animal was rarely to be seen. However, let there be a battle or an advance and strays would be running all over the place. It was at times like those that temptation proved stronger than regulations and many an instance occurred where a 'better one' was gathered in and the 'original' turned loose in its place. Everybody believed that the rank and file of the military police, who were invariably to be seen riding splendid chargers, came to their good fortune by these means.

Army Form O. 1640.
(In books of 50.)

Report of Transfer of Officers' or Troop Horses and Mules.

(To accompany the animal or to be despatched not later than the day on which the animal leaves the unit.)

(a) Unit from which transferred.
(b) Unit to which transferred.
(c) Army numbers.
(Mules should be distinguished from horses.)
(d) Date last shod.
(e) Date last foraged.
(f) Height and Class.
(i.e., charger, cob, troop horse, &c.)

Date............ .... Officer Commanding.

Certificate of Veterinary Officer.

I certify that I have inspected the animals about to proceed to............ and that they are properly shod and free from disease.

I further certify that these animals have not been in contact with any animals affected with contagious or infectious diseases.

Date............ .... Veterinary Officer.

This portion to be completed by the Receiving Officer.

I certify that the............animals have been brought on charge in my account on ....*being the day following that shewn at (e) above.

Name............
Date............ Rank............

* Horse billets will, in accordance with Allowance Regulations, be shewn on the F. 718 of the unit at the station of arrival and not of departure.

INSTRUCTIONS

(1) This Form is to be prepared in *duplicate* by Officers Commanding units in every case in which animals are struck off on Army Forms F. 718 or P. 1927 and brought on charge in another Army Form F. 718 or P. 1927.
(2) The Officer Commanding the unit *receiving* the animals will complete the Form and return one copy of the unit from which the animals were sent.
(3) The respective copies will be attached as sub-vouchers to the Army Forms F. 718 or P. 1927 concerned.
(4) The certificate of the Veterinary Officer should be completed when animals are moved from one station ...er.

W9367 M934 5000 bks. 11/16s 173 G & S E.583 Forms O. 1640 / 20

Figure 8.11. Army Form O.1640, 'Report of Transfer of Officers' or Troop Horses and Mules'. (*French Papers, NAC*)

Moreover, every veterinary officer was aware (unofficially, of course) that at all times one or two surplus animals were being held on the quiet within the lines of his unit, but he would have been something less than human to have enquired too closely into such matters. Of course, it would not have done to have allowed the practice to be indulged in to any extent because the question of forage had to be considered. Forage was issued only for as many animals as were officially known to be on the strength and any unauthorized increase in the latter would have meant a corresponding reduction of fodder all round, which with a none too free supply would have meant a certain deterioration in condition. But the practice was pursued, or as one would say, was 'winked at' by unit commanders, and for these reasons the returns of animal strength which the veterinary officers were called on to render, were only relatively accurate. They started in the first instance with a known definite number and continued the record according to the changes that were officially brought to their notice.

DECORATIONS The executive officers who were awarded decorations for their consistent devotion to duty in the field were:
Captains A.E. Cameron, M.P. Kennedy, and E.L.E. Taylor, each of whom received the Military Cross.
Captains W.A. Robertson, M.J. Preston, and W.F. Towill, who were awarded the Order of the British Empire.
Captain R.G. Matthew, on whom was bestowed the Croix de Guerre by the Belgian Government.
Captains N.G. Beaver, H. Colebourn, T.A. Girling, F.G. Liddle, M.J. Preston, R.G. Matthew, W.A. Robertson, P.P. Souillard, A.D. McAllister and W.F. Towill, were Mentioned in Despatches.

Of the non-commissioned officers, Sergeant F.A. Scott, attached to the Seventh Infantry Brigade, who was always in the forward area, fearlessly carrying on his work, received the Military Medal; Sergeant A.M.I. Billie, attached to the Fifth Infantry Brigade, the Meritorious Service Medal; Sergeant G.L. Black, attached to the Second Brigade, C.F.A., the Military Medal.

IN LIGHTER VEIN Nobody, not even the proverbial schoolboy with his fondness for attending his grandmother's funeral, can surpass the soldier in the latter's fertility of mind at inventing excuses to clear himself of predicaments. The stories of that nature that had their origin in the war would fill a small-sized volume but it is pertinent only to our purpose to recount one or two in which animal interests or the interests of the veterinary corps were concerned. For pure subtlety it would be difficult to excel the following exhibition of ready wit:

On one occasion, when the 27th Canadian Infantry Battalion was out of the line at rest at Camblain l'Abbé with Major E. C. Complin in command, rations of bully beef were coming up with rather provoking persistency. Some of the men, whose appetites were whetted for something that would remind them more of home, started to forage on their own account, and soon there were numerous complaints from nearby peasants of the disappearance of their sheep. Not that the peasants were particularly distressed at such losses, for they invariably put in claims for three or four times the value of the animals and received twice the value in compensation, but discipline had to be maintained and the commanding officer judged it was time to put a stop to the depredations. So he caused an order to be issued to the effect that anyone caught killing a sheep would be severely dealt with. One day, shortly thereafter, he was rummaging round the country when he suddenly came upon a secluded spot where two of his men had just despatched a sheep. At the same moment, the more self-possessed of the two, far from being perturbed at the major's unexpected appearance, exclaimed, as he turned and kicked the carcass: "That will teach you to snap at me!"

This story is also claimed by the Imperials. One of the veterinary officers, Captain -----, a man of convivial tendencies, once treated the personnel of his command to a dinner, at which a goodly supply of the liquid products of the country were provided, by which the guests were inspired to overstay their passes with a consequent appearance next day in the orderly room. Major -----, on whom fell the duty of dealing with the offenders, addressed a communication to the Captain, couched in the following terms:

"Captain -----, if you paid half as much attention to your military duties as you do to your social affairs, you would be a mighty good soldier".

To which Captain ----- returned the following rejoinder: "Major -----, respectfully submitted that if you were half as good at your social obligations as you are at your military duties, you would be a damned good fellow." There is no record of what followed.

One morning, Trooper H.T.V. Prosser, whilst attached to the Remount Depot at Hautot, had to appear in the orderly room on a charge of absenting himself from his beat on sentry duty the previous night. The officer before whom the case was tried, who enjoyed the reputation of being rather long-winded, prolonged the proceedings by delivering himself of some preliminary remarks that had no bearing on the "crime" with which the accused was charged. The latter was becoming visibly uneasy and when finally called upon to offer an explanation of his dereliction of duty, exclaimed: "Sir, I admit the correctness of the charge, but it was on account of circumstances over which I had no control, and what is more, Sir, if these proceedings are drawn out much longer, I shall be under the necessity of absenting myself once more for the same reason."

Lance Corporal M ----- was a genuinely frugal Scotsman. One day at Shorncliffe, he approached Sergeant Major Moore with an application for leave of absence in order that he might visit his "cousin, an officer in the Royal Flying Corps, just home on leave from the front". He was informed that his application would be duly considered. An hour or so later, a sergeant brought to the sergeant major an envelope which had been picked up and which contained 2s. (50 cents) with a message signed by the lance corporal addressed to a friend in Folkestone begging the latter to dispatch without delay a telegram to a Miss---- requesting her to telegraph to him the following communication: "Jack home on leave from France. Come at once if you want to see him". The sergeant major pinned the message to the application, sent for the lance corporal and exhibiting the two papers to the latter, asked if they both belonged to him. Said the lance corporal, "The bottom one does, Sir, but I don't know that the top one does". "If that is the case" laconically remarked the sergeant major, "I guess the 2s. belongs to me". The shock was too great for the Scotsman, who, on going out, reported sick to the medical officer and was sent to the hospital.

The following story is also recorded in Imperial annals, but whether or not it had its origin in Canadian circles, it is good enough for bringing our little diversion to a close:

One of the veterinary officers was much given to sending in written suggestions for the betterment of the service. One of his effusions had evidently wearied the reviewing authority, a Latin scholar, who disposed of it by returning it, endorsed "Nil damnedum bonum".

TERRIFYING EXPERIENCES It has been stated in the introduction to this work that the veterinary personnel performed duties which, strictly speaking, were of a rear line or noncombatant character. Nevertheless, they were at times, equally with their combatant comrades, exposed to experiences which were severe enough to try the stoutest hearts. This was particularly true at the Battle of Amiens where the veterinary officers and first aid sergeants attached to the artillery were forced to lie in 'funk-holes' a great deal of the time.[1] How strenuous these experiences were may be gauged from a remark made by an orderly sent back to deliver a message, from the front lines area to the transport lines at dusk when the enemy aircraft were particularly busy, and who was obliged to lie in a prone position for 3 1/2 hours ere he could move without certainty of annihilation: "Well, I thought the front line bad enough, but if this is the rear, me for the trenches. We have protection there at any rate."

PERSONNEL KILLED In the chapter giving the Roll of Honour, we learn how two officers and one sergeant of the veterinary corps lost their lives from long-distance shelling whilst engaged at their duties in the rear lines.

FIRST AID SERGEANTS WOUNDED Besides these casualties, several of the first aid sergeants sustained wounds at different periods of the war, amongst them being Sergeant A. Brewer, attached to the Second Divisional Ammunition Column; Sergeant R. Miller, struck by a fragment of a bomb on August 3rd, 1916; Sergeant H. Doak, attached to the Second Brigade, C.F.A., wounded on the Somme in September, 1916; and Sergeant G.L. Black, who earned his stripe on August 29th, 1918.

CASUALTIES TO HORSES An idea of the risk attendant on duties performed in the transport lines, which might be two or three miles back from the actual battle front, may be gathered from the losses amongst the animals. At Breilen, 1915, the Third Artillery Brigade lost 124 animals from shellfire, and during the night of August 10-11th, 1918, there were heavy casualties from bombing which lasted from dusk till daybreak, the Third Divisional Ammunition Column alone losing 110 killed and 54 wounded. The highest number of animals in the Canadian Army Corps to lose their lives in any one week, that ending October 3rd, 1918, was 586, of which 489 were killed by shells and bombs and 97 had to be destroyed. Such figures, of course, represented extraordinary losses, such as might be sustained during active operations. Usually, during periods of quiet, losses occurred in comparatively small numbers.

HORSES GOING OVER THE TOP There was only one instance recorded in the war of horses and mules being called on to engage in an attack in the very front lines. This was at the beginning of the Battle of Amiens, where occurred the unique spectacle of pack animals laden with small arms ammunition being led 'over the top' with the Canadian infantry.

COMPARATIVE ANIMAL WASTAGE The functions of the veterinary services as a whole in the field were chiefly directed to reducing to the lowest possible figure wastage of animal strength, and Canadians have ample reason to

Figure 8.12. Personnel of the C.A.V.C. bandaging a horse hit by shrapnel, France, August 1917. Officer on left is Capt. F.A. Daigneault. (*NAC PA 1680*)

be satisfied with the accomplishment of their own veterinary service when they learn that the Canadian Army Corps showed a percentage of wastage during the months of December, 1917 and January, February and March, 1918, considerably lower than that of the other corps of the army of which it formed a part. Following are the figures:

Percentage of Wastage Canadian Army Corps	Percentage of Wastage Total Army
0.55%	0.74%

TOTAL CANADIAN ANIMAL WASTAGE There was much speculation on the part of the people at home, during the war, as to the actual losses in animal life incurred by the Canadian forces, the range of conjecture having varied widely. The reader will be interested to be enlightened on this point and many will no doubt be surprised to learn that the average losses were by no means as startling as they supposed. In every hundred horses doing duty at the front, slightly over two were put out of action from all causes combined in the course of a month, and the actual deaths did not amount to one per hundred per month. Or, looking at the matter from another point of view, we may say that in the course of four years of such warfare, the equivalent of the entire original strength of horses would be placed *hors de combat* either temporarily or permanently, but it would take ten years for it to be completely effaced.

The accompanying table (Figure 8.13) gives the yearly wastage percentage of Canadian animals in France, covering the period 1915-1918. It should be noted that the term 'gross wastage' includes animals missing and evacuated to hospital as well as those that died or were killed or destroyed, whilst the term 'dead wastage' applies only to those that died or were killed or destroyed, from which it will be seen that the yearly gross wastage was 26.10% and the yearly dead wastage 9.56%.

FEAR EXHIBITED BY ANIMALS The question whether horses or mules realize the danger of shellfire must be answered in the affirmative. When bombs and shells exploded in proximity to the transport lines, both horses and mules would neigh with fright and exhibit all the signs of terror. They seldom stampeded but appeared stupefied

YEARLY WASTAGE PERCENTAGE OF CANADIAN ANIMALS IN FRANCE 1915- 1918.

FORMATION	Admitted to Sick Lines for Treatment.	Cured	Evacuated.	DEAD WASTAGE Died	Destroyed	Missing	Found	Average Strength	Cast	Yearly Wastage Percentage Gross.	REMARKS.
Can. Cavalry (R.C.H.A.)	249	90	107	1	8	-	-	718	-	27.84	Covering 6 months April to September, 1916.
Can. Corps Troops.	2165	1430	555	82	68	-	-	3470	3	24.24	Covering 8 months June - July, 1916, July, - December, 1917. Sept.16/1915 - March 2/1916. Included in 1st Division.
1st Can. Division	14757	9843	3407	933	413	87	4	5353	44	25.99	Covering 27½ months, incl. Corps troops from Sept.16/15, to March 2nd, 1916.
2nd Can. Division	8001	5190	1974	426	229	14	22	5028	3	21.64	Covering 19 months. Sept.23- December 30th/15. Jan.- Sept. 1916. June - December, 1917.
3rd Can. Division	11124	4620	4834	648	994	50	-	4619	2	29.27	Covering 24 months Jan. 1916 to December, 1917.
4th Can. Division	6451	3246	1867	646	535	1	21	5130	-	29.70	Covering 15 months. August - October, 1916. January - December, 1917.
All Corps 1918, to May 9th,	5058	2651	1551	160	160	4	48	4022	-	24.03	Covering 4½ months. Jan. 1st - May 9th, 1918.
5th Div'l. Arty.											
GRAND TOTAL	47,805	27,070	14,295	2896	2407	156	95	28,340	52	(26.10 (9.56	(Wastage) Including Evacuations (Gross. Excluding Evacuations (Dead.

Figure 8.13. Yearly wastage of Canadian animals, France, 1915-1918. (*French Papers, NAC*)

from fright.

HORSE SAGACITY On the other hand, an incident witnessed by Lieutenant-Colonel Tamblyn and regarded by him as a display of sagacity may be mentioned. A bomb was dropped from an aeroplane on a road in front of a mess cart of the Ninth Brigade, C.F.A., drawn by two horses. The bomb killed the driver and wounded both animals, one mortally. The animals proceeded of their own accord to their wagon lines some 800 yards distant, having to make several turns at crossroads, with their driver lying dead in the cart.

WITH THE NONCOMBATANT BRANCHES

The Canadian Railway Troops and the Canadian Forestry Corps in France were organized as Imperial troops. That is to say, all their material, including their horses and excepting only their technical equipment, were of Imperial ownership, but the personnel was provided and paid by Canada. It was a state of affairs exactly similar to that which prevailed at No. 1 Canadian Veterinary Hospital, which, as we have seen, arose from a recognition of Canada's obligation to maintain the equivalent of the number of troops on the lines of communication deemed necessary to serve its fighting units in the field.

WITH THE CANADIAN RAILWAY TROOPS This corps, whose specialty was the construction of standard and light gauge railways, was composed of 13 battalions which continually moved from one army area to another, or from army areas to lines of communication or to French or Belgian areas, wherever their services were required. The war establishment called for a veterinary officer and an assistant sergeant per battalion and the Imperial veterinary authorities endeavored to persuade Canadian veterinary headquarters in London to make provision accordingly. But it was pointed out by Colonel Neill that there were only some 350 animals per battalion and that the usual number of animals held to require the undivided services of a veterinary officer was anything over 500, and furthermore, that inasmuch as 90% of the work of the battalions was done on behalf of Imperial troops and only 10% for the Canadian Army Corps, and the Canadian authorities had all they could do to find sufficient veterinary officers to keep our own Canadian units up to strength, no greater number could be allocated to this unit than 6 officers and 13 sergeants. These were distributed as circumstances required, each officer having charge of the veterinary interests of one or more battalions. Returns were made to the Deputy Directors of Veterinary Services (Imperial) of the areas in which they happened to be working. Otherwise, their work was similar to that of the veterinary officers and sergeants with the divisions.

Figure 8.14. Capt. W.F.R. 'Buckie' Stubbs, C.A.V.C. (seated, left) with members of the segregated black 2nd Construction Battalion, at Canadian Forestry Corps District 5, La Joux, in the Jura Mountains, France, c. January 1918.[2] (*Stubbs Collection*)

WITH THE CANADIAN FORESTRY CORPS The work of this corps was carried on in nine different districts in France. With the exception of two, the districts were well away from the fighting zone. Of the two, one was employed in the army area and moved from time to time wherever its services were needed whilst the other was attached to the Royal Air Force with which it moved whenever required. With each district was one veterinary officer and with each company, of which there might be from 4 to 13 composing a district, was a first aid sergeant.

The job was quite an isolated one and did not appeal to an active man, for the companies, each with from 70 to 100 horses, were situated far apart in camps in the back woods, some running mills, some doing bush work and others looking after transportation. On account of difficulties of transportation, it was impracticable to make other than infrequent evacuations to the base hospitals, so the veterinary officer with each district conducted his own local hospital with accommodation for about 30 cases and with a 2-wheeled ambulance. The veterinary officer made his rounds about two or three times a week and had to traverse a very considerable extent of territory, the companies being sometimes scattered over an area of 70 miles. He usually lived with the company situated nearest to his hospital, and there were about six officers to the mess. The only recreation to relieve the deadly monotony was fishing, cards and frequent weekend trips to the nearest cities.

The work was very hard on the horses, which were mostly old and of B category, the only end in view being production. So true was this that at the final disposal of the army horses at the end of the war, many of these particular animals were deemed only fit for conversion into meat for human consumption. Many totally blind animals quite useless for work at the front, were employed to advantage for straight hauls on good roads. The work being of such a strenuous character, a much larger forage ration was supplied to these horses, 16 pounds each of oats and hay being allowed. The principal troubles were calks, collar injuries from straining and jostling, and snagging, together with a great deal of debility from overwork. There were plenty of lice and more or less mange prevalent, attributed in some districts to the employment of infested animals on the trails by French civilians and in others to arrival of infested remounts and neglected grooming.

In fact, the grooming problem was a more difficult one in the Forestry Corps than in the army areas, proper attention in this respect being sometimes totally neglected. Here, as in the army areas, the employment of men who were good teamsters was largely the determining factor in the maintenance of condition and this was very evident where a team was tended and driven by the same teamster throughout. It was noticed that the animals employed at the sawmills, where there was an abundance of sawdust for bedding, had more incentive to rest, and thereby maintain their condition than those working in the bush where the transportation problem rendered the provision of bedding impracticable. Shoeing and general smith work were done conjointly by the same workers. Captain W.G. Walks and Lieutenant O.V. Gunning considered this system a very disadvantageous one for when pressing repair work was needed by the company, the shoeing was neglected.

Stabling was one of the first considerations in forestry camp construction and even the companies working in the bush, isolated high up on the mountains, possessed stabling which, excepting the finer points of finish, would have done credit to a Canadian farm. Mange was controlled by means of hand scrubbing with calcium sulphide solution, there being no facilities for dipping, excepting in the case of No. 5 District at La Joux, where a dipping tank was erected at the instigation of, and under the supervision of, Captain W.F.R. Stubbs (Figure 8.14). Veterinary officers made their returns to the Deputy Director of Veterinary Services (Imperial) of the area in which they were working.

CHAPTER 9

MOBILE VETERINARY SECTIONS
CORPS VETERINARY EVACUATING STATION

DESCRIPTION A mobile veterinary section was a small self-contained unit, which acted as a central collecting and clearing station for the sick, lame and wounded animals of all the units composing a division. It was the branch of the veterinary corps that worked as a unit in the field. There was a separate section for each of the four divisions that formed the Canadian Corps, besides another that did duty with the mounted regiments forming the Canadian Cavalry Brigade and working apart from the Corps in conjunction with the Imperial cavalry. There was a fifth section formed for duty with the Fifth Division which, however, was disbanded without seeing overseas service when the latter division was broken up at Witley.

FUNCTIONS Each section formed the connecting link between the veterinary officers working in the field with combatant units and the hospitals at the bases. It made evacuations direct to the hospitals until the middle of April, 1918, when there was organized for the whole corps a central evacuating station, to which all divisional mobile sections thereafter transferred the hospital cases and which took over the work of forwarding to the hospitals[1].

LOCATION It accompanied its division from place to place whenever a movement was made and during important actions sometimes found it necessary to establish advanced collecting posts in charge of a non-commissioned officer and one or more men.

ADVANCED COLLECTING POSTS These advanced posts formed an important feature of the mobile service during active operations, particularly in the open warfare that characterized the later stages of the war. They carried on their duties in the actual battle area, often under heavy shelling, always moving with the headquarters of another unit, usually the divisional ammunition column, by which their whereabouts could be located by the fighting units which they relieved of the care and responsibility of sick and wounded animals. Keeping in touch with the mobile section in the rear, they sent thither the casualties to rest and receive first aid treatment before proceeding on the journey to the base hospitals.

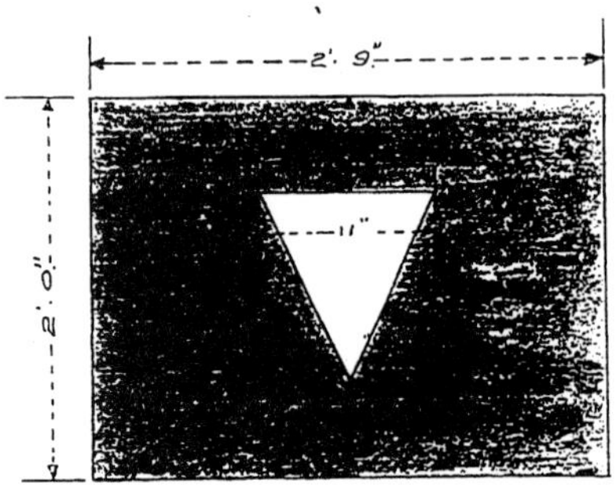

Figure 9.1. Flag (white on red) flown to mark location of Mobile Veterinary Section. *(French Papers, NAC)*

Generally, during inactive warfare, the mobile section was allotted a position at some central point within the divisional area as near as possible to the units disposing of the greatest number of horses, but with due regard to proximity to the nearest railhead, and its location was always indicated by its distinguishing flag formed of an inverted white triangle on a red base (Figure 9.1). It was invariably within the shell area and on more than one occasion became the recipient of unwelcome enemy projectiles and bombs. Excepting when buildings or covered standings were available, the horses had to be picketed in the open, entirely unprotected from the elements (Figure 9.2), often in bad weather, knee-deep in mud. After the setting up of the new veterinary evacuating station in 1918, it was located, with due regard to watering facilities, available cover, etc., in the most advantageous position taking into consideration the distance from the evacuating station and the battle area, forming a sort of halfway depot.

MOBILITY It had to be ready to move at short notice. At the Second Battle of Ypres, No. 1 Section had taken up a position near Elverdinghe in front of a battery which soon received the attention of the enemy's guns. The shells began to burst every three or four minutes in increasingly unpleasant proximity, and one having wiped out a score of horses in the immediate vicinity, Captain O'Gogarty decided to move off about half a mile to the right, the getting away being effected within ten minutes. During the critical days of March, 1918, just after reaching Basseux, No. 2 Section had to stand to for several days with wagons laden, in momentary expectation of an order to retreat.

Figure 9.2. No. 2 Canadian Mobile Veterinary Section, O.C. Capt. F.A. Daigneault (right), caring for horses wounded at Hill 70, August, 1917. Horses are tethered in the open to a picket line about 3 feet off the ground; hay nets were hung from the line along the top of the posts (*NAC PA 1763*)

Duties The duties of a mobile section were primarily to collect and to evacuate, but to a limited extent it also acted as a field hospital. Its work was not confined merely to handling the horses belonging to its own division; on the contrary, all mobile sections, whether Imperial or Dominion, worked hand in hand with one another for the benefit of all animals of all the Entente armies, whether they were of Imperial, Dominion, Belgian, French, Portuguese or American ownership. Upon an animal coming under the care of the section, it was assigned an identification number which was either stenciled or clipped with curved scissors on the neck or rump of the near side (Figure 9.3), a descriptive roll was taken and the case duly entered on the records. The length of stay at the section depended on several factors, amongst which were the length of time to be spent by the section in any particular locality, the prospect of an early cure and the availability of transport facilities to the base hospitals. If it was a case that could be treated with certainty of successful outcome within a reasonable length of time, the animal was kept till recovery ensued, when it was returned to its unit, unless there was an overwhelming number of wounded, when one and all were passed on.

Figure 9.3. "2CMVS" (2nd Canadian Veterinary Mobile Section) being stenciled to the near side (left) rump of a wounded horse. The outcome is visible on the rump of the horse on the left. France, 1917. (*NAC PA 1711*)

9. MOBILE VETERINARY SECTIONS

EVACUATIONS The final authority to decide on the need of evacuation was the Deputy Assistant Director of Veterinary Services of the division concerned, and until an animal was passed by that officer, it was not considered as having been struck off the strength of the unit from which it had come. On the other hand, if it was a case requiring hospital treatment, the animal was passed along with a number of others similarly circumstanced in charge of a non-commissioned officer and the necessary number of men to the nearest available base hospital. The hospitals that served this purpose were all Imperial and were situated at Neuchâtel, Abbeville, Forges-les-Aux, Romescamps and St. Omer. In the chapter on No. 1 Canadian Veterinary Hospital, the reader is informed why Canadian horses were not sent directly to the latter institution, as might be supposed, and elsewhere it is shown how, when horses passed off the strength of Canadian units, they became Imperial property.

Before an animal was moved, it was categorized or ticketed with a colored diagnostic label attached to a few plaited hairs at the root of the tail, red serving to distinguish specific cases, green surgical cases and white medical ones. These colored labels formed a means for quick recognition and classification at the receiving hospitals. Still another color, namely blue, was employed by the Remount Department to indicate animals that had been set aside to be cast for being no longer serviceable to the army. Transportation to hospitals was usually effected by rail from the nearest railhead, but in some instances a convoy was sent over the roads. All animals able to proceed on foot were led, but if too lame to walk were moved by ambulance.

STRAY ANIMALS Another duty was to take in stray, surplus and captured animals. Horses at the front often broke loose and wandered off, perhaps into another unit's lines, and during an action a great many stray animals would be wandering about. Under such circumstances, it was the duty of the unit making the find to turn the animal over to the nearest mobile section, though more often than not the unit contrived to retain the animal if it was a good one, turning in one of its own animals of which it wished to rid itself. Under the regulations, if there were no distinguishing marks to admit of identification, the section kept the stray a week, meanwhile advertising it, and if no claimant turned up, issued it impartially to any unit short of an animal.

MINOR FUNCTIONS Amongst the minor functions was the manufacture of sulphide of lime for distribution to the different veterinary officers working with the divisional units for use as a preventive measure against the spread of mange in the lines. The sections were also called upon at times to dispose of unserviceable animals at public auction to local butchers at prices varying from Frcs. 150 to Frcs. 250 (approximately $30 to $50). And from the beginning of 1917 they were allotted the task of collecting and forwarding to the bases the hides of all animals that succumbed.

DISTRIBUTION OF REMOUNTS At one period the sections performed the duty of bringing up and distributing remounts to take the place of animals that had been evacuated, but later on they were relieved of this duty when the Remount Department made distribution direct, though during the march into Germany, they were again called upon to function in this respect.

AID TO INHABITANTS The mobile sections found, as did the individual veterinary officers working in the field, many opportunities for rendering timely assistance to those unfortunates amongst the peasants who had been caught in the maelstrom of war. Indeed, it was a headquarters order that the cattle and flocks of the inhabitants were to be given every attention which circumstances would permit.

COLLECTION OF ABANDONED ANIMALS Still another duty consisted of the collection from peasants and farmers of such animals as the veterinary officers had been forced to 'abandon' from lack of moving facilities. In the early days, the section, upon production by the inhabitant of the horse recovery form that had been left by the veterinary officer along with the animal, settled for all indebtedness arising in this manner with ready cash from an imprest account with which it was entrusted. The allowance at first was Frcs. 1.75 (35 cents) and later Frcs. 2 (40 cents) per horse per day, and it was a system that worked with eminent satisfaction to the inhabitant as it ensured to him payment in reward for his labors. But later the system was modified by the introduction of an additional formality which worked to the subsequent disadvantage of the service. The change consisted in the making of payments from the base through the mayor of the commune in which the peasant resided, the section on taking over the 'abandoned' animals taking also the recovery form and leaving in the place of the latter a second form or receipt note (Figure 9.4) which served as evidence of the claim of the peasant.

Now, it usually happened that the inhabitant was very much in debt to the mayor, who might also be a not over-scrupulous man, and when the farmer in due time presented his receipt for payment, it was treated as a credit against his indebtedness, or some other excuse for non-payment was made, and the mayor put into his pocket the money that was intended to be transferred to the inhabitant. Hence it came about that the inhabitants developed a decided disinclination to receive on billet horses that it was necessary to 'abandon' as they could never be certain about being reimbursed for their trouble. It was true that under the law the inhabitant could be forced by the mayor to take in such animals after application had been made, but the manner in which the animals fared under such conditions may be better imagined than described.

During the march towards Germany, the allowance was raised to Frcs. 5 ($1.00) in Belgium, to enable the inhabitants to meet the increased cost of all commodities, and all animals it had been necessary to leave behind were collected by the evacuating station instead of by the mobile sections.

Receipt Note.

To be left with Inhabitant when collecting a sick horse or mule.

M......................................

Having considered the present condition of the animal left in your charge and compared it with that stated on the note by the English Army Authorities I assess the amount due to you for its maintenance at the rate, per diem, as stated against each animal below :—

Animal say whether horse or mule.	Unit to which animal belonged.	Date left.	Date collected.	Date died. *	Number of days.	Rate assessed.		Amount due to Inhabitant.	
						frs.	cts.	frs.	cts.

Signed......................................

O.C. No....... Mobile Veterinary Section.

Instructions.

1.* The circumstances of the death of an animal will be enquired into by the Veterinary Officer collecting and verified by any reasonable means and a certificate or statement to corroborate the statement given to the inhabitant.

2. A notification of horses collected should be forwarded by O.C. Mobile Veterinary Section to the A.D.V.S. Division for forwarding to the O. i/c Branch Requisition Office, Headquarters, 2nd Army.

AVERTISSEMENT.

1. Dans le certificat ci-dessus l'officier de l'armée anglaise chargé de ramener l'animal, a déterminé ce qui vous est du pour son entretien. Vous devez remettre, sans retard, ce certificat au Maire (ou Bourgmestre) de votre commune pour qu'on puisse vous en payer le montant.

2. Au cas où l'animal mourrait, il vous faudrait montrer les preuves de sa mort à l'officier qui vous donnera un certificat qui doit être annexé à ce reçu.

VERMAENING.

1. In het voorgenoemd getuigschrift heeft de officier van het Engelsch Leger, welke het dier komt halen, de onderhoudskosten aan u verschuldigd aangeduid. Dit getuigschrift moet zonder verwijl aan den Burgemeester, of den Maire, overhandigd worden, opdat deze bovengemelde som uitbetalen kunne.

2. In het geval dat het dier sterft, moet u hiervan een bewijs voortbrengen waarna de officier u een bewijsschrift zal geven welk aan dit ontvangstbewijs te hechten is, alvorens hetzelve aan den Burgemeester, of Maire, af te geven.

1st Printing Co. R.E. 2nd Army [illegible]

Figure 9.4. Receipt Note issued to farmers from whom "abandoned" horses were recovered. (*French Papers, NAC*)

A self-imposed obligation assumed by the mobile sections must not be forgotten. With the arrival of the First Canadian Division in the field, a number of requests was received from farmers throughout the area asking for assistance for their sick animals. Realizing the great hardship under which the agriculturists were laboring, since the latter had been left quite helpless in the matter of veterinary aid through the calling to the colors of all fit and capable veterinarians, the sections made every endeavor to equalize the situation, commensurate with their military duties. Eventually, regular weekly free clinics were held at the lines to which civilian animals suffering from all sorts of troubles were brought for examination and treatment. In fact, these clinics now and then resembled a county fair or market day by the number of farmers brought together. It was heart to heart actions such as these that helped so much to cement the bonds of friendships between France and Canada.

AMBULANCES When the first sections went to France they did not possess any form of conveyance for the transportation of incapacitated animals and the need of some sort of vehicle soon made itself felt. The first steps

Figure 9.5. No. 2 Canadian Mobile Veterinary Section, Bizet, Belgium, March, 1919. Capt. R.J. Vickers is beside the Belgian farm ambulance (left); Lieut J.W. Heppelston is beside the British civilian horse ambulance (right). Compare the ground clearance of the two vehicles. (*NAC PA 4228*)

towards correcting this deficiency were taken by hiring low carts from the inhabitants. Captain Daigneault of No. 2 Section obtained a Belgian farm ambulance (Figures 8.2, 9.5), which through its usefulness to all concerned, became celebrated throughout the Second Division. This vehicle, simply and strongly constructed, easily accommodated two patients and when the unit moved, it was capable of carrying as much equipment as a general service wagon and was very much easier to load.

The civilian carts were replaced by regular horse drawn ambulances obtained through the Imperial Base Veterinary Hospital at Abbeville. The first of these arrived on May 12, 1916, the gift of friends in Canada, and eventually ambulances were supplied to the Second, Third and Fourth Sections by the Royal Society for the Prevention of Cruelty to Animals, and to the Second Section by the Blue Cross. But, ambulances constructed for civilian use were found to be ill-adapted to military needs, being cumbersome and with but five inches road clearance (see Figure 9.5), and on account of their tendency to rack themselves to pieces on the rough roads. Whenever anything went wrong, there was always difficulty in getting repairs effected either by sending the vehicle to the base or by undergoing a long wait for the necessary authority to have the new parts made in civilian shops, the military shops not being able to undertake the work. Moreover, a single horse drawn ambulance per section was found to be quite inadequate to meet the requirements; as many as three per section could have been kept busy in times of active operations.

The employment of horse drawn ambulances came in for general condemnation as being too slow and retarding the work of the sections, and had motor vehicles been part of the establishment and been freely used, they would have paid for themselves over and over again in the saving of animals which at times had to be abandoned in numbers for mere lack of transportation facilities. Late in the war each Imperial army headquarters was supplied by the Royal Society for the Prevention of Cruelty to Animals with a motor ambulance capable of accommodating two animals, which vehicle, however, remained under the direction of the Deputy Director of Veterinary Services, where its need was not urgent and where it was of little service to the divisions. Though, at times, it helped in the removal of the lame and wounded, appeals for its use were mostly unheeded, it being represented, though on an erroneous assumption, that the cost of operating the same, viz. 1 shilling (24 cents) per mile, did not pay, thereby defeating the main object intended to be accomplished, viz. the relief of suffering animals. Eventually, the

Canadian Corps Evacuating Station came into possession of one motor ambulance, which arrived on September 13th, 1918.

MOBILE SURGERY NEEDED Captain Vickers pointed out the difficulty experienced by the mobile sections in transporting surgical equipment and the surplus feed that it was always necessary to carry as a provision against all emergencies, and suggested that to meet this want there should be added to the establishment a light vehicle fitted up as a combined field surgery and pharmacy and which would also be capable of carrying a measure of provender.

SPECIAL SIGN POSTS When a division moved into a new area, its component units were spread over a considerable extent of territory and needless to say some time would elapse before the various mounted units learned of the exact whereabouts of the mobile section. The men detailed to conduct thither the sick and wounded horses that were walking cases would be instructed in the general direction, but, being strangers in the new territory, would sometimes have difficulty in bringing up at the exact location, hidden away, as it might be, in some isolated farmyard. The section invariably flew its distinguishing flag, but the latter was only observable from a comparatively short distance. Naturally, it was particularly desirable that the animals should be brought to their destination by the shortest possible route and that they should not have their chances of recovery jeopardized by unnecessary wandering about. To obviate this difficulty, Lieutenant-Colonel Edgett devised a special signpost with an indicator which could be turned to point towards the exact locality in which the section had taken up its quarters. A number of these posts were placed at the corners of roads and on paths through fields and were the means of saving to the wearied animals many a long and aimless tramp. This system was afterwards generally adopted in the other divisions.

PERSONNEL As the command of a section was a post of considerable importance, an effort was always made to allocate to it none but the best amongst the veterinary officers. In commenting on this point, the Deputy Director of Veterinary Services (Imperial) of the Second Army wrote Colonel Neill, in January, 1916: *An O.C. Mobile Veterinary Section is a difficult Officer to find.*

The original strength of each section comprised 27 hands, all told, consisting of a veterinary officer in command, a staff sergeant, two sergeants, two corporals, one shoeing smith and twenty men, of whom one acted as cook and two as batmen, but upon the organization of the evacuating station and consequent reduction of duties, the number was decreased by doing away with the staff sergeant and six men, the latter being transferred to form part of the personnel of the evacuating station. The entire strength was rarely in the lines at one time, since parties would be absent for a day or two at a time, usually in charge of one of the non-commissioned officers, engaged in conducting casualties to the base hospitals. Recruits as needed were obtained from No. 1 Canadian Veterinary Hospital at Havre. As the section was a mounted one, every member was a specialist in horsemanship, and it was invariably extolled as an object lesson to all ranks who had as duties the care and management of horses in the field. It was a very busy unit, its personnel ever on the move, covering a broad extent of territory and coping with a multitude of ever-occurring situations. On one occasion, in November, 1916, some of the men of No. 4 Section were called upon to go up to the trenches to act as stretcher bearers, but usually conditions operated in the opposite direction and it was necessary to call for details from other units to assist in conducting horses to railheads.

LET US NOW CONSIDER EACH INDIVIDUAL SECTION:

NO. 1 MOBILE VETERINARY SECTION

The first of the mobile sections was organized and trained at Salisbury Plain. It left Netheravon on February 7th, 1915, entrained at Amesbury and embarking at Avonmouth, landed at St. Nazaire on the 11th. Thence it proceeded by train to Strazelle. The section was commanded in order of sequence by the following officers:

COMMANDING OFFICERS

Captain M.G. O'Gogarty from date of organization till January, 1916

Figure 9.6. No. 1 Canadian Mobile Veterinary Section, Huy, France, March, 1919. Officer Commanding (front centre) Capt. P.P. Souillard, N.C.O.'s and men. (*NAC PA 4203*)

Captain A.E. Coulombe from January, 1916 till November, 1917
Captain E.M. Dixon from November, 1917 till August, 1918
Captain P.P. Souillard[2] (Figure 9.6) from August, 1918 till demobilization
Captain J.H. Burnet performed acting duty during the absence of the commanding officer on leave.

ACTIVITIES In the beginning this unit was kept very busy receiving and treating the horses of the Belgian army and of the Australian divisional mounted troops, its average admissions being five per day which had increased by July, 1916, to sixteen per day, whilst in April, 1917, when it was functioning as an evacuating station for the other divisions during active operations, it was receiving as many as 150 in a day. Under the latter conditions its resources were sorely tried for not only did the enormous amount of extra work thrust upon it entail the absence of a corresponding number of its personnel to act as conducting parties to the base hospitals, but wounded animals were dying in large numbers and these had to be buried.

EXTRA HELP WANTED At times but one or two men were left at the section, and there being from 140 to 300 horses on the lines to be fed, watered and have their wounds dressed, the unit was quite unable to deal effectively with the situation. It was not until an appeal for extra help had been made and 50 additional men had been sent up for temporary duty that the situation was relieved.

MANUFACTURE OF SULPHIDE OF LIME This unit started the manufacture of sulphide of lime in the field on July 24th, 1916, and within ten days was making nearly 50 gallons per day, which afforded an ample quantity for treating mange in its own lines as well as keeping Belgian and several other units supplied.

In the winter of 1917-1918, whilst at Barlin, it superintended the operations at the dipping tank at that point, putting through in one day upwards of 700 animals.

FIRST MAN WOUNDED The first man in the corps to be wounded, Trooper R. Miller, belonged to No. 1 Section; he was hit in the arm by a fragment of shell at the Second Battle of Ypres, the same shell killing the two horses he was leading.

APPRECIATION OF SERVICES The following Divisional Routine Order appeared on December 4th, 1918: *The G.O.C. is pleased to state that he has received a letter from the Mayor of Fenain expressing appreciation of the fine work done by the First Canadian Mobile Veterinary Section whilst in the Fenain area.*

LOCATION During its movements from place to place, this section operated in the following localities: Bac St. Maur, Meteren, Croix du Bac, Steenvoorde, Elverdinghe, Poperinghe, Nieppe, Busnes, Neuve Eglise, La Crêche, Tilques, Albert, Frésnicourt, Bruay, Barlin, Estrée Cauchie, Ecurie, Mazingarbe Fosse, Bouvigny-Boyeffles, Eturn, Tincquette, Agnes-les-Duisans, Arras, Heninel, Hendecourt, Agnes-les Suisans, Quéant, Cherisy, Etaing, Fenain, Aubry Elonges, Flénu, Neufvillers Station, Braine-le-Comte, Thines, Gembloux, Vezin, Gives, Borlon, Haute Bodeux, Petit Thier (across the German frontier at 7:50 a. m., December 7th, 1918), Mirfeld, Murringen, Kirschseiffen, Weibkirchen, Pingsdorf, Rodenkirchen, through Cologne (across the Rhine at 10:45 a. m., December 13th, 1918), Heumar, and back to Cologne, where artillery barracks on Marionbergstrasse were occupied. On the homeward journey, it went to Huy and thence to Bramshott via Havre and Southampton.

NO. 2 MOBILE VETERINARY SECTION

This section assumed its functions at Shorncliffe in June, 1915, and after spending a few weeks at Sandling and St. Martin's Plain in training with the Second Division, left on September 16th, and proceeding by way of Southampton and Havre, joined the division at Caestre on the 19th of the same month. The officers who commanded were:

COMMANDING OFFICERS

Captain F.A. Daigneault (Figure 9.7) from date of organization till April, 1918
Captain R. Vickers from April, 1918 till demobilization
Captains A.H. Hunter, J.G. Harvey, T.A. Girling, A.E. Cameron and Lieutenant J.W. Heppleston carried on in acting capacity during different periods of absence of the commanding officer on leave or duty.

Figure 9.7.
Capt. F.A. Daigneault.
(*From NAC PA 1763*)

ACTIVITIES During the time No. 2 Section was in the field, about 8,300 sick and injured animals were evacuated by it to base hospitals, and hundreds of cases of minor ailments such as colic, dental troubles, etc., were treated and the animals returned to their units. About Frcs. 15,000 (approximately $3,000) were received for animals sold for butchery and the money remitted to the field cashiers. Over 200 horse hides were despatched to the base. The personnel operated the dipping tank erected at Fosse 10, which was one of the most successful of the series operated by the Canadians, as many as 900 animals being passed through in a day.

MILITARY CROSS AWARDED The Military Cross was bestowed on Captain Vickers towards the close of the war for his consistent devotion to duty both as an executive officer and as officer in command of the section.

MERITORIOUS SERVICES AWARDED Of the non-commissioned officers, Staff Sergeant J.H. Gosselin and Sergeant F.B. Kendall were awarded the Meritorious Service Medal for valuable services, the latter being also Mentioned in Despatches for consistent devotion to duty while in the field.

TROOPERS INJURED Two troopers, W. Hannah and D. Watson, sustained accidental wounds towards the latter part of the war. They were in proximity to a pile of refuse burning in a yard when two explosions emanated from the same, supposedly caused by grenades.

PRE-EMINENCE No. 2 Section, throughout the war, was reputed to be the best conducted of the four Canadian divisional mobile sections. Lieutenant-Colonel Edgett recorded in his war diary at Reninghelst, August 28th, 1916, that:

The Hospital and convalescent arrangements of No. 2 C.M.V.S., together with the appearance of the lines in general, are the best I have seen in the field and reflect great credit on Captain Daigneault, the C.O.

It should have been added that Captain Vickers, who succeeded Captain Daigneault, took care to maintain this well-earned reputation. Captain Vickers, who had previously served as veterinary officer of the Sixth Brigade, C.F.A., was the author of a useful little brochure entitled 'Veterinary Notes', which embodied his observations in the wagon lines and in which he expressed some very apposite maxims. Here are two:

If you hear a driver say his horse has no brains, he is most probably unconsciously describing his own case.
A driver who does not honestly feel that his team are his best pals in the battery is not worth calling a driver.

LOCATION Amongst the places at which the unit during its wanderings spent longer or shorter periods were: Westoutre, Bruay, La Targette, Oradelles, Poperinghe, Bajus, Aux Rietz, Fontes, Petit Servins, Basseux, Ignocourt, Cagny, Caix, Wailly, Petit Château, Hendecourt, Sains les Marquion, Raillencourt, Marquette, La Sentinelle, St. Saulve, Quievrechain, Frameries, Maurage, Gosselies, Fleurus, Rhisne, Barvaux-Condroz, Heyd, Malempre, Rodt (across the German frontier at 11:30 a. m., December 7th, 1918), Schoenberg, Stadtkyll, Schonau, Florzheim (across the Rhine December 13th, 1918), Sieglar, Sieburg, and homeward by train via Auvelais, Tamines, and Buzet.

NO. 3 MOBILE VETERINARY SECTION

Having undergone but three weeks of training ere it was called upon to proceed to France and there join the Third Division, this unit arrived at Havre on March 2nd, 1916.

COMMANDING OFFICERS

Captain R. Waddy - from date of organization till August, 1916
Captain H.S. Clapp - from August, 1916 till May, 1917
Captain L.E.L. Taylor - from May, 1917 till demobilization.
Captain A. Cowan acted in place of Captain Taylor whilst the latter was absent from duty suffering from shellshock.

COMMANDING OFFICER WOUNDED Captain Taylor (Figure 9.8) enjoyed the distinction of being placed *hors de combat* through enemy shellfire on two separate occasions, besides having been severely wounded whilst serving at Gallipoli as a lieutenant in the Imperial army, on which account he had been invalided home. He subsequently rejoined as a farrier sergeant in the Canadian artillery and was transferred to the veterinary corps with a commission.

The first of the two occasions referred to was at Brandhoek on November 14th, 1917, when a high explosive shell fell in the lines of the section at 11:30 p.m. as he was proceeding to his billet, the concussion throwing him to the ground and causing him to become shocked, though animals in close proximity escaped without wounds. He was evacuated next day to hospital but returned on December 15th, 1917. Much has been recounted concerning the vagaries of exploding shells, of which this particular one afforded a striking example. It dropped in front of a row of mules, not one of which was wounded, whereas some horses standing at a distance were killed and wounded. So close did the shell drop in front of the mules that their heads actually overhung the resultant hole, and Captain Taylor himself was 200 yards away.

The next occasion was at Le Quesnel on August 13th, 1918, when he was slightly wounded by a fragment of shell while supervising the removal of sick and wounded animals from his sick lines when the

Figure 9.8. Capt. Lionel E.L. Taylor (*NAC PA 203589*)

Figure 9.9. Dressers of a Mobile Veterinary section fixing a boot on the foot of a horse hit during the Canadian advance on Hill 70, August, 1917. (*NAC PA 1710*)

enemy was shelling areas in close proximity to his section. His coolness and presence of mind were recorded by his immediate superior, Lieutenant-Colonel Tamblyn, as being very commendable. This officer handled his section with such consummate skill during the Battle of Amiens that he was able to assist not only his own division but the First and Fourth Divisions and several Imperial units.

MILITARY CROSS AWARDED For his work in this connection, he was awarded the Military Cross, the only instance of an immediate award being granted to a Canadian veterinary officer in the war, a distinction of which he had ample reason to be proud.

MILITARY MEDAL AWARDED For his splendid work at Passchendaele, Staff Sergeant H.B. Kenner was awarded the Military Medal and received mention in the following terms:

A great deal of the success with which the section was operated was due to Staff Sergeant H.B. Kenner, who is worthy of mention.

ACTIVITIES During the difficult days of October-November, 1917,[3] this section rendered utmost benefit in first aid treatment and collection of ambulance cases, but being unable to cope with the situation the whole of No. 1 Section and five men of No. 2 Section were moved up to assist it.

LOCATION It spent varying periods at Fletre, Poperinghe, Albert, Aubigny, Bruay, Barlin, Carency, Aux Rietz, Ouderdom, Hazebrouck, Fontes, Petit Servins, Hurionville, Basseux, Quesnel, Laresset, Vis en Artois, Inchy en Artois, Somain, La Choque, Raismes, Onnaing, Jemappes, Mons, Manage, Limal, Ohain, Alsemberg, Gandinière and Ramequies.

NO. 4 MOBILE VETERINARY SECTION

No. 4 Section was really the fifth to be formed under the original nomenclature, but upon its immediate predecessor

Figure 9.10. "A" Mobile Veterinary Section, Canadian Cavalry Brigade, France, February, 1919. The Officer Commanding (front, centre, with moustache) is Capt. J.R.J. Duhault C.P.A.V.C., with N.C.O.'s and men. (*NAC PA 4166*)

going to join the Cavalry Brigade and later receiving the designation 'A', it became the Section of the Fourth Division. It left Bramshott on August 13th, 1916, and arrived at Havre on the 16th. It was commanded as follows:

COMMANDING OFFICERS
Captain W.W. Forsyth from date of organization till October, 1917
Captain R.M. Lee from October, 1917 till October, 1918
Captain A.C. Wagner from October, 1918 till demobilization.
Captains W.E.S. West, W.A. Robertson and A.T. McLean carried on in acting capacity at different times.

ACTIVITIES This unit had a very busy time. On one occasion whilst camped in the open mud with the 5th Army in the Somme area, between the 1st and 27th of November, 1916, it collected, treated as far as possible, fed, watered and evacuated to the base, over 600 horses belonging to other divisions (Imperial) in addition to taking care of its own division. On this occasion, its total personnel was 23 and all the help it sought was a few men to act as conducting parties to the trains. Its splendid work brought forth appreciative comment from the General Officer Commanding the Division and the Deputy Director of Veterinary Services (Imperial) of the Fifth Army in a letter which was read to the section on parade.

Again, when the unit was relieving the 3rd Australian Mobile Veterinary Section in October, 1917, four men were kept constantly dressing wounds from early morning till late at night under great difficulties on account of the weather and the condition of the standings, and one evening, whilst shipping was going on, Staff Sergeant J.W. Johnston and two men fed and watered 100 animals. Staff Sergeant Johnston was Mentioned in Despatches for his work at Passchendaele.

RECORD PERFORMANCE During the Amiens push in August, 1918, this section under Captain Lee was ordered to take up a position near railhead and to function on behalf of, and until the arrival of, the regular corps evacuating station. It selected a site at Saleux, and during five days received 926 animals and evacuated 917, a record performance. The majority of the animals arriving during the night and having to be loaded on the trains during the day, the personnel got very little rest, but one and all rose to the occasion and worked under the most trying conditions without a word of complaint.

Figure 9.11. "A" Cavalry Mobile Veterinary Section, mounted. The Mobile Veterinary Section flag (inverted white triangle on red) is flying to left behind Capt. J.R.J. Duhault's head. The horses are wearing face guards to ward off flies. (*NAC unnumbered*)

AID TO INHABITANTS No. 4 Section was a great favorite with the agriculturists of one locality, through the kindly interest displayed by its commanding officer in the care of their sick animals, not without its humorous side, for nothing could have been more mirth provoking than the sight of Captain Lee, standing in the midst of a group of gesticulating natives with his coat off and sleeves rolled up, handing out advice in his very best French.

LOCATION Places at which this unit spent longer or shorter periods were: Poperinghe, Westoutre, Albert, Bruay, Fresnicourt, Petit Servins, Carency, Aux Rietz, Savy, Dieval, Ecoivres, Saleux, Cayeux, Bernaville, Agny, Croiselles, Queant, Inchy-en-Artois, Anzin St. Aubin, St. Quentin, Denain, La Sentinelle, Elonges, Cusmes, Grand Rosières and Hevillers.

'A' MOBILE VETERINARY SECTION

This, the original fourth section, went to the front for service with the Canadian Cavalry Brigade, and as already explained, later received a separate designation. It was trained at Shorncliffe, part of its personnel coming from No. 2 Veterinary Hospital and part from the cavalry training depot. It left on April 3rd, 1916, for Southampton, where it embarked the same day for Havre, but on approaching the latter port, the vessel was ordered back to Southampton on account of submarine activity and it was not till April 7th that the unit disembarked. After one night spent at the rest camp at Havre, it proceeded to the St. Pel area, where it joined the Cavalry Brigade.

COMMANDING OFFICERS

Captain J.H. Hennan, from date of organization till Sept., 1917
Captain M.G. O'Gogarty[4] from September, 1917 till November, 1917
Captain J.R.J. Duhault (Figures 9.10, 9.11) from November, 1917 till demobilization.

ACTIVITIES 'A' Section, in addition to handling horses from the entire Canadian Cavalry Brigade, also frequently received horses from the Indian cavalry divisions as well as from many other formations.

During the Cambrai operations, Captain Duhault established a series of three collecting stations - an advanced, a central and a rear - whereby there was a connecting chain between the troops in action and the veterinary evacuating station. This enabled wounded animals to be attended to at the earliest possible moment and a large percentage was thereby saved, which would otherwise have been a complete loss.

During the operations in March, 1918, there being at that time no arrangements for the disposal of wounded animals from his unit, Captain Duhault proceeded to establish at Saleux a temporary casualty clearing station by which he was enabled to dispose of a large number which had been collected by his section. This station discharged its particular function for a period of ten days during which time 500 wounded horses passed through and were evacuated, in addition to 300 which were placed directly on trains.[6]

An idea of the task that fell to this section may be gathered from the following data for the period beginning April 9th, 1916, and up till June 30th, 1918: animals received for treatment - 4,203; evacuated to hospital units - 3,648; cured and returned units - 494; died and destroyed - 61; total - 4,203.

PERSONNEL WOUNDED During the section's period of service, Acting Corporal E.O. Hancox and Trooper J. Meloche sustained wounds.

O.B.E. AWARDED Captain Duhault, who was an officer of the Permanent Corps, was awarded the Order of the British Empire for his very efficient services whilst in command of the section.

COURAGEOUS ACTS In August, 1918, a brigade routine order was issued under the heading 'Acts of Courage' in the following terms:

The General Officer Commanding wishes to express his appreciation of the following acts of courage: On the night of 11th of August, a party of 20 horses was being evacuated from 'A' Canadian Mobile Section to No. 14 Mobile Veterinary Section (Imperial) by Sergeant Williamson, Troopers Macdonald, Davis and Beattie, from Caix to Hourges. This party was severely bombed by enemy aircraft which threw flare lights on them. The shock of the bombs so terrified the horses, causing the lead rope to break, that a stampede was only averted by these men sticking to their posts. After getting the animals down which was done under great difficulties in the darkness and during the continuance of bombing in the vicinity, they were able to proceed and delivered all the horses at their destination.

On another occasion, Troopers J. Turner and R. Scheising were mentioned under similar circumstances.

DEMOBILIZATION On March 18th, 1919, the personnel were sent to various units of the Canadian Cavalry Brigade for demobilization purposes and on that date the section ceased to exist.

LOCATION 'A' Section moved about a great deal and in the course of the war was stationed at many places, amongst which may be mentioned: Blangy, Souez, Daours, Ville-sur-Corbie, Neslette, Querrien, Tully, Moislain, Montecourt, Cappy, Croix, Bouchy, Mereaucourt, Guyencourt, Boves, Camon, St. Ouen, Hangest, Hautecote, Blangermont, Coulincourt, Vermand, Ytres, Avelin, Maubray, Herrines, Mont-St-André, Perwez, Rimière Château, Ehein, Thon-Samson, Bèthencourt-sur-mer and Dargnies.

SECTION DISBANDED WITHOUT SERVICE

NO. 5 MOBILE VETERINARY SECTION The last section to be organized was created for service with the Fifth Division, which, after attaining a high degree of efficiency at Witley, was disbanded in March, 1918, without seeing service in France. This section was trained at Shorncliffe and went, in February, 1917, under command of Captain J.F. Wood, to take up its duties at Witley. Captain Wood, falling ill, was succeeded by Captain A.T. McLean, who remained in command till disbandment took place.

CORPS VETERINARY EVACUATING STATION

The evacuating station of the Canadian corps, one of several similar establishments formed throughout the British armies, came into being for the better handling of the work of evacuation to the base hospitals by centralization of the same.

Inadequacy of Mobile Sections From what has been already stated, the reader will gather that whilst the mobile sections did invaluable work throughout the entire period of the war, they did not altogether measure up to what was demanded of them, not from any lack of efficiency or devotion to duty on the part of the personnel, but solely because the whole scheme of mobile sections was inadequate to meet the requirements of the situation at times of extraordinary military activity. During important actions it was found that they were unable to carry out, unaided, the task allotted to them, owing to the circumstances under which they had to operate, and there was, consequently, more or less dislocation of arrangements.

Each section possessed 24 horses on its own establishment which had to be fed, watered, groomed and exercised, and of the total available personnel of 24, as many as from six to twelve might be absent as conducting parties, whilst three others might be manning the advanced collecting post; then with 100 or more animals coming in daily, it was faced with a tremendous problem. The men could not perform miracles, yet as far as was humanly possible, they accomplished marvels in the face of unanticipated difficulties. Besides, the great object of the service was being defeated on account of the enforced delay in treatment to which the animals were subjected, owing to the fact that they had to be held two or three days until a trainload could be made up for shipment to the base, this delay in some instances entailing the eventual destruction.

Lack of Dental Equipment Another factor that militated against complete efficiency of the service was the entire lack of equipment for dental work. None of the sections had been provided with any sort of dental implements with the exception of a rasp, and only the possession of a few privately owned instruments enabled a modicum of dental work to be done. This was a great shortcoming for it usually necessitated the complete evacuation to the base of all cases having irregularities not amenable to simple corrective measures, a procedure that resulted in the loss to the divisions of many a hardened animal. It should be understood in this connection that the Canadian mobile sections had to be organized and equipped according to the establishment in vogue in the Imperial service; and to the fact that veterinary dentistry in Europe has never attained the importance that characterizes it on this side of the Atlantic is to be attributed the inadequate provision of dental appliances made by the Imperial authorities, a shortcoming which struck the Canadian veterinary officers with astonishment.

Temporary Veterinary Detachment An attempt to cope with the afore-mentioned difficulties was made in September, 1917, when a new veterinary detachment was created for the Canadian Corps under the late Captain T.A. Girling, which it was intended should act as a forward hospital for debility and light surgical cases that could be returned to their units within four weeks, and for dental work. It was particularly felt that some such post was needed for the purpose of bringing surgical cases under treatment with the least possible delay and thereby reducing the seriousness of wound infection. It was to accommodate 50 animals from each division and during its existence it operated the corps dipping tank at Barlin, putting through approximately 2500 animals. But the advent of the Passchendaele operations led to its disbandment within little more than a month.

Canadian Veterinary Authorities First to Suggest Betterment The Passchendaele operations more than ever emphasized the great need of a reorganization of the evacuating system and this led to the Canadian veterinary authorities in the field strongly urging the establishment by the Imperial authorities of an advanced veterinary hospital at railheads with each corps to act as: Temporary hospital; Dental clinic; Evacuating station.

Origin The outcome was the establishment of a chain of corps evacuating stations, included amongst which was one formed by the Canadian veterinary authorities for service with the Canadian corps.

Duties The work of this unit did not differ from that which had hitherto been performed individually by the mobile sections, except that its function being to deal mainly with the latter, admissions from individual units were restricted and infrequent.

Commanding Officer It began operations at Ecoivres on April 16th, 1918, under Captain F.A. Daigneault, who, till then, had been in charge of No. 2 Mobile Section and who was now selected as commanding officer, with promotion to the rank of major, in recognition of the fact that he had always maintained the best conducted of all the Canadian mobile sections.[5]

PERSONNEL The personnel was made up of withdrawals from the mobile sections and a few reinforcements from No. 1 Canadian Veterinary Hospital, and consisted of one staff sergeant, one sergeant, two corporals, one shoeing smith corporal, one shoeing smith and 32 men, of whom four acted as dressers, one as cook, one as batman, and the rest as grooms, and all were supposed to be of a medical category slightly lower than the highest.

ACTIVITIES It began receiving cases on April 17th, from the Canadian division and from two Imperial divisions and made its first evacuation of 232 animals by train on April 20th. Thenceforth, the different mobile sections ceased to carry on evacuations themselves, but instead sent all evacuation cases at once to the new station after first dressing wounds. Owing to the reduced personnel of the mobile sections, this work was surrounded with considerable difficulty during major operations when there were large numbers of animals to be evacuated. The usual method of one man leading two animals was quite out of the question and resort had to be made to the cable system as practised for exercising at No. 1 Canadian Veterinary Hospital. But the apparatus being only of an improvised nature and without rings or fixtures at regular intervals to which the halter ropes might be made secure, such as was used at Havre, led to some difficulty in the animals slipping their halter ropes backwards and forwards along the rope. Captain Vickers suggested chains for this purpose instead of ropes on the ground that they would be practically indestructible and take up less room.

MOTOR AMBULANCE Though an earlier effort on the part of the Blue Cross to supply a motor ambulance to the Canadians had proven abortive, for reasons stated elsewhere, such a vehicle finally came into the possession of the evacuating station on September 14th, 1918. Though rather late in the war, it was of immense help in facilitating the work during the march into Germany.[7]

ACTIVITIES The extent of the station's activities during a period of combat is indicated by the returns for the week ending August 15th, 1918: Strength of animals in corps area 25,512 horses
5,583 mules
Total: 31,095

Sick and injured admitted - 1,818; cured and returned to duty - 242; evacuated to hospital - 363; died or destroyed (593 due to enemy fire) - 616; remaining under treatment - 597.

VISITS FROM AMERICAN OFFICERS On August 14th, 1918, Major Knowles of the American Expeditionary Force visited the station for the purpose of having explained to him the new method of receiving and evacuating sick and wounded animals and a similar visit was paid on September 21st, 1918, by the senior veterinary officer of the same force.

LOCATION Localities in which the station operated were as follows: Ecoivres, Achiecourt, Quéant, Auberchicourt, Raismes, Jemappes, Mons, Namur, by rail to Bonn, where it arrived at 8 a.m. on December 24th, 1918. On February 2nd, 1919, it entrained at Bonn for Andenne, homeward bound.

NO. 6 MOBILE VETERINARY SECTION

This section was organized at Petawawa, Canada towards the latter part of 1918 for service with the Siberian Expeditionary Force. Throughout the short period of its existence, it was commanded by Captain C.J. Cooper.

Though 1632 horses were purchased for the force, but 291 crossed the Pacific, owing to lack of shipping facilities. Native Siberian horses, small, undersized animals possessing about half the working capacity of Canadian horses, supplemented the force. In the absence of contagious diseases and a minimal number of minor injuries and sickness, the Canadian horses did remarkably well and were the admiration of the native people. The unit returned to Canada the following summer.

CHAPTER 10

THE HEADQUARTERS STAFF

Throughout the war, the headquarters or administrative offices of the Canadian Army Veterinary Corps were stationed in England. In the early days of the first contingent, there were no regularly organized headquarters but they came into being as a result of the demands occasioned by the expansion of the service, developing step by step in pace with the growth of the latter.

LIEUTENANT-COLONEL W.J. NEILL The first officer to command the corps was Lieutenant-Colonel W.J. Neill. Born in Omemee, Ontario, in 1876, he began his military career in 1893 as a private in the ranks of the 45th Regiment of Militia, and being commissioned in the same unit in 1897, rose to the rank of major. In 1909 he was transferred to the Reserve of Officers. He graduated at the Ontario Veterinary College in 1902 and shortly afterwards went to the South African War as Veterinary Captain to the 3rd Regiment of Mounted Rifles, arriving there towards the suspension of hostilities. He was then given command of Details of Camp at Signal Hill, near Johannesburg. On the termination of the war, he remained in South Africa, acting as District Commissioner of Lands in N.W. Transvaal from 1902 until 1903, when he returned to Canada. He then went to the United States where he spent most of the time until, in January, 1914, he was called by Major-General Sam Hughes, Minister of Militia, to assume a commission in the permanent forces with the rank of major and appointment as Principal Veterinary Officer of Military District No.3 at Kingston, Ontario, and upon the outbreak of the war was appointed Director of Veterinary Services, Canadian Militia, with the rank of lieutenant-colonel. It is not known that he had any special qualifications for this appointment other than his previous military training as he was comparatively unknown in Canadian veterinary circles.[1] Nevertheless, he manifested considerable ability in the handling of the intricate and variable problems that confronted him and had he at all times received from administrative officers in the field the support that was due him, it is possible he would have remained at his post till the end of the war.

AS A.D.V.S., C.E.F. When the war broke out, he was the logical candidate for the veterinary administrative position with the first contingent and went overseas as Assistant Director of Veterinary Services, going later to France in the same capacity with the First Division. Certain remnants of the First Division, consisting of odds and ends of brigades, remained behind in England in more or less divided state until the arrival of the second contingent in April, 1916. In the interim, the threads of the Canadian Veterinary Service in England were held together by Major J.H. Wilson, to whom Lieutenant-Colonel Neill had turned over the command when he left Salisbury Plain for France.

APPOINTED D.V.S. Meanwhile, Lieutenant-Colonel Neill, who had been appointed Director of Veterinary Services, Canadian contingents, with the rank of temporary colonel, by the War Office Order of February 11th, 1915, returned from France in the middle of March and at once proceeded to organize a corps headquarters, in which he was ably assisted by Honorary Lieutenant A.E. Frape, who had been holding the post of officer commanding the Base Depot of Veterinary Supplies (Canadian), with Sergeant W. Denton in a clerical capacity.

LOCATION OF HEADQUARTERS It was on May 1st, 1915, that corps headquarters went into premises at 36 Victoria Street, London, S.W., but in September of the same year, upon the organization of the Second Division at Shorncliffe, a move was made to 41 Grimstone Avenue, Folkestone. A year was spent at Folkestone, when on September 16th, 1916, a move was made back to London, where Cleveland House, St. James's Square, gave shelter for a couple of months till offices in Argyll House, the seat of Canadian general headquarters, were ready for occupancy on November 16th. Still another move was made on May 17th, 1917, when the third floor of Oxford Circus House was acquired, and a final move was made back to Argyll House in May, 1918, where veterinary headquarters remained till the conclusion of the war.

COLONEL NEILL, ACTING Q.M.G. Colonel Neill continued to administer his office until the 28th of September, 1916, when he was directed to assume the acting appointment of Quartermaster-General of the Canadian Forces in England, in the absence of Colonel Murphy in Canada. He relinquished this position on the 5th of December, when he went back to his original one. On the occasion when he was absent on duty, Lieutenant-Colonel H.D.

Figure 10.1. Brigadier-General W.J. Neill and Canadian Veterinary Service Headquarters staff,[2] London, England, undated. (*NAC PA 5206*)

Smith worthily filled the post.

APPPOINTED DIRECTOR OF REMOUNTS In July, 1915, he was appointed director of remounts, making his title the combined one of Director of Veterinary Services and Remounts.

MISSION TO CANADA AND PROMOTION TO BRIGADIER-GENERAL In May, 1917, he was detailed by the War Office to proceed to Canada in connection with the Imperial Remount Commission, and before going was promoted to the substantive rank of brigadier-general (Figure 10.1), the War Office authorities wishing him to carry with him the enhanced prestige that the advance to this rank would bring with it. He returned from Canada in August, Lieutenant-Colonel Smith having carried on as acting director during his absence.

HONORARY CAPTAIN A.E. FRAPE During the whole tenure of Brigadier-General Neill's command, Honorary Lieutenant Frape, promoted to captain July 1st, 1915, acted as his right-hand man. Captain Frape was an able, energetic officer, who through faithful and efficient service had worked his way upwards and qualified himself for commissioned rank. He had served nearly 14 years in the ranks and had gained his stripes in the Royal Canadian Horse Artillery, where as farrier, he proved himself second to none in Canada. For three years prior to the war, he had served in the Canadian Permanent Army Veterinary Corps and at the outbreak of war was promoted to honorary lieutenant and quartermaster.

APPOINTMENT ADVERSELY REGARDED But, his appointment to a staff position at veterinary headquarters was looked at askance by many of the officers of the veterinary corps, for the reason that he was not a qualified veterinarian, and it cannot be denied that from this point of view, Colonel Neill, when he selected him as his assistant, fell into somewhat of an error, from the effects of which he never fully recovered the early popularity he had enjoyed with his officers. Most of the latter thought he should have taken his assistant from amongst themselves and thereby obtained someone able to bring to bear not only technical knowledge but experience gained under actual service conditions in the field, for it must be remembered that Colonel Neill himself had spent but little over one month at the front ere he was recalled. But, the veterinary officers overlooked the fact that it is an unquestionable privilege of a commanding officer to surround his immediate person with those he considers best fitted to carry out his policies, and it is not to be doubted that the urgent need for continued employment in the field of every available veterinarian in a service that was never overburdened with a surplus of qualified practitioners, was an important factor in determining Colonel Neill's course of action. Captain Frape was gazetted Assistant Director of Remounts in April, 1917; he could not be appointed an Assistant Director of Veterinary Services, because he was not a qualified veterinarian, but he was graded for pay as such.

In every organized body of men, no less in a military organization, there exists the desire to look up to some individual to personify its ideals, someone who shall be the embodiment of those ideals, and Colonel Neill, in feeling obliged to ignore the susceptibilities of his officers, lost, in some measure, the whole-hearted support of the latter.

Figure 10.2. Captain Arthur E. Frape. (*NAC PA 203425*)

HONORARY LIEUTENANT DENTON From the same viewpoint, he did not make things any better when he took to himself a second helper, also not a veterinarian, in the person of Sergeant W. Denton (promoted in due course to honorary lieutenant) despite the fact that the latter officer was most capable and steady and did exceptionally good work. Lieutenant Denton had the onus of keeping all the statistics, records and accounting until the arrival later of Staff Sergeant Meers. Owing to the frequent removals of headquarters to new offices, this was a labor of no little difficulty, which, however he surmounted by virtue of a marvelous memory and consistent devotion to duty. On Colonel Edgett's arrival, he was transferred to the Base Depot where he acted as quartermaster.

DUTIES OF HEADQUARTERS VETERINARY DEPARTMENT Following is a compilation of the duties performed by veterinary headquarters:

<u>Veterinary Officers</u>

(1) General supervision of, and instruction issued to, relative to the proper administration of their duties

(2) Issuing of orders and circular letters to, directing the proper course of procedure for the prevention and combatting of contagious diseases, etc., when same broke out

<u>Veterinary Services - General</u>

(l) Filing and recording all data with reference to officer and other ranks, posting officers for different duties

(2) Routine correspondence in connection with the department

(3) Compiling and issuing daily corps orders. Filing and indexing miscellaneous correspondence in connection

(4) Attending to requirements for reinforcements for service with the British Expeditionary Force

<u>Veterinary Supplies</u>

(l) Obtaining of veterinary medicines, instruments, veterinary chests, wallets, etc., and supervising distribution of same

(2) Keeping ledger accounts of all veterinary supplies bought and to where and to whom issued

(3) Keeping ledger accounts of veterinary supplies used by each individual veterinary officer or organization

<u>Veterinary School</u>

(1) Receiving nominal rolls of men passing instructional courses for farriers, shoeing smiths and first aid sergeants. Correspondence in connection

(2) Appointing suitable men to take instructional course for first aid sergeants
(3) Posting first aid sergeants to various units to meet requirements

REMOUNT DEPARTMENT

Remount account between War Office and Canadian Remount Department

(1) Information collected from reports sent periodically by the administrative veterinary officer of the Canadian Army Corps showing remounts received from, and evacuations made to, the Imperials, in France
(2) Remounts received from, and evacuations made to, the Imperials in England
(3) Compiling monthly statements, in connection, showing monthly debit or credit balance

Routine

(l) Returns. Receiving and checking semimonthly returns from each individual veterinary officer, showing strength, remounts received, casualties, etc., of each unit, to be entered in unit account. Correspondence in connection with same
(2) Indents. Receiving indents for remounts from units newly arrived from Canada, from units organizing in England. Indenting on War Office or transferring from Canadian temporary remount depot, to cover same. Correspondence in connection with same
(3) Miscellaneous. Filing and compiling miscellaneous forms and reports

DIFFICULTIES OF OFFICE There is no gainsaying the fact that Brigadier-General Neill, in the exercise of the duties of his office had an exceptionally difficult road to travel, meeting many unexpected obstacles which made his position a very trying one. Every fair-minded person will sympathize with him at finding himself in the embarrassing situation of having to be responsible in his capacity as Director of Veterinary Services and Remounts for the compiling of statistical veterinary returns and the correct accounting of remount obligations between the Canadian authorities and the War Office, and yet being denied the authority for having direct communication with the administrative veterinary officers of the Canadian corps in the field, the individuals from whom the requisite information had to be derived.[3]

It may well be questioned whether Brigadier-General Neill had a square deal and whether official red tape was not pushed to an absurd degree and made to overstep the bounds of reason. At first, he had no difficulty in this respect but there came a time when the spectre of red tape reared its ugly head and by its intrusion impaired the efficiency and smooth running of the Canadian service. The channels of communication of which he might then make use were three, namely: the Military Secretary, the Adjutant-General and the Quartermaster-General, but they were hedged with much delay and frequently failed to be productive of result; and when, as actually came about, he got out of tune with his immediate superiors, the situation became well-nigh intolerable for him and he felt it incumbent on him, in the interests of the service, to tender his resignation, which he did on the 18th of March, 1918.

The most important of Brigadier-General Neill's functions was the compilation of remount returns and it seems incredible that a high administrative officer appointed to handle a situation that involved millions of dollars of Canadian taxpayers' money should have been subjected to such inconsiderate treatment and been obliged to carry on his duties under such extraordinary difficulties. He pointed out that the responsibilities of his department, involving the accounting of large sums of money, were great, and that there were at the time no less than 38 Canadian units in France, unattached to the Canadian Army Corps, scattered amongst Imperial formations, which units were constantly receiving horses on Canadian charge and with which his office in London was not in touch, there being no Canadian officer authorized to act as intermediary. He went on to state that prior to July, 1916, copies of all returns were submitted to his office by the administrative veterinary officers, but that, in accordance with an army corps order issued about that time, this procedure was discontinued, the result being that the very necessary information required by his department filtered through in a desultory manner and consequently the settlement of accounts with the War Office had to be held up owing to impossibility of verification.

It was absolutely essential for the adjustment of accounts and maintenance of records that he be in possession of information dealing with the horse strength and various increases and decreases due to casualties that occurred from time to time, which he was not at that time (May, 1917), owing to the fact that he was not in regular receipt of copies of Army Form A2000, strength distribution and increase and decrease reports. He urged that it was advisable to establish a representative (either himself or a deputy) in France at an advantageous point to supervise indents for the receipt and distribution of remounts to Canadian formations and to keep in touch with the Director of Remounts (Imperial) in order to protect Canadian interests, pointing out that the Australians had recognized the wisdom of making such provision by placing a representative at General Headquarters in France.

To cite but one concrete instance of discrepancy of figures arising from the then lack of system, he mentioned where the War Office figures for issue of remounts to Canadian units for the first quarter of 1917 were given only in bulk and were found to exceed the total accounted for by some 1200 horses, which it was presumed had been issued to Imperial units attached to Canadian divisions as had happened previously in 1916, when animals had been demanded by the different Canadian divisions without it being specified that some were intended for attached Imperial units. They were consigned to the Canadian divisions but, on arrival, were re-allotted to Imperial units, without the fact being brought to the knowledge of the issuing depot and thus, inadvertently, charged to Canada. The absence of returns from Canadian sources in the field left him entirely dependent upon the War Office for figures regarding evacuations and issues of remounts without an opportunity of checking the same.

IMPROVEMENT IN CONDITIONS Things improved somewhat when the change was made in the administrative service of the Canadian Army Corps in France in July, 1917, and the centrally situated Assistant Director of Veterinary Services was made responsible for collecting returns and information from all the divisions and submitting them under one covering letter. It was then that Lieutenant-Colonel Edgett, upon assuming the new position, instituted a system of making consolidated returns whereby the information required for statistics and accounting could be compiled.

LACK OF COOPERATION BY C.A.V.C. OFFICERS[4] The reader, in referring to the chapter in which the table of yearly wastage percentage is stated, will observe certain omissions noted, the result of which, of course, has been to invalidate the strict accuracy of the estimate in respect to the horses in the Canadian service. These omissions represent the nonreceipt by London headquarters of certain of the monthly returns, a delinquency due partly to the obstructive formalities now under discussion and partly to incapability of comprehension on the part of some of our own administrative officers.

The original cause of the temporary absolute stoppage of the returns was an unfortunate step taken by the Assistant Director of Veterinary Services of one of the divisions who complained to his divisional headquarters that too many returns were being demanded of him. Divisional headquarters failed to appreciate the importance of the matter or to perceive what the Director of Veterinary Services in London had to do with the Canadian veterinary services in the field, which, of course, was an entirely sophistical view to take of the matter, and as a result, the administrative veterinary officers of all the divisions were instructed to cease sending returns direct, it being ruled that that was not a proper channel of communication.

There still remained available two channels of transmission, had the administrative officers all been imaginative enough to make use of them, namely: Canadian Army Corps Headquarters and a more roundabout way through the Director of Veterinary Services (Imperial). Two of the administrative officers, Majors Tamblyn and Edgett, alert to the desideratum, did actually take advantage of the latter channel and forwarded their returns with a request that they be transmitted to the Director of Veterinary Services (Canadian) in London. But the other administrative officers took advantage of the attitude assumed by their divisional headquarters and refrained from continuing their aid to the end in view, and so little importance was attached to the matter by those in authority in Canadian Army Corps Headquarters that for a period of several weeks no returns whatever, outside of those already referred to, came through. It was not till Colonel Neill took over the acting appointment of Quartermaster-General in September, 1916, till December, 1916, and was enabled to make direct application himself that the returns began to filter through, but far from satisfactorily.

There was still lack of a centralized system of gathering the returns which persisted till Lieutenant-Colonel Edgett had assumed the administrative position already referred to.

Nor were conditions any better with respect to the matter of the personnel of the veterinary corps. At no time during Brigadier-General Neill's incumbency was the London office enabled to maintain an accurate record of the whereabouts in France of even the veterinary officers, not to speak of other ranks. It is to this fact that any shortcomings in recording the names of members of the veterinary corps in the pages of this work must be ascribed. It was part of the duty of the Canadian veterinary directorate to produce such reinforcements as were needed, but when the latter passed on to the strength of the forces in France, they came practically wholly under the direction of the Imperial authorities and for the time being were lost to the control and ken of the Canadian directorate.

OBSTRUCTIVE TACTICS OF C.A.V.C. OFFICERS The difficulty that was experienced in getting returns impelled Colonel Neill to have a letter written to the Assistant Director of Veterinary Services of one of the divisions requesting that he transmit to the London office on the last day of each month a nominal roll of both officers and other ranks, but evidently this officer[5] was no more disposed to cooperate with the chief in London, from whose control he was detached whilst in France, than in the matter of the statistical veterinary and remount returns, for in the following month of August, it was again found necessary to repeat the request.

Apparently, the officer in question was determined to be relieved from supplying the desired information, for in September, a communication emanated from Lieutenant-General Sir Julian Byng, at that time commander of the Canadian Army Corps, who also did not seem to grasp the importance of the matter from the Canadian viewpoint, to the effect that the necessity for forwarding a nominal roll of personnel of the Canadian Army Veterinary Corps was not apparent, and requesting that authority might be given to discontinue the submission of these rolls, and that the Director of Veterinary Services and Remounts (Canadian) might be instructed to submit his requests through the proper channel to the Deputy Adjutant-General at the base, instead of direct to units of staff officers of the army corps.

The result was that the administrative veterinary officers of all the divisions were ordered by the Canadian Army Corps authorities to cease rendering the desired information.

PROTEST OFFERED In the meantime, Brigadier-General Neill was being asked for this very information from different sources and was quite unable to supply it. Accordingly, he sought the intervention of the Quartermaster-General (Canadian), one of the channels through which he was authorized to communicate with the forces in France.

Under date of December 24th, 1917, he pointed out that under arrangements in force, no correspondence or requests for returns being permitted to emanate from his office direct to the various branches of the veterinary corps in France, it was impossible for him to keep an accurate record of the strength, interchanges and repostings of the personnel in France. He stated that he did not receive a report, nor was he advised or considered when an officer was reposted or became a casualty, excepting when the latter arrived or reported to the general depot at Shorncliffe. He requested that steps might be taken and arrangements made whereby his department would come into possession of facts pertaining to its personnel doing duty with the various units of the Overseas Military Forces of Canada.

MAKING OF APPOINTMENTS AND PROMOTIONS The question of controlling the presence of veterinary officers in France gave rise to some misunderstanding at the outset. Colonel Neill, as chief administrative officer of the Canadian veterinary service, and on the presumption that nobody than himself was better qualified to know the capabilities of his subordinate officers, naturally thought that he should have the main voice in their disposal and selection and promotion to the higher positions. Moreover, as provided in the home establishment of the Canadian Army Veterinary Corps, it was specifically laid down that the senior officer was charged with the recommendation for appointments and promotions. That this was Colonel Neill's view was exemplified by the case of Captain L.M. Grignon, who having ineffectually applied to his immediate superior in France for leave of absence to proceed to Canada for 6 weeks to settle up his father's estate, made a further application to Colonel Neill in England. The case gave rise to some correspondence in which the latter made the observation that the application should originally have been forwarded to his office, as he was responsible for the personnel of the veterinary corps, to maintain a complete establishment.

Colonel Neill was undoubtedly correct in his attitude, but circumstances alter cases, and he was expected to modify his viewpoint, the authorities in France taking the extreme stand that all personnel passed beyond the sphere of control of the Home Command as soon as taken on the strength of the British Expeditionary Force, when, in fact, it was only as regards executive duties. The matter was brought to a head in a letter addressed by Colonel Neill to the administrative veterinary officer of the First Canadian Division on August 16th, 1916, requesting him to forward as soon as possible the names of veterinary officers in his division whom he considered capable of filling the position of Assistant Director of Veterinary Services. This brought forth a communication from the General Officer Commanding-in-Chief, dated September, 1916, directing that the procedure adopted by the D.V.S. & R. (Canadian contingents) whereby he corresponded directly with the Assistant Director of Veterinary Services of one of the Canadian divisions should cease.

Brigadier-General Moore, Director of Veterinary Services (Imperial) in a letter dated September 2nd, 1916, also observed that recommendations for administrative veterinary appointments at the front should be made by the Director of Veterinary Services in France, whilst the Deputy Director of Veterinary Services (Imperial) of the Second Army wrote to Brigadier-General Moore on August 29th, that if Colonel Neill wished to make recommendations for officers to hold special or administrative appointments, it would appear preferable for the demand to be made through the proper channels.

IMPERIAL AUTHORITIES ACTING ARBITRARILY The next step along these lines was taken in the case of Captain A.E. Watson. Captain Watson, before the war, had attained to eminence by reason of his original contribution to veterinary science whilst in charge of the Dominion Veterinary Research Laboratory at Lethbridge, and because of his unusual qualifications had been specially employed on microscopical work at Folkestone, investigating an outbreak of mange which occurred at Shorncliffe in December, 1915.

Whilst acting as veterinary officer of the Second Divisional Artillery, he was, in January, 1917, moved from the Canadian corps and detailed for duty in establishing the Imperial Veterinary Laboratory at Rouen without the matter being referred to Canadian veterinary headquarters in London. His selection occurred by reason of his training and experience as a bacteriologist, there being no officer in the Imperial service available for the position, and it was approved by the War Office in April, 1917. In a sense, he was responsible for the action taken, for it was on receipt of a circular sent to units at the front, pointing out the need of a bacteriologist to deal with contagious diseases, that he applied for the appointment through his administrative officer. When the Quartermaster-General (Canadian) heard about it, he wrote the Assistant Military Secretary, under date of December 22nd, 1917, suggesting that the Imperial authorities be asked to state their authority for detailing Captain Watson for duty outside the Canadian service.

After the usual exchange of correspondence, the matter ended in Captain Watson being recommended to be formally seconded to the Imperial service in January, 1918, a year after he had been appropriated. Later, after the armistice, Colonel Edgett applied for his return to the Canadian forces as he felt that Canada should have some benefit of his scientific observations, particularly as he had been in the pay of Canada all the time, but the Imperial authorities at first strenuously opposed the application, claiming that the war was not yet terminated and that the General Officer Commanding-in-Chief considered that the British Expeditionary Force still had need of his services. However, his release was effected in March, 1919, and he returned to his own service in London.

HOW QUESTION OF AUTHORITY WAS SETTLED The question still remained in the air and was not decisively settled until the summer of 1918, after the establishment of the Canadian Section at General Headquarters in France and the advent to Canadian Headquarters in London of Lieutenant-Colonel Edgett, who drew up a fixed policy to govern all such procedure, got it approved by the Canadian authorities and accepted, though with a certain amount of reluctance, by the Imperial authorities.

But the extent to which Colonel Neill was able to exercise his own authority in making selections from amongst his officers for the higher positions showed that with one, or possibly two, exceptions, his judgment was sound and fully justified by results. Where he slipped up, it was due to placing too great reliance on the recommendations of others.

IMPERIAL AUTHORITIES APPROPRIATING SERVICES OF CANADIAN OFFICER It has been explained in the chapter on The Veterinary Officer, that the supply of British veterinarians was insufficient to meet the demands of the new armies and that the Old Country, in her dilemma, turned to Canada, which provided over 200 qualified practitioners to become officers in the Army Veterinary Corps (Imperial).

It was intended by the Canadian authorities that the services of all those who went over as officers of the Canadian Army Veterinary Corps should be confined to the Canadian forces, but very early in the war, the Imperial authorities exhibited a tendency to make use of them in connection with Imperial units. Thus it was that Captain W.G. Stedman, who happened to have been sent to No. 1 Canadian Veterinary Hospital at Havre in excess of the authorized establishment of officers, was moved away from there in October, 1915, on the authority of Brigadier-General Moore, and posted to the 25th Division (Imperial) for duty, without the consent of Colonel Neill having been obtained. When the matter came to the notice of the latter, he enquired the reason for the procedure and was informed that Captain Stedman had only been attached to the Imperial unit temporarily, pending a vacancy in a Canadian unit, and that he would be returned to England if it were desired. Whereupon, Colonel Neill expressed his willingness that he should remain where he was as other officers were momentarily expected from Canada and that from these the services of still another would be cheerfully loaned for a couple of months or more. Captain Stedman was soon afterwards transferred to First Canadian Division. About the same time, a communication was received by Colonel Neill from Brigadier-General Moore, who stated that he had been on the point of writing to ask if it would be possible to reduce the establishment of Canadian divisions in point of officers, lending some of them to the Army Veterinary Corps (Imperial), on account of shortage in the latter force.

CANADIAN AUTHORITIES INTERVENE It was felt by the Canadian authorities that to accede to such an all-embracing claim would be inimical to Canadian interests and steps were taken to effect an arrangement of the nature of a compromise but with Canadian prerogative paramount. It was pointed out that all administrative appointments in the Imperial service were made by the branches concerned without reference to the corps commander, but it was felt that as there was but one Canadian corps in France, it would be better for the service if the corps commander were consulted unofficially, as in that way the administrative services would get the benefit of his knowledge and he would be able to put forward his views before any definite action was taken. Although all recommendations for the fighting forces would naturally emanate from the corps commander, the administrative services were responsible for their organization outside of the corps as well as in it, and the final decision as to their respective branches should, therefore, be with them. Consequently, no changes should be made in the corps, so far as appointments were concerned or otherwise by either the Imperial authorities or Canadian Headquarters in the British Isles, without first of all being referred to the corps commander for his approval, through the office of the Military Secretary (Canadian).

IMPERIAL AUTHORITIES STILL ACTING ARBITRARILY Later, the Imperial authorities disregarded the understood procedure, which entailed reference to, and approval by, the Director of Veterinary Services (Canadian) before any appointment was made, by transferring Major Saunders from the command of No. 1 Canadian Veterinary Hospital at Havre to the administrative position of the First Division on their own initiative, to which act Colonel Neill was impelled to offer a protest, though without prejudice, to the officer concerned.

EFFORTS TO OBTAIN RECOGNITION OF V.O.'S SERVICES Colonel Neill made more than one effort to obtain due recognition of the services of the Canadian Army Veterinary Corps. Whilst still at Folkestone, in January, 1916, he wrote to Brigadier-General Wood in France, calling the attention of the latter to the fact that up till that time not one officer, non-commissioned officer, or man of the Canadian Army Veterinary Corps serving in the First or Second Divisions had been Mentioned in Despatches, whilst some of the Canadian veterinarians serving as officers in the Army Veterinary Corps (Imperial) had been mentioned and received the Military Cross. He went on to state that it would be much appreciated if it were seen fit to have some of these officers mentioned in order to give them all the encouragement possible to maintain the record they had held up till that time.

To which communication Brigadier-General Wood replied that he had brought the matter before the Canadian Army Corps commander, Sir Edwin Alderson, who promised to give the matter consideration the next time Despatches were called for from the corps.

Eventually, and particularly at the close of the war, a substantial list of honours and awards was forthcoming so that the Canadian Army Veterinary Corps had no cause to complain of insufficient recognition.[6]

VETERINARY INTERESTS IN ENGLAND WANING From the time when the first Canadian troops arrived in England and during the period of getting the earliest and subsequent arrivals into being as a coherent fighting force, the veterinary and remount interests of the Canadian forces in Great Britain assumed a growing importance. But, by the time the transfer of the four divisions to France to form the Canadian Army Corps had been completed, veterinary activities were on the wane and when the Fifth Division was disbanded, had dwindled to insignificant proportions. There remained practically only the accounting of remounts to be carried along and the maintenance of the reinforcing and training base.

VETERINARY BASE DEPOT DISBANDED Canadian Headquarters thought the veterinary corps could get along without a separate base of its own, the personnel to come under the General Base Depot, and put this decision into effect.

BRIGADIER-GENERAL NEILL RESIGNS Meanwhile, as has already been pointed out, Brigadier-General Neill relinquished his appointment, and the desire being to make a clean sweep of headquarters administration, Captain Frape, who had recently left for Canada on leave, was retained at home.[7]

ARRIVAL OF LIEUTENANT-COLONEL C.E. EDGETT - APPOINTED D.V.S. It was at this stage that Lieutenant-Colonel C.E. Edgett (see Fig. 7.6) assumed charge, he having arrived from France and been taken on the strength of the corps in England on the 14th of April, 1918, with appointment as Assistant Director of Veterinary Services, which led to his advance to the appointment of Director of Veterinary Services and rank of acting colonel. He did not receive the title of Director of Remounts, although he carried on the duties of that department.

BIOGRAPHICAL SKETCH[8] Born in Moncton, New Brunswick, in 1882, he first saw service as a trooper in the North West Mounted Police from 1900 to 1904. In 1906 he was graduated from the Ontario Veterinary College and later took a postgraduate course at the Chicago Veterinary College. He was from 1907 till 1912 in the employ of the Department of Agriculture as meat inspector and practised in his own town and later at Aneroid, Saskatchewan. He served as a veterinary lieutenant in the militia from 1906 till the outbreak of the war. He went to Valcartier with the original Winnipeg section, was posted as veterinary officer to the First Divisional Ammunition Column and later to the Third Infantry Brigade. His work in France, together with his subsequent promotions and appointments is stated in the chapter on The Administrative Veterinary Officer in the Field. He was twice Mentioned in Despatches and was awarded the Distinguished Service Order.

AFFAIRS IN DISORGANIZED STATE Upon his arrival in England, he found Canadian veterinary affairs in a state bordering on disorganization, owing to the mistake made by Canadian Headquarters in endeavoring to minimize the existence and importance of the veterinary corps. There were no longer in effect any arrangements for reinforcing the service in France or any base for the training of reinforcements, yet the call from France was persistent.

RESUSCITATION OF VETERINARY BASE DEPOT All his energies had to be devoted to resuscitating the almost extinguished efficiency of the mainspring of the corps. He had to find officers and men and provide for the training of the same. But, in this officer, the corps could not have had a more resourceful, uniformly efficient, yet prudent commander, and though the work was of a laborious uphill character, by dint of application and perseverance he soon mastered the problem and induced Canadian Headquarters to alter its views, with the result that the base, in a modified form, was reestablished at Shorncliffe and arrangements made with the Imperial authorities to take advantage of the existing army veterinary school at Woolwich for the training it was necessary to give the newcomers. But, here again, as during his predecessor's incumbency, one of his greatest difficulties was the matter of suitable officer reinforcements.

DIFFICULTIES SURMOUNTED Thanks to the adoption of a well-thought-out and definite policy and the tactful handling of all outstanding difficulties, the course of Colonel Edgett's administration ran with delightful smoothness. This policy provided for the elimination of most of the difficulties that had beset Brigadier-General Neill by controlling the appointments and postings of officers through the recently established Canadian Section at General Headquarters in France, and was still further improved at the beginning of 1919 by the placing there of his personal representative, Lieutenant-Colonel Tamblyn, as D.D.V.S.

FOLLOWING ARE THE SALIENT FEATURES OF THE NEW POLICY:

PROCEDURE C.A.V.C. FRANCE - Officer Personnel

Reinforcements

All officer reinforcements will be demanded direct on the Canadian Section by Canadian Corps, Canadian Cavalry Brigade, Canadian Forestry Corps, Canadian Railway Troops, and Canadian Veterinary Hospital.

Reinforcements will be despatched from England to No. 1 Canadian Veterinary Hospital, and nominal rolls will be forwarded by D.V.S., H.Q., O.M.F.C., to Canadian Section, G.H.Q., 1st Echelon, who will instruct as to posting.

In demanding officer reinforcements the class of unit for which the reinforcement is required should, in each case, be stated.

The new establishment for the veterinary hospital at Havre provides for 7 officers. This will permit of a permanent cadre of 5 officers being regularly employed, and still enable an exchange to be frequently made of at least 2 officers from the hospital with officers from the forward areas.

Reposting

In the case of officers attached to units in the Canadian corps, the corps will make the necessary reposting on the recommendation of the A.D.V.S. Corps, notice being forwarded to the Canadian Section in each instance. Canadian Section will forward copy of Move List to D.V.S., B.E.F.

In the case of officers outside the Canadian corps, or between the Canadian corps and units on the lines of communication, the Canadian Section will issue instructions for reposting, giving the D.V.S., B.E.F., ample notification.

Officers between England and units in the field will be reposted by Canadian Section, G.H.Q., 1st Echelon, on the recommendation of D.V.S., H.Q., O.M.F.C., due notification of these postings being forwarded to the D.V.S., B.E.F.

Canadian Section will forward a weekly move list and nominal roll of C.A.V.C., officers in France to H.Q., O.M.F.C., and D.V.S., B.E.F.

Appointments

All new appointments in the field in the C.A.V.C., will receive the final approval of H.Q., O.M.F.C., after being recommended by the usual authorities through Canadian Section, G.H.Q., 1st Echelon.

Promotions

All C.A.V.C. officer promotions will be made by H.Q., O.M.F.C.

(a) Promotions and appointments of non-commissioned rank of C.A.V.C. units in France will, up to and including that of corporal, be made by the A.A.G.'s office at the base, on recommendation of O.C. units on whose nominal roll the soldier is carried.

(b) Promotions and appointments to warrant and non-commissioned rank will only be promulgated in Pt. II Orders after recommendation of such promotion, or appointment, has been concurred in by the Canadian Section, G.H.Q., lst Echelon.

(c) As soon as a substantive vacancy exists in the unit for an appointment above that of corporal or sergeant, the O.C. will advise Canadian Section, G.H.Q., 1st Echelon, through the usual channels, who, if senior warrant officer or non-commissioned officer, is not serving in the unit in which the vacancy exists will, after reviewing the circumstances and taking primary into consideration, the desirability of promotion within the unit, either approve of recommendation, or arrange that the senior recommended N.C.O. be posted and given acting rank for a probationary period of 30 days. If at the end of 30 days, it is not considered that he can suitably fill the appointment, a detailed report as to in which respect he is considered unable to perform the duties of the higher rank will be submitted to Canadian Section, G.H.Q., 1st Echelon, and instructions issued as to disposal.

(d) Artificer N.C.O's may be considered for promotion if they are the senior in their rank, and are recommended as suitable for promotion.

(e) The officer commanding who recommends N.C.O. as being suitable for promotion to a higher grade must be prepared to accept such N.C.O. in the higher grade in his own unit.

Reinforcements

(a) Demands for reinforcements will continue to be made in the usual way by A.A.G. base, Canadian Section, G.H.Q., 3rd Echelon, classification and number of each to be stated.

(b) Confirmed N.C.O's from England who have had service in the field to be disposed of in accordance with special instructions in each case from Headquarters, O.M.F.C.

PART II ORDERS

A new copy of all Part II Orders affecting C.A.V.C. personnel in France will be forwarded to H.Q., O.M.F.C., by A.A.G. Canadian Section, 3rd Echelon, regularly.

MAJOR W.G. STEDMAN DOING DUTY During the period between Brigadier-General Neill's departure and Lieutenant-Colonel Edgett's arrival, Major W.G. Stedman performed the duties of the headquarters offices.

THE SUB-STAFF This chapter must not be brought to a close without a brief reference to those who formed the sub-staff at headquarters.

Sergeant-Major G.l. Brodie, who gained his promotion to the rank of warrant officer (first class) at the end of 1918, went over as corporal with the original section of Winnipeg. After serving for a time with No. 1 Mobile Section and later at Third Divisional Headquarters, he was called to London by Colonel Neill to maintain the records and perform clerical duties. He had been awarded the Meritorious Service Medal "in recognition of valuable services rendered with the armies in the field whilst employed with 3rd Divisional Headquarters Sub-staff".

Staff Sergeant D. H. Meers originally served in the Twenty-Ninth Battalion of Infantry and being severely wounded at the Battle of St. Eloi, was invalided to England. He went to headquarters in June, 1917, where he was placed in charge of accounts and statistics. Being an expert accountant, he proved himself of great value in straightening out the entangled state into which, for a time, remount matters were precipitated. After the armistice, he was sent to France to reduce to exact figures the outstanding obligations of the Canadian government in respect to this matter and was completely successful in adjusting the remount account for 1917-1918-1919 for which he was highly commended.

Staff Sergeants L.W. Raines, L.P. Dusart and J. Bailey came as sergeants from the disbanded remount department and acted in a clerical capacity. The two former were transferred in the same capacity in the summer of 1917 to the Witley and Shorncliffe areas respectively, whilst the latter was posted to the Forestry Corps in the spring of 1918. None of these saw service in France.

Sergeant C.W. Niemeyer enlisted originally in the Remount Department at Valcartier. He was taken on the strength of the sub-staff in March, 1916, when, on account of his remarkable record for securing enlistments in the British army, he was returned to Canada the following May to become recruiting officer in Military District No. 2. He was a journalist by profession and had seen 15 years of varied military service, part of which was in Nigeria. It was claimed that he held the record for individual recruiting in Great Britain, with no less than 8,331 attested men, all obtained without reward of any kind.

Trooper H. Harrison came from No. 2 Mobile Section and acted as orderly to both Brigadier-General Neill and Colonel Edgett.

Three women stenographers were successively employed in the office, namely: **Miss Phyllis Hammond** of Toronto and **Mrs. P. Mitchell-Eadon** and **Miss Edith Evans,** both of London, England.

HONOURS AND AWARDS[9]
OFFICERS - CANADIAN ARMY VETERINARY CORPS.

Rank	Name	Honours and Awards		Gazette
Captain	Beaver, N.G.	Mentioned in Despatches	31-12-18	L.G. 31089
Captain	Bowler, E.	D.C.M.		
Captain	Cameron, A.E.	M.C.	1-1-17	L.G.
Captain	Colebourn, H.	Mentioned in Despatches	1-6-17	L.G. 30107
Lieut.-Col.	Cutcliffe, A.B.	D.S.O.	3-6-18	L.G. 30716
		Recommended for gallant and distinguished service	30-11-15	L.G. 27116
		Mentioned in Despatches	28-5-18	L.G. 30706
Major	Daigneault, F.A.	Mentioned in Despatches	11-7-19	L.G. 31448
Lieut.	Denton, W.	Services noted		W.O.L.107817
Major	Duhault, J.R.J.	Mentioned in Despatches	11-7-19	L.G. 31448
		O.B.E.	3-6-19	
Colonel	Edgett, C.E.	D.S.O.	3-6-18	L.G. 30716
		Mentioned in Despatches	1-6-17	L.G. 30107
		Mentioned in Despatches	28-5-19	L.G. 30706
Lieut.-Col.	Evans, T.C.	M.C.	1-1-16	
		Mentioned in Despatches	1-1-16	L.G.
		Mentioned in Despatches		L.G. 30448
		Mentioned in Despatches	11-7-19	L.G. 31448
Captain	Frape, A.E.	Services noted		W.O.L.107817
Captain	Girling, T.A.	Mentioned in Despatches	1-6-17	L.G. 30107
Captain	Hunter, A.H.	Services noted		W.O.L.241217
Captain	Kennedy, H.P.	M.C.	3-6-18	L.G. 30716
Captain	Liddle, F.G.	Mentioned in Despatches	11-7-19	L.G. 31448
Captain	Matthew, R.G.	Mentioned in Despatches	28-5-18	L.G. 30706
		Belgium Croix de Guerre	5-4-19	L.G. 31275
Captain	McAlister, A.D.	Mentioned in Despatches	11-7-19	L.G. 31448
Hon. Lt.	Newell, A.	Services noted		W.O.L.24217
Captain	Preston, H.J.	O.B.E.	3-6-19	L.G. 31370
		Mentioned in Despatches	11-7-19	L.G. 31448
Lieut.	Prinn, W.J.	Services noted		W.O.L.107817
Major	Richards, S.C.	O.B.E.	1-1-19	L.G. 31092
		Mentioned in Despatches		L.G. 30345
Captain	Robertson, W.A. (Fig. 10.3)	O.B.E.	3-6-18	L.G. 31092
		Mentioned in Despatches	31-12-18	L.G. 31089
Major	Saunders, G.C.	D.S.O.	3-6-18	L.G. 30716
		Mentioned in Despatches	15-6-16	L.G.
		Mentioned in Despatches		L.G. 30448
		Mentioned in Despatches	28-5-18	L.G. 30706

Rank	Name	Honours and Awards		Gazette
Captain	Souillard, P.P.	Mentioned in Despatches	1-6-17	L.G. 30107
Lieut.-Col.	Tamblyn, D.S.	O.B.E.	3-6-19	L.G. 31370
		D.S.O.	1-1-18	L.G. 30450
		Mentioned in Despatches	2-1-17	L.G.
		Mentioned in Despatches	1-6-17	L.G. 30107
		Mentioned in Despatches		L.G. 30448
		Ordre de Leopold	18-10-19	
Captain	Taylor, L.E.L.	M.C.	11-1-19	L.G. 31119
Captain	Towill, W.F.	O.B.E.	3-6-19	L.G. 31370
		Mentioned in Despatches	11-7-19	L.G. 31448
Captain	Vickers, R.J.	M.C.	1-1-19	L.G. 31092
Major	Walsh, F.A.	Mentioned in Despatches	2-1-17	L.G.
Lieut.-Col.	Wilson, J.H.	Mentioned in Despatches	1-6-17	L.G. 30107
Captain	Woods, J.F.	Services noted		W.O.L.24217

Figure 10.3. Capt. W.A. Robertson[10] leaving Buckingham Palace with his sister and his mother from Scotland, after receiving his O.B.E. from King George V, 1 January, 1919. (*C.A.V. Barker Museum*)

CHAPTER 11

THE VETERINARY OFFICER

OFFICERS IN C.A.V.C. QUALIFIED VETERINARIANS Conforming to the regulations, commissions in the Canadian Army Veterinary Corps were restricted to qualified veterinarians who were either graduates of the Canadian veterinary colleges, licentiates of the Royal College of Veterinary Surgeons of Great Britain, or holders of diplomas granted by veterinary colleges of the other British countries or by veterinary colleges in the United States which had been duly recognized by the United States Department of Agriculture as competent places of learning. No qualification test other than the possession of a diploma of the sort mentioned was required in the expeditionary force, a condition quite different from that which holds good in the militia, where a subaltern must pass successive qualification tests not only in veterinary attainments, but in military proficiency, and spend a certain period in each grade before being advanced to a higher one. There was no time for anything of that kind and the demand for officers was too urgent to permit of dallying with peace-time conventionalities.

EXCEPTIONS Practically all rules have their exceptions and in regard to purely veterinary qualifications, as the war progressed, it was found expedient to make a few promotions of non-graduates to honorary commissioned rank for the carrying on of the administrative work or interior economy of the corps. One of the exceptions, Captain A.E. Frape, was on the headquarters staff during the incumbency of Brigadier-General Neill, and the others were mainly in the quartermaster branches of the two veterinary hospitals and bases where Honorary Captain F.T. Sear functioned at Havre and Honorary Lieutenants A. Newell and W. Denton at Shorncliffe. Lieutenant Denton was also stationed for a considerable period at headquarters in London. There was another officer in charge of the School of Farriery at Shorncliffe, Lieutenant W.J. Prinn, who, though possessing the particular knowledge and skill fitting him for the post of instructor in that important line of work, did not happen to be a qualified veterinarian. Finally, there were one or two other officers who performed duties in the veterinary service for longer or shorter periods. These were: Captain A. Turnbull, of the Canadian Army Service Corps, who went over in the early days as quartermaster to the hospital at Havre and served there for a short time, Captain C.E. Shirley, an infantry officer, who, having been wounded and invalided from France in the spring of 1916, was appointed to act as quartermaster at the hospital at Shorncliffe, and Captain F.D. Shaver, who, when the Canadian Remount Department was disbanded, assumed charge successively of the temporary Canadian remount depots conducted by the veterinary service at Shorncliffe and Witley till the middle of 1917.

It is not quite true to state that the veterinary officers were all graduates at the time of receiving their commissions. There was the case of Captain C.L. Edwards, not yet through his final year at college, who turned up at Valcartier during the early rush and on the recommendation of Lieutenant-Colonel Neill was commissioned without the qualification being insisted upon, but who was later given his diploma and who turned out to be a very efficient officer.

DIFFICULTY IN PROCURING As time went on and new veterinarians were needed to replace those who from one cause or another had been obliged to return home, considerable difficulty was experienced in securing the services of available graduates. The call for such men in the earlier days, coupled with an urgent demand that had also come from the Imperial Army Veterinary Corps, had left the country pretty well denuded of practitioners fit for military service overseas.[1] Consequently, a strict adherence to the regulations could not be persisted in and it became necessary to anticipate eventualities and to enter into an arrangement with the authorities of the Ontario Veterinary College whereby were released a number of final year students who were at a prospective stage of graduation and whose progress in studies had rendered them presumably eligible for qualification. These men, some 14 in all (Figure 11.1), were taken on the commissioned strength of the corps and in due course were awarded their diplomas, a procedure quite irregular but justified under the circumstances.

TRANSFERS FROM RANKS Mention must also be made of a few qualified veterinarians who in the first instance enlisted in the ranks not only of the veterinary corps but of fighting units and who later applied for and were given commissions. Amongst these were Corporal W.A. Robertson and Trooper R.M. Lee, who were undergraduates of

Figure 11.1. Final year students of the Ontario Veterinary College, Year '15, who went overseas prior to graduation, to be commissioned as Veterinary Officers and ultimately awarded a diploma. L-r: J. Bovaird, D.V. Reed, T. Childs, A.R. Cameron, A.B. Gibson, M. Carson, F. Parmiter, H. McGee, W.E. Armstrong, J.A. Stanford, M.I. Neely, and G.A. Rose. Bovaird was not commissioned. Of the remainder, only Cameron joined the C.A.V.C. The others were commissioned in the Army Veterinary Corps (Imperial). *(C.A.V. Barker Museum)*

the Ontario Veterinary College and who, in their patriotic zeal to serve their country, renounced their opportunity to complete their final year, without which they were not entitled to present themselves for examination for qualification, who came over as reinforcements, spent a few months in training, were permitted to go back to Toronto in October, 1915, to complete their course and returned to Shorncliffe duly commissioned. Others were: Farrier Sergeant W.M. Parsons, of the cavalry, Acting Farrier Sergeant L.E.L. Taylor of the artillery, Privates A.W. Busselle and W.C. Batty of the railway troops, Privates F.H. Cassels and A.P. Chambers of the infantry, Sergeant T.H. Hungerford of the Machine Gun Corps, Trooper J.J. O'Gorman who had been transferred from the 35th Infantry Battalion to the veterinary hospital at Shorncliffe, Trooper J.B. Williams serving in the same unit, Sergeant H.W. Craig, serving in No. 1 Mobile Section, to which he had been transferred after having spent a year in the trenches as a private in the 5th Infantry Battalion, Farrier Sergeant A.H. Hughes and Trooper O.V. Gunning of the Reserve Cavalry Regiment, Private H. Bowler, D.C.M., one of the immortal 'Princess Pats' and Gunner J.D. Macdonald, who, having ineffectually applied to authorities at Ottawa in July, 1917, enlisted in, and came over as a reinforcement for the artillery and succeeded in getting transferred in England.

TRANSFERS FROM OTHER UNITS There were also one or two instances of veterinarians commissioned as combatant officers in other units and who were allowed to transfer to the veterinary corps, namely: Lieutenant H. Sproston, from the 31st Infantry Battalion, Lieutenant J.D. McGillivray from the 184th Infantry Battalion and Major A.T. McLean from the 193rd Infantry Battalion.

GOVERNMENT VETERINARIANS Not all who were already qualified were in actual practice and proficient as general practitioners; some had long before entered government employment as pathologists or meat inspectors, specialized occupations hardly calculated to keep a man fit to practise the healing art but rather to lead him to forget the greater part of the general training he had received in his collegiate course, whilst others had spent the intervening years since their graduation in the pursuit of special lines of endeavour. Both of these classes were naturally somewhat out of gear with the sort of work that was looming up before them, but that fact did not deter them from resolving to reawaken their latent capabilities and to place such talents as they possessed at the disposal of the army.[2]

DEMAND FROM BRITISH ARMY Reference has been made to a demand that had come from the Imperial Army Veterinary Corps for qualified men to act as officers, the supply for the British army from the British Isles being totally inadequate to meet the demand. This fact, to a certain extent, placed the two corps in a state of competition which, however, was more apparent than real, for at all times the recruiting authorities worked in the interest of both services and directed applicants to throw in their lot where they were most needed. Four, namely: Lieutanants F.D. Early, T.R.R. Hoggan, A. Cowan and H. H. Bishop, were commissioned in the first instance in the Imperial corps but terminated their connection therewith on the expiration of a year's service and then entered the Canadian corps, whilst two made a change in a contrary sense, namely: Captain M.G. O'Gogarty and Lieutenant J.B. Williams. Altogether, 203 were passed into the Imperial service, whilst 148 were enrolled in the Canadian service.[3]

TERMS OF ENGAGEMENT The terms of engagement offered to the veterinarian as an inducement for him to enter the Imperial Army Veterinary Corps comprised an undertaking to serve for a period of one year with the rank of lieutenant and remuneration to the extent indicated in the comparative table below. If, on the expiration of the year's service, he elected to continue, he was gazetted to a captaincy with increased pay and allowances and a bonus.

On the other hand, the applicant for service with the Canadian corps was required to make declaration on attestation that he agreed to serve in the Canadian Overseas Expeditionary Force, and to be attached to any arm of the service therein, for the term of one year, or during the war then existing between Great Britain and Germany should that war last longer than one year, and for six months after the termination of that war provided his services were so long required, or until legally discharged.

RATES OF PAY & ALLOWANCES

Pay and Allowances of the Officers of the Canadian Army Veterinary Corps

	Pay Allowance	Field Allowance	Messing
Lieutenant			
prior to 11-9-18	$2.00	$ .60	$1.00
from 12-9-18	$2.00	$1.00	$1.00
Captain			
prior to 11-9-18	$3.00	$ .75	$1.00
from 12-9-18	$3.00	$1.00	$1.00
Captain (brigade veterinary officer)			
prior to 31-3-16	$3.00	$3.00*	$1.00
from 1-7-16 to 31-3-17	$3.00	$1.25*	$1.00

*Staff field allowance of $3.00 was reduced to $1.25 from 1-4-16 and was discontinued from 1-4-17, but an officer appointed in 1915 or 1916 and authorized to receive staff field allowance of $3.00 and $1.25 respectively was entitled still to receive the same provided he had held the appointment continuously.

From the above statement it will be seen that an extra emolument known as 'staff pay' was accorded to those who were originally attached to infantry brigades, in spite of the fact that they might not have any more horses to look after than officers attached to artillery brigades or other units. This anomalous state of affairs continued in two or three cases right up till the end of the war, but automatically ceased in the case of those who were absorbed into higher appointments with increased pay.

We may now take a glance at the comparative rates of pay in the two services and wherein the Canadian officer in the Imperial service was better off than his comrade in the Canadian service (Figure 11.2). From the foregoing statement it will be noted that the executive officer in the service of the Imperial veterinary corps was far better off in a financial sense than his comrade in the Canadian veterinary corps, not only during the first year of his service, unless the latter happened to be married, but for every succeeding year until the rates for field

Rate $4.86⅔ to £1. 0. 0.

COMPARATIVE STATEMENT.

Pay and Allowances of Excutive Officers of the A.V.C. & C.A.V.C.

Rank.	OFFICERS (Imperial Service)								OFFICERS (Canadian Service)			
	Pay. £. s. d.	Field Allce. s. d.	Lodging Allce. s. d.	Fuel Allowance. Winter. s. d.	Fuel Allowance. Summer. s. d.	Total Winter. £. s. d.	Total Summer £. s. d.	Total Average. £. s. d.	Pay.	Field Allce.	Messing Allce.	Total.
Lieutenant.	£250 a year 13.8.	3. 0.	2. 3.	11.	7.	19.10.	19. 6.	19. 8½	$2.00	.60¢	$1.00	$3.60 14/9½
Captain.	Capt. 15.6.					1. 3. 5.	1. 2. 8.	1. 3. 0½				
	Bt.Mj. 18.3.	3. 6.	3. 0.	1. 5.	8.	1. 6. 2.	1. 5. 5.	1. 5. 9½	$3.00	.75¢	$1.00	$4.75 19/6¼d.
Higher Rates.	Capt. 17.6.					1. 5. 5.	1. 4. 8.	1. 5. 0½				
	Bt.Mj. 1. 0.3.					1. 8. 2.	1. 7. 5.	1. 7. 9½				

Figure 11.2. Comparison of pay and Allowances of Executive officers in the (British) Army Veterinary Corps and the Canadian Army Veterinary Corps. (*French Papers, NAC*)

allowance were slightly raised towards the close of the war. The difference, expressed in dollars was as follows:

Difference in Pay and Allowances for First Year

Imperial	£398.0.0	$1,936.93	as lieutenant
Canadian		1,733.75	as captain
Difference		$ 203.18	in favor of Imperial lieutenant over Canadian captain.

Difference in Pay and Allowances for Succeeding Years

Imperial	£498.0.0	$2,423.60	as lieutenant
Canadian		1,733.75	as captain
Difference		$ 689.85	in favor of Imperial captain over Canadian captain

NOTE:- The difference in pay for the first year was not that between the rate for a Canadian lieutenant against an Imperial lieutenant, all officers appointed to the Canadian veterinary services after the first few months having been granted the rank of captain upon appointment.

In comparing the above-stated differences, it must not be forgotten that a married captain in the Canadian service was in receipt of an additional $480 as separation allowance, which was not the case in the Imperial service. Consequently, a married captain in the Canadian service was better off in the first year of his service than a lieutenant, married or unmarried, in the Imperial service, but less well off than a captain, married or unmarried, in the Imperial service.

Newly joined officers in the Canadian service received $250 outfit allowance, whilst those in the Imperial service received £37.10s.0d ($182.50).

The pay and allowances for the higher officers depended on their appointments irrespective of their rank (Figure 11.3).

UNREST OVER PAY These differences in emoluments were the cause of considerable unsettlement in the minds of some of the officers. Thus, Captain J.F. Wood, whilst in command of the hospital at Shorncliffe, Captain V.C.

Appointment.	1915 (to 31-3-16) Pay.	Field Allowance.	Messing Allowance	Subsistence Allowance.	1916 (to 31-3-17) Pay.	Field Allowance.	Ration Allowance.	1917 (to 31-3-18) Pay.	Subs. Allce. if stationed in London	1918 (from 1-4-18) Pay.	Subs. Allce. if stationed in London.
	$.c.	$.c.	$.c.	$.c.	$.c.	$.c.	s.d.	$.c.	$.c.	$.c.	$.c.
D.A.D.V.S.								8.00	1.00	8.00	1.00
A.D.V.S.	8.00	3.00	1.00	.50	7.00	2.00	1/9	9.00	1.00	9.00	1.00
D.V.S.	9.00	3.00	1.00	.50	9.00	3.00	1/9	12.00	1.00	12.00	1.00

NOTE. An Officer appointed in 1915, who was in receipt of 1915 rates and who had held the appointment continuously was entitled to continue on such rates if they were more beneficial.

Figure 11.3. Pay and Allowances of Senior Officers in the Canadian Army Veterinary Corps. (*French Papers, NAC*)

Best, Captain T.C. Evans and Lieutenant L.E.L. Taylor, individually wrote to Colonel Neill requesting to be permitted to transfer to the Imperial service. Captain Evans was fretting as late as June, 1916, that little chance appeared to exist in the Canadian service for promotion with a consequent increase of pay, an apprehension from which, in his own particular case, he was not long thereafter to be disillusioned. At that period he was veterinary officer with the Fifth Brigade, C.F.A., and the reply he received from Colonel Neill was flattering if not promising:

With regard to your transferring to the A.V.C., I really don't see my way clear to recommending your transfer, as you are one of my most capable officers. I have every confidence in you and want to retain your services in the C.A.V.C.

In March, 1916, the executive veterinary officers of the First Division sent a collective note to their administrative veterinary officer for transmission to the Director of Veterinary Services (Canadian) in England, expressing their sense of grievance on the question of pay and praying that the latter might be increased to correspond with the rates received by veterinary officers from Canada serving with the Imperial veterinary corps.

In the last year of the war, the rates of pay for officers of the medical corps were appreciably increased, which fact impelled Colonel Edgett to request that the same benefit be extended to officers of the veterinary corps. The application was recommended by the Quartermaster-General and the Chief of the General Staff and forwarded to the Minister, but no action was taken.

LACK OF PROPER TRAINING In the early days, when reinforcing veterinary units were being formed in Canada, the newly-commissioned officer was straightway attached to one of such units with which he went to England, but later on, when the organization of veterinary units was no longer carried out in Canada but at the base depot in England, he was sent across in an individual capacity and upon arrival was posted to the base depot at Shorncliffe. At Shorncliffe he was supposed to undergo a certain period of training in the duties pertaining to his office, but it would be the grossest misrepresentation of facts to state that he received from superior officers any attention that could be dignified by the term 'instruction'. A few desultory lectures were given with occasional drills. He was merely told to take charge of the welfare of a certain number of horses within the hospital lines or of units in adjacent territory. He was practically turned loose without a word of counsel to guide him in the performance of his military duties. He simply muddled through and all he learned of military duties was gained by reading and in the school of hard experience with stray bits of advice picked up here and there from the sergeant-major or the few old soldiers that were to be found amongst the non-commissioned officers of the corps. These remarks do not apply, of course, to the question of horsemastership or veterinary science in both of which he was supposed to be proficient on entering the service, an assumption that was far from justified in the case of the younger and recent graduates, some of whom could not ride. It must be remembered that the newly-commissioned officers for the most part had come direct from civil life and were utterly devoid of knowledge of the military calling, and still less were they familiar with the make-up of the veterinary corps or the scope of its work in the war. They were the individuals upon whom the responsibility for the effectiveness and smooth-working of the service corps was soon to devolve, and as such they should have been given abundant opportunity for an insight into the machinery and working of the corps. But too often the junior officers were left groping in the dark, so to speak, with the inevitable consequence that, being unable to get at facts, they often acquired a faulty view of their duties. It cannot be said that the responsible authorities, at any stage of the war caused to emerge from the Canadian Army Veterinary Corps the ideal type of officer for the command of a veterinary training base.[4]

QUEER IDEAS OF NOVICES The need of guidance in the exercise of the very limited authority that is permitted to a veterinary officer was exemplified by the belief expressed by one of the newly-commissioned youths possessed of an inflated idea of his importance, to the effect that if his judgment on veterinary grounds warranted the procedure, he had the right to order even a general to dismount from his horse, a remark indicating that whatever zeal prompted it sadly needed tempering with discretion!

Experience is said to be the best teacher, but much valuable time was lost which might well have been spent in acquiring the necessary knowledge imparted in a systematic manner.

The instruction given to the privates of the corps both in regimental duties and in animal management, left little to be desired, but the almost entire absence of anything resembling training on military duties, drill, the use of arms, interior economy and higher administration in the case of the officers remained a glaring defect in the direction of the training base.

USE OF ARMS It scarcely admits of argument that every individual wearing the uniform, whether he belonged to the strictly combatant forces or to a semi or noncombatant unit, such as the veterinary corps, should have familiarized himself in some measure with the use of arms, but there was a tendency amongst the veterinary officers to regard that art in their case as superfluous on the assumption that they would not be likely to participate in actual fighting.[5] Not manifesting any particular desire to acquire instruction and no influence being brought to bear on them to awaken their interest, they remained untrained. On the other hand, the officers who were subsequently sent to Witley to be attached to the Fifth Division, under the direction of Major Stedman, were afforded by the latter ample opportunity to acquire a fair knowledge of arms and the employment of the same, 'potted' courses in musketry, bombing, Lewis gun and bayonet fighting being made available to all who wished to make themselves proficient.

COMPETENCE ACQUIRED When the war came to a close, the veterinary officers who had served in the field were well versed in the military profession. Four years or less of actual warfare had made them veritable experts at the game. But, at the outset, scarcely one had more than a smattering of military knowledge and looking backward to those early days, many will smile at the remembrance of the mistakes, some of them almost ludicrous, that were made in 'learning the rules'.

SHORTAGE OF AVAILABLE OFFICERS At no stage of the war did the veterinary corps have at its disposal an excessive number of veterinary officers, excepting just prior to the armistice. It usually happened that as soon as the establishment called for by existing units had been provided for, a fresh demand arose, either on account of the formation of new units or because of casualties, and steps had to be taken to increase the supply. In the beginning, the Canadian veterinary corps was in a far better position than the Imperial veterinary corps, in which a shortage was felt from the start and which prompted the Director of Veterinary Services (Imperial) to ask Lieutenant-Colonel Neill in October, 1914, that any qualified veterinarians serving in the ranks of the first contingent might be permitted to transfer to the Imperial veterinary service in consideration of being appointed lieutenants. Already in the fall of 1915, it was deemed advisable to conserve for the Canadian forces all potential resources in veterinary officers and, with that end in view, the privilege of returning to Canada was extended to all veterinary undergraduates serving in the ranks. In January, 1916, the veterinary officers in the different divisions were asked for names of veterinarians in Canada who would be likely to join up upon it being represented to them that their services were needed. During that year reinforcements went over in some numbers but in November Colonel Neill wrote that he was urgently in need of the services of more officers. Practically all these reinforcements were recent graduates and utterly devoid of military training, which hindered to a great extent the adjustment of the problems that had to be faced. In July, 1916, the Quartermaster-General at Ottawa cabled that it was impossible to secure the veterinary officers with military experience.

The Quartermaster-General in London suggested having veterinary officers without military experience sent over, in view of the fact that there was quite a number willing to go, whereupon Colonel Neill wrote to the Military Secretary in London, under date of July 16th, 1916, that if it were impossible to get veterinary officers with military experience, he recommended great care to be taken in selecting these officers as to character, habits and physical fitness, and that he preferred officers who had practised 3 or 4 years, adding a rider that men who have just graduated from college are of no use.

In November, 1916, Lieutenant-Colonel Smith, who was then acting as Director of Veterinary Services, wrote to the Military Secretary requesting that 6 more veterinary officers be cabled for from Canada, to meet present requirements. A cabled message to Canada resulted in the reply that the authorities at home were unable to secure the number asked for. Again in December, 1916, Lieutenant-Colonel Smith requested of the Quartermaster-General in London that application be made to Headquarters, Ottawa, for 6 veterinary officers,. urgently required. The reply received was that it was impossible to get veterinarians with 3 years' experience and that only recent graduates were available. All attempts at getting reinforcements with practical experience having failed and there being no choice in the matter, the Quartermaster-General at Ottawa was requested to have recent graduates sent over.

In March, 1917, the shortage was more acute than ever. At that time there were required the following:

Needed reinforcements in France	7
To complete Fifth Division in training at Witley	2
For railway battalions in France	4
Total:	13

In order to provide a surplus of 2, a total of 15 was asked for. It was at this stage that 14 near-graduates were sent over.[6]

UNSATISFACTORY REINFORCEMENTS That the whole question of reinforcements considerably exercised the mind of Colonel Neill may be judged from the following letter he wrote to the Military Secretary under date of September, 1916:

Several conditions existent in the administration of the veterinary services in Canada have caused a great amount of inconveniece and unnecessary trouble. We want veterinary surgeons with at least 3 or 4 years' experience to reinforce Canadian Army Veterinary Corps units overseas. Military experience is not an absolute essential, but veterinary experience is demanded. Headquarters, Ottawa, complied with our request by sending young graduates without any practical knowledge of their profession, who required long training under competent Veterinary Officers before they were fit for duty in the field. The majority sent over of late have been French Canadians with very little knowledge of English.[7] *In one instance, the most recent one, a colored gentleman, was sent, but being rejected, is now awaiting return to Canada, incurring unnecessary expense to the Department.*[8] *Officers have been sent over from Canada without definite instructions as to where they should report and to whom, and having no papers of identification or attestation in their possession, necessitating a great deal of inconvenience in establishing them on the strength of the Canadian Army Veterinary Corps.*

To which the officer administering Canadian Army Veterinary Services in Canada, after a copy had been forwarded to him, replied:

All requests were given every consideration and referred to the District Officers Commanding with regard to selection. It has been difficult to secure the services of veterinary surgeons of at least 3 years' experience and practice, for the reason that the majority had already proceeded overseas with mounted units. Where possible, the services of veterinary surgeons with experience have been secured and where not available, veterinary surgeons with less experience have been accepted.

The fact was that the difficulties in respect to officer reinforcements for the veterinary corps were insurmountable except by the slow process of adaptation of available material which consisted for the most part of recent graduates totally unacquainted with military organization, routine and veterinary duties and responsibilities. They had received no military training in Canada and could not be employed on active service upon their arrival in England until they had acquired a certain amount of experience at the training base.

In 1918, after Colonel Edgett had assumed direction of veterinary services, the question of reinforcements became as acute as ever, which impelled him to address a letter to the Quartermaster-General, under date of April 23rd, requesting that authority be obtained to have an insertion put into Canadian Corps Orders in France, calling for veterinary surgeons who might be serving in the ranks with a view to granting a limited number of commissions in the Canadian Army Veterinary Corps. The result was the following Corps Routine Order which appeared on May 10th, 1918:

Vacancies for temporary commissions as V.O., in C.A.V.C.

Applications by personnel holding Veterinary Surgeons' Certificates or who have practised as V.S's in civil life and who are recommended for temporary commissions in the C.A.V.C., should be forwarded on Army Form H.Q.C. 32 through the regular channels to A.D.V.S., Canadian Corps, not later than 20th inst.

PROFICIENCY OF C.A.V.C. THREATENED The careless wording of the above order threw consternation into the commissioned ranks of the corps. It looked as if the authorities were about to permit the entry of non-graduates into the veterinary service with commissions, and in fact, one or two of the first aid sergeants actually made application on the strength of the certificates they had received at the hands of Brigadier-General Neill at the completion of their short course of training at Shorncliffe. But Lieutenant-Colonels Evans and Tamblyn, administrative officers of the Second and Third Divisions respectively, ever mindful of the uplift of the profession and that any such measure would mean a blow to the proficiency of the corps from which it would take long to recover, voiced the feelings of the veterinary officers in an energetic manner,[9] by writing letters of protest to Lieutenant-Colonel Cutcliffe at Corps headquarters, who took steps to head off the impending calamity.

UNDERGRADUATES PERMITTED TO RETURN HOME At the same time, the privilege formerly extended to undergraduates in the ranks of the veterinary, medical and dental professions, to return home to complete their studies, which had been discontinued in 1916, again came into effect and one of the first aid sergeants, Sergeant E.G. Ungar, who had passed a period at college before joining the corps, took advantage of the opportunity.

CONTINUED UNSATISFACTORY REINFORCEMENTS In the meantime, the Military Service Act had come into force and Colonel Edgett proceeded to make known the names of certain veterinarians of experience in Canada who had so far failed to come forward in the hour of their country's need and who, it was hoped, would be compelled to serve. But the authorities at Ottawa were only able to send over 20 recent graduates of which only 8 proved themselves on arrival to be competent. The rest had to be sent to undergo training at the Imperial veterinary depot at Woolwich, when the armistice coming into effect, they were returned to Canada to be demobilized.

FREAK APPLICATIONS FOR COMMISSIONS As might have been expected, the shortage of veterinary officers soon got noised about and resulted in all sorts of queer applications. When the later original battalions from Canada were being broken up in England, many attempts were made to obtain commissions in the veterinary corps on the ground of wide experience with horses. One of the most amusing applications came from one A. Woollard of Chesham, who wrote asking if he might be taken into the corps because he held a diploma from the 'Veterinary Science Association of London, Ontario',[10] but who was informed that the regulations did not recognize that institution as a veterinary college.

Some, whose service in the Imperial veterinary corps had been terminated on account of inebriety or inefficiency, tried to enter the Canadian veterinary corps, but were prevented from doing so through their record becoming known from the War Office.

MISREPRESENTATION Only one or two individuals succeeded in getting past the 'professional barrier' and by misrepresentation obtained commissions, but they did not last long in their ill-acquired position for the truth was soon revealed. One, a sergeant of the veterinary corps, had proved himself an excellent first aid dresser at the hospital at Shorncliffe, where he was employed, and where he frequently had given out that he had been qualified at Edinburgh. His pretensions were not enquired into, as they should have been, until he had proceeded to France as veterinary officer of the Second Divisional Train. But, upon the truth becoming known, he was promptly recalled and after failing to justify his claim and upon the college authorities being interrogated with negative result, he was placed under close arrest and underwent trial by court-martial by which he was sentenced to dismissal from the service.[11]

INFLUENCE IN APPOINTMENTS AND PROMOTIONS In the beginning, there was no settled policy governing the rank assigned to veterinary officers on their being commissioned. Some were appointed to the rank of lieutenant and others to higher rank, this depending in large measure on the amount of influence that could be wielded by each one in his own favor. As late as November, 1915, Colonel Neill felt impelled to express his view to the General Officer Commanding Canadians that administrative appointments in any new divisions coming over should be left open till arrival in England as by that time he had a number of capable officers thoroughly trained to fill those positions and he considered it proper that their services should be recognized. In the case of those holding the lower rank, Colonel Neill had already, in August, 1915, recommended that they be promoted to the rank of captain to bring their rate of pay up nearer to the standard in the Imperial service. But it was not till the middle of 1916, that Colonel Neill was informed that the Department of Militia and Defence had ruled that officers of the medical and veterinary services, should receive the higher rank when taken on the strength of the overseas forces, such rank being temporary and not affecting the rank in the Militia List.[12]

DISCONTENT THROUGH UNFAIR CONDITIONS The discontent of the officers in France was intensified when, in June, 1916, there arrived from Canada, as reinforcements, 5 new officers, some not yet in uniform but with the rank of captain already conferred on them whilst there were 5 still serving in the field and holding their original rank of lieutenant. The anxiety of the latter, however, was soon appeased by the desired promotion.

Even with a captain's pay, our officers were behind the Imperials and as late as January, 1917, Brigadier-General Neill was urging an adjustment and incidentally pointing out the difficulty of attracting men to the Canadian service when such inequalities confronted the applicant for a commission in either service.

FIXED POLICY It has been stated that it was decided that newly joined officers in the Canadian veterinary corps of the overseas forces should automatically receive the rank and pay of captain. It was, however, customary to allow such officers, on their appointment to carry on for a few months as lieutenants, prior to their appointment to the higher rank, to prove their efficiency, when they were antedated to the original date of their appointment. Colonel Edgett held slightly different ideas on the subject, and when he took over the direction of the corps, arranged that thereafter a captaincy should only be attainable after a year's service in the case of recent graduates who had not had a year's experience in civil practice.[13]

SCARCITY OF PROMOTION The immediate bestowal of the rank of captain on the later arrivals from Canada opened up a difficulty in another direction. It proved reactive on those who had seen service from the beginning but who had no prospect for further advancement on account of the relative slowness of promotion in a noncombatant unit. Accordingly, in April, 1917, Colonel Neill recommended for promotion to the rank of major Captains Evans, Dixon, Edwards, O'Gogarty, Colebourn, Coulombe, Stedman, Douglas, Grignon, Souillard, Elliott, Daigneault and Frape, all of whom had gone over with the first contingent, on the grounds that they had rendered faithful and prolonged service and that they were entitled to advancement to rank superior to that accorded to more recent arrivals from home, but nothing was done since there was no provision in the establishment for such action. Colonel Edgett made a similar recommendation towards the close of the war, but without avail, it being pointed out by the Military Secretary that there would be created an undesirable precedent which would affect all units in the overseas forces.

The only promotions open to officers of the veterinary corps were to the administrative appointment in each division of the army Corps and of the training areas in England, to the command of No. 1 Canadian Veterinary Hospital at Havre and, after the spring of 1917, to the command of the new Evacuation Station of the Army Corps. It has been pointed out elsewhere that prior to the reorganization of the veterinary service in midsummer, 1917, each division had an Assistant Director of Veterinary Services, an appointment which in the Imperial establishment carried with it the rank of major, but that after that time the administrative post was reduced to that of Deputy Assistant Director of Veterinary Services. Because of the additional duties in connection with remounts assumed by the veterinary service in the Canadian Army Corps, Colonel Neill secured an advance in rank to Lieutenant-Colonel for those officers who held the appointment. When the aforesaid reduction went into effect, only the administrative officer of the entire army corps continued to retain the status of an Assistant Director of Veterinary Services. The officer, appointed to the latter post naturally continued to hold the higher rank and the others should automatically have reverted to the lower rank. But the cause of the latter was championed by Lieutenant-General Sir Arthur Currie, who held that such a proposition would be unfair so all officers who had held appointments with headquarters of divisions prior to June 27th, 1917, when the change came into effect, were allowed to retain the higher rank, but officers who might subsequently receive appointments were to hold the lower rank. Thus it came about that Lieutenant-Colonels Edgett, Tamblyn and Evans continued to hold the higher rank whilst serving in administrative capacity with divisions and the same ruling was made to apply in England to Major Walsh, who became lieutenant-colonel, whilst serving as administrative officer of the Shorncliffe area.

MERIT TO THE FORE The procedure by which appointments with corresponding increase in rank were made is described in the chapter on The Headquarters Staff. It remains to be stated here that after the early method of advancement had had its day, it was supplanted by the system of promotion based on seniority of service, but even then the claims of merit could not be entirely overlooked and there were a few exceptions, conspicuous amongst which were the instances of selection in the cases of Lieutenant-Colonel Edgett to the direction of veterinary services (Canadian) and in that of Captain Richards to the command of No. 1 Canadian Veterinary Hospital, before whom stood 22 other officers in point of seniority of service. Nevertheless, neither of these officers might assume more than acting capacity in the next higher ranks of colonel and major respectively, on account of the army rule that seniority of service is entitled to prior recognition in point of substantive rank. It is a system that is supposed to do away with intrigue and jealousy, but is one that cannot be rigorously applied without the service being made to suffer.

CHARACTER AND COMPETENCE The character and competence of officers are always topics of interest. It can fairly be stated that every man who joined the corps for overseas service was actuated by purely patriotic motives, or in the case of our comrades of American citizenship, from an overwhelming sense of duty to aid in the suppression of the evil forces that menaced the liberties of the world. Indeed, without including the two or three who formed the extent of the permanent or regular branch of the corps, every man was a volunteer and, with a few exceptions, strove throughout the entire period of the war, to uphold the dignity of the calling he had felt constrained to embrace. The lapses from the standard of deportment were few and far between and consisted mainly of one or two lamentable instances of downfall through the evil influence of drink. Three officers of the corps were court-martialed and cashiered on this account.[14]

It is a *sine qua non* in the army that an officer must be a gentleman, one whose example may inspire others to so order their lives that the interests of the service may at all times be advanced and never hindered. George Bernard Shaw once wrote that "a gentleman is a man who tries not to take out of life more than he puts in". Applying this standard to our officers, it is a pleasure to record that nearly every one gave to the service more than he could ever hope to gain in return. Two also gave their lives, and most of the others were ready to answer the selfsame call had the Fates so decreed.

Most of the officers in the higher stations inspired confidence in those they were called upon to direct and control. It is true that one or two at the start found themselves 'in the right church but the wrong pew' but those made good when they were eventually transferred to their proper sphere. Amongst those so advanced there was perhaps only one glaring instance of ineptitude. The particular individual to whom reference is made was regarded by his confreres as a sad misfit and quite incompetent for the higher position.[15]

CANADIAN V.O. COMPARED WITH BRITISH V.O. Contrasted with his British brother in the Imperial service, in point of efficiency, the Canadian veterinary officer was in no way behind. Indeed, in the employment of modern methods of operative procedure, in dentistry, in the use of the emasculator in surgical operations, he outclassed the British veterinary officer. The latter was a splendid fellow, an excellent horseman as a rule, and better perhaps in animal management, but too prone to conservatism from the Canadian viewpoint. It must be concluded that Canadian veterinarians were held in high esteem by the Director-General of Veterinary Services (Imperial), who, on Lieutenant-Colonel Edgett's assumption of the direction of Canadian veterinary services, asked the latter if any more were available, remarking that they exhibited a more serious regard for duty and paid closer attention to prophylactic measures than their British comrades and that at the refresher courses they displayed more interest and applied themselves with greater zeal.

REFRESHER COURSES The refresher courses consisted of instructional classes lasting a few days and conducted at the base hospitals designed to afford veterinary officers serving in the field an opportunity to observe the methods practised in the treatment of the cases sent down from the front. When the Canadian veterinary school was disbanded at Shorncliffe, Brigadier-General Neill endeavored to have it set up at Havre, one of his ideas being that its presence at that point might serve to make of the Canadian veterinary hospital a particular place of resort for Canadian officers from up the line, where they might enjoy a temporary change of work and surroundings amidst their own people, instead of going to the Imperial establishments, a suggestion that was not adopted by the authorities, though it met with the unqualified approval of those who would thereby have benefitted.

IMPERIALS LEARNING FROM CANADIANS The Imperials learned much from the Canadians as did the Canadians from the Imperials. We have seen elsewhere how necessity compelled them to appropriate to their own use Captain Watson for the carrying on of laboratory work. The employment of the dipping tank by all the armies for the control of mange, a method of treatment commonly made use of in the range districts of North America and which, throughout the war, turned out to be of such inestimable benefit in keeping down this scourge, was due to the initiative of Canadians, though at first in the face of great prejudice on the part of the Imperials. This prejudice was most extraordinary in view of the successful experiences of the governments of Canada, Australia, South Africa and the United States in the use of dipping vats for the eradication of skin diseases due to any kind of parasite.

It was through the representations of a Canadian veterinarian who had elected to accept a commission in the Imperial Veterinary Corps that the method of combating mange eventually adopted by the Imperial authorities came into operation. The story shall be given in the words of Lieutenant-Colonel Evans, who, in recalling the occurrence which took place during his sojourn at No. 5 General Hospital at Abbeville, related it as follows:

I met at Abbeville Lieutenant F. V. Perry who was from Western Canada and who for many years had acted as veterinarian with the North West Mounted Police. When the Army (Imperial) Veterinary Corps called for Canadian graduates to accept commissions in its service, Perry was one who volunteered and when I met him he was in charge of a ward in the hospital. At that time all mange was being treated with sulphur ointment applied locally by hand. This not only was expensive, but extremely tedious, requiring a huge staff for a moderately small ward. Perry suggested the calcium sulphide solution to supplement the ointment and vouched for its efficacy to the Director of Veterinary Services (Imperial). Perry had his reputation at stake for he gave his word that it was the authorized Canadian dip for the treatment of mange in the West and that it would be effectual if properly prepared. The old formula was the one adopted, consisting of 10 lbs. of good quick lime, 22 1/2 lbs. of flowers of sulphur and 100 gallons of rain water. This happened in July, 1915, eleven months after the commencement of the war. The fact that this dip produced results and was accepted as a specific in the treatment of mange is vouched for in the publishing of the V.D.S. Circular Memo No. 77, under 'Notes on the preparation of calcium sulphide solution for the treatment and prevention of mange' as follows: "Of all the remedies used in this country in the treatment of mange, both sarcoptic and psoroptic varieties, calcium sulphide solution has proved the most generally satisfactory. One of its greatest advantages is that, if properly prepared and applied, it is not in any way harmful to the skin or to the general condition of the animal affected."

Whilst on this subject, it will not be amiss to refer to a point that intimately concerns Canadian veterinarians, namely, the non recognition hitherto by the Royal College of Veterinary Surgeons, the licensing body of Great Britain, of graduates of colonial and foreign veterinary colleges, resulting in the latter being barred from practising in the United Kingdom should they so desire. It was felt by the Canadian veterinary officers that since Great Britain in her extremity had been only too glad to avail herself of the services of some 200 Canadian veterinarians, she could afford to make a special concession by granting a measure of recognition to those who had served in the war. The result was that under the auspices of the Khaki University there was effected an arrangment whereby graduates of certain colleges might obtain extended leave for the purpose of attending a course of two terms of one session at one of the British veterinary colleges to prepare themselves for the examination for the M.R.C.V.S. diploma. The candidates who took advantage of the opportunity were:

Major C.G. Saunders; Captain E.L. Brown; Captain H. Colebourne; Captain R.M. Lee; Captain R.J. Vickers, Lieutenant O.V. Gunning.

SCOPE OF AUTHORITY A few remarks as to the scope of authority vested in a veterinary officer will not be out of place here, since the reader may wish to be enlightened on this point.

As regards the power of command, it is expressly laid down in the King's Regulations and Orders for the Army (paragraph 231) that officers of the army veterinary service will not "exercise any military command outside that service except over such officers and soldiers as may be attached thereto for duty". Thus, be it noted, his right to command extends only to the members of his own corps under ordinary circumstances, and with the exception stated, it is not within the sphere of duty contemplated for the veterinary officer that he should give military orders to the soldiers of units other than his own, though under extraordinary circumstances and in the absence of the officers of other units, it might be incumbent on him to take charge. But, this very limitation of authority has its own limitation and does not mean that a veterinary officer is to stand idly by and refrain from correcting an obvious breach of discipline or act of negligence on the part of any soldier or even officer, especially when veterinary interests are involved, for the aforesaid regulations and orders (paragraph 440) point out that "an officer is at all times responsible for the maintenance of good order and the rules and discipline of the service", and that "it is his duty to notice, repress, and instantly report, any negligence or impropriety of conduct of N.C.O.s and private soldiers whether on or off duty, and whether the offenders do or do not belong to his particular unit".

Neither has he, in point of fact, authority over any horses except such as are patients in, or on the strength of, veterinary hospitals, nor even over the horses of any unit to which he may be attached for veterinary supervision, until such horses have been formally placed with the consent of the commanding officer on the sick list and under his professional care in regimental sick lines or elsewhere. It is the duty of a veterinary officer attached to a unit to advise and recommend to the officer commanding the unit in all matters pertaining to veterinary control, for in the latter must rest the ultimate decision. The limitation of authority is made quite clear in the Veterinary Manual (War), 1914, of which the following is an extract:

A veterinary officer attached to a unit is responsible for the treatment of all sick and injured animals which are able to remain with it. He will also advise commanders of units which animals should be transferred to mobile sections for conveyance to the veterinary hospitals. Those not likely to be fit for duty at an early date should be so dealt with, as their retention with the field army hampers mobility, and in the end increases wastage.

He will immediately bring to the notice of commanders of units any points which may bear upon the health and condition, or affect wastage of the animals under his professional care.

He must be ever on the alert to prevent the introduction or spread of contagious diseases; prompt advice regarding prophylactic measures materially influences wastage from this cause. This necessitates frequent and careful inspections, which should be carried out as opportunities are offered by the military situation.

He will inspect all horses joining the unit, and will immediately report all suspicious cases and outbreaks of contagious diseases to commanders of units and to the Assistant Director of Veterinary Services of the formation.

RESPONSIBILITY FOR CORRECT SHOEING Furthermore, in respect even to another important matter, namely, the shoeing, it is laid down in the Regulations and Orders (paragraph 1254) and in Regulations for Army Veterinary Services, that "a squadron commander is responsible to the C.O. that the shoeing is correct", that "the veterinary officer is responsible for representing to the general, or other officer commanding, any faults or bad workmanship", and that the veterinary officer will "specially note that attention is paid to all regulations in all details". Even when an animal is incurably injured or diseased, it is doubtful whether a veterinary officer should take on himself the responsibility of actually causing its destruction, for the regulations state (K.R. & O., paragraphs 1239 and 1240, amendments under A.O. 135, 1916) that "animals certified by a veterinary officer to be incurably injured may be destroyed forthwith. In other cases where destruction is considered necessary, the previous sanction of the G.O.C., or O.C. station will be obtained" and "the giving of authority for the destruction of an animal, whether on the veterinary officer's certificate referred to ...., or otherwise, does not dispense with inquiry into the circumstances of its loss .... except when the veterinary officer is able to certify that death from natural disease would otherwise have ensued". Running all through the aforequoted regulations is an implication that the function of the veterinary officer is but to recommend and certify and not to assume authority himself.

TRANSPORT AND WAGON LINES OFFICERS The authority over the horses of a unit rests in the commanding officer, but the time of the latter being largely occupied in attending to other regimental duties, the daily routine of supervising all matters pertaining to the horse transport of a unit, including the rationing and stabling of the animals, care of harness, vehicles, etc., was delegated to a subordinate officer, who was usually a lieutenant but sometimes a captain. Consequently, the duties of the latter were closely interwoven with those of the veterinary officer and it was necessary for smooth working that the two should cooperate on all occasions and by mutual exercise of tact and courtesy avoid misunderstandings and friction. Of course, the officer in charge of the horse lines was not concerned with purely veterinary matters, other than to act on the advice of the veterinary officer, and the opinion of the latter in cases of a transitory nature that did not involve evacuation was generally treated as an 'order' in the same sense that the public is pleased to regard the opinion of a physician in civil life. On the other hand, when it became necessary to evacuate an animal for unfitness, the matter assumed a different aspect. Any commanding officer of a unit who took an interest in the animals under his command was invariably keen to have his authority recognized and would have had just cause for resentment had his veterinary officer, without reference to himself or his representative, undertaken to 'order' the evacuation of a horse of his command for lameness or other nonspecific unfitness. Moreover, as has already been pointed out, the actual responsibility in a pecuniary sense for the horses on charge to any unit rested in the officer commanding the unit, and it was necessary that the latter should be kept fully advised of any changes and receive his due in the form of a receipt for every animal that was disposed of in this manner.

WISDOM OF CAUTION Therefore, the wise veterinary officer, after having decided on the advisability of getting rid of an animal that was unfit for further service, would go no further than to make a recommendation to that effect and await the commanding officer's concurrence, which was invariably forthcoming. Only in cases of extreme urgency, such an as outbreak of mange or other contagious disease, did the situation warrant immediate action on the part of the veterinary officer and subsequent reporting of the facts, and in that event, no reasonable commanding officer was ever known to take exception, but on the contrary commended the zeal which could but redound to the benefit of the whole command.

V.O. PROTECTED From the foregoing remarks, it might be inferred that the veterinary officer was in the unenviable situation of being shorn of that authority which he needed to enforce such hygienic measures as he was charged, in his judgment, to see were carried out and that if he was unfortuante enough to work under a commanding officer who saw fit to disregard his advice, he ran the risk of incurring censure for failure in the performance of a duty which he was prevented from carrying out. But, in such event, he could always protect himself by recording his opinion and recommendation in writing to the obstructing commanding officer and at the same time bringing the facts of the case to the notice of his superior officer in his own corps, who in turn would take the matter up with the higher authorities through the proper channels for rectification.

'SWAPPING' OF HORSES A case in point that occurred at Witley Camp arising out of indiscriminate inter unit 'swapping' of horses may be mentioned. Theoretically, the horses on the strength of a unit, whether for officer or trooper, for riding or draft purposes, were allocated to it from the Remount Department according to establishment as laid down by the War Office, after they had been requisitioned by the officer commanding the unit, and were not supposed to be thereafter evacuated from the unit excepting for veterinary reasons on the recommendation of the attached veterinary officer. Horsemen have ever enjoyed a reputation for indulging in a good trade at a favorable opportunity and in this respect mounted army officers are no exception; moreover, it not infrequently happened that one unit became possessed of certain animals that were found to be not as well adapted to the work in hand as certain animals in some other unit and *vice versa*, in which event it was to the best interests of the service that an interchange should be effected. There was a proper way to bring this about, but some of the officers were inclined to put the leveling up process into effect by the informal method of offhand 'swapping' without making the veterinary officer or even their own commanding officer privy to the transaction, a procedure that could not be countenanced by the former if he was to carry on his duties in a satisfactory manner, especially with such a disease as mange prevalent in the area.

RIGHT OF APPEAL In the case referred to, the veterinary officer brought the matter to the notice of the commanding officer of his brigade with a request that an order might be promulgated that the practice must cease. The request was negatived on the ground that it was desired that the officers of the different units should have every opportunity without obstruction to be suited with respect to their mounts. It need hardly be remarked that there was no desire on the part of the veterinary officer concerned to do otherwise than have everybody satisfied, but it was necessary that he should be made aware of what was going on, if only for veterinary reasons. Consequently, to put himself right, he appealed to his administrative officer, who in turn took the matter up with the General Staff of the division, whence an order was issued to the officers commanding brigades that the practice must cease and that the latter would be held personally responsible that the order was not infringed.

DESCRIPTIVE ROLLS The reader may want to know how a veterinary officer could recognize all the horses under his supervision, particularly if the number ran into hundreds. In reality, this was quite simple. The cautious veterinary officer, on taking over the supervision of the horses of a unit, for instance, immediately proceeded to make a descriptive roll of all the animals; that is to say, he took note of the sex, age, height, class, color, presence or absence of white on parts of the body where it is usually found, together with any other distinguishing markings. It is practically impossible to find any two animals, even amongst hundreds, bearing exactly similar markings, so a ready and easy means of recognition was thereby afforded. There was, however, a lack of uniformity in the manner of making these descriptive rolls, there being no really satisfactory authorized model to serve as a guide. Each officer followed his own inclination and used all sorts of terms and abbreviations which, whilst serving as a reminder to himself, were not always intelligible to others. To obviate this inconsistency, the form on the following page was devised by one of the officers towards the close of the war, and received the approval of Colonel Edgett with a view to its general adoption.

CONDITIONS IN FRANCE AND ENGLAND DIFFERED Having reviewed the regulations, it is only necessary to add that under training conditions in England they were usually adhered to, but that under the exigencies of service in France and Belgium, a very different state of affairs prevailed, where neither time nor opportunity occurred for the observance of usual formalities, so that it came about that vastly more authority was left in the hands of the veterinary officer.

NOMINAL ROLL Appendix A is a list of all those who served on the commissioned strength of the Canadian Army Veterinary Corps, in alphabetical order, together with a few particulars of interest concerning their qualifications, etc. It will be noticed that the majority were graduates of the Ontario Veterinary College, whilst McGill and Laval universities are represented as well as the British colleges and one or two of the numerous institutions of the United States. Many were born in Canada, but a large proportion came originally from the British Isles. Four or five, namely Captains Hanagan, Beaven, Boswell and Brown, were born in the United States, and though under the

British Army Act, those other than British subjects were ineligible for commissioned rank in the Imperial forces, and this ruling was advanced as a reason for turning down the application of a non-commissioned officer of the corps, Corporal Kline, for permission to transfer to commissioned rank in another unit, these particular officers were asked no questions as to their citizenship at the time of attestation, and none proved to be more loyal and efficient than they.[16] The rule seems generally to have been disregarded in the Canadian forces, where other units possessed a certain quota of officers who were Americans.

CANADIAN V.O.'S IN IMPERIAL SERVICES Appendix B is a roll of officers, Canadian veterinary surgeons who were commissioned in the Imperial army for service in the Royal Army Veterinary Corps.[17]

V.O.'S JOB SUMMED UP When all the pros and cons have been weighed, it may assuredly be stated that the veterinary officer had a job in the war about as pleasant as anybody's could have been under the circumstances. He enjoyed a considerable degree of independence and exerted no small amount of authority, he did not have to suffer the uncommon hardships or run the extreme risks of his comrades in the trenches, and the element of sport was ever present to lend colour to his work. These factors all combined to make his life a fairly tolerable one.

DESCRIPTIVE ROLL

Color	Sex	Class	Age	Height	Brands
B	M	HD	8	15.3	V NR

MARKING	Head	Collar	Saddle	Legs	Elsewhere
	St Ra Sn UL LL	N O	N	NFF pt NHO sp OFC OHC pt	Patch OR Wd NShl

Hoof Numbers	22 NF	153 OF
Rump Numbers		

Date____________________ (Signed)____________________

Index to Abbreviations

Color		Sex		Class
B	Bay	M	Mare	R Rider
B	Brown	G	Gelding	LD Light Draft
Bl	Black	Jk	Jack	HD Heavy Draft
G	Grey	JN	Jenny	P Pack

Head Markings		Leg Markings		Body	
St	Star	F	Fore	Shl	Shoulder
Ra	Race	H	Hind	Fl	Flank
Sn	Snip	F	Fetlock	Rp	Rump
UL	Upper Lip	P	Pastern		
LL	Lower Lip	C	Coronet	**General**	
		pt	partly	N	Near
		sp	spotted	O	Off
				Wd	Wound scar

CHAPTER 12

ROLL OF HONOUR

Figure 12.1. Funeral cortège of Capt. Theodore A. Girling, poet of the Canadian Army Veterinary Corps. Died of influenza pneumonia, Belgium, March 1919. (*NAC PA 203436*)

Of the 145 officers of the Canadian Veterinary Service during the war, two, Captains T.Z. Woods and B.R. Poole, made the supreme sacrifice as a result of direct enemy action; two, Captains E.M. Dixon and T.A. Girling, died on active service in France and two, Captain C.W. Baker and Lieutenant R.H. Wilson, died in England. One, Captain F.D. Early, died after having been invalided home.[1,2,3]

Of the non-commissioned officers, one, Sergeant G.R. Matthew, was killed in action in France. Other non-commissioned officers and men, who had served part of their time in the veterinary corps but had been drafted to other units, also lost their lives, but as they were at the time no longer connected with the veterinary corps, they do not come within our purview.

Figure 12.2. Vet.-Lieut. T.Z. Woods.[4] (*NAC PA 203590*)

Captain T.Z. Woods (Figure 12.2), veterinary officer attached to the Second Infantry Brigade, was grievously wounded by shrapnel on the evening of April 6th, 1916, whilst attending to his duties in the transport lines of the Fifth Battalion in Dickebusch Wood near Hooggroof. His horse was killed at the same time. He was taken to No. 10 Casualty Clearing Station, where the injured limb was amputated but he succumbed on April 9th. He lies in Lizssenhoek Military Cemetery, 3000 yards southwest of Poperinghe. Captain Woods had an enviable record. He had served with the Winnipeg Light Infantry in the North-West Rebellion in 1885 and with the Strathcona Horse in the South African War. At the outbreak of the Great War he was over 50 years of age and on that account would have been justified in holding back. But, he was made of sterner stuff as his career in the militia had shown. It is noteworthy that in 1909 and again in 1912 it was questioned by the department whether to retain his services, in view of the fact that he had

Figure 12.3. Capt. B.R. Poole.
(*NAC PA 203430*)

reached the age limit of his rank, but on the recommendation of Colonel Sam Steele that he be retained in his appointment by virtue of his South African services, his fitness, and the difficulty in getting officers of his training and capability, an extension of his period of service was granted.

Captain B.R. Poole (Figure 12.3), attached to the Fifth Battalion, Canadian Railway Troops, was killed instantaneously. On the 3rd of May, 1917, battalion headquarters were situated in the courtyard of a house (33 rue Meaulins) in Arras. On the morning of that day the enemy was shelling the town heavily. Captain Poole was standing in front of his tent which was pitched in the yard when he was instantly killed by a shell which struck the wall. The quartermaster and battalion sergeant-major were in their tents close by but were uninjured, though two men working nearby were wounded by the same shell. Captain Poole was interred in the Arras Military Cemetery, plot 4, row E, grave 29. His son, Corporal Kenneth G. Poole, was serving in the corps at the time. Lieutenant-Colonel Smith, acting as Director of Veterinary Services (Canadian) at the time wrote to the Military Secretary under date of May 10th, 1917, that the corps deeply regretted the loss of this officer as his services had been of inestimable value, that he was highly efficient and the senior of his rank in the corps and in every way eligible for promotion to the rank of major.

Figure 12.4. Capt. E.M. Dixon.
(*NAC PA 203423*)

Captain E.M. Dixon (Figure 12.4) was Acting Deputy Assistant Director of Veterinary Services of the Second Division at the time of his death. He was proceeding to England and had embarked on the ambulance transport at about 10 a.m., on the 27th of September, 1918, at Calais as a 'walking' patient, suffering from chronic gastritis. He was speaking to other patients when he suddenly collapsed on the deck about 11:45 a.m. The sergeant-major who witnessed the occurrence proceeded immediately to his assistance and, recognizing that the case was serious, sent for the deck medical officer who arrived almost immediately but only to find that he had expired. He was buried in Les Baracques British Cemetery at Sangatte.

Figure 12.5. Capt. F.D. Early.[5]
(*NAC PA 203424*)

Captain F.D. Early (Figure 12.5) had served with the Royal Army Veterinary Corps from January, 1915 till February, 1916, when, his engagement having ended, he joined the Canadian service and after short periods spent at the two Canadian veterinary hospitals, was attached as veterinary officer to the Strathcona Horse. Disability, from sarcoma, arose in June, 1917 and he was invalided to Canada in April,

1918 only to pass away at Queen's Military Hospital, Kingston, Ontario on the fifteenth of the following month.

Sergeant G.R. Matthew (Figure 12.6) was a brother of Captain R.G. Matthew. He qualified as a first aid sergeant at Shorncliffe in the fall of 1916 and was then attached to the Fifth Division at Witley till its disbandment. He went to France in June, 1918, and was there attached to the Eighth Brigade, Army Field Artillery. On the 30th of September, 1918, he was proceeding from his dugout at the old German railhead of Bourlon village to the Canadian Y.M.C.A. in order to see his brother and make some purchases and while on the way, an enemy high velocity shell burst on the cobble stone road nearby, pieces of which striking him, caused injuries which resulted in instant death. He rests in the Ontario Military Cemetery near Bourlon Wood.

Figure 12.6. Sgt. G.R. Matthew. (*NAC PA 203429*)

Figure 12.7. Capt. C.W. Baker. (*NAC PA 203421*)

Captain C.W. Baker (Figure 12.7) sustained a fracture of both legs at Aubigny in November, 1916, when his horse fell on him. Whilst lying in the First London General Hospital at Camberwell he died on the 10th of January, 1917. He was interred in Nunhead Cemetery.

Trooper A.S. Young, of No. 1 Mobile Section, was stricken with appendicitis and died on November 9th, 1916.

Lieutenant R.H. Wilson was a veterinary graduate serving in the ranks and had just received a commission in the veterinary corps when, on the morning of October 19th, 1917, he was admitted to St. Thomas's Hospital in London suffering from corrosive sublimate poisoning. He died on October 21st. The verdict at the coroner's inquest was: "Suicide during temporary insanity". He was buried in the Canadian Military Plot in Brookwood Cemetery, Surrey, with military honors, but his remains were later disinterred and conveyed to Toronto at the wish of his wife.

Captain T.A. Girling (Figure 12.8) had come safely through the war since November, 1915, and, as veterinary officer of the Fourth Infantry Brigade, was looking forward to an early return to his home at Saskatoon, when he was stricken with influenza and pneumonia,[6] to which he succumbed in No. 48 Casualty Clearing Station, on March 1st, 1919. Captain Girling achieved fame as the poet of the veterinary corps, being author of a set of poems, entitled: 'The Salient and other Poems', composed in France and Flanders.[7] He was interred at Namur.

Figure 12.8. Capt. T.A. Girling.[5] (*NAC PA 203426*)

CHAPTER 13

REMOUNTS

Remount And Veterinary Services Separate In the British army, there are two separate and distinct departments that are concerned with the care of animals, namely: The Remount Department and the Veterinary Service. The former has to do with purchase and issue to units whilst the latter concerns itself solely with hygiene, sickness and injury.

Canada made provision for an identically similar organization to serve the expeditionary force, so that in addition to the veterinary corps there was, at the beginning, an entirely separate and self-contained unit for remount purposes which, however, as will be disclosed, proved to be but a short-lived affair.

Organization at Valcartier During the organization of the first Canadian contingent at Valcartier, the principle of mobilizing units and completing their establishment in horses at their local headquarters was carried out wherever practicable - a system which proved to be very satisfactory. But there was a large number of units in the force which were not so fortunate owing to the difficulties experienced in procuring in their vicinity horses to meet the requirements with the limited time at the disposal of the Purchasing Commission, formed May 5th, 1914. Consequently, horses had to be purchased in outside localities and shipped into Valcartier Camp, where many of them did not arrive until after the first general outward move had been made. It was, therefore, found necessary to establish a remount depot, capable of accommodating about 2000 horses. Considerable difficulty was experienced in arranging on such short notice all the details for the satisfactory accommodation of this number of animals, principally on account of the lack of available picketing material, for it must be borne in mind that there were no comfortable stables or well laid horse lines in existence. But, by the adoption of the system of open corrals and the construction of the same by employment of stakes hand cut from the bush on the camp site, matters soon righted themselves.

Figure 13.1. Cap Badge, No. 100 Remount Squadron, Canadian Expeditionary Force. *(C.A.V. Barker Museum)*

Remount Squadrons A squadron, known as No. 100, was formed at Valcartier to handle remounts for the first contingent (Figure 13.1). It went over in the early days and took up its quarters on Salisbury Plain where it performed the role of Canadian remount depot and continued to act in that capacity till the departure of the First Division to France. Thereafter, its functions as a purely Canadian remount depot ceased on its being amalgamated with the Imperial remount service and on being transferred overseas in May, 1915, for duty at the Imperial remount depot at Hautot, France. It was still a Canadian unit in receipt of Canadian pay but discharging Imperial duties, which it continued to do until it was finally disbanded in the early summer of 1916. Two other squadrons, known respectively as Nos. 101 and 102 were mobilized at St. John's, P.Q. No. 101 was recruited principally at Calgary and No. 102 in Montreal. The former went across in May, the latter in June, both landing at Plymouth and entraining there for Romsey, where they spent about a week and then joined No. 100 at Hautot. As all three squadrons were practically carrying on work that properly belonged to the Imperial forces and as they were of no assistance to the Canadian forces, it was decided to withdraw them. This decision was put into effect in October, 1915, though the original squadron was allowed to continue till May, 1916, when it also was disbanded, some 200 of its personnel going to reinforce No. 1 Canadian Veterinary Hospital at Havre.

Shipment of Remounts In the meantime, Colonel Neill had been recalled from the First Canadian Division in France, about the middle of March, 1915, to assume control of the disembarkation of horses arriving from

Canada.

HELP FROM IMPERIALS The first shipment of horses as reinforcements arrived in England on March 20th, 1915. These and subsequent arrivals on landing were accommodated in a temporary remount depot, on the racetrack at the exhibition grounds at Plymouth. Two detachments of men, from Imperial remount depots, were loaned to care for these horses, such as were fit being shipped direct to units of the Second Division. Incapacitated animals were looked after in a rest camp, situated in some brickfields near the station, and as soon as fit to move were taken over by the Imperial remount depots and rationed for Canadian account at a flat rate of 2s.0d - *per diem.* These were later issued to Canadian units on requisition. Strict account was kept of all horses handed over, convalescents to farms and evacuations to hospitals being charged back and credit received for them. The total number brought over by steamers and handed over to the Imperials from March, 1915 till August, 1915 was 11,155; the total number of evacuations to convalescent farms was 605; whilst the total number of Canadian horses handed over to the Imperials, from different sources and cared for by them from March 1st, 1915 till March 15th, 1916, when Canada's credit in horses became exhausted, was 16,916.

It will be understood that all this time Canada had been purchasing these horses and shipping them to Europe as reinforcements to meet the requirements of her troops, but lacking facilities in England, found it more convenient and profitable to take advantage of existing Imperial machinery than to enter into an undertaking of that kind on her own account.

REMOUNT PROBLEM SOLVED The question then presented itself whether it would not be better to dispose of the whole remount problem by acquiring fresh supplies of horses as needed from the British remount department at a definite figure and leaving the field for purchase in Canadian markets and transportation to Europe entirely free to the Imperial authorities. Accordingly, in March, 1916, at a meeting held at the War Office, at which the Director of Remounts (Imperial), the Assistant Director of Remounts (Imperial), the Director of Veterinary Services and Remounts (Canadian) and an official representing the British financial department were present, an agreement was come to that all remounts required by the Canadian forces in both England and France would be supplied as demanded at a uniform flat rate of £56 per animal, horse or mule, delivery to be effected at unit railheads. The advantage of this arrangement will become apparent from a glance at the following estimate made by Colonel Neill in justification of the new policy:

Horses purchased in Canada	$200.00
Cost of transportation to England	75.00
Cost to acclimatize and condition	50.00
Total:	$325.00
$325 at $4.86 to £	£66.17s.5d
Purchase price from Imperial government	£56.0s.0d
Approximate amount saved	£10.17s.5d

PRICE SETTLED The above-mentioned price, viz. £56, was, thereafter, paid by Canada until the beginning of 1917 for all remounts furnished in England and France, and at the same time credit was given to Canada at the same rate for all horses evacuated to Imperial hospitals, irrespective of the degree of disability of the latter.

METHOD OF SETTLEMENT Settlement was made by the issue of quarterly statements recording remount issues to Canadian units and including also credits for animals returned to the Imperials (evacuations). These statements were jointly certified to by the Remount Department (Imperial) and the Director of Veterinary Services and Remounts (Canadian) and passed for payment to the Chief Paymaster as certificates of Imperial remount charge against Canada for the period specified. Once in a while there was some difficulty in getting correct statements. On one occasion, this was due to Imperial units attached to Canadian divisions receiving their remounts through Canadian headquarters in the field. A mixup resulted which was thereafter obviated by requiring Imperial units in a similar situation to indent direct on the Imperial Remount Department.

SAVING MONEY Colonel Neill estimated that by pursuing the new policy, when he took over the direction of Canadian remount affairs in August, 1915, enormous sums of money would be saved to the Canadian taxpayer. His figures at the expiration of 22 months are interesting and give one a good idea of the magnitude of the transactions involved.

ESTIMATE OF COST
TO ESTABLISH REMOUNT DEPOT FOR 5000 HORSES

ENGLAND		
	Buildings	£90,000.0s.0d
	Equipment	13,536.4s.8d
	Horses for personnel	6,856.0s.0d
FRANCE	Base depot	40,000.0s.0d
	Advanced depot	20,000.0s.0d
EXPENSES FOR 22 MONTHS		
	Horse rations @ £620.0s.0d *per diem*	415,090.0s.0d
	Pay (personnel) @ £511.0s.0d *per diem*	342,298.15s.0d
	Men's rations @ £150.0s.0d *per diem*	100,425.0s.0d
	Veterinary medicines @ £77.10s.0d *per diem*	51,886.5s.5d
		£1,080,092.4s.8d
Estimated amount saved on horses purchased from the Imperial government		
	5,500 at £10.17s.5d	59,789.11s.6d
		£1,139,881.16s.2d
	Less settlement for ration account	45,615.3s.6d
Total amount saved		£1,094,266.12s.8d
	at ($4.97 2/3) =	$5,325,430.94

CANADA'S REMOUNT REQUIREMENTS SUPPLIED FROM HOME At the aforesaid meeting the question of the source of supply of the number of remounts required by the Canadian forces came up for discussion. It was pointed out by the Imperial authorities that from the purely departmental point of view, it was convenient, economical and altogether satisfactory to ship both horses and mules purchased on the North American continent from one port and to draw the supply as required from one firm of dealers, but on Colonel Neill representing that the Canadian people would expect the wastage in the Canadian Army Corps to be supplied from Canada, the Imperials expressed their hearty concurrence and announced their intention to instruct their purchasing representative to obtain in Canada the number of animals required for that purpose, estimated to be approximately 900 monthly (about half the number eventually required) for the four divisions.

BRIGADIER-GENERAL NEILL IN CANADA On May 4th, 1917, Brigadier-General Neill, upon instructions received from the War Office, temporarily relinquished his duties as Director of Veterinary Services and Remounts and proceeded to Canada for the purpose of opening up the Canadian remount market and to increase the purchase of Canadian horses for the Imperial armies. He visited the different provinces and went into the question of supplying remounts with the various provincial governments, which arranged inspections and meetings with the large dealers. The type of animal sought[1] was for field artillery (Figure 13.2) and heavy draft purposes, the prices to be paid being limited to $190 for the former and $220 for the latter. The results of his trip were shown in his report, the main features of which were as follows:

In Ontario The class of horse shown was good and very serviceable. In Toronto, a meeting was called by the Horse Breed Association and a committee formed for the purpose of assembling the horses. A meeting of dealers

Figure 13.2. A heavy artillery piece being drawn into action by a team of 12 horses hitched in tandem pairs, aided by men. A light draft horse was sought for such work with the field artillery. (*Imperial War Museum D 405, courtesy Guelph Museums, McConkey Collection*)

was also held and all details explained to them regarding the requirements. Strange to relate, the death rate in Canadian horses retained in the yards pending embarkation was higher than amongst American horses similarly situated. The only explanation offered was that the disease from which the animals suffered was conveyed from the United States and became very virulent in Canadian horses. As a measure of avoidance of the infection, it was arranged that the city stockyards, which were capable of accommodating from 600 to 700 animals, should be used for the purpose of isolation and as soon as this was done the losses practically ceased.

In Quebec The outlook was not very encouraging in this province owing to the fact that the type of horse desired was not available, a smaller horse being mostly in use and breeding not carried on to any extent, necessitating the importation of horses into the province. Consequently, the prices offered did not attract and the class shown was poor.

In Nova Scotia Here a certain number of field artillery type was obtainable, but animals of a heavier type were not procurable at the price offered as they could command from $40 to $50 higher locally.

In New Brunswick The conditions were similar to those in Nova Scotia.

In Manitoba There was more or less of a scarcity of the right type, especially of heavy horses, which in any case were realizing from $25 to $50 more than the remount purchase price.

In Saskatchewan Field artillery horses were available but those weighing over 1500 lbs. were scarce. There was a large number of unbroken horses in the Maple Creek district. The prices offered were satisfactory for field artillery animals, but very few of 1500 lbs. and over were offered at the remount figure, this class being in demand locally and eagerly picked up at from $235 to $250.

In Alberta Conditions in this province were very similar to those in the two foregoing.

In British Columbia Some of very good serviceable type were secured at Kamloops, but there was no prospect of obtaining many at any other district.

BRITISH REMOUNT COMMISSION IN CANADA The British Remount Commission went on buying horses in Canada till August, 1917, when, ostensibly on account of financial reasons, it ceased, but continued to buy in the United States. There was naturally some anxiety on the part of Canadian horse breeders at this turn of events, especially in view of the much discussed policy of keeping trade within the Empire, and it was considered hardly fair that there should be discrimination against Canadian horses. The War Office then suggested that Canada should buy horses herself and after specially marking them, turn them into British army depots in America at the same time promising that every care would be taken to deliver them to Canadian troops, but the proposition was not adopted as it was not considered likely by our Quartermaster-General in London that they would ever reach Canadian units.

Besides the British Remount Commission there were also commissions from the French and Italian governments buying horses in Canada. They all held a meeting in Montreal on June 7th, 1917, in order to arrange for cooperation.

NUMBER PURCHASED IN CANADA Up till the end of July, 1917, the number of horses purchased by the different remount commissions in Canada was approximately as follows:

British	41,000
French	15,000
Canadian	25,000
	81,000

and the different commissions estimated their expenditure in Canada for horses, maintenance, transportation, etc., at:

COST	British	$17,000,000
	French	3,000,000
	Canadian	4,300,000
		$24,300,000

CANADIAN AND AMERICAN HORSES COMPARED The Imperial authorities frankly stated that the horses shipped by the remount commission from the United States were generally superior to those shipped by the Canadian government, they being particularly sound and well constitutioned. It should be noted that when the first exportations were made from the North American continent they were shipped from Canadian ports and it became the habit to speak of them, irrespective of their origin, as 'Canadians'. Horses obtained from Australia did not appear favorably as a purchase with those obtained from North American areas.

TOTAL NUMBER PURCHASED At the outbreak of the war, the British army possessed 19,000 horses. After mobilization, 468,000 were purchased in the United Kingdom and no fewer than 688,000 of which 269,000 were mules, were bought and shipped from North America. The Imperial authorities aimed to maintain the strength of the remounts at 6% of the animals in the field.

Losses that occurred on shipboard were practically all due to contact with infection in the yards before going on board.[2] In one shipload the losses went as high as 7%. Consequently, it was found advisable to employ the clinical thermometer freely and to reject all animals showing an elevated temperature prior to shipment. On the westward voyage, the ships were thoroughly cleansed, disinfected, aired and limewashed with a mixture containing 5% of a reliable disinfectant, so that all decks and holds were presumably sterile for the reception of the next shipment.

In England, the Imperial authorities maintained three large reception depots and one large export depot, with a number of smaller depots scattered about the country to which the imported animals were passed to be conditioned before issue to units.

ARRANGEMENTS IN ENGLAND Whilst Canada received full credit for all horses evacuated in France, the same arrangement was not applicable to the United Kingdom, the Imperial authorities reserving the right to reject any animals they did not wish turned into their depots, thereby necessitating their disposal to outside dealers. In that way the difference between the rate of £56 per head and the amount realized from the sale of cast horses was lost.

At the same time, remounts drawn from Imperial depots in England might be returned if found unsuitable. Of 200 surplus horses inspected by a War Office representative in company with Lieutenant-Colonel Smith in June, 1917, at Shorncliffe, only 25 were accepted as fit to transfer. Of thc rest, 29 were sent to London and sold at public auction, realizing an average of £21.13.6 ($105.48), whilst the remainder were distributed amongst Canadian units in England. Some of the latter, which went to the Fifth Division at Witley, eventually found their way into Imperial depots, in spite of their nonacceptance in the ordinary way. This method of disposal was possible because the Imperial authorities made a practice of accepting into their hospitals as evacuations any animals from Canadian units organizing to proceed overseas. But all animals belonging to Canadian training formations which were admitted into Imperial veterinary hospitals for treatment and forage at Imperial expense were charged for at the daily rate of 2s 6d (60 cents), 2s - of which was for the forage and - 6d to cover cost of medicine.

INCREASE IN COST By the beginning of 1917, the cost of providing remounts had undergone a considerable advance and the Imperial authorities held that the understanding originally arrived at should be reconsidered with a view to Canada bearing her share of the increase. Apparently there had been no definite agreement or contract that the price originally decided on should not be subject to revision and Colonel Neill was under the impression that it was to hold good for the duration of the war. It would seem to have been a singular oversight on the part of the responsible authorities that no definite agreement was drawn up and properly authorized and signed. It is true that Colonel Neill represented Canada's interests in the arrangement but he was not the official upon whom the responsibility for signing such an agreement devolved and one is tempted to ask why some high official with authority to conclude an undertaking of that nature was not present at the meeting or why the transaction did not officially pass through his hands.

The War Office proceeded to show what the actual cost had risen to for delivery of horses both in England and France, according to the following table:

War Office Estimate of March, 1917 showing actual cost per animal from North America landed in England at that time spent in North America to 30th September, 1916 £21.995.0s.0d

Animals purchased	481,726
Remaining in yards	25,611
Died or sold	24,879
Shipped	431,236
Lost on voyage	5,636
Landed in England	425,600
In yards	25,611
	451,211
Average cost	£48.15s.0d
Freight	13.10s.0d
	£62.5s.0d

This allowed nothing for conditioning in the United Kingdom or for transport expenses after landing.

STANDARD OF EFFICIENCY Until midsummer of 1918, the standard of efficiency of animals at the front was maintained at a high level, but at that time it became necessary slightly to reduce it and to get more service out of animals of a category that till then had usually been disposed of, on account of the prevailing shortage of horses, a shortage that was intensified by the requirements of the American Expeditionary Force. For instance, blind or defective vision cases, instead of being evacuated, were placed with units behind the fighting line where they might continue to do useful work, particularly on smooth roads where there were no shell holes into which they might fall. 'Workably sound' was the order of the day, little notice being taken of such as were technically unsound from bone disease. Aged animals, many of which were to be found amongst heavy drafts, were continued in service and none was evacuated till thoroughly tried and proved to be of no use.

SHORTAGE At the period mentioned, the Director of Remounts reported that there were 12,000 outstanding indents for animals in the British armies that could not be filled, and to meet this state of affairs and at the same time to provide mounts for the American forces, the War Office ordered certain reductions in the establishment of horses of some of the field artillery units. At this time, when horses were so badly needed at the front, there were both officers and men, constantly exposed to danger and hardships, who were entitled to be mounted yet could not be accommodated, and at the same time there were officers enjoying safe and comfortable situations at the base hospitals who were carrying on certain practices that hardly reflected credit on the system that made such a thing possible. By devious means, these officers contrived to hold back a not inconsiderable number of animals to enable them to indulge in the pastime of polo. The officer in command of a hospital practically controlled the movements of an animal when once it had come under his supervision. Under pretext of continued sickness, it was possible for him to retain it 'under treatment' for an indefinite period. In this manner such animals as were desired for polo were held back and when inspections by higher officers took place, of which due notice was invariably given, their presence was disguised by the simple expedient of mixing them in with the genuine cases. One hospital was known to have a string of a dozen polo ponies, a fact which, under the conditions then existing at the front, amounted to little short of a scandal.

COMPLAINT AT QUALITY At times, there was considerable complaint on the part of our veterinary officers as to the quality of remounts supplied to Canadian units. It was even boldly asserted that Imperial units invariably got the pick of the animals. As early as June, 1916, Captain O'Gogarty, then in command of No. 1 Mobile Section, was complaining of the condition of the remounts sent from the base and pointing out that certain units had been obliged to turn over to him newly arrived animals for evacuation to hospital on account of debility, mange, lameness and unhealed wounds. All the administrative officers made similar comment. Major Saunders at Bruay in August, 1917, recorded in his diary that the majority of the 110 remounts recently received were in very poor condition and unfit for issue. Lieutenant-Colonel Evans, at Basseux, in April, 1918, noted that all the animals received at that time for light draft purposes by the Second Division were mules whilst Imperial artillery units which were offloading from the same train, were getting horses. Lieutenant-Colonel Tamblyn was complaining of the riders and light drafts sent to his division at Bernaville in October, 1916, and again at Barlin, in August, 1917. On the latter occasion he wrote that in the divisional ammunition column he had found many animals recently received from the base as remounts not of the conformation desired for that class of work, they being long-backed. He pointed out that the issue of that class of animal only tended to make unnecessary transportation and expense as they rarely withstood the strain that was put on them for more than a month when they once more had to be evacuated. Again in September of the same year, he reported that in shipments of remounts received during the few preceding months, a large percentage of the animals had subsequently been evacuated owing to want of proper selection at the base prior to shipment. To overcome that difficulty he suggested there was only one alternative and that was to appoint a thoroughly good horseman at the base to represent Canadian units, such representative to pass all animals sent to the front.

By the time the march into Germany started, the Remount Department was hard pushed to supply the Canadians with suitable animals. Lieutenant-Colonel Tamblyn at Raismes, took over 88 remounts, all of which were of a poor type and undersized and of which a number had to be evacuated at once on account of debility.

Most of the complaint in the divisions was directed against the animals supplied for riding purposes and it was only natural that the best of this class should have been sent to cavalry units.

NO DISCRIMINATION Although the quality and adaptability of all classes of remounts supplied to the Canadian divisions left much to be desired, the fact was that Imperial units were no better off and the Remount Department did the best it could under the circumstances. This fact was recognized by Lieutenant-Colonel Edgett (and by Lieutenant-Colonel Tamblyn), who, when acting as Assistant Director of Veterinary Services at Corps Headquarters in July, 1918, had an opportunity to look over the remounts intended for Imperial units at Army Field Remount Section and wrote that he did not think any discrimination was taking place, but that he felt satisfied that the Director of Remounts was doing his best to supply the Canadian corps with the best possible and moreover, the Deputy Director of Remounts had intimated that he would exchange any not found suitable.

REMOUNTS DRAWN FROM CANADIAN UNITS IN ENGLAND The arrangements with the Imperial authorities did not debar Canada from obtaining remounts for units in the field from other sources. In August, 1918, some 40 horses were selected from amongst different Canadian training areas in England as suitable for officers' chargers and were despatched to the Canadian Cavalry Brigade in France.[3]

LACK OF MEDICAL HISTORY In the Chapter on No. 1 Canadian Veterinary Hospital, reference has been made to the medical history card that accompanied each horse on its passage through a base hospital. These cards did not accompany a horse to form part of its record upon its discharge from hospital unless it was transferred to another hospital, but were filed away and the animal, on its transfer to a remount depot, treated as a new-comer to the army.

It is to be regretted that the Imperial authorities did not see fit to perpetuate the medical history of each horse on active service for some very interesting information might have been obtained as to comparative freedom from, or liability to, disease from the point of view of country of origin.

CANADA'S 'OLD CONTEMPTIBLES' We know that many horses originally from Canada, particularly those of Percheron blood, passed through the whole period of the war without suffering any disorder sufficient to necessitate their evacuation. Indeed, in some units the need of remounts was quite exceptional. Lieutenant-Colonel Cutcliffe, when inspecting the horses of the First Infantry Brigade in March, 1918, found that one battalion still had all its original horses save two, which it had brought from Canada in 1914.

UNFIT TYPE On the other hand, British animals of the heavy Shire type failed to prove their fitness for the hardships expected of horses on active service. Every unit that had them experienced a great deal of sickness amongst them, over 60% belonging to the First Division being left behind in hospital at Netheravon. Moreover, it was known to all that throughout the war a not inconsiderable number of animals were chronic frequenters of the hospitals, which rendered them not only comparatively useless to the service but a financial burden to the public besides. Had a continuous medical record been kept, all such undesirables could have been weeded out and otherwise disposed of. The omission of such record was regarded by the Canadian service as a great defect in an otherwise remarkably competent organization.

The following table shows the original number of horses taken by units of the Second Division from England to France and the number still remaining on the strength at the end of operations in 1919, comprising some that were originally taken over from Canada:

Unit	Establishment of horses taken to France		Number of original animals still on strength		Remarks
4th C.I.Bde.,H.Q	23		13		
18th Bn.	55		28		
19th Bn.	55		27		
20th Bn.	55		21		*12 of these taken
21st Bn.	55	243	*25	114	from Canada
5th C.I.Bde., H.Q.	23		18		
22nd Bn.	55		23		
24th Bn.	55		20		
25th Bn.	55		15		
26th Bn.	55	243	25	101	
6th C.I.Bde., H.Q	23		8		
27th Bn.	55		28		
28th Bn.	55		26		*20 of these were
29th Bn.	55		15		wounded once,
31st Bn.	55	243	*31	108	2 twice & 1 thrice

5th Bde., C.F.A., H.Q.	33				
17th Bty.	128				
18th Bty.	128		12		
20th Bty.	128				
23rd Bty.	128	545	12	24	
6th Bde., C.F.A.,H.Q.	33				
15th Bty.	128		22		
16th Bty.	128		30		
22nd Bty.	128		29		
25th Bty.	128	545	12	93	
4th Fld Amb.	45		28		
5th Fld. Amb.	45		*21		*6 of these taken from Canada
6th Fld. Amb.	45	135	18	67	
Divisional Train	398	398	111	111	
Total:	**2352**		**618**		

THE AMERICAN MULE The American mule, of course, maintained its reputation of being a highly useful and economical animal.[4] Some commanding officers who at first were averse to their employment became such ardent admirers that later they would on no account exchange them for horses. One battery commander, a facetious individual, was so enamored of them that he gave out he had conferred the rank of 'brevet horse' on every one in his unit!

Most commanding officers preferred small mules to large in view of their greater agility in action and on the march. Some of the artillery commanders liked a 6-mule hitch (Figure 13.3) to every subsection as it led to economy in forage for the benefit of the remaining horses. Mules were very useful in routine work, but as they proved to be extremely stubborn under shell fire and tended to neigh when silence was desirable, during an action they would usually be relegated to the rear.

RETURN PRIVILEGE FOR OFFICERS' CHARGERS Whilst all animals evacuated to hospital were struck off the strength of the Canadian forces and there was little likelihood that they would ever again come into Canadian ownership, if they happened to be choice specimens an exception was made in the case of officers' chargers. Provision was made for the eventual return of the latter provided a label bearing the name and unit of the owner was securely attached to the head collar or clipped in the hair of the back or quarter and the fact that return was desired was notified to the officer commanding the receiving hospital on the evacuation roll or by special memorandum.

CANADIAN VETERINARY OFFICERS' EXTRA WORK In one respect the veterinary officers, both administrative and executive, in the Canadian service were required to perform just double the duties of their comrades in the Imperial service. In the latter, all work pertaining to remount matters was carried on under the remount branch in no way connected with the veterinary service. But in the Canadian service, though remount matters constituted a separate department and entailed a great deal of accounting, they were included in the daily routine of the veterinary officers. And, not only did the administrative veterinary officers have to carry on their remount dealings with the Imperial authorities, but in addition, were required to make a thorough set of returns of a purely Canadian nature, setting out every item of animal decrease and increase in detail for the Quartermaster-General's Branch (Canadian) in London.

PROCEDURE FOR OBTAINING REMOUNTS The procedure for obtaining remounts was as follows: The weekly returns of the executive officers in the field indicated shortage, if any, to the administrative officer at Divisional

Figure 13.3. Six-mule team drawing ammunition on a light railway track near Petit Vimy, France, April 1917.[5] (*NAC PA 1135*)

Headquarters. The latter twice monthly prepared a consolidated indent of requirements, which was transmitted through the Quartermaster Branch at Divisional Headquarters to the Assistant Director of Veterinary Services at Corps Headquarters, who sent it to the Deputy Director of Remounts (Imperial) of the army concerned. The latter passed it on to the Director of Remounts (Imperial), who drew the animals of the number and classes required from the remount depot best able to make delivery, the Director keeping in touch by wire every morning with the different depots to post himself on the available strength by classes. When the shipment was started, the Deputy Director of Remounts wired the fact through the same channels to the administrative veterinary officer, whose duty it was to inspect the animals on their arrival. On arrival at railhead, a conducting party from the division was present to take over, the animals being allotted by the administrative veterinary officer to the units in need. In some cases, the unit officers, who came for the purpose, were allowed to make selection by turn.

During the Battle of Amiens, where there were heavy losses, special trains of remounts had to be rushed up from the depots, but though the battle began on August 8th, the first trainload of 352 did not arrive on the scene till 6 days later on account of the difficulties of transportation on the railways.

EVACUATION FOR 'REMOUNT REASONS' Whilst the evacuation of animals for peculiarly veterinary reasons lay within the province of the veterinary officer, there were certain conditions under which he had no authority to act, the so-called 'remount reasons'. These comprised all cases of vice, aged and worn-out animals, faulty conformation, wind sucking, and, if the animal's condition warranted it, for being unsafe to ride. The sole authority for evacuation for the aforesaid reasons was the Remount Department and in such cases commanding officers were required to send in by the 28th of each month a descriptive roll with full particulars, when a date and place for inspection were appointed and such action taken as the circumstances warranted. This duty was generally delegated by commanding officers to the veterinary officers so that in reality the latter became the functionaries for both remount and veterinary reasons.

DISPOSAL OF HORSES IN FRANCE TO BELGIUM[6] On the declaration of the armistice, the problem presented itself of disposing of the horses in the Canadian service in France to the best advantage. Colonel Edgett proceeded to get busy and approached representatives of the Belgian government with an offer of the entire lot and after a certain amount of discussion, the Belgian government agreed to take over at a flat rate of £40 per head, as soon as the Canadians were ready to make delivery. In view of the fact that the Belgian government was unable to make full cash payment, Canada established a ten year credit on its behalf bearing interest at the rate of 5% per annum. Delivery was effected when the troops were withdrawn through a demobilization camp established at Ronaix with Lieutenant-Colonel Tamblyn in charge. All the animals were malleined before being turned over.

This method of disposing of the horses *en bloc* at a flat rate turned out to have been a very shrewd procedure as is indicated by a letter to the Canadian Section at General Headquarters from Brigadier-General H.H. Panet, appointed to represent Canada at Brussels in the transaction with the Belgian government in which he demonstrated the difficulties encountered in disposing of the animals by auction sales would have been enormous by reason of the fact that the British army was placing on the market 110,000 animals, apart from 75,000 sold to butchers, and that in all probability the Canadian animals, under such circumstances, would not have been disposed of till July. He considered that the deal with the Belgian government was one that could not have been improved on for the whole of the Canadian animals (approximately 20,000) would be turned over to the Belgian government by the 31st of July.

REPATRIATION OF HORSES The Overseas Military Council of Canada, under authority of the government, provided that certain animals on the strength of the Canadian forces might be brought back to Canada. The privilege was accorded only to general officers under the following Order:

1. General officers on the strength of the Overseas Military Forces of Canada on the 11th of November, 1918, who, during the war, as general officers, had filled an appointment on an establishment in the field for which said appointment the establishment provided chargers, might, if they so desired, have returned to Canada, chargers up to the maximum:

(a) General officers of the rank of brigadier-general - 2 horses
(b) General officers of the rank of major-general - 3 horses
(c) Lieutenant-generals - 4 horses

This decision caused great dissatisfaction amongst those to whom the privilege was denied, many regarding it as unjust class discrimination and the return of any horses at all being regarded by the veterinary service with considerable apprehension. There were some at the close of the war still in possession of the animals originally allotted to them which had faithfully shared with them all the hardships and dangers through which they had passed. A mutual attachment had been formed and many had looked forward to being accorded the privilege of buying their chargers with a view to continuing the relationship at home. Moreover, there were certain instances where an obligation had been assumed by the authorities to allow the eventual repurchase by former owners of horses that had been taken over from Canada as personal property. When the forces went to France, the War Office laid down that none but government owned animals should accompany the troops and each officer possessing a privately owned mount and wishing to take it with him was obliged to dispose of it to the army, though he might still continue to ride it, for the price that was being paid in Canada, viz. $175, with the understanding that at the end of the war he might repurchase the animal if he so desired. But, in justification of the attitude of the Council, it should be remarked that there were good and sufficient reasons which could not be overlooked.

On the termination of hostilities the object of paramount importance was to get the troops home as soon as possible and it was believed that any attempt at the same time to transport a number of horses would only lead to confusion and delay. Moreover, there were questions of quarantine to be considered and the Director of Veterinary Services (Canadian) was strongly opposed to the return of any horse whatever, for fear of introducing into Canada, with far-reaching evil results, the infectious disorders which the veterinary service had learned to dread, though in a matter of this kind he had no jurisdiction. In the meantime, the Overseas Council had not figured on the attitude the Department of Agriculture might assume, and as a matter of fact, there was a standing order of the Department of Agriculture prohibiting the importation of horses from all European countries, excepting purebred animals for propagation purposes. The Department of Agriculture was not consulted on the matter and the first shipment of 60 animals was already on the water before it became aware of the situation. It was only through intervention on the part of the Minister of Militia that special arrangements were made for the landing and isolation under quarantine for a period of not less than six months in order that periodic tests for freedom from disease might be conducted. A second shipment of 50 animals was started when the Department of Agriculture refused to consent to a further relaxation of the regulations.

On the other hand, owing to serious inroads on the horse strength of Great Britain, which the demands of the war had brought about, the British government was obliged to repatriate a large number of its own animals. The original intention was to return 100,000, consisting chiefly of selected mares suitable for breeding purposes, together with a few special geldings of superior type, but eventually about half this number were repatriated.

DISPOSAL OF HORSES IN ENGLAND Meanwhile, there were the animals in England that had also to be disposed of and no time was lost as soon as the armistice was declared, by Colonel Edgett, ably assisted by Captain F. Doyle, C.A.S.C., in getting them on the market for sale at public auction. The first lot comprised some choice specimens from the Canadian Army Service Corps at Shorncliffe, which were offered on November 18th and fetched an average price of £73 ($355.27) as follows:

Saddle	£35.2s.4d ($170.89)
Light draft	£70.0s.0d ($340.67)
Heavy draft	£89.7s.7d ($435.97)

Another lot from Witley brought:

Saddle	£34.13s.0d ($168.62)
Light draft	£69.6s.0d ($337.24)
Heavy draft	£89.5s.0d ($434.34)

In December the prices had fallen to the following:

Saddle	£26.6s.3d ($128.05)
Light draft	£26.6s.3d ($128.05)
Heavy draft	£65.4s.8d ($317.47)

UPKEEP COST OF HORSES IN O.M.F.C. The following figures showing the cost of upkeep of the horses in the Canadian forces in the month of November, 1916, will prove interesting:

IN NOVEMBER, 1916 - ORGANIZATION OF A DIVISION

			Total
Headquarters, division	70		70
Infantry brigade	23	3 brigades	69
Infantry battalion	56	12 battalions	672
Pioneer battalion	98		98
Machine gun section (brigade)	53	3 brigades	159
Divisional train	457		457
Engineer headquarters	7		7
Engineer company	78	3 companies	234
Field ambulance	54	3 ambulances	162
Signal company	107		107
Headquarters, artillery	19		19
Artillery brigade	537	4 brigades	2,148
Divisional ammunition column	1,015		1,015
Total:			5,417

Cost of organizing a division (horses): 5,417 horses @ £56 each = £303,352

Maintenance Of A Division

The wastage of a division worked out at a pro rata figure of approximately 25%, viz.:

Organization strength	5,417
Wastage	1,300

As the Canadian forces were allowed credit for horses evacuated (about 65% of the total wastage of 1,300 horses) there was left an approximate specific wastage of 455 horses per division. Therefore, the total approximate cost of upkeep per division was 455 horses @ £56 each . . . . = £25,480

The estimated cost of upkeep of drugs per division was 1,330

Total yearly expenditure of division . . . . = £26,810

The estimated horse strength in France equalled about the strength of five divisions.

Cost of maintenance of one division . . . . = £26,810

Cost of maintenance of whole of Canadian force in France . . . . = £134,050

Horse strength in England equivalent to one division. . . . . = £26,810

Total cost of maintenance of Canadian forces in France & England . . . . = £160,860

'Evacuated To Hospital'

What are these straggling scarecrows,
Marching with limping pace?
'Tis a train-load of wounded horses,
For a Hospital down at the Base.

Two hundred and eighty cripples,
With every variety of ill,
If you called 'em a mile of misery,
It would pretty well fill the bill.

With coats like a moth-eaten hearthrug,
With hips that projected like a rack,
And ribs that a blind man could number,
Sunken eyes and a razor-like back.

With bandages bloody and pus-stained.
Wounds gaping or packed up with wool.
It's a sight to make pitying angels
Turn away with a sigh, and eyes full.

"Fall in! fall in! for admissions,
Detail ten men from each troop.
Single file, left! through the gateway
For classification and group."

"Bay gelding, light draught, and age seven,
Wound, gunshot near hind, post to 'C',
Through the dip, then mallein.
Tell the dressers to get him ready for me."

"Black mare, heavy draught, age twenty,
Debility, ringbones both fore.
Walk her up to the slab, and shoot her.
She'll never be workable more."

Chloroform, scalpel, and forceps,
Bistoury, probe and curette;
Crushed oats, and linseed, and locusts,
And a Calcium sulphide dip.

So the horse that was limping and lousy,
And thin, and wracked with pain,
Once more gets his head and tail up,
And -- goes back to the front again.

Back to the toil and exposure,
Back to the seas of mud,
Back to the gas and the shrapnel,
And the snow, and the rain, and the blood.

We are told there's a God counts the sparrows,
And knows when each one of them fall;
But He must have forgotten the horses,
Though His Son was born in a stall.

France, 27/12/17. A.L. Wilson.

The Veterinary Record, 7 February, 1918, p. 331.
Reprinted with permission.

CHAPTER 14

ANIMAL HYGIENE AT THE FRONT

IMPORTANCE OF QUALITY AND REGULARITY - WATERING An adequate and regular supply of good water proved to be an important factor for maintaining the horses in condition. The source of supply usually depended on some rivulet in the vicinity of the horse lines though quite often a considerable distance had to be travelled between the two positions, which circumstance, particularly when there might be a shortage of men for stable duties, led to many horses being irregularly watered, which resulted in the development of more or less debility. Debility resulting from improper watering facilities was a marked experience on the Somme in 1916.

CARE TAKEN OF SUPPLY Horses ordinarily were not allowed to enter streams for drinking in order to avoid contamination of those coming immediately after, but the water was pumped up by means of portable hand pumps, a supply of which was carried by all units, into portable canvas troughs. These were 30 feet long, two placed end to end, permitting the watering of 25 animals at one time. Where positions were continuously being occupied, the engineers often rigged up permanent troughs, usually constructed of corrugated iron, and where the fall of water permitted it, even supplied metal pipes and spigots. At the Battle of Amiens, the water situation in the forward area became very serious, the animals in some instanccs having to be watered at dirty ponds or from shell holes, though occasionally wells were available. Water from shell holes was avoided as far as possible because it was generally contaminated with lyddite and other poisonous gases and whilst not known to cause death, seriously affected digestion. Sometimes animals going up to the forward area would have to exist from l a.m. until 4 p.m. without drinking.

WATERING PARADES When things were running smoothly, the watering assumed the function of a formal parade, which, under the supervision of a unit officer, as was always supposed to be the case, was quite an interesting event to behold. The animals were walked to the troughs in files, an attendant conducting two, one of which he sat astride bareback. On approaching the troughs, they would be lined up in rows facing the latter (Figure 14.1). At the word of command, the first row stepped forward to take its fill, the men meanwhile having

Figure 14.1. Watering horses of the Canadian Artillery at the front. November, 1916. (*NAC, PA 849*)

dismounted and removed the bits. There they remained until the last horse had finished, when, on command, they filed to one side, to be rebitted and remounted and moved off at a walk, the next row taking the place of the first and so on.

At one time, in 1917, considerable slackness prevailed as a result of unit officers neglecting their duty to be in attendance and leaving the superintendence to junior non-commissioned officers. The animals were being led to the troughs at a pace that exceeded the walk and were not halted until in the immediate vicinity of the troughs when it was impossible to remove the bits from anxious ones, and the men, by shouting at the troughs, were disturbing the quietude which should have prevailed. Lieutenant-Colonel Evans, ever mindful of the welfare of the horses, observing these disquieting conditions, reported the matter to the Assistant Director of Veterinary Services at Corps Headquarters and pointed out the urgent necessity of a stricter supervision of the watering parades. The result was a promulgation of an order requiring unit officers to attend, and thereafter there was a great improvement. This incident is mentioned to show wherein an alert veterinary service could be of immense value in promoting efficiency and guarding the health of the animals.

DIFFICULTY OF WATERING ON HOSPITAL TRAINS There was always some difficulty in providing proper watering facilities for horses in trains en route to hospitals. The animals were always watered before loading but at first no provision was made for the trains to stop long enough to enable the men in attendance to give them adequate attention in this respect. Often 24 or even 36 hours would elapse before the animals got a chance to drink, and as a general rule, it took 48 hours to make the journey to Neuchâtel. So many animals arrived at their destination in such deplorable condition that the authorities were prompted to investigate the cause and upon discovering the same, took effectual steps to remedy the evil. Empty shell cases of the largest calibre, which in any case were destined for the bases, were made use of as fixed troughs in the cars and could easily be filled from the outside. These were gathered together at the supply railheads by the divisional ammunition column teams on return from the forward areas.

IMPROVISATION AGAINST SHORTAGE During the great retreat in March, 1918, the animals suffered from lack of water during forced marches, and it was realized that something would have to be done in future even if only for the moistening of parched throats. As there was a plentiful supply of empty gasoline cans of 2-gallon capacity on all fronts, it was decided that a certain number of these should be carried on the wagons and gun limbers which could easily be done by having the farriers construct and attach racks to the same. In the case of the 18 pounders, the arrangement was as follows:

<u>On gun limber</u>	
1 strapped to each guardrail	2
<u>On lst line wagon</u>	
limber 1 strapped to each guardrail	2
body 1 strapped to each guardrail	2
4 on rack attached to foot board	4
<u>On battery firing wagon</u>	
limber 1 strapped to each guardrail	2
body 1 strapped to each guardrail	2
4 on rack attached to foot board	4
Total:	18

This afforded a total capacity of 36 gallons for from 18 to 20 animals.

In the case of the howitzers, which being heavier, had a greater carrying capacity, the arrangement was as follows:

<u>On gun limber</u>	2 strapped to each guardrail	2
<u>On lst line wagon</u>	8 on rack across top of body	8
<u>On battery-firing wagon</u>	8 on rack across top of body	8
	Total:	18

This afforded a total capacity of 40 gallons for from 22 to 24 animals.

The scheme did not work out as successfully as had been anticipated as the severe jolting to which the cans were subjected when the wagons went over rough ground caused the seams to open from the soldering, giving way with consequent leakage. Moreover, the cans rusted a good deal on the inside, so that the water had to be changed frequently. Consequently the cans were generally discarded.

FORAGE AND FEEDING The sustenance of the great number of horses employed in the war was a matter of vast dimensions. It was not done in a haphazard manner, but each animal was carefully provided for on an authorized scale which varied from time to time according to the supplies available. The reader elsewhere has been informed that horses and mules to the number of 26,000 were usually employed at one time in the service of the Canadian troops in both England and France and that these were apart from the still greater number in the service of the Imperial forces. When one remembers that to properly nourish each animal there is needed every day of the year not less than an average of some 25 lbs. of foodstuffs, half of which must be of a bulky nature to enable it to maintain its digestion unimpaired, some idea of the immensity of the problem of feeding the horses of the army may be grasped. Taking the above-mentioned number of animals, we arrive at the grand figure of 650,000 lbs., or approximately 290 tons (at 2240 lbs. to the ton) for the horses of the Canadians alone, which had to be provided every day, after it had been obtained from original sources of supply, often across the seas, and stored at bases to be finally moved up and distributed by steam, motor and horse transport in the zones of the army.

SYSTEM IN ENGLAND In England, where Canada maintained her own horses on an independent basis, supplies were procured by purchase from the Imperial authorities. At Shorncliffe, Witley and other Canadian stations in England, indents were made for the requisite quantities on the nearest Imperial bases, whence the provender was despatched by rail to the camps, where it was taken in hand by the transport units and removed to the storage depots, to be delivered as needed on indent received from the various units disposing of horses. In this manner there was a constant flow of supplies and it was only towards the summer of 1917, when there were indications of an impending difficulty of transportation of hay and straw, that the Canadian Army Service Corps at Shorncliffe received instructions to lay in a 2 months' stock of the former commodity, which it did in every way possible, even by hauling it from nearby farms, until it had accumulated a reserve which at one time amounted to 385,000 lbs. Oats were always forthcoming, but there was occasionally a shortage of bran when the Canadian Army Service Corps was obliged to seek a supply on its own account, purchasing this commodity by the ton in the open market. From the period mentioned onward, no straw could be had for bedding, but instead, peat moss was procured. The latter substance was not liked by the veterinary service for it was found to be associated with a decided increase in the prevalence of lice on the horses.

METHOD OF OBTAINING SUPPLIES The method of obtaining supplies on the part of each individual unit was as follows: The commanding officer sent in his requisition, according to the authorized scale, for as many horses as would appear on his parade statement the following day, each unit being supposed to receive notice from headquarters of any contemplated change in its horse strength some 48 hours in advance. To provide against unforeseen occurrence, it did not matter if the amount of fodder allowed per horse was exceeded on any one day, provided the total number of rations drawn in any one month tallied with the parade statement of the month of the horses on charge to that unit in that particular month.

AT NO. 2 C.V.H. But it may occur to the reader that whilst this system of rationing from day to day would be comparatively easy to carry out in units in which the number of horses was fairly constant, some difficulty might be experienced in a unit of the nature of a veterinary hospital where horses in any number might have to be admitted on an emergency without any previous warning. This difficulty was supposed to be met by sending with the animal the unconsumed portion of the day's rations, but as a matter of fact, such procedure was rarely followed, as the commanding officer of the hospital at Shorncliffe always contrived to have a considerable supply of provender in reserve, regulations to the contrary notwithstanding. Indeed, it could hardly have been otherwise because a period of 48 hours was required for an indent for fodder to pass through official channels ere it resulted in delivery of the required articles, during which time the animals would have been without sustenance.

Whilst each horse admitted to hospital was entitled to the full authorized ration, many such animals from the necessity of reducing the quantity of stimulating elements of their food, such as oats, as part of their treatment, or because they were standing in comparative idleness, did not consume anything like the quantity that was drawn for them, so that a surplus accumulated, particularly in summer when there was a certain amount of green food available. This surplus, consisting mainly of grain, amounted usually to about 1500 lbs., but at one time rose as high as 2700 lbs. When the surplus assumed undue proportions, it was customary to refrain from indenting for a day or two until it was reduced to reasonable proportions. Thus, at all times, the animals admitted to No. 2 Canadian Veterinary Hospital were assured of a hospitable welcome.

The prewar issue of forage in Canada was as follows:

Horses	Oats (lbs.)	Hay (lbs.)	Straw (lbs.)
Heavy draft	12	16	8
Light draft	10	15	8
Riding	10	12	8

This may be compared with the authorized scale in England in June, 1917:

(1) Hay and oats

Horses	Oats	Hay	Chaff
Heavy draft	15	10	5
Light draft	10	8	4
Riding	10	7	3

(2) Hay and corn

Mules	Corn	Hay	Chaff
Draft	12	10	6
Pack	6	6	4

Chaff might consist of all straw or mixed hay and straw, according to what was available, but where it was mixed, the quantity of straw it contained had to be not less than 20%.

(3) Rock salt

An issue of rock salt, not exceeding 2 lbs. per horse per week, was authorized when ordered in writing by the veterinary service.

(4) Bedding

Straw was not allowed to be used for bedding. Instead, peat moss was supplied in bales at the rate of 112 lbs. per animal for the first issue and 5 lbs. per animal per day in subsequent issues.

(5) Equivalents

The scale of forage ration equivalents was as follows:

Oats	1 lb.	Corn 1 lb.	Barley 1 lb.
Bran	1 1/8 lb.	Linseed 1 1/2 lb.	Oatmeal 1/3 lb.
Malt	3/7 lb.	Hay or chaff 1 3/4 lb.	

(6) Green forage

Issues of green forage, when available, were made on the basis of 3 lbs. of green forage in lieu of 1 lb. of hay or oats.

(7) Grazing

When horses were turned out to graze during the day, not more than 1/3 of the forage ration was issued for the day on which they were turned out.

The method of feeding employed at the Shorncliffe hospital was the giving of a considerable quantity of oats and linseed in the boiled state. Every animal in the lines was given one feed of boiled food daily, those moderately debilitated were fed two such feeds, whilst the extremely debilitated received their entire grain portion in the boiled state. Large farm boilers were kept going, the oats and linseed being put into the boilers with sufficient water and the fires started at 8:30 a. m. The mixture was slowly heated, meanwhile being frequently stirred, until it boiled about noon. Thereafter, it was kept simmering until 5 p.m., when the fires were banked for the night. The resultant mixture was used next day, after it had been thoroughly mixed with the authorized amount of chaff, moistened with hot water, to assure proper mastication. Sometimes about 1/2 lb. of bran was added, but this article being very scarce, it was used only occasionally as a laxative and not as a constant part of the ration. Long hay was given three times daily and dry oats when boiled food was not given at every feed.

SYSTEM IN FRANCE In France, the foraging arrangements were on a different basis. The Imperial authorities undertook all responsibility and made all provision up to delivery to the Canadian railheads, whence it was distributed by Canadian transport, the cost of the service being included in the arrangement entered into between the two governments that Canada should pay 6s. ($1.50) per day for the support of each Canadian soldier in the British Expeditionary Force.

AT HAVRE At Havre, where the Canadians were naturally interested in the foraging arrangements, a reserve of 60,000 complete rations was maintained by the Imperial authorities for the provision of some 7,500 horses which were at all times on hand, distributed as follows:

Return of April 15th, 1918

At No. 1 Canadian Veterinary Hospital	1,529 animals
At No. 2 Imperial Veterinary Hospital	1,645
At Imperial Remount Depot	4,097
At Army Service Corps Depot	288
	7,559

The forage was brought in barges from England and the average issue daily amounted to some 70 tons. Some observations made by one of the Canadian veterinary officers on the quality and origin of the same may be mentioned at this juncture:

Hay Mostly English, of mixed meadow and timothy and second growth clover. Occasionally Canadian timothy of uniformly good quality, being better cured, cleaner and baled in more convenient size and not so compressed.

Straw Oat straw sometimes issued in lieu of hay. Clean and excellent for chaffing.

Oats From Canada and Argentine. Canadian far superior and clean, with full body and little husk. Argentine long-whiskered and mixed with wild oats and mustard.

Bran English and Canadian. English larger, harder flake. Canadian softer and in smaller sacks, easier to handle.

Linseed Crushed cake.

Roots Mangold wurzel and white turnip.

AT NO. 1 C.V.H. At No. 1 Canadian Veterinary Hospital, about two days' rations were always kept on hand. Rations were indented for two days ahead and drawn the day previously. Supposing that a horse was sent to the remount depot on a Wednesday, its rations would be surplus on Thursday, and incoming horses from up the line would be accompanied with rations for the succeeding 24 hours, though horses transferred from No. 2 Imperial Hospital came without rations. But the latter could always be fed with the surplus arising from the horses that had gone to the remount depot in the morning and, when necessary, a supplementary indent for the morrow would always be honoured.

The scale of rations in 1918, when every economy in the use of forage had to be observed, was as follows:

	Hay (lbs.)			Oats (lbs.)		
	Heavy draft	Light draft	Mules	Heavy draft	Light draft	Mules draft
Debility cases	14	11	11	15	10	10
All others	14	11	11	12 3/4	9	9

The following, when available, were issued in lieu of oats:

2 lbs. beans	per animal	9 lb. equalling	8 lb. oats
4 lbs. locust beans	" "	3 lb. "	2 lb. oats
Linseed cake	" "	2 lb. "	3 lb. oats
Linseed meal	" "	1 lb. "	3 lb. oats
2 lbs. roots			

The organization that ensured the regular feeding of the animals at the front was one of the marvels of the war. Forage was obtained as much as possible in France from civilians, each army having its own purchasing board which formed depots for the distribution. These depots maintained threshing machines which went and threshed the crops of the farmers and got the straw which was drawn to a central point and trussed for distribution to the different divisions, the latter doing their own hauling. A certain margin was figured on for wastage on account of wet and this margin found its way to units having the most enterprising officers who would send extra wagons, if need be, 20 miles to the rear. This straw formed a valuable substitute for hay.

SHORTAGE Only occasionally was there actual shortage, confined mostly to hay, and then it was usually due to local conditions such as the necessity for employing all available transport for the bringing up of munitions. For instance, at Materen in February, 1915, Lieutenant-Colonel Neill recorded a shortage of hay and the feeding of straw in its place and in the early part of 1916 the forage ration was reduced to 5 lbs. hay and 6 lbs to 7 lbs. oats on account of the movement of big guns. To cope with the situation, the men of some of the units handed over their own hardtack for the benefit of their horses, buying bread from the local French bakers for their own use in its place.

During the advance into Germany, the Army Service Corps was unable to keep up its deliveries to coincide with the rapidity of the movements of the troops and, as a consequence, the horses suffered greatly from shortage of rations. The hay shortage persisted even after the army had settled down on the Rhine. Major Saunders recorded inspecting 63 remounts during the march, at Jemappes, at 9 p. m. on November 17th, and finding the animals exhausted through not having been fed since noon of the day before. When the Germans first retired, they left behind a considerable amount of forage and all the horses and cattle of the inhabitants having been previously removed by the enemy, these supplies, especially the hay, proved of immense benefit to our animals, then cut down to 4 lbs. hay, supplemented by from 4 to 6 lbs. straw, so that they began picking up flesh rapidly.

CHAFF CUTTING MACHINES ISSUED The authorities began issuing hand driven chaff cutting machines in the winter of 1916-1917, but most units, on account of their limited transport facilities, looked upon them as a nuisance, which meant that in many cases they were seldom in use and sooner or later would be discarded. On this account, Lieutenant-Colonel Tamblyn, with his ever practical ideas, suggested the institution of a conveniently located central chaff cutting and oat crushing plant for each division, to be run with a small gasoline engine after the same manner as his central clipping stations, which would have required but ten men to operate it, whereas it needed from 3 to 4 men in each unit to manipulate individual machines. The suggestion, though eminently practical, was not adopted till October, 1918, when a power machine was received for the Canadian Army Corps.

ENEMY AGENTS TAMPERING WITH FORAGE Early in 1916, it was reported by the Imperial authorities that small steel hooks and croton oil beans had been found amongst the oats purchased in the United States and which were believed to have been placed there by German agents. Everybody was warned and soon an instance came to light in the Third Infantry Brigade. These hooks were from 1/2 inch to 3/4 inch long and were shaped like arrow heads; they looked as if they might have been fashioned from the ends of horseshoe nails.

FORAGE POISONING In the latter part of the same year, cases of forage poisoning occurred. Lieutenant-Colonel Edgett at Albert reported 32 typical cases, of which 11 proved fatal, but though all feed was carefully inspected, the source of the trouble could not be located.

SYSTEMS OF FEEDING One of two systems of forage control was practised in artillery units, when in line, according to the ideas of the officers in charge, and both might be going on at one time amongst the different batteries composing a brigade. They were known respectively as the 'central feed system' and thc 'subsectional system'.

Each had its advocates but the former found most favor on the ground that it prevented wastage by affording regularity and systematization, all the feed for the battery being pooled and protected from pilfering by forming a sort of strong room placed in charge of a non-commissioned officer who rarely favored anybody's horse but his own. A line orderly from each subsection worked in the feed room (usually a shack or tent), helping to chaff and fill hay nets, etc.

Under this system, poor horses needing extra feed were segregated into a 'rest line' which was more amenable to control than by any other system. A list of all animals needing special feed was posted and issues made accordingly to the line orderlies who were held responsible to the sergeants in charge of subsections that the special feeds reached the horses needing them. Drivers were at all times prone to 'pinch' from the rations of other men's horses or to switch special feeds to their own animals, so it was found best to defer handing out the special feeds till the hour of feeding and constant watchfulness was necessary to prevent one animal from getting more than its share. This tendency to departure from rectitude was, of course, due to the eagerness of the men to maintain their own particular animals in the best condition and for that reason one felt constrained to regard it as a virtue rather than a vice. There being only sufficient portable boilers and chaff cutting machines for the batteries as a whole, this feature fitted in very nicely with the central idea.

The procedure in the feed room was as follows: The hay was shaken over a 2-inch sieve on to a tarpaulin, all the short portions, seeds and clover tops being collected and put in a tub and soaked for from 12 to 24 hours. An idea of the type of sieve employed may be gathered from likening it to a large double bedstead having a spring of the same mesh. Great care was taken to avoid waste of hay seed, the fact being ever kept in mind that it formed the most nutritious part of the hay ration, comparable with ripe oats to the straw of the latter. This is a point that is commended as a measure of economy to the consideration of the Canadian farmer who is not noted for utilizing as fodder the abundant supply of seed that collects on the floor of his hay barn and which is too often regarded by him as waste sweepings to be relegated to the manure pile. A certain portion of the oats was boiled and mixed with this hay seed and the resulting mixture set aside and fed to the poor horses at the discretion of the wagon lines officer on the advice of the veterinary officer. The straw was chaffed to the extent of 50% if the issue was large, or in its entirely if the issue was small, a certain proportion of green fodder being chaffed and mixed with it when obtainable. When the issue of straw was very small, hay would be chaffcd. Oil cake, when forthcoming, was fed either dry or boiled with the oats.

In the subsectional system, the feed, when delivered to the battery lines, was divided pro rata amongst the component sub-sections and each of the latter looked after its own horses. A permanent line orderly was appointed who was supposed to take a special interest in looking after the horses of his own sub-section and to give the thin ones a little more by taking from those in good condition. He watched that no man took undue advantage over another and as a further protection slept in the feed depository at night time. If he happened to be a sound sleeper, the night pickets, being drivers with teams of their own, would sometimes pay a visit and help themselves to an extra supply for the latter.

As an example of feeding, watering, grooming and exercising routine, we may take that as practised in summer by the 15th Battery where the horses showed up to advantage. In this battery, the feed ration, both hay and oats, was divided up into four equal portions which were fed four times daily, excepting in winter when the grain only was fed three times daily. Grazing, in the inhabited areas, was permitted at the roadside only, unless by arrangement with the peasants, who usually needed available pasturage for their own cattle, but the horses were often taken up to the forward areas, in range of enemy long-distance fire, whence the inhabitants had taken their departure and the territory was considered abandoned. It is noteworthy that the community instinct manifested itself strongly in the battery horses when grazing under these conditions. They would be turned loose and herded by a few of the men, but each seemed to recognize the group to which it belonged, never mixing with the other or wandering far afield.

Routine observed by the 15th Battery in summer time:

6:30 a.m.	Grooming, one man to 3 horses
7:30	Watering parade
7:45	Feeding
9-10	Grooming
10-10:30	Cleaning lines and harness
10:30-11:30	Exercising and grazing
11:30	Watering parade
12 noon	Feeding
2 -3:30 p.m.	Exercising and grazing
3:30-4:30	Grooming
4:30	Watering parade
5:00	Feeding
8:00	Watering parade
8:30	Feeding

Another battery observed the following schedule:

6-6:45 a.m.	Exercising - 3 to 4 miles
6:45	Watering parade
7:00	Hay and rub down
7:20	Oats and chaff
9-10:45	Exercising and grazing
10:45	Watering parade
11-12	Grooming
12 noon	Oats and chaff
2-4 p.m.	Exercising and grazing
4:00	Watering parade
4-4:45	Oats and chaff
7:00	Hay
8:00	Watering parade
8:15	Oats and chaff

When on the move it was necessary to have recourse to the subsectional system, each subsection having to look after itself, and the procedure was somewhat modified. That followed in the 16th Battery under Major Baker, a remarkably all-round proficient artillery officer, was as follows: Supposing a move was to be made early next morning, it was found best to feed at midnight and again at 4 a.m., and if any hay was left over, it was carried in bales on the footboards of the 1st line wagons rather than in nets swinging at the horses' sides, which was found to be wasteful when the hay had not been subjected to the sieving process. A double feed of oats was put in the nosebags and the remainder carried in sacks on the footboards of the gun limbers and firing battery wagons. A series of short halts was made at 10 kilometer distances, when a portion of the oats in the nosebags would be fed, the bags being taken off before all was eaten, and immediately on arrival at billets the animals were watered and fed the unexpended portion of hay and oats. If moving the next day, the same procedure was followed as on the previous night, but if the unit went into line again, the procedure reverted to central battery control with the chaff cutting machine in operation.

In the Light Horse, the system partook of the central character, when lying well back from the line, each squadron receiving its forage in bulk and issuing it to the different troops from a central feed room in charge of a non-commissioned officer, the thin animals being taken care of in a similar manner.

HAYNETS When horses are picketed in the open, it is necessary to provide some device to prevent their hay from being blown away from in front of them in windy weather. This fact became very evident in the early days on Salisbury Plain, where the wind prevailed forcefully and almost continuously. The difficulty was overcome by the employment of the haynet, a simple and practical device in general use in the British army. At first, the haynet was used only in windy weather but it was soon found that not only did it serve this particular purpose, but it was of great importance in preventing wastage from the hay being trampled underfoot into the mud. Thereafter, it was universally employed excepting when the supply fell short. It could also be used slung to a horse's side on the march for the purpose of carrying the day's ration, though, as already pointed out, this method of portage was avoided as far as possible as it proved wasteful when there had been no opportunity to sieve the hay.

Constructed of stout cord or cotton, in 4 inch mesh and bag shaped, it had a capacity of about 3/4 of a bushel and would hold from 7 to 8 lbs. of hay. When in use, it was secured to the picket line within easy reach of the animal, the latter prehending the hay through the meshes. One net was usually made to serve two horses tethered opposite each other to the picket line, by slinging it between them. But the method of securing the net to the picket line was far from perfect and was susceptible of improvement. The bottom of the net still rested on the ground and the horses, in pawing, frequently got the whole contrivance underfoot and destroyed it.

OVERHEAD SYSTEM This led Lieutenant-Colonel Tamblyn to devise an important modification in the method of its employment, namely the overhead system, a system to the importance of which the army authorities remained strangely indifferent. He advised that the picket line be strung at the usual height, but between posts 6 feet in height above the ground at intervals of 15 feet, and that a second line be strung between the tops of the posts, from which the nets should be suspended (see Figures 9.2, 9.3 and 14.4). He went so far as to state that this method had been proved to save not less than 2/5 of the hay ration over the old one, the balance being usually trampled underfoot, not to speak of the great destruction of the nets themselves, and in his report of August, 1917, strongly advocated the general enforcement of the overhead system. However, his advice was not heeded by the High Command, a remissness that was difficult to comprehend, though most unit commanders were quick to perceive the advantage and acted on it of their own accord. Where the nets were not forthcoming, he suggested that screens of chicken wire staked 3 feet in front of the picketing line would prevent the hay from being blown out of reach of the animals.

We have seen in the chapter on No. 1 Canadian Veterinary Hospital at Havre, that an alternative scheme was put into operation whereby hay cages were constructed of discarded baling wire as a provision of economy against wastage of the nets. These, of course, being non collapsible, could not have been made use of in the field, but Captain Vickers suggested that the nets could well be made of chain, by which wastage would have been reduced to a minimum. Captain Vickers also advocated that the picket lines be constructed of chain of suitable weight with tie rings at proper intervals, on the ground that they would give better satisfaction, would be less bulky to carry, and prove more economical than the usual ropes.

DISPOSAL OF MANURE In most units, the disposal of manure was effected in a systematic manner according to regulations. Dumps were established in certain fields to suit the convenience of the peasantry with due respect to proper distance from camp. The manure was piled in a regular manner to form immense heaps, shaped oblong with gabled top, ranging from 4 to 5 feet in height. To obviate the fly nuisance, the entire heap was covered with earth to a depth of about 8 inches, taken from a trench dug all about it. The manure left behind by the armies will be advantageous to the agricultural communities of the war zones, a valuable legacy, from which the surrounding lands will benefit for many years to come.

In some instances, during the summer times, the manure was raked back to a distance of from 15 to 20 feet, allowed to dry for a day or two and then set on fire, the fire smouldering continuously till everything was consumed. The smoke did not disturb the horses and helped to keep the flies away.

CLIPPING, GROOMING AND BLANKETING

DIFFERENCE OF OPINION ON CLIPPING The experience gained during the period covered by the war under actual campaigning conditions lasting five consecutive winters, one of which was of exceptional severity, enabled the veterinary services to arrive at definite conclusions with respect to the question of clipping. At the outset, there had been considerable diversity of opinion as to its advisability, a circumstance not to be wondered at when one remembers that those in whom the responsibility for decision was vested came from practically all parts of the world, comprising Australia, New Zealand, India, South Africa, the British Isles and eastern and western Canada, bringing with them ingrained ideas suitable to their local climatic conditions, which were not to be lightly thrown aside.

The average horsemaster is usually very set in his ideas on animal hygiene and it took the experience of more than one winter to break down many previously acquired convictions. Then again, each of the five winters had its own peculiarities so that what suited the conditions met with in 1914-1915 was incompatible with those of 1916-1917 or 1918-1919. Nobody foresaw the extraordinary cold that characterized the winter of 1916-1917, otherwise the order issued that season to clip the entire coat, and the completion of which was allowed to be prolonged well into the cold months regardless of stabling facilities, with disastrous results, would never have been promulgated, or at least would have been modified to trace-high clipping.

OBJECT OF CLIPPING The prime object of clipping was the prevention, by both direct and indirect means, of parasitic skin disease. When large numbers of horses were herded together, as perforce had to be the case, and with the mange parasite known to be dormant or lurking when not actively pathogenic, it necessitated the practice of every precaution calculated to render nugatory the conditions that were ever existent for the outbreak of dreaded skin disease.

In the first place, incipient mange is most difficult to detect in animals with thick, heavy coats, and under such conditions will often gain enough headway to become a focus for further spreading of the infestation before its presence is detected. Clipping exposed to view suspicious lesions and enabled the veterinary officers promptly to isolate and treat such cases. Secondly, it made the task of grooming infinitely easier and more attractive to the men and thereby prevented the spread of the disease in units where laxity in grooming had prevailed. On the other hand, Lieutenant-Colonel Evans observed that there was less tendency in the unclipped horse to contract mange than in the clipped one, and that clipping did not encourage naturally lazy grooms to take any extra pains with their work, for clipped horses were often found to be the dirtiest in the lines. A good man would groom a horse in 15 minutes when the coat was in condition, and from 15 to 20 minutes three times daily were usually allotted to the task.

GROOMING EQUIPMENT The only equipment regularly issued for grooming consisted of the body brush and dandy brush. The employment of the currycomb on the skin was prohibited in the British army, for fear that its use in a rough manner might result in cutting of the hair and irritation to the skin.

DIFFERENCE OF OPINION ON USE OF CURRYCOMB In the early days of the Fourth Division, before it had left England, a horsemaster from the Imperial Remount Department was sent to the camp at Bramshott to lecture on grooming. This officer declared that the currycomb was never intended to be used on the skin but that its purpose was solely to keep the body brush clean, despite the fact that in civil life the article is freely used for the former purpose by some of the best professional grooms. To this teaching, Major Edgett demurred with the result that the lectures were discontinued. Major Edgett held that the body brush issued by the army authorities was insufficient for stimulating the skin, the most important object to be aimed at in grooming. The currycomb is employed in the North West Mounted Police without any detriment to the animals. In any case, the article was not issued in France, though how the men, in its absence, were expected to effectually remove 'the mud that made the war famous' was never satisfactorily explained and the questionable restriction was generally ignored amongst the Canadians.

IMPROVISATION OF GROOMING CONTRIVANCES The Canadian is nothing if not able to improvise and necessity soon compelled him to originate a variety of contrivances to meet the pressing want. At the request of some of the officers of artillery units, the artificers in the engineers constructed a very serviceable 'rose' currycomb of corrugated metal which they supplied at Frcs. 2 (40 cents) apiece (Figure 14.2). These were paid for by funds of the battery canteens and were retailed to the men at the same price, the idea being to induce the latter to take proper care of them. Another very ingenious and serviceable comb was improvised out of crown-stoppers from empty beer bottles. Of these 12 were nailed to a block of wood made from the end of an ammunition box, cut oval-shaped and measuring 6 inches long by 3 1/2 inches wide and having a handstrap nailed on its back. The corrugated edges of the crown stoppers answered the same purpose as the more elaborate article made by the engineers. Still another type was constructed of superimposed empty shoepaste tins of graduated sizes nailed on to a similar block of wood. As a result of these activities on the part of the Canadians, the Deputy Director of Veterinary Services (Imperial) of the First Army made enquiry of Lieutenant-Colonel Cutcliffe in December, 1917, as to the types of improvisations made use of by them with a view to recommending the general use of currycombs throughout the Imperial armies. Several samples made by our men were forwarded to him.

IMPORTANCE OF GROOMING It was abundantly proven that neither the mange parasite nor the louse would thrive on animals that were well groomed, and it is not overstating a fact to say that mange only made its appearance in those units where indifferent grooming was permitted. But, the ever present problem was to get proper grooming carried out. No phase of animal management gave the veterinary officers more cause for anxiety than this particular

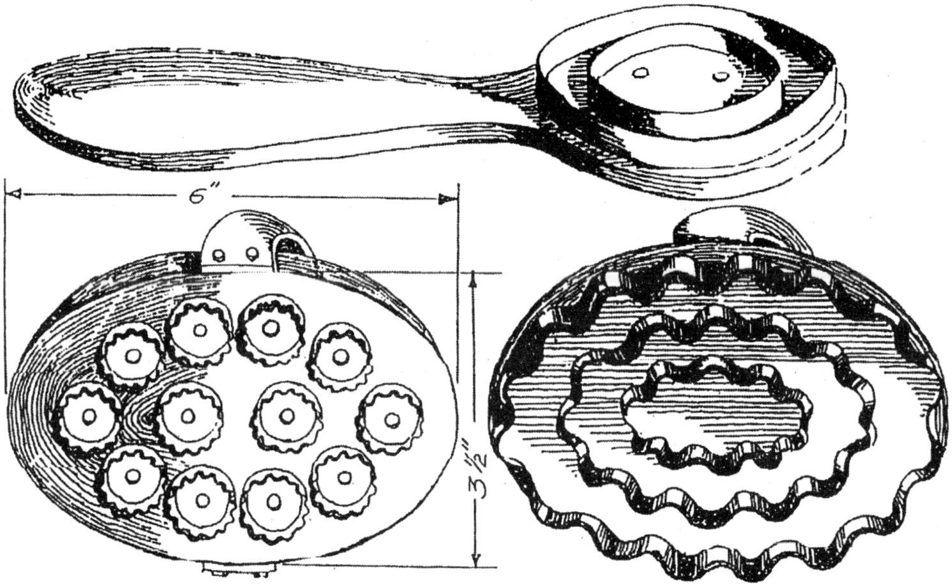

Figure 14.2. Curry combs improvised by Canadian troops, using lids of shoe paste tins (top), beer bottle caps (bottom left) and corrugated iron (bottom right). (*French Papers, NAC*)

matter. Its importance was a point most difficult to get either the unit officers in charge of horse lines or the men whose duty it was to do the actual work, to comprehend. Generally speaking, the average Canadian soldier was an indifferent horseman, omitting always the cavalrymen, not that the Imperials were much better off in this respect, for the bulk of all the new armies was made up of men who in that sense were 'not to the manner born'; by which is meant that the old-time professional horseman and groom, the man who always contrived to have his horses' coats shining with a marvelous gloss, was an individual rare to find and when he turned up was usually appropriated by the officers to tend to their own particular mounts, which were always well groomed and for that reason never required clipping.

EFFICIENCY Nevertheless, there were to be seen individuals scattered here and there throughout the different units and even some entire individual units who in this respect stood high in efficiency. For instance, so excellent was the care of the 75 animals belonging to No. 3 Company of the Fourth Divisional Trains, that over a period of 10 months it was unnecessary to evacuate a single animal. And at the end of the war might be seen men not only still tending to the horses originally allotted to them before leaving Canada but maintaining the latter in the pink of condition.

NEGLIGENCE The difficulties that confronted the veterinary officer over the grooming question dated from the start and continued till the end. In the early days on Salisbury Plain, Lieutenant-Colonel Neill found cause to complain at negligence and in June, 1915, at Dieppe, Captain Cutcliffe pointed out that at the time there was a shortage of grooming kits in the First Division and that officers and men were forced to provide themselves with a supply with their own money. Many and varied were the excuses always advanced for the lack of proper grooming. The most frequent one offered by unit officers was that owing to the time occupied in training that was constantly going on, together with the building of shelters and standings for the horses, there was not enough time available for properly attending to the stable duties. But, on the other hand, it was frequently noticed that unit officers would fail to satisfy themselves that the animals were clean before dismissing the men, and that they always managed to have the animals cleaned for a previously announced inspection. Too much attention was given to the furbishing of steel, and lack of interest arising from ignorance on the part of commanding officers was often responsible, for it was not an uncommon sight to see such officers when making their periodical inspections closely examine the metal parts of the harness but scarcely look at the horses.

CONTROL OF CLIPPING For the first three years the decision as to clipping and the time of year it should be undertaken remained more or less subject to the whim of officers commanding units and it was not till the cumulative evil results of the indiscriminate pursuit of this practice made themselves evident in the startling mortality that occurred amongst the horses during the awful winter of 1916-1917 that the High Command began to realize that the matter was properly one for coordinated control under the direction of the veterinary service. Thereafter, definite regulations were promulgated with a view to checking the evil. But even then unit commanders were allowed discretion in the matter as to the months of October and November, though after the last day of November clipping might only be undertaken with the sanction of the administrative veterinary officer of the division concerned.

REGULATION ENFORCED This regulation was strictly enforced. Only a few unit officers gave trouble to the extent of having their chargers' legs clipped and when one of the executive veterinary officers caused the clipping of 100 animals of the unit to which he was attached, in the month of March, without first having obtained permission from his administrative officer, the offense was considered serious enough to warrant his being returned to the base. In the previous year, clipping had been going on indiscriminately well into the winter and the war diaries of the administrative veterinary officers are teeming with entries foreboding and commenting on the evil results that might be expected or those that were already evident.

Had it been possible to ensure that every horse in the army could have been efficiently groomed, the necessity for clipping would never have arisen, but where it was not possible to attain that state of perfection, the alternative practice had to be resorted to. There was, however, a limit to which the practice could be pursued with safety. It was found that the best results in a climate like that of northern France were obtained by confining operations to the month of October, and in no instance to carry on the work later than the middle of November unless for actual mange.

WINTER CLIPPING - TRACE HIGH ONLY In some cases, clipping was absolutely essential during winter; for instance in the divisional trains, where the horses worked hard every day and sweated excessively and could not be properly cleaned without it. But in those cases clipping might only be done trace high, as a compromise between the need for warmth and the loss of condition that resulted from sweating when the whole coat was left on. In fact, it was noticed that there was usually a rapid improvement in condition in animals that were clipped trace high, by which method removal of the coat is confined to the areas of the skin which function most actively in sweating. When, during cold weather, a thick, heavy coat becomes wet from the skin outward through the process of sweating, water being a good conductor, there is rapid radiation of body heat with resultant tissue wastage. This loss may be compensated for if there is sufficient food available, but when there is no provision for an increase in the supply of the latter, the organism has to suffer. The same condition does not apply so forcibly to wetting of the coat by rain which takes place in a contrary direction. Many horsemasters who were prejudiced against any form of clipping were struck with the improvement that followed the trace high method when it was necessary to practise the latter during the winter months and thereafter became ardent adherents to the idea.

In no case might the legs of either riding or draft animals be clipped below the elbow or stifle after September 1st, but manes might be hogged.

RAPID GROWTH OF COAT It was noticed and recorded by both Lieutenant-Colonels Cutcliffe and Edgett that horses clipped in the early part of October had in 6 weeks' time grown exceptionally thick, heavy coats, which enabled them to withstand the severe weather conditions of January, February and March.

Lieutenant-Colonel Tamblyn was a strong advocate of the systematic control of clipping. He urged that the policy of permitting unit commanders to decide on such a question was erroneous as the matter was one of a purely veterinary nature to be properly decided by the Assistant Director of Veterinary Services at Corps Headquarters and by administrative veterinary officers of the divisions who were responsible for the health of the animals. Moreover, he was decidedly against the indiscriminate use of clipping machines by individual units. He pointed out that machines left with units were not cared for and not in use half the time and that none but men known to be experienced should be detailed to carry on the work.

Figure 14.3. Canadian Artillery watering their horses and mules in winter snow and ice, December, 1916. (*NAC PA 2321*)

CENTRAL CLIPPING STATIONS ESTABLISHED In September, 1917, he was enabled to put his scheme of central stations into operation, to the number of 3 to a division, one being placed at divisional headquarters, one in the artillery lines and one at the mobile section. Each station had 7 clipping machines and one sharpening machine, with a non-commissioned officer in charge and a second non-commissioned officer and 28 experienced men supplied from the units, the whole under the supervision of a veterinary officer. This detail could handle 6 horses per machine per day. Animals that arrived in a dirty condition were sent back to their units to be washed with soap and warm water the day before it was intended to send them again, so that the knives would not be damaged by dirt.

This system proved highly satisfactory, the advantages accruing being the avoidance of delay, the permitting of a thorough supervision, the maintenance of the machines in good condition, the affording of individual inspection for skin disease of each animal by a veterinary officer, and immediate isolation in case of necessity, and the disposal of every vestige of clipped hair by burning to prevent the spread of mange. Similar arrangements were also introduced in the Fourth Division by Lieutenant-Colonel Edgett.

NECESSITY OF ONE BLANKET It is scarcely necessary to point out that the growth of the coat on the approach of winter is nature's method of providing against inordinate radiation of body heat during the coming months of cold. But when the animals, living as they often did in the open and exposed to the elements, were suddenly deprived of their natural protection by clipping, provision had to be made to meet the changed conditions, otherwise they would have suffered greatly and the door been opened to disastrous consequences. It was realized that in view of the extreme sensibility of the horse's system to variations in temperature, it would be the height of folly to try to 'harden' it by exposure. Only by a considerable increase in forage allowance which may be used by the organism in producing more heat can the same result be obtained as by the natural coat or an artificial substitute. And where the situation required that every economy be practised in the use of forage, the only alternative to fall back on was the blanket. Accordingly, the blanket formed a very important adjunct to the equipment, but it was not allowed to be used until clipping had taken place in order that the animals might derive full benefit therefrom.

HEAVY MORTALITY FROM THE COLD Reference has been made to the extreme cold of the winter of 1916-1917 (Figure 14.3) and the heavy mortality that occurred that season. The mortality was particularly high at Vimy towards the end of the winter. Many of the horses had been in stables all winter and had been clipped in December and January, and then put in the open in mud knee-deep. The poor creatures would stand all day and night treading up and down till they sank from sheer exhaustion. So many from the different units perished that they had to be dumped into big holes, 24 in a lot. This mortality was believed by many of the veterinary officers to have been due to clipping. For instance, few horses died that winter in the 16th Battery where clipping had not been done, whilst many succumbed in the 15th Battery where clipping had been done.

But Lieutenant-Colonel Tamblyn, who through his position as administrative officer of his division could review the situation as a whole, whilst recognizing that late clipping had undoubtedly been a contributing factor, ascribed the wastage in the main to fast and heavy work, lack of supervision on the part of unit officers in feeding, and poor forage, all these factors working in conjunction with the inordinate cold. Moreover, one adversity seemed to follow close upon the heels of another, for to make matters worse, there was an outbreak of ulcerative stomatitis, a painful malady affecting the mouth, which prevented many animals from partaking of even the scant supply of food that was so urgently needed by the system for the maintenance of body heat if they were not to perish from the rigors of the cold. Lieutenant-Colonel Tamblyn pointed out that in some units which had not clipped, results exactly opposite to those that occurred in the two batteries mentioned above took place, as many as 80% of the animals being lost.[1]

HEAVY EVACUATIONS FOR DEBILITY An idea of the deplorable state of affairs may be gained from the following table of evacuations for debility which it was necessary to make from the units of one division alone, in the early months of 1917:

Feb. 25th	164 animals
March 28th	76 "
April 2nd	78 "
April 12th	60 "
April 21st	134 "

HORSES DEVOURING BLANKETS The low temperature of that winter gave rise to some remarkable circumstances. Though rations might at times be normal, which, however, was far from being the usual condition, so strong was the craving for anything that would serve as a means for producing body heat, that the horses actually nibbled one another's tails and ate the blankets. In some units 75% of the blankets would be used up in this manner, a new blanket put on at night being completely devoured by morning. In fact, the issue of blankets could not keep up with the destruction. Resort was sometimes had to numnahs, but even these were eaten.

On one occasion, some of the men whose love of their horses moved them to compassion, gave up of their own scant supply of blankets, one apiece, though they were sleeping in barns without straw or fires. The blankets had disappeared in the morning! They then tried tarpaulins; the horses started in on these, but not finding them palatable, desisted and the situation was saved for a couple of weeks till the weather got warmer. As a result of this wasteful experience with blankets, Lieutenant-Colonel Edgett recommended that they be sewn in front so that the animals could not pick up the loose ends, whilst Lieutenant Colonel Tamblyn suggested that they should be issued in at least two sizes, pointing out that the one size made to fit the larger animals hung loosely on the smaller, thereby affording the latter a better opportunity to lay hold of the same than if they had been made to fit tightly round the neck.

Lieutenant-Colonel Evans pointed out that the very thick hair which grew on unrugged animals and which the grooms found such a heartbreaking task to keep clean, did not grow on either horses or mules which were kept continuously rugged, day and night.

During the march into Germany, some trouble was experienced in getting the unit officers and men to make use of blankets. For some unexplained reason the impression prevailed that this very necessary article of equipment was not to be taken along and many blankets were discarded and left lying on the ground. It was not till repeated representations were made to the unit officers that attention was paid to the matter.

STABLING AND STANDINGS - BACK TO NATURE Generally speaking, all units, when at the front, picketed their horses in the open, both summer and winter (Figure 14.4). Only in certain billets well to the rear and in veterinary

Figure 14.4. Picket lines of the Fort Garry Horse, in the open, June 1916. Note that no overhead line for haynets has been strung. (*NAC PA 51*)

hospitals and remount depots at the bases was general stabling accommodation obtainable, though even up near the front, buildings in varying degrees of damage from shellfire were made use of. Officers, particularly, endeavored to secure stalls for their chargers in civilian stables though this procedure at all times gave concern to the veterinary service on account of the risk of contagion in buildings which could not be adequately controlled. The possibility of buildings harboring infection was always a source of anxiety. Even during the march of the troops to Germany and after their arrival in the latter country, the veterinary service had to be particularly alert to guard against the more dangerous disorders. It was ascertained that foot-and-mouth disease was prevalent at Libois and Lieutenant-Colonel Cutcliffe, upon inspecting 1027 animals belonging to civilians in Bonn, found amongst them one case of farcy and 70 of mange. The former was ordered to be destroyed and the latter all quarantined and their stables disinfected.

AVOIDING THE MUD In the open, the problem that always presented itself was the provision of solid standings in an effort to avoid the awful mud which caused a great deal of mud fever[2] and scratches[3]. More often than not unit commanders, neglecting to consult the veterinary officers, had these constructed at too great a distance from the roads, the intervening space in wet weather soon becoming churned into a veritable quagmire, sometimes to such an extent as to be rendered impossible. In such cases, it became necessary to construct roads leading to the standings, thereby using up enormous quantities of material not to speak of labor on the part of the engineers. All this resulted in a lot of animal wastage which might have been avoided had the veterinary service had direction of such matters. Standings were generally constructed of brick salvaged from buildings destroyed by shellfire. One layer of brick was useless. It was found best to provide a foundation of 6 inches of limestone, with which the country abounded, topped with a coating of 4 inches of fine slag to level the same. On this, the brick were laid edgewise and filled in with fine slag and water, the whole forming a more or less solid mass, which, however, often required repairing. But it was found that some horses would not lie down on cold brick and those that did continually received abrasions on their necks, fetlocks and hocks by coming in contact with the sharp edges of the brick. Others would go to sleep standing and, falling, bruise their legs and bodies. Consequently, it was decided at one of the weekly conferences of the administrative veterinary officers that flooring of earth or slag was preferable to stone or brick.

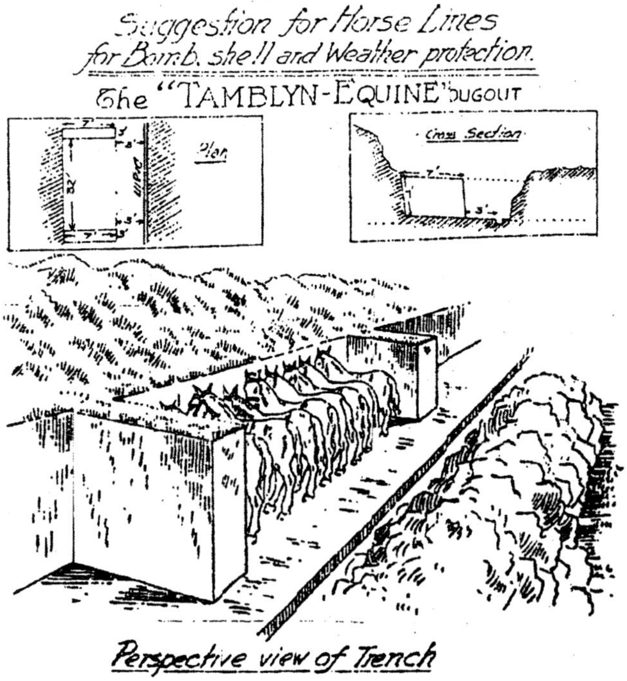

Figure 14.5. Trench to shelter horses from shell blasts. Traverses provide protection from blasts down the trench. (*French Papers, NAC*)[4]

PROTECTION FROM SHELLFIRE AND BOMBS

CASUALTIES Towards the summer of 1917, the casualties from long distance shellfire and night bombing assumed such proportions that a general order was promulgated requiring the erection of protections for the horses around their standings. How necessary this was may be judged from a single instance where one of the sections of the ammunition column of the Third Division, three-quarters of an hour after it had moved into a new location and before it had time to construct shelters, sustained casualties to 110 animals, all of which were either killed outright or had to be destroyed from the effects of two bombs dropped in their midst. The bombs used on that occasion were known as 'razor' bombs, a type which in exploding, cut a wide swath as a scythe does grass, the injuries in nearly every instance being about the legs.

TRENCHES FOR HORSES In constructing shelters, advantage was often taken of sunken roads or old abandoned trenches which were widened to about 12 feet at the top and 6 to 8 feet at the bottom. A stretch of trench 250 feet long would comfortably hold from 70 to 80 animals. Entrances were made alongside to minimize risk and traverses were constructed at intervals of 50 or 60 feet. Where animals were picketed in the open, anti-bomb traverses of turf and earth were erected round the standings (Figure 14.5). Regulations required that these, to be effective, should have a height of 6 feet and be 7 1/2 feet thick at the base and 3 feet thick at the top.

DUGOUTS FOR HORSES Lieutenant-Colonel Tamblyn suggested the adoption of dugouts which would not only act as a protection against bombs but also against severe climatic conditions. He showed that such standings could be constructed in practically any area and easily be roofed and camouflaged (Figure 14.6). This officer also suggested the utilization of shell holes by advancing transport as a means of protection. The idea was to square the shell holes, as depicted in the accompanying plan (Figure 14.7), so as to hold two animals each. This means of protection would not only scatter the animals, which was a very important point, but it would also prevent them from being wounded by fragments. A direct hit could only be fatal to the one or two occupants, instead of to a large number as was frequently the case when the animals were picketed closely together.

Figure 14.6. Plan for roofing and camouflage of horse trenches. (*French Papers, NAC*)[4]

SPACIOUS DOG'S DUGOUT Whilst on this subject, mention shall be made of a remarkable instance of animal intelligence exhibited in the summer of 1918 by a dog belonging to the 15th Battery, Sixth Brigade, C.F.A. The dog was of the old English sheepdog breed, a race well known for its sagacity and, with the exception of the poodle, reputed to be the quickest of all at understanding and obeying human signals. There had been some increasingly frequent shelling in the neighborhood of the horse lines and the order had gone forth to dig the horses in. As usual, the animal was much in evidence as when anything out of the ordinary was going on and after the men had completed their labors, it proceeded to dig its own dugout and not only that but with the entrance in correct position away from the direction of the Huns. It dug into the face of a bank, 2 or 3 feet downwards in a sloping direction till it reached chalk which barred its further progress, or there is no knowing how far into the ground it might have continued to tunnel. Afterwards, whenever the shells began to come over in that direction it ran to its funkhole and remained there till quiet and safety again prevailed.

PROTECTION FROM INJURIES TO THE FEET

DANGER FROM NAILS A matter of the greatest concern to the veterinary service, throughout the war was the frequency of injury to the horses from P.U.N., a term used to imply 'picked up nail', as well as from the adventitious casting of shoes.

CAUSE Aside from the prevalence of the actual causative factor, a prolific predisposing cause was the evil practice on the part of many of the shoeing smiths in removing the hard, horny flakes of the sole, a practice that was very difficult to correct. An astonishingly large number of nails was to be found lying about everywhere at all points frequented by the troops, but particularly in the vicinity of ammunition dumps and places where packing cases were opened in large numbers. The average man in opening a case gave little thought to the potentiality for evil that reposed in the carelessly littered nail; to him a nail was a superfluous article to be got rid of in the most expeditious manner possible, viz. by casting it from him, whilst to the horse it became a lurking menace that might easily lead to its death. Another way that nails got scattered was by the men throwing ashes from burned boxes outside the doors of their billets and still another way was by the cooks burning wood from brokenup boxes in their field kitchens, without withdrawing the nails, and as the kitchens passed along the highways with open dampers a trail of nails was left behind.

Lieutenant-Colonel Edgett on examining the main road between Château de la Haie and Carency, estimated there was a derelict nail to every lineal yard of road which impelled him to impress on the authorities the importance of unit commanders realizing the seriousness of this state of affairs to the end that steps might be taken to correct the evil. In like manner, Captain W.W. Forsyth detailed a non-commissioned officer and two men to pick up nails and other articles liable to cause injury to the feet on the road between his mobile section at Carency and Villers-au-Bois station. In 2 1/2 hours, the following articles were picked up:

Nails (wire and iron)	200
Small arms ammunition cartridges	46

Numerous pieces of tin, metal, wire and worn-out shoes.

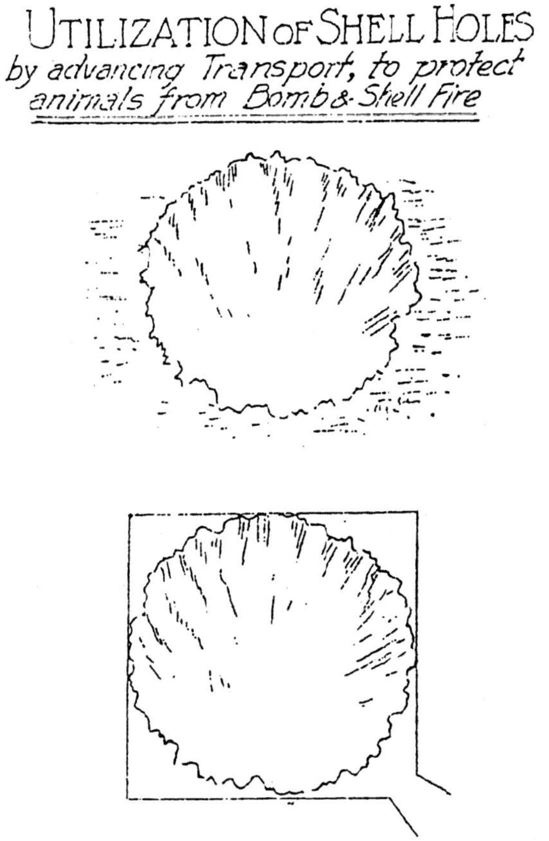

Figure 14.7. Modification of shell-holes to shelter horses near the front. (*French Papers, NAC*)[4]

NAIL GATHERING PATROLS Regular patrols were inaugurated for the sole purpose of picking up nails in order to reduce casualties from this cause. Strange to relate, 80% of nail pricks took place in the hindfeet and the reason for the relative immunity for the forefeet was found, upon investigation, to be quite remarkable. Nails mostly lay flat on the surface of the mud, and in that position were not likely to penetrate the foot. The forefoot of the horse, in the act of coming down on and being withdrawn from a nail, caused the latter to assume a perpendicular position and the hindfoot of the animal being almost immediately afterwards implanted at the same spot, the nail was 'picked up' by the latter and driven further into the tissues at each succeeding step.

Shoes Torn Off At Albert, in October, 1916, the mud was of such a sticky character that it required great exertion to withdraw the feet, which caused a great many shoes to be pulled off with considerable portions of the wall. Fascined roads and tracks were responsible for a good many animals losing their shoes.

Protective Shoeing Different forms of protective shoeing against 'picked up' nails and bruised soles were attempted. Insertions of double thickness of biscuit tin were of no avail, nor was leather any more successful. Lieutenant-Colonel Tamblyn's device of corrugated iron, pounded flat and cut out to the shape of the foot with a posterior projection to be afterwards turned up, punched and applied between the sole and the shoe, the intervening space being first packed with tow, proved very effective though attended with certain disadvantages. Dirt tended to collect between the foot and the plate and becoming very hard led to bruising of the sole and consequent lameness; and the depression made to receive the frog would not fit all frogs, making it necessary to cut the latter. Animals suffering from P.U.N. wounds had similar plates applied out on the ground surface of the shoe and rendered detachable for dressing by screw calks. Animals so fitted continued to work with no bad results. It was suggested that plates of a metal somewhat lighter than iron, cut and numbered according to the different sizes of shoes, be supplied from the base to save the time and trouble of improvising the same at the front. As a result, two sizes of such plates were supplied from the base.

German Crippling Weapon A 4 pointed steel spike, this diabolical contrivance was scattered broadcast by the Germans on Vimy Ridge. Its purpose was to cripple horses and men. It varied from 3 to 8 inches in length and no matter how it was thrown to the ground, it always rested with one spike upright. A few casualties resulted.

Means of Identification

Linen Tags When animals were shipped from one point to another, as for instance from the front to hospital, it was very important that they should bear some mark of identification. The authorities provided the mobile sections with linen tags for this purpose but these did not prove a success in that they were frequently destroyed.

Metal Tags The substitution of other means was, throughout the war, left to the devices of the officers in command of the field units who had to improvise metal tags which could have been manufactured cheaply, quickly and more suitably at the base. Three types were employed at No. 1 Canadian Veterinary Hospital, and a fourth, of German origin, was picked up at Bonn by Captain Vickers and suggested by him as being suitable for use on the head gear of animals evacuated from mobile sections. No. 1 was used to wrap around the check strap of the head gear, No. 2 to attach to the buckle of the same, and No. 3 (split) for attachment to the tail, it being bent round a few plaited hairs. The small one, No. 4, had a pin at one end and a button at the other. When bent over and the pin point made to enter the button, the former came against a piece of hard metal within the latter, which caused it to be bent inside so that it could not be withdrawn and the tag remained firmly clamped.

CHAPTER 15

AID EXTENDED BY HUMANE AND KINDRED SOCIETIES[1]

It has been considered advisable to treat this subject rather fully for it is felt that the people at home who so generously gave to the cause of the war horses are entitled to be freely informed as to the result of the action taken for the accomplishment of their beneficent purpose. Not only they, but also the members of the Canadian Army Veterinary Corps, who considered themselves peculiarly concerned with the matter, will be afforded an opportunity to satisfy a justifiable curiosity which was continually being roused but never satisfied throughout the whole period of the war. Strange as it may seem the members of the corps were never kept posted on these particular events. There is an entry in Major Saunders' diary, made at Bruay on August 25th, 1917, to the effect that at a conference of the administrative veterinary officers of the Canadian corps the question was raised by Major Evans as to what was being done with the funds which it was well known were being collected in Canada for the aid of the veterinary service, but no information was available.

The story is not as edifying as one might wish to see unfolded, for unhappily, on the one hand there was exhibited a certain amount of misdirected zeal and on the other a blighting influence cast by the Imperial veterinary authorities. The latter lent themselves to what many have regarded as an ill-judged interference with a well organized effort to give effect to the endeavour of a number of people at home to back up the Canadian veterinary service in the field. They could hardly have been aware of the extensive Canadian interests involved, otherwise it is difficult to believe they would have adopted a policy by which they made themselves instrumental in thwarting the kind intentions of many of our people in the home land.

The question of supplementary aid from outside sources remained from the beginning until the end a sore point within the Canadian veterinary service. How this unfortunate state of affairs came about will now be related, but before proceeding any further, it must be frankly admitted, in justice to all concerned, that there are two sides to every question and that it has only been found possible in these pages to state the Canadian viewpoint.

The two important societies in London devoted to the welfare of animals are: The Royal Society for the Prevention of Cruelty to Animals, located at 10b Jermyn Street, S.W., and Our Dumb Friends League with offices at 58 Victoria Street, S.W. Both societies command the support of many people of prominence, but sad to relate, do not, or did not at that time, carry on their great and good work in harmonious relationships. It would be discourteous and entirely out of place in a work of this nature to enter into a discussion of the pros and cons that have brought about this unfortunate difference, for the Canadian Army Veterinary Corps will ever entertain a deep regard and gratitude for the unstinted and splendid assistance it received from both organizations throughout the whole period of the war. But to afford a clear insight into the subject under review, it will be impossible to avoid stating a few facts, introduced, be it understood, solely by way of explanation and without the slightest wish to take sides.

There was a third society in London, named the Animal Defence Society, which also conducted a war fund for army horses and which received valuable monetary aid from Canadian sources, chiefly from Montreal, but as far as known, did not extend its ministrations to Canadian horses or to the Canadian Army Veterinary Corps. How the Montreal branch of this society eventually became interested in the Veterinary Corps will be related further along in this chapter.

It should be borne in mind that in the early stages of the war there was no organized effort in Canada on a noteworthy scale to lend support to the equine interests of the purely Canadian overseas forces, excepting that of the horsebreed societies. The money that was sent to Europe in the early days to help in alleviating the sufferings of the war horses was not raised under projects that contemplated limiting its disbursement solely for the benefit of the horses of the Canadian forces. The underlying motive that inspired the collection of the considerable total amount subscribed was a sympathetic regard on the part of Canadian horse lovers for the welfare of all dumb creatures which had no choice but sacrifice themselves in the cause of human liberty, irrespective of their ownership. At the same time, there was a very general understanding that Canadian units would be made the chief beneficiaries.

Unfortunately, through lack of information of prevailing conditions, want of both cooperation and systematic administration together with expenditure that was not always judicious, a good deal of the well-meant effort was dissipated without the end aimed at being achieved. Looking backward in the light of the experiences of the Veterinary Corps and remembering the old adage that charity properly begins at home, we can appreciate how infinitely more helpful and satisfactory it would have been had the effort been directed into a single channel by a country-wide coordinated movement in the establishment and administration of a purely Canadian fund for the benefit of the animals in the service of the Canadian forces. Such a fund, recognized by the Canadian military authorities, would perforce have received official sanction by the British Army Council to the immeasurable benefit of Canadian units.

THE BLUE CROSS FUND

Our Dumb Friends League is a society which exists for the encouragement of kindness to animals. In 1912, at the time of the Balkan War, it extended its activities and organized, for the benefit of the horses employed in that conflict, a fund to which it applied the highly appropriate name 'Blue Cross'. When the Great War broke out, this society quickly realized that there was great scope for important work in the prevention of suffering in animals. It proceeded to organize its forces and vigorously setting to work, became throughout the war, the means of alleviating untold suffering to thousands of dumb creatures. Its intimate relationship with Canadians came about in the following manner:

Soon after the arrival of the first Canadian contingent in England, Captain J.R.J. Duhault, one of the veterinary officers, becoming aware of the readiness of the society to extend aid, applied for the donation of a light cart to enable him to get about more expeditiously in the discharge of his duties. This request had been shortly before preceded by another for an ambulance for one of the combatant units. Both requests were promptly acceded to and an order placed for the construction of the two vehicles. About the same time, Mrs. E. Hathaway Turnbull, a woman of American birth married to a member of the well-known New Brunswick family of that name, and one of the 'livewire' members of the committee of the Blue Cross Fund, hearing of the plight of the horses of the first contingent at Salisbury Plain, procured a letter of introduction from General Sir Ian Hay to Major-General Alderson, C.B., and motored thence to see herself the actual conditions. According to Mrs. Turnbull, Major-General Alderson remarked: *I am more interested in what you can do for my horses than for my men; the latter are provided for but not the former*. Immediately on the return of this woman to London, and at her request, the Blue Cross sent everything that had been asked for.

On January 2nd, 1915, Lieutenant-Colonel Neill interviewed the officials of the society with respect to further donations of much needed supplies. It was then decided that inasmuch as Captain Duhault in the meantime had been moved from his former sphere of duty to one where the cart would not be needed, the latter, together with the ambulance, should be sent to No. 2 Canadian Veterinary Hospital at Shorncliffe, where both vehicles arrived the following July. The good news quickly spread amongst the other Canadian units and soon there was a regular stream of requests for aid pouring in on the Blue Cross Fund.

In the meanwhile, the society was casting about for ways and means to enable it to keep pace with the rapid growth of the demands made upon its resources. It began appealing for monetary help by advertising in the overseas editions of the Times and Daily Mail and also in a few of the American newspapers, receiving at the same time several valuable 'write-ups' at the hands of the editorial staffs. It should be mentioned at this juncture that the society already had regular subscribers in Canada, mostly amongst Britishers who had come here before the war, but also from a few Torontonians. In response to the special call, the first person to help was Mrs. D.L. McCarthy of Toronto, who, with characteristic promptitude, set to work to organize a local branch of the Blue Cross Fund. The next were Miss Dora Kitte, Mrs. Lilian Guy, Mrs. Hewlings and Mrs. Dennis Cox of Victoria; Mrs. Blackwood Wileman, of Cowichan, B. C.; Mrs. Coombes of Winnipeg; Miss Louise Kerr of Toronto and Mrs. Tuxford of Moose Jaw, all of whom organized local branches of the fund, whereby important sums of money were collected. Numerous women and men in other parts of Canada came to the fore and soon there was in the hands of the parent fund in London a sum which by the end of 1918 had risen to no less a total than $26,684.50.[2]

The above sum was by far the largest of any subscribed in Canada for the purpose that passed through any one channel. It is difficult to believe that the donors for the most part did not hope, nay intend, that their contributions should be administered for the benefit of the horses in the service of the Canadian troops or to assist the Canadian Army Veterinary Corps in the discharge of its duties, though it is but fair to add that the officials of the fund, when soliciting contributions, made no statement, either implied or expressed, to lead the public to such conclusion. We know, indeed, that the intent was uppermost in the minds of the S.P.C.A. of Regina.[3] In any case, the Canadian veterinary officers looked upon the Canadian subscriptions in the light of a resource upon which it was intended they should have a prior claim, a feeling that was loyally recognized by the custodians of the same. Yet this entirely legitimate, and under the circumstances, very natural aspiration, was in large measure frustrated by the unsympathetic attitude of the Imperial veterinary authorities.

It has more than once been pointed out in this work that the Canadian forces, as long as they were stationed in England, practically enjoyed a full measure of 'home rule', but that as soon as they went to France they became, to all intents and purposes, part of the Imperial forces and under the control of the latter. During the whole period of the war, all Canadian units and particularly the Canadian Army Veterinary Corps, whilst in England, were subjected to no interference in seeking aid from the Blue Cross and other societies, and of this they did not fail to take every advantage. No attempt was made by the Imperial authorities at any time to say them nay. Until the latter part of 1916, veterinary officers and units in France continued to receive from this and other societies all they asked for without a word of formal dissent on the part of the Imperial authorities.

All sorts of appliances and materials, consisting of bandages, medicines, horseblankets, pads, clipping machines, portable forges, protective boots, brushes, stable utensils, veterinary instruments, etc., were provided, not only for the horses of the Canadian troops training in England, but for those serving with Canadian units in France. Besides the cart and ambulance already referred to, two other ambulances were forthcoming, one going to the Fifth Division at Witley and the other to the Second Canadian Mobile Section in France towards the close of the war, and as we shall see, even a motor ambulance was offered.

Amongst the units that profited from time to time in this manner were:

No. 1 Canadian Veterinary Hospital at Havre
No. 2 Canadian Veterinary Hospital at Shorncliffe
All the Canadian mobile veterinary sections
All the regiments of cavalry, both active and in reserve
Several battalions of infantry, both active and in reserve
Several battalions of engineers
Several batteries of field artillery
Several divisional trains
Several battalions of machine gunners
Several companies of the Forestry Corps
Several of the lesser units.

It would be impossible adequately to estimate the enormous benefit that resulted to Canadian units from the help almost lavishly bestowed on them by this very estimable organization. It can only be said that Canadians will ever hold in tender memory the kindly ministrations of the Blue Cross.

For reasons best known to themselves, the Imperial veterinary authorities refused to 'recognize' the Blue Cross Fund, and there came a time when they began to take cognizance of its activities and to decide upon a policy of suppression with all the means in their power. At first a circular letter was sent to the veterinary officers in the field forbidding them to accept unauthorized assistance. But the officers of combatant units, not having been included in the admonition, continued to 'carry on'. The Imperial authorities then adopted a more comprehensive method of stopping the 'traffic' by issuing a General Routine Order, first under date of January 21st, 1917, and by amendment on November 29th, 1918, applicable to all alike couched in the following terms: *As full provision is made for the supply to all units of veterinary medicines, necessaries and equipment through Base and Advanced Depots of Veterinary Stores, articles for the treatment of animals will only be obtained through this channel or on the authority of the Director of Veterinary Services. Applications to the Royal Society for the Prevention of Cruelty to Animals or to other societies of a similar nature, firms, or private persons, are prohibited.*

Likewise, at the Canadian Veterinary Hospital at Havre, an order was issued on January 11th, 1918, worded as follows: *Officers, non-commissioned officers and men of the Army Veterinary Corps are forbidden to make application to private individuals, firms, societies or friends for veterinary stores of any description.*

The wording of the first of the above-mentioned orders did not constitute an accurate statement of the facts. It was far from the truth to state that "full provision was made for the supply of necessaries and equipment" as understood by the Canadian veterinary officers. The instruments alone, as supplied by the Imperial authorities, were considered by our officers to be inadequate and antiquated and time and again when requests were sent in for something more up-to-date and serviceable, no response was forthcoming. For instance, from beginning to end, there was an almost entire lack of proper dental instruments such as Canadian veterinarians are familiar with and which they regard as absolutely essential to the proper carrying on of their work.

Practically the whole body of Canadian veterinary officers looked upon this action of the Imperial veterinary authorities as high-handed and an unwarrantable interference with their personal liberty. They had amongst them individuals possessing scientific attainments superior to any to be found amongst officers of the Imperial Veterinary Corps (see letter of the Secretary of War concerning Lieutenant-Colonel Evans in the chapter on The Administrative Officer), and did not relish being treated like a lot of untutored school lads.[4] Nearly all ignored the order and continued to solicit and receive instruments and other much needed paraphernalia till the end of the war.

The methods by which it was sought to restrain these activities are both interesting and amusing. On one occasion, at No. 1 Canadian Veterinary Hospital, one of the officers was anxious to demonstrate the application of an improved suture for which a fully curved needle was indispensable. Curved needles at that time were not available as part of the veterinary equipment supplied by the authorities. The officer, undeterred by the awful menace of Imperial wrath, wrote to the Blue Cross for a supply and (for obvious reasons) instructed that the package should be addressed to 'The officer in charge of surgical work'. Within a few days the package arrived and was deposited by the mail carrier on the desk of the commanding officer, who, be it added, was not privy to the transaction. A few minutes later, in walked the Deputy Director of Veterinary Services (Imperial) on his regular tour of inspection and upon espying the package bearing a Blue Cross label, immediately demanded to be informed of the identity of the culprit. The commanding officer, blissfully ignorant of the matter, was unable to satisfy him, whereupon he proceeded to confiscate the articles by putting them in his own pocket!

Two letters, written a week apart by the Director of Veterinary Services (Imperial) to the Director of Veterinary Services and Remounts (Canadian) in March, 1916, threw a flood of light on the mental workings of the Imperial veterinary authorities. The letters concerned three horsedrawn ambulances one of which had been offered by the Blue Cross and two others, the cost of which had been defrayed by the humane societies of the cities of Kingston and Hamilton. Respecting the former, it was announced to Colonel Neill in the first letter that it would not be required in France, the reason given being that the Blue Cross Society was not recognized by the War Office! In the second letter, it was stated that arrangements would be made to have the two vehicles presented by the two Canadian societies placed in the service of the First and Third Canadian Divisions, and the enquiry was made whether Colonel Neill could arrange for an ambulance for the Second Canadian Division or whether it should be left to the Imperial veterinary authorities to supply it, being again remarked that the Blue Cross ambulance was not required. Here we are treated to the extraordinary spectacle of the Imperial authorities asking Colonel Neill to find an ambulance for one of the Canadian divisions and at the same time refusing to permit him to make use of one which had virtually been paid for by our own people at home, simply because the channel through which it was proffered had not been 'recognized' by the War Office.

Mr. H.P. Biggar, representative in Europe of Canadian Archives, whilst on an official visit to Paris, had occasion to pass through Havre and incidentally paid a visit to the Canadian veterinary hospital. Being of an observant nature, he noticed a certain lack of much needed requisites, particularly in the operating theatre. On his return to London, he brought this fact to the attention of the Blue Cross officials, who, with their usual promptitude, responded in the manner disclosed in the following correspondence:

From Mr. Arthur J. Coke, Secretary, Blue Cross Fund, to Major Richards, Officer Commanding No. 1 Canadian Veterinary Hospital, Havre:

58 Victoria Street
London, S.W.
December 30th, 1917.

I have had a visit from Mr. H.P. Biggar of the Canadian government, and I understand from him that you are in need of veterinary requisites for your hospital. I need hardly say that the committee of the Blue Cross Fund will be most pleased to offer you all the help in their power on behalf of the horses, and if you would let me hear from you the best means by which we can assist, the matter shall have our immediate attention.

From Major Richards to the Secretary, Blue Cross Fund:

Havre,
January 5th, 1918.

Your communication of the 30th December received. I wish to thank you most sincerely for your kind suggestions. I am in communication with Brigadier-General Neill, our Director of Veterinary Services in England, regarding requirements at this hospital and shall ask him to communicate directly with you.

Major Richards transmitted to Brigadier-General Neill copies of the foregoing correspondence and suggested in connection therewith that it would be a great advantage to the hospital to have an operating table at an estimated cost of two thousand Francs (approximately $400.00) together with an up-to-date set of American dental instruments. He mentioned that officers then serving with his unit had purchased with their own funds various instruments and appliances necessary for use there which could not be obtained from government sources and that those instruments were in constant use, and asked that the cost be refunded.

In the meantime, the Blue Cross forwarded the cheque to Major Richards, who, not wanting to jeopardize his position as commanding officer of what was virtually an Imperial veterinary hospital in the face of explicit orders issued by the Imperial authorities, reluctantly felt constrained to return it.

From Major Richards to General Sir Leslie Rundle, G.C.B.

Havre, January 12th, 1918.

I am in receipt of your letter of the 5th inst. forwarding by cheque the generous donation of £100.0.0 from the Blue Cross Fund for the use of No. 1 Canadian Veterinary Hospital, at the instance of the Canadian High Commissioner.

To comply with regulations and orders, I very much regret to have to appear ungrateful in returning your cheque, which is enclosed herewith, with the request that the amount may be forwarded and made payable to Brigadier-General W.J. Neill, the Head of the Canadian Overseas Services, who will doubtless see that it is properly applied.

Kindly convey my sincere thanks to the Blue Cross Fund for the interest shown by the society in the veterinary hospital under my command.

From General Sir Leslie Rundle, G.C.B., Honorary Treasurer, Blue Cross Fund, to Captain A.E. Frape:

88 Victoria St.,
London, S.W.
January 17th, 1918.

I understand that Mr. Biggar has spoken to you today with reference to a cheque for £100.0.0 which my committee wish expended on No. 1 Canadian Veterinary Hospital at Havre. This cheque was sent to Major Richards, Commanding Officer, but he returned it saying it should be forwarded to Brigadier-General W. J. Neill, head of the Canadian veterinary service. I should like to explain that the objects of the Blue Cross are to supplement the issue of veterinary supplies of the different governments, and as we were given to understand that No. 1 Canadian Veterinary Hospital was in need of a particular kind of operating table, and also that there were several things that could be purchased for the extra comfort of the horses, my committee granted this sum. I understand from Mr. Biggar you will see that this amount is spent on this particular hospital for the benefit of the horses.

From Captain A.E. Frape to Mr. Arthur J. Coke:

Oxford Circus House,
London W.,
January 18th, 1918.

I beg to acknowledge receipt of your cheque for the sum of £100. On behalf of General Neill, who is at present in France, I return sincere thanks for this generous gift, and assure you that it will be devoted to the requirements of No. 1 Canadian Veterinary Hospital, at Havre, for veterinary appliances and equipment. Whilst in France, General Neill will visit No. 1 Canadian Veterinary Hospital and will no doubt acquaint himself with their wants and will, on his return, be in a position to expend the money for actual requirements. In the meantime, the cheque will be placed in safe custody awaiting General Neill's return from France.

In another letter to Brigadier-General Neill, Major Richards asked whether some of the money that was being collected throughout Canada for the Blue Cross, could not be diverted to the Canadian veterinary hospital where it could be utilized to the best advantage and enable the officers to pursue bacteriological and research work.

It is gratifying to know that Captains Savage and Hunter, the two officers who had devoted their own money to the purchase of instruments and other much needed laboratory equipment, were duly reimbursed from this donation.

The crowning act of official apathy was the rejection by the Imperial authorities of the offer of a motor ambulance for the Canadian veterinary service. In the chapter on the Mobile Sections, it has been pointed out how much the need of a quick ambulance service had been felt by the Canadian veterinary service.

In February, 1918, Brigadier-General Neill took up the matter in the following manner:

From Brigadier-General Neill to the Secretary, Blue Cross Fund:

Oxford Circus House,
London W.
February 4th, 1918.

The Canadian corps at the front have requested me to enquire if it is possible for you to furnish us with a motor ambulance for carrying horses, for service in France.

The committee of the Blue Cross Fund held a meeting and authorized the construction of such a vehicle at a cost of £1000 (approximately $5000). Brigadier-General Neill then wrote to the Quartermaster-General stating that he had received a notice from the Blue Cross to the effect that it was willing to provide a motor ambulance for two horses, for the use of the Canadian forces in France, and asking to be informed whether there would be any objection to the acceptance of such a gift. He went on to state that such an ambulance would be of great service under the new organization of the corps and would be the means of saving a great number of horses as no delay would take place in moving them to the clearing depot. He anticipated that permission would have to be obtained from the authorities in France before such a vehicle would be allowed to be moved over there.

The Quartermaster-General lost no time in advising the Secretary of War of the proposed donation and that it was desired to accept the same if the vehicle could be used to advantage in the field and to employ it in connection with the work of the Canadian veterinary service.

How the generous offer was treated may be appreciated from the following letter which the Quartermaster-General found necessary to write to the secretary of the Blue Cross Fund:

Argyll House
London, W.
May 2nd, 1918

I am directed to inform you that the Field Marshal Commanding-in-Chief British Armies in France, much appreciates the generous offer of your committee to supply a motor horse ambulance to the Canadian forces in the field, but that same cannot be accepted, as all arrangements have been made or are being met in this respect. I can assure you that the Canadian authorities appreciate very much, and regret under the circumstances, being unable to accept the very liberal offer of the Blue Cross committee.

It is to be regretted that our own Quartermaster-General did not push this matter to the limit and insist that the Imperial authorities should change their attitude in a matter that so intimately concerned our people both at home and at the front.

The ambulance, which in the meantime had been constructed and paid for with funds which had been provided by people in Canada, lay in London unutilized. However, the incident seems to have aroused the Imperial authorities from their apathetic attitude for soon afterwards a motor ambulance was actually supplied by them from their 'authorized' source, namely, the Royal Society for the Prevention of Cruelty to Animals.

It is interesting to note that even six months later, the R.S.P.C.A. was advertising in the British press for contributions to enable it to supply motor ambulances. Herewith is reproduced an appeal that appeared in the columns of the London Morning Post on November 13th, 1918 (Figure 15.1).

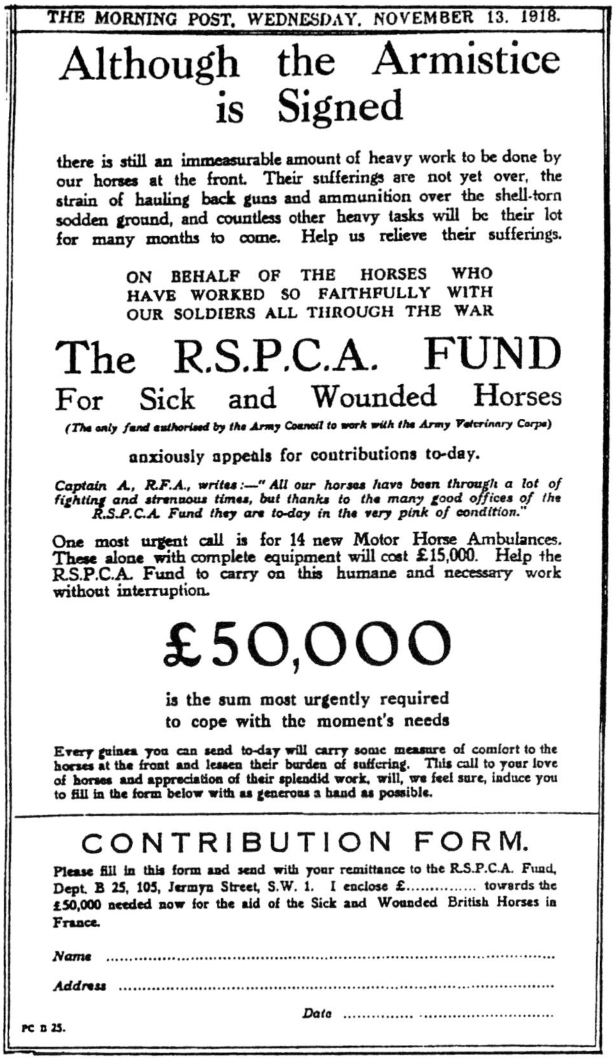

THE MORNING POST, WEDNESDAY, NOVEMBER 13, 1918.

Although the Armistice is Signed

there is still an immeasurable amount of heavy work to be done by our horses at the front. Their sufferings are not yet over, the strain of hauling back guns and ammunition over the shell-torn sodden ground, and countless other heavy tasks will be their lot for many months to come. Help us relieve their sufferings.

ON BEHALF OF THE HORSES WHO HAVE WORKED SO FAITHFULLY WITH OUR SOLDIERS ALL THROUGH THE WAR

The R.S.P.C.A. FUND
For Sick and Wounded Horses

(The only fund authorised by the Army Council to work with the Army Veterinary Corps)

anxiously appeals for contributions to-day.

Captain A., R.F.A., writes:—"All our horses have been through a lot of fighting and strenuous times, but thanks to the many good offices of the R.S.P.C.A. Fund they are to-day in the very pink of condition."

One most urgent call is for 14 new Motor Horse Ambulances. These alone with complete equipment will cost £15,000. Help the R.S.P.C.A. Fund to carry on this humane and necessary work without interruption.

£50,000

is the sum most urgently required to cope with the moment's needs

Every guinea you can send to-day will carry some measure of comfort to the horses at the front and lessen their burden of suffering. This call to your love of horses and appreciation of their splendid work, will, we feel sure, induce you to fill in the form below with as generous a hand as possible.

CONTRIBUTION FORM.

Please fill in this form and send with your remittance to the R.S.P.C.A. Fund, Dept. B 25, 105, Jermyn Street, S.W. 1. I enclose £............. towards the £50,000 needed now for the aid of the Sick and Wounded British Horses in France.

Name ....

Address ....

Date ....

PC B 25.

Figure 15.1. Advertisement placed by the Royal Society for the Prevention of Cruelty to Animals after the armistice soliciting funds to build motor horse ambulances. (*French Papers, NAC*)

From what has been related, the reader will doubtless have come to the conclusion that the whole matter was most clumsily handled. There was no risk of any vital national interest being involved and had the Imperial veterinary authorities but treated the matter of Canadian donations as a thing apart and not sought to restrain the Canadians from managing what was their own affair, there would have been no wounding of Canadian susceptibilities and vis-à-vis the R.S.P.C.A., which they chose to employ to suit their own convenience, there could have been no question of transgressing the most delicate standard of chivalrous etiquette.

The expenditure of the Blue Cross on behalf of the horses of the Canadian forces as compared with the income from Canadian sources stood as follows:

Received from Canadian sources
£5,483.2s.4d 1/2 at $4.86 2/3 = $26,684.50
Expended on behalf of Canadian units
£1,500.0s.0d at $4.86 2/3 = $7,299.90

The latter figure does not include the £1000 which was expended on the motor horse ambulance.

Just prior to the armistice, Captain Vickers, in command of No. 2 Mobile Section, being greatly in need of another horsedrawn ambulance, applied to the Blue Cross for assistance. A vehicle of this kind was sent to him, and strange to relate, reached him without any opposition on the part of the Imperial authorities. It served a good purpose for the few weeks the horses were still on hand, and when the latter were finally disposed of to the Belgians, it was, with the concurrence of the Blue Cross, presented to one of the Belgian humane societies.

At the beginning of the war, Brigadier-General Neill had taken with him from Canada a remarkably intelligent trick horse, named 'Chatham'. 'Chatham' was a Kentucky-bred animal and had been trained by Mrs. Davis of Unionville, Ontario, who had also ridden him at the Toronto Exhibition. He had a varied career in France, being present at several battles and coming through unscathed, until his beauty was unfortunately marred by the loss of an eye through an accident. As was the case with all other privately owned horses, Brigadier-General Neill eventually had to accept for him from the government the sum of $175, though his value was scarcely less than $600 or $700 on account of his accomplishments. Amongst the latter, he would, at the word of command, bend low to be mounted, lie down mounted or otherwise, do the turkey trot, fox trot, single foot, cross step, fast trot and canter, and would bow and pick up a handkerchief. Mrs. Turnbull, to whom reference has already been made, conceived a great admiration for this beautiful creature and used his picture and accomplishments to illustrate the lantern slide lectures she gave in many places for the benefit of the Blue Cross. 'Chatham' had remained on the strength of the Veterinary Corps and at the end of the war, when the horses were being disposed of, Colonel Edgett thought it would be a graceful act of courtesy and an excellent opportunity to show the appreciation of the Veterinary Corps for the good work done on behalf of the Canadian horses by the Blue Cross, to present 'Chatham' to Mrs. Turnbull, which intention, being approved by the higher authorities, was duly carried out.

We shall close our reference to the activities of the Blue Cross by informing the public that the efforts of this very worthy society found grateful appreciation at the hands of the French military authorities, to whom the help intended for the Canadian veterinary service in France was in the main eventually diverted. Indeed, the Victoria branch, conducted by Miss Kitte, continued to maintain a Blue Cross hospital with one of the French armies till the close of the war.

THE ROYAL SOCIETY FOR THE PREVENTION OF CRUELTY TO ANIMALS FUND

The great and good work accomplished in the past by this society in the defense of the rights of animals is too well-known to need any laudatory remarks. Its war effort consisted of the establishment of a fund for sick and wounded horses, for which it was accorded official recognition by the Army Council with authority to act for, and supplement the activities of, the Army Veterinary Corps (Imperial). Its services were accepted on condition that all its servants practically enlisted, and its secretary enjoyed a commission with the rank of captain.

In thus associating itself with the army authorities, the R.S.P.C.A. virtually surrendered its independence of action and in reality became the agent of the War Department in procuring from the charitable public, funds for the construction and maintenance of veterinary hospitals and for the supply of veterinary requisites in the war zone and at military training centres at home, which, strictly speaking, should have been part of the public charge. It naturally followed that the application of these resources was at the behest of the Imperial veterinary authorities. If the latter decided on a certain line of expenditure, the money was spent; if their approval for a projected expenditure was not secured, the matter lapsed.[5]

In big undertakings, such as the extension of the facilities at the hospital at Havre, the system worked very well, but when it came to a question of the needs of the individual veterinary officers and units of the Canadian forces in the field, these fared badly. The Canadian veterinary officers in France were never in touch with this society and until the order forbidding intercourse with it was promulgated, many of them did not even know of the existence of the R.S.P.C.A. fund. Consequently, after vain efforts at securing aid through interminable official channels, our veterinary officers gave up bothering themselves about the matter and turned to other sources, the existence of which they were well aware and where they knew a heart-to-heart and prompt response awaited them. It is not for one instant to be doubted that had the existence of this fund been brought to the knowledge of the veterinary officers generally, and had the latter been permitted to make direct appeals, the society would have done everything possible in the circumstances. But the society, having tied itself up with the authorities and having relinquished its right to enter into relationship with individual officers of the British Expeditionary Force, did not succeed in making a hit with our people.

On the other hand, in England, as with the Blue Cross, so with the R.S.P.C.A., conditions all round were on a different footing. There, both societies and the corps retained their independence of action and the rule of no intercourse did not apply.

The line of action followed by the R.S.P.C.A. in no wise differed from that followed in the case of the Red Cross, which, as is well-known, supported numerous hospitals for soldiers at the bases in a semiprivate but officially recognized capacity. It is, of course, true that from whatever standpoint one may look at the matter, the money in some way or other was expended in the alleviation of suffering, and the above mentioned facts are merely stated to show that the Imperial veterinary authorities, in endeavouring to take unto themselves the sole control of a single resource of this kind, to the exclusion of other similar and equally meritorious resources, only succeeded in bringing about a state of affairs that resulted almost wholly in 'mis-fires' as between the R.S.P.C.A. fund and the Canadian veterinary officers and a strong sense of grievance on the part of the latter that obstacles should have been put in their way to hinder them from procuring aid from another fund liberally supported by their own people at home. It was, of course, this policy of 'sole control' that explains the hostile attitude that was exhibited towards the activities of the Blue Cross.

A very substantial sum, namely some $40,000 was expended in making improvements at the Canadian veterinary hospital at Havre, which, despite the fact that this institution was virtually an Imperial veterinary hospital (as has been explained elsewhere) resulted in immeasurable benefit to the Canadian personnel employed there. Other sums, as we shall see, were devoted to providing a number of requisites to certain Canadian units.

The society collected a vast amount of money for its special fund, largely through advertisements, a very small amount of which, however, came from Canada.[6]

The income and expenditure of the R.S.P.C.A., as between the Canadians and itself, stood as follows:

Received from Canadian sources	£ 505.14s.2d	@ $4.86 2/3 = $2,461.10
Expended on behalf of Canadian units	£1,800.0s.0d	@ $4.86 2/3 = $8,760.00
Expended on behalf of Canadian veterinary hospital at Havre	£8,200.0s.	@ $4.86 2/3 = $39,906.67[7]

Had the war continued longer, there is no doubt that the R.S.P.C.A. would have entered into closer relationship with our officers in the field through the intermediary of Colonel Edgett, who, when he had taken over the direction of veterinary services in England, interviewed the officials of the society and requested that a supply of instruments and books be sent to France. These were readily forthcoming and were duly forwarded. An x-ray apparatus for the hospital at Havre was also asked for and the society undertook to supply the same, but the armistice intervening, the project was laid aside.

KINGSTON HUMANE SOCIETY

Early in the war, the Kingston Humane Society became actively engaged in relief work for the benefit of the war horses at the front. By means of subscriptions, collections and entertainments, it raised a total amount of $2,651.50, of which $834.67 was contributed by the Hamilton Humane Society. At the suggestion of Colonel A.E. Ross of Kingston, the money was mainly expended in remitting to the War Office in October, 1915, the sum of $1,858.19 to cover the cost of 3 ambulances. These vehicles became available at a time when all the veterinary mobile sections, Imperial as well as Canadian, were being equipped with a much needed form of conveyance. In connection with this matter the Director of Veterinary Services (Imperial) wrote to Major Saunders at Havre in December, 1915, to the effect that he was equipping all mobile sections at the front with a light horsedrawn ambulance, of which there would be about 50, many of them presented by the Royal Society for the Prevention of Cruelty to Animals and including the two provided by the humane society of Kingston, Ontario. The type was a light float such as was used for transporting cattle in France which it was believed would be better than the heavier vehicles, the idea being to use them for carrying equipment when the mobile veterinary section was on the march and to use them for ambulance purposes when the troops were more or less stationary. He added that he would have 5 motor ambulances for lines of communication by the middle of the following month but that he considered them too big and unwieldy for the narrow roads at the front, and moreover, some commanders would object to them on account of liability to block roads, etc.

In the opinion of the Canadian veterinary service, Brigadier-General Moore erred in his ideas as to the adaptability of these floats. They proved to be unsatisfactory though, for lack of something better, were put to considerable use. They were built with only 5 inches of road clearance and consequently could only go on good roads. Many horses had to be destroyed through having fallen in places inaccessible to these vehicles and others succumbed through having to be dragged to them on the main roads. As ambulances they were scarcely worth the money that was paid for them and they were not what the Humane Society expected they would be when it ordered them.

After the ambulances had been provided for, there came a call for bandages for wounded animals and under the leadership of Miss Mary Going a Blue Cross Society was formed as an auxiliary to the humane society. This Blue Cross Society had no connection with the Blue Cross Fund of London, England.

About 30,000 bandages were rolled and packed entirely by young local boys, who also collected a quantity of sphagnum moss with which they made additional dressings. The bandages and moss dressings were sent for the most part direct to Captain F.A. Walsh, veterinary officer attached to the First Canadian Infantry Brigade, who caused them to be used behind the principal battle fronts at Vimy, Ypres, etc. Brigadier-General Perreau, Commandant of the Royal Military College, was a strong supporter of the work of the society and the cadets of the college gave largely to its funds. Mr. J.R.C. Dobbs, secretary-treasurer of the Kingston Humane Society, spent a great deal of his time and energy in promoting the success of the work.[8]

Regina Society For The Prevention of Cruelty to Animals

The continually unsatisfied wants of the Canadian veterinary officers in the field, even as late as 1918, induced Lieutenant-Colonel Tamblyn, Deputy Assistant Director of Veterinary Services of the Third Division, to disregard the Imperial order on the subject and to direct to the above named society a request for certain requisites to the value of $350 with the following remarks:

These instruments are urgently required, especially for the coming winter campaign. They are not supplied for army use, so that their provision through a private source would be a godsend to the veterinarians in the field, and incidentally, to the animals.

The S.P.C.A. of Regina, which, as we have seen, had already sent nearly $3,000 to the Blue Cross Fund, promptly responded to the new call made upon it and was preparing to forward these requisites when the armistice intervened.

Horse Breed Societies and Kindred Associations of Toronto

Dr. E.A.A. Grange, Principal of the Ontario Veterinary College, wrote early in the war asking if any special equipment were needed at Havre to make the work at the Canadian veterinary hospital easier and more efficient and requested information. He then made a definite offer on behalf of the Canadian horse breed societies for anything the hospital needed. Major C.G. Saunders, who was then actively engaged on the surgical work of the institution, pointed out that an operating table, such as every progressive veterinarian in Canada considers indispensable to a properly conducted veterinary establishment, would be most useful. But, the Director of Veterinary Services (Imperial) in France, with a singularly antiquated idea on the subject, did not approve, though the association was most anxious to supply such equipment and the need of which throughout the entire period of the war, made itself forcibly felt by every officer who carried on the surgical work. In a letter to Major Saunders, the director made some remarks on the acceptance of supplementary articles, which are noteworthy in view of the treatment subsequently meted out to the Blue Cross Fund. He expressed his appreciation of the offer of the horse breed societies to provide so much equipment for the Canadian veterinary hospital at Havre and asked that his thanks be transmitted. He remarked that though there was the Base Depot of Veterinary Stores at Havre, for the supply of requisite medicines and necessaries, there would be no harm in accepting any article deemed necessary to supplement supplies obtained therefrom. But, he opined that an operating table would not be necessary and that the mattresses that had been devised would be more suitable.

A fund amounting to $6,000 was subscribed by these societies and devoted to the purchase of 20 horses, harness complete for the same, an ambulance and a transport wagon, with the understanding that these should go to the front as a unit. But at this stage occurred a hitch.

It was quite impracticable to send the horses to Europe as a Canadian transaction, for the reason that the Canadian authorities had long ere that given up shipping remounts to Canadian units, the Imperial authorities having taken over the entire undertaking for the combined forces. Consequently, it was necessary for the department to divert the 20 horses and distribute them amongst units in Canada, 12 riders being sent to the Royal Military College at Kingston, 4 riders to the Riding School at Quebec and 4 draft animals to the Citadel at Quebec.[9]

PURPLE CROSS FUND OF MONTREAL

We now come to the donation of $1,322.11 (£276.12s.0d) given by the Montreal branch of the Purple Cross Service for wounded and sick army horses.

The Purple Cross Service was founded in London, England, by the Animal Defence Society, with offices at 170 Piccadilly W., with the object of rendering practical voluntary assistance to horses in warfare. Like the Blue Cross Fund, it was not accorded recognition by the British Army Council and consequently directed its energies towards working in conjunction with the French army authorities under authorization by the French Minister of War. It maintained 3 hospitals in the zone of the armies, besides providing a staff of veterinary surgeons and assistants, ambulances, hospital equipment, forage, drugs and instruments.

The Montreal branch of this very worthy organization was inaugurated at a meeting held at the residence of Lady Meredith, 526 Pine Avenue West, on March 9th, 1915. The meeting was called at the instigation of Miss E.T. Macleod, who had been in communication with Miss Lind-af-Hageby, Honorary Secretary and founder of the Purple Cross Service in England and France.

Frequent meetings were held, many contributing members secured and several important subscriptions obtained. A great deal of propaganda work was accomplished and in September a branch was formed in Halifax, N. S., with Mrs. A.W. Jamieson as president and Miss Helen Stairs as secretary. The Halifax branch did excellent work, raising $300. Very generous responses also came from Prescott, Brockville, Sherbrooke, St. Lambert, Quebec, Charlottetown, Moncton and Amherst, and a large case of bandages from Calgary, but none of these towns formed any organized branches. The boys of the Westmount Athletic Association showed great generosity and patriotism by giving up their prizes and sending a cheque for $100.

A few supplies, consisting of nearly 6,000 bandages, some wither pads and ointment, were shipped to England, but in the main, money was transmitted overseas to help in equipping the hospitals with much needed instruments, anaesthetics, etc., a total sum of $2,445 being sent.[10]

About the middle of the war, the parent service was obliged to suspend operations on account of insufficient home support and returned to the Montreal branch the sum of $820.97. This sum, together with a balance on hand of $501.14, totaling $1,322.11, thereby became a disposable fund without any contemplated outlet, when the needs of the Canadian Army Veterinary Corps being brought to the notice of Lady Meredith, she very graciously remitted a draft in its favor to England. The draft was duly received but owing to the money not being directed by veterinary headquarters into the channels provided for by army regulations, only a small part was made to serve the original purpose of its kindly intentioned donors.

Army regulations require that all contributions of such a nature shall be managed under the direction of committees and all accounts audited by a regimental board of 3 officers. This is a laudable provision for there is no gainsaying the fact that the direction of expenditure by collective minds is better than by a single mind, and moreover, it ensures proper accounting from a public standpoint. On the other hand, it is a method of procedure which is often cumbersome, slow-moving and extremely trying to anybody animated by a wish to get prompt results. Brigadier-General Neill, in his zeal to avoid red tape, chose a course of action which would have enabled him virtually to control the expenditure of the fund. He arranged that the money should lie in the London branch of the Bank of Montreal and be used by the manager in the payment of accounts forwarded by him with vouchers for purchases made. Approximately $250 (£52.15s.2d) had been put to use in this manner in the purchase of pocket instrument cases, dental instruments and magnifying lenses, which were mostly despatched to the administrative veterinary officers of the different divisions, when the matter coming to the notice of the Quartermaster-General, the latter proceeded to raise objections with the result that there was an impasse and the fund became 'short-circuited' and tied up.

There was a good deal of correspondence on the subject,[11] in which the Adjutant-General took a hand suggesting that the fund be transferred to the Chief Paymaster to be paid out on the request of Brigadier-General Neill for expenditures made in the manner arranged for. But it was pointed out that the suggestion was untenable in view of the conditions under which the money had been deposited in the bank, namely that it was outside the scope of the military authorities and that the bank was without authority to make the proposed transfer.

By that time, the whole matter had become so distasteful to Brigadier-General Neill that he decided to wash his hands of the affair and have nothing further to do with it. Consequently, the end of the war found an unexpended balance in the bank of £233.16s.10d of Purple Cross funds, which, but for the unfortunate mixup which occurred, might have been applied to the benefit of the sick and wounded horses of the Canadian forces.

PARKE, DAVIS AND COMPANY

The London branch of this well-known firm on several occasions donated free of charge, upon application by the veterinary officers and also of its own volition, consignments of bacterins, phylacogens and other pharmaceutical products for experimental purposes, action that was greatly appreciated by the corps.

GIFTS TO THE PERSONNEL OF THE CANADIAN ARMY VETERINARY CORPS

It is appropriate, in this chapter, to acknowledge on behalf of the personnel of the corps, the receipt from time to time from friends at home of many gifts of luxuries and comforts, the arrival of which served as a reminder that the home-fires were still burning and helped to dispel many a pang of homesickness.

From H.R.H. The Duchess of Connaught, in December, 1914, each man of the corps in the first contingent received a box of maple sugar. From the Montreal Gazette Tobacco Fund, in August, 1916, came a case of tobacco and cigarettes, which were distributed at No. 2 Canadian Veterinary Hospital at Shorncliffe, whilst the mobile veterinary sections in France also participated in the kindly remembrance of this journal. Both the Canadian Field Comforts Commission and the Canadian War Contingent Association included the Veterinary Corps amongst the units to which they made their periodical distribution of good things from home. From British sources also came many useful gifts, through Colonel E.E. Martin, C.M.G., Deputy Director of Veterinary Services (Imperial) of the First Army at the instigation of Mrs. Moore, wife of Major-General Moore, Director of Veterinary Services (Imperial) on behalf of the Army Veterinary Corps (Imperial) Auxiliary.

CHAPTER 16

SOME WAR DISEASES AND METHODS OF TREATMENT

It is not intended to offer the reader a technical discourse on the diseases encountered in the war and the methods adopted to combat the same. For one thing, sufficient information at the present time is not available for the reason that the experience gained by the Canadian veterinary officers was limited to their own environment and reports on which had to be made to the Imperial authorities, who alone came into possession of complete data.[1] Accordingly, but a few matters of more or less general interest will be touched on.

MANGE No disease gave the veterinary service more cause for anxiety than mange. It was met with, off and on, in practically every unit and from the beginning of the war till the end. The Canadian veterinary officers had much to do with it, not only in England, but in the war zones in Belgium and France, not to speak of the many cases handled at the Canadian veterinary hospital at Havre, where, as has been stated in the chapter on that institution, a specialty was made of treating skin diseases.

Mange made its appearance in the early days at Shorncliffe (Figure 16.1) and continued to crop out as long as the Canadians occupied the area, and it is known that horses in which the disease had not been entirely eradicated were shipped thence to both Canterbury and Witley. From this it must not be considered that mange was introduced by Canadian animals, for the horses of both first and second contingents arrived in England entirely free from the disease.

The sarcoptic form was the one that gave most trouble at Shorncliffe and one reason why it was so difficult to keep in subjection was undoubtedly due to the lack of dipping facilities, which necessitated all treatment being carried out by hand.

The rather interesting but scarcely tenable theory was advanced by Captain V.C. Best that rats were responsible for the spread of the infestation. At his request, and by permission of the medical authorities, Private

Figure 16.1. Mange treatment using lime-sulphur applied with a hand-operated spray pump, No. 2 Canadian Army Veterinary Hospital, Shorncliffe, England, ca. 1915-1916. (*NAC PA 5002*)

Mitchell, of the Canadian Army Medical Corps, in private life a professional rat catcher, was detailed to carry out regular measures throughout the area for extermination of the rodents by means of ferrets and dogs. Within 21 days were caught some 1,200 rats, 60% of which showed evidence of parasitic skin disease and in a period of 12 months over 12,000 were destroyed. It is a remarkable fact that with the extermination of the rodents, mange, ringworm, strangles and influenza disappeared from the area for a period of 5 months. Captain Best's figures showed that in the Reserve Cavalry Brigade there was a decrease in the sick list of from 26% to 2.4% and that the Canadian Army Service Corps horses exhibited no parasitic cases from October, 1916 till July, 1917, though in the previous year there had been a showing of 16%, whilst the Field Artillery experienced a decrease from 17% to 1.9% in 8 months during 1916-1917.

At Witley, towards the end of 1916, when the Third Divisional Artillery was getting ready to proceed to France, there was an outbreak, caused, it was believed, by some of the horses, on a trek, being put in infested stables at Lark Hill, whence 8 cases had been moved a few hours previously, as the unit had hitherto been free from the disease. Two weeks after the return to Witley, the first cases developed, about a hundred animals in all subsequently becoming infested. Prompt action for checking the spread was necessary in order that the unit might proceed to France without delay, so a temporary makeshift dipping tank was hastily constructed and the animals passed through under supervision of Captain A. Savage. A steam road engine was installed to keep the solution at the proper temperature of 100 degrees. Later, under instructions from Colonel Neill, a more solid tank was constructed at a preliminary cost of £26 ($126.53) and a subsequent one of £5.18s.0d ($28.71), with the aid of the engineers. That the action taken was a wise one was shown by the report rendered by Major Edgett, under date of September 20th, 1916, after the unit had arrived in France: "There has not been a case of mange in the 3rd C.F.A., which speaks well for the dip and Captain Savage's work before leaving England."

Afterwards, this dip was freely used for the horses of the 5th Divisional Artillery, 7000 immersions being made between April and September, 1917.

On the continent, the first two suspected cases amongst Canadian horses were reported by Lieutenant-Colonel Neill in the First Brigade, C.F.A., in February, 1915, to be followed by two others seen by Major Cutcliffe the following June, one of which was in a remount received 12 days previously. There is no doubt that much of the mange experienced later by the Canadians was by incompletely cured remounts, for the diaries of the administrative officers of the different divisions often recorded observations to that effect. But the havoc that can be wrought by contact with a single infested animal was forcibly demonstrated by an experience in the Fourth Division, where an officer, in exchanging one horse for another, caused the introduction of the disease to a unit from which it was subsequently necessary to make no less than 48 evacuations of the finest animals.

After the Imperial authorities had been convinced of the efficacy and advantages of the dip method of treating mange, first brought to their attention by Lieutenant F.V. Perry of western Canada, the construction of many dipping tanks was authorized, not only at the veterinary hospitals but throughout the army areas (see Appendix F). Those made use of by the Canadians were situated at Reninghelst, Hooggraaf, Barlin, Fosse 10, Fresnicourt, and Boyeffles. Some of them were of a very temporary character and constantly needed repairing whilst others were more pretentious. By evacuating infested animals and passing all contact ones through one or the other of these tanks periodically, the disease was kept in check and usually eradicated until it was reintroduced by the arrival of infested remounts or by contact with existing foci of infestation during a move. At No. 1 Canadian Veterinary Hospital, the presence of living parasites was not demonstrable after the second time of passing through the calcium sulphide solution.

To ensure effective results it was found to be absolutely necessary to clip all over before subjecting an animal to treatment and the use of blankets was avoided as far as possible.

In May, 1918, Lieutenant-Colonel Cutcliffe reported that mange was practically stamped out and that no difficulty would be experienced in keeping it so in the Canadian Army Corps if the same care and supervision were taken of the animals and standings in other army corps, etc.

In areas where a dipping tank was not available, it was decided in May, 1917, to distribute quicklime and sulphur to the veterinary officers to enable them to treat parasitic diseases within the lines, rather than to resort to evacuation of cases which were suspects only.

The first aid sergeants of the veterinary corps attached to units generally contrived to possess portable

Figure 16.2. Treating a mule with mange using lime-sulphur scrubbed into skin with a brush, No. 2 Mobile Veterinary Section, France, August, 1917. (*NAC PA 1706*)

boilers whereby they were enabled to prepare the solution or the mobile sections would prepare and distribute it.

The method of preparing and using the solution in the lines was as follows:

Formula: Sulphur - 2-1/4 pounds; Quicklime - l pound; Water - 2 gallons

Directions for preparing: Have two containers (galvanized buckets). Put the 2 gallons of water in one and boil. In the other container, spread the sulphur evenly on the bottom and the quicklime on top. Add sufficient water from the first container to slake the lime and continue stirring in more water till rendered into a paste.

When the water in the first container has come to a boil, stir in the paste and continue stirring till the solid matter is dissolved. This should take 2 to 3 hours, if properly finished, and the mixture should be of a dark chocolate color. When finished, enough water should be added to make up for evaporation, bringing the quantity to 2 gallons again.

Directions for application: Mix 1 part of the solution with 2 1/2 to 3 parts water. Apply to the clipped animal at a temperature of 150°F by means of a bottle and scrub in with a dandy brush (Figure 16.2). Repeat in from 5 to 10 days.

N.B. The fingers of the person making the application are apt to get sore after a time, which may be prevented to a great extent by applying grease around the finger nails or by using gloves.

For scrubbing the skin in the field, in order to thoroughly clean it and assist exfoliation in old standing cases showing coarseness and corrugation, the following formula was found very useful:

Soft soap -1 pound; Coal oil - 1 quart; Water - 5 gallons; Boiled to an emulsion.

This was scrubbed in and left on for 24 hours when the old hair, dirt and skin debris came away freely. About 8 or 10 gallons sufficed to treat 25 animals.

Lieutenant-Colonel Tamblyn suggested a plan for a field dipping tank, which proved very successful, its chief features being its adaptability to field conditions, the securing of complete immersion and cheapness of construction. As many as 120 animals could be passed through it hourly, when worked at full pressure, but the ordinary capacity was about 400 animals daily.

LICE In the eradication of this pest, when nicotine was not available, a general clipping and resort to the calcium sulphide dip, as for mange, proved very effective. At Shorncliffe, the sulphur fume box was employed with success.

TETANUS Tetanus was encountered more frequently in Belgium than in northern France. Animals with deep gunshot and foot wounds were given preventive doses of from 1500 to 3000 units of antitetanic serum.

NECROTIC DERMATITIS From time to time a good deal of trouble was experienced with this disease. It was a condition akin to that of 'trench feet' amongst the troops, due to stasis of the circulation and infection from the infected mud of the surroundings either automatically or through abrasions of the skin. It led to large sloughs of the skin and connective tissues. Lieutenant-Colonel Smith remarked on the number of cases (fully 75%) which developed in animals standing in the mud at Westoutre in December, 1915. In November, 1917, there were many cases amongst horses of the Third Divisional Artillery, when Lieutenant-Colonel Tamblyn noticed that it was developing in animals travelling on fascine made roads but not in those traveling on plank roads, owing to the former snagging themselves with the sharp ends of the sticks that were used to make up the fascines (see Figure 7.5) or sustaining abrasions from constantly placing their feet between the fascines.

THRUSH[2] This condition was very commonly met with in certain localities, whether the animals were standing in the open or in floored stables, and at times assumed the character of a general local infection. By far the most effective treatment was thorough cleansing of the parts and free application of tincture of iodine twice daily, which would often clean up the trouble within a day or two.

INJURIES FROM KICKS There was a great deal of trouble from this cause, particularly at feeding time and the only effectual way of dealing with it was to picket the habitual kickers away from the line.

CONTAGIOUS PUSTULAR STOMATITIS[3] There were one or two outbreaks of this disorder. It was a condition that closely resembled foot-and-mouth disease in cattle, the mucous membrane of the tongue, lips and gums exhibiting ulcerated patches, with occasional development of pustules on the lips in addition. There were more or less salivation, twitching and smacking of the lips, and indisposition to feed. All the cases did well under treatment consisting of mouth washes with a weak solution of iodine whilst rigid isolation of infected animals under military guard prevented further spread.

ULCERATIVE CELLULITIS[4] Few of the so-called 'war diseases' of animals gave rise to so much work, interest, controversy, research and investigation, or caused such serious losses, as this disease.

Before the war, it was not known to exist either in Great Britain, Canada or the United States, and was practically unknown to English speaking veterinarians. In France, however, it had long been known and had been described by Professor Nocard in 1892. When it first made its appearance amongst the horses of the British army in 1916, it was not recognized as the infectious disorder described by Nocard, but was regarded as a new disease of an entirely different nature. From 70 to 100 cases were recorded weekly from all units of the British Expeditionary Force. In midsummer of 1918, 920 horses and 150 mules were undergoing treatment in the different hospitals at the base, but by that time the disease was on the wane. Nearly 60% of all cases had to be destroyed, but of those placed under treatment 50% were returned to duty.

It was an ulcerative condition of the skin and subcutis usually confined to the legs below the knee and hock and much commoner in the hind legs than in the fore. As the disease progressed, the animal would get fairly accustomed to it and might continue to work in the usual manner unless a large area of skin sloughed away or an important structure became involved. The course was most irregular and annoying as some animals would appear to have recovered only to develop a new crop of ulcers after a lapse of weeks, which in the course of time might reduce them to a pitiable condition.

Captain Watson was ordered to make a thorough bacteriological investigation with the result that he established the identity of the disease with that described by Nocard. His report, submitted to the Director of Veterinary Services (Imperial) was published in the Veterinary Journal of November, 1917.

Veterinary officers in the Canadian service were allowed to treat the disease but were obliged to evacuate all cases to the base hospitals.

PERIODIC OPHTHALMIA[5] From the veterinarian's viewpoint, periodic ophthalmia was one of the most regrettable features of the war. It ruined the eyes of hundreds of otherwise perfectly sound horses.
We knew very little about it, though we had known of 'moonblindness' all our lives, and, to be honest, that was about as much as we knew concerning it. The English language contains no sane description of the cause, pathology or treatment of this disease.

In France, however, such was not the case. As long ago as 1861, Renaud estimated that 70% of the horses in the Departments of Pas de Calais, Nord, Somme and Seine Inferieure, were affected. With that fact before us, it is easy to understand why the disease was widespread in the British armies in France.

The treatment at No. 1 Canadian Veterinary Hospital was directed towards keeping the animal in the dark, dilating the pupil so as to prevent intraocular changes and lessening the pain by means of atropine or cocaine ointment. The prescribed army treatment as set forth in an official circular, consisted of injecting Lugol's solution of iodine (22 grains iodine, 33 grains potassium iodide, l ounce distilled water) into the periorbital tissues by means of a hypodermic syringe.

DEBILITY Debility was responsible for a great deal of wastage of animal strength. It was mostly attributed to the necessity of overworking the animals on insufficiency of rations coupled with exposure to excessive cold. This was particularly true during the Passchendaele operations when horses and mules were reduced to such a low degree of vitality that numbers lay down in their tracks and died. But there is no doubt that under ordinary conditions many cases resulted from indigestion directly due to irregularities of the teeth, which, owing to the lack of dental instruments provided by the authorities, could not be remedied in the lines. And it may be added that there were indications in certain instances of infestation of the intestinal canal by bloodsucking verminous parasites, a condition which is not unknown in certain parts of Canada.

GAS POISONING[6]

CHLORINE AND PHOSGENE GAS These two gases affected the respiratory passages throughout but mainly irritated the lining membrane of the bronchial tubes. According to the degree of poisoning, the pathological changes went on to static pneumonia, bronchial pneumonia, lobar pneumonia and gangrene. Fat and thin animals suffered more than those in good condition. At the outset the signs exhibited were: very distressed and rapid respiration, a yellowish discharge from the nostrils, a frothy one from the mouth, considerable prostration, increased pulsation, elevation of temperature, a very persistent cough and difficulty in swallowing with consequent indisposition to eat. After the twelfth hour, the signs increased in severity until about the forty-eighth hour, when the animal either rapidly succumbed or recovery ensued. The majority of those affected had to be evacuated for rest and recuperation.

MUSTARD GAS This form of gas did not affect animals so extensively as the chlorine and required to be in high concentration to cause serious damage. It produced a painful blistering effect wherever it came in contact with the skin, particularly of those areas of the body devoid of hair and such parts as the conjunctiva and the mucous membrane of the mouth and nostrils. Where the eyes were affected, they were swollen and closed and discharged freely, whilst the mucous membrane of the mouth turned a darkish blue and in severe cases was covered with watery vesicles. The animal exhibited dullness, had more or less rise of temperature and was disinclined to eat for several hours.

TREATMENT The prime essentials were complete rest in the open air, plenty of fresh water, mashes and access to green forage when the latter was available. The medicinal agents made use of were anodynes and bicarbonate of soda solution for washing affected parts in cases of mustard poisoning.

Figure 16.3. Canadian Army Veterinary Corps Captain with mount and anti-gas mask, 1918. (*NAC PA 5001*)

Employment of Anti-gas Respirators From the accompanying illustration (Figure 16.3), one might be led to the idea that the respirator or helmet was used on horses to the same extent as by the soldiers. But as a matter of fact, though such an article was manufactured soon after the first gas attacks and supplied to some of the units on a basis of 10% of the horse strength of the same, and later in a quota of 1500 per division, it was not generally employed for reasons to be set forth.

In the first place, the effect of the gas on animals was not nearly as severe as on the men, for there were instances where the latter were seriously affected whilst the former revealed no signs beyond slight dullness. But it must not be inferred from this that the casualties amongst animals were infrequent, for such was not the case.

Lieutenant-Colonel D.S. Tamblyn reported that to require the adjustment of respirators to animals during a gas attack, whether by shell or cloud, was an injustice to the men in charge and impracticable. During a cloud of chlorine gas attack at Ypres, in 1916, no respirators were adjusted to such animals as came within reach of the same, and though 150 were affected only one had to be subsequently destroyed, the rest recovering in from 5 to 15 days and returning to duty. In two subsequent shell chlorine gas attacks at Vimy Ridge, an attempt was made by the drivers to adjust the respirators to their horses, with the result that a number of men and horses died from gas poisoning, while a number were killed by shellfire. It was believed that had these drivers adjusted their own respirators and driven their teams to the high ground, no casualties would have taken place.

In the Ypres gas attack mentioned, there is no doubt that a large number of casualties was brought about through transport officers permitting their animals to halt amongst the ruins of that town, which was a mistake, as gas only settles in such places which should, therefore, have been avoided.

The respirator pictured in the accompanying illustration (Figure 16.3) was impracticable because it did not meet requirements. It was constructed on the order of the old P.H. helmet, supplied in the early days to the troops and which was discarded when the very efficient Box respirator came into general use. It was practically useless for animals on the move as it impeded breathing, and the gunners would rather risk having a few horses gassed than be hampered in quick movement.

The Method of Chloral Hydrate Anaesthesia as Practised at No. 1 Canadian Veterinary Hospital

Contributed by Captain A. Savage[7]

A glance through the veterinary literature pertaining to anaesthetics shows that the opinion of prominent surgeons is anything but conclusive on the subject of chloral hydrate. Nocard and Kaufmann support it vigorously; Cadiot and Almy and Hobday condemn it, whilst most writers of books refer to it in terms of great personal unfamiliarity.

At the Canadian veterinary hospital, it was tried and liked and its use soon became a routine. The only reason it was not used almost exclusively was because the drug became unobtainable. But if one may draw conclusions from the hundred odd cases on which it was tried according to the method described, the same would be that it is safe, simple and effective.

Chloral hydrate being a powerful depressant of the central nervous system, including the many centres in the medulla, as well as the heart muscle, it was to counteract its undesired effects on the processes of circulation and respiration that the other drugs mentioned were brought into use.

Figure 16.4. Lieut. Alfred Savage, C.A.V.C., June, 1916. (*NAC P296*)

The animal was led into the operating room and given hypodermically 1/4 grain atropine sulphate. An area about 3 by 4 inches directly over the jugular vein was shaved and disinfected with tincture of iodine. While waiting for the atropine to act (as judged by the dilation of the pupil) the operator prepared a solution of chloral hydrate according to the following formula: For each 100 lbs. weight of the horse, 5 to 6 grams of chloral were allowed. This had to be fresh and of the best quality. The total amount was dissolved in sufficient warm (previously boiled) water to make a 3% solution and filtered carefully through cotton, wool or filter paper and poured into an irrigator or other suitable apparatus. This solution at approximately blood heat was injected by gravity into the jugular vein of the standing animal through a trocar or large needle. The patient might stagger and fall over before the full amount had been administered, in which case, provided it was not sufficiently narcotized for the purpose in view, it was given enough of the balance to produce the desired effect in the recumbent position. No bad effects were experienced from some of the solution getting outside the jugular vein or under the skin.

Some animals were not completely anaesthetized by this procedure, whereupon they were given either a local anaesthetic of cocaine and adrenalin or inhalations of chloroform. Others were completely narcotized, even the corneal reflex being absent. This stage, however, began to pass off in about 15 minutes, when, if the operation was a protracted one, additional measures had to be taken. As a precaution against too sudden a revival, thc animal, once down, was kept in hobbles.

Cyanosis, sweating, or a feeble pulse, were indications that the circulatory disturbance was dangerously great, in which event, resort was had to camphorated oil (10%). This was injected hypodermically in doses of from 30 cc to 50 cc, care being taken that not more than 10 cc were given at any one place. If the circulatory depression called for more immediate action, warmed spirits of camphor (10%) were given intravenously.

The time required for recovery varied, some animals not regaining their feet for 3 hours. Strychnine was a great help in this respect.

No fatalities occurred in spite of the fact that some horses were given more than 3 ounces of the drug in the manner indicated.

TREATMENT OF WOUNDS AT NO. 1 CANADIAN VETERINARY HOSPITAL

Contributed by Captain A. Savage

The majority of wounds treated in the hospital were those caused by high explosive shells. Such wounds had a definite character and, in a general way, were susceptible to routine treatment.

Surface wounds were accepted at 'face value'. Deep ones in heavily muscled or highly vascular regions, unless the animal's history showed quite definitely that a foreign body had been extracted from them, were explored as soon as possible and the metal, if any, removed.[8] This procedure was accompanied by provision of the necessary drainage and for many reasons was usually done under total anaesthesia. The region of the wound was clipped, shaved and treated with tincture of iodine, these preliminary steps being followed by packing or tamponading and treatment of the more usual sort beginning from 24 to 48 hours later when the surgical dressing was removed (Figure 16.5).

It was accepted that bacteria and their products were deleterious to the healing process. In fact, aside from providing rest, comfort and mechanical cleanliness, the question of wound treatment resolved itself mostly into a fight against existing infection and taking the needful steps to preclude further invasion by microorganisms.[9] Existing infection might be combated in many ways, briefly outlined as follows:

1. Destruction of the infection by antiseptics, heat, etc.
2. Neutralization of the infectious products by
   (a) Dakin's solution locally
   (b) Vaccines, bacterins, sera, etc., injected into the animal
3. Mechanical removal of the infection by
   (a) Surgical means
   (b) Wright's hypertonic saline lymph flow
   (c) Bier's hyperaemic method
4. 'Biological' removal of the infection by

Figure 16.5. Irrigation of a shrapnel wound of the shoulder with disinfectant at a Canadian Mobile Veterinary Section, France, August, 1917. (*NAC PA 1709*)

(a) Wright's opsonic method of phagocytosis
(b) Bier's hyperaemic method

All the above-mentioned methods were tried, but the method which became a standard routine was the frequent use of a 2% warm saline solution as an irrigation. A case was led into the dressing shed. Suspended overhead was a 2 gallon irrigator filled with warm saline solution and fitted with a length of rubber tubing. The dresser made use of a previously prepared and sterile cotton swab and the saline stream. The wound was cleaned and thoroughly irrigated without being touched by hand. It was a simple procedure but proved most effective, not only as a treatment but as a method of preventing infection from wound to wound and of minimizing the risk of such specific infections as ulcerative or epizootic lymphangitis.

The discharge from every wound was examined microscopically at least once in two weeks as a check against the slow developing signs of the latter diseases.

It was found that bandages could be largely replaced by a thick smear of vaseline as a dust and fly protectant, and that many wounds, particularly lacerated muscle wounds, healed best if unhampered even by a gauze covering.

QUITTOR OPERATION AT NO. 1 CANADIAN VETERINARY HOSPITAL

Contributed by Captain A. Savage

The surgical treatment of quittor[10] has been attempted with varying degrees of success by prominent veterinary surgeons the world over. Their object in all cases has been to remove at least the necrotic portion, if not all, of the lateral cartilage. The number of methods of gaining access to the diseased part, however, shows quite clearly that none of them possesses outstanding merit. For example, the operations of Bayer, Merrilat, Cadiot and Almy mutilate the hoof, and that of Johne, while avoiding this, not only leaves a deep wound and prominent scar, but is technically difficult to perform.

At the Canadian Veterinary Hospital a method was followed which was a modification of the Johne operation and depended largely upon the French 'renette' for actually removing the cartilage. Its effectiveness may be judged by the fact that of nearly 500 cases operated upon between the spring of 1915 and 1918, 80% were discharged to remounts.

The leg was clipped, if necessary, and the field of operation shaved. On account of the subsequent rapid growth of horn, the foot, if not quite short, was well cut down and reshod.

Casting the animal with hobbles and chloroform anaesthesia were the rule (Figure 16.6). The affected foot was released and brought approximately into the position assumed when standing by means of a rope around the pastern. A strong rubber tourniquet was then applied above the fetlock. The field was disinfected with tincture of iodine and an antiseptic or sterile pack placed over the hoof to prevent soiling the wound unnecessarily.

An incision the length of the lateral cartilage was made through the skin and subcutis immediately above the coronary band and parallel to it. Small retractors held by an assistant were made to apply traction to the upper (proximal) flap of the wound. A right-handed sage knife was then used to separate this from the underlying tissues up to the dorsal margin of the cartilage. Any inflammatory tissue overlying the cartilage was removed by a few well-directed strokes of the sage knife until the cartilage was exposed. This might then be largely removed by means of the right and left sage knives, but a preferable instrument was the 'renette' which enabled the operator to work between the coronary band and the joint capsule without much danger of injuring either, provided he was reasonably careful. As much cartilage as possible was removed.

Cases in which ossification of the cartilage accompanied necrosis had to be specially dealt with and where there was a sinus discharging at the sole of the foot, the latter was enlarged and curetted.

The wound was cleansed with dry cotton, flooded with tincture of iodine and firmly packed with gauze. A small gauze pad was placed over it. Owing to the severe hemorrhage which would otherwise have ensued, bandaging was firm and thoroughly done before the tourniquet was removed. That done, the animal was released.

Subsequent treatment of the wound began in 48 hours and consisted of antiseptic or saline irrigation, repacking with gauze and bandaging lightly. Healing occurred by granulation, but if the daily dressing was up to standard the ultimate scar was nearly invisible.

Figure 16.6. Capt. G.A. Rose (white gown) a Canadian serving with the Army Veterinary Corps (Imperial), and assistants, illustrating equine surgery in 1916. The horse has been hobbled, cast on a soft mat, and is anesthetized using a chloroform mask. (*C.A.V. Barker Museum*)

Following the operation, the animal might be markedly lame for 2 or 3 weeks. This was particularly the case with heavy drafters; light horses and mules often did not limp a step.

The average time of recovery was from 6 to 8 weeks. A second operation was rarely necessary and had only to be performed when a portion of cartilage had been left unremoved.

SKIN REGENERATION Captain Savage did some very good work at Havre in effecting the regeneration of skin without the formation of scar tissue. In one instance, a horse developed a large hematoma of the neck as a result of a bite. The whole of the tumor with the skin covering the same was excised, leaving a denuded triangular-shaped space measuring 7 x 12 x 12 inches. The edges of the skin were lightly cauterized at the time with a dull red iron and the raw surface powdered with boric acid. The subsequent treatment was directed towards continually removing the beginnings of scab formation by cleaning the raw surface once daily by means of a stream of saline solution and a swab, whilst the edges were anointed with biniodide of mercury ointment (1:16). In 10 weeks' time, the raw surface had been reduced to a space measuring 6 1/2 X 5 X 4 inches, the whole being surrounded by encroaching new skin together with hair follicles, and eventually the regenerative process involved the entire surface.

DENTISTRY As has been stated elsewhere, one of the conditions with which the Canadian veterinary officers always had difficulty in contending was the almost entire absence of equipment for correcting dental irregularities in the horses at the front. The Canadian service had to depend for its equipment on what was supplied by the Imperial authorities and for this purpose there was almost next to nothing. Through this lack of provision, many

Figure 16.7. Horse standing in a water bath to ease the pain of laminitis. No. 2 Canadian Veterinary Hospital, Shorncliffe, 1918. (*NAC PA 5004*)

an otherwise husky animal had to be evacuated to a base hospital, thereby largely adding to the expense of army upkeep, when, had a few necessary instruments been available in the mobile sections, they might have been fixed up on the spot with comparative ease and retained in the line. The Canadian military authorities throughout the war recognized the importance of caring for the soldiers' teeth, yet little was done in this direction in respect to the animals, in spite of many recommendations from the veterinary service that veterinary dentistry was a no less important factor in preventing animal wastage.

How the matter appeared to a very observant officer of the Canadian Army Service Corps, Lieutenant-Colonel J.A. Shaw, in a report made by him to Colonel Edgett, is of more than passing interest:

.....I am now sending forward what I have been able to pick up re horse dentistry.

It has been, in my opinion, one of the greatest savers of horse flesh that has been employed in the army and has made such a difference in the condition of our horses, that I have made it a rule to have every horse's teeth inspected periodically, and this is one of the first things that I have done with any new horses coming into the unit. This examination has proved that every horse needs some attention, perhaps minor, but which had to be attended to.

Easily 75% required urgent attention; 15% required cutting or extracting, and it might be interesting to note that 25% of my grey horses required cutting or extracting so that the percentage amongst the other colours was considerably below 15.

We have found many cases of discharge from the nostrils directly due to decayed or split teeth and the discharge has ceased when the teeth were properly attended to.

Practically all of our colic cases were found to be suffering from bad teeth, and the percentage of colic cases amongst the horses whose teeth have been properly attended to has been almost nil.

Several cases of animals, which were supposed to be beyond conditioning, turned out exceptionally fine after their teeth had been properly treated. In fact, I considered horse dentistry to be such an important factor in the maintaining of horse flesh, that when we were unable to secure a complete kit of dental tools, I had these purchased regimentally. I believe that this was the only set of dental instruments that existed in this area, with the result that practically all horses of the area, with the exception of the artillery, were sent here for treatment.

THE VETERINARY BACTERIOLOGICAL LABORATORY OF THE ARMY VETERINARY CORPS

This institution, which came into being about the middle of the war, was not, properly speaking, a Canadian one, but as the Imperial authorities were obliged to turn to the Canadian Army Veterinary Corps to find a bacteriologist qualified to direct its activities, and Captain E.A. Watson[11] was detailed to fill the position, it is appropriate that it should receive consideration in the body of this work.

Towards the end of 1916, certain diseases of a contagious but obscure or unidentified nature made their appearance and became increasingly prevalent among the army horses in France. The Director of Veterinary Service (Imperial) sent out a circular worded as follows:

It is intended to ask for the services of an expert bacteriologist to be attached to a veterinary hospital at the advanced base to whom slides or material for microscopic examination can be sent and to assist in investigation of all contagious diseases.

The services of Captain E.A. Watson, then veterinary officer attached to the Seventh Brigade, C.F.A., were considered indispensable for this purpose and he was ordered to relinquish his appointment in the line and report at Abbeville. In the chapter on The Headquarters Staff, it is pointed out how the Imperial authorities took this action without consulting the Canadian authorities. After making some preliminary investigations, Captain Watson made his recommendations for necessary equipment and his plans and suggestions being favorably considered, he was instructed to fit out a laboratory at No. 6 (Imperial) Veterinary Hospital at Rouen, this particular hospital being chosen as a central and convenient station where animals could be collected for observation and experiment and specimens and material received from the various units in the field.

Research and general laboratory work were begun in March, 1917, and considerable progress was made during the next few months. The causative agent of a very troublesome disease known as ulcerative cellulitis was isolated and identified, vaccines and immunizing sera were prepared and a satisfactory method of treatment devised. The work of the laboratory grew from day to day and it was soon evident that a much larger institution and an increased staff were necessary to meet the growing demands.

A scheme was drawn up detailing the requirements in equipment and personnel. A grant of money from the R.S.P.C.A. allowed for the purchase of the equipment, search was made for premises in the city of Rouen, and a suitable building being found, it was leased and adequate water, gas and electric light and power installations put in.

Though handicapped with insufficient and untrained personnel, Captain Watson was able to accomplish a great deal of useful work as is indicated in the following summary:

(1) Large quantities of vaccines and sera were prepared - 100,000 doses - and issued out to veterinary units for the treatment of ulcerative lymphangitis.

(2) Over 1,000 specimens were received, examined and reported on. These included examinations for glanders, anthrax, rabies, ulcerative lymphangitis, epizootic lymphangitis, sporothricosis, etc.

(3) Biological tests of the action of various antiseptic disinfectants and parasiticides, and the determination of their phenol coefficients.

(4) Tests of samples of oil cakes for crotin and poisonous alkaloids.

(5) Separate individual courses of instruction in bacteriological, microscopical and general laboratory methods were given to 10 Army Veterinary Corps officers and 6 other ranks.

(6) Laboratory research work and observations and experiments in the field in connection with:
   (a) Ulcerative cellulitis
   (b) Epizootic lymphangitis
   (c) Ophthalmia

CHAPTER 17

EPILOGUE: 1919-1940[1]

THE CANADIAN ARMY BETWEEN THE WORLD WARS The fortunes of the Canadian Army Veterinary Corps and its successors between 1919 and 1939 in most ways reflected the circumstances prevailing generally in the Canadian Army. However, they were modified by the Corps' bond with the horse as the instrument of military mobility and motive power. The ultimate disbandment of the Veterinary Corps likely was partly a function of lack of vision by its commanding officers, or of their inability to free the image and role of the Canadian military veterinarian from this stereotype as the army mechanized. The small size of the army, its limited roles, and associated logistical constraints probably also affected the opportunity for the Veterinary Corps to diversify its functions.

During the period 1919-1921, the Canadian Army was re-established with a Permanent Force of professional soldiers, and a Non-permanent Active Militia of citizen-soldiers, neither on a scale capable of significant military preparedness.[2] The Permanent Force infantry, cavalry and artillery were supported by service units, among which was the Canadian Permanent Army Veterinary Corps, renamed in November 1919 the Royal Canadian Army Veterinary Corps, in recognition of the work done in World War I.

Throughout the inter-war period the Permanent Force received niggardly parliamentary appropriations and initially was at least schizophrenic, and probably delusional, about its mandate. Was it preparation for the defence of Canada against the United States, or for participation in a major European war as part of a British Imperial Force?[3] In the words of J.L. Granatstein "the pay, conditions of service, and the state of weaponry and training were simply pathetic",[4] and the army a "backward-looking organization...devoted to its own survival as its primary task".[5] There was little public support or respect for the Permanent Force; its budget was $4.9 million in 1930-31, $5 million in 1936-36, and $6 million in 1938-39.[6] The Bennett Government cut pay by 10% in the early years of the Depression; in 1937, Lieut.-Col. D.S. Tamblyn, O.A.C.A.V.S. earned $4745 in pay and allowances.[7] In March 1939, the Permanent Force numbered just over 4100, of whom 446 were officers.[8] While some were hard-working and endeavoured to prepare themselves against the possibility of war, other officers were "...time-servers and hangers-on, those who counted the years until their pensions came due".[9]

After World War I, outstanding officers had been encouraged to join the Permanent Force, usually at their wartime rank. Although not all of the older Permanent Force officers were replaced, an officer caste of relatively high rank for age was produced, which, with promotion by seniority, and little turnover within the higher echelons, stagnated. Majors and above often aged in rank, in a force with few small units to command, and a retirement policy that did not create opportunities for promotion. "Provided an officer, no matter how lazy or incompetent, could avoid sudden death or grave misbehaviour, he could look forward to a ripe old age in the service."[10] Junior officers turned over more rapidly, resigning out of frustration with the lifestyle of frequent moves, sanctions on marriage, bad pay and low chance of promotion, or as a result of failing examinations for promotion due to inexperience and lack of training.

Opportunities for training were poor for the Permanent Force regiments of infantry - Royal Canadian Regiment, Royal 22e Régiment, and Princess Patricia's Canadian Light Infantry; cavalry - Royal Canadian Dragoons, Lord Strathcona's Horse (Royal Canadians); and the Royal Canadian Artillery and Royal Canadian Horse Artillery. Summer combined exercises usually were cancelled through lack of funds. Since most regiments were distributed over several bases spread across the country, even single units lacked the opportunity to train cohesively.[11] A major function of the Permanent Force was the supply of officers and N.C.O.s to train Non-Permanent Militia units weekly in the various military districts.

The Non-Permanent Active Militia also was starved of funds and equipment, and such basic items as uniforms and boots often were in short supply. However, as before the war, membership in the militia conferred some social status, especially for officers, and after World War I units persisted in large and smaller urban centres throughout the country. The opportunity for the Non-Permanent Militia to train was limited to weekly drill with two-week summer camps, which, like the Permanent Forces exercises, more-often-than-not were cancelled. Although in 1938 the Non-Permanent Militia nominally had over 50,000 men, including over 6,000 officers, real strength may not have been half that, and, in most units the standard of military training was low.[12]

THE CANADIAN ARMY VETERINARY SERVICE IN TRANSITION 1919-1922 Demobilization of C.A.V.C. (C.E.F.) personnel overseas proceeded through the spring and summer of 1919. Lieut.-Col. Edgett returned to Canada in July, 1919, as did Tamblyn, Evans and Cutcliffe, while Saunders retired in England.[13] With the departure of these senior officers, the organization ceased to exist in fact, although it was not officially disbanded until 1920.[14]

In April 1919, the Canadian Permanent Army Veterinary Corps was reconstituted as the Royal Canadian Army Veterinary Corps, and the number of officers (7) and other ranks (23), and distribution by Military District were established,[15] although the title 'Royal' was not officially granted until November 1919.[16] Meanwhile, in January 1919, Brig.-Gen. William Neill had resigned his commission in the C.P.A.V.C., as did Arthur Frape, his Staff Captain overseas and the C.P.A.V.C. Quartermaster.[17] That left only two veterinary officers in the Permanent Force in July 1919, Lieut.-Col. T.J. de Montarville Taschereau, and Capt. J.R.J. Duhault.[18] The former was with the Siberian Expeditionary Force until May 1919; upon returning he was stationed in Kingston as the A.D.V.S. Military District 3, Neill's former post.[19] Duhault was not returned from C.E.F. service overseas until September 1919; in April 1920, he was gazetted Major in the R.C.A.V.C., rejoined 'A' Squadron, Lord Strathcona's Horse (Royal Canadians) and became S.V.O. Military District 10, Winnipeg.[20]

Figure 17.1. Lieut.-Col. T.J.deM. Taschereau, c. 1917. (*NAC PA 203432*)

During this period, someone, perhaps Taschereau, or superiors in the Directorate of Transport and Supply, engaged in recruiting to fill the establishment of the R.C.A.V.C. In late 1919 Lieut.-Col. Marcelin A. Piché C.A.V.C. returned from London, where he had been assisting with demobilization of the C.E.F. On 1 April 1920, he was gazetted Lieutenant-Colonel in the R.C.A.V.C., S.V.O. Military District 4, Montreal which was later moved to St. Jean, and became veterinarian to 'A' Squadron, Royal Canadian Dragoons, St. Jean.[21] At the same time, Lieut.-Col. David S. Tamblyn, Lieut.-Col. T. Charles Evans and Capt. F.S. Macdonald were also gazetted in the R.C.A.V.C. Tamblyn was recruited from a field position with the Health of Animals Branch of the Dominion Department of Agriculture in Saskatchewan, to which he had returned briefly after demobilization. He was stationed in Calgary, S.V.O. Military District 13 and provided veterinary care to the horses of 'B' Squadron, Lord Strathcona's Horse (R.C).[22] Evans had returned briefly to his post in Ottawa as pathologist with Health of Animals Branch, before re-joining the R.C.A.V.C. He was stationed at Stanley Barracks in Toronto, S.V.O. Military District 2, and veterinary officer to 'B' Squadron, Royal Canadian Dragoons.[23] Macdonald was S.V.O. Military District 5, Quebec City.[24] In December 1920, Capt. Fred. Walsh was gazetted in the R.C.A.V.C., completing its complement; he was S.V.O. Military District 3, Kingston and the Royal Canadian Horse Artillery, with Taschereau's move to Ottawa (see below).[25]

Figure 17.2. Lieut.-Col. M.A. Piché c. 1913. (*Steele, 1914*)

Concurrently, the establishment of officers in the R.C.A.V.C. was amended to accommodate the appointments made (from 2 Colonels and Lieut.-Colonels, 1 Major, 2 Captains and 2 Lieutenants, to 4 Lieut.-Colonels, 2 Majors and 1 Captain).[26] The R.C.A.V.C. thus began the interwar period as a small unit top-heavy with senior officers, a classic example of the demographic problem in the Permanent Force as a whole, although that clearly had not been the intent, given the distribution of ranks promulgated in the original 1919 establishment. In 1920 the youngest officer (Duhault) was 32, the eldest (Piché) 54, with the others, except Tamblyn, who was 39, in their 40's or early 50's. None had been graduated less than 10 years, and while they had a wealth of experience as military veterinarians, from the U.S. Cavalry in the far west (Piché) to the mud of Flanders, they were, at best, a 'mature' group.[27]

In November 1920, Lieut-Col. T.J.deM. Taschereau assumed command of the Canadian Army Veterinary Services, the administration of which was transferred from the Director of Transport and Supplies, where it had resided since Neill went overseas with the C.E.F. in 1914.[28] Subsequently, the senior veterinary officer held the command until the service was disbanded. Taschereau moved to Militia Headquarters, Ottawa, but effective August 1922 he retired. Lieut.-Col. Piché, also a French-Canadian, succeeded him as Administrator of Veterinary Services in June 1922.[29]

The organization of the Canadian Army Veterinary Corps (N.P.A.M.) was amended in June 1920 to include Mobile Veterinary Sections, which were not contemplated in the original pre-war establishment.[30] Effective January 1921, the C.A.V.C. was disbanded for reorganization, and a new establishment was set at 140 Officers, 49 senior N.C.O.s, and 211 rank and file, for a total of 400 men, plus 140 riding horses for the officers. These were dispersed among the 11 Military Districts in 11 Sections, 7 Mobile Veterinary Sections, 2 Cavalry Mobile Veterinary Sections, and as regimental veterinary officers with horsed units.[31] Between late 1920 and early 1922, R.C.A.V.C. officers, as S.V.O.s, sorted through the over 360 officers nominally in the C.A.V.C. based on the Militia List, seeking those in their Military District, correcting names that had been mis-spelled for years, determining who was still alive, where they were, and rating their qualities. Veterinarians selected from those who had served in the C.A.V.C. (N.P.A.M.) or overseas, in the R.A.V.C., or in the Regimental Veterinary Service were canvassed. Those willing to serve actively were assigned to fill vacancies as veterinary officers in the C.A.V.C.; the remainder were placed on the reserve list or retired.[32] By late 1922, there were 96 veterinary officers in the C.A.V.C.: 31 with N.P.A.M. cavalry regiments, 23 with artillery batteries, 13 assigned to divisional transportation trains or engineer companies, 5 with mobile veterinary sections, 3 administrative, 20 unassigned, and 1 on the Corps Reserve.[33]

The terms of initial appointment and advancement in both the R.C.A.V.C. and the C.A.V.C. were amended in 1922. Initial appointments were at the rank of Lieutenant, with promotion to Captain after a year's service, if qualified. Promotion to Major and Lieut.-Colonel would be subject to qualification and establishment (i.e. a vacancy at the higher rank due to turn-over).[34]

By the end of 1922, the organization of the post-war Canadian Army Veterinary Service was complete, and many of the officers who would carry it through the next decade were in place.[35] *Regulations for The Canadian Army Veterinary Service, 1923* summarizes the organization and *modus operandi* of the Veterinary Service at this stage. Other than updating of minor regulations, and including photographs of identifying markings on horses, they vary little from the earlier 1912 and 1916 Regulations. Already the fiscal trend for the next 18 years had been established. "...August 1921 the strength of the Permanent Army Veterinary Services was reduced from 7 officers and 22 [sic] other ranks to 7 officers and 7 other ranks in order to effect necessary economy."[36] And in mid-1922, Taschereau's retirement reduced the number of officers in the R.C.A.V.C. to six.

UNIFORMS AND TRADITIONS With the exception of service dress, introduced in 1903 under *General Order 49 - 1903,* to replace the undress uniform for every day wear, Veterinary Surgeons/Officers wore the uniform of the regiment to which they were attached (see Figures 1.1, 1.2), since until 1905 there was no Veterinary Service to necessitate a common uniform. *The Canadian Militia Dress Regulations 1907*,[37] developed to reform the uniform following lessons learned in the Boer War, then established the uniforms of The Army Veterinary Department and its successors until 1938.[38] Full dress, undress, mess dress and service dress uniforms were prescribed for officers. However, until the C.A.V.C. was introduced, some veterinary officers still wore the uniform of the unit to which they were attached (Figure 12.2), and members of the Regimental Veterinary Service may have continued to.

The full dress uniform for officers of The Army Veterinary Department ranking below Colonel (Figure 17.3) was comprised of a blue cloth tunic with maroon cloth collar and cuffs, with lace trim around the collar and gold Russia braid at the bottom. The cuffs of the tunic were edged with gold cord, forming an Austrian knot traced with gold Russia braid. Buttons had an indented pattern of 'Army Veterinary Department' in a circle on an 8-

Figure 17.3. Full Dress Uniform, Officer, Royal Canadian Army Veterinary Corps.[39] (*A.H. Bowling*)

pointed star, surmounted by a crown, and within the circle the Royal Cipher.[40] A shoulder belt of gold lace two inches wide, the gold lace sword belt 1 ½ inches wide, and sword slings, had a maroon stripe down the centre. A twisted round gold shouldercord lined with blue was also worn. On the waist belt was a gilt metal frosted plate with the Royal Cipher and Crown in silver, encircled with maple leaves, and on the bottom of the wreath a scroll inscribed 'Dieu et mon Droit'. The trousers or pantaloons (riding breeches) were blue cloth, with two maroon stipes 3/4 of an inch wide and 1/8 inch apart down the side seem. High jacked boots with silver spurs were worn when riding, Wellington boots with boxes for spurs when dismounted. A gold ornamented maroon cloth pouch was worn on the waist belt. Gloves were of white buckskin. A universal pattern white cloth-covered cork helmet was worn, surmounted with a ball in a leaf cup, extending 1 3/4 inches from the centre of the top of the helmet. The helmet plate had the monogrammed initials 'AVD' in silver on a ground of green enamel. A cavalry pattern sword about 3 ft. 5' long, with slightly curved blade, and scabbard, was worn at the waist.

The undress uniform was a frock coat (required for permanent force officers only) or 'patrol jacket universal', the former double breasted (Figure 17.2), the latter single breasted (Figures 1.3, 1.4, 3.3), in blue cloth or serge. Both had a stand up collar, and shoulder straps, the latter the colour of the regimental facings, maroon for the Veterinary Department, with the badges of rank embroidered in gold. White buckskin gloves were to be worn with the tunic. The sword belt was as for the full dress uniform, as were belt plates, buttons, trousers or pantaloons, boots etc. A blue cloth peaked universal pattern forage or naval pattern cap, with band and welts of maroon cloth, was worn. A cap badge in gilt metal, with a wreath surmounted by a crown, and within the wreath a monogram 'A.V.D.' in silver was worn, as was a pair of similar but smaller collar badges. This badge pattern was superceded about 1912 by the C.A.V.C. pattern, with a wreath of maple leaves, topped by a beaver, and the contained monogram 'CVC' (see figure page v).[41] A uniform similar to the officer's undress uniform with 'patrol jacket universal' was worn by N.C.O.s and Other Ranks of the C.A.V.C and C.P.A.V.C, once they were formed, after 1910-12.

The mess kit was comprised of a universal pattern blue cloth mess jacket with maroon roll collar, blue shoulder straps with embroidered badges of rank, pointed maroon cloth cuffs, no buttons, braid or piping. Collar badges as on the tunic, miniature decorations and medals were to be worn. Alternatively, a blue cloth mess waistcoat could be worn, cloth, no collar, open in front, fastened with four buttons. A linen collar and black necktie was prescribed. Trousers and boots were as full dress uniform.

The service dress (Figures 3.1, 3.3), worn at camp, on manoeuvres etc., had a drab (khaki) serge single-breasted jacket, with turn down lapel collar on which collar badges of the corps were worn, and shoulder straps edged with white cloth, and with a loop of maroon braid, on which bronze badges of rank were worn. The cuffs had a flap edged with chevron lace, and rings of worsted chevron lace and braid were worn according to rank. Buttons were as for the dress tunic. In 1912 the design was changed slightly and after that it was worn with a drab collar and black knotted tie on parade, while in 1914, a drab shirt, collar and tie were made regulation. A Sam Browne leather belt was worn, with a sword-frog, an ammunition pouch, and a pistol case; veterinary officers carried their instrument case in the breast pocket of their jacket. Riding breeches of khaki Bedford cord were worn with brown leather leggings or woolen putties, and brown ankle boots with steel jack spurs. A khaki forage cap was worn with the cap badge in the pattern described for the undress uniform, but in bronze. Cork helmets, Stetson hats, and straw hats were also uniform issue (Figure 3.1). Service dress, with the tunic buttoned at the neck, also was worn by N.C.O.s and Other Ranks of the C.A.V.C. and C.P.A.V.C after they were formed.

In 1912 the Wolseley pattern helmet replaced the universal pattern helmet. In 1913, C.A.V.C. officers, as part of Winter Dress, were authorized to wear a black Persian lamb fur cap with a puggaree badge (cap badge) in front, and a maroon cloth bag on the right side.[42]

Overseas in the Canadian Expeditionary Force during World War I, veterinary officers wore the service dress prescribed for mounted officers.[43] It resembled that in the C.A.V.C. at home, with a lapeled jacket and breeches, shirt, collar and tie, Sam Browne belt, and high lace-up riding boots, or ankle boots with leather leggings or puttees. Officers were responsible for purchasing their own kit, and some wore highly-tailored uniforms (see Figures 7.1 and 10.3), while others made do with less well-fitted apparel (Figure 8.1). The forage cap came in 'stiff', or 'semi-stiff' forms, though some may have worn the prohibited softer British pattern trench cap (Figure 12.5). The cap badge could vary markedly.[44] Many used the 1912 C.A.V.C. badge (see Figures p. v, and 12.3), while later in the war, some wore the C.E.F. style maple leaf C.A.V.C. badge (Figures p. xi and 6.6), or, rarely, the general issue C.E.F. badge (Figure 17.8). Others wore what appears to be an Army Veterinary Corps (Imperial) cap badge (see Figures 7.2, 17.1). Smaller matching collar badges were to be worn, but often they did not match, and sometimes were not worn (Fig. 12.3). The permutations and combinations arising from the variations in headwear, badges, legwear and boots sometimes made for a very non-uniform uniform (see Figure 7.3 for a variety of expressions of officers' service dress).

N.C.O.s and Other Ranks wore Canadian 7 button khaki tunics with stand-up collars, or British pattern 5 button tunics with roll collars, which sometimes were Canadianized by being converted to a stand-up collar type (Figures 5.10, 6. 9, 7.3 and 9.6). Brass 'CAVC' shoulder titles were worn above the 'CANADA' title on the upper part of the sleeve. Men in France seem to have worn the plain C.E.F. non-corps maple leaf cap badge (Figure 9.6), or the C.E.F. style maple leaf C.A.V.C. badge, but in England the 1912 pattern C.A.V.C. badge commonly was used (Figure 5.10). Pantaloons, puttees, ankle boots and spurs were worn, as were leather bandoliers by junior N.C.O.s and privates or troopers (Figures 9.6, 9.10). Warrant Officers Class 1 wore a Sam Browne belt and some Warrant Officers and Staff Sergeants wore high riding boots (Figures 7.3, 9.10).

However, until 1938, when 'battledress' was introduced, the Permanent Force and N.P.A.M. units in Canada continued to wear the 1907 uniform as modified slightly from time-to-time, despite strong commentary from some quarters agitating for more practical clothing. Peaked forage caps, Sam Browne belts, breeches and brass buttons attracted particular ire for their impracticality.[45] Until the late 1930's, the Royal Canadian Dragoons were still wearing cork helmets and carrying swords on manoeuvres (Figure 17.5).[46] The major change of significance to the Veterinary Service was the authorization in 1922 of the use by the R.C.A.V.C. of a new cap and collar badge (Figure 17.4), based on the post-war British R.A.V.C. Centaur pattern badge.[41] Members of the N.P.A.M. were authorized to use the same badge when the C.A.V.C. was renamed Royal Canadian Army Veterinary Corps

Figure 17.4. Centaur pattern Royal Canadian Army Veterinary Corps cap badge, 1922. (*C.A.V. Barker Museum*)

Figure 17.5. A machine gun troop of Royal Canadian Dragoons on exercises at Camp Borden, 1937. In the absence of an actual machine gun, the banner with the arrow signifies their role. The men wear cork helmets, and swords are carried in a scabbard on the saddle. Lurking on the road in the right background are several motor vehicles. (*Archives, Royal Canadian Dragoons*)

(Non-Permanent) in 1936.[47] An R.C.A.V.C. style button was promulgated in 1923; it resembled the original 1907 button, but 'RCAVC' replaced 'AVD' around the outside.[48]

Each unit in the Canadian Militia had a Regimental March. That of the R.C.A.V.C. was The Royal Army Ordnance Corps March, 'The Village Blacksmith'.[49]

In 1930, the R.C.A.V.C. and the C.A.V.C. were allied officially with the Royal Army Veterinary Corps of the British Army.[50]

MECHANIZATION Conditions in the Canadian Army peaked with reorganization in 1920-21, and rapidly went downhill, with little financial respite but for a slight increase in spending in the late 1930's, and only token mechanization. The Veterinary Service was no exception to the general pattern, but rather than rejuvenation, it experienced extinction at the end of this period. In fact, its demise probably was hastened by World War II, which forced the army to mechanize.

Mechanization was adopted by or imposed on military forces world-wide during the inter-war period. Motor vehicles had failed as transport at the front in the First War to a large extent because of their inability to cope with mud, but further in the rear, hundreds of thousands were in use on the Allied side by the end of the conflict. Other than some crawler tractors, automotive power seems rarely to have been used to draw guns, the hitches, wheels and suspension of which could not cope with towing at high speed until modified for the purpose. The promise of armour had been glimpsed during W.W. I in the success of numerous but rather primitive tanks and armoured machine gun cars. The significance of air superiority, though not its full potential, had been appreciated. However, from May 1915 to January 1916, the Canadian Cavalry Brigade had fought dismounted, since there was little tactical opportunity for its use on a static entrenched front. Mounted, cavalry was vulnerable to the machine gun, shrapnel from artillery air bursts, and strafing by fighter planes, ending its use as a shock force, and restricting its function to reconnaissance, exploitation of breakthroughs, and pursuit.[51] Even then it was exposed.

Hence, as was the case in civilian life, at the end of World War I the days of the horse in a military role seemed numbered. Yet some armies, including the Germans, went into the Second War with mounted units and much horse transport. As late as 1936, the German Army had only one Panzer Regiment operational; the Soviet Red Army had two mechanized corps in 1932, the French army had formed an armoured division in 1934, while it was 1939 before the British had a comparable formation.[52] The rate of mechanization was a function of the degree of conservatism of major decision-makers in the army in question; the trial-and-error mode of development of armoured and other military vehicles, and the tactics for their use; and the political priorities and financial resources of the country, necessary to justify and fund the development and acquisition of equipment which, with

Figure 17.6. 'The Modern Horse Gunners' was the title for this photo of the March Past of 'A' Battery, Royal Canadian Horse Artillery, c. 1933. Guns (hidden) are hauled by six-wheel Leyland trucks acquired in 1930. Bandsmen are just visible on the right. (*Canadian Defence Quarterly Vol. 10, p. 393, 1932-33*)

relatively rapid evolution in the area, might quickly become outmoded or obsolete.[53]

In the Canadian army, with some exceptions, notably E.L.M. Burns,[54] there were few early open advocates of mechanization. He published 'The Mechanicalization of Cavalry' in 1924[55], and for the next 15 years The Canadian Defence Quarterly contained articles advocating mechanization.[56] Counter-balancing the thinkers and dreamers were the traditionalists and die-hards, who described or extolled the place of the horse in the military.[57] Even a better hitch for securing loads to pack animals was reported.[58] The 1931 International Jumping Team, organized by Lieut.-Col. R.S. Timmis, O.C. Royal Canadian Dragoons, rated more space in the 'Military Notes' of one issue than 'Mechanization', though the latter was top of the page.[59] And it was reassuring to learn from a recently-mechanized British cavalry officer that "The moral and physical deterioration which some pessimists prophesied when the order to mechanize was first received has certainly not yet begun to set in...Our polo team has...won the Inter-regimental in Egypt for the past three years..."[60]

Mechanization outside the Motor Machine Gun Brigade crept into the Canadian Army with the artillery. Non-Permanent Militia field batteries had originally hired horses for use during training at Camp Petawawa, but with budget reductions, after 1923 they were supplied by the Royal Canadian Horse Artillery, a Permanent Force unit. However, in 1925 the R.C.H.A. was called out to control strikers in Cape Breton, and that year, Field Artillery guns at Petawawa had to be hauled by tractors. In 1928, trials were conducted to select a truck for army use, and in 1929, the 3rd Medium Battery, Royal Canadian Artillery, Kingston was equipped with Leyland six-wheel trucks for hauling artillery. In March 1930, 'A' and 'B' Batteries of the Royal Canadian Horse Artillery Brigade, Kingston paraded as mounted units for the last time. They retained a riding establishment for training and ceremonial purposes, but the remainder of the horses were sorted at the Artillery Park (quite likely by Lieut.-Col. David Tamblyn) and dispersed to 'C' Battery R.C.H.A. in Winnipeg, and other Permanent Force Units. The Leyland trucks (Figure 7.6) and six-wheel Crossley cars that replaced them were received in May 1930. Mechanization of the R.C.H.A. was completed when 'C' Battery in Winnipeg converted to gun tractors in 1935. An Artillery Field Brigade, comprised of a headquarters and four batteries of four guns, had 402 horses which had to be fed, groomed and exercised 365 days of the year; they were replaced by 16 gun tractors, 14 staff cars, 5 light lorries and 5 bicycles. However, effective mechanization of other artillery elements of the Permanent or Non-Permanent Militia did not occur prior to World War II, although all were officially authorized the reduced manpower of 'mechanized' establishments in 1938.[61]

The shortage of money prevented official training camps for N.P.A.M. artillery units for much of the 1930's, but some batteries did cobble together summer field exercises, necessarily without horses, which they would have had to hire. Rather, they improvised, using borrowed or rented private automobiles and trucks to carry men and supplies, and to haul guns.[62] So straitened circumstances forced functional, if not official, mechanization of the N.P.A.M. artillery; a veterinary officer obviously was not required to attend their camps!

Mechanization of the cavalry was even more tentative. In 1930, a few small tracked Carden-Lloyd 'tankettes' were purchased for training, and in 1934, two experimental armoured cars, a Ford and a Chevrolet, were obtained. One was eventually placed with 'A' Squadron, Royal Canadian Dragoons, in St. Jean, and one with 'A'

Figure 17.7. Veterans of W.W. I still serving with the Royal Canadian Dragoons, Camp Petawawa, 1937. Lieut.-Col. J.R.J. Duhault, O.B.E, R.C.A.V.C. is front row, fourth from left, in shorts; Tpt. Maj. A.E. Galloway is back row, left.[66] (*Royal Canadian Dragoons Archives, CFB Petawawa*)

Squadron, Lord Strathcona's Horse in Winnipeg. Along with several Ford 'reconnaissance' vehicles and private automobiles, they first took part in combined training with the cavalry in 1936;[63] other units not so equipped had been practising combined cavalry and mechanized operations with civilian vehicles.[64] In 1937, the Royal Canadian Dragoons conducted a 300 mile route march from St. Jean to Camp Petawawa accompanied by their armoured car and mechanized support vehicles, including a float to transport tired or injured horses. The good condition of the horses during this journey "...of course, was due in large measure to the attentive services of our Veterinary Officer, Lt.-Col. J. Duhault, R.C.A.V.C."[65] (Figure 17.7). In 1938, 'A' Squadron Royal Canadian Dragoons conducted combined manoeuvres with cavalry, recce cars, the armoured car, the Carden-Lloyds and airplanes. Meanwhile, the Canadian Armoured Fighting Vehicle School had been established at Camp Borden, equipped, by 1939, with several light tanks in addition to the armoured car. After war was declared in September 1939, the Canadian Army was forced to take a decision about mechanization, and in mid-1940, it lurched out of the horse age. By June the Permanent Force cavalry regiments had been dismounted; they were saved from dispersal by their erstwhile nemesis, E.L.M. Burns, and incorporated into the Canadian Armoured Corps when it was formed in August 1940.[67]

DOWNHILL COURSE 1923-1940 The vacancy in the R.C.A.V.C. created by Taschereau's retirement had been filled in May 1923 by Capt. William J. Morgan (Figure 17.8), who was stationed in Montreal. He also was a 'mature' officer, 54 years old, a veteran of the Boer War and, briefly, the C.A.V.C. in France, with about 30 years in the Regimental Veterinary Service, N.P.A.M., attending artillery units in the Kingston area. He even had commanded the 32nd 'Kingston' Battery C.F.A.[68] But after his departure in 1924 the R.C.A.V.C. was allowed to run down; retirements were not replaced. In March 1923, Duhault, who had been promoted to Lieut.-Col. in 1922, and Macdonald exchanged postings; the former moved to Quebec City, and the latter to Winnipeg.[69] In August 1925, Tamblyn and Walsh did the same, the former transferring to Kingston, the latter to Calgary.[70] Macdonald left the service in 1929,[71] and when Piché retired in June 1930, Tamblyn replaced him as Officer Administering the Canadian Army Veterinary Services.[72] Duhault returned to Winnipeg in 1930, and Walsh retired December 1934.[73] In April 1936, Tamblyn suffered a near-fatal heart attack and Evans became Acting Officer Administering Army Veterinary Services.[74] Later that year Duhault was posted to M.D. No. 4, at St. Jean, with 'A' Squadron of the Royal Canadian Dragoons, probably to compensate for Tamblyn's absence, and he remained there for the rest of his career.[75] When Tamblyn was forced to retire on medical grounds in March 1937, Evans succeeded him as the last O.A.C.A.V.S., Duhault his remaining Permanent Force officer.[76] Although Corps headquarters and records were in Kingston, Evans remained in Toronto. Tamblyn was appointed Honorary Lieut.-Col., R.C.A.V.C. in October 1937.[77]

Figure 17.8. Capt. W.J. Morgan c. 1918. (*NAC PA 7737*)

Counter-intuitively, in 1928 the Peace Establishment of the R.C.A.V.C. had been increased, to 12 officers and 38 Other Ranks,[78] neither of which was approached during the decline of the Corps. Revised regulations governing administration of the Veterinary Service dated 1930 were drafted in 1929.[79] They are not mentioned in General Orders, and may not have been officially promulgated, but a subsequent description of the Army Veterinary Service by Tamblyn follows them closely.[80] They updated instructions for executive veterinary officers with respect to managing routine duties. The lists of diseases, especially infectious diseases, as well as the lists of drugs and instruments, also were updated. Appointments to the R.C.A.V.C. (hypothetical, since no more were made) were to be at the rank of Lieutenant, with eligibility for promotion to captain after 8 years, and to major after a total of 15 years commissioned service. Appointments to the C.A.V.C. were to be at the rank of Lieutenant, with eligibility for promotion to Captain after two years; higher promotion was to be based on qualification and establishment.

During this period, R.C.A.V.C. officers saw to the horses of the Permanent Force cavalry squadrons in St. Jean, Toronto, Winnipeg and Calgary, to the Royal Canadian Horse Artillery in Kingston and Winnipeg, and at Permanent Force and N.P.A.M. concentrations at Sarcee Camp in Alberta; Camp Hughes in Manitoba; Camp Borden; Niagara-on-the-Lake; Camp Petawawa; Barriefield, near Kingston; St. Jean; Sussex N.B.; and Aldershot in Nova Scotia.[81] At the 1929 Sarcee Camp exercises, "the Veterinary Hospital provided treatment for the horses of 'C' Battery, R.C.H.A. Winnipeg, 'A' Squadron Lord Strathcona Horse (Royal Canadians), and a couple of animals from No. 13 Detachment, Royal Canadian Army Service Corps of Calgary. The horse lines for these units were on opposite sides of a road with the Veterinary Hospital adjacent."[82]

Veterinary Stores, such as medications, dressings, instruments etc. (Figure 17.9) were inspected and inventoried by D.V.O.s, all horses in Permanent Force units were inspected annually, and occasionally a remount was purchased (at least 15.2 hands, 5 years old, maximum price $200, and subject to mallein test).[84] D.V.O.s, some of whom were Non-Permanent, also recommended appointments and supervised personnel and training matters in the Non-Permanent arm of the service. They inspected all horses taken on strength for camps, dispensed Veterinary Field Chests to unit veterinary officers involved in camps, and audited the status of horses and drugs during camps.

As the number of Permanent Force officers dwindled, they covered broader areas. For instance, after Piché's retirement in 1930, Tamblyn, at Kingston, was O.A.C.A.V.S. and D.V.O. M.D. No. 3, but also served as executive veterinary officer to 'A' Squadron, Royal Canadian Dragoons, St. Jean Quebec, in M.D. No. 4,[85] the Royal Canadian Horse Artillery in Kingston having largely mechanized. This involved care for sick horses, as well as implementing preventative measures and ensuring good husbandry and horsemanship, in stables and at camp. In 1934, one of the horses at St. Jean was mallein test positive; 20 animals were ordered destroyed by the Dominion Department of Agriculture, and glanders was confirmed at autopsy by Tamblyn. During the Depression, R.C.A.V.C. officers also attended at sites where workers on the Unemployment Relief Scheme, administered by A.G.L. McNaughton, Chief of General Staff, were constructing military bases, presumably using draft horses.[86] If Permanent Force veterinary officers were unavailable temporarily, or, as the Corps was run down, permanently, C.A.V.C. officers were contracted to cover for them at camps and as regimental veterinary officers.[87]

Reflecting its financial woes, the army was frugal to the point of being miserly and oppressive in its administration of the Veterinary Service. From November 1929-February 1930 Tamblyn was attached to the R.A.V.C. Headquarters at Aldershot, England, in order to familiarize himself and the Corps with current British methods; in return for the opportunity, he had to sign a bond of 10 years further service.[88] Local travel on legitimate

Figure 17.9. Veterinary Stores, Fort Osborne Barracks, Winnipeg, attended by Quartermaster Sergeant Farrier Fred C. Rush. Although this is a C.P.A.V.C. store in 1912, little would have changed in an R.C.A.V.C. store in 1922, or 1932.[83]
(Lord Strathcona's Horse (Royal Canadians) Museum, Calgary Alberta)

business, even by an officer of Tamblyn's seniority, needed formal application and higher approval, and often was refused, "owing to paucity of funds", for such short distances as Kingston-Ottawa.[89] Travel claims were examined in minute detail and petty questions asked.[90]

Consonant with difficulties in other arms of the N.P.A.M., the C.A.V.C. often seems to have had problems in establishing effective units and training. In 1924, Lieut.-Col. Angus Tracy, O.C. No. 4 Veterinary Section, wrote apologetically to Piché, indicating that the economic conditions had driven most of his men to seek work elsewhere. "Unemployment is the bane of all units in Sherbrooke and we are all carrying men...that are on leave away working or looking for work...My senior N.C.O. is at present in Lewistown Me." However, he hoped that if they were required for camp that summer, "...I will be able to turn out a good section as I did in days gone by."[91]

In 1928, due to financial constraints and lack of opportunity for meaningful training, the C.A.V.C. Mobile Veterinary Sections and the Cavalry Mobile Veterinary Section were constituted 'Reserve' units, to be mobilized in time of need. However, the 11 Veterinary Sections established in 1921 were retained.[92] These would form the basis for veterinary hospitals on mobilization, but had very low establishments of Other Ranks. Most C.A.V.C. officers, as executive veterinary officers of cavalry regiments or artillery batteries, performed their main duties, and had opportunity for training, only if their units went to camp.[93] They were responsible for inspection of hire horses prior to and during camp; describing and reporting to the D.V.O. on the status and well-being of horses in their charge; treatment of any illness or injury during camp; and disposition of horse claims arising from mishap or disease in camp. Ideally, they would carry on demonstrations and exercises for C.A.V.C. Other Ranks when they were not required on scheduled duty in camp. During the off-season, lectures on topics such as management, first aid, destruction of animals, and functions of mobile veterinary sections, evacuation stations and veterinary base hospitals in war were to be arranged.[94] The limitations on training opportunities imposed by regulations, and the low frequency of camps, with decreasing use of horses due to cost, necessarily compromised C.A.V.C. preparedness, and cannot have contributed to morale.

Although appointments of C.A.V.C. officers to regimental posts were to be for five years, renewable if in the interests of the service, renewal was the norm, turnover was rare, and many officers served for 10 or more years with the same unit. In December 1922, the C.A.V.C. had 9 Lieutenant-Colonels, 23 Majors, 48 Captains and 15 Lieutenants (95 active list);[95] in 1935, before Militia re-organization, the corresponding numbers were 7, 22, 17 and 15 (61 active list),[96] relative accumulation occurring at the higher ranks in an organization declining in numbers, though not in establishment; stagnation in rank was obvious. In 1935, 9/17 captains were veterans of W.W. I. Although recruitment of junior officers was continuous, it did not keep up with attrition. Tamblyn recognized this problem, stating "Retarded promotion...by the retention of senior officers who have reached the age limit, is not conducive to maintaining interest for the junior officer."[97] After becoming O.A.C.A.V.S. in 1930 he may have engineered the synchronous turnover of many senior C.A.V.C. officers that occurred in October 1931, when over half the Lieutenant-Colonels and Majors remaining in the service in 1932 were gazetted to rank, following promotions formerly blocked by elderly incumbents.[98]

In 1935-36 the Non-Permanent Active Militia was radically reorganized, the effect of which was to reduce markedly the number of cavalry regiments and infantry battalions, to maintain the number of artillery units, to increase engineer units, and to create armoured units[99] (although equipment and mechanization did not accompany reorganization). The effect on the now R.C.A.V.C.(N.P.) was a reduction in establishment to 50 veterinary officers,[100] in recognition of staffing reality and the reduction in requirement for horse transport, horse-drawn artillery and cavalry operations. This was accompanied by a re-alignment of the skeletal reserve veterinary units to more realistically reflect the structure of a corps mobilized for war. Thus, the old Veterinary Sections, which served as elements of veterinary base hospitals, were abolished, and the Mobile Veterinary Sections, which had been reduced to a reserve role in 1928, were resurrected as the major operational entity, with seven in the establishment, along with two Cavalry Mobile Veterinary Sections, a single Veterinary Evacuating Station, and a single Veterinary Hospital.[101] Veterinary officers were distributed among the formed units of the R.C.A.V.C.(N.P.), not all of which were fully manned, and attached to mounted units.

In December, 1936, just prior to reorganization taking effect, there were 55 veterinary officers on the active list,[102] of whom 28 were attached to cavalry regiments, 9 to artillery batteries, 4 to engineer companies, and the remainder to veterinary divisional sections, or unassigned. At reorganization, with the loss or mechanization of units, many officers of all ranks retired, possibly for reasons of seniority, morale, or because they could not be re-deployed readily due to their location. Twenty-four of the 55 officers in the Corps in December 1936 were not on the active list in November 1939, two months after the declaration of war. However, active recruiting had gone on, and at that time there were 44 veterinary officers;[103] of the 13 of who had joined since 1937, 6 did so in 1939. Nineteen were attached to cavalry regiments (mergers and mechanization mandated in 1936 had not taken effect), 24 to R.C.A.V.C.(N.P.) units, and one to an engineer company. One of the Provisional Lieutenants was a member of the Canadian Officer Training Corps. In 1939, a revision of the Regulations for the Canadian Army Veterinary Services which reflected these changes was drafted, but apparently never promulgated or published.[104]

Thus at the outbreak of war, the R.C.A.V.C.(N.P.) seemed to have reorganized successfully, rationalizing its mission and rejuvenating its officer corps with young blood. But it was hitched to the dying horse.

CANADIAN OFFICER TRAINING CORPS The Canadian Officer Training Corps was organized to provide military training to university students, so that they might later serve as officers in the Permanent Force or N.P.A.M. Although a veterinary platoon had been on the establishment of the C.O.T.C. contingent at Guelph since 1923, it was activated only in 1935.[105] The first three candidates, already C.O.T.C. infantry Lieutenants, trained themselves in the 'R.C.A.V.C.' component of the examination, and qualified as C.O.T.C. Captains in 1935, eligible for a Veterinary Service commission upon graduation. In 1936, two others successfully followed the same path. In 1937, Lieut. A.A. Kingscote, R.C.A., ex-R.N.W.M.P. and Professor of Parasitology at the Ontario Veterinary College, tutored candidates in the 'common-to-all-arms' subjects, and beginning in 1938 Capt. George Cairns, R.C.A.V.C.(N.P.), also a faculty member, tutored in army equitation using hired horses, and dealt with Veterinary Service organization, regulations, and treatment of army horses and mules.[106] These cohorts of students were very successful officer candidates. At least six, and probably over a dozen candidates passed the examinations qualifying them for a commission in the R.C.A.V.C.(N.P.) at graduation.[107]

After the Second World War began, most male O.V.C. students joined the wartime C.O.T.C. 'Auxiliary Battalion'. Ontario Agricultural College students formed Platoons A, B, and C, while veterinary students drilled in Platoon D, under 2nd Lieutenants T.L. Jones and V.R. Brown, with regular C.O.T.C. Cadets as N.C.O.s. They even formed a band. Such drill fulfilled half the wartime military training obligation of students, and qualified those who wished to join for entrance into the regular C.O.T.C. program.[108]

Although the R.C.A.V.C. was not to be the vehicle of service, many of these men entered the armed forces in W.W. II, and a number died in the cause of peace.[109]

DISBANDMENT The senior officers in the R.C.A.V.C. in the inter-war period clearly were backward-looking and horse-oriented, and if they saw the writing on the wall for the Corps in relation to mechanization, they seem to have ignored the message.

Evans, as editor of *The Canadian Veterinary Record* in the early 1920's, published numerous items on the Veterinary Service, and on the place of the horse in the world. His equine orientation and wishful thinking is reflected in articles such as: 'The Horse Still Thrives';[110] a review of Moore's 'Army Veterinary Service in War';[111] 'Back to Horses in England';[112] 'A Study of the Horse versus Tractor' (authored by Evans; the horse wins the comparison);[113] and 'The Australian Horse in the War'.[114] 'Famous Horse at Stanley Barracks'[115] reported the feats of 'Bucephalus', a jumper purchased by Evans, ridden by Q.M.S. Charles Lyne of the R.C.A.V.C. at the Royal Winter Fair, and later to achieve international success when ridden by Lieut.-Col. R.S. Timmis.[59] Evans published a letter by Timmis on breeding better horses for cavalry remounts,[116] while Taschereau contributed comments on the shoeing of horses and on the breeding of good horses.[117]

Tamblyn was the probable author of 'Instructional Value of the Canadian Army Veterinary Corps',[118] and in 1932 he produced a small book, '*The Horse in War*',[119] in which he memorialized the equine contribution in the First War. The strength of Tamblyn's belief in the horse, but perhaps not his insight and objectivity, is exemplified by an earlier presentation to the Veterinary Association of Alberta, also entitled 'The Horse in War', in which he "pointed out the superiority of the horse over the tank and motor-driven vehicles in actual warfare."[120]

There is limited information with which to evaluate the mindset in the R.C.A.V.C. later in the interwar period. But even in the face of inexorable, albeit slow, mechanization, Tamblyn maintained his faith in the horse: "To me, complete mechanization is not possible if efficiency and economy are to be maintained...not until war is made impossible will the horse be replaced in war".[121] However, he was aware of alternative roles for army veterinarians, alluding to "food inspection, remounts, and others" in that same article, and to war dogs in his book. An R.C.A.V.C. N.C.O. during his tenure as O.A.C.A.V.S. felt that "Tamblyn fought hard to improve the status of the Veterinary Corp [sic] but time was running out on the use of horses in the army."[122] In other words, Tamblyn fought a rearguard action in the face of mechanization, rather than actively seeking to re-orient his organization.

The only concrete evidence we have for an internal attempt to expand or refocus the role of the Veterinary Service prior to its demise is a lengthy letter from T.C. Evans to The Secretary, Department of National Defence, Ottawa, dated 21 March, 1940.[123] In it he referred to enquiries from a number of prominent veterinarians as to whether the services of the profession could be put to good use in a mechanized army. He went on to make a case for use of the Veterinary Service in food hygiene, as well as dealing with the threat of disease in captured horses and mules, cattle, sheep and goats, and swine. He used the U.S. Army Veterinary Corps as an example of such employment of veterinarians, and noted also their involvement in research. And he concluded that "there may be some place...for veterinary officers...apart from a fighting arm in the Services...although up to the present time no information has been received as to whether or not their services will ever be required."

This plaintive conclusion, and indeed the entire circumstance of the letter, suggest that up to that time Evans had been passive in dealing with the future of the Corps. He failed to enlist the external lobbyists, such as those communicating with him, to petition the government. He failed to realize how marginalized he was in the decision-making machinery, a fact implicit in his last statement. And he was too naive to recognize that such a supplicant letter sent to a nameless individual in a large organization struggling to fight a war could have little impact. One is left to believe that Evans, lacking in personal political 'pull' himself, also had no influential contacts at higher levels upon whom he could call for assistance. We have no idea what response, if any, was engendered by this letter; none is found in the file. Perhaps Evans had spent too many decades in the backwaters of provincial barracks life, administering a minuscule establishment with little profile or prestige, and meekly applying to superiors for permission to travel 50 miles, to have the self-confidence or even the capability to act more forthrightly as an advocate for his Corps and his profession. It seems not to have occurred to him to have rallied the organized profession to his cause, though it later demonstrated its willingness to act on behalf of the then-disbanded Corps. Perhaps he really was too much a 'P.F.er' to deal effectively with the challenge.

At about the same time that Evans was sending his letter off into the administrative abyss, his lone Permanent Force colleague, Duhault, was central to the ritual of permanently unhorsing the army. On 8 April, 1940, Lieut.-Col. Duhault was called upon to destroy humanely 10 horses of 'A' Squadron, Royal Canadian Dragoons at St. Jean that were unsuitable for auction or for further use. The carcasses were sold to a local dead stock dealer for $3.50 each.[124]

But one war-horse too old to be auctioned off did not take that route.[125] 'Teddy', a grey, foaled in 1910, and a Dragoon horse since 1916, was the Squadron mascot. He was groomed impeccably, and led past the entire Squadron formed up in the Barrack Square, through the gate to the drill field. One story has it that at this point he bolted, and the Squadron had to break ranks to recapture him, then form up again. He was despatched with a pistol shot fired by Lieut.-Col. Duhault. Trumpet-Major A.E. Galloway (Figure 17.7), who had ridden Teddy during the First War, sounded Last Post. After two minutes of silence, the trumpeter sounded Reveille. "...There was not a dry eye among those hardened war veterans". Teddy was buried in the earthworks at St. Jean.

The Dragoons had their last public mounted parade in June 1940. The horses still with Lord Strathcona's Horse and the Dragoons were auctioned off between June and October 1940.[126] With them went the era of the Horse Soldier in the Canadian Army, and also that of the Horse Doctor.

The Royal Canadian Dragoons, Lord Strathcona's Horse, and many N.P.A.M. cavalry units were eventually remounted, on motor-cycles, armoured cars and tanks, as units of the Canadian Armoured Corps. But the Army Veterinary Corps was not to be resurrected or reincarnated in a new rôle.

On 17 October, 1940, The Governor-General, The Earl of Athlone, signed Privy Council Order P.C. 5724 approving a Treasury Board recommendation that the Royal Canadian Army Veterinary Corps Permanent Active Militia and Non-Permanent Active Militia be disbanded, effective 1st November, 1940.[127] A saving of $10,334 was projected for the 1940-41 fiscal year (Figures 17.10 and 17.11).

Disbandment of the R.C.A.V.C. and the R.C.A.V.C.(N.P.) was effected by General Order 240-1940, 25 October, 1940: "...the Governor in Council authorizes the disbandment of the undermentioned Corps of the Active Militia effective 1st November, 1940...". One wonders whether or not this was a surprise to Evans, as Officer Administering the Veterinary Service.

At disbandment, Evans and Duhault were placed on the Supplementary List of Officers, permanently employed, but not borne on regimental establishments, while Tamblyn was required to relinquish his appointment as Honorary Lieut.-Colonel of the R.C.A.V.C.[128] Lieut.-Col. Evans became a Liaison Officer for Military District 2, in charge of recruiting locally for the Canadian Womens' Army Corps. He distributed Veterinary Corps instruments, equipment and stores to the veterinary colleges before retiring to Victoria B.C. in 1943.[129] Lieut.-Col. Duhault became Officer Commanding Military District 4, and retired by 1943.[130] Non-Commissioned Officers in the R.C.A.V.C were similarly redeployed or retired.[131] Officers of the R.C.A.V.C.(N.P.) presumably were retired, although some took a reduction in rank and stayed with their regiments in another rôle, or volunteered for active service.[132]

In 1940, the R.C.A.V.C. was one of only two national Canadian veterinary institutions, the second being the fledgeling Canadian Journal of Comparative Medicine, edited by Charles A. Mitchell. The latter strongly leapt to the defence of, or at least led the lament for, the former. In a series of editorials and opinion pieces extending over the next three years, it hammered at the disbandment of the Corps.[133] The major thrust of these arguments was that the federal government was ignorant of the contribution that veterinarians could make in areas other than 'doctoring horses', particularly in the areas of sanitation, public health and food inspection. They concluded that the decision had been made by "someone incompetent to value the veterinary profession in the light of modern times".[134] It was pointed out that the judgement whether or not to retain the Royal Army Veterinary Corps had been

T. 199009 B.

NATIONAL DEFENCE

50

N.P.

The Board recommend that the following Order be authorized. The estimated saving for the balance of the fiscal year is $10,334.

23 rd OCTOBER 1940

ORDER

VETERINARY SERVICES - DISBANDMENT

Pursuant to Section 20(2) of the Militia Act, His Excellency the Governor-in-Council, authorizes the disbandment of the undermentioned Corps of the Active Militia, effective 1st November, 1940:-

The Royal Canadian Army Veterinary Corps, Permanent Active Militia.

The Royal Canadian Army Veterinary Corps, Non-Permanent Active Militia.

(H.Q. 1-84-1)
(H.Q. 621-3-12)

Figure 17.10. Treasury Board recommendation to disband the Royal Canadian Army Veterinary Corps. (*National Archives of Canada*)

in favour of retention, and that the Corps was then deployed in traditional and new roles. The broad array of activities undertaken by the U.S. Army Veterinary Corps was noted.[135] (For example, they cleaned up the milk supply serving American personnel in Newfoundland, where mastitis, brucellosis and bovine tuberculosis were then common, and established quality control on the raw milk supply and dairies in Edmonton Alta. which served troops constructing the Alaska Highway and Canol pipeline).[136] The fact was highlighted that, in Europe, on both the Axis and Allied sides, the horse was far from rare on the field of battle. A plea was made for the establishment of a core cadre of veterinary officers, carrying out food inspection and sanitation duties, but which might, if the circumstances demanded, act as the nidus upon which a larger corps could grow to deal with animal health problems.

Disbandment of the R.C.A.V.C. was for the profession a national issue and a rallying point, symbolizing the perceived governmental disregard of, or contempt for, the contributions of veterinarians to animal agriculture and public health in time of war. Other federal policy matters, such as failure of the Wartime Bureau of Technical Personnel to exempt veterinarians from conscription for home service, contributed to the sense of grievance. But regulation of professional affairs was a provincial matter, and there was no national veterinary voice to which the federal government had to pay attention. Partly in response to the concern engendered in the profession nationally by disbandment, Mitchell convened in June 1943 the first meeting of the Dominion Veterinary Medical Council, which drew delegates from every provincial veterinary association. This session helped lay the groundwork for the ultimate incorporation of the Canadian Veterinary Medical Association, in 1948.[137] Thus, the demise in 1940 of the moribund R.C.A.V.C., at the time the only national Canadian veterinary organization, contributed to the birth eight years later of what has become an effective national voice for the veterinary profession in Canada.

Since decision-makers in Ottawa were unlikely to encounter material published in the Canadian Journal

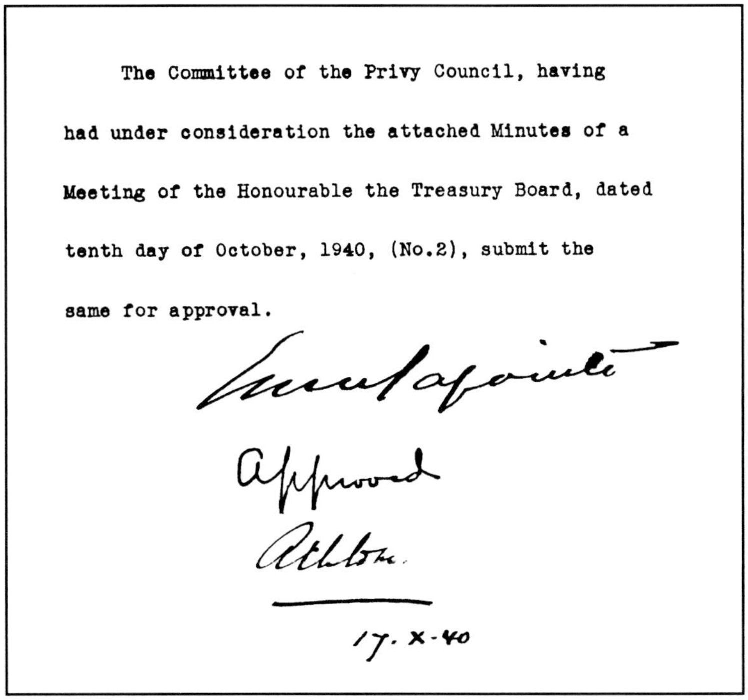
The Committee of the Privy Council, having had under consideration the attached Minutes of a Meeting of the Honourable the Treasury Board, dated tenth day of October, 1940, (No.2), submit the same for approval.

Approved

17.X.40

Figure 17.11. Privy Council of Canada approval of the Treasury Board recommendation to disband the Royal Canadian Army Veterinary Corps, signed by Ernest Lapointe, Minister of Justice (top), and The Earl of Athlone, Governor General (bottom), 17 October, 1940. (*National Archives of Canada*)

of Comparative Medicine, there was a need for direct access to them. In the absence of a national voice, provincial veterinary associations petitioned the federal government individually regarding re-institution of the Veterinary Corps, or at least recognition of the professional skills that might qualify veterinarians for commissions in which their capabilities might best be utilized. As matters stood, a veterinarian volunteering for service might be enrolled as an enlisted man in any of the military arms, or be commissioned, but in no case was his professional skill recognized or exploited. Veterinarians could become infantry privates, bomber pilots, truck drivers, artillery officers or seamen, but they had no outlet for their professional competencies.[138]

Perhaps the strongest lobby was mounted by the Ontario Veterinary Association, which had the advantage of relative size and proximity to Ottawa. Presidential addresses were made and resolutions were passed deploring the disbandment of the Veterinary Service,[139] but letters to J.L. Ralston, the Minister of National Defence, were being filed without action. In 1942 a committee to further the lobbying was established, chaired by Dr. W.J. Rumney, a former Captain in the R.C.A.V.C.(N.P.), and including in its membership Drs. George Cairns and A.E. Cameron, both ex-Veterinary Corps and the latter the Veterinary Director General of Canada, Lieut.-Col. T.C. Evans, A.L. McNabb, of the Ontario Ministry of Health, C.A. Mitchell and G. Rose, of the Dominion Department of Agriculture, the latter also ex-Veterinary Corps, and W. Roberts, a recent graduate. The Minister of Defence finally acknowledged a memorandum of facts submitted by the committee, but again filed it without action.

However, through the agency of Members of Parliament, Rumney, who was politically well-connected, gained an audience for himself, Cairns and Roberts with the Quartermaster General, and representatives of the Adjutant General, the Army Medical Corps, the Army Service Corps, and the Department of Agriculture. The military officials in attendance were surprised at the education and qualifications of veterinarians, and that their credentials were unrecognized in the armed forces. Further statements of fact were lodged, and after several more meetings with representatives of the military and the Selective Service Board, assurances were given in early 1943 that some veterinarians would be taken on as officers in the Medical Corps to carry out sanitation and food hygiene work.[140] In the meantime, Lieut.-Col. Evans had sent the Director of Medical Services a reworked version of his

1940 letter,[141] and C.D. McGilvray, Principal of O.V.C., prepared a brief entitled 'The Value and Usefulness of the Veterinary Profession' for the Wartime Bureau of Technical Personnel.[142] That the latter brief needed to be written speaks volumes about the low profile of the profession nationally at the time.

Despite the intensity of this lobbying, and the apparently positive response, there had been no action by March 1944. Rumney wrote Ralston, enquiring as to reasons for failure to act, when the press was reporting efforts to free up Medical Officers from non-medical duties.[143] The reply gave procedural excuses for the delay, but did presage appointment of veterinarians to the Medical Corps as commissioned assistants to Hygiene Officers, and as Non-Medical Bacteriologists. A few such appointments did eventuate, later that year.[144]

Although the Canadian Army had been unhorsed, the British Army was purchasing remounts in Canada, some of which were shipped overseas under the care of former R.C.A.V.C. officers, such as Cairns and Rumney. They returned with the observation that Canada was the only major participant in the war to have abolished its Veterinary Corps.[145] Both the American and British Armies maintained Veterinary Corps activity across a broad front, including care of horse transport, war dogs and carrier pigeons, sanitation and food inspection, and biomedical research.[146] The Canadian Army was a major burden to the R.A.V.C. in Sicily and Italy because it lacked Veterinary Corps elements to care for the pack animals necessary to carry supplies in the mountainous terrain.[147] Australia, with a narrow range of wartime activity requiring veterinarians, comparable to Canada, maintained a core of A.A.V.C. officers for sanitation and some animal health and welfare functions until 1946.[148]

Ultimately, during World War II Canadian veterinarians became involved in all of the sorts of wartime activities in which members of Veterinary Corps participated in other countries. But their skills were not as readily obvious, nor the men as accessible for exploitation in the national cause, as if they had been part of an organized Veterinary Corps, which, familiar with the profession, could target recruiting for specific purposes; be tasked with various appropriate functions; or from which officers could be seconded, as needed. As it was, the commissioned sanitary and medical bacteriology roles in the Medical Corps came late during the war. In 1952, Capt. N.V. Sanderson, a public health veterinarian, was commissioned in the Royal Canadian Army Medical Corps, the last Canadian military veterinarian.[149] Practitioners contracted with the British Remount authorities, buying and transporting horses, and several Canadian army veterinarians accompanied shiploads of mules from the U.S.A. overseas.[150] Veterinarians were heavily involved in biological and chemical warfare research, as officers seconded to secret projects,[151] or as civilian public servants, similarly seconded.[152] Canadian veterinarians living in the U.S.A. were among the over 2,000 veterinary officers in the U.S.A.V.C. in W.W. II,[153] but to our knowledge none went to the U.S. specifically to enlist in the Veterinary Corps.

The demise of the Royal Canadian Army Veterinary Corps resulted from a combination of circumstances. Paramount was the narrow-mindedness and tunnel vision of the few senior officers of the Permanent Force during the critical period of mechanization. However, their outlook and the opportunity to adapt the role of the Corps no doubt were confined by many years of extreme financial stringency imposed at the national political level, and by the narrow and very conventional range of activities considered or carried out by the small and conservative armed forces establishment, itself non-innovative and struggling to survive. There were no war dogs or carrier pigeons. The army did not contemplate governance of occupied territory and replacement of civilian services, or participation in foreign aid endeavours that would require expertise in animal health. It was not required to generate food for itself or for the civilian population, as occurred in British colonies and in territory occupied by the Allies in war. Biomedical research, when it was done, was contracted to the universities, the Department of Agriculture, or later, after the Second War, to the Defence Research Board. And in unusual or unique circumstances, the resources or authority of the British Army could be called upon, rather than seeking or developing expertise in house.

It is ironic that the factor that rendered the U.S. Army Veterinary Corps almost impotent in World War I, its organization under the Surgeon General, was the trait that conferred upon it the diversity of roles and the professional recognition that permitted it to persist in more recent times, as A.E. Cameron observed in a cogent and dispassionate analysis of the disbandment of the R.C.A.V.C.[154] In the British military tradition, the Veterinary Corps, under the Quartermaster General, had been pitted against the cavalryman and farrier of the Remount Service for professional recognition and independence in the early part of the century. And it restricted its subsequent opportunities to adapt by abandoning the field of sanitation and food inspection to the Medical Corps, who would not surrender it, and failed to recognize and exploit the professional competence of veterinarians in those domains.

Appendix A

NOMINAL ROLL, OFFICERS OF THE C.A.V.C.[1]

Nominal Roll Interpretation

Reading from left to right; Name - Place of Birth - Date of Birth - College where Graduated[2] - Graduation year- Highest Temporary Rank attained in C.A.V.C., O.M.F.C. - Date Taken on Strength of C.A.V.C., O.M.F.C. - Units in which Service was rendered as C.A.V.C. Officer O.M.F.C. - Honours and Awards - Ultimate Disposal - Previous Military Service - Previous War Service - Location of Civil Practice prior to the War - Previous Government or Civic Appointment.

Part 1- Officers of the Canadian Army Veterinary Corps who served as such in England, or in the North Russian or Siberian Expeditionary Forces

Bowler, Ernest; Australia, 1870; Sydney University 1891; Capt. 7.4.16; S.V.O. Seaford area; Wounded, D.C.M.; Demob.; Lieut. N.S.W. Mtd. Rifles in S.A. War; Sgt. P.P.C.L.I., B.E.F. in France.

Boyes, Nelson R.; Huntsville, Ont., 1897; O.V.C. 1918; Lieut. 29.8.18; Base Depot; Demob.

Campbell, James A.; British India, 1880; O.V.C. 1900; Maj. 17.11.18; V.O. 16th C.I. Bde., S.E.F.; Demob.; Vet. Capt. Gov. General's Bodyguard 1905-1910; Capt. to Maj., C.A.V.C. C.M. 1910-1918; St. John's, Newfoundland 1900-1905; Toronto, Ont., 1905-1918.

Christian, Oscar; Drayton, Ont., 1887; O.V.C. 1915; Lieut 3.9.18; Base Depot; Demob.; Pvte. 103rd Calgary Rifles; Prvnl. Lieut. C.A.V.C., C.M.; Milden and Conquest, Sask.; Meat Inspector Dept. of Agriculture 1915.

Cooper, Clarence J.; Bermuda Islands, 1880; O.V.C. 1902; Capt. 27.2.17; O.C. No. 6 C.M.V.S.; A/A.D.V.S., S.E.F.; Demob.; Pvte. to Sgt., Bermuda Vol. Rifle Corps; Lieut. 31st Inf. Regt, C.M.; Prvnl. Lieut. C.A.V.C., C.M.; Bermuda; Meaford, Ont.; New York City, U.S.A.; Inspector British Remount Commission 1914-1916.

Denton, Wilfred; Lancashire, Engl., 1890; Hon. Lieut. and Quartermaster 1.4.17; H.Q., O.M.F.C.; Q.M. Base Depots Shorncliffe and Witley; Brought to the attention of the Secretary of State for War for valuable service in connection with the War; Demob.; Staff Sgt., C.A.V.C., C.M.

Eckert, Henry A.; Sebringville, Ont., 1891; O.V.C. 1912; Lieut. 12.8.18; Base Depot; Returned Invalided 16.10.18;[3] Crediton, Ont.

Frape, Arthur E.; Bristol, Engl., 1876; Capt. and Asst. Dir. of Remounts 22.9.14; O.i/c Records and A.D.R., H.Q., O.M.F.C.; Brought to the attention of Secretary of State for War for valuable services rendered 7.8.17; Returned on leave 12.3.18, retained in Canada 22.3.18;[4] Hon. Lieut. and Q.M., C.P.A.V.C., C.M.

Hungerford, Thomas E.; Bandon, Ireland, 1890; United States College of Veterinary Surgeons 1912; Capt. 6.8.18; V. O. 16th Bde. C.F.A., N.R.E.F.; Demob.; Washington, D.C., U.S.A.

Lajoie, Leon G.; Three Rivers, P.Q., 1889; Laval 1916; Lieut. 29.7.18; Base Depot; Demob.; Three Rivers, P.Q.

Lapointe, Joseph A.; Batiscan, P.Q., 1894; Laval 1917; Lieut. 29.7.18; Base Depot; Demob.; St. Jerome, P.Q.

Laroche, Philippe; Montreal, P.Q., 1886; Laval 1914; Lieut. 29.7.18; Base Depot; Demob.; Montreal, P.Q.

Maynard, Earl R.; Savannah, N.Y., U.S.A. 1884; O.V.C. 1911; Lieut. 8.1.16; V.O. 85th Bty and Am. Coln.; V. O. C.A.S.C. unit, S.E.F.; Demob.; Gunner 76th Bty., C.F.A.

McCarrey, John J.; Montreal, P.Q., 1877; McGill University 1896; Capt. 22.9.14; No. 2 C.V.H.; Returned and Resigned 7.5.15;[5] Montreal, P.Q.; Chief Food Inspector, City of Montreal.

McCarthy, Nathanial; London, Engl., 1869; O.V.C. 1906; Capt. 6.3.17; No. 2 C.V.H.; V.O. 14th C.I. Bde.; Returned Invalided 14.8.17;[6] Lieut. C.A.V.C., C.M.; Castor, Alta.

McKelvie, Silas A.; Alliston, Ont., 1892; O.V.C. 1918; Lieut. 29.8.18; Base Depot; Demob.

Newell, Alfred; Portsmouth, Engl., 1879; Hon. Lieut. and Quartermaster 22.13.17; Q.M. No. 2 C.V.H.; Brought to the notice of the Secretary of State for War for valued service in the War; Returned Invalided 18.10.17;[7] Pvte., Kent Arty Militia and 1st and 2nd Bns. Engl. Gren. Gds. 1896-1900; Pvte. to Coy. Sgt. Maj., R.C.G.A. 1906-1913; Sgt., C.P.A.V.C., C.M. 1913-1914; Pvte., 2nd Bn. Gren. Gds. and S.A. Constaby. in S. A. War 1900-1902; Q.M. Sgt., C.A.V.C., O.M.F.C., 1914-1917.

Prinn, William J.; Truro, Engl., 1870; Lieut. and Chief Instructor in Farriery 28.11.16; No. 2 C.V.H.; A/O. C. No. 2 C.V.H.; Brought to the attention of the Secretary of State for War for service rendered in the War; Returned Surplus 9.14.18.[8]

Rainville, Joseph H.; St. Hyacinthe, P.Q., 1887; Laval 1915; Lieut. 29.7.18; Base Depot; Demob.; Actonvale, P.Q.

Secord, James B.A.; Cathcart, Ont., 1894; O.V.C. 1917; Capt. 25.3.17; No. 2 C.V.H.; Returned Invalided 14.6.17.[9]

Shaver, Floyd D.; Brantford, Ont., 1885; Capt. and Remount Officer 4.9.16; Temporary Remount Depot, Shorncliffe; Temporary Remount Depot, Witley; Brought to notice of the Secretary of State for War for service rendered in connection with the War 24.2.17; Returned Surplus 18.10.17;[10] Pvte., 38th Reg., C.M.; Pvte. 96th Regt, C.M.; Capt. Remount Dept., O.M.F.C.; Attd. Imperial Remount Dept., Romsey; Livestock specialist, Ont. Dept. of Agriculture.

Shirley, Charles E.; Staffordshire, Engl., 1886; Capt. and Quartermaster 1.4.16; Q.M. No. 2 C.V.H.; Wounded whilst serving with 3rd C.I. Bn. 17.6.15; Transferred to C.O.C. 1.8.17; Tpr to Sgt. Maj. 10th, 17th and 6th Hussars, C.M. 1899-1907; Tpr 2nd C.M.Rs. in S. A. War; Lieut. 3rd C. I. Bn., B.E.F. in France; Capt. 23rd. Res. Bn. O.M.F.C.

Taschereau, Thomas J. de M.; Charlesbourg, P.Q., 1869; Ecole vét. de Québec 1890; Lieut.-Col. to England 28.9.14, to Siberia 11.10.18; V.O. R.C.Ds.; V.O. i/c Imperial Home Countries Divn Art.; A.D.V.S. Bramshott Area; A.D.V.S. Shorncliffe Area; Returned from Europe 26.9.16; A.D.V.S. S.E.F.; Returned from Russia at General Demobilization; Bugler C.M. 1884; Lieut. 17th and 87th Regts. C.M. 1887-1888; Maj. to Lieut.-Col. 23rd Regt, C.M. 1894-1898; Capt. to Maj. 3rd R.C.R. 1899-1902; O.C. 92nd Regt, C.M. 1902-1906; Vet. Capt. R.C.Ds 1907-1911; Capt. to Maj., C.A.V.C., C.M. 1911-1914; A.D.V.S., C.E.F. 1914; Nicolet, P.Q.; Ste. Marie de Beauce, P.Q.

Touchette, Joseph A.O.; Valleyfield, P.Q., 1894; Laval 1918; Lieut. 29.7.18; Base Depot; Demob.

Vining, Alonzo; Thorndale, Ont., 1891; O.V.C. 1918; Lieut. 29.8.18; Base Depot; Demob.

Williams, James B.; Dublin, Ireland, 1880; San Francisco Veterinary College, 1916; Lieut. 1.9.17; V.O. 5th C.D. Trn.; Returned Surplus 12.3.18;[11] Pvte., 24th Res. Bn.; Tpr, C.A.V.C., O.M.F.C.

Wilson, Robert H.; Toronto, Ont., 1883; Grand Rapids Veterinary College 1906; Lieut. 1.9.17; Died 21.10.17.[12]

Wood, John F.; Hamilton, Ont., 1886; O.V.C. 1913; Capt. 11.7.15; Remount Depot; O.C. No. 2 C.V.H.; O.C. No. 5 C.M.V.S; Brought to the attention of the Secretary of State for War for valuable service rendered in connection with the War 24.2.17; Returned Invalided 14.8.17;[13] Prvnl. Lieut. C.A.V.C., C.M.; London, Ont.

Part 2 - Officers of the Canadian Army Veterinary Corps who served as such in both England and France.

Baker, Charles W.; Queensville, Ont., 1871; O.V.C. 1892; Capt., 19.6.16; V.O. 11th C. I. Bde; No. 2 C.V.H.; V.O. 12th Bde. C.F.A.; Died 10.1.17.[14]

Batty, William C.; Saddle Lake, Alta., 1891; McKillip V.C. 1915; Capt. 6.8.18; No. 1 C.V.H.; V.O. 5th C.D.A.C.; V.O. lst Bde C.F.A.; Demob.; Pvte., 10th Bn. C. Ry Trps B.E.F. France; Roundup, Montana.

Beaven, Clarence T.; South Berwick, Maine, U.S.A.; 1893; O.V.C. 1917; Capt. 25.3.17; No. 2 C.V.H., No. 1 C.V.H.; V. O. 5th Bde C.F.A.; Demob.

Beaver, Norman C.; Morriston, Ont.; 1884; O.V.C. 1914; Capt. 27.9.16; No. 2 C.V.H.; V.O. 8th C.I. Bde; M.i.D. 1.12.18; Demob; Lieut. C.A.V.C., C.M.; Woodstock, Ont.

Best, Victor C.; London, Engl.; 1885; McKillip V.C. 1913; Capt. 10.2.15; V.O. 2nd C.D. Trn.; Invalided 17.10.17;[15] Prvnl. Lieut. C.A.V.C., C.M.

Biron, Jean; d'Israeli, P.Q., 1893; Laval U. 1914; Capt. 21.8.16; No. 2 C.V.H.; No. 1 C.V.H.; V.O. 6th C. I. Bde; V. O. Shoreham area; V.O. 1st C.D.A.C.; Demob; Prvnl. Lieut. C.A.V.C., C.M.

Bishop, Henry H.; Ottawa, Ont., 1888; O.V.C. 1915; Capt. 9.8.16; No. 1 C.V.H.; No. 2 C.V.H.; V.O. 12th Bde, C.F.A.; V.O. 15th C.I. Bde.; V.O. 5th Bde., C.F.A.; Invalided 9.14.18;[16] Prvnl. Lieut., C.A.V.C., C.M.; Lieut. A.V.C., B.E.F. in Egypt and Salonika, 1915-1916.

Boswell, John F.; Westboro, Mass., U.S.A., 1890; O.V.C. 1917; Capt. 23.5.17; No. 2 C.V.H.; No. 1 C.V.H.; V.O. 5th Dist., C.F.C.; V.O. 2nd C.D. Trn; V. O. 1st. Bde., C.F.A.; Demob.

Brown, Elmer L.; Welch, Oklahoma, U.S.A., 1895; O.V.C. 1917; Capt. 23.5.17; No. 2 C.V.H.; V.O. 2nd C.I. Bde; Demob.

Brown, Herbert A.; Victoria, B.C., 1887; Chicago Vet. College 1908; Capt. 11.9.16; No. 2 C.V.H.; V.O. 14th Bde., C.F.A.; Demob.; Lieut. C.A.V.C., C. M.; Victoria, B.C.

Brun, Charles E.; St. Sebastian, P.Q., 1878; Laval 1911; Capt. 6.13.17; No. 2 C.V.H.; No. 1 C.V.H.; V.O. 7th C.I. Bde.;

V.O., C. Ry Trps; V.O. 2nd Bde., C.F.A.; Demob.; Prvnl. Lieut. C.A.V.C., C.M.; Richmond, P.Q.

Brunet, Octave; Quebec, P.Q., 1881; O.V.C. 1910; Capt., 13.5.15; V. O. 2nd C. Res. Pk; No. 1 C.V.H.; V.O. 12th Bde., C.F.A.; V.O. 3rd Bde., C.F.A.; Demob.; Capt. C.A.V.C, C.M.; Ste. Anne de Bellevue, P.Q.; Meat Inspector Dept. Agriculture 1912-1914.

Burnet, James H.; Sidmouth, Engl., 1870; Royal Vet. College, London 1896; Capt., 13.2.15; V.O. 2nd C. Res. Pk.; No. 2 C.V.H.; Returned as surplus 12.3.18[17]; Prvnl. Lieut. C.A.V.C., C.M.

Busselle, Albert W.; Walkerton, Ont., 1872; O.V.C. 1903; Capt. 17.3.17; V.O., C. Ry Trps; No. 1 C.V.H.; Demob.; Field Inspector, Dept. of Agriculture 1907.

Cameron, Alne E.; Broughty Ferry, Scotland 1878; O.V.C. 1908; Capt., 1.7.15; V.O. 6th C.I. Bde.; A/A.D.V.S. 2nd C. Divn; A/O.C. No. 2 C.M.V.S; Military Cross, 1.1.17; Demob.; Pvte., London Scottish; Prvnl. Lieut. C.A.V.C., C.M.; Tpr, Rhodesian Mtd. Police in S. A. War; Lost Mountain Sask.; Field Inspector, Dept.. of Agriculture. 1908.

Cameron, Allan R.; Toronto, Ont., 1889; O.V.C. 1915; Capt. 5.2.16; V.O. 8th Bde., C.F.A.; No. 1 C.V.H.; V.O. 9th Bde, C.F.A.; V.O. 10th, Bde., C.F.A.; Demob.; Lieut. C.A.V.C., C.M.; Vegreville, Alta.

Cassels, Frederick H.; Paisley, Ont., 1870; O.V.C. 1893; Capt., 14.11.16; No. 2, C.V.H.; V.O. 13th C.I. Bde.; No. 1 C.V.H.; V.O. 12th Dist., C.F.C.; V.O. C. Ry Trps; Demob.; Prvnl. Lieut., C.A.V.C., C.M.; V.S. for U. S. Govt. in Phillipine War, 1902; Pvte. 103rd. C.I. Bn., O.M.F.C.; Tacoma, Washington; Chehalis, Washington; Assist. State Veterinarian, Washington; State Dairy Commissioner, Washington.

Chambers, Alexander; Treherne, Man., 1893; O.V.C. 1918; Lieut., 29.8.18; No. 1 C.V.H.; No. 2 C.V.H.; Demob.

Chambers, Preston, A.; Ormstown, P.Q., 1879; O.V.C. 1908; Capt., 24.10.16; No. 1 C.V.H.; V.O. 8th Bde., C.F.A.; Returned 5.4.17;[18] Prvnl. Lieut., C.A.V.C., C.M.; Pvte. 194th C.I. Bn., O.M.F.C.; Ormstown, P.Q.

Church, Wiley G.; Kentville, N.S., 1880; O.V.C. 1914; Capt., 13.6.15; V.O. 2nd C.D.A.C.; V.O. 5th Bde., C.F.A.; No. 2, C.V.H.; Returned Invalided 17.5.17;[19] Lieut., C.A.V.C., C.M., Aylesford, N.S.

Clapp, Harry S.; Picton, Ont., 1886; O.V.C. 1907; Capt., 9.10.15; No. 2 C.V.H.; O.C. No. 3 C.M.V.S.; V.O. 3rd C.D. Trn.; No. 1 C.V.H.; Demob.; Prvnl. Lieut. C.A.V.C., C.M.; Belleville, Ont.

Cleveland, Harry R.; Danville, P.Q., 1873; McGill University 1894; Capt., 20.7.15; V.O. 5th C.M. Rs.; V.O. 8th C.I. Bde.; A/A.D.V.S. 3rd C. Divn; Returned Invalided 26.5.17;[20] Vet. Capt. (R. of Os.), 11th Hussars.

Colebourn, Harry; Birmingham, Engl., 1887; O.V.C. 1911; Capt., 22.9.14; No. 1 C.V.H.; V.O. 4th C.I. Bde.; No. 2 C.V.H.; V.O. 11th Dist. C.F.C.; S.V.O. Bramshott area; M.i.D. 1.6.17; Demob; Meat Inspector, Dept.. of Agriculture 1911.

Coleman, Norman J.; Forrester's Falls, Ont., 1887; O.V.C. 1918; Lieut. 30.8.18; No. 1 C.V.H.; V.O. 2nd Bde. C.F.A.; Demob.

Coulombe, Aime E.; Quebec, 1882; Laval 1913; Capt., 22.9.14; V. O. 2nd Bde., C.F.A.; O.C. No. 1 C.M.V.S.; V.O. 1st C.D. Trn.; A/D.A.D.V.S. 1st C. Divn; Demob; Prvnl. Lieut. C.A.V.C., C.M.; Montreal, P.Q.

Cowan, Alexander; Montreal, P.Q., 1873; McGill University 1895; Capt., 11.9.16; V. O. 11th Bde., C.F.A.; No. 1 C.V.H.; O.C. No 3 C.M.V.S.; V.O. 9th C.I. Bde.; Demob; Lieut., C.A.V.C., C.M.; Lieut., A.V.C., B.E.F. in France 1915-1916; Westmount, P.Q.; City Dairy Inspection P.Q. 1900-1905.

Craig, Harold W.; Darlingford, Man., 1883; O.V.C. 1914; Capt., 11.2.16; No. 1 C.V.H.; V.O. 5th Bde., C.F.A.; V.O. F.G.H.; Demob.; Prvnl. Lieut., C.A.V.C., C.M.; Pvte. 5th C.I. Bn., B.E.F. in France; No. 1 C.M.V.S. in France; Vanguard, Sask.

Cutcliffe, Ashton B.; Swansea, Wales, 1867; O.V.C. 1892; Lieut.-Col., 22.9.14; V. O. 1st C. Divn Engs.; A.D.V.S. 1st Divn; A.D.V.S., H.Q., C.A.C.; Recommended for gallant and distinguished service 30.11.15; M.i.D. 28.5.18; Distinguished Service Order, 3.6.18; Demob.; Lieut. C.A.V.C., C.M.; Brantford, Ont.

Daigneault, Frederick A.; Lawrenceville, P.Q., 1871; Laval 1908; Maj., 22.9.14; O.C. No. 2 C.M.V.S.; O.C., C.C.V.E.S.; M.i.D. 11.7.19; Demob.; Lieut. C.A.V.C., C.M.; St. Jerome, P.Q.; Meat Inspector, Dept. of Agriculture 1912.

Dixon, Elijah M.; Manchester, Engl., 1871; Royal Veterinary College, London, 1892; Capt. 22.9.14; V. O. 1st Bde., C.F.A.; No. 1 C.V.H.; V.O. lst C.O. Trn.; O.C. No. 1 C.M.V.S.; A/D.A.V.S., 2nd C. Div; Died 27.9.18;[21] V. O. in S. A. War.

Douglas, Kenneth L.; Stratford, Ont., 1872; O.V.C. 1913; Capt., 22.9.14; V. O. 1st C. Res. Pk.; V. O. C.L.H.; Demob,; Prvnl. Lieut., C.A.V.C., C.M.; Stratford, Ont.; Meat Inspector, Dept. of Agriculture 1913.

Duchêne, Hewet D.J.; Chicoutimi, P.Q., 1888; Laval 1912; Capt. 7.10.14; V. O. 1st C. Fld. Ambl.; No. 2 C.V.H., V. O. 9th C.I. Bde.; No. 1 C.V.H.; Returned 26.1.17;[22] Capt., C.A.V.C., C.M.

Duhault, Joseph R.J.; Montreal, P.Q., 1888; Laval 1910; Capt. 22.9.14; V. O. L.S.H.; No. 1 C.V.H.; A/O.C. No. 2 C.V.H.; O.C. 'A' C.M.V.S.; Order of the British Empire 3.6.19; M.i.D. 11.7.19; Demob.; Lieut. 85th Bn., C.M. 1907-1911; Capt., C.P.A.V.C., C.M.; Montreal, P.Q.; Meat Inspector, Dept. of Agriculture 1910-1911.

Durkin, Lewis H.; Grand Valley, Ont., 1887; O.V.C. 1908; Capt., 1.7.15; V.O. 1st C.M.Rs.; V.O. 1st C.D.A.C.; Returned Invalided 7.12.17;[23] Prvnl. Lieut. C.A.V.C., C.M.; Grand Valley, Ont.

Early, Frank D.; Brampton, Ont., 1889; O.V.C. 1913; Capt., 15.3.17; V.O. No. 2 C.V.H.; No. 1 C.V.H.; V.O., L.S.H.; Returned Invalided 15.4.18;[24] Prvnl. Lieut. C.A.V.C., C.M.; Lieut. A.V.C., B.E.F. in France 1915-1916; Saskatoon, Sask.

Edgett, Charles E.; Moncton, N.B., 1882; O.V.C. 1906; Chicago Veterinary College, Special Course Student 1907; Colonel, 22.9.14; V.O. 1st C.D.A.C.; V.O. 3rd C.I. Bde., A.D.V.S. 4th Cdn. Divn; D.A.D.V.S. 4th C. Divn; A.D.V.S. C.A.C.; A.D.V.S., O.M.F.C.; D.V.S., O.M.F.C.; M.i.D. 1.6.17 and 28.5.18; Distinguished Service Order 3.6.18; Demob.; Tpr, N.W.M.P.; Lieut. C.A.V.C., C.M.; Moncton, N.B.; Aneroid, Sask.; Meat Inspector, Dept. of Agriculture 1907-1913.

Edwards, Charles L.; Souris, Man., 1890; O.V.C. 1915; Capt., 22.9.14; No. 2 C.V.H.; V.O. 1st C.I. Bde; V.O. 1st C.D.A.C.; Returned on leave 26.5.17; Retained in Canada 26.8.17;[25] Prvnl. Lieut. C.A.V.C., C.M.

Elliott, Harry J.; Port Hope, Ont., 1874; McKillip Veterinary College 1900; Capt., 22.9.14; V.O. 4th C.I. Bde.; A/O. C. No. 2 C.V.H.; S.V.O. Bramshott area; S.V.O. Witley area; V.O. i/c Crowborough Camp; V.O. No. 4 Dist., C.F.C.; Demob.; Capt., C.A.V.C., C.M.; Brandon, Man.; Meat Inspector, Dept. of Agriculture 1910.

Evans, Thomas C.; Ealing, Engl., 1879; O.V.C. 1908; University of Toronto 1910; Lieut. Col. 22.9.14; O.C. No. 1 C.V.H.; V.O. 5th Bde., C.F.A.; V.O. 2nd C.D.A.C.; D.A.D.V.S. 2nd C. Divn; Imp. A. Veterinary School, Aldershot; Military Cross 1.1.16; M.i.D. 1.1.16, 28.12.17 and 11.7.19, Demob.; Capt., C.A.V.C., C.M.; Wingham, Ont.; Pathologist, Biology Lab., Dept. of Agriculture, Ottawa, Ont.

Evely, Claude C.; St. Thomas, Ont., 1880; O.V.C. 1901; Capt., 12.5.15; V.O. 3rd C.M.Rs; V.O. 2nd C.D. Trn.; Returned 15.9.16;[26] Prvnl. Lieut. C.A.V.C., C.M.; St. Thomas, Ont., Meat Inspector, Dept. of Agriculture 1907-1909.

Ferguson, [Fergusson] Charles D.; Ingersoll, Ont., 1897; O.V.C. 1918; Lieut. 29.8.18; V.O., L.S.H.; Returned at General Demobilization.

Foreman, Harold O.; Sault Ste. Marie, Michigan, U.S.A. 1893; O.V.C. 1918; Lieut. 29.8.18; No. 1 C.V.H., Khaki University (Lecturer); Returned at General Demobilization.

Forsyth, Wilfred W.; Brera, Scotland, 1885; O.V.C. 1913; Capt., 1.7.15; No. 2 C.V.H.; O.C. No. 4 C.M.V.S.; V.O. 4th Bde., C.F.A.; V.O. 4th C.D. Trn.; Demob.; Lieut. C.A.V.C., C.M.; Dairy Inspector, Toronto Public Health Dept., Toronto, Ont.

French, Cecil; London, Engl., 1871; McGill University 1894; Royal Veterinary College, Munich (Special Student); Capt., 17.4.17; No. 2 C.V.H.; V.O. 15th C.I. Bde.; No. 1 C.V.H.; V.O. 6th Bde., C.F.A.; Cdn. War Records; Demob.; Pvte., 3rd Bn. Vict. Rifles 1892-1894.

Galbraith, William T.; Gorrie, Ont., 1895; O.V.C. 1917; Capt., 25.3.17; No. 2 C.V.H.; V.O. 14th C.I. Bde.; V.O. 5th Bde., C.F.A.; V.O. 4th Bde., C.F.A.; No. 1 C.V.H.; Demob.

Gaudry, Martin T.A.; Montreal, P.Q., 1869; Laval 1892; Capt. 15.10.14; No. 2 C.V.H.; No. 1 C.V.H.; Returned Surplus; Resigned 2.7.17.[27]

Geoffroy, Joseph T.M.; St. Jean, P.Q., 1893; Laval 1917; Lieut. 29.8.18; No. 1 C.V.H.; Demob.

Girling, Theodore A.; Huddersfield, Engl., 1876; O.V.C. 1904; McKillip Veterinary College (Special Student); Capt., 23.11.15; No. 2 C.V.H.; V.O. 9th C.I. Bde.; V.O. 4th C.I. Bde.; O.C. Temp. Vet. Det. C.A.C.; A/O.C. No. 2 C.V.H.; A/O.C No. 2 C.M.V.S.; M.i.D. 1.16.17; Died 1.3.19;[28] Prvnl. Lieut. C.A.V.C., C.M.; Saskatoon, Sask.; City Veterinarian, Saskatoon Dept. of Health 1911-1915.

Gough, William E.; Birmingham, Engl., 1868; O.V.C. 1913; Capt., 14.11.16; No. 2 C.V.H.; No. 1 C.V.H.; V.O. No. 2 Dist., C.F.C.; Demob.; Toronto, Ont.

Grignon, Louis M.; Quebec, P.Q., 1892; Laval 1914; Capt., 22.9.14; V.O. 1st C.H. By.; No. 1 C.V.H.; V.O. No. 12 Dist., C.F.C.; Demob.; Prvnl. Lieut. C.A.V.C., C.M.; St. Adele, P.Q.

Gunning, Oscar V.; Loughton, Essex, Engl., 1886; Ohio State University 1917; Lieut. 29.4.18; No. 1 C.V.H.; V.O. No. 6 Dist., C.F.C.; V.O. F.G.H.; Demob.; Tpr, C.R.C.R., O.M.F.C.; Casseltown, North Dakota, U.S.A.

Halbert, Samuel F.T.; Markdale, Ont. 1894; O.V.C. 1918; Lieut. 11.8.18; No. 1 C.V.H.; V.O. F.G.H.; Demob.

Hanagan, Ray; Vernon, N.Y., U.S.A., 1894; O.V.C. 1917; Capt., 25.3.17; No. 2 C.V.H.; No 1 C.V.H.; V.O. 1st C.I. Bde.; V.O. 1st Dist., C.F.C.; Demob.; Vernon, N.Y., U.S.A.

Hanmore, Gerald S.; Vesta, Ont., 1892; O.V.C. 1912; Capt., 25.5.15; No. 2 C.V.H.; No. 1 C.V.H.; V.O. 3rd C.D. Trn; Returned 17.2.17;[29] Lieut. C.A.V.C., C.M.

Harrington, James; Ancaster, Ont., 1884; O.V.C. 1912; Capt., 24.3.17; No. 2 C.V.H.; V.O. C. Ry Trps; Returned Invalided 10.12.18;[30] Lieut. C.A.V.C., C.M., Ancaster, Ont.

Harvey, James G.; Guelph, Ont., 1885; O.V.C. 1902/1910; Capt., 18.9.16; V.O. 13 Bde., C.F.A.; V.O. 6th C.I. Bde; V.O. 2nd C.D.A.C.; A/O. C. No. 2, C.M.V.S.; Demob.; Prvnl. Lieut. C.A.V.C., C.M.; Morrisburg, Ont.

Hennan, James H.; Roland, Man., 1888; O.V.C. 1912; Capt., 1.7.15; No. 2, C.V.H.; V.O. C.C.M.G.Sq.; O.C. 'A' C.M.V.S.; Demob.; Prvnl. Lieut. C.A.V.C., C.M.; Crystal City, Man.

Heppleston, John W.; Yorkshire, Engl., 1890; O.V.C. 1918; Lieut. 29.8.18; A/O.C. No. 2 C.M.V.S.; Demob.

Hogan, John D.; Ottawa, Ont., 1894; O.V.C. 1917; Capt. 25.3.17; No. 2 C.V.H.; No. 1 C.V.H.; V.O. 6th Dist., C.F.C.; Returned on leave 19.1.18; Retained in Canada 19.3.18.[31]

Hoggan, Thomas R.R.; Dumfrieshire, Scotland 1870; Royal (Dick) Veterinary College, Edinburgh 1892; Capt., 28.9.16; V.O. i/c Crowborough Camp; No. 2 C.V.H.; V.O., C. Ry Trps; V.O., 7th C.I. Bde; Demob.; Prvnl. Lieut. C.A.V.C., C.M.; V.O. in S. A. War; Lieut. A.V.C., B.E.F., in Dardanelles & Egypt 1915.1916. England, Scotland; Vancouver, B.C.

Hopkins, Arthur W.; Yorkton, Sask., 1892; O.V.C. 1917; Capt., 25.3.17; No. 2 C.V.H.; V.O. No. 6 Dist., C.F.C.; Demob.

Hughes, Arthur H.; Liverpool, Engl., 1883; Kansas City Veterinary College 1914; Capt., 1.9.17; No. 2 C.V.H.; V.O. 13th C.I. Bde.; No. 1 C.V.H.; V.O., C. Ry Trps; V.O. 2nd C. Res. Pk.; V.O. 5th C. Res. Pk.; Demob.; Pvte., Rifle Bde. 1898-1899; Driver, A. S. C. in S. A. War; Tpr, 7th C.M.Rs., O.M.F.C.; Farrier Sgt., C.R.C.R., O.M.F.C.; Gardner, Kansas, U.S.A.; San Antonio, Texas U.S.A.; Veterinarian to Livestock Sanitary Commission, Kansas, 1915.

Hughes, John T.M.; Tenby, South Wales, 1881; Royal Veterinary College, London 1904; Capt., 9.10.15; No. 2 C.V.H.; V.O., F.G.H., A/O. C. No. 2 C.V.H.; V.O., C.R.C.R.; V.O., R.C.Ds.; Demob.; Capt., C.A.V.C., C.M.; Gleichen, Alta.; Strathcona, Alta.; Stock Inspector, Dept. of Agriculture 1908.

Hunter, Alfred H.; Belleville, Ont., 1892; O.V.C. 1914; Capt., 1.7.15; V.O. 4th Bde., C.F.A.; V.O. 2nd C.D. Trn; A/O. C. No, 2, C.M.V.S.; No. 1 C.V.H.; Brought to the attention of the Secretary of State for War for valuable service rendered in connection with the War, 24.12.17; Demob.; Lieut. C.A.V.C., C.M.; Province of Ont. Research Laboratory 1914.

Kennedy, Michael P.; Warsaw, Ont., 1882; O.V.C. 1912; Capt. 19.5.16; No. 2 C.V.H.; No. 1 C.V.H. ; V.O. 5th C.I. Bde,; Military Cross 3.6.18; Demob.; Lieut. C.A.V.C., C.M.; Lakefield, Ont.

Lee, Richard M.; Crowe, Engl., 1892; O.V.C. 1916; Capt., 19.5.16; No. 2 C.V.H.; No. 1 C.V.H.; V.O. 4th Bde., C.F.A.: O.C. No. 4 C.M.V.S.; Demob.; Corporal, C.A.V.C., C.M.; Tpr, C.A.V.C., O.M.F.C.

Liddle, Francis G.; Newport, Engl., 1875; Royal Veterinary College, London 1896; Capt., 24.4.15; No. 1 C.V.H.; V.O. 3rd Bde., C.F.A.; Demob.; Prvnl. Lieut. C.A.V.C, C.M.; Mission City, B.C.

MacDonald, John D.; London, Engl., 1873; O.V.C. 1896; Capt., 6.8.18; No. 1 C.V.H.; V.O. No. 5 Dist, C.F.C.; Demob.; Far. Sergt., Man. Drgns. & 5th B.C. Regt, Gar. Art.; Corporal Sh. Smith, 68th By., C.F.A., O.M.F.C.; Oak Lake, Man.; Sooke, B.C.

McAllister, Archibald D.; Shelburne, Ont., 1894; O.V.C. 1917; Capt., 25.3.17; No. 2 C.V.H.; V.O. 15th C.I. Bde.; No. 1 C.V.H.; V.O. 4th C.D.A.C.; M.i.D. 11.7.19; Demob.

McGillivray, John D.; Dalkeith, Ont. 1871; McGill University 1894, McKillip Veterinary College (Special Course Student); Capt., 24.11.16; No. 2 C.V.H.; V.O. 5th C.D.A.C.; No. 1 C.V.H.; V.O. 4th C.D.A.C.; V.O. No. 9 Dist. C.F.C.; V.O. 1st Bde., C.F.A.; Returned Invalided 25.5.18;[32] Prvnl. Lieut. C.A.V.C., C.M.; Transport Officer, 184th C.I. Bn., O.M.F.C.; Manitou, Man.; Winnipeg, Man.

McKinnon, Kenneth W.; Summerside, P.E.I. 1897; O.V.C. 1918; Lieut. 29.8.18; No. 1 C.V.H.; V.O. 3rd C. Divn H.Q.; Demob.

McLean, Adam T.; McLean's, N.B., 1883; O.V.C. 1910; Capt., 5.2.17; V.O. 5th C.D. Trn.; O.C. No. 5 C.M.V.S.; No. 1 C.V.H; V.O. 2nd C.D. Trn.; V.O. 6th Bde., C.F.A.; V.O. 3rd Bde., C.F.A.; V.O. 10th C.I. Bde.; A/O C. No. 4 C.M.V.S.; Demob.; Trumpeter to Capt., 8th Hussars, C.M. 1897-1914; Temporary Maj., 193rd C.I. Bn, O.M.F.C.; Moncton, N.B.; Truro, N.S.; Town Food Inspector, Truro, N.S. 1913-1915.

McLellan, David J.; Wyoming, Ont., 1893; O.V.C. 1917; Capt., 25.3.17; No. 2 C.V.H.; V.O. 5th C.D.A.C.; V.O. 5th C.D. Trn.; V.O. 13th Bde., C.F.A.; Demob.; Corporal 1st Hussars, C.M.

Matthew, Robert G.; Lysander, P.Q., 1874; McGill University 1897; Capt., 24.9.16; V.O. 14th Bde., C.F.A.; V.O. 8th

Bde., C.F.A.; V.O. 9th Bde. C.F.A.; A/O.C. No. 3 C.M.V.S.: A/D.A.D.V.S. 3rd C. Divn; Belgian Croix de Guerre; M.i.D.; Demob.; V.S./Sgt. N.W.M.P.; Regina, Sask.; Netherhill, Sask.

Morgan, William J.; Kingston, Ont., 1866; O.V.C. 1893; Chicago Veterinary College (Special Student) 1908; Capt., 29.8.18; No. 1 C.V.H.; V.O. C. Ry Trps; Demob.; Vet. Lieut-Col. 9th Bde. C.F.A., C.M.; Tpr, S. A. Constaby. in S. A. War; Kingston, Ont.; Meat Inspector, Dept. of Agriculture 1907.

Neill, William J.; Omemee, Ont., 1876; O.V.C. 1902; Brig.-Gen., 22.9.14; A.D.V.S. 1st Cont.; A.D.V.S. 1st C. Divn; D.V.S. and R., O.M.F.C.; Relinquished appointment 12.3.18; Returned Invalided 26.6.18;[33] Pvte. to Maj. 45th Regt C.M. 1893-1914; Maj. C.P.A.V.C. 1914; Lieut. Col. and D.V.S., C.M. 1914; Vet. Capt. 3rd C.M.Rs. and Command of Details of Camp at Signal Hill in S. A. War.

O'Gogarty, Maurice G.; Ireland, 1877; O.V.C. 1912; Capt., 22.9.14; V.O. R.C. Ds.; O.C. No. 1 C.M.V.S.; O.C. 'A' C.M.V.S.: O. C. No. 2 C.V.H.: Resigned on transfer to A.V.S. 10.3.18; Tpr Ceylon M. I.: Prvnl. Lieut., C.A.V.C., C.M.: in S. A. Constaby. in S. A. War.

O'Gorman, James J.; Cardiff, Wales, 1873; Glasgow Veterinary College 1894; Capt. 14.11.16; No. 2 C.V.H.: V.O. C. Rly. Trps; Demob.; Tpr, C.A.V.C., O.M.F.C.; S. A. War; Cardiff and Merthyr, Wales; Rhodesian Government 1896-1904.

Parsons, Williams M.; Lewes, Engl., 1887; O.V.C. 1912; Capt., 23.6.16; No. 2 C.V.H.: V.O. 10th C.I.Bde.; V.O. 4th C.D.A.C.: V.O. L.S.H.; Resigned 11.1.19.[34]

Poole, Bernard R.; Peshawar, India, 1869; O.V.C. 1891; Capt., 4.5.16; V.O. 3rd Bde.; C.F.A.; No. 2 C.V.H.; V.O. Rly. Trps; Killed in Action 3.5.17;[35] Capt. C.A.V.C., C.M.; Field Inspector Dept. of Agriculture 1909-1916.

Preston, Marvin J.; Iona, Ont., 1884; O.V.C. 1911; Capt., 5.12.16; V.O. 10th Bde., C.F.A.; V.O. 9th Bde., C.F.A.; Order of the British Empire; M.i.D.; Demob.; Prvnl. Lieut., C.A.V.C., C.M.; Moosomin, Sask.

Rich, John L.; Brookbury, P.Q., 1886; O.V.C. 1913; Capt., 19.5.16; No. 2 C.V.H.; V.O. 3rd C.D.A.C.; Demob.; Lieut. C.A.V.C., C.M.; Thedford Mines, P.Q.

Richards, Samuel C.; Carmarthenshire, Wales, 1873; McGill University 1896; Maj. 25.4.15; No. 2 C.V.H.; V.O. 1st C.D. Trn.; V.O. 8th Bde., C.F.A.; O.C. No. 1 C.V.H.; M.i.D.; O.B.E.; R.N.W.M.P.; Prvnl. Lieut. C.A.V.C., C.M.; Boston, Massachusetts, U.S.A.; Victoria, B.C.; Stock Inspector, Dept. of Agriculture 1906-1907.

Roberston, William A.; Elgin, Scotland 1888; O.V.C. 1916; Capt., 19.5.15; No. 2 C.V.H.; V.O. 12th C.I. Bde.; A/O. C. No. 4 C.M.V.S.; A/D.A.D.V.S. 4th C. Divn; M.i.D. 31.12.18; Order of the British Empire 1.1.19; Demob; Pvte. 3rd. V. Bn. Seaforth Highlanders 1904-1906; S/Sgt. C.A.V.C., C.M.; Corporal C.A.V.C., O.M.F.C.

Rogers, William T.; Durham County, Ont., 1872; O.V.C. 1900; Capt., 7.2.15; A/O.C. No. 2 C.V.H.; V.O. C. Ry Trps; Returned Invalided 5.10.18;[36] Capt. C.A.V.C., C.M.; Toronto, Ont.

Roy, John A.; Campbellton, N.B., 1893; O.V.C. 1914; Capt., 17.1.15; No. 2 C.V.H.; V.O. 3rd. C.D. Trn.; Returned Invalided 23.7.16;[37] Prvnl. Lieut. C.A.V.C., C.M.

Roy Joseph D.; St. Ephraim, P.Q., 1890; Laval 1911; Capt., 7.8.16; No. 2 C.V.H.; No. 1 C.V.H.; V.O. 7th C. I. Bde.; Returned 17.2.17;[38] Prvnl. Lieut. C.A.V.C., C.M.

Ruttan, Charles, W.; Wingham, Ont., 1887; O.V.C. 1906; Capt., 1.3.16; V.O. 11th C.I. Bde.; V.O. 4th C.D. Trn.; V.O. 13th C.I. Bde.; No. 1 C.V.H.; V.O. C. Ry Trps; Returned on leave 7.9.17; Retained in Canada 15.12.17;[39] Prvnl. Lieut. C.A.V.C., C.M.; Wingham, Ont.

Saunders, Charles G.; Cuckfield, Engl., 1875; O.V.C. 1907; University of Toronto 1910; Maj., 14.10.14; V.O. 3rd. Bde.; C.F.A.; O.C. No. 1 C.V.H.; D.A.D.V.S. 1st C. Divn; M.i.D. 15.6.16 and 28.5.18; Distinguished Service Order 1.6.16; Demob.; Capt. C.A.V.C., C.M.; Toronto, Ont.

Savage, Alfred; Montreal, P.Q., 1889; Cornell University 1914; Capt., 15.2.16; No. 2 C.V.H.; V.O. 11th Bde., C.F.A.; No. 1 C.V.H.; Demob.; Prvnl. Lieut., C.A.V.C., C.M.; Ste. Anne de Bellevue, P.Q.

Sear, Frederick T.; Leighton Buzzard, Engl., 1862; Hon. Capt. and Quartermaster, 28.7.16; Q.M. and A/Adjt., No. 1 C.V.H.; Demob.; R.Q.M.S., Bed. Regt and 43rd. D.C.O. Rifles, 1914-1915; Isazai Campaign, India, 1892.

Sharp, Herbert R.; Walkerton, Ont., 1884; O.V.C. 1906; Capt., 23.3.17; No. 2 C.V.H.; V.O. 14th C. I. Bde.; No. 1 C.V.H.; V.O. 1st Bde., C.F.A.; Returned 23.9.18;[40] Prvnl. Lieut. C.A.V.C, C.M.

Sheppard, James A.; Elora, Ont., 1891; O.V.C. 1918; Lieut. 29.8.18; No. 1 C.V.H.; V.O. No. 12 Dist. C.F.C.; V.O. No. 4 Dist. C.F.C.; V.O.R.C.Ds.; V.O. C.M.G.Sq; Demob.

Simon, William H.; St. John, N.B., 1872; O.V.C. 1890; Capt., 7.5.15; V.O. 2nd C.D. Trn; V.O. 5th C. I. Bde; No. 2 C.V.H.; No. 1 C.V.H.; V.O. 8th C. I. Bde; Returned 9.3.17;[41] Vet. Capt. 8th P.L.N.B. Hussars.

Simpson, Hugh W.; Orangeville, Ont., 1893; O.V.C. 1917; Capt., 25.3.17; No. 2 C.V.H.; V.O. C. Ry Trps;, No. 1

C.V.H.; V.O. 2nd C. Res. Pk.; V.O. 8th Bde., C.F.A.; V.O. 3rd Bde., C.F.A.; Demob.

Smith, Henry D.; Montreal, P.Q., 1866; McGill University 1888; Lieut.-Col., 1.5.16; A.D.V.S. 2nd C. Divn; A.D.V.S. Shorncliff area; A.D.V.S. Witley area; A/D.V.S. & R., O.M.F.C.; Relinquished Appointment and Returned 15.9.17. Retained in Canada, 15.12.17;[42] Pvte. Mont. Gar. Art., 1878-1882; Reg. V.O. 13th C.F.A. 1904-1911; Capt. to Maj. C.A.V.C., C.M. 1911-1915; Winnipeg, Man.

Souillard, Pierre P.; Le Havre, France, 1887; Laval 1912; Capt., 22.9.14; V.O., R.C.H.A.; V.O. 2nd Bde., C.F.A.; O.C. No. 1 C.M.V.S.; M.i.D. 1.6.17; Demob.; Lieut. C.A.V.C., C.M.; Richmond, P.Q.

Spearman, Harold; Stittsville, Ont., 1880; O.V.C. 1917; Capt., 25.3.17; No. 2 C.V.H.; V.O. 5th C.D.A.C.; Demob.

Sproston, Henry; British Guiana, 1882; Royal Veterinary College, London 1904; Capt., 2.6.16; V.O. 3rd C. Divn H.Q; No. 1 C.V.H.; V.O. 4th C.D. Trn.; V.O. C. Ry Trps; Demob.; Pvte., London Scottish, 1902-1904; Prvnl. Lieut. C.A.V.C., C.M.; Lieut., 31st C. I. Bn., O.M.F.C.; Nokomis, Sask.; Youngstown, Alta.

Stedman, William G.; Mcleod, Alta., 1886; O.V.C. 1907; Maj., 22.9.14; No. 2 Imp. V.H.; V.O. 25th Imp. Divn; H.Q. 1st C. Divn; No. 1 C.V.H. A/Adjt.; D.A.D.V.S. 5th C. Divn; Duty D. V. S. Office, H. Q., O. M. F. C.; D.A.D.V.S. 4th C. Divn; Demob.; Vet. Lieut. 23rd Alberta Rangers, Calgary, Alta.

Stevenson, Charles H.A.; Pitlochry, Scotland, 1868; O.V.C. 1898; Capt., 27.4.16; No. 2 C.V.H.; V.O. 9th Bde., C.F.A.; Returned Invalided 4.4.17;[43] Reston, Man.

Stubbs, William F.R.; Caledon, Ont. 1891; O.V.C. 1913; Capt., 24.3.17; V.O. No. 5 Dist. C.F.C.; No. 1 C.V.H.; V.O. 6h Bde., C.F.A.; Demob.; Prvnl. Lieut., C.A.V.C., C.M.; Caledon, Ont., Meat Inspector, Dept. of Agriculture 1915-1916.

Tamblyn, David S.; Callington, Cornwall, Engl., 1881; McGill University 1901; Lieut.-Col., 12.6.15; V.O. 1st C.M.Rs.; V.O. 7th C. I. Bde.; A.D.V.S. 3rd C. Divn; D.A.D.V.S. 3rd. C. Divn; Duty D.V.S., Office H.Q., O.M.F.C.; D.A.D.V.S., Can. Sect., G.H.Q.; M.i.D. 2.1.17, 1.6.17 and 1.1.18; Distinguished Service Order 1.1.18; Order of the British Empire 3.6.19; Chevalier of the Order of Leopold (Belgian) 1.6.19; Demob.; Lieut. C.A.V.C., C.M.; Vet. Lieut. in W. Lt. Horse and Vet. Capt. in Imp. Lt. Horse in S. A. War; Chief Veterinary Inspector for Saskatchewan Dept. of Agriculture 1905.

Taylor, Lionel E. L.; Windermere, Engl., 1887; McKillip Veterinary College 1909; Capt., 3.10.16; No. 2 C.V.H.; No. 1 C.V.H.; V.O. 3rd C.D. Trn.; O.C. No. 3 C.M.V.S.; Military Cross 11.1.19; Wounded Twice; Demob.; A/Far. Sgt., C.F.A., O.M.F.C.; Edmonton, Alta.; Regina Sask.

Thurston, Ernest C.; Montreal, P.Q., 1873; McGill University 1896; Maj., 22.9.14; V.O. R.C.H.A.; S.V.O. C.C. Bde.; A.D.V.S. Bramshott area; S.V.O. Witley area; Duty D.V.S. Office H.Q.; O.M.F.C.; S.V.O. Bramshott area; S.V.O. Borden area; Demob.; Vet. Lieut. to Vet Maj., 3rd Bde., C.F.A., C.M., 1903-1914; Sydney, N.S.; Port Inspector, Dept. of Agriculture 1906.

Titus, Ralph C.; Trenton, Ont. 1875; O.V.C. 1901; Capt., 20.2.15; No. 2 C.V.H.; No. 1 C.V.H.; V.O. R. C. Ds.; V.O. 1st C.I. Bde.; Returned on leave, retained in Canada 2.10.17.[44]

Vickers, Reginald J.; Brighton, Engl. 1883; O.V.C. 1912; University of Toronto 1912; Capt., 1.7.15; V.O. 6th Bde. C.F.A.; O.C. No. 2 C.M.V.S.; A/D. A.D.V.S. 2nd C. Divn; Military Cross 1.1.19; Demob.; Pvte., Royal Gloucester Gar. Art.; Tpr Buluwayo Scouts, Rhodesia; Far. Sgt. 12th Man. Drgns.; Prvnl. Lieut., C.A.V.C., C.M.; The Plains, Virginia, U.S.A.; Govt. Veterinary Inspector for State of Virginia.

Waddy, Richard; Wexford, Ireland, 1886; Edinburgh 1896; Capt., 9.3.15; O.C. No. 2 C.V.H.; O.C. No. 3 C.M.V.S.; Returned 5.9.16.[45]

Wagner, Allan C.; London, Ont., 1890; O.V.C. 1917; Capt., 25.3.17; No. 2 C.V.H.; V.O. 10th C. I. Bde.; O.C. No. 4 C.M.V.S.; Demob.

Walks, William G.; Chesley, Ont., 1888; O.V.C. 1917; Capt., 25.3.17; No. 2 C.V.H.; V.O. 13th C. I. Bde.; V.O. No. 10, Dist. C.F.C.; No. 1 C.V.H.; V.O. 3rd C. D. Trn.; V.O. 2nd C.D. Trn.; Demob.

Walsh, Frederick A.; Acrington, Engl., 1878; O.V.C. 1894; Chicago Veterinary Collage (Special Course Student); Lieut.-Col., 22.9.14; V.O. 1st C. I. Bde.; A.D.V.S. 3rd C. Divn; A.D.V.S. Shorncliffe area; S.V.O. Shorncliffe area; M.i.D. 2.1.17; Relinquished Appointment and Returned 4.10.18;[45] Prvnl. Lieut. C.A.V.C., C.M.; Meat Inspector Deptartment of Agriculture 1908.

Watson, Edward A.; Newton Abbot, Engl., 1879; O.V.C. 1904; Capt., 10.8.15; O. C. No. 2 C.V.H.; V.O. 3rd Bde., C.F.A.; V.O. 7th Bde., C.F.A.; O.C. R.A.V.C Lab., Rouen; Demob.; Capt., C.A.V.C., C.M.; Tpr and Sgt., Imp. Yeomy.; C. M. Rs., & Transvaal Consty. in S. A. War; Pathologist, Vet. Research Lab., Lethbridge, Alta.; Dept. of Agriculture 1905.

Welch, John W[47].; Cayuga, Ont., 1867; O.V.C. 1894; Capt., 21.11.16; No. 2 C.V.H.; V.O. H.Q., C.F.C.; No. 1 C.V.H.; S.V.O. Bramshott area; Demob.; Toronto, Ont.

West, William E. S.; Madoc, Ont., 1894; O.V.C. 1914; Capt., 19.5.16; No. 2 V.H.; V.O. 11th C. I. Bde.; A/O. C. No. 4 C.M.V.S.; Demob.; Prvnl. Lieut. C.A.V.C., C.M.; Campbellford, Ont.

Wilson, John H.; London, Ont., 1870; O.V.C. 1890; Lieut.-Col., 7.10.14; V.O. R.C.H.A.; O.C. No. 2 C.V.H.; A.D.V.S. Shorncliffe area; A.D.V.S. Bramshott area; A.D.V.S. 2nd C. Divn; A/D.D.V.S. 1st Army; Brought to notice of Secretary of State for War for valuable service rendered in connection with the War, 24.2.17; M.i.D. 1.6.17; Returned in 12.5.17. Resigned 15.8.17;[48] Pvte. to Vet. Capt. 1st Hussars 1887-1911; Capt. to Maj., C.A.V.C., C.M. 1911-1914; London, Ont.; Meat Inspector, Dept. of Agriculture 1907.

Woods, Thomas Z.; Brantford, Ont., 1864; O.V.C. 1904; McKillip Vet. College (Post Grad.) 1905; Capt., 1.4.15; V.O. 1st C. D. Trn; V.O. 2nd C.I. Bde.; Mortally wounded-died of wounds 9.4.16;[49] Vet. Lieut., C. A., S.C. C.M.; Pvte. Winnipeg Light Infantry in N.W. Rebellion 1885; Tpr, Strathcona Horse in S.A. War; Winnipeg, Man.

Appendix B

NOMINAL ROLL OF CANADIAN VETERINARY SURGEONS WHO SERVED AS VETERINARY OFFICERS IN THE IMPERIAL ARMY VETERINARY SERVICE

At the outbreak of The Great War in August 1914, the Imperial Army Veterinary Corps was organized on the lines described in Chapters 7-9, ready to mobilize and function. But it was comprised of only about 165 regular veterinary officers,[1] and 208 other ranks. The British Expeditionary Force landed in France in August 1914 with 6 veterinary hospitals, each for 250 horses; 11 mobile veterinary sections; and 2 base depots, manned by 122 administrative and executive veterinary officers and 797 other ranks.[2] By war's end, the then Royal Army Veterinary Corps was comprised of 651 officers and 15,000 other ranks, and operated 18 veterinary hospitals and 4 convalescent depots housing 39,800 horses; 17 veterinary evacuating stations; 66 mobile veterinary sections; 5 stores depots; 1 bacteriology laboratory; and 7 horse carcass economizers. Six Indian Army mobile veterinary sections and 2 veterinary hospitals were also active.[3] These were supplemented by a Canadian and an Australian veterinary hospital which were integrated into the Imperial hospital system, 2 veterinary evacuating stations (1 Canadian, 1 Australian), and 11 mobile veterinary sections supplied by overseas and dominion governments (Canada - 5, Australia - 5, New Zealand - 1), with a total complement of 114 officers and 1446 other ranks.[4]

Over the course of the war, a total of 1668 officers and 41,755 other ranks served in the Imperial Army Veterinary Corps.[5] According to Moore,[6] the overseas and dominion veterinary services, among which the C.A.V.C. was the largest, supplied about 15% of the 765 veterinary officers on the ground in France. The Australian Army Veterinary Corps was almost as large as the C.A.V.C.; 125 veterinary officers, 95 of whom were graduates of Australian schools, served overseas during the course of the war, many in theatres other than France.[7]

The demand for veterinary officers in the Imperial Army Veterinary Service could not be met from Great Britain alone; it was necessary to seek veterinarians from overseas.[8] As a result, as French noted in Chapter 11, more Canadians served in the Imperial Army Veterinary Corps (203) than in the C.A.V.C. (148).[9] The Canadians listed here comprised over 12% of the officers who were in the Imperial Service over the course of the war.

Captain Rose of the A.V.C. (Figure B.1) is representative of this group of Canadians. He was one of over a dozen members of the Class of OVC '15 who were recruited out of final year (Chapter 11; Figure 11.1), only one of whom entered the C.A.V.C.

Figure B.1. Capt. G.A. Rose, Picton, Ontario (standing with cane, left centre), Admissions Officer at the Receiving Office of No. 4 Reserve Veterinary Hospital, Imperial Army Veterinary Corps, Bulford, England, 1915. (*C.A.V. Barker Museum*)

Interpretation[10]
Number after name means year of graduation and graduation from the Ontario Veterinary College or the University of Toronto - e.g., Adams, F.J., '11. Graduates of other Colleges are identified as follows: Montreal (Lav); McGill (Mc); Queens (Qu); Chicago (Ch); San Francisco (SF); London (Lo); Edinburgh (Ed); Glasgow (Gl); Unknown (?)

Name	**Rank**	**Enlisted**	**Discharged**
Adams, F.J., '11	Capt.	20.7.15	Demobilization
Aikenhead, R.C., '?	Capt.	24.3.15	Demobilization
Andrew, A.T., '16	Capt.	6.7.16	
Andrews, J.R.C., '13	Capt.	3.9.15	
Armstrong, W.E., '15	Capt.	19.7.15	
Atmore, B.R., '17	Lieut.	24.7.18	Demobilization
Bailey, A.E., '07	Capt.	20.2.15	Demobilization
Baker, C.W., '92	Lieut.	4.2.15	Contract term. 19.2.16
Banks, V.L., '13	Capt.	9.5.16	Demobilization
Barnes, F.M., '91	Lieut.	17.5.15	Relinq. Comm. 11.8.15
Bennett, J.E., '11	Capt.	18.2.15	Demobilization
Bentham, W.G., '16	Capt.	1.4.17	
Bidlake, H., '92 (Lo)	Lieut.	3.6.15	Relinq. Comm. 15.1.16
Birkin, F., '14	Capt.	1.5.15	
Bishop, H.H., '15	Lieut.	0.7.15	Contract term. 8.8.16 Returned
Black, A.S., '16	Capt.	6.7.16	
Blanchard, W.H., '89	Capt.	24.3.15	Invalided 31.7.17
Boast, C.R., '11	Lieut.	23.7.17	
Brand, J.M., '15	Capt.	24.3.15	
Brand, W.D., '98	Capt.	13.1.15	Demobilization
Braund, F.J., '96	Capt.	29.3.16	
Bright, S.G., '11	Capt.	6.7.15	Demobilization
Brinsmead, H., '16	Capt.	4.8.16	
Brown, B.A., '96	Capt.	9.7.15	Demobilization
Brown, J.H., '82	Capt.	25.3.16	Demobilization
Brydon, A.B., '12	Capt.	27.3.16	Demobilization
Buchan, J.A., '94 (Mc)	Lieut.	12.1.15	Relinq. Comm. 24.5.15
Buckle, F.W., '01	Lieut.	8.8.18	Demobilization
Buie, J., '06	Capt.	20.2.15	
Bunnell, W.G., '96	Capt.		
Burt, A.C., '11	Capt.	28.3.16	Demobilization
Caldwell, H.L., '17	Capt.	11.4.17	Demobilization
Cameron, W.R., '12	Capt.	29.3.16	Demobilization
Carmichael, B.T., '17	Lieut.	24.7.18	
Caron, W.L.J., '17 (Lav)	Lieut.	1.16.18	
Carson, M., '15	Lieut.	24.3.15	Contract term. 13.4.16
Catt, R.B., '16	Lieut.	16.8.18	
Chagnon, H., '14 (Lav)	Capt.	1.3.15	Demobilization
Chalk, F., '08	Capt.	29.7.15	
Childs, T., '15	Capt.	10.3.15	Demobilization
Clark, J.L., '96	Capt.	27.3.16	Died--Egypt 16.2.18[11]
Collett, H.B., '11	Capt.		
Colthurst, R., '94	Lieut.	17.7.15	Relinq. Comm. 4.13.16
Coombes, F.M., '09	Capt.	22.2.15	
Corbett, C.C., '16	Capt.		Died--France 3.3.18[11]
Corbett, E.R., '16	Capt.	6.7.16	Demobilization

Coutts, R.B., '98	Capt.	2.8.15	Demobilization
Cowan, A., '95	Lieut.	25.3.15	Contract term. 19.4.16
Crawford, N.M., '18	Lieut.	7.8.16	
Croken, I.E., '12	Capt.	13.11.16	
Cunningham, C.G., '15	Lieut.	24.3.15	Returned 12.3.16
Cunningham, J.R., '16	Capt.	11.3.15	
Davidson, W.B., '18	Lieut.		
Delaine, F.L., '02	Capt.	14.1.15	Died - Canada 21.3.18[11]
D'Esmarteau, W.B.,'88 (Lav)	Lieut.	16.2.15	Relinq. Comm. 5.9.15
Deyell, J.D., '?	Lieut.	13.7.15	Contract term. 29.7.16
Dill, W.I., '16	Capt.	30.5.16	Demobilization
Doll, T.B., '12	Lieut.	5.6.28	
Donne, F., '?	Capt.	23.7.17	
Donnelly, J.F., '07	Capt.	3.8.15	Resigned 16.5.19
Donovan, L.A., '16	Capt.	22.5.16	
Dufresne, J.B.A., '09 (Lav)	Lieut.	27.8.18	Demobilization
Dunn, J., '15	Capt.	29.3.16	Demobilization
Dunn, T.L., '?	Lieut.	18.10.18	Demobilization
Earle, F.D., '13	Lieut.	18.10.15	Contract term. 29.1.16
Edmunds, J.A., '16	Capt.	28.5.16	Invalided 31.12.17
Ellah, J.N., '15	Capt.	11.4.17	
Ellsworth, L.H., '15	Lieut.	24.3.15	Contact term. 5.4.16
Farrel, J.J., '13	Capt.	26.3.15	
Farrell, M.I., '17	Capt.	11.4.17	Demobilization
Flanders, C.M., '15	Capt.	29.3.16	
Forbes, H.L., '16	Capt.	11.4.17	
Frayne, G., '15	Capt.	3.6.16	
Gibson, A.B., '15	Lieut.	10.3.15	Contract term. 2.4.16
Gokey, F.W., '95	Lieut.	30.1.15	Cancelled Comm. 12.9.16
Graham, H.W., '06	Lieut.	24.7.18	
Gray, R.G., '12	Capt.	17.8.15	Contract term. 13.9.16
Grogan, W.S., '14	Lieut.	28.5.18	
Guertin, J.O., '10 (Lav)	Capt.	14.1.15	Transfer Australian 13.12.18
Hall, R.J., '86	Capt.	15.2.15	Demobilization
Hanna, J.E., '13	Capt.	29.3.16	
Harries, T.B., '04	Capt.	23.5.15	Demobilization
Hayter, G.P., '98	Capt.	2.2.15	Resigned 19.8.17
Heffron, J.L., '16	Lieut.	24.7.18	
Heron, E.W., '10	Capt.		
Heslop, C.H., '16	Lieut.	24.7.18	Demobilization
Hill, E.M., '16	Lieut.	24.7.18	
Hill, S.A., '15	Capt.	22.9.16	
Hill, W.R., '15	Capt.	24.3.15	
Hobson, G.K., '13	Capt.	11.1.15	Demobilization
Hoggan, T.R.R., '92 (Ed)	Lieut.	30.1.15	Contract term. 14.5.16
Hotchkis, T.F., '15	Capt.	26.5.15	Invalided 10.10.17
Houde, J.A.A., '04 (Lav)	Capt.	8.12.17	Demobilization
Howell, H.N., '18	Lieut.	24.7.18	
Huston, W., '15	Capt.	24.3.15	Killed in France 6.12.17[11]
Hyslop, H.T., '13	Capt.	11.1.15	Demobilization
James, R.T., '15	Capt.	23.5.15	Demobilization
James, N.V., '09	Capt.	24.3.16	Twice wounded

Jaques, J., '15	Capt.	28.3.16	Demobilization
Jull, G.N., '16	Capt.	6.7.16	Demobilization
Kee, W.J., '16	Capt.	29.5.16	Died - London 20.12.18[11]
Kelleher, J.S., '17	Lieut.	11.4.17	Resigned 16.6.18
Kenney, W.G.C., '15	Capt.	24.3.15	
Kerr, S.S., '15	Capt.	24.3.15	Demobilization
Kesten, S.H., '? (Ch)	Capt.	4.7.15	Demobilization
Kilpatrick, W.A.M., '98 (Gl)	Lieut.	28.3.15	Relinq. Comm. 2.12.15
Laurie, J.H., '13	Capt.	13.1.15	
Lavery, J.F., '87	Capt.	11.4.17	Demobilization
Lawrence, G.C., '16	Capt.	14.12.17	
Lay, G.E., '18	Lieut.	7.8.18	Demobilization
Lay, R.H., '16	Capt.	6.7.16	Demobilization
Lefebvre, H.H., '13 (Lav)	Lieut.	17.6.17	Died - Mesopotamia 15.12.17[11]
Lenton, W., '05	Capt.	10.6.16	
Love, B.I., '15	Lieut.	24.10.18	Demobilization
MacDonald, R.W., '98	Capt.	19.2.15	
Macdougall, W.F., '12	Capt.	31.8.15	
MacIntosh, R.D., '12	Capt.	14.1.15	Demobilization
Mackie, C., '16	Capt.	15.1.17	
MacLeod, A.H., '16	Capt.	6.7.16	
MacLeod, N., '?	Lieut.	17.9.18	
Maconachie, C.O., '06	Capt.	23.5.15	Demobilization
MacQueen, L.H., '96 (Gl)	Major		13.2.15
McCormack, W.D., '02	Lieut.	14.9.18	
McCullough, H., '10	Lieut.	13.1.15	Contract term 29.1.16
McFarlane, A.McP., '15	Capt.	19.9.16	
McGee, H.E., '15	Capt.	10.3.15	
McGill, W.A., '? [Qu '99]	Lieut.	24.2.16 [?15]	Contract term 18.3.16
McKee, S.C., '16	Lieut.	22.5.18	
McLachlan, E.J., '17	Capt.	11.4.17	
McLeod, M.M., '13	Capt.	28.12.16	Invalided 2.7.18
McMahon, T.W., '14	Capt.	2.9.15	
McManus, J.H., '12	Capt.	8.3.18	Demobilization
McPhatter, M., '?	Lieut.	19.5.15	Contract term 12.6.16
Medd, W.H.B., '93	Lieut.	27.2.15	Contract term. 23.3.16
Melanson, J.T., '18	Lieut.	7.8.18	Demobilization
Millar, J.L., '13	Lieut.	27.8.18	Demobilization
Miller, A.S., '06	Lieut.	11.4.17	Demobilization
Miller, J.C., '?	Capt.	29.8.15	
Milner, R.J., '11	Capt.	20.12.16	Demobilization
Mitchell, A.F., '16	Capt.	25.5.16	Demobilization
Morrin, W.A., '95 (Mc)	Capt.	14.1.15	Killed in France 1.8.18[11]
Morrison, W.L., '16	Capt.	29.5.16	Demobilization
Morrow, J.J., '08	Capt.	18.2.15	
Morphy, F., '05	Lieut.	29.3.16	Invalided 8.9.17
Nagle, J., '90	Lieut.	20.7.16	Relinq. Comm. 18.5.16
Nedeau, H. McC., '13	Capt.	28.3.16	Invalided 15.12.17
Neely, M.I., '15	Capt.	10.3.15	
Notting, E.S., '18	Lieut.	8.8.18	Demobilization
O'Brien, G.J., '10	Capt.	10.6.17	Demobilization
O'Gogarty, M.G. '12	Capt.	11.3.18	

Olsen, N.P., ‘05	Capt.	25.1.17	Demobilization
Page, F.R., ‘12	Capt.	29.3.16	Demobilization
Parmiter, F., ‘15	Capt.	10.3.15	
Perry, F.V., ‘02	Capt.	11.1.15	Resigned 10.3.18
Pilkey, M., ‘12	Capt.	12.1.15	
Pook, G.G., ‘14	Capt.	25.7.15	
Purcell, J.T., ‘11	Capt.	13.2.17	Wounded
Reed, D.V., ‘15	Capt.	10.3.15	Demobilization
Richmond, A.R.B., ‘11	Capt.		
Robins, W.P., ‘83	Lieut.	25.3.16	Contract term. 24.4.17
Robinson, P.A., ‘96	Lieut.	11.1.15	Relinq. Comm. 6.10.15
Robson, I., ‘18	Lieut.	7.8.18	
Rose, G.A., ’15	Capt.	10.3.15	Demobilization
Salisbury, E., ‘16	Capt.	7.7.16	Invalided 5.10.18
Scott, J.D., ’15	Capt.	24.3.15	Demobilization
Seim, A., ‘97	Lieut.	11.1.15	Contract term. 5.2.16
Sénécal, L., ‘16	Lieut.	22.5.16	
Sewell, K.D.A., ‘14	Capt.	26.4.16	
Sharpe, W.G., ‘13	Capt.	12.2.15	Invalided 7.10.17
Simpson, J., ‘12	Capt.	26.7.15	
Simpson, T.V., ‘96	Lieut.	12.2.15	Contract term. 27.2.16
Skelton,R.T., ‘12	Capt.	10.7.15	
Smith, F.D., ‘15	Capt.	2.7.15	
Smith, W.H., ‘94	Lieut.	25.3.16	Relinq. Comm. 5.5.17
Snyder, O.A.K., ‘16	Lieut.	24.7.18	
Sparrow, M., ‘12	Capt.	1.8.15	Demobilization
Spurr, S.F., ‘16	Capt.	6.7.16	Demobilization
Stanford, J.A., ‘15	Capt.	24.3.15	Demobilization
Steele, M.B., ‘06	Lieut.	22.3.16	Relinq. Comm.
Steiner, E.S., ‘17	Hon. Capt.	11.4.17	Demobilization
Stewart, C.D., ‘?	Lieut.	14.1.15	Relinq. Comm. 3.6.15
Stuart, J.McL., ‘14	Capt.	3.2.15	
Sullivan, J.L., ‘14	Capt.	24.3.16	Demobilization
Swenerton, L.D., ‘02	Lieut.	18.6.15	Termination 29.7.16
Thompson, C.F., ‘15	Capt.	24.3.15	Demobilization
Thompson, W.S., ‘06	Capt.	12.2.15	Died[11]
Thornewill, G.S., ‘06	Capt.	18.2.15	Demobilization
Tomlinson, G.N., ‘95	Capt.	28.3.15	Returned 7.6.17
Trudel, H.A., ‘11	Capt.	1.3.15	
Tummonds, W.H., ‘08	Lieut.	8.8.15	Contract term. 27.9.15
Tweedley, H., ‘?	Lieut.	16.10.15	Relinq. Comm. 15.7.16
Vulliamy, H.F., ‘91	Capt.	7.3.18	Demobilization
Walters, P.K., ‘05	Capt.	24.3.16	
Watt, H.J., ‘17	Capt.	11.4.17	Demobilization
Welbanks, H.P., ‘15	Capt.	16.10.16	
Welsh, J.W.[12]	Lieut.	1.9.15	Contract term. 3.9.16
Whitehead, G., ‘11	Capt.	31.8.15	
Whyte, J., ‘05	Capt.	14.5.17	Relinq. Comm. 20.12.17
Williams, J.E. ‘15	Capt.	24.3.15	Demobilization
Williams, R.N.M., ‘07	Capt.	15.3.15	Invalided
Wilson, R.G., ‘10	Lieut.	30.4.16	Relinq. Comm. 31.7.17
Wolfe, C.E., ‘13	Capt.	13.1.15	

Wolff, H.H., '17	Lieut.	16.5.16	
Wood, W.H., '16	Capt.	19.8.16	
Wright, N., '07	Capt.	25.3.16	Invalided 15.4.19
Younie, A.R., '14	Capt.	19.2.15	Demobilization
Zealand, H.W.A., '17	Capt.	11.4.17	Demobilization
Zinck, K.D., '18	Lieut.	1.8.18	Demobilization

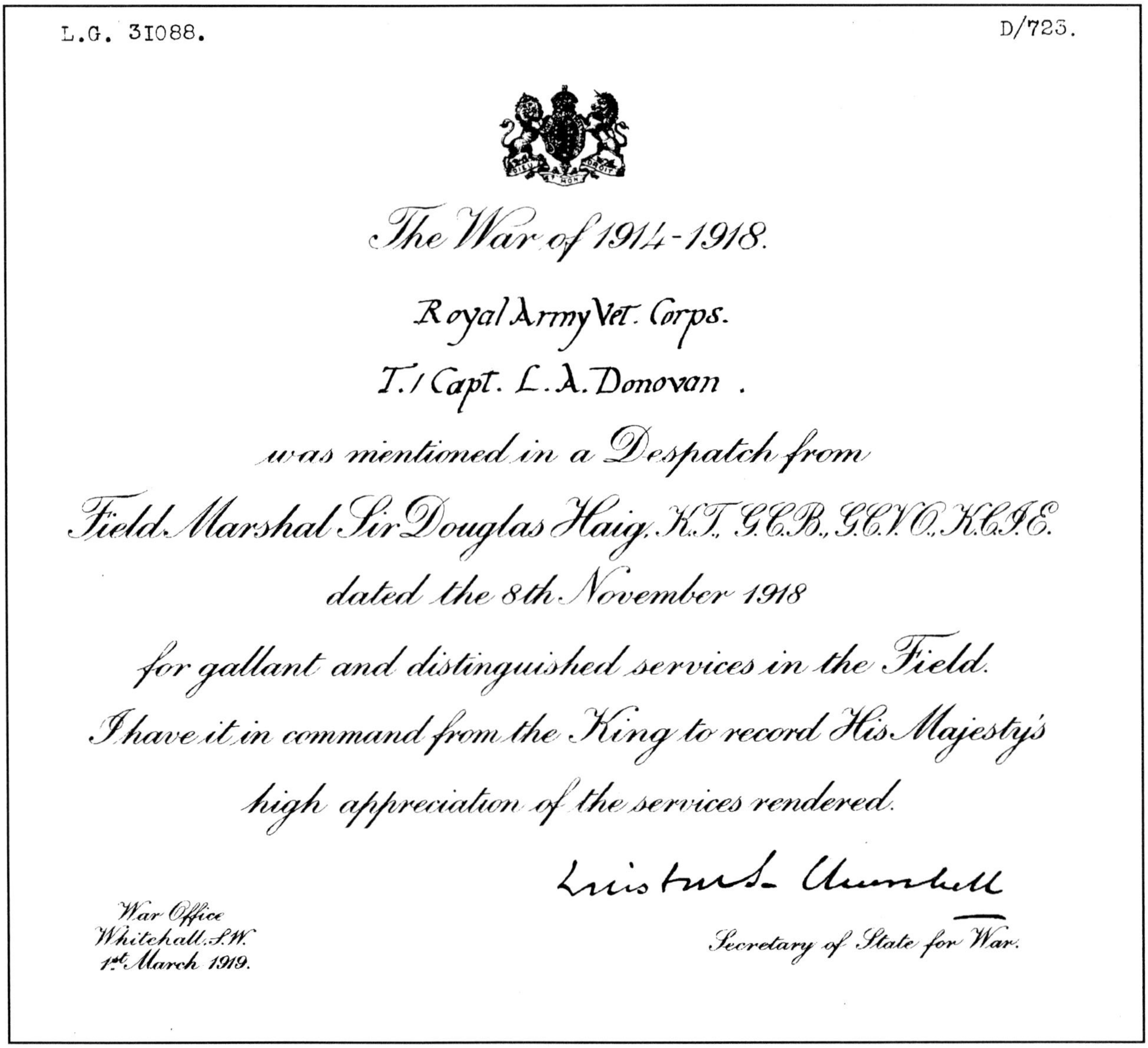
L.G. 31088. D/723.

The War of 1914-1918.

Royal Army Vet. Corps.

T./Capt. L.A. Donovan.

was mentioned in a Despatch from

Field Marshal Sir Douglas Haig, K.T., G.C.B., G.C.V.O., K.C.I.E.

dated the 8th November 1918

for gallant and distinguished services in the Field.

I have it in command from the King to record His Majesty's high appreciation of the services rendered.

Winston S. Churchill

Secretary of State for War.

War Office
Whitehall, S.W.
1st March 1919.

Figure C.1. Certificate recording that Capt. L.A. Donovan, New Brunswick,[1] who served in the R.A.V.C., was mentioned in Despatches. Signed by Winston S. Churchill, Secretary of State for War. (*C.A.V. Barker Museum*)

Appendix C

CANADIAN VETERINARY OFFICERS WHO SERVED IN THE IMPERIAL ARMY VETERINARY SERVICE AND RECEIVED AWARDS[2]

A total of 381 Officers of the Imperial Army Veterinary Service were decorated and 857 were Mentioned in Despatches.[3] The Canadians among these are listed below. All graduated from the Ontario Veterinary College except Major MacQueen (Glasgow). The year of graduation is denoted by the apostrophe and number after each name.

M.C. - Military Cross
M.i.D. - Mentioned in Despatches
O.B.E. - Order of the British Empire
Belgian Croix de Guerre

Name	Rank	Enlisted	Award
Brand, J.M., '15	Capt.	24.3.15	M.i.D. 27.7.17
Brand, W.D., '98	Capt.	13.1.15	M.i.D.
Childs, T., '15	Capt.	10.3.15	M.i.D.
Coombs, F.M., '08	Capt.	22.2.15	M.i.D. 25.5.18
Coutts, R.B., '98	Capt.	2.8.15	M.i.D. 7.11.17
Cunningham, J.E., '16	Capt.	11.3.15	M.i.D.
Donovan, L.A.,'16	Capt.	22.5.16	M.i.D. 30.12.18
Dunn, J., '15	Capt.	29.3.16	M.i.D. 30.12.18
Ellah, J.N., '15	Capt.	11.4.17	M.i.D. 22.1.19
Hanna, J.E., '13	Capt.	29.3.16	M.i.D. 30.12.18
Harries, T.B., '04	Capt.	23.5.15	M.i.D. 30.1.19
Jull, G.N., '16	Capt.	6.7.16	M.i.D. 30.1.19
Laurie, J.H., '13	Capt.	13.1.15	M.i.D. 2.1.17
Maconachie, C.O., '06	Capt.	23.5.15	M.i.D. 30.12.18
McGee, H.E., '15	Capt.	10.3.15	M.i.D. 11.12.17
Miller, J.C., '?	Capt.	29.8.15	M.i.D. 30.12.18
Neely, M.I., '15	Capt.	10.3.15	M.i.D. 7.6.18
Skelton, R.T., '12	Capt.	10.7.15	M.i.D. 7.11.17
Thompson, W.S., '02	Capt.	12.2.15	M.i.D. 11.12.17
Wright, N., '07	Capt.	25.3.16	M.i.D. 23.8.18
Hanna, J.E., '13	Capt.	29.3.16	M.C. 16.11.17
Laurie, J.H., '13	Capt.	13.1.15	M.C. 01.01.18
Maconachie, C.O., '06	Capt.	23.5.15	M.C. 1.1.18
McMahon, T.W., '14	Capt.	29.9.15	M.C. 15.9.18
Stuart, J. McL., '14	Capt.	3.2.15	M.C. 16.9.18
Coombs, F.M., '08	Capt.	22.2.15	O.B.E. 20.7.20
Maconachie, C.O., '06	Capt.	23.5.15	O.B.E. 1.6.19
MacQueen, L.H., '96	Capt.	13.2.15	O.B.E.
James, N.V., '09	Capt.	24.3.16	Belgian Croix de Guerre

Appendix D

NOMINAL ROLL - OTHER RANKS, C.A.V.C.[1]

Abbott, H.H.
Abbott, W.A.A.
Ackers, C.
Adamson, A.B.
Addyman, E.
Adkins, F.
Agland, R.H.
Aird, A.
Alcock, A.E.
Alexander, G.
Alexander, M.
Allen, A.
Allen, E.W.
Allen J.
Allen, J.C.
Allen, W.B.
Almas, J.F.
Anderson, G.
Anderson, G.W.
Anderson, L.G.
Anderson, T.
Andrews, H.
Angell, F.G.
Anson, F.I.
Archibald, W.
Arkley, C.
Arnott, F.W.
Ash, J.E.
Ashmore, C.F.
Aston, W.
Atherton, R.
Atkinson, C.H.
Atkinson, G.
Attewell, G.
Aubert, C.F.
Austin, J.
Austin, W.E.

Bagrie, J.
Bailes, G.
Baillie, J.
Bain, C.S.
Baird, J.
Baker, T.C.S.
Baker, W.
Balcombe, W.R.
Baldwin, H.
Ball, J.
Banks, G.N.
Bannister, H.
Barben, J.E.
Barber, J.
Barbour, R.
Barlow, A.
Barnard, A.
Barnes, A.E.
Barrow, J.
Barry, H.E.
Bartlett, F.H.C.
Barton, W.
Bateman, N.C.
Bates, R.F.
Battist, A.S.
Baynham, E.C.
Beadle, A.W.
Beale, H.
Bearpark, H.F.
Beaton, P.
Beaulac, A.
Beecher, G.
Beer, T.
Bellas J.
Bennett, F.J.
Bennett, G.
Bennett, P.G.
Bentley, J.H.
Berger, E.
Bergstrom, A.
Bernard, F.
Berry, J.
Besse, S.
Bew, J.C.J.
Bick, W.H.
Bickerstaff, H.
Biggs, J.
Bignell, H.
Bigny, J.
Bilot, A.
Bintcliffe, N.
Birch, J.
Bird, E.
Biscoe, C.H.
Bissil, W.H.
Black, G.L.
Black, N.A.
Black, T.
Blacklaws, D.
Blake, J.T.
Blanchette, A.
Bleach, E.
Bligden, W.
Blouin, E.
Blouin, J.
Bolin, B.W.
Bond, W.
Bonnett, F.
Bonneville
Booker, J.
Booth, A.E.
Bosanko, A.
Bosely, E.
Botting, S.A.
Bottomly, T.H.
Bourgeau, V.
Boushey, F.
Boutillier, N.
Bowditch, A.G.
Bowerman, R.
Boyce, L.H.
Bradbury, F.M.
Bradley, W.
Bradshaw, S.
Brault, J.T.
Brean, R.
Brenchley, G.B.
Brethour, J.E.
Briden, H.B.
Broadhurst, W.
Broadway, S.
Brodie, A.
Brookbank, G.
Brooks, G.W.
Brooks, W.H.
Brown, A.W.
Brown, J.
Brown, W.M.
Browning, J.
Brownrigg, W.A.
Bruce, H.G.
Buchanan, W.
Buckpitt, T.A.J.C.
Budd, A.E.
Buller, W.
Burbar, G.B.
Burden, G.
Burdette, R.F.
Burgess, A.
Burke, W.J.
Burn, J.
Byers, T.W.

Caddy, W.
Cafe, B.F.
Cairney, J.
Cairns, J.H.
Cameron, J.
Cameron, J.A.F.
Campbell, A.S.
Campbell, J.A.
Campbell, J.E.
Canham, R.S.
Carpenter, G.
Carter, F.
Case, R.
Casey, J.A.
Casserly, J.J.
Chamberlain, E.
Champion, J.
Chappelle, G.N.D.
Chapman, L.
Chatterton, G.
Chauvin, F.
Chessman, W.
Cheval, M.
Childs, B.F.
Chown, J.
Christianson, G.
Christie, R.V.
Clake, G.
Clare, L.J.
Clark, F.
Clark, J.D.
Clark, R.
Clark, W.H.
Clarke, J.J.
Clausen, A.
Cloke, R.W.
Cocklin, D.
Cocks, H.
Cocks, W.E.
Coe, A.R.
Coghlan, M.J.
Coles, E.N.
Coley, J.P.
Collins, T.
Collinson, F.
Colvin J.
Connors, R.
Conroy, A.J.
Cook, A.A.
Cook, C.
Cooke, R.S.
Cookson, C.N.
Coolen, R.C.
Coppell, W.H.
Cooper, P.H.
Cooper, W.J.
Corbett, M.
Cordonier, A.J.
Cossette, E.
Course, J.F.
Court, J.E.
Coutu, J.E.
Couture, E.
Coveyduck, A.
Cox, F.
Craddock, V.C.
Craig, D.W.
Cramer, F.H.
Crawford, C.
Creasey, A.J.
Cregeen, S.G.
Cretney, J.H.
Crippen, N.D.
Croft, E.
Cross, A.L.
Cross, J.
Crosslew, J.
Crossley, H.
Crowe, G.
Cruickshanks, J.
Cruickshanks, R.
Cubitt, F.W.
Cundall, G.
Cundall, R.C.
Cunningham, G.E.
Cussen, T.
Cutts, A.G.

Daly, J.
Danis, A.
Dann, J.
Darby, W.A.
Darby, W.S.
Davis, J.
Davis, T.
Dawes, R.H.
Deal, L.B.
Dean, F.E.
Dear, W.
Delelly, F.J.
Delves, G.E.
Demmans, A.T.
Denis, A.
Denley, J.E.
Derynck, H.
Descoteau, W.
De Soto, G.
De Ville, R.F.
Dick, E.
Dickie, G.
Dickman, J.
Dickson, R.L.
Dickson, R.L.C.
Ditchburn, W.M.
Doak, A.H.
Dodd, E.H.
Dodds, A.
Dodds, W.
Dodson, F.
Dolan, D.
Dolan, E.
Dolson, C.
Dorward, J.
Dougherty, S.
Doughty, F.
Douglas, W.
Doust, T.S.
Dow, D.
Dowling, J.F.
Downing, F.H.
Downs, R.
Doyle, E.
Draper, A.G.
Drew, L.T.
Drew, C.
Drinkwater, C.
Driscoll, W.
Dryburgh, S.G.
Drysdale, G.R.

Drysdale, G.S.
Dubé, M.
Duddlestone, P.G.
Dufour, H.
Dugal, L.
Duggan, P.
Dugmore, W.H.
Dukeshire, C.
Duley, A.
Duncan, B.
Duncannson, D.
Dundas, C.
Dunford, J.
Dunkley, T.
Dunnam, J.
Dunne, J.
Dunnett, J.
Dunning, S.J.
Dunsmore, G.R.
Dupas, D.
Dupernault, V.
Duplain, R.H.
Durand, J.
Durand, S.H.
Durkee, W.J.
Dutton, H.
Dwyer, J.
Dyer, A.W.
Dyer, W.
Dyke, D.

Eagle, J.W.
Earl, D.
Earthy, C.V.D.
Eckensweiler, J.
Eeles, A.W.
Egen, B.
Egen, H.W.
Elder, T.G.
Elgar, W.H.
Ellery, G.J.
Elsom, C.
Endersby, C.
Erskine, J.L.
Erwin, A.E.
Escott, E.
Eskdale, W.M.
Eslinger, A.
Etheridge, E.P.J.
Evans, A.G.
Evans, F.G.
Evans, W.J.
Everitt, A.G.
Everitt, J.

Fairbrass, A.W. ?
Fairlie, D.
Farley, A.F.M.
Feeley, J.
Ferguson, J.
Fern, W.
Ficht, H.R.
Fittes, H.
Fitzsimmons, M.
Fleming, G.C.
Fletcher, E.
Flynn, D.
Foley, H.G.
Foley, W.
Forrester, D.S.
Forsyth, N.S.
Fountain, H.
Fournin, H.
Foster, D.P.
Foster, J.
Foster, W.
Fowler, A.
Fowler, T.
Fox, W.P.
Franzman, W.J.
Frape, A.E.
Fraser, A.
Fraser, H.
Fraser, J.
Fraser, G.W.
Fraser, J.H.
Fraser, W.J.
Frazier, P.
Fredette, G.
Freeman, E.H.
Fregin, W.
French, C.
Frost, H.
Fudger, R.A.
Fuley, J.
Fulton, A.
Furnish, J.
Fyffe, A.
Fysh, C.

Gagnon, N.
Gagnon, V.
Gallagher, J.A.
Gales, S.G.
Gamble, E.
Gardner, J.
Gatenby, W.
Gates, H.B.
Gauthier, F.J.
Gauthier, U.
Geary, E.
Geddes, J.
Geldart, C.P.
George, N.
George, W.
Gibb, G.
Gibb, J.
Gibbs, H.
Gibbon, L.L.
Gibbons, R.
Gibson, W.
Gilchrist, J.
Giles, C.H.
Gillot, J.G.
Gireaux, J.A.
Gladwin, F.
Glanville, R.
Glass, C.H.
Glendennen, J.
Glew, S.
Glover, J.S.
Glynn, T.
Goddard, F.E.
Godley, J.
Goldsmith, J.B.
Goldson, F.E.
Golics, A.C.
Gonella, C.
Gore, G.
Graham, A.C.
Graham, C.J.
Graham, J.A.
Grant, F.M.
Grant, W.
Gray, H.C.
Gray, W.F.
Greaves, A.E.
Green, E.
Green J.W.
Green W.W.
Greening, A.
Greenly, H.
Grice, H.
Griffin, J.W.
Griffiths, T.
Grimmer, P.H.
Grossart, W.J.
Groves, A.E.
Grubb, W.
Guerard, G.
Guerin, J.L.
Gunian, J.W.
Guptell, H.H.

Haddleton, F.
Hadwin, T.
Hague, A.
Haig, D.W.
Halder, T.E.
Hales, H.
Hales, W.
Hall, F.
Hall, J.R.
Hall, L.
Hallis, G.H.
Halls, E.
Halstead, H.
Hancock, N.H.
Hand, H.
Hannah, W.
Hannant, P.J.
Hanrahan, W.
Hanson, F.
Harbert, G.
Harbury, C.
Harcourt, H.F.
Hardy, W.
Harding, W.
Harley, J.
Harris, G.
Harrison, A.
Harrison, H.
Harrison, H.J.
Harrison H.P.
Harvey, A.H.
Harvey, J.W.
Harvey, R.H.
Harwood, W.
Hasledon, M.B.
Hatfield, E.J.
Haughey, J.
Hawkins, A.
Hay, W.J.
Haylett, A.
Hayman, P.W.
Hazle, A.
Hazle, J.D.
Heath, T.
Heaven, W.
Hebert, D.
Hebner, M.H.
Hemstock, P.
Henderson, A.
Henderson D.
Henham, A.L.S.
Henningson, C.
Hermon, W.A.
Hesford, J.
Hewer, S.
Heysett, W.
Hickey, D.
Hickman, W.
Hickmott, T.
Higgins, A.C.
Hill, A.
Hill, J.C.
Hill, J.R.
Hindle, J.M.
Hipkiss, W.J.
Hodgson, J.W.
Hogarth, G.
Hogarth, W.H.
Hogue, H.
Holder, J.W.
Holing, J.
Holland, S.L.
Hollands, D.
Hollenbeck, A.J.
Hollinshead, M.
Holroyd, W.
Hooper, A.C.
Hooper, P.J.
Hopkins, J.
Horne, L.
Houghton, F.E.W.
Houle, O.O.
Howard, A.E.
Howard, P.J.L.
Howe, E.J.
Howe, J.
Huddlestone, H.
Hudson, D.
Hudson, J.W.
Hudson, W.F.
Huggins, F.
Hughes, F.
Hughes, H.
Hughes, J.
Hughes, T.
Hull, R.
Hunt, W.
Hunter, G.
Hurst, A.G.
Hutson, D.
Hyatt, M.

Ibbotson, A.
Inall, E.

Jackman, G.
Jackson, C.R.
Jackson, F.
Jackson, H.E.
Jackson, H.G.
Jackson, H.L.
Jackson, W.
Jacobson, M.
Jacobson, W.
Jeggers, S.H.
Jenkins
Jennings, S.J.
Jennings, T.W.
Jessop, T.
Jewell, H.
Johnson, H.
Johnston, A.C.
Johnstone, A.
Jolliffe, S.C.
Jones, A.
Jones, A.R.
Jones, S.
Jutras, E.

Keamo, W.
Keen, T.J.
Keep, G.
Keir, A.
Kellaway, H.
Keller, B.
Kelly, A.
Kelly, A.D.
Kendall, H.G.
Kenny, E.F.
Kenny, T.F.
Kernan, A.
Kerridge, P.L.
Kerslake, G.
Kilgallon, M.
Kilpin, W.E.
Kimber, B.H.

King, A.H.
King, B.
King, J.
King, T.
Kings, H.
Kinmond, W.
Kirby, F.D.
Kirk, W.C.
Kline, C.C.
Knowles, W.E.

Lackay, J.
Lacost, N.
Lacost, N.L.
Lafleur, M.
Lafond, A.
Lamb, J.J.
Lancaster, A.W.
Lang, T.B.
Langfield, A.
Lansberry, A.
Lantz, F.
Lapiere, A.
Larkin, G.
Larmour, G.
Larock, N.
Lascarmure, A.
Lawrence, G.
Lawson, C.
Leach, F.
Leahy, P.
Leaman, G.W.
Lear, G.
Leclerc, J.B.
Leduc, J.O.
Lee, P.R.
Lee, J.
Leeds, C.
Lemarsh, R.
Leonard, R.
Leslie, W.D.
Lessard, W.
Levesgne, C.
Lewis, T.W.
Lewitt, W.E.
Lippiatt, A.
Little, T.
Lodge, C.D.
Loomer, N.F.
Love, J.
Love, W.C.
Lovean, D.M.
Lovell, R.G.
Lowe, K.
Lowry, B.
Luker, W.
Lundy, E.O.U.
Lush, A.J.
Lymburner, A.
Lyons, C.H.
Lyons, J.

Mack, J.
Madden, J.J.
Madden, J.W.
Mallette, A.
Malley, W.
Mann, J.T.
Maracle, M.
Margerison, F.W.
Marks, J.
Marlow, C.
Marquardt, M.
Marshall, B.
Marshall, H.
Martin, A.E.
Martin, C.T.
Martin, E.
Martin, J.
Masson, J.
Mathers, W.
May, C.H.
Mayor, A.
Mazler, M.
Macdonald, J.R.
Macdonald, R.
Macgregor, R.F.
Maclean, R.
Macpherson, G.
McArthur, E.
McBeth, E.
McCall, G.
McCarthy, L.J.
McClenaghan, J.
McCreery, W.J.
McDermott, C.R.
McDonagh, E.
McDonald, A.
McDonald, A.E.
McDonald, C.
McDonald, H.
McDonald, J.
McDonald, L.
McDonald, M.
McDonald, N.
McDougall, J.A.
McDowell, H.
McEvers, H.
McFarlane, A.
McGall, W.
McGarr, J.
McGeary, T.
McGee, D.
McGibbon, H.B.
McGillivray, A.
McGillivray, C.J.
McGovern, H.T.
McGregor A.R.
McHugh, J.
McIlroy, J.
McInnes, I.
McInnes, J.
McIntosh, J.
McKay, D.J.

McKay, W.D.
McKay, W.H.
McKee, J.C.
McKee, R.
McKenzie, A.
McKenzie, J.
McKenzie, K.J.
McKenzie, N.
McKey, B.
McKinnon, A.
McKinnon, J.
McKnight, D.M.
McLaren, T.
McLaughlin, J.
McLaurin, N.
McLean, J.
McLean, J.A.
McLeod, W.L.
McMillan, A.
McNabb, G.H.
McNairn, G.J.
McNall, W.G.
McNeill, N.L.
McPherson, G.
McPherson, R.
McRitchie, G.
McTaggart, T.
Meehan, B.
Mellish, A.
Meloche, J.
Menard, C.
Merriman, A.D.
Merritt, A.J.
Metherall, P.L.
Middledith, H.J.
Miles, A.
Millard, F.
Miller, G.
Miller, G.S.
Miller, H.
Miller, J.
Millicent, T.J.
Milligan, J.
Millington, E.
Miles, J.
Milne, A.C.
Milner, R.R.
Milkiman, J.R.
Mitchell, A.H.
Mizar, M.
Moisan, R.
Mole, W.
Moody, J.T.
Mooney, W.
Morgan, F.
Morgan, W.O.
Morris, J.J.
Morrison, J.H.
Morrison, J.R.
Morrow, H.C.
Morton, E.
Mosely, J.C.

Mounce, L.
Muddyman, A.
Muir, J.D.
Muir, J.E.
Muir, R.A.
Mullin, F.
Mullin, N.J.
Mulraine, E.
Murdock, J.
Murphey, F.
Murphey, J.
Murphey, T.
Murray, H.
Murray, J.
Murray, J.J.T.
Myatt, T.
Myers, E.

Nadeau, P.
Neilson, R.A.
Nettleton, A.
Neville, W.
Newett, H. [?Newell, A.]
Newman, E.
Nichol, W.R.
Nichols, B.
Nicholson, J.A.
Nickle
Nickle, J.
Nielsen, P.E.
Nixon, H.T.H.
Nixon, W.H.
Noel, N.
Norton, W.

O'Connor, J.
O'Donnell, J.
O'Hanley, R.T.
O'Keefe, J.
O'Kell, F.E.
Oliver, H.
O'Mara, J.
O'Malley, C.
O'Neil, V.V.
O'Neill, I.L.
O'Rourke, P.F.
Osborne, S.
Osborne, W.

Pace, P.B.
Page, J.
Pagee, J.
Palmer, G.F.
Papine, P.
Park, J.
Parker, E.
Parkin, W.
Patis, G.
Patrick, C.
Patterson, A.E.
Patterson, T.
Pattison, E.F.

Paul, C.E.
Paul W.
Pauline, J.
Peacock, W.
Pearce, F.H.
Pearce, W.R.
Pearson, E.
Pendleton, W.J.
Penney, W.H.
Penrose, G.M.
Pepper, E.F.
Perkins, F.A.
Perkins, S.J.
Person, K.
Phillips, J.
Phillips, J.W.
Pike, H.
Pilon, L
Pilot, J.
Pinkerton, A.
Pipe, 0.
Pittman, J.F.
Pocock, A.S.
Poland, J.
Poole, F.
Port, L.
Preston, A.E.
Preston, J.
Prichard, T.
Pringle, R.W.
Prinn, W.C.V.
Privé, J.
Proctor, J.
Prosser, H.T.
Prothero, W.
Prouse, T.
Prout, J.H.
Pryor, H.
Purvis, G.
Puttick, W.C.
Pynn, J.

Radford, T.
Rae, J.D.
Rainford, F.
Rainnie, J.
Rame, W.J.
Ramsay, W.H.
Rapley, F.
Rathwell, F.
Rattray, C.
Rault, P.M.
Ray, E.W.
Read, H.
Reardon, A.
Reddy, W.
Rees, D.H.
Reeves, C.
Reid, D.F.
Reid, E.H.
Reid, G.
Reid, G.P.

Reid, J.F.
Reid, J.L.
Reidy, J.P.
Rendles, W.
Reynolds, A.S.
Reynolds, R.
Rhodes, W.
Rhoode, H.E.
Richards, H.
Richards, J.W.
Richardson, J.
Rickards, A.
Riddell, W.G.
Riley, W.
Rioux, E.
Ritchie, A.
Roantree, H.W.
Robbins, J.J.
Robert, H.
Roberts, F.
Roberts, M.
Roberts, S.J.
Robertson, F.
Robinson, F.
Robinson, F.E.
Robinson, J.A.
Robinson, R.W.
Rochan, P.
Roggeveen, P.A.
Rollins, L.
Romanik, D.
Romeo, H.
Rose, C.
Rose, W.G.
Rosson, H.
Rotchell, T.C.
Roy, C.
Ruddy, J.J.
Rumming, T.C.
Ruse, R.
Russell, G.R.
Rutherford, J.W.
Rutter, J.E.
Ryan, E.
Ryan, J.
Ryan, W.

Saddler, W.H.
Sallis, J.
Salmon, J.
Samways, T.
Sanderson, N.A.
Sanguiner, O.
Sargent, W.
Saunders, O.M.
Savard, G.
Sayer, J.T.
Scarman, M.G.
Scheiding, R.
Schellinck, C.
Schofield, A.
Schofield, D.
Schofield, W.
Scholes, J.F.
Scobie, R.
Scollen, T.B.
Scott, G.C.
Scott, W.
Scott, W.H.
Scoular, J.
Seaborn, H.
Seal, G.T.
Sealy, A.G.
Seppanen, K.
Shaw, A.W.
Shaw, G.
Shaw, W.R.
Shea, T.
Shepheard, F.G.
Sheridan, W.R.
Sherrard, A.J.
Sherwood, T.
Shields W.
Short, W.
Shurety, F.T.
Shuttleworth, H.
Siford, A.
Siford, R.
Simes, E.
Simmonds, G.
Simmons, H.W.
Simpson, C.G.
Slade, G.
Smart, R.F.
Smith, E.
Smith, F.C.
Smith, G.A.
Smith, H.
Smith, J.
Smith, J.S.
Smith, J.T.
Smith, J.W.
Smith, M.
Smith, S.B.
Smith, W.
Smith, W.F.
Smith, W.H.
Smith, W.J.
Smyth, B.J.
Snow, W.P.
Sorrie, W.
Speakman, J.R.
Spencer, J.
Spindler, R.J.
Spinney, G.A.
Spyker, C.
Stairman, F.
Stanley, R.
Stark, S.G.
Starnes, J.A.
Stevens, H.
Stevens, H.G.
Stevens, P.
Stevens, W.
Stevenson, F.
Stewart, E.
Stewart, J.
Stewart, W.M.
Stigliani, A.M.
Still, A.W.H.
Stinton, H.
Stobbart, J.B.
Stobie, G.
Stock, P.A.
Stoddart, W.J.
Stoodley, G.
Storer, J.A.
Stratford, J.J.
Stretton, W.
Stubbs, G.H.
Sturdy, J.
Sulear, A.
Sullivan, G.
Sullivan, J.W.
Sutherland, D.H.
Sutherland, W.
Swan, H.J.
Swanson, J.
Swanson, W.
Sweet, J.
Swift, J.R.

Tapp, J.
Tappin, P.J.
Taschereau, R.
Taschereau, R.H.
Taylor, A.J.
Taylor, C.
Taylor, E.
Taylor, F.A.
Taylor, G.B.
Taylor, H.G.
Taylor, J.
Taylor, J.D.
Taylor, R.H.
Taylor, W.
Theriault, W.C.
Third, W.
Thomas, N.
Thompson, R.T.
Thompson, W.
Thornton, J.R.
Thorpe, J.
Tilley, R.
Tomer, F.
Tooth, W.A.
Torrance, H.S.
Touchette, J.J.
Tournout, R.
Trapnell, D.
Trebble, J.
Trotman, J.
Tudball, J.T.
Turner, J.
Turner, J.A.
Turner, L.
Turner, W.

Underwood, J.
Upwood, S.
Utas, C.

Vacher, P.
Vance, J.
Vance, J.J.
Vanwart, J.A.
Vasseur, L.J.
Vernon, F.
Vince, W.A.L.
Vincent, J.E.
Vine, R.S.
Vinson, A.
Vosburgh, G.

Walker, C.H.
Walker, W.F.
Wallace, G.W.
Wallace, R.
Wallace, R.H.
Walling, H.
Walmsley, J.
Walre, C.
Walton, R.J.
Walton, W.
Waplington, L.
Ward, C.
Ward, J.S.
Wareing, F.
Wares, D.
Warnica, J.F.
Warwick, H.
Waterbury, B.
Waters, F.
Watkins, G.A.
Watkins, J.T.
Watson, D.
Watson, E.
Watson, G.
Watson, R.B.
Watts, E.
Watts, J.
Webster, J.
Weir, E.F.
Weir, R.
Wenham, W.
West, S.H.A.
Westerman, W.
Westwater, F.
Westwood, W.
Weter, P.
Wey, J.K.
Wey, K.L.
Wey, L.J.L.
Whatley, E.
Wheeler, C.W.
Wheeler, E.H.
Whelpton, G.S.
White, F.
White, J.S.
White, W.
Whittaker, W.
Whittal, J.L.
Whittick, W.W.
Whyte, G.
Wiggins, F.
Wilkie, C.
Wilkins, J.E.
Wilkinson, J.
Wilkinson, N.D.
Willie, T.
Williams, R.
Williams, T.
Williamson, E.B.
Wilson, A.B.
Wilson, C.A.
Wilson, J.
Wilson, J.D.
Wilson, W.
Winter, W.
Wiseman, N.
Wiseman, S.
Wood, H.J.
Wood, P.G.
Woodley, A.
Woods, P.
Wooliscroft, J.S.
Wooster, W.J.
Wright, H.R.
Wyer, A.

York, T.C.
York, T.
Yorston, A.B.
Young, A.F.
Young, G.
Young, H.R.
Young, R.
Young, T.
Youngman, R.H.

Appendix E

Part 1[1]

VETERINARY OFFICERS OF THE 1ST CANADIAN CONTINGENT B.E.F. - 1914

Assistant Director of Veterinary Services	Lieutenant-Colonel W.J. Neill
3rd Infantry Brigade - H.Q.	Lieutenant E. Souter
4th Infantry Brigade	Captain Harry Elliott
Divisional Cavalry	Captain W.G. Stedman
Royal Canadian Dragoons	Major T.J. Taschereau
Lord Strathcona's Horse	Captain J.R.J. Duhault
1st Artillery Brigade and Ammunition Column	Captain E.M. Dixon
3rd Brigade Canadian Field Artillery	Captain C.G. Saunders
No. 1 Heavy Battery Artillery	Lieutenant M.R.A. Gaudry
Royal Canadian Horse Artillery	
'A' Battery	Major John H. Wilson
'B' Battery	Lieutenant P.P. Souillard
Divisional Engineers	Lieutenant A.B. Cutcliffe
Divisional Train	Captain T.Z. Woods
No. 1 Reserve Park	Lieutenant K.L. Douglas
Canadian Army Veterinary Corps	
No. 1 Section[2]	Captain T.C. Evans
	Lieutenant J.J. McCarrey
No. 2 Section[3]	Captain T.A. Daigneault
	Lieutenant L.M. Grignon
Canadian Mobile Veterinary Section	
No. 1	Lieutenant M.G. O'Gogarty
No. 2	Lieutenant C.L. Edwards
Canadian Veterinary Base	
Supply Depot	Lieutenant and Quartermaster A.E. Frape
Remount Depot	Lieutenant H.D.J. Duchêne

Part 2[4]

CANADIAN ARMY VETERINARY CORPS

The Canadian Army Veterinary Corps was mobilized about the middle of October, 1914, by Lieut.-Col. M. A. Piché, Montreal, under orders from the Dominion Government, and sailed for England on November 10th, 1914. The corps consists of 230 men under four officers, and includes Veterinary Surgeons and qualified dressers.

It is understood that this corps will be attached to the First Canadian Contingent, and will form a Hospital behind the firing line where all wounded animals will receive attention. All the men, with the exception of thirty from Sherbrooke, are Montrealers.

No. 3 Section - C.A.V.C.

CAPTAIN

T. C. Evans, C.A.V.C., Officer Commanding

LIEUTENANT

J.J. McCarrey, C.A.V.C.

STAFF SERGEANT

Shirt, A. J.

SERGEANTS: Buttling, W.J.; Kenner, H.B.; Moores, W; Smith, W.; White, O.C.

CORPORALS: Cave, C.A.; Feeley, J.; Hurst, A.G.; Sullivan, J.; Vosburgh, G.; Wenham, W.

TROOPERS

Achton, F.G.
Anderson, T.
Atkinson, G.
Bates, B.
Beer, T.
Bilot, A.
Biscoe, C.H.
Bottomley, T.H.
Brownrigg, W.A.
Burden, G.
Burn, J.
Casey, J.A.
Champion, Jos.
Cheval, M.T.
Clark, F
Clark, T.O.
Clark, W.H.
Clisdell, J.
Collins, T.
Coveyduck, A.
Cox, H.
Creasey, A.J.
Croft, E.F.
Cross, James
Crossley, H.
Cutts, A.G.
David, G.A.
Dodds, W.
Doughty, F.
Elder, T.G.
Escott, B.
Fall, F.
Fredette, G.
Fritzsimmons, M
Galcs, J.S.
George, N.
George, W.
Graham, J.A.
Grahame, H.
Green, G.E.
Hamilton, R.I.
Hancock, R.H.
Harbury, C.
Hennimgsen, C.
Hill, A.
Huestis, R.R.
Insall, B.A.
Jupp, G.
Kendall, H.G.
Kernan, A.
Kilpin, W.E.
Larkin, G.
Leeds, Chas.
Macpherson, G.
McBeth, N.
McClintock, R.
McDonagh, A.G.
McIlroy, J.
McLaurin, N.
Merritt, A.J.
Millicent, T.J.
Miller, J.W.
Millington, E.
Mole, U.
Moore, J.
Murray, A.T.
Nickle, J.
Norton, W.
Noury, A.
O'Keefe, J.
O'Malley, C.
Papinie, P.
Perkins, W.E.
Pilot, J.
Poole, F.
Pritchard, T.
Pynn, J.
Reddy, A.E.
Richardson, J.
Ricketts, A.
Russell, G.R.
Scheiding, R.
Shaw, A.W.
Sheridan, W.R.
Stames, J.A.
Stark, A.C.
Stewart, Jas.
Sweet, J.
Taylor, J.F.A.
Trapnell, D.
Tuggey, H.A.
Upwood, S.
Vance, J.
Wallace, R.
Wallace, R.A.B.
Watley, E.
Webster, J.
Wilson, C.
Wilson, J.
Wooster, W.J.
Young, R.
Young, Thos.

No. 4 Section - C.A.V.C.

CAPTAIN

F.A. Daigneault, C.A.V.C., Officer Commanding

LIEUTENANT

L. Grignon, C.A.V.C.

STAFF SERGEANT

Foster, H.

SERGEANTS: Akerman, A.; Cotton, J.; Gosselin, J.F.; Hay, J.; Turner, S.R.J.

CORPORALS: Bennett, C.; Hyatt, M.; Kendall, F.; Stevens, J.R.; Threffall, M.S.; Turner, J.B.

TROOPERS

Attewell, A.J.
Attewell, G.
Austin, Joseph
Baker, W.
Barton, W.
Baynham, E.C.
Beecher, G.
Biggs, J.
Blencowe, B.
Bradburn, R.M.
Brereton, T.
Brown, W.
Buller, W.
Charvin, F.
Cordonniere, J.
Couture, E.
Dennis, A.
Donaldson, C.
Doust, T.S.
Drysdale, G.
Dugmore, W.H.
Dunkley, W.
Duperrault, V.
Durand, J.
Durand, S.T.
Edridge, G.
Ellis, A.
Erskine, J.
Flynn, D.
Fowler, T.
Gatenby, W.
Gauthier, F.T.
Gauthier, U.
Gaves, L.
Geary, E.
Gibbs, J.L.
Gill, E.
Glendeven, J.A.
Goldsmith, J.B.
Gore, A.J.
Greenhough, J.
Guinan, J.
Hackett, J.
Harburt, G.
Harrison, H.
Hatfield, E.J.
Hayes, C. J.
Hull, R.H.
Humble, E.A.
Jones, A.R.
Jutrand, E.
Keir, A.
Lapierre, A.
Laviolette, O.
Leahy, P.
Lebrit, A.
Lessard, W.
Lovell, F.
Machan, W.C.
Madden, J.J.
Martin, E.
McCall, G.
McDonald, A.
McDonald, E.G.
McDonald, H.
Mead, D.
Meloche, J.
Menard, C.
Mills, J.
Montgomery, G.
Morton, E.
Murphy, F.
Murphy, T.
Myers, Ed.
Nockle, J.
O'Rourke, P.
Pallett, A.
Pavey, H.
Pearce, W.R.
Pepper, E. J.
Perkins, E.F.
Phillips, J.
Plunkett, A.
Poulton, A.
Richardson, J.
Rioux, E.
Scott, W.
Scrivener, G.
Shaw, G.
Stewart, A.
Stratton, W.F.
Tournour, R.
Val-de-Ver, A.
Valiquette, G.
Vier, R.
Wales, C.A.
Walker, P.G.
Wallace, D.
Williams, H.H.
Winwood, A.

Appendix F

TRANSMISSIBLE DISEASES OF HORSES[1]

Mange

Mange is a contagious disease caused by mites. Prominent signs of mange are a skin eruption, itching and loss of hair, which can be very debilitating. Several kinds of mites affect horses; one (*Sarcoptes)* burrows into the epithelium, while the others (*Psoroptes* and *Chorioptes*, the latter the cause of so-called symbiotic mange[2]) feed more superficially. In World War I the most severe and widespread form was sarcoptic mange, the scourge of army horses. Mites usually are acquired by contact with an infected animal, stabling, blankets, or harness. Mixing of animals, and poor grooming, hygiene, and nutrition predisposed to outbreaks in army horses. Inflammation initiated by the presence of mites results in itching, which causes the animal to rub, producing bare patches of skin. As the disease progresses there is extensive loss of hair, and the denuded skin becomes covered by crusts and scabs.

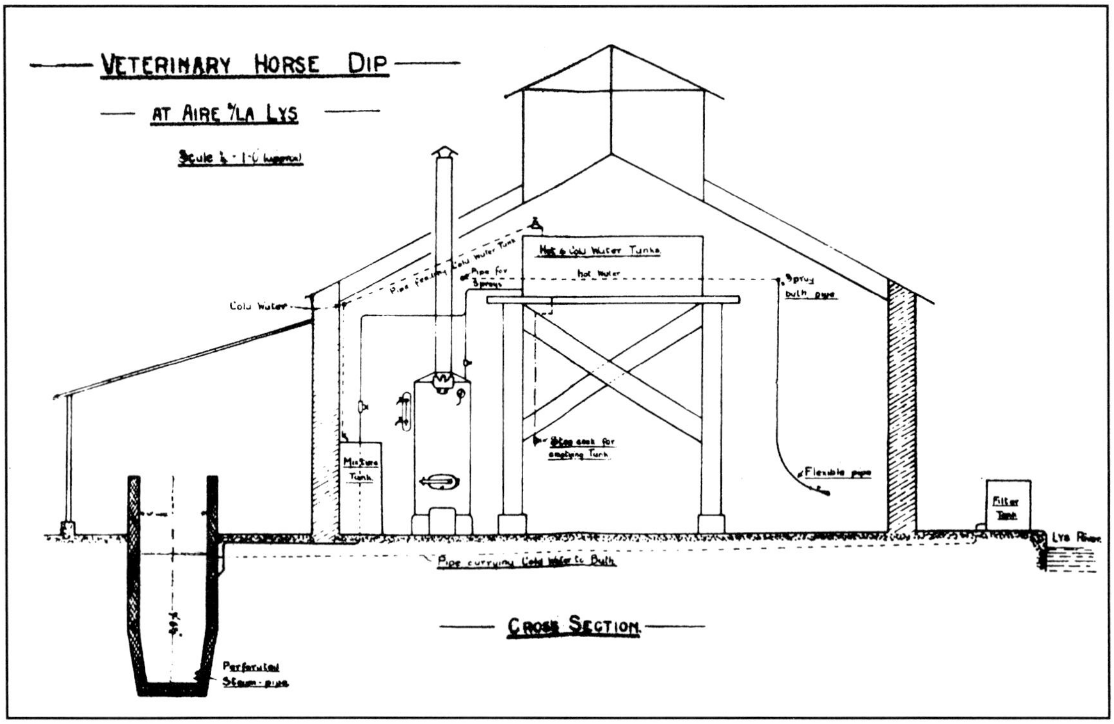

Figure F.1. Plan for horse dip at Aire á là Lys, France. Water from the river, right, is filtered, and is pumped to the bath or dip, in section at left, and into an elevated pressure tank on the stand in the centre of the building. Steam from the boiler, with chimney, on the left in the building, is piped to the dip, where thermostatically-controlled steam jets below the surface maintain the temperature of the solution at about 100°F. Hot water from the boiler is stored in an elevated tank, which feeds the 'mixture tank' containing the lime-sulphur solution, at left in the building. Hot lime-sulphur solution is piped from there to the dip, and to flexible overhead spray lines, in the bay on the right of the building. Horses were treated by a plunge in the dip, or by spraying. (*French Papers, NAC*)

A diagnosis is readily made by finding mites in a microscopic examination of skin scrapings from a recently infected area. Mange is prevented by segregation and treatment of infected horses, and by preventing horses from contacting infected animals, horse blankets, grooming instruments, housing etc. This was obviously difficult to accomplish in times of war. While mange is treated currently with effective acaricidal drugs, in The Great War, the main treatment employed was application of hot lime-sulphur (calcium sulphide) by dip (Figures 6.15, F.1), by spray (Figures 16.1, F.1) or by hand (Figure 6.12). In some circumstances, a sulphuration chamber, in which the horse was placed for fumigation, was used.[3]

Glanders

Glanders is a chronic infectious disease of horses caused by *Pseudomonas mallei*, a bacterial organism which is transmissible to humans.[4] Glanders was extremely important during World War I, since wars produce conditions that favour the distribution of infected animals. Effective methods of detection and control of this disease under war conditions were not known until early in the war. Antibiotics had not yet been discovered, and since there was no effective treatment, affected animals were destroyed.

The disease is characterized by the formation of nodules, abscesses and ulcers in the lungs, nasal membranes and other body organs and tissues. The term 'farcy' is applied to nodular and ulcerative skin lesions. Transmission of the infection is usually through lung or nasal discharges, which contaminate community water troughs, pails, mangers, harness and feed.

Under war conditions, with a large population of horses intermingling because of the nature of their work, it was necessary to subject potential carriers to a reliable diagnostic test proven in peace time, the mallein test, which in principle resembles the tuberculin test. This consisted of the injection of 0.1 mL. of concentrated mallein into the skin of the lower eyelid of the right eye, followed by observation of the site over a period of 48 hours. A marked swelling of the lid, purulent discharge and photophobia was classed as a positive test of a carrier animal (Figure 5.3). Mallein testing and the destruction of all reactors was established as a routine procedure in all remount depots and veterinary hospitals.

Contagious Stomatitis

This disease in horses is characterized by the formation of vesicles and pustules on the swollen mucous membrane of the cheeks, lips, gums and tongue. The cause is a pox virus occurring as a stable enzootic in young horses. There is slight salivation and sometimes an odour. The disease may be confused with vesicular stomatitis in which there are no nodules or pustules. Another name for this disease is horsepox.

Vesicular Stomatitis

This viral disease in horses is marked by large vesicles (blisters) chiefly on the upper surface of the tongue. In 1916 it occurred in remount depots in France soon after the introduction of horses originating in the United States. Segregation of affected animals, disinfection of premises and treatment with mild antiseptics usually controled an outbreak.

Strangles

Strangles, (distemper) is a severe infectious bacterial disease of horses caused by *Streptococcus equi*, which localizes in the nasal passages and throat. It is characterized by fever, inflammation of the lining of the throat, rhinitis, and abscessation of the lymph nodes in the region. It is foremost among the acute infections of army horses, remounts and stockyard horses. The disease is acquired naturally through contaminated food or water. Young horses are most susceptible; old animals are seldom affected.

The signs are difficulty swallowing, regurgitation, swelling of the lymph nodes of the throat, and abscessation. Multiple abscesses in many organs is usually fatal. Treatment depends on the severity and signs. Drainage of abscesses usually is required, and antibiotics, unavailable to veterinarians during W.W. I, are used therapeutically. Affected animals are isolated, and contaminated areas must be disinfected.

Appendix G

DESTRUCTION OF ANIMALS[1]

Moore, in discussing the economic and other realities of war, reflected on the unfortunate necessity to kill animals which, by reason of disease, injury or debility posed a threat to the heath and welfare of other animals, or had suffering which could not be mitigated. "I only ask that readers not mark down the Veterinary Service and myself as butchers, instead of a community of experts whose mission is to cure and not to kill. I can safely say that the act of destruction is distasteful to the Veterinary Officer, but some one of his Corps must do the deed, and the responsibility for the execution of it in a proper and humane manner devolves on the Veterinary Officer."[2]

Figure G.1. Point of aim for pistol shot to humanely destroy a horse. (*French Papers, NAC*)

The proper method to follow is to hold the horse by the head-rope with the left hand then bring the right hand up pointing the revolver about one foot from the head. When releasing the trigger aim slightly upwards at the centre of the forehead well above the level of the eyes, just below where the lowest hairs of the forelock grow. See that no one stands directly behind the horse. One shot should be sufficient.[3]

Appendix H

CANADIAN MILITARY VETERINARIANS 1855-1940

The military careers of over 600 Canadian veterinarians can be traced by use of this Appendix, in association with Appendices A and B. Use Appendix H for officers who served as Veterinary Surgeons or Veterinary Officers in the North West Rebellion of 1885, the Boer War, or in the Active Militia between 1855 and 1939. Use Appendices A and B for officers who served in the C.A.V.C. (C.E.F./O.M.F.C.), or in the Imperial Army Veterinary Corps in W.W. I. Veterinarians who served in the Non-Permanent or Permanent Active Militia and who also went overseas in W.W. I will be found in Appendix H and in one or both of Appendices A and B, so their pre-and/or post-war careers can be followed.[1] Veterinarians who served in the Canadian Armed Forces in W.W. II and subsequently are in the Notes to Chapter 17.

Name; college of graduation;[2] dates of commissioning, seniority, or promotion; rank; unit; locality; date last listed or retired. Assume continuity of appointment at rank and/or in unit between dates, unless indicated otherwise.
MP = veterinarian in North West Mounted Police or Royal N.W.M.P.; NW = in Northwest Rebellion,[3] 1885; BW = in Canadian or British unit in Boer War,[4] 1899-1902; CEF/SEF = C.A.V.C. in Canadian Expeditionary Force or Siberian Expeditionary Force in W.W. I [Appendix A]; IMP = in Imperial Army Veterinary Corps in W.W. I [Appendix B]; *Permanent Active Militia.

Ager, E.E., O.V.C. 1914; 17.8.15, Lieut., C.A.V.C., M.D. No. 10 - 1919.

Alexander, J.G., O.V.C. 1874; 17.6.12, Lieut., C.A.V.C.; 1914, No. 2 Coy C.A.S.C., Toronto Ont. - 1919.

Allan, A.W., O.V.C. 1934; 20.9.34, Lieut., C.A.V.C., No. 3 Section, Kingston Ont; 1.12.36, Lieut., R.C.A.V.C.(N.P.), No. 2 M.V.S.; Reserve List, 1939.

Alloway, Arthur, ? grad.;16.10.56, Vet. Surg., 1st Wentworth Troop of Cavalry, Hamilton Ont.; 1863; 1865.

Alloway, Clement J., M.V.C. 1869; 2.7.80, Vet. Surg., 6th Prvnl. Regt of Cavalry, Montréal P.Q. - 1887.

Anderson, H.H., O.V.C. 1922; 1.9.26, Lieut., C.A.V.C., 2nd Reg., Alberta Mounted Rifles, Pincher Creek Alta.; 3.11.30, Reserve List; 1.12.36, Lieut., R.C.A.V.C.(N.P.), Reserve List - 1939.

Anderson, J.G., O.V.C. 1924; 9.3.25, Lieut., C.A.V.C., 13th Divn Trn, Calgary Alta.; 1932, 19th Bde. C.F.A., Calgary, Alta.; 25.2.33, Capt.; 1.12.36, Capt., R.C.A.V.C.(N.P.), 2nd Cavalry M.V.S., Calgary Alta. - 1939.

Andrews, J.R.C., IMP; 15.1.21, Reserve List; 20.9.26, Capt., C.A.V.C., 11th Hussars, Richmond P.Q.; 15.6.30, 2nd Reserve Regt, 11th Hussars; 1.12.36, Capt., R.C.A.V.C.(N.P.), Reserve List - 1939.

Aubry, J.H., Laval 1917; 13.4.18, Lieut., C.A.V.C., M.D. No. 4; indicated IMP, but not in Appendix B; - 1919.

Bailey, A.E., IMP; 15.1.21, Capt., C.A.V.C., M.D. No. 12, Saskatchewan; 1.1.28, Maj.; 19.4.33, died Wynyard Sask.

Baker, C.B., O.V.C. 1923; 20.9.33, Lieut., C.A.V.C., 17th Duke of York's Royal Canadian Hussars, Montreal P.Q. - 1936; 28.1.37, R.C.A.V.C.(N.P.), Capt., 17th Hussars - 1939.

Baker, C.W., 1.2.15, Lieut., C.A.V.C.; IMP; CEF; 10.1.17, died overseas.[5]

Baker, G.P., McGill 1894; 15.5.12, Lieut., C.A.V.C., 32nd Manitoba Horse, Roblin Man. - 1919.

Ball, E.P., M.V.C. 1884; 20.6.92, Vet. Surg., 5th Dragoons, Cookshire P.Q.; 1897, Vet.-Lieut. - 1899.

Banks, V.L., IMP; 15.1.21, Capt., C.A.V.C., 2nd Divn Trn, Toronto Ont. - 1930.

Barker, M., O.V.C. 1907; 25.4.13, Lieut., C.A.V.C., 22nd Saskatchewan Light Horse, Lloydminster Sask.; 1915, M.D. No. 10 - 1919.

Barlow, B.E., O.V.C. 1918; 1.3.37, Lieut., R.C.A.V.C.(N.P.), D.V.O., M.D. No. 13, Alberta; unattached - 1939.

Barton, J., ? grad.; 20.6.90, Vet. Surg., 5th Regt of Cavalry, Cookshire P.Q. - 1892.

Bean, J.A., O.V.C. 1895; 11.6.97, Vet.-Lieut., 8th Fld. Bty., Gananoque Ont.; 11.6.02, Vet.-Capt. - 1908.

Beaver, N., CEF; 2.8.22, Capt., C.A.V.C., 4th Bty. C.F.A., Peterborough Ont.; 4.4.29, No. 3 Reserve M.V.S. - 1936.

Bédard, J.A.E. [J.-E.-A.], Laval 1915; 1.1.23, Lieut., C.A.V.C., No. 5 M.V.S., Québec P.Q.; 1930, 13th Bde. C.F.A., Québec P.Q.; 1.12.36, Lieut., R.C.A.V.C.(N.P.), Reserve List - 1939.

Beggs, R.E., O.V.C. 1916; 14.2.38, Lieut., R.C.A.V.C.(N.P.), No. 1. M.V.S., London, Ont. - 1939.

Bennett, J.E., IMP; 19.4.37, Lieut., R.C.A.V.C.(N.P.), No. 7 M.V.S., Victoria, B.C. - 1939.

Benson, D.R., O.V.C. 1907; 15.1.21, Lieut., C.A.V.C., No. 2 Coy, 3rd Divn Trn, Kingston Ont. - 1924.

Bentham, W.G., IMP; 19.6.25, Capt., C.A.V.C., 3rd Bde. C.F.A., Toronto Ont.; 1.5.34, Maj., No. 2 Section, Toronto Ont.; 1.12.36, Maj., R.C.A.V.C.(N.P.), Reserve List - 1939.

Berry, R.G., O.V.C. 1888; 22.5.99, Vet.-Lieut., 5th Dragoons, Cookshire P.Q. - 1902; not in list 1903-1905; 25.5.06, Vet.-Lieut., C Squadron, Canadian Mounted Rifles, Fort Saskatchewan Alta. - 1908.

Berubé, J.A., Laval 1919; 15.1.21, Lieut., C.A.V.C.; 1.5.24, Capt., No. 4 M.V.S., Montréal P.Q.; 1.9.28, No. 4 Reserve

M.V.S.; 1.12.36, Capt., R.C.A.V.C.(N.P.), Reserve List - 1939.

Best, V.C., CEF; 15.1.21, Capt., C.A.V.C., S.V.O., M.D No. 11, Victoria B.C. - 1924.

Bett, A.W., O.V.C. 1930; 13.3.31, Lieut., C.A.V.C., No. 2 Section, Toronto Ont. - 1932.

Bishop, F.C., ? grad.; 1.6.28, Lieut., C.A.V.C., M.D. No. 2, Toronto Ont.; 1.6.29, Lieut. Manitoba Horse, Dauphin Man.; 30.6.30, Capt. - 1935.

Blacklock, T.A., ? grad.; 18.3.21, Lieut., C.A.V.C., 8th Bde. C.F.A., Hamilton Ont. - 1925.

Blanchard, W.H., O.V.C. 1889; BW - Cpl., 2nd Canadian Mounted Rifles; 14.5.06, Vet.-Lieut., 24th Bty. C.F.A., Peterborough Ont. - 1909.

Bland, J.W., O.V.C. 1888; 5.5.93, Vet. Surg., 3rd Hussars, Cobourg Ont.; Vet.-Lieut. - 1899.

Boast, R.D., 2.3.13, Lieut., C.A.V.C. - 1913.

Bond, John Pratt, O.V.C. 1873; 5.9.79, Vet. Surg., Governor General's Body Guard, Toronto Ont. - 1887.

Boucher, W.W., O.V.C. 1889; 8.6.14, Lieut., C.A.V.C., 29th Light Horse, Saskatoon Sask.; 15.1.21, Maj., 10th Bde. C.F.A., Saskatoon Sask. - 1928.

Bovaird, J., O.V.C. 1915; 1.6.33, Lieut., C.A.V.C., 1st Hussars, London Ont.; 7.6.35, Capt.; 1.12.36, Capt., R.C.A.V.C.(N.P.), 1st Hussars - 1939.

Bowlby, G.H., ? grad.; 18.2.09, Vet.-Lieut.,[6] 24th Regt, Grey's Horse, Woodstock Ont. - 1909.

Bradley, J.E., O.V.C. 1888; 1.6.88, Vet. Surg., Gananoque Fld. Bty., Gananoque Ont.; No. 8 'Gananoque' Fld. Bty. - 1896.

Brazenall, F., O.V.C. 1919; 1.11.25, Lieut., C.A.V.C., 44th Bty. C.F.A., Prince Albert, Sask. - 1930.

Brock, A.M., O.V.C. 1896; 16.12.07, Vet.-Lieut., 16th Light Horse, Regina, Sask. - 1912.

Brother, A.H., O.V.C. 1905; 28.3.08, Vet.-Lieut., 9th Mississauga Horse, Toronto, Ont. - 1914.

Brown, James, ? grad.; 20.8.79, Vet. Surg., Newcastle Fld. Bty., Newcastle N.B. - 1886.

Brun, C.E., 1.5.12, Lieut., C.A.V.C. - 1914; CEF; not in list 1922-1928; 15.4.29, Capt., C.A.V.C., unattached; 1931, 6th Duke of Connaught's Royal Canadian Hussars, St. Hilaire P.Q.; 1932, 17th Duke of York's Royal Canadian Hussars, Montréal P.Q.; 1934, No. 4 Section, Montréal; 1.12.36, Capt., R.C.A.V.C.(N.P.), No. 3 M.V.S., Montréal; 15.1.38, Maj. - 1939.

Brunet, O., 1.10.13, Lieut., C.A.V.C.; CEF; 15.1.21, Maj., 13th Scottish Light Dragoons, Waterloo P.Q.; 1.10.31, Lieut.-Col.; 1934, 6th Duke of Connaught's Royal Canadian Hussars, St. Hilaire P.Q.; 1.12.36, Lieut.-Col., R.C.A.V.C.(N.P.), 17th Duke of York's Royal Canadian Hussars, Montréal P.Q. - 1939.

Bruyns, A.G.M., O.V.C. 1932; 10.1.39, Lieut., R.C.A.V.C.(N.P.), Governor-General's Horse Guards, Toronto Ont. - 1939.

Buckle, F.W., 19.4.06, Vet.-Lieut., No. 2 Coy, C.A.S.C., Toronto Ont. - 1912; not in list 1913-1917; IMP.

Busselle, A.W., MP - Vet. Staff Sgt., R.N.W.M.P., Sask. 1905;[7] CEF; 15.1.21, Capt., C.A.V.C., Alberta Mounted Rifles, Pincher Creek Alta. - 1925.

Caesar, John S., O.V.C. 1870; 11.6.75, Vet. Surg., 3rd Prvnl. Regt of Cavalry, Cobourg Ont. - 1885.

Cairns, G., O.V.C. 1925; 1.5.27, Lieut., C.A.V.C., No. 2 M.V.S., Toronto Ont.; 1928, No. 2 Reserve M.V.S.; 1931, No. 2 Divn Trn, Toronto; 25.5.31, Capt.; 1934, No. 2 Section, Toronto; 1.12.36, Capt., R.C.A.V.C.(N.P.), No. 1 Veterinary Hospital, Toronto - 1939.

Cameron, A.E., 1.6.13, Lieut., C.A.V.C.; 1914, 27th Horse, Moose Jaw Sask.; CEF; 15.1.21, Maj., 18th Bde. C.F.A., Lethbridge Alta.; 1926, 32nd 'Kingston' Bty. C.F.A., Kingston Ont.; 1930, No. 3 Divn Eng., Kingston; 1.10.31, Lieut.-Col.; 1.12.36, Lieut.-Col., R.C.A.V.C.(N.P.), No. 2 M.V.S., Kingston - 1939.

Cameron, A.R., CEF; not in list 1922-1927; 19.3.28, Capt., C.A.V.C., 20th Bde. C.F.A., Edmonton Alta.; 1.12.36, Capt., R.C.A.V.C.(N.P.), Reserve List - 1939.

Campbell, Frank Alexander, O.V.C. 1874; 23.12.87, Vet. Surg., The Governor-General's Body Guard, Toronto Ont.; 1897, Vet.-Capt.; 1.4.03, Vet.-Maj. - 1905.

Campbell, J.A., 14.11.05, Vet.-Lieut., The Governor-General's Body Guard, Toronto Ont.; 12.2.12, Capt., C.A.V.C.; 1.1.15, Maj.; SEF; 3.1.21, Lieut.-Col., C.A.V.C.; 1.03.27 to Reserve List; 1.12.36, Lieut.-Col., R.C.A.V.C.(N.P.), Reserve List - 1939.

Caron, W.L.J., IMP; 15.1.21, Capt., C.A.V.C., 1st Bde. C.F.A., Ottawa Ont. - 1930.

Carson, M., IMP; 15.1.21, Capt., C.A.V.C., The Manitoba Horse, Russell Man.; 1925, M.D. No. 13, Alberta; 1926, Manitoba Horse; 1930, 5th Bde. C.F.A., Winnipeg Man. - 1932.

Carpenter, W.H., ? grad.; 14.11.55, Vet. Surg.; 1863, Québec Fld. Bty., Québec P.Q.; 1865.

Cassels, F.H., CEF; 15.1.21, Capt., C.A.V.C., No. 1 Coy, 11th Divn Trn, Vancouver B.C. - 1922.

Catley, S.L.C., O.V.C. 1930; 13.10.38, Lieut., R.C.A.V.C.(N.P.), No. 1 M.V.S., London. Ont. - 1939.

Chambers, A., O.V.C. 1918; 1.7.18, Lieut.; indicated CEF, and also indicated in 1925 Reserve List, but not in Appendix A; 15.1.21, Reserve List; 1.2.37, Capt., R.C.A.V.C.(N.P.), 1st Cavalry M.V.S., Regina Sask. - 1939.

Chipman, G.R., O.V.C. 1913; 12.5.13, Lieut., C.A.V.C., 14th King's Canadian Hussars, Middleton N.S. - 1919.

Church, W.G.,[8] 23.3.08, Vet.-Lieut., 14th King's Canadian Hussars, Cannington N.S. - 1912; not in list 1913 - 1914; CEF; 15.1.21, Capt., C.A.V.C., No. 6 M.V.S., Summerside P.E.I.; 1.9.26, Maj.; 1930, P.E.I. Medium Arty. Charlottetown P.E.I. - 1930.

Clairmont, M., ? grad.; 23.1.39, Lieut., R.C.A.V.C.(N.P.), No. 3 M.V.S., Kingston Ont. - 1939.

Clark, G.M., O.V.C. 1923; 1.3.24, Lieut., C.A.V.C., 12th Manitoba Dragoons, Brandon Man.; 1.11.29, Capt.; 1.12.36, Capt., R.C.A.V.C.(N.P.), 12th Manitoba Dragoons - 1938.

Clark, W.F., O.V.C. 1887; 8.5.13, Lieut., C.A.V.C., 31 Fld. Bty., Aylmer Ont. - 1919.

Clarkson, W., O.V.C. 1921; 7.3.24, Lieut., C.A.V.C., No. 2 M.V.S., Toronto Ont. - 1926.

Clegg, R., O.V.C. 1914; 29.1.16, Lieut., C.A.V.C., M.D. No. 2 - 1919.

Cleveland, H.R., 1.9.03, Vet.-Lieut., 11th Hussars, Richmond P.Q.; 1.9.08, Vet.-Capt. - 1913; CEF.

Cober, A., O.V.C. 1911; 3.6.12, Lieut., C.A.V.C.; 1914, 19th Alberta Dragoons, Edmonton Alta. - 1914.

Colebourn, H., 22.5.13, Lieut., C.A.V.C.; 1914, 34th Fort Garry Horse, Winnipeg Man.; CEF; 15.1.21, Maj., C.A.V.C., Fort Garry Horse - 1928.

Coleman, Arthur Owen, O.V.C. 1868; 27.12.78, Vet. Surg., Princess Louise Dragoon Guards, Ottawa Ont. - 1893.

Coleman, N.J., O.V.C. 1918; CEF; not in list 1922-1926; 17.3.27, Capt., C.A.V.C., 8th Divn Trn, Hamilton Ont.; 1931, No. 2 Section, Toronto Ont.; 1932, No. 2 Divn Eng., Toronto Ont. - 1935.

Colgan, R., O.V.C. 1892; 9.7.01, Vet.-Lieut., 7th Fld. Bty., St. Catharines Ont. - 1908.

Colman, A.R., O.V.C. 1904; 15.1.21, Lieut., C.A.V.C., 18th Canadian Light Horse, Kindersley Sask. - 1930.

Connolly, M.G., O.V.C. 1902; 4.11.17, Lieut., C.A.V.C., M.D. No. 13; indicated IMP but not in Appendix B - 1919.

Cooper, C.J., 1.2.17, Lieut., C.A.V.C., M.D. No. 2; SEF; 15.1.21, Capt., C.A.V.C., No. 2 M.V.S., Toronto Ont. - 1922.

Coté, T.A., Laval 1900; 9.4.13, Lieut., C.A.VC., 5th Fld. Bde. C.F.A., Québec P.Q. - 1919.

Coulombe, A.E., 8.8.14, Lieut., C.A.V.C.; CEF; 15.1.21, Maj., C.A.V.C., 2nd Bde. C.F.A., Montréal P.Q. - 1925.

Couture, J.A., M.V.C. 1873, McGill, 1890; 30.6.87, Vet. Surg., Quebec Fld. Bty., Québec P.Q.; 1897, Vet.-Capt. - 1898.

Couture, Joseph E., ? grad; *6.4.96, Vet. Surg., 'B' Bty. R.C.A., Québec P.Q.; 1897, *Vet.-Lieut. - 1897.

Cowan, A.D., 19.6.03, Vet.-Lieut., 3rd 'Montréal' Fld. Bty., Montréal P.Q. - 1909; 24.11.09, Vet.-Lieut., 6th Bde. C.F.A., Montréal; 15.6.11, Lieut., C.A.V.C.; No. 4 Coy C.A.S.C., Montréal; IMP; CEF.

Craig, H.W., CEF; 25.5.27, Capt., C.A.V.C., Manitoba Mounted Rifles, Morden Man. - 1936.

Craig, Joseph, O.V.C. 1870; 5.12.79, Vet. Surg., Hamilton Fld. Bty., Hamilton Ont. - 1883.

Croken, I.E., IMP; 15.1.21, C.A.V.C., Maj., Prince Edward Island Light Horse, Charlottetown P.E.I.; 1.1.36, Lieut.-Col., R.C.A.V.C.(N.P.), Prince Edward Island Light Horse - 1939.

Cromwell, A.J., O.V.C. 1898; 16.6.03, Vet.-Lieut., 7th Hussars, Bury P.Q.; 16.6.08, Vet.-Capt.; 1910, 26th Stanstead Dragoons; 15.1.21, Maj., C.A.V.C., Eastern Townships Mounted Rifles, Coaticook P.Q.; 2.5.27, Lieut.-Col. - 1936.

Cummins [Cummings], P.H., M.V.C. 1880/ McGill 1891; 17.6.87, Vet. Surg., Queen's Own Canadian Hussars, Québec P.Q. - 1896.

Cutcliffe, A.B., 5.4.09, Vet.-Lieut., 25th Brant Dragoons, Brantford Ont.; 6.2.12, Lieut., C.A.V.C.; CEF; 1.10.20, Brevet Lieut.-Col., 10th Brant Dragoons, Brantford Ont.; 15.1.21, Lieut.-Col., C.A.V.C. - 1931.

Daignault [Daigneault], F.A., 1.11.12, Lieut., C.A.V.C; CEF; 15.1.21, Maj., C.A.V.C., 6th Bde. C.F.A., Sherbrooke P.Q.; 1.10.30, Lieut.-Col.; 1934, 6th Duke of Connaught's Royal Canadian Hussars, St. Hilaire P.Q.; 1.12.36, Lieut.-Col., R.C.A.V.C.(N.P.), No. 3 M.V.S., Montréal P.Q. - 1939.

Davidson, W.B., IMP; 15.1.21, Reserve List; 1.9.28, Lieut., C.A.V.C., No. 1 Reserve Cavalry M.V.S., Winnipeg Man.; 9.3.31, Capt., No. 10 Section, Winnipeg; 1.12.36, Capt., R.C.A.V.C.(N.P.), M.D. No. 12, Saskatchewan; 1.5.38, Maj., 14th Horse, Climax, Sask. - 1939.

Davis, H.J., O.V.C. 1919; 12.10.31, Lieut., C.A.V.C., 7th Bde. C.F.A., London, Ont.; 1936, 1st Hussars, London; 1.12.36, Lieut., R.C.A.V.C.(N.P.), 1st Hussars - 1939.

Derome, C.E. [?W.], ?1904 Laval; 22.4.10, Vet.-Lieut.; 15.3.13, Lieut., C.A.V.C.; 1914, 6th Duke of Connaught's Royal Canadian Hussars, St. Hilaire P.Q., - 1914.

Dickinson [Dickenson], S.S., O.V.C. 1883; 29.5.85, Vet. Surg., Durham Fld. Bty., Port Hope, Ont. - 1892.

Domville, H., O.V.C. 1893; 20.6.92, Vet. Surg., 8th Princess Louise's New Brunswick Hussars, Rothesay N.B. - 1893; 1893, No. 10 Fld. Bty., Woodstock N.B.; 1897, Vet.-Lieut. - 1899.

Donovan, L.A., IMP; 15.1.21, Capt., C.A.V.C., S.V.O. M.D. No. 7, Saint John, N.B.; 1925, D.V.O., M.D. No. 7; 10.31, Maj., New Brunswick Dragoons, Saint John N.B. - 1936.

Douglas, K.L., 10.8.14, Lieut., C.A.V.C.; CEF; 5.1.21, Maj., C.A.V.C., 4th Divn Trn, Montréal P.Q.; 1925, Reserve List; 1930, 2nd Reserve Regt, Princess Louise Dragoon Guards; 1.5.31, Maj., Princess Louise Dragoon Guards; 1.12.36, Maj., R.C.A.V.C.(N.P.), Princess Louise Dragoon Guards - 1939.

Doyle, L.S., O.V.C. 1902; 9.5.07, Vet.-Lieut., Prince Edward Island Light Horse, Charlottetown P.E.I.; 10.5.09, Vet.-Lieut., 19th Bty., Moncton, N.B. - 1913; 13.6.13, Vet.-Capt.; 15.1.21, Maj., C.A.V.C., 12th Bde. C.F.A., Moncton N.B.; 21.6.27, Lieut.-Col. - 1936.

Duchêne, H.D.J., Laval 1912; 2.5.12, Lieut., C.A.V.C.; 1914, 15th 'Shefford' Bty., Granby P.Q.; 9.4.14, Capt.; CEF.

Duchene, J.D., Laval 1891; 11.4.96, Vet.-Lieut., Queen's Own Canadian Hussars, Québec P.Q.; *18.11.97, Vet.-Lieut., 'B' Bty., R.C.A., Québec P.Q. - 1902; 29.4.02, 10th Queen's Own Canadian Hussars; 26.11.03, Vet.-Capt.; 1.7.11, Maj., C.A.V.C.; 1914, P.V.O. M.D. No. 5, Québec P.Q. - 1919; 14.1.34, died Québec P.Q.

Dufresne, J., Cornell 1936; 1.7.38, Lieut., R.C.A.V.C.(N.P.), No. 3 M.V.S., Montréal P.Q. - 1939.

Duhault, R.J.R., Laval 1910; 20.9.11, Lieut., C.P.A.V.C., No. 5 Det., LdS.H.(R.C.), Winnipeg Man., - 1914; CEF; 1.4.20, Maj., R.C.A.V.C., No. 10 Det., Winnipeg; 21.12.22, Lieut.-Col.; 1924, No. 5 Det., Québec P.Q.; 1931, No. 10 Det., Winnipeg; 1936, No. 4 Det., St. Jean Québec - 1940; ? O.C., M.D. No. 4, St. Jean - c. 1942.

Duncan, John A., M.V.C. 1884; NW - 1885, North West Rebellion, Medical Officer and Vet. Surg., attached 'A' Bty.

Dunn, J., IMP; 15.1.21, Capt., C.A.V.C., No. 2 Section, Toronto Ont.; 1.10.31, Maj.; 1.4.32, No. 2 Reserve M.V.S.; 1.12.36, Maj., R.C.A.V.C.(N.P.), Reserve List - 1939.

Duthie, R.C., O.V.C. 1914; 6.5.14, Lieut., C.A.V.C., 23rd Alberta Rangers, Pincher Creek Alta.; indicated IMP, but not in Appendix B; 15.1.21, Capt., C.A.V.C., 92nd Bty. C.F.A., Edmonton Alta. - 1924.

Eckert, H.A., CEF; 15.1.21, Capt., M.D. No. 1, London, Ont.; 1928, 1st Divn Eng., London, Ont.; 1.12.36, Capt., R.C.A.V.C.(N.P.), 1st District Eng. - 1938.

Edgett, C.E., 1.4.06, Vet.-Lieut., No. 7 Coy, C.A.S.C., Saint John N.B.; 12.3.13, Lieut., C.A.V.C., No. 18 Coy C.A.S.C, Winnipeg Man.; CEF; 15.1.21, Maj., M.D. No. 11, British Columbia; 23.1.31, Reserve List; 1.12.36, Maj., R.C.A.V.C.(N.P.), Reserve List - 1939.

Elliott, Charles, O.V.C. 1870; 10.5.72, Vet. Surg., 2nd Regt of Cavalry, Oak Ridges Ont.; 1893, 2nd Dragoons, St. Catharines, Ont.; 10.9.96, Vet.-Maj.; retired 1.11.07.

Elliott, H.J., 4.6.08, Vet.-Lieut., 18th Mounted Rifles, Winnipeg, Man.; 13.11.11, Lieut., C.A.V.C., unattached; 25.11.13, Capt., 18th Mounted Rifles, Portage la Prairie Man.; 21.8.16, Maj.; CEF; - 1922.

Etienne, A.A., Laval 1890; 25.9.12, Lieut., C.A.V.C ; 9.8.13, Capt., 6th Bde. C.F.A. - 1919.

Evans, T.C., 1.6.11, Lieut., C.A.V.C.; 17.12.13, Capt., 8th Bde. C.F.A., Ottawa Ont.; CEF; 1.4.20, Lieut.-Col., R.C.A.V.C., No. 2 Det., D.V.O. M.D. No. 2,Toronto Ont.; May 1936, A.O.A.C.A.V.S.; Mar. 1937, O.A.C.A.V.S. - 1940; 1940, Lieut.-Col., Liaison Officer, M.D. No. 2, Toronto; 1943, retired.

Evely, C.C., 10.6.14, Lieut., C.A.V.C.; CEF.

Farrant, A.L., ? grad.; 1.4.14, Capt., C.A.V.C., 30th British Columbia Horse, Vernon, B.C.; indicated CEF but not in Appendix A - 1919

Farrell, J.J., IMP; not in list 1922-1930; 14.4.31, Capt., C.A.V.C., No. 6 Reserve M.V.S., Summerside P.E.I. - 1935.

Fisher, J.W., O.V.C. 1883; 8.9.91, Vet. Surg., 'Durham' Fld. Bty., Port Hope Ont.; 1895, No. 14 'Midland' Fld. Bty., Port Hope; 1897, Vet.-Lieut.; 1897, Vet.-Capt.; 23.9.05, Vet.-Capt., 10th Bde. C.F.A., Cobourg Ont.; 24.9.06, Vet.-Maj.; 12.8.11, Maj., C.A.V.C.; 1.11.12, Lieut.-Col.; 15.1.21, Lieut.-Col., C.A.V.C., 4th Bde. C.F.A., Coburg Ont. - 1922.

Forbes, H.L., IMP; 15.1.21, Capt., C.A.V.C., No. 1 M.V.S., London Ont. - 1922.

Forsyth, W.D., O.V.C. 1901; 6.1.16, Lieut., C.A.V.C., M.D. No. 2 - 1919.

Forsyth, W.W., 23.8.13, Lieut., C.A.V.C., M.D. No. 2, Toronto Ont.; CEF; 15.1.21, Capt., C.A.V.C., Mississauga Horse, Toronto; 15.12.28, Maj.; 1.1.36, Lieut.-Col.; 1.12.36, Lieut.-Col., R.C.A.V.C.(N.P.), Governor-General's Horse Guards, Toronto - 1939.

Fortier, J.A. [?A], ?Laval 1896; 4.8.11, Lieut., C.A.V.C., M.D. No. 5, Québec P.Q.; indicated IMP but not in Appendix B. - 1916.

Frame, R., O.V.C. 1900; 11.5.04, Vet.-Lieut., 12th Manitoba Dragoons, Brandon Man. - 1906.
Fraser, J.H., O.V.C. 1910; 15.10.31, Lieut., C.A.V.C., No. 6 Section, Halifax N.S. - 1936.
Frédette, L.G., Laval 1898; 12.6.99, Vet.-Lieut., 15th Fld. Bty., Shefford P.Q. - 1903; 1904-1908, not in list; 1.6.09, Vet.-Lieut., 19th Alberta Mounted Rifles, Edmonton Alta. - 1910.
Frew, A.G., O.V.C. 1920; 20.6.33, Lieut., C.A.V.C., 10th Brant Dragoons, Brantford Ont.; 20.6.35, Capt.; 1.12.36, Capt., R.C.A.V.C.(N.P.), 2/10 Dragoons - 1939.
Frink, James Henry, O.V.C. 1879; 7.5.80, Vet. Surg., 8th Regt of Cavalry, Apohaqui N.B. - 1891; 2.6.93, Vet. Surg., 8th Hussars, Rothesay N.B.; 1897, Vet.-Lieut.; 16.12.99, Vet.-Capt. - 1901.
Galbraith, W.C., O.V.C. 1891; 1.6.14, Lieut., C.A.V.C., 1st Howitzer Bde., Fld. Artillery, Guelph Ont. - 1919.
Gariépy, E.V. [V.-E.], Laval 1918; 14.5.18, Lieut., C.A.V.C., M.D. No. 4; indicated IMP but not in Appendix B - 1919.
Gauthier, J.L. Laval 1913; 12.8.1913, Lieut., C.A.V.C., 5th Bde. C.F.A., Québec P.Q.; 1914, MD No. 4., Montréal P.Q.; indicated CEF but not in Appendix A - 1919.
Gauvin, C.J.H., Laval 1904; 20.6.08, Vet.-Lieut., No. 10 Coy C.A.S.C., Québec P.Q.; 31.7.11, Lieut., C.A.V.C., No. 10 Coy C.A.S.C., Québec ; 7.9.17, Capt.; 15.1.21, Maj., C.A.V.C., M.D. No. 5, Québec P.Q.; 1924, No. 5 Section, Québec P.Q.; 1.10.31, Lieut.-Col.; 1.12.36, Lieut.-Col., R.C.A.V.C.(N.P.), No. 4 M.V.S., Québec P.Q. - 1939.
Gaw, E.C., O.V.C. 1907; 1.4.12, Lieut., C.A.V.C.; 1914, 15th 'Shefford' Fld. Artillery, Granby P.Q.; 25.6.14, Capt. - 1921.
George, H.H.S., ? grad; 1.4.08, Vet.-Lieut., Canadian Mounted Rifles Independent Squadron/British Columbia Horse, Kamloops B.C. - 1910.
Gilpin, W.G., O.V.C. 1890; 20.4.05, Vet.-Lieut., No. 5 Coy, C.A.S.C. Ottawa, Ont.; 20.4.10, Vet.-Capt.; 2.4.12, Capt., C.A.V.C., No 5 Coy C.A.S.C., Ottawa; 2.7.15, Maj.; 15.1.21, Lieut.-Col., C.A.V.C., No. 1 Coy 3rd Divn Trn, Ottawa - 1925.
Girard, J.U.G., Laval 1939; 9.5.39, Lieut., R.C.A.V.C.(N.P.), No. 4 M.V.S., Montréal P.Q. - 1939.
Girling, T.A., 2.3.08, Vet.-Lieut., 22nd Saskatchewan Light Horse, Saskatoon, Sask. - 1911; not in list 1912-1915; CEF; died overseas.[9]
Gohn, G.A., O.V.C. 1902; 23.2.16, Lieut., C.A.V.C., M.D. No. 2 - 1919.
Graham, H.W., 20.5.09, Vet.-Lieut., 7th Bty. C.F.A., St. Catharines Ont. - 1911; not in list 1912-1918; IMP; 12.1.23, Capt., C.A.V.C., 2nd Dragoons, St. Catharines Ont. - 1931.
Grange, Edward Alexander Andrew, O.V.C. 1873; 13.8.75, Vet. Surg.; 7.5.80, 1st Prvnl. Bde. Fld. Artillery, Guelph Ont. - 1881.
Gray, R.G., IMP; 15.1.21, Capt., C.A.V.C., M.D. No. 10, Manitoba - 1925.
Greene, M.P., ? grad.; 11.7.73, Vet. Surg., 8th Regt of Cavalry, Apohaqui N.B. - 1876.
Grignon, L.M., CEF, 15.1.21, Maj., C.A.V.C., No. 4 M.V.S., Montréal P.Q.; 1925, No. 4 Divn Trn, Montréal - 1932.
Guertin, J.O., IMP; 15.1.21, Capt., C.A.V.C., Alberta Mounted Rifles, Medicine Hat Alta. - 1926.
Hadwen, S., McGill 1902; BW - May-July 1902, Vet.-Capt., 6th Canadian Mounted Rifles.
Hall, A.H., McGill 1894; 15.6.06, Vet.-Lieut., No. 10 Coy C.A.S.C., Québec P.Q.; 5.6.11, Lieut., C.A.V.C., No. 12 Coy C.A.S.C., Toronto Ont.; 1914, 13th Bde. C.F.A., Toronto - 1916.
Hall, William B., M.V.C. 1877; 22.6.77, Quebec Fld. Bty., Québec P.Q.; *29.1.87, 'B' Bty. R.C.A., Québec P.Q.; *1.7.93, Royal Canadian Dragoons, Toronto Ont.; *27.6.96, Hon. Vet.-Maj.; BW - *Dec. 99-Jan. 01, Hon. Vet.-Maj., Royal Canadian Dragoons; *1.4.03, Vet.-Maj.; *1.5.05, Hon. Veterinary Lieut.-Col., P.V.O., Western Ontario Command; *22.3.10, Veterinary Lieut.-Col.; *1.4.11, Lieut.-Col., C.P.A.V.C.; retired 1913.
Halsey, A.B., O.V.C. 1911; 14.6.11, Lieut., C.A.V.C., M.D. No. 4, Montréal P.Q. - 1919.
Hamilton, R., ? grad.; 15.1.21, Capt., C.A.V.C., M.D. No. 11, British Columbia - 1925.
Hanmore, G.S., CEF; 15.1.21, Capt., C.A.V.C., M.D. No. 2, Toronto, Ont. - 1927.
Harries, T.B., IMP; 15.1.21, Capt., C.A.V.C., No. 2 Cavalry M.V.S., Calgary, Alta.; 12.1.28, Maj.; 1928, No. 2 Reserve Cavalry M.V.S. - 1934.
Harrington, A.D., McGill 1902; BW - May-July 02, Vet.-Capt., 4th Canadian Mounted Rifles.
Harrington, J., O.V.C. 1912; 1.5.12, Lieut., C.A.V.C.; 1914, 2nd Dragoons, St. Catharines, Ont.; CEF; not in list 1922-1926; 21.1.27, Capt., C.A.V.C., 8th Bde. C.F.A., St. Catharines Ont. - 1927.
Harris, A.W.,[10] M.V.C. 1880, McGill 1890; 18.4.84, Vet. Surg., Ottawa Fld. Bty., Ottawa Ont.; No. 2 Fld. Bty., Ottawa; 18.4.97, Hon. Vet.-Maj.; 1.4.03, Vet.-Maj.; 25.10.04, 5th The Princess Louise Dragoon Guards, Ottawa; 18.4.08, Hon. Vet.-Lieut.-Col.; 29.6.11, Lieut.-Col., C.A.V.C., M.D. No. 3, Ottawa; 2.3.22, retired.

Harris, James, ? grad.; 13.8.75, Vet. Surg., Ottawa Fld. Bty., Ottawa Ont. - 1883.
Harris, J.G., O.V.C. 1887; 1.6.88, Vet. Surg., Welland Canal Fld. Bty., Welland Canal Ont. - 1890.
Harvey, J. Gardiner, 22.1.03, Vet.-Lieut., 1st Bde. C.F.A., Guelph Ont.; 22.2.05, No. 1 Coy, C.A.S.C., Guelph; 23.1.08, Vet.-Capt.; CEF; 15.1.21, Capt., C.A.V.C., 11th Bde. C.F.A. - 1930.
Hawke, W.R., O.V.C. 1905; 5.2.09, Vet.-Lieut., 21st Alberta Hussars, Medicine Hat Alta. - 1912.
Hay, A.H., ? grad.; 1.4.12, Lieut., C.A.V.C., No. 12 Coy, C.A.S.C., Toronto Ont. - 1912.
Hayes, C.E., O.V.C. 1906; 6.4.12, Lieut., C.A.V.C.; 1914, 13th Scottish Light Dragoons, Waterloo P.Q. - 1919.
Hibert [Hébert], H.G., Laval 1917; 20.4.18, Lieut., C.A.V.C., M.D. No. 4; indicated IMP but not in Appendix B - 1919.
Heighway, E.W., O.V.C. 1894; 1.5.13, Lieut., C.A.V.C.; 1914, No. 16 Coy C.A.S.C., London Ont. - 1919.
Henderson, C.McP., ? grad.; 31.7.12, Lieut., C.A.V.C., No. 11 Coy C.A.S.C., Vancouver B.C.; 1914, No. 19 Coy C.A.S.C., Vancouver B.C. - 1921.
Hennan, J.H., CEF; 15.1.21, Capt., C.A.V.C., No. 7 M.V.S., Winnipeg Man.; 1.9.28, No. 7 Reserve M.V.S.; 1.12.36, Capt., R.C.A.V.C.(N.P.), Reserve List - 1939.
Henry, R.H., O.V.C. 1931; 6.5.36, Capt., C.A.V.C., Mississauga Horse, Toronto Ont.; 3.7.37, Capt., R.C.A.V.C.(N.P.), The Governor-General's Horse Guards - 1939.
Hewitt, L.LeB., ? grad.; 24.12.26, Lieut., C.A.V.C., 12th Divn Trn, Regina Sask. - 1928.
Higgins, C.H., McGill 1896; 1.4.11, Lieut., C.A.V.C.; 17.12.13, Capt., M.D. No. 3, Ottawa Ont.; 21.8.16, Maj. - 1921.
Hilliard, W.A., McGill 1897; 1.6.06, Vet.-Lieut., 12th Manitoba Dragoons, Brandon Man. - 1909.
Hinman, Willett James, O.V.C. 1875; 13.8.75, Vet. Surg., Durham Fld. Bty., Port Hope Ont. - 1876; not in list 1877-1879; 17.12.80.- 1883; not in list 1884-1885; 30.7.86 - 1888; not in list 1889-1891; 20.6.92, Vet. Surg., Winnipeg Fld. Bty., Winnipeg Man.; 1895, 13th Winnipeg Fld. Bty., Winnipeg; 1897, Vet.-Lieut.; 7.5.98.Vet.-Capt. - 1903.
Hobson, G.K., IMP; 15.1.21, Capt., C.A.V.C., M.D. No. 10, Manitoba; 15.3.26, Maj., M.D. No. 11, British Columbia; 1.1.36, Lieut.-Col.; 1.12. 36, Lieut.-Col., R.C.A.V.C.(N.P.), No. 7.M.V.S., Victoria B.C. - 1939.
Hodgson, R.K., O.V.C. 1909; 7.4.13, Lieut., C.A.V.C.; 1914, No. 12 Coy C.A.S.C., Toronto, Ont. - 1919.
Hogan, J.D., CEF; 1922-1926 not in list; 6.1.27, Capt., C.A.V.C., 2nd Divn Eng., Toronto Ont.; 1930, 4th Hussars, Kingston Ont.; 1.12.36, Capt., R.C.A.V.C.(N.P.), Reserve List - 1939.
Hoggan, T.R.R., IMP; CEF; 15.7.20, Brevet Capt., C.A.V.C., 15th Bde. C.F.A., Vancouver B.C.; 15.1.21, Capt., C.A.V.C. - 1931.
Holloway, S.H., O.V.C. 1929; 1.1.31, Lieut., C.A.V.C., 18th Light Horse, Rosetown Sask.; 1934, unattached; 4th Divn Eng., Montréal P.Q.; 1.12.36, Lieut., R.C.A.V.C.(N.P.), No. 4 District Eng., Montréal; 15.1.38, Capt. - 1939.
Hood, A.J.G., ? grad.; 28.9.12, Lieut., C.A.V.C.; 9.8.13, Capt.; 1914, Montreal Heavy Bde. Arty. - 1921.
Hopkins, A.G., O.V.C. 1891; 21.4.13, Lieut., C.A.V.C.; 29th Light Horse, Saskatoon, Sask., - 1914; not in list 1915; 1916, M.D. No. 10 - 1919.
Hotchkis, T.F., IMP; 15.1.21, Capt., C.A.V.C., Kings (Nova Scotia) Mounted Rifles; 1926, King's County Horse; 1927, M.D. No. 6, Nova Scotia; 10.31, Maj., 14th Bde. C.F.A., Dartmouth N.S. - 1936.
Howard, Edward, ? grad.; 29.1.57, Vet. Surg., The Napanee Troop of Cavalry, Napanee Ont.; 1870.
Howe, E.E., O.V.C. 1912; 22.9.13, Lieut., C.A.V.C., M.D. No. 3, Kingston Ont. - 1914.
Hurd, C.L., O.V.C. 1912; 18.2.13, Lieut., C.A.V.C. - 1913.
Hutton, F.G.H., O.V.C. 1889; 12.6.93, Vet. Surg., No. 7 Fld. Bty., Welland Canal Ont.; Vet.-Lieut. - 1898.
Ilsley, B.R., O.V.C. 1893; 8.9.96, Vet.-Lieut., King's Canadian Hussars, Canning, N.S.; 8.9.01, Vet.-Capt.; 15.7.05, Vet.-Capt. - 1908; 1909, Vet.-Capt., Canadian Mounted Rifles Independent Squadron/British Columbia Horse, Vernon, B.C. - 1912.
Irwin, J.J., O.V.C. 1896; 1.9.03, Vet.-Lieut., 15th 'Shefford' Fld. Bty., Granby P.Q.; 1.9.08, Vet.-Capt., 7th Bde. C.F.A., Montréal P.Q.; 16.8.13, Capt., C.A.V.C., 7th Bde. C.F.A., Sherbrooke P.Q. - 1919.
Jakeman, W., M.V.C. 1880, McGill 1890; 16.8.99, Vet.-Lieut., 17th Bty. C.F.A., Sydney, N.S. - 1902.
James, Alfred E., O.V.C. 1888; BW - Jan. 02-Jul. 02, Vet.-Lieut., 2nd Canadian Mounted Rifles; 1903-1904, not in list; 10.3.05, Vet.-Lieut., 2nd Ottawa Bty. C.F.A., Ottawa Ont.; 30.3.06, Vet.-Lieut., 8th Bde. C.F.A., Ottawa - 1912.
James, W.H., O.V.C. 1905; 10.5.12, Lieut., C.A.V.C.; 1914, 30th British Columbia Horse, Vernon, B.C. - 1914.
Johnston [Johnson], A.M., O.V.C. 1930; 10.6.32, Lieut., C.A.V.C., 3rd The Prince of Wales Canadian Dragoons, Peterborough, Ont.; 1.12.36, Lieut., R.C.A.V.C.(N.P.), Reserve List - 1939.
Johnston, T.F., O.V.C. 1902; 7.4.05, Vet.-Lieut., No. 7.Coy, C.A.S.C., Saint John, N.B. - 1906.

Jull, G.N., IMP; 15.1.21, Capt., C.A.V.C., 2nd Divn Trn, Toronto Ont. - 1926.

Kennedy, G.A., McGill 1902; 14.6.04, Vet.-Lieut., 6th Duke of Connaught's Royal Canadian Hussars, Montreal P.Q. - 1909.

Kennedy, M.P., O.V.C. 1912; 4.2.13, Lieut., C.A.V.C., C Heavy Bty., Coburg Ont.; CEF; 15.5.20, 2nd Heavy Bty., Coburg - 1921.

Kenney, W.G.C., IMP; 28.3.24, Lieut., C.A.V.C., Reserve List, not posted - 1926.

Kesten, S.H., IMP; 15.1.21, Capt., C.A.V.C., 10th Divn Trn, Winnipeg, Man.; 31.3.26, Maj. - 1928.

Kilpatrick, W.A., 23.5.14, Lieut., C.A.V.C., M.D. No. 13, Alberta; IMP - 1919.

Kinney, G.G., O.V.C. 1910; 15.1.21, Lieut., C.A.V.C., 4th Hussars, Kingston Ont. - 1928.

Labelle, E.C., Laval 1916; 15.1.21, Lieut., C.A.V.C., 82nd Bty. C.F.A., Gaspé P.Q. - 1926.

Labelle, G.T., Laval 1917; 18.4.18, Lieut., C.A.V.C., M.D. No. 2.; indicated IMP but not in Appendix B - 1919.

Laberge, N., Laval 1908; 16.5.12, Lieut., C.A.V.C., No. 6 Coy C.A.S.C., Sherbrooke P.Q. - 1914.

Lafleche, O.R., ? grad.; 30.7.13, Lieut., C.A.V.C., M.D. No. 4, Montréal P.Q.; 22.5.15, Capt., No. 4 Coy C.A.S.C., Montréal P.Q. - 1919.

Lamaire, W., ? grad.[?Lemaire, J.W., Laval 1910]; 8.3.13, Lieut., C.A.V.C., 1st Howitzer Bde. Guelph Ont.; 1914, 36th Bty. C.F.A., St. Boniface Man. - 1919.

Langevin, J.O., Laval 1910; 20.2.13, Lieut., C.A.V.C., M.D. No. 3, Kingston Ont. - 1919.

Langlois, J.S.R., Laval 1917; 12.4.18, Lieut., C.A.V.C., M.D. No. 4, Montréal P.Q., indicated IMP but not in Appendix B - 1921.

LaRoque [LaRocque], N.d'A., Laval 1912; 1.3.13, Lieut., C.A.V.C., No. 5.Sect., Québec P.Q.; 9.4.15, Capt., M.D. No. 5, Québec P.Q. - 1921.

Laurie, J.H., IMP; 15.1.21, Capt., C.A.V.C., 2nd Divn Trn, Toronto Ont.; 1927, No. 3 M.V.S., Kingston Ont.; 15.11.28, Maj., Governor General's Body Guard, Toronto; 1.1.36, Lieut.-Col.; 1.12.36, Lieut.-Col., R.C.A.V.C.(N.P.), No. 1 Vet. Hosp., Toronto - 1939.

Lavery, J.F. IMP; 21.3.24, Capt., C.A.V.C., Reserve List, not posted - 1926.

Lee, J., [?W.J.] ?O.V.C. 1903; 19.7.15, Lieut., C.A.V.C., M.D. No. 13 - 1919.

Lee, W.H.T., O.V.C. 1906; 10.7.15, Lieut., C.A.V.C., M.D. No. 10 - 1919.

Lefebvre, F., Laval 1913; 22.5.13, Lieut., C.A.V.C., M.D. No. 13, Alberta - 1919.

Lefebvre, H.H. [?A.-A.], 23.5.13, Lieut., C.A.V.C., M.D. No. 4, Montréal P.Q.; IMP; died overseas.

Leslie, F.J., O.V.C. 1935; 23.11.37, Lieut., R.C.A.V.C.(N.P.), No. 1 M.V.S., London Ont. - 1939.

Loughman, J., O.V.C. 1880; 15.6.88, Vet. Surg., Winnipeg Fld. Bty. - 1892.

Love, B.I,, IMP; not in list 1922; 18.1.23, Lieut., C.A.V.C., 13 Divn Trn, Calgary Alta.; 1.10.25, Capt., 20th Bde. C.F.A., Edmonton Alta.; 1928, 13th District Eng., Calgary; 10.12.34, Maj.; 1.12.36, Maj., R.C.A.V.C.(N.P.), 19th Alberta Dragoons, Edmonton - 1939.

Lyster, A.T., O.V.C. 1900; 1.8.11, Lieut., C.A.V.C. - 1913.

MacCormack, W.D., O.V.C. 1902; 16.3.08, Vet.-Lieut., 5th 'Kingston' Bty., Kingston Ont. - 1914.

Macdonald, C.S., O.V.C. 1897; 11.6.01, Vet.-Lieut., Canadian Mounted Rifles, Toronto Ont.; 1.4.03, Vet.-Lieut., 9th Toronto Light Horse; 9th Mississauga Horse, Toronto Ont.; 1.4.08, Vet.-Capt.; 1.1.12, Capt., C.A.V.C., 9th Mississauga Horse; *1.4.14, Capt., C.P.A.V.C., Det. No. 1, P.V.O. M.D. No. 2, Toronto Ont. - 1916.

Macdonald, F.S., O.V.C. 1888; MP - c. 1895; 24.12.15, Lieut., C.A.V.C., M.D. No. 2; *1.4.20, Capt., R.C.A.V.C., Det. No. 5, Québec P.Q.; *1922, Det. No. 10, Winnipeg Man. - 1929.

Macdonald, J.D., CEF; 15.1.21, Capt., C.A.V.C., British Columbia Mounted Rifles, Vernon B.C.; 1930, British Columbia Dragoons, Vernon; 10.31, Maj. - 1932.

Macdonald, R., BW - Civilian Veterinary Surgeon, Imperial Army Veterinary Dept., 1st Mounted Infantry;[11] not in Militia List; IMP.

Macdougall, W.F., IMP; 15.1.21, Capt., C.A.V.C., 15th Light Horse, Calgary Alta.; 1.10.31, Maj.; 1.12.36, Maj., R.C.A.V.C.(N.P.), 15th Light Horse - 1939.

MacIsaac, D.A., O.V.C. 1911; 15.2.26, Lieut., C.A.V.C., 16th Bde. C.F.A., Sydney Mines N.S. - 1935.

MacMaster, J.D., O.V.C. 1912; 12.6.16, Lieut., C.A.V.C., M.D. No. 3 - 1919.

MacQueen, L.H., IMP; 1.7.24, Lieut., C.A.V.C., M.D. No. 11, British Columbia; 1.5.24, Capt.; 1928.D.V.O. M.D. No. 11 - 1931.

McCarthy, N., ? grad.; 7.8.16, Lieut., C.A.V.C., M.D. No. 13 - 1919.

McCoy, C.G. [G.C.], O.V.C. 1912; 1.2.13, Lieut., C.A.V.C.; 1914, 28th New Brunswick Dragoons, Saint John N.B. - 1914.

McCuaig, D., O.V.C. 1892; 15.6.07, Vet.-Lieut., 19th Bty., Moncton N.B. - 1909.

McEachran, Charles, M.V.C. 1884, McGill 1890; 27.8.86, Vet. Surg., Montreal Fld. Bty., Montréal P.Q.; No. 3 'Montreal' Fld. Bty.; 1897, Vet.-Capt.; 27.8.01, Vet.-Maj. - 1903.

McEachran, Duncan, 'Dick' Edinburgh 1862; 22.6.77, Vet. Surg., Montreal Fld. Bty., Montréal P.Q. - 1886.

McEwan, F.A., O.V.C. 1908; 26.9.13, Lieut., C.A.V.C., 35th Central Alberta Horse, Red Deer Alta. - 1919.

McFarlane, A.M., IMP; 13.2.22, Lieut., C.A.V.C., Reserve List, not posted - 1926.

McFatridge, H.S., O.V.C. 1898; 1.5.07, Vet.-Lieut., 7th Nova Scotia Regt Heavy Bde. Arty., Halifax N.S.; 10.3.12, Lieut., C.A.V.C.; 1914, 11th Bde. C.F.A., Halifax; 30.1.14, Capt., 11th Bde C.F.A. and P.V.O. M.D. No. 6; 9.9.14, Maj., P.V.O. M.D. No. 6; 15.1.21, Lieut.-Col., C.A.V.C.; 1924, D.V.O. M.D. No. 6, Halifax, N.S. - 1930.

McGill, W.A., 1.2.05, Vet.-Lieut., No. 3 Coy, C.A.S.C., Kingston, Ont. - 1910; not in list 1910-1916; IMP.

McKeon, W.J., ? grad.; 12.6.15, Lieut., C.A.V.C., M.D. No. 11 - 1919.

McKinnon, K.W., CEF; 15.1.21, Capt., C.A.V.C., Prince Edward Island Heavy Bde. Arty., Charlottetown P.E.I. - 1925.

McLaren, C.E., ? grad.; 18.5.99, Vet.-Lieut., Queens Own Canadian Hussars, Québec P.Q. - 1901.

McLellan, D.J., CEF; not in list 1922-1925; 7.10.26, Lieut., C.A.V.C., 8th Princess Louise's New Brunswick Hussars, Sussex N.B.; 1.11.29, Capt.; 1.12.36, Capt., R.C.A.V.C.(N.P.), 8th Hussars; 1939, No. 2 M.V.S., Kingston, Ont. - 1939.

McMahon, B.M., ? grad.; 30.6.15, Lieut., C.A.V.C., M.D. No. 10 - 1919.

McManus, J.H., O.V.C. 1912; 1.6.13, Lieut., C.A.V.C., M.D. No. 10, Manitoba - 1917.

McMillan, Adam, O.V.C. 1890; BW - Dec. 99-Mar. 01, May-Jul. 02, Far. Q.M.S. Canadian Mounted Rifles, Acting Vet.-Lieut. Lord Strathcona's Horse, Vet.-Lieut. 5th Canadian Mounted Rifles; not in list 1903-1908; 27.5.09, Vet.-Lieut., 12th Manitoba Dragoons, Brandon Man. - 1911.

M'Intosh [McIntosh], Daniel, O.V.C. 1869; 30.6.70, Vet. Surg., Frontenac Squadron of Cavalry, Kingston Ont.; 1880, 4th Prvnl. Regt of Cavalry (4th Hussars), Kingston Ont. - 1881.

M'Nee [McNee], Archibald, O.V.C. 1867; 7.9.76, Vet. Surg., Winnipeg Fld. Bty. - 1876.

Mader, C.K., O.V.C. 1932; 7.4.36, Lieut., C.A.V.C., unattached; 1.12.36, Lieut., R.C.A.V.C.(N.P.), No. 1 M.V.S., London, Ont. - 1939.

Maguire, H.E., O.V.C. 1904; 28.6.04, Vet.-Lieut., 13th Scottish Light Dragoons, Waterloo P.Q.; 1.2.12, Lieut., C.A.V.C. - 1912.

Manchester, W., O.V.C. 1889; 16.6.05, Vet.-Lieut., 8th Princess Louise's New Brunswick Hussars, Sussex N.B. - 1909.

Markham, H.V.O., O.V.C. 1912; 1.3.13, Lieut., C.A.V.C.; 16th Light Horse, Regina Sask. - 1919.

Marquis, N.L., Laval 1898; 12.12.11, Lieut., C.A.V.C., M.D. No. 5, Québec P.Q.; indicated IMP but not in Appendix B; 15.1.21, Maj., C.A.V.C., M.D. No. 5; 15.11.30, Reserve List - 1931.

Marsden, H.W., O.V.C. 1919; 11.1.22, Lieut., C.A.V.C., 19th Alberta Dragoons, Edmonton Alta. - 1925.

Massie, James, O.V.C. 1879; 13.5.81, Vet. Surg., 4th Prvnl. Regt of Cavalry (4th Hussars), Kingston Ont.; *9.5.87, 'A' Bty., R.C.A., Kingston; *27.7.96, Hon. Vet.-Maj.; BW - *Dec. 99-Jan. 01, Hon. Vet.-Maj., R.C.F.A.; *1.4.03, Vet.-Maj.; *1.5.05, Hon. Vet.-Lieut.-Col., P.V.O., Eastern Ontario Command; *18.8.10, Vet.-Lieut.-Col.; *1.4.11, Lieut.-Col., C.P.A.V.C.; retired 1913.

Maynard, E.R., O.V.C. 1911; 7.2.16, Lieut., C.A.V.C., M.D. No. 10 - 1919.

Milner, R.J., IMP; 15.1.21, Capt., C.A.V.C., 9th (Grey's) Horse, Wingham Ont. - 1928.

Ming, E., O.V.C. 1884; 15.6.88, Vet. Surg., 4th Regt of Cavalry, Kingston Ont.; 1893, 4th Hussars, Kingston; 1897, Vet.-Capt.; 15.6.03, Vet.-Maj.; 30.6.11, Lieut.-Col., C.A.V.C., 4th Hussars; 15.1.21, retired.

Morgan, W.J., O.V.C. 1893; 2.6.93, Vet. Surg., No. 5.Fld. Bty., Kingston Ont.; 1897, Vet.-Lieut.; 2.6.98, Hon. Vet.-Capt.; BW - 6.4.01, seconded - Dec. 1901, Hon. Vet.-Capt., R.C.F.A.; 2.6.03, Vet.-Capt.; 8.3.06, Vet.-Capt., 9th Bde. C.F.A., Deseronto Ont.; 3.6.08, Vet.-Maj.; 3.6.13, Vet.-Lieut.-Col.; CEF; 4.4.19, Reserve of Officers; 15.2.21, Prvnl. Maj., 32nd 'Kingston' Bty. C.F.A.; *1.5.23, Capt., R.C.A.V.C.; 3.4.24, Reserve of Officers.

Morrissey, J., ? grad.; 18.6.86, Vet. Surg., Newcastle Fld. Bty./No. 12 'Newcastle' Fld. Bty., Newcastle N.B.; 1897, Vet.-Capt. - 1899.

Morrow, J.J., IMP; 15.1.21, Capt., C.A.V.C. ,3rd Bde. C.F.A., Toronto Ont.; 1925, Reserve List, not posted; 2nd Reserve Divn Trn, Toronto - 1931.

Muma, A.E., O.V.C. 1907; 17.9.13; Lieut., C.A.V.C., 30th Bty. C.F.A., Aylmer Ont. - 1917.

Murphy, A.C., O.V.C. 1894; 23.6.93, Vet. Surg., 17th Fld. Bty., Sydney N.S.; 1897, Vet.-Lieut. - 1898.

Murphy, H., O.V.C. 1911; 12.4.12, Lieut., C.A.V.C., No. 15.Coy C.A.S.C. Montréal P.Q.; 18.5.22, Lieut., C.A.V.C., 3rd Divn Eng., Kingston Ont.; 27.8.24, Capt.; 1930, 4th Hussars, Kingston, Ont.; 1931, No. 3 Section, Kingston, Ont.; 1.4.32, Maj.; 1.12.36, Maj., R.C.A.V.C.(N.P.), No. 2 M.V.S., Kingston, Ont. - 1938.

Murray, J.G., O.V.C. 1908; 12.4.12, Lieut., C.A.V.C., 24th Regt Grey's Horse, Ingersoll, Ont. - 1919.

Murray, Robert, ? grad.; NW - 1885, Vet. Surg., Boulton's Mounted Infantry (Boulton's Scouts), Manitoba.

Neill/Neil, W.J., BW - May-July 1902, Vet.-Lieut., 3rd Canadian Mounted Rifles; 1903-1913 not in list; 16.1.14, Maj., C.P.A.V.C., No. 2 Det., Kingston Ont.; 11.8.14, Lieut.-Col.; CEF; 1.1.19, to Reserve of Officers.

Noble, I.B., O.V.C. 1919; 22.6.22, Lieut., C.A.V.C., 14th Canadian Light Horse, Swift Current Sask.; 1.6.26, Capt.; 1.5.34, Maj.; 1.12.36, Maj., R.C.A.V.C.(N.P.), 14th Canadian Light Horse, Climax Sask. - 1939.

Northmore, E.J. [?W.],?Queens ' 99; 18.4.01, Vet.-Lieut., 5th Fld. Bty., Kingston Ont. - 1903.

Notting, E.S., IMP; 15.1.21, Reserve List; 15.12.31, Capt., C.A.V.C., 1st P.E.I. Medium Bty., Charlottetown P.E.I.; 1.12.36, Capt., R.C.A.V.C.(N.P.), P.E.I. Light Horse, Charlottetown P.E.I. - 1939.

Nyblett, R.M., O.V.C. 1902; 4.5.12, Lieut., C.A.V.C., 15th Canadian Light Horse, Calgary Alta. - 1914.

O'Gogarty, M.G., CEF; IMP; 15.1.21, Maj., C.A.V.C., M.D. No. 2, Toronto Ont.; 25.2.24, Reserve List - 1926.

O'Neill, J.J., O.V.C. 1919; 15.1.21, Lieut., C.A.V.C., 13th Bde. C.F.A., Québec P.Q. - 1926.

Pallister, P.E., O.V.C. 1903; 11.3.08, Vet.-Lieut., 5th Princess Louise Dragoon Guards, Ottawa Ont.; 15.1.21, Maj., C.A.V.C., Princess Louise Dragoon Guards; 30.9.25, Lieut.-Col.; 1.5.31, 2nd Reserve Regt, Princess Louise Dragoon Guards; 1.12.36, Lieut.-Col., R.C.A.V.C.(N.P.), Reserve List - 1938.

Paquette, G.H., O.V.C. 1911; 18.12.15, Lieut., C.A.V.C., M.D. No. 3 - 1919.

Paquette, R.S., O.V.C. 1915; 27.12.15, Lieut., C.A.V.C., M.D. No. 3 - 1919.

Parker, John M., M.V.C. 1889, McGill 1890; BW - 1899-1902, Civilian Vet. Surg., Army Veterinary Dept..

Parmiter, F., IMP; not in list 1922-1924; 1.10.25, Capt., C.A.V.C., No. 13 Dist. Eng., Edmonton Alta.; 1930, 19th Alberta Dragoons, Edmonton; 1.4.32, Maj.; 1.12.36, Maj., R.C.A.V.C.(N.P.), 19th Alberta Dragoons - 1939.

Patterson, W.J.H., M.V.C. 1869; 2.2.04, Vet.-Lieut., The 17th Duke of York's Royal Canadian Hussars, Montréal P.Q.; 28.7.08, Vet.-Capt.; 1.5.14, Vet.-Maj.; 15.1.21, Major, C.A.V.C.; 17.10.21, retired.

Perley, H.S., O.V.C. 1893; 26.7.98, Vet.-Lieut., Princess Louise Dragoon Guards, Ottawa Ont. - 1901.

Piché, M.A., ?E.M.v.M. 1885, ?Laval ?1887, 1892; 30.8.97, Vet.-Lieut., Duke of York's Royal Canadian Hussars, Montréal P.Q. - 1898; 1898-1904, Capt. to Maj. (Fld. Officer) and 2 I.C., 6th Duke of Connaught Hussars, Montreal; 1905, P.V.O., Quebec Command, Army Veterinary Dept., Montréal P.Q.; 1.7.11, Lieut.-Col., C.A.V.C., P.V.O. 4th Divn, Montréal P.Q.; 15.1.19, Overseas Representative, Director of Records, M.H.Q., London England; *1.4.20, Lieut.-Col. R.C.A.V.C., No. 4 Det., Montréal P.Q.; *Aug. 22, O.A.C.A.V.S., Montréal; 31.8.30, retired.

Pilkey, M., IMP; not in list 1920-1930; 6.2.31, Capt., C.A.V.C., 4th Bde. C.F.A., Peterborough Ont. - 1934.

Pilon, J.G.A., Laval 1913; 13.4.18, Lieut., C.A.V.C., M.D. No. 4; indicated IMP but not in Appendix B - 1921.

Poole, B.R, 16.5.98, Vet.-Lieut., 3rd The Prince of Wales Canadian Dragoons, Peterborough Ont.; 16.5.03, Vet.-Capt.; 1.8.11, Capt., C.A.V.C., 3rd The Prince of Wales Canadian Dragoons - 1914; CEF; 3.5.17, Killed in Action.[12]

Porter, C.H., O.V.C. 1907; 7.2.16, Lieut., C.A.V.C., M.D. No. 2 - 1919.

Porter, J.W., O.V.C. 1888; 1.5.11, Lieut., C.A.V.C., 28th New Brunswick Dragoons, Saint John N.B. - 1912.

Post, H.H., O.V.C. 1893; 15.8.11, Lieut., C.A.V.C., 3rd Prince of Wales Canadian Dragoons, Peterborough Ont. - 1919.

Poulin, L., ? grad.; 27.6.98, Vet.-Lieut., 1st 'Quebec' Fld. Bty., Québec P.Q.; 27.6.03, Vet.-Capt.; 1.8.11, Capt., C.A.V.C., 5th Divn Area, Québec P.Q. - 1916.

Price, W.B., O.V.C. 1911; 1.3.14, Lieut., C.A.V.C., 15th Canadian Light Horse, Calgary Alta. - 1915; 1916, not in list; 20.2.17, Lieut., M.D. No. 13; 15.1.21, Capt., C.A.V.C., M.D. No. 13, Calgary; 10.31, Maj.; 1932, D.V.O. M.D. No. 13 - 1935.

Provost, George W., ? grad.; 2.7.80, Vet. Surg., 5th Prvnl. Regt of Cavalry, Cookshire P.Q. - 1890.

Pugsley, H.J., O.V.C. 1899; 1.9.99, Vet.-Lieut., 10th Fld. Bty., Woodstock N.B.; 18.5.06, Vet.-Capt., 4th Bde. C.F.A., Woodstock; 15.1.21, Maj., C.A.V.C., 89th 'Woodstock' Bty. C.F.A., Woodstock N.B.; 1927, M.D. No. 7 - 1931.

Quinn, J.F., O.V.C. 1883; 17.5.89, Vet. Surg., Hamilton Fld. Bty., Hamilton Ont.; 1894, No. 4 Fld. Bty., Hamilton; 1897, Vet.-Capt.; 17.5.04, Vet.-Maj., 4th Bty., 2nd Bde. C.F.A.; 26.3.07, Vet.-Maj., 2nd Bde. C.F.A. - 1911.

Rasberry, S.J., O.V.C. 1894; 31.3.08, Vet.-Lieut., No. 9 Coy C.A.S.C., Hamilton Ont.; 11.3.12, Lieut., C.A.V.C., No.

9 Coy C.A.S.C., Hamilton Ont. - 1919.

Reed, D.V., IMP; not in list 1922-1925; 2.12.26, Capt., C.A.V.C., 3rd Reserve Regt, Mississauga Horse; 1.12.36, Capt., R.C.A.V.C.(N.P.), Reserve List - 1939.

Reed, J.H., O.V.C. 1882; 16.9.82, Vet. Surg., 1st Prvnl. Bde. Fld. Arty., Guelph Ont.; 1st Bde. C.F.A.; 1897, Vet.-Capt.; 8.5.99, Vet.-Maj.; 1.4.03, Vet.-Maj.; 16.9.07, Hon. Veterinary Lieut.-Col; 11.5.12, retired.

Rich, J.L., 1.5.13, Lieut., C.A.V.C., 7th Hussars, Bury P.Q.; CEF; 15.1.21, Maj., C.A.V.C., 7th Hussars; 1.10.31, Lieut.-Col.; 1936, 2nd Reserve Regt, 7th Hussars - 1936.

Richmond, A.R.B., O.V.C. 1911; 12.3.12, Lieut., C.A.V.C. - 1913.

Riddell, R., O.V.C. 1880; MP - 1884-1886 Veterinary Staff Sgt., N.W.M.P.; NW - 1885, N.W.M.P. contingent, North West Rebellion; 1886-1887, Vet. Surg., N.W.M.P.; BW - Dec. 99-Jul. 02, Vet.-Lieut., 1st Canadian Mounted Rifles, Vet.-Capt., 2nd Canadian Mounted Rifles; 1903-1904, not in list; 23.8.05, Vet.-Capt., 15th Light Horse, Calgary Alta.; 15.4.12, Capt., C.A.V.C.; 1914, No. 11 Sect., Victoria B.C. - 1919.

Robertson, D.M., O.V.C. 1912; 27.7.31, Lieut., C.A.V.C., No. 3 Section, Kingston Ont. - 1936.

Robinson, S., O.V.C. 1904; 4.4.12, Lieut., C.A.V.C., 12th Manitoba Dragoons, Brandon Man.; 10.6.14, Capt. - 1919.

Rogers, W.T., 27.4.09, Vet.-Lieut., 24th Bty., C.F.A., Peterborough Ont.; 11.8.11, Lieut., C.A.V.C., M.D. No. 3; CEF; 15.1.21, Maj., C.A.V.C., 3rd Prince of Wales' Canadian Dragoons, Peterborough; 1.7.32, died.

Rooks, A.L., O.V.C. 1916; 22.7.16, Lieut., C.A.V.C.,, M.D. No. 2; indicated IMP but not in Appendix B - 1919.

Rose, G.A., IMP; 15.1.21, Capt., C.A.V.C., M.D. No. 2, Toronto Ont.; 1926, No. 2 Section, Toronto; 16.3.30, Maj.; 1.12.36, R.C.A.V.C.(N.P.), Maj., No. 1 Vet. Hosp., Toronto - 1939.

Ross, H.H., O.V.C. 1905; 19.10.18, Lieut., C.A.V.C., M.D. No. 10; 15.1.21, Reserve List; 20.2.31, Lieut., C.A.V.C., No. 10 Section, Manitoba; 6.10.32, Capt.; 1.12.36, Capt., R.C.A.V.C.(N.P.), No. 1 Veterinary Evacuating Station, Winnipeg, Man. - 1939.

Roy, J.A., CEF; 15.1.21, Capt., 8th Princess Louise's New Brunswick Hussars, Sussex N.B.; 1927, M.D. No. 7, Saint John N.B.; 1.10.31, Maj. - 1936.

Rudd, S.C., O.V.C. 1887; 1.7.08, Vet.-Lieut.; not in list 1909; 1910, 24th Regt, Grey's Horse, Woodstock Ont. - 1912.

Rumney, W.J., O.V.C. 1925; 30.5.30, Lieut., C.A.V.C., 8th Divn Trn, Hamilton Ont.; 12.7.33, Capt., 2nd Dragoons, St. Catharines Ont.; 1.12.36, Capt., R.C.A.V.C.(N.P.), 2/10 Dragoons, St. Catharines - 1939.

Rutherford, John Gunyon, O.V.C. 1879; NW - 17.4.85, Vet. Surg., Winnipeg Fld. Bty. - 1885.

Sangster, G., M.V.C. 1886, McGill 1890; 17.6.87, Vet. Surg., 6th Regt of Cavalry, Toronto Ont. - 1892.

Sargent, R.E.L., O.V.C. 1936; 23.8.39, Lieut., R.C.A.V.C.(N.P.), No. 7.M.V.S., Victoria, B.C. - 1939.

Saunders, C.G., 4.5.08, Vet.-Lieut., 9th Bty., 2nd Bde. C.F.A., Toronto Ont.; 1.11.11, Lieut., C.A.V.C., 2nd Bde. C.F.A.; 15.12.13, Capt.; CEF - 1919.

Schnell, F.H., ? grad.; 15.6.23, Lieut., C.A.V.C., Border Horse, Virden Man.; 30.9.32, Capt.; 1935, 12th Manitoba Dragoons, Brandon; 1.12.36, Capt., R.C.A.V.C.(N.P.), Fort Garry Horse, Winnipeg Man; 6.3.39, Maj. - 1939.

Scott, J.D., IMP; not in list 1922-1935; 15.6.36, Capt., R.C.A.V.C.(N.P.), 7/11 Hussars, Bury P.Q. - 1936.

Scott, W.F., M.V.C. 1884; 22.6.89, Shefford Fld. Bty., Granby P.Q.; 15th 'Shefford' Fld. Bty.; Vet.-Capt. - 1899.

Seim, A., IMP; 15.1.21, Maj., C.A.V.C., 1st Divn Trn, London Ont. - 1927.

Seymour, W., O.V.C. 1913; 1.4.16, Lieut., C.A.V.C., M.D. No. 10; 15.1.21, Lieut., C.A.V.C., unattached - 1924.

Sewell, K.D., IMP; 21.1.22, Capt., C.A.V.C., 12th Manitoba Dragoons, Brandon, Man. - 1924.

Sharp, H.R., O.V.C. 1906; 15.12.16, Lieut., C.A.V.C., M.D. No. 12 - 1919.

Sharpe, W.G., IMP; 15.1.21, Capt., C.A.V.C., 16th Canadian Light Horse, Yorkton, Sask. - 1931.

Shearer, W.A., O.V.C. 1905; 11.1.32, Capt., C.A.V.C., Fort Garry Horse, Winnipeg Man.; 1936, Fort Garry Horse and P.V.O. M.D. No. 10; 1.12.36, Capt., R.C.A.V.C.(N.P.), D.V.O. M.D. 10; 26.7.38, Maj. - 1939.

Simard, P.E., Laval 1915; 1.7.16, Lieut., C.A.V.C., M.D. No. 13; indicated IMP but not in Appendix B - 1919.

Simon, W.H., 30.8.01, Vet.-Lieut., 8th Princess Louise's New Brunswick Hussars, Sussex N.B.; 9.3.05, Vet.-Capt.; 1.5.05, P.V.O., Maritime Provinces Command; 1910, Vet.-Capt.; CEF - 1919.

Simpson, T.C., McGill 1891; 20.6.92, 6th Duke of Connaught Hussars, Montreal P.Q.; 1897, Vet.-Lieut. - 1904.

Simpson, T.V., IMP; 1.7.26, Capt., C.A.V.C., 16th Light Horse, Yorkton Sask. - 1932.

Sims, C.B., OVC 1914; 24.7.26, Lieut., C.A.V.C., 11th Hussars, Richmond P.Q.; 1931, King's Canadian Hussars, Kentville, N.S. - 1935.

Sine, M.W., O.V.C. 1883; 4.2.87, Vet. Surg., Kingston Fld. Bty., Kingston Ont. - 1889.

Smith, Andrew, 'Dick' Edinburgh 1861; 10.5.72, Vet. Surg., Toronto Fld. Bty., Toronto Ont.; No. 9 'Toronto' Fld. Bty.;

27.7.96, Hon. Vet.-Maj.; 1.4.03, Vet.-Maj.; 1905, 9th Bty., 2nd Bde. C.F.A.; 30.4.06, retired.

Smith, J.C., ? grad; 31.5.13, Lieut., C.A.V.C., No. 14 Coy C.A.S.C., Calgary Alta. - 1914; 10.10.15, Lieut., C.A.V.C., M.D. No. 13, Calgary Alta.; 1916, No. 14 Coy C.A.S.C. - 1916.

Smith, H.D., 26.4.04, Vet.-Lieut., 13th 'Winnipeg' Fld. Bty.; 26.4.09, Vet.-Capt.; 1.7.11, Capt., C.A.V.C.; 10.7.13, No. 10 Sect., Winnipeg Man.; 1914, P.V.O. M.D. No. 10, Winnipeg - Aug. 14; CEF; 15.1.21, Lieut.-Col., C.A.V.C., S.V.O. M.D. No. 10; 1924, 5th Bde. C.F.A., Winnipeg - 1927.

Smith, J.W., O.V.C. 1919; 15.1.21, Lieut., C.A.V.C., Manitoba Mounted Rifles, Morden Man.; 2.4.28, 18th Bty. C.F.A., Regina Sask.; 1930, 12th Divn Trn, Regina; 1932, 10th Bde. C.F.A., Regina - 1936.

Smith, W.H., 1.3.13, Lieut., C.A.V.C.; IMP - 1917.

Souillard, P.P., 7.11.12, Lieut., C.A.V.C., 11th Hussars, Richmond P.Q.; CEF - 1919.

Souter, E.S., ? grad.; 16.9.14, Lieut., C.A.V.C., M.D. No. 11 - 1919.

Spanton, J.P., McGill 1898; 24.6.99, Vet.-Lieut., Duke of York's Royal Canadian Hussars, Montreal P.Q.; BW - Mar. 1900-Oct. 1902, Capt. V.O., 1st Battalion, Imperial Yeomanry, British Army; 1902, Vet.-Lieut., Duke of York's Royal Canadian Hussars, Montreal - 1903.

Sparrow, M., IMP; 22.10.22, Lieut., C.A.V.C., 11th Divn Trn, Vancouver B.C.; 1.4.32, Reserve List, unattached - 1934.

Spearman, W., O.V.C. 1915; 15.1.21, Lieut., C.A.V.C., M.D. No. 3, Kingston Ont. - 1928.

Stanford, J.A., IMP; 15.1.21, Capt., C.A.V.C., 14th Bde. CFA, Halifax N.S.; 1.6.30, Maj.; 1931, M.D. No. 4; 1934, New Brunswick Dragoons, Saint John N.B. - 1936.

Stedman, W.G., 2.4.06, Vet.-Lieut., The 23rd Alberta Rangers, Macleod Alta.; 1912, Pincher Creek Alta.; CEF; 15.1.21, Maj., C.A.V.C., 23rd Bty. C.F.A., Calgary Alta.; 1925, 19th Bde. C.F.A. Calgary; 21.5.31, died Calgary.

Steeves, H.W., O.V.C. 1915; 12.2.16, Lieut., C.A.V.C., M.D. No. 13 - 1919.

Stephenson, A.R., [?A.K. Stevenson, O.V.C. 1878]; 10.4.85, Vet. Surg., 3rd Prvnl. Regt of Cavalry, Cobourg/ Peterborough Ont. - 1892.

Stevenson, George T., McGill 1897; BW - Mar. 1900-Jan.1901, Vet.-Lieut., Lord Strathcona's Horse.

Stewart, D.A., O.V.C. 1896; 30.8.15, Lieut., C.A.V.C., 30th Bty. C.F.A., Aylmer Ont.; 15.1.21, Capt., C.A.V.C., 1st Divn Trn, London Ont. - 1931.

Strong, Z., O.V.C. 1896; 4.1.15, Lieut., C.A.V.C., M.D. No. 10; indicated IMP but not in Appendix B - 1919.

Stuart, J.McL., IMP; not in list 1920-1925; 1.2.26, Capt., C.A.V.C., 3rd Divn Trn, Kingston Ont.; 1932, No. 3 Section, Kingston Ont.; 1.5.34, Maj.; 1935, 4th Hussars, Kingston; 1.12.36, Maj., R.C.A.V.C.(N.P.), Reserve List - 1939.

Sullivan, J.L., IMP; 15.1.21, Capt., C.A.V.C., New Brunswick Dragoons, Saint John N.B.; 1930, 6th Divn Trn, Halifax N.S.; 10.31, Maj., 6th Divn Eng., Halifax; 1.12.36, R.C.A.V.C.(N.P.), Maj., 6th District Eng., Halifax - 1938.

Swenerton, L.D., IMP; 15.1.21, Capt., C.A.V.C., 5th British Columbia Light Horse, Kamloops B.C. - 1934.

Swinburn[e], George, ? grad.; 17.1.56, Vet. Surg.; 1863, 2nd Troop of Cavalry, Montréal P.Q.; 1865, Vet. Surg. to Montreal Squadron of Cavalry; 1866; 1867. George Swinburn, probably Jr., Montréal, graduated O.V.C. 1875.

Sylvain, L.A. [L.-J.-A.], Laval 1918; 3.5.18, Lieut., C.A.V.C., M.D. No. 4; indicated IMP but not in Appendix B - 1919.

Symington, W.W., O.V.C. 1913; 1.9.20, Lieut., C.A.V.C., Saskatchewan Mounted Rifles, Lloydminster Sask.; 1.6.25, Capt. - 1928.

Tamblyn, D.S., BW - Jul. 1901-Jan. 1905, Civilian Vet. Surg. Army Vet. Dept., Lieut. V.O. Western Light Horse, Capt. V.O. Left Wing Imperial Light Horse, Capt. V.O. Western Rifles; 1906-1908, not in list; 6.4.09, Vet.-Lieut., Reserve of Officers; 16.8.13, Lieut., C.A.V.C., 26th Bty. C.F.A., Regina Sask.; CEF; *1.4.20, Lieut.-Col., R.C.A.V.C., Det. No. 13, Calgary, Alta., P.V.O. M.D. No. 13; *1925, Det. No. 3, Kingston; P.V.O. M.D. No. 3; *30.6.30, O.A. C.A.V.S.; Apr.1936 invalided; 15.3.37, retired; 27.10.37, Hon. Lieut.-Col., R.C.A.V.C.; 1.11.40, required to relinquish appointment.

Tamlin, C.S., O.V.C. 1888; 31.5.89, Vet. Surg., 'London' Fld. Bty., London Ont.; 1896, 6th 'London' Bty. C.F.A.; 1897, Vet.-Lieut.; 18.5.05, Vet.-Lieut., 6th 'London' Bty.; 11.11.11, Capt., C.A.V.C., 6th Bty. C.F.A; 26.11.14, Maj.; 15.1.21, Lieut.-Col., 12th Bty. C.F.A., London Ont.; 1925, 7th Bde. C.F.A., London - 1931.

Tanner, A.C., O.V.C. 1911; 11.9.16, Lieut., C.A.V.C., M.D. No. 2 - 1919.

Taschereau, T.J. de M.,[13] *1.11.07, Vet.-Capt., Royal Canadian Dragoons, St. Jean P.Q.; *1.4.11, Capt., C.P.A.V.C., Royal Canadian Dragoons; *1.4.14, Maj.; CEF; SEF; *May 1919, Lieut.-Col., C.P.A.V.C., Det. No. 3, A.D.V.S, M.D. No. 3, Kingston, Ont.; *Nov. 1920, O.A.C.A.V.S., Ottawa, Ont.; 31.8.22, retired.

Taylor, H.A., O.V.C. 1913; 3.2.15, Lieut., C.A.V.C., M.D. No. 10 - 1919.

Taylor, W.R., O.V.C. 1891; 22.12.98, Vet.-Lieut., Manitoba Dragoons, Virden Man. - 1902; 1903, not in list; 1904, Vet.-

Lieut., The Canadian Mounted Rifles, Medicine Hat, Alta.; 1907, Reserve of Officers.

Tennet [Tennent], James, O.V.C. 1874; 10.9.75, Vet. Surg., London Fld. Bty., London Ont. - 1889.

Théoret, J.-A., Laval 1913; 21.5.13, Lieut., C.A.V.C., M.D. No. 4, Montréal P.Q. - 1919.

Thompson, S.N., O.V.C. 1936; 20.7.39, Lieut., R.C.A.V.C.(N.P.), 12 Manitoba Dragoons, Brandon Man. - 1939.

Thurston, E.C., 24.8.03, Vet.-Lieut., 17th Sydney Fld. Bty., Sydney N.S., ; 5.1.07, Vet.-Lieut., 3rd Bde. C.F.A., Sydney N.S.; 24.8.08, Vet.-Capt. - 1910; 18.4.14, Vet.-Maj.; CEF; 15.1.21, Maj., C.A.V.C., 16th Bde. CFA, Sydney N.S.; 15.9.25, Lieut.-Col., M.D. No. 4, Montréal P.Q.; 1927, 2nd Bde. C.F.A.; 1931, D.V.O. M.D. No. 4; 4.5.35, died Montréal.

Titus, R.C., 4.8.11, Lieut., C.A.V.C., No. 3 Coy C.A.S.C., Kingston Ont.; CEF - 1919.

Touchette, J.A.O., CEF; 1.7.22, Lieut., C.A.V.C., 17th Duke of York's Royal Canadian Hussars, Montréal P.Q.; 1.10.23, Capt.; 16.6.31, 2nd Reserve Regt, 17th Hussars; 1.12.36, Capt., R.C.A.V.C.(N.P.), Reserve List - 1939.

Towill, W.F., O.V.C. 1917; 16.3.17, Lieut., C.A.V.C., M.D. No. 2; indicated CEF but not in Appendix A - 1919.

Tracey/Tracy, A.W., McGill 1893; MP; BW - 1900, Far. Sgt., 2nd Bn., Royal Canadian Rifles; 3.4.05, Vet.-Lieut., No. 6 Coy, C.A.S.C., Sherbrooke P.Q.; 3.4.10, Vet.-Capt.; 1.4.11, Capt., C.A.V.C., No. 4 Section, Montréal P.Q.; 25.2.14, Maj.; 15.1.21, Lieut.-Col., C.A.V.C., M.D. No. 4 - 1930.

Trudel, H.A., IMP; 15.1.21, Capt., C.A.V.C., No. 1 Co., 5th Divn Trn, Québec P.Q. - 1926.

Tuthill, John, ? grad.; 27.12.55, 1st York Troop of Cavalry, Toronto Ont. - 1863.

Viau, J.A., Laval 1912; 27.11.13, Lieut., C.A.V.C., M.D. No. 4, Montréal P.Q. - 1919.

Vittie, George, ? grad.; 3.9.75, Vet. Surg., 'Shefford' Fld. Bty., Granby P.Q. - 1889.

Waddy, C.E., ? grad; 2.1.15, Lieut., C.A.V.C., M.D. No. 10 - 1919.

Waldie, John, ? grad.; 5.11.75, Vet. Surg., Gananoque Fld. Bty. - 1888.

Walker, R.V.L., O.V.C. 1926; 22.3.35, Lieut., C.A.V.C., 9th Bde. C.F.A., Belleville Ont. - 1936; 1937, not in list; 1.4.38, Lieut., R.C.A.V.C.(N.P.), Princess Louise Dragoon Guards, Ottawa, Ont. - 1939.

Walks, W.G., CEF; 15.1.21, Capt., C.A.V.C., M.D. No. 1, London Ont. - 1927.

Wall, S.L., O.V.C. 1914; 1.2.15, Lieut., C.A.V.C., M.D. No. 2 - 1919.

Wallis, W.B., McGill 1898; BW - Feb. 1900-Jan. 1904, Capt. V.O., Imperial Yeomy., British Army.

Walsh, F., 1.5.14, Lieut., C.A.V.C.; CEF; 8.5.19, retired; *21.12.20, Capt., R.C.A.V.C., Kingston Ont.; *1926, Det. No. 13, Calgary Alta.; 2.12.34, retired.; 10.2.36, died Kingston.

Watson, E.A., BW - Tpr., Canadian Mounted Rifles; 1.4.11, Lieut., C.A.V.C., 25th Bty. CFA, Lethbridge Alta.; 29.4.14, Capt., M.D. No. 13, Lethbridge Alta.; CEF - 1921.

Watson, T.E., O.V.C. 1893; 7.11.07, Vet.-Lieut., 2nd Dragoons, St. Catharines Ont. - 1910.

Weale, O.C., O.V.C. 1918; 3.1.21, Lieut., C.A.V.C., No. 14 Coy, C.A.S.C. - 1921.

Weaver, C.H., O.V.C. 1911; 1.3.13, Lieut., C.A.V.C., M.D. No. 4, Montréal P.Q. - 1914.

Welbanks, H.P., IMP; 15.1.21, Capt., C.A.V.C., 9th Bde. C.F.A., Belleville Ont. - 1930.

Welch, J.W., CEF; 15.1.21, Capt., C.A.V.C., 2nd Dragoons, St. Catharines Ont. - 1922.

White, S.A.K., O.V.C. 1900; 16.4.01, Vet.-Lieut., 5th Princess Louise Dragoon Guards, Ottawa Ont. - 1904.

Wilson, James A. [James H./J.H. Sr.], O.V.C. 1868; 31.5.72, Vet. Surg., 1st Regt of Cavalry, London Ont.; 1893, 1st Hussars, London; 1897, Vet.-Capt.; 25.8.97, Vet.-Maj., retired.

Wilson, John H. [J.H. Jr.], 1.12.97, Vet.-Lieut., 1st Hussars, London Ont.; 23.2.03, Hon. Vet.-Capt.; 29.7.11, Capt., C.A.V.C., 1st Hussars; 1.4.13, Maj.; 1914, PVO 1st Divn; CEF; 15.1.21, Lieut.-Col., C.A.V.C., S.V.O. M.D. No. 1, London, Ont.; 1924, D.V.O. M.D. No. 1; 1927, D.V.O. M.D. No. 1, and 1st Hussars; 1928, D.V.O. M.D. No. 1; 1932, 1st Hussars - 1932.

Wolff, H.H., IMP; 15.1.21, Capt., C.A.V.C., 11th Hussars, Richmond P.Q.; 1927, 5th Divn Trn, Québec P.Q.; 1.10.31, Maj.; 1936, 2nd Reserve Regt, 7/11 Hussars; 1.12.36, Maj., R.C.A.V.C.(N.P.), Reserve List - 1939.

Wood, J.F., 27.5.13, Lieut., C.A.V.C.; No. 8 Coy C.A.S.C., Kentville N.S.; CEF; 15.1.21, Maj., M.D. No. 1, London, Ont. - 1927.

Wood, W.R., O.V.C. 1915; 1.5.16, Lieut., C.A.V.C., M.D. No. 4 - 1916.

Woods, T.Z., NW - 1885, Pvte. 90th Winnipeg Bn. (Winnipeg Light Infantry); BW - 1900-1901, Tpr. Lord Strathcona's Horse; 4.4.07, Vet.-Lieut., No. 11 Coy, C.A.S.C., Winnipeg Man.; 10.7.11, Lieut., C.A.V.C., No. 11 Coy C.A.S.C., Winnipeg Man.; 9.12.13, Capt.; CEF; 9.4.16, died of wounds.[14]

Wright, N., IMP; not in list 1920-1924; 29.4.25, Capt., C.A.V.C., 17th Bde. C.F.A., Saskatoon Sask.; 1.6.32, Maj. - 1936.

Wrightman, J.H., O.V.C. 1939; 8.7.39, Lieut., R.C.A.V.C.(N.P.), No. 1 M.V.S., London Ont. - 1939.

Appendix I

ABBREVIATIONS[1]

A/A.D.V.S.	Acting Assistant Director of Veterinary Services
A.A.G.	Assistant Adjutant General
A./D.A.A.G.	Acting Deputy Assistant Adjutant-General
A.A.V.C.	Australian Army Veterinary Corps
A/D.A.D.V.S.	Acting Deputy Assistant Director of Veterinary Services
A.D.V.S.	Assistant Director of Veterinary Services
A. Coln.	Ammunition Column
A./O.C.	Acting Officer Commanding
Arty.	Artillery
Attd.	Attached
A.V.C.	Army Veterinary Corps (British/Imperial)
A.V.D.	Army Veterinary Department
B.C.	British Columbia
Bde.	Brigade
B.E.F.	British Expeditionary Force
Bn.	Battalion
Bty.	Battery
B.V.Sc.	Bachelor of Veterinary Science
C.A.C.	Canadian Ammunition Column
Capt.	Captain
C.A.S.C.	Canadian Army Service Corps
C.A.V.C.	Canadian Army Veterinary Corps
C.C.M.G.Sq.	Canadian Corps Machine Gun Squadron
C.C.V.E.S.	Canadian Corps Veterinary Evacuation Station
C.D.	Canadian Division
C.D.A.C.	Canadian Divisional Ammunition Column
C.D. Trn.	Canadian Divisional Train
C.E.F.	Canadian Expeditionary Force
C. Fld. Ambl.	Canadian Field Ambulance
C.F.C.	Canadian Forestry Corps
C.F.A.	Canadian Field Artillery
C.I.	Canadian Infantry
C.M.	Canadian Militia
Comm.	Commission
C.M.Rs.	Canadian Mounted Rifles
C.M.V.S.	Canadian Mobile Veterinary Section
C.O.C.	Canadian Ordnance Corps
Constaby.	Constabulary
C.O. Trn.	Canadian Ordnance Train
C.O.T.C.	Canadian Officer Training Corps
Coy	Company
C.P.A.V.C.	Canadian Permanent Army Veterinary Corps
C.R.A.	Commanding Royal Artillery
C. Res. Pk.	Canadian Reserve Park
C. Ry	Canadian Railway
C.V.H.	Canadian Veterinary Hospital
C.W.R.O.	Canadian War Records Office
D.A.D.V.S.	Deputy Assistant Director Veterinary Services
D.C.M.	Distinguished Conduct Medal
D.D.V.S.	Deputy Director Veterinary Services
Demob.	Demobilization
Det.	Detachment
Divn	Division
Divn Trn	Divisional Train
D.H.H.	Directorate of History and Heritage
D.N.D.	Department of National Defence
D.O.C.	Deputy Officer Commanding
Drgns.	Dragoons
D.S.O.	Distinguished Service Order
D.V.O.	District Veterinary Officer
D.V.S.	Doctor of Veterinary Science <u>or</u> Director of Veterinary Services
D.V.S. & R.	Director of Veterinary Services and Remounts
D.V.Sc.	Doctor of Veterinary Science
E.M.v.M.	Ecole Médecine vétérinaire de Montréal
Engl.	English
E.v.f.M.	Ecole vétérinaire française de Montréal
Far.	Farrier
F.G.H.	Fort Garry Horse
Fld.	Field
F.Q.M.S.	Farrier Quartermaster Sergeant
F.R.C.V.S.	Fellow, Royal College of Veterinary Surgeons
Gar.	Garrison
Gds.	Guards
G.H.Q.	General Headquarters
G.O.	General Order
Gov.	Governor
Gren.	Grenadier
H.A.R.C.V.S.	Honorary Associate, Royal College of Veterinary Surgeons

H.Q.	Headquarters
i/c	In Charge
IMP	Imperial
K.I.A.	Killed in Action
K.R. & O.	King's Regulations and Orders
Lieut.	Lieutenant
LdS.H.(R.C.)	Lord Strathcona's Horse (Royal Canadians)
Maj.	Major
Man. Drgns.	Manchester Dragoons
M.C.	Military Cross
M.D.	Military District
M.i.D.	Mentioned in Despatches
M.R.C.V.S.	Member Royal College of Veterinary Surgeons
Mtd.	Mounted
M.V.	Médecin vétérinaire
M.V.C.	Montreal Veterinary College
M.V.S.	Mobile Veterinary Section
NAC	National Archives of Canada
N.C.O.	Non-Commissioned Officer
N.D.H.Q.	National Defence Headquarters
No.	Number
N.P.A.M.	Non-Permanent Active Militia
N.R.E.F.	North Russian Expeditionary Force
N.S.W.	New South Wales
O.A. C.A.V.S.	Officer Administering Canadian Army Veterinary Service
O.B.E.	Officer Order of the British Empire
O.C.	Officer Commanding
O.i/c	Officer In Charge
O.M.F.C.	Overseas Military Forces of Canada
O.V.C.	Ontario Veterinary College
P.C.	Privy Council
P.F.	Permanent Force (Permanent Active Miltia)
P.O.W.	Prisoner of War
P.P.C.L.I.	Princess Patricia's Canadian Light Infantry
Prvnl.	Provisional
P.V.O.	Principal Veterinary Officer
Pvte.	Private
Q.M.	Quartermaster
Q.M.G.	Quartermaster-General
Q.M.S.	Quartermaster Sergeant
R.A.V.C.	Royal Army Veterinary Corps
R.C.A.	Royal Canadian Artillery
R.C.A.V.C.	Royal Canadian Army Veterinary Corps
R.C.A.V.C.(N.P.)	Royal Canadian Army Veterinary Corps (Non-Permanent)
R.C.D.	Royal Canadian Dragoons
R.C.H.A.	Royal Canadian Horse Artillery
Regt.	Regiment
Res.	Reserve
R.N.W.M.P.	Royal North West Mounted Police
R.Q.M.S.	Regimental Quartermaster Sergeant
R.S.M.	Regimental Sergeant-Major
R.S.P.C.A.	Royal Society for the Prevention of Cruelty to Animals
R.V.S.	Regimental Veterinary Service
S.A.	South African
Sgt.	Sergeant
Sect.	Section
S.E.F.	Siberian Expeditionary Force
Sh.	Shoeing
S.M.I.	Sergeant-Major 1st Class
S.V.O.	Senior Veterinary Officer
Tpr	Trooper
Trps	Troops
Tpt. Maj.	Trumpet-Major
U.S.	United States (America)
U.S.A.V.C.	U.S. Army Veterinary Corps
Vet. Surg.	Veterinary Surgeon
V.O.	Veterinary Officer
V.S.	Veterinary Surgeon (diploma)
W.W. I	World War I
W.W. II	World War II
Yeomy.	Yeomanry

NOTES

Pages v-xiii.

1. This cap badge was authorized for use by the Canadian Permanent Army Veterinary Corps and Canadian Army Veterinary Corps in *G.O.s 65 and 66-1912*, and was used by the C.A.V.C. (N.P.A.M.) until 1936. A vaulted wreath of maple leaves, surmounted by a beaver, within the wreath a cutout with a monogram or cypher of an intertwined 'CVC'. Original size 1¾" across, in various metals, including brass, copper, or gilt on silver (officers). Collar badges were smaller, and were worn with the beavers facing each other. The collar badge was improperly worn on the cap by some officers (Vickers, Fig. 7.3). Depending on the manufacturer, the beaver may be head up or head down, facing left or right, and the wreath of maple leaves may be vaulted (open at the top, the usual form, seen here) or closed. *Cross, 1995, pp. 2-3.*

   Prior to the formation of the Army Veterinary Department in 1905, Veterinary Surgeons/Officers wore the insignia of the regiment or unit to which they were attached, and some continued to do so up until at least 1910 (Fig. 12.2). Between 1907 and the introduction of the C.A.V.C. badge in 1912, the cap badge of the Army Veterinary Department was a gilt or gilding metal maple wreath surmounted by a crown, within the wreath a monogram 'AVD' in silver *Ross & Chartand, 1977.* This badge presumably continued to be worn by members of the Regimental Veterinary Service (see Ch. 1). Confirmed illustrations or examples are unknown *Harper, 1999a*, but Capt. A.E. Cameron, photographed overseas after January 1917, may have been wearing such a cap badge in NAC PA 7235, not published here. Since he was commissioned in the C.A.V.C. (N.P.A.M.) in 1913, and was not a member of the R.V.S., it seems unusual that he would wear an obsolete badge. He wore C.A.V.C./C.E.F.-style maple leaf collar badges (see below) in the same photo.

   A cap badge commonly worn 1915-1919 by C.A.V.C. officers is surmounted by a crown. The wreath is laurel, rather than maple, in those in which that point is discernable in the original (eg. Figs. 7.2, 7.7, 12.5), with an internal monogram of intertwined 'AVC', clearly the Imperial Army Veterinary Corps badge of the 1903-1918 era *Kipling & King, 1973, pp. 258-259.* Tracy's and Duhault's pre-1914 badges (Figs. 1.3, 1.4) also are surmounted by a crown, and Tracy's has an 'AVC' monogram indicating that they too are Imperial A.V.C. badges, rather than the Canadian A.V.D. badge.

   Under *Dress Regulations for Canadian Units, 1916* a C.E.F. pattern cap badge was mandated to be worn by C.A.V.C. members serving in the Canadian Expeditionary Force, "as issued", but no official description or approval has been found *Harper-Barker, 1998, 1999a; Harper, 1999b.* It was comprised of an emblem resembling the 1903-1918 British Army Veterinary Corps badge (laurel wreath, surmounted by a crown, containing the monogram or cypher 'AVC'), the whole, in browning or blackened copper or brass (officers - sterling silver *Cross, 1995, p. 1*), mounted on the background of a large asymmetric maple leaf (see Figs. p. xi, 6.6); the smaller collar badges were similar.

   However, the maple leaf C.E.F. badge seems not to have supplanted the 1912 badge, and photos of overseas C.A.V.C. officers from the period 1917-1919 show some wearing the 1912 badge, less commonly the maple leaf badge, and most commonly the Imperial A.V.C. badge, sometimes with lapel badges which do not match the cap badge. Rarely, the generic C.E.F. maple leaf cap badge was worn by an officer (Fig. 17.8), and, occasionally, no cap badge is evident (Figs. 6.9, 6.11, 8.14). Badges were issued to N.C.O.s and lower ranks by the Ordnance Office, C.E.F., but officers had to supply their own *NAC RG9, III, B.1, Vol. 3364, B-4-45: Director of Clothing and Equipment - Director of Veterinary Services, 1916*, which may explain in part the individuality shown in style worn. The interpretation *Case, 1996* that the various styles of badge reflected the C.E.F. Division to which the officer was posted, we believe to be erroneous.

   The maple leaf badge was worn only by members of the C.A.V.C. serving in the C.E.F. Officers of the C.P.A.V.C. and C.A.V.C. in Canada wore the 1912 badge, which remained uniform for the C.A.V.C. (N.P.A.M.) until 1936.

   The C.P.A.V.C. was renamed the Royal Canadian Army Veterinary Corps in 1919, and in 1922, under *G.O. 46-1922*, the R.C.A.V.C. cap and lapel badges were modified to the Centaur pattern (see Fig. 17.4: in gilt, with Centaur in silver; a Centaur encircled by a wreath of maple leaves surmounted by a crown; below a riband inscribed 'R.C.A.V.C.'), after the badge of the Royal Army Veterinary Corps, which had been promulgated in 1920. The Centaur, half horse, half human, represented Chiron of Greek mythology, who taught the art of healing to Asclepius, and was a wise, just, temperate being, the noblest example of the combined human and animal form. He was also an expert hunter, gymnast, musician and prophet. The figure of Chiron had long been associated with the Royal College of Veterinary Surgeons in Great Britain. In 1936, the C.A.V.C. N.P.A.M. was renamed the Royal Canadian Army Veterinary Corps (N.P.) under *G.O. 75-1936*, and its officers and men henceforth wore the Centaur pattern badges *Anon., Vet. Rec., 1920; Curson, 1933a; G.O. 46-1922 - Appendix J; G.O. 75-1936.*

2. Algernon M. Talmage R.A., 1871-1939, an English artist, was one of a group of British and Canadian painters recruited by Sir Max Aitken, Lord Beaverbrook, through the Canadian War Memorials Fund, to paint war scenes depicting Canadian forces *Who Was Who, Volume III, 2nd ed, 1967 p. 1324; Johnson & Greutzner, 1976, p. 492; Tippett, 1984.*

   On June 18, 1918, Capt. Alfred Savage C.A.V.C. wrote "Some sort of a 'war artist' turns up from England to paint things here [No. 1 Canadian Veterinary Hospital, Le Havre, France]. He cannot draw rations, but helps us eat ours." However, Talmage won Savage's confidence quickly, since by mid-July they were socializing heavily. On 3 September,

1918, Talmage, "who expects to leave us at any time now and go to Canadian Corps for a session", threw a mess dinner for the officers of No. 1 Canadian Veterinary Hospital, and on Thursday, 5 September, 1918, he left, "a jolly good fellow". Savage renewed his friendship with Talmage while he was on leave, staying at the Savoy Hotel in London immediately after the armistice. He dined out several times with "Algy", at Boodles, The Arts Club, and at The Chelsea Arts Club. Savage enjoyed meeting a number of Talmage's artist friends, going "...home v. late and not quite sober" *Savage Diary, 18 Jun., 19, 29 July, 3 Aug., 3 Sept., 5 Sept., 17, 18, 21 Nov. 1918.*

About the time that Talmage left to join the Canadian Corps, it was consolidating its position at the Canal du Nord, followed by the advance on Cambrai and environs over the period September 27-October 11, 1918 *Nicholson, 1962, pp. 436-460*; *Morton and Granatstein, 1989, pp. 218-233.* It is likely the evacuation of horses from that battle which is shown in the painting on the cover.

This painting, completed in 1919, was originally exhibited that year in The Canadian War Memorials Exhibition, at the Royal Academy of Arts in London, and at the Anderson Galleries in New York and subsequently in Montreal and Toronto, as No. 53, 'The Road to Hénin' with the caption "Germans shelling the ridge". It is under that name that it was catalogued by *Wodehouse, 1968, pp. 56-57* in the 'Check List of the War Collections', correctly, not mistakenly, as *Halliday 1995* suggests. However, in the catalogue of the *Canadian War Memorials Paintings Exhibition, New Series - The Last Phase, 1920* (Fig. p. vi.), it was illustrated as Exhibit No. 156, 'A Mobile Veterinary Unit in France', and captioned "Wounded horses being brought from front line, road to Heminel, Cambrai front. The picture is an incident of the work of the Canadian Veterinary Services in France. A Mobile Unit taking wounded horses back to an evacuating station after having received first aid dressings." Hénin-Beaumont is a village about 25 km northwest of Cambrai; 'Heminel' cannot be found. The name of this painting likely changed due to an error in the 1920 exhibition, which has been perpetuated *Canadian War Memorials Exhibition, London, 1919; Canadian War Memorials Exhibition, New York, Montreal and Toronto, 1919; Canadian War Memorials Paintings Exhibition, Toronto, 1920.*

Oil on canvas, 284.5 x 360.7 cm (112 x 142 in., about 9 x 12 ft.) in size, it was hung in the Senate Chamber of the Parliament Buildings, Ottawa in 1921 as 'A Mobile Veterinary Unit in France', and it remains on display there under that name *Clement, 1999.* A colour print was among the reproductions of works by official war artists distributed to schools in 1926 by the Imperial Order Daughters of the Empire *I.O.D.E., 'A Mobile Veterinary Unit in France'.*

Talmage depicted the activities of the Canadian Army Veterinary Corps in 24 smaller paintings, now held by the Canadian War Museum, which also were exhibited in London in 1919: 'A Mobile Veterinary Unit In France' (a different painting from that on the cover, but probably the one with which it was confused in 1920), 'Dawn on the Hindenburg Line', 'Camp at Agny', 'The Church at Quéant', 'The Blacksmith's Shop', 'Écoust', 'A German Camp', 'On the March', 'Near Wancourt', 'Evacuating Station Hindenburg Line', 'Ruins at Inchy', 'The Wood at Quéant', 'Sunset', 'A Mobile Veterinary Unit Near Quéant', 'At an Evacuating Station', 'Wounded Horses', 'Feeding Mules in the Corral', 'Convalescents', 'Convalescents in the Corral', 'The Sulphur Dip for Mange', 'Mud Baths for Tender Feet', 'The Water Cure for Laminitis Cases', 'In the Mud', and 'Exercising in the Corral'. 'The Road to Hénin' is not found. *Canadian War Museum Catalogue.*

Most depict scenes near the Cambrai front, but the last 5 were done at No. 1 Canadian Veterinary Hospital, Le Havre. The catalogue stated "The Canadian Veterinary Services have played a great part in the preservation and recuperation of horse power during the war. The Veterinary Hospital at Havre is one of the most successful and up-to-date hospitals in France. Thousands of horses pass through the hands of Major Richards and his staff yearly,... Mr. Talmage's pictures deal with cases of horses at the hospitals and also with the mobile veterinary units in the field which collect and give first-aid to wounded and over-worked horses before entraining them from the various railheads back to the base hospitals". *Canadian War Memorials Exhibition, New York, Montreal and Toronto, 1919.*

3. Richard Caton Woodville was a British artist who had a long career as an illustrator for the 'Illustrated London News'. Born 7 January 1856, he established a reputation as a 'battle painter', and as a magazine writer on sport and travel. He took risks on the battlefield while covering conflicts in the Middle East, Asia Minor and the Balkans, as well as in The Great War. He also did several large paintings for Queen Victoria which were hung in Windsor Castle. His sports were listed as shooting, big game hunting and travel, suitable pastimes for a venturesome British observer and correspondent of his era. He died 17 August, 1927 *Who Was Who 1916-1928, Vol. II, 4th Ed., pp. 1146-1157, 1967; Morton and Granatstein, 1992, caption to figure, plate following p. 32.*
4. See Chapter 12 and Note 12.5 for information on Capt. Girling.
5. Donated to the C.A.V. Barker Museum by Ross Irwin.
6. Certificates of Sgt. M.S. Knight donated to the C.A.V. Barker Museum by his son Morgan Knight.
7. Donated to the C.A.V. Barker Museum by Dr. D.J. McLellan.
8. Capt. W.F.R. Stubbs' photos donated to the C.A.V. Barker Museum by his niece Mrs. June Raeburn.
9. Medal presented to Sgt. W. Dugmore donated to the C.A.V. Barker Museum by his son J.D. Dugmore.

10 Photos of Lieut.-Col. A.B. Cutcliffe donated to the C.A.V. Barker Museum by his daughter Mrs. R.B. Woodland.
11. Donated to the C.A.V. Barker Museum by Dr. W.A. Robertson.
12. Donated to the C.A.V. Barker Museum by Dr. G.A. Rose.
13. Badge of Sgt. W. Luker donated to the C.A.V. Barker Museum by his son Sam Luker.
14. Donated to the C.A.V. Barker Museum by Mr. W.E. Wight.
15. Certificate of Capt. L. A. Donovan donated to the C.A.V. Barker Museum by his son Dr. Larry Donovan Jr.
16. Worn by all ranks of the C.A.V.C.in the C.E.F. after 1916-17. For discussion of cap badges, see Note ii-xiii.1 above.
17. Letter from Major-General John Moore R.A.V.C., Director, Veterinary Services, to C.A.V.C. officers and men in the British Expeditionary Force at demobilization, February 25, 1919. *French Papers, NAC MG30, E14, C, Vol. 1.*
18. Letter from Colonel C.E. Edgett, Director of Veterinary Services, C.A.V.C., to the officers of the C.A.V.C. on demobilization, 10 February, 1919. *French Papers, NAC MG30, E14, C, Vol. 1.*

Foreword

1. Lieut. E.H. Wylie, quoted from the 'Veterinary Journal', *Blenkinsop & Rainey, 1925, p. 550.*
2. Lieut.-Col. C.E. Edgett, while Police Chief of Vancouver, gave a newspaper interview that recorded his graduation from the University of Toronto, and war service, decorations and army rank, without mentioning that he was a veterinarian or that it was the C.A.V.C. that he had commanded. *Anon., Vancouver Province, 20 Mar. 1932.*
3. *Kesten, 1939; Gattinger, 1962, p. 78.*
4. *Duguid, 1938.* Duguid, Director of the Historical Section, General Staff, Canadian Army, had the advantage of access to all war records, and to the manuscript that French had prepared.
5. *Nicholson, 1962.* He also gives little attention to many of the other non-combatant units, though the Railway Corps, the Forestry Corps, Tunneling Companies and certain other engineering units are highlighted.
6. *Macphail, 1925.* Relatively rapid publication of the official history of the Canadian Army Medical Corps under the auspices of the Minister of Defence reflects the political influence of the medical profession at the time. Note French's envious comment in his Preface on the resources devoted to that work by the Military History Section.
7. *Nicholson, 1967* makes no reference to veterinary care of horses, as is the case with *Fraser, 1976* and other histories of Lord Strathcona's Horse (Royal Canadians). *Greenhous, 1983* makes incidental reference to an attached veterinary officer.
8. *Smith, 1927.* Little of Smith's book is devoted to the events of the First War, but it provides some summary statistical information and useful context on the culture and pre-war preparations of the Army Veterinary Corps.
9. *Blenkinsop & Rainey, 1925.* This is a comprehensive treatment of the organization and administration of Imperial Army Veterinary Corps activity in all theatres of the war. Major-General Sir L.J. Blenkinsop, was Colonel-Commandant of the Royal Army Veterinary Corps. Prepared under some difficulty 6 years after war's end, it seems deficient in material regarding the Western Front. Moore's small volume somewhat makes up for this short-fall. However, *Blenkinsop & Rainey* is the definitive source on administration of Imperial Veterinary Services (and therefore the C.A.V.C. in France), on veterinary hospitals, on remount and transportation problems, on animal diseases, surgery, and animal disposal.
10. *Moore, 1921.* Written by the Director of Veterinary Services of the British Expeditionary Force, France, whose command included the C.A.V.C., despite its small size it contains much to inform interpretation of circumstances in the C.A.V.C. The author used as the cover design the inverted white triangle against a red background found on the flag flown by a Mobile Veterinary Section to signal its location for those evacuating injured horses (see Figs. 8.4, 9.1 and 9.11).
11. No official history of the Australian Army Veterinary Corps was published, and there is scant reference to the A.A.V.C. in the numerous volumes of the otherwise excellent official history of the Australian Imperial Force in W.W. I, written/edited by C.E.W. Bean. *Whitfield, 1951* and *Taylor, 1990, 1994* provide historical overviews of the Australian military Veterinary Service from its inception in the colonial forces of the 1870's to its disbandment in 1946, an evolution that parallels the Canadian situation. *Henry, 1929, 1931, 1932* recounts experiences with the A.A.V.C. in the Middle East and on the Western Front in Europe during W.W. I. Transport of horses, the effects of gas on horses, and efficient activities of a veterinary officer of the time are described in *Henry, 1933* and *Henry, 1935* (2 papers). *Curson, 1933*a describes decorations and badges of the A.A.V.C.
12. *Merillat & Campbell, 1935.* The copy of Volume 1 of this book found in the University of Guelph Library is inscribed "To my Alma Mater, from L.A. Merillat '88, June 26th 1938". Merillat was prominent in American veterinary professional and educational affairs for over 50 years, and became a Lieutenant-Colonel in the U.S. Army Veterinary Corps in the Great War *Evans & Barker 1976, p. 125.* This is an extremely detailed, well-informed and frank account of the evolution of the veterinary service in the American army, set against a rich background of American veterinary history. It has excellent accounts of disease problems, and is very well-illustrated. A brief historical overview is found in *Miller, 1961.* *Riordan, 1983* is a personal reminiscence of life in the U.S. Army Veterinary Corps in the First War.
13. *Leclainche, 1936; L'état-major de l'armée - Les armées françaises dans la grande guerre, 1922-1939,* was unavailable.

14. *Donnell, 1920.* It is a superficial but accurate survey of the activities of the corps, studded with just enough facts to convince the reader of its authority. Lieut.-Col. T.C. Evans, and Capt. Cecil French are thanked by the author for much of the data, and Donnell alluded to the fact that French was preparing an official history.
15. *Tamblyn, 1920.* This paper summarized the organization of the C.A.V.C. in France, and provided a civilian vehicle for many of his practical suggestions for veterinary management of army horses, not all of which had been accepted by higher authorities in France during the war. At the time, Tamblyn was employed by the Dominion Department of Agriculture. It was the text of a presentation made at the 56th Annual Meeting of the American Veterinary Medical Association, New Orleans, Louisiana, November, 1919.

    There was no Canadian national veterinary organization until 1948, and therefor no national venue at the time for Canadian veterinarians to meet and exchange professional or scientific information *Barker & Crowley, 1989.* Nor were there Canadian veterinary periodicals prior to 1920, when *The Canadian Veterinary Record* commenced publication, initially under the editorship of students at the Ontario Veterinary College. It folded at the end of 1925. Another veterinary journal of substance was not published in Canada until, in 1937, C.A. Mitchell founded the *Canadian Journal of Comparative Medicine*, now the *Canadian Journal of Veterinary Research. Evans & Barker, 1976, pp. 140-146.*

    American publications such as the *Journal of the American Veterinary Medical Association*, the *American Journal of Veterinary Medicine*, and the earlier *Journal of Comparative Medicine and Veterinary Archives* served Canadian veterinarians as the medium for professional communication. Hence, the limited documentation of Canadian Army Veterinary Corps activities in the periodical literature often is found in American journals, sometimes with American authors (see *Steele, 1914a,b*). During W.W. I, and the early post-war period, promotions and decorations of Canadian veterinary officers are found in the *London Gazette* and they and some social notes also are found in *The Veterinary Record*, published by the British Veterinary Association.
16. *'Biscum', 1921.* This article summarizes lessons to be learned about management of horses in war, based on the experience of the C.A.V.C. The identity of the author is unknown to the editors; no former officers of the C.A.V.C. ever practiced in Medicine Hat, the purported address of the author, based on *Love, 1965* and personal research. The topics and opinions, the style of the article, its authority, and the attitude to horses, strongly suggest that the author was Lieut.-Col. David Tamblyn, then with the R.C.A.V.C. in Calgary. As an Associate Editor, he would have known of The Canadian Veterinary Record, not a widely-circulated vehicle for veterinary opinion at the time. Quite possibly he was asked to write an opinion piece by the then Editor, Lieut.-Col. T.C. Evans R.C.A.V.C. Tamblyn's commission in the R.C.A.V.C. may have compelled him to publish under a pseudonym, or it may be that his opinions were well-known, and he felt that the message would be strengthened by seeming to come from another source.
17. French's articles in *The Canadian Veterinary Record* (*French, C., 1922, 1923a, b*) were extracted with limited abridgement from Chapter 15, which was published more-or-less completely, and from Chapter 11, which was left incomplete. The material in Chapter 15 relating to the disposition of the funds collected by Canadian animal welfare societies is arguably the most controversial, if not scandalous, in the book. On those grounds, and perhaps because he sensed a grievance related to this matter on the part of both the public and C.A.V.C. officers, French may have published Chapter 15 first.

    The fact that the later installments on 'The Veterinary Officer' did not appear may signify that he or the journal was actively prevented from publishing the remainder, but we have no proof. The original manuscript was apparently suppressed by the Historical Section of the Militia Department in Ottawa (see Author's Preface), and they may have objected to an alternative route of publication on grounds of Crown copyright.
18. *Tamblyn, c. 1932.* This book, undated, but cited by *Duguid, 1938* as published in 1932, served as a vehicle for expression of the author's romantic view of the horse in war, for a series of portraits of chargers belonging to Canadian officers in World War I, accompanied by short essays on each, and for a chapter on war dogs. It offers insights on the attitudes of the author, but little of substance on the unit in which he served, and which he ultimately commanded. *The Tamblyn Papers*, including material relevant to this book, are in *NAC MG30, E, Vol. 454.*
19. Having had access to some of the same sources, including *Timmis, 1962*, and others cited in the notes to Chapter 3 of *Gattinger, 1962*, it is clear that Gattinger embellished a little for effect, and occasionally was inaccurate.
20. *Dukes, 1993* provides a useful but very succinct and occasionally slightly inaccurate historical overview of veterinary activity in the Canadian army from 1855.
21. See *Chisholm & Davie, 1992* for a recent biography of Aitken, and *Morton, 1982* for a description of the overseas administration of the Canadian war effort, with many references to Aitken's involvement.
22. Numerous form letters from the Historical Section, Canadian War Records Office, dated as early as February 1917, and encouraging compliance, are filed with the questionnaires completed by officers commanding the various elements of the C.A.V.C. in France. Follow-up letters to mid 1918 also are found *NAC RG9, III, D1, Vol. 4717, Files 5-10.*
23. Neill was ignorant of Higgins' reputation and position; he was Chief of the Biological Laboratory in the Health of Animals Branch of the Dominion Department of Agriculture. His outline seems reasonable, though slanted heavily toward the

equine economy in war. *French Papers, NAC MG30, E14, C, Vol. 1: Correspondence 2 Mar. 1917-3 Apr. 1917, to and from Major T.T. Kirkby, Dept. of Militia and Defence, Ottawa, and Brigadier-General MacRae, Quartermaster-General O.M.F.C., London, with attached proposal by Higgins; Higgins, 1942/1943; Saunders, 1996, pp. 63-66.*

24. Such questionnaires can be found with submissions by various C.A.V.C. units in *NAC RG9, III, D1, Vol. 4717.*
25. Examples of suggested content include alleged attempts by Germans to poison forage, the "life of a horse in France,...in fact anything that is of popular character." *French Papers NAC MG30, E14, C, Vol. 1, Folder 4: 11 May 1917, Major H.T. Cock, H.Q., O.M.F.C., London, to Director of Veterinary Services.*
26. *French Papers, NAC MG30, E14, C, Vol. 1, Folder 4.*
27. Untitled, 24 double-spaced typewritten foolscap pages including an appendix, marked "The original copy as compiled by Sgt. Kelly". Apparently revised; an accompanying note says "The revised copy of the C.A.V.C. History as compiled from copy written by Sergt. Kelly was taken by Gen. Neill, 1-4-18, [signed] Bailey". This was 2 weeks after Neill's resignation. *French Papers, NAC MG30, E14, Volume 1: Kelly, Sgt. A. Untitled narrative of C.A.V.C. history, prepared 1917, to H.Q. O.M.F.C., London, Sept. 1917.*
28. A letter from Beaverbrook to Neill, with the salutation "My dear Billy" and signed "Max", 13 Nov. 1917, introduced Moyse to Neill for the purpose of obtaining information from C.A.V.C. Headquarters for his history. Neill gave him a copy of Sgt. Kelly's narrative. Within the previous week or two, Neill had commissioned French to produce a history of the C.A.V.C. (see Note 30 below), so the two efforts seem briefly to have been at cross purposes. Neill must have contacted Beaverbrook regarding French, because on 14 November, Beaverbrook informed Moyse of French's activity, and the correspondence cited in Note 32 below seems to have established French's role vis-a-vis Moyse's. *NAC RG9, III, D1, Vol. 4747, File 1: 13 Nov. 1917, Beaverbrook to Neill; 14 Nov. 1917, Beaverbrook to Moyse; 16 Nov. 1917, Moyse.*
29. The copy of Cecil French's *Surgical Diseases and Surgery of the Dog* in the University of Guelph Library is stamped "D.V.S.& R., Apr 27, 1917" (Director of Veterinary Services and Remounts), with the handwritten notation "Rec'd By Capt. A.E. Frape, C.P.A.V.C.", Staff Officer at C.A.V.C. Headquarters in London, England. The date suggests that French presented this book to the C.A.V.C. at the time of his enlistment in April, 1917.
30. *NAC RG9, III, D1, Vol. 4717, Folder 112, File 1: 10 Nov. 1917, French to Lima.* See Note 15.11, about correspondence between Neill and Lady Meredith related to use of Purple Cross Fund moneys to finance the History of the C.A.V.C. In associated text, French commented that it was about this time that Neill approached him to write the history. The response to the request for Purple Cross Fund sponsorship was negative, but the plan to publish still involved any profits being donated to the Purple Cross Fund. Ultimately, French did convince Lady Meredith to agree that Purple Cross funds might be used for the book, provided the profits accrued to the Society.

    Lieut.-Col. T.C. Evans offered to buy a subscription for a 'deluxe' edition of the book, but hoped that a cheaper version would be printed to satisfy the needs of officers and men not-so-well-off. *French Papers, NAC MG30, E14, Vol. I: 13 Feb. 1919, T.C. Evans to C. French.*
31. *French Papers, NAC MG30, E14, Vol. 1: 22 Nov. 1917, French to Neill and reply.*
32. *NAC RG9, III, D1, Vol. 4717, Folder 112, File 1: 10 Nov. 1917, French to Lima; 13 Nov. 1917, French to O.I.C. C.W.R.O.; 14 Nov. 1917, Beaverbrook to Lima; 14 Nov. 1917, Beaverbrook to Moyse; 26 Nov. 1917, Hastings to French; 14 Dec. 1917, Hastings to French.*
33. *NAC RG9, III, D1, Vol. 4717, Folder 112, File 1: 10 Apr. 1918, French to Hastings; 12 Apr. 1918, Hastings to Beaverbrook; 19 Apr. 1918, Hastings to French; undated ms., Brief Historical Report of the Administration and Organization of the Canadian Army Veterinary Corps and Remounts.*
34. *French Papers, NAC MG30, E14, Vol. 1, DVSR No. 557-34/862: 1 May 1918, C.E. Edgett, Memorandum to C. French, re progress on C.A.V.P. History; undated, A.E. Frape, Confidential Circular Memorandum, re C.A.V.C. history, 3 pp.*
35. *Savage Diary, 13 Nov. 1918.*
36. Lieut.-Col. T.C. Evans, D.A.D.V.S 2nd Canadian Division, who strongly supported French's efforts, wrote "Out of our Veterinary Officers we have obtained practically nothing...lack of interest or deficient in a literary cranial convolution; either this or being abundantly modest...all we can obtain is just sufficient to compile a sort of C.A.V.C. stud book. I know everyone appreciates what you are doing and believe that they are all entirely sympathetic, but we cannot exalt [sic] them to a degree of purpose to cause them to write anything." However, his officers, especially Capt. R. Vickers and Capt. J.G. Harvey, were as forthcoming as any in supplying material to French, though only a few paragraphs could be coerced from Major F.A. Daigneault. *French Papers, NAC MG30, E14, Vol. I: 13 Feb. 1919, T.C. Evans to C. French.*

    Lieut.-Col. D. Tamblyn, D.A.D.V.S. 3rd Canadian Division contributed greatly, and much is reflected in the final text. *French Papers, NAC MG30, E14, Vol. I: 'Notes for Consideration', 'Canadian Army Veterinary Corps', undated.*

    French was most active in soliciting contributions from C.A.V.C. officers during late 1918 and the first 2-3 months of 1919. Many of the group photographs of C.A.V.C. units in this book were taken during that period, probably to illustrate French's work. At the time the C.A.V.C. was supporting the military occupation in Germany, or was otherwise caring for the horses of the military and civilian populace in war-torn parts of France and Belgium, while awaiting disposal of the horses and demobilization themselves. Such activity was less hectic than war, but units were still on the move, and there were tens of thousands of horses to deal with and categorize for disposal.

37. *Stacey, c.1983, p. 65.*

38. *French Papers, NAC MG30, E14, Vol. 2: 25 April 1933, A.F. Duguid to D.S. Tamblyn, re Evaluation of French history of C.A.V.C.*

39. Tamblyn's comments on the author's preface reveal his intense dislike for particular individuals, and his projection of that dislike, perhaps unjustifiably, on French and his work:

"Later recordings in this chapter show a bias opinion [sic] of a few who desire limelight.

The reasons for non-official recognition at Ottawa was [sic] no doubt due to the critical material submitted.

Lack of recognition of the N.D.H.Q., in regard to its efforts to assist during the Mobilization period and subsequent thereto.

Inability to co-operate on the part of the Senior Officers C.A.V.C., due to lack of respect for persons of higher rank and the total indifference by those responsible for the compilation of the so credited History.

The material as a whole shows the hold Neill, Edgett, and Frape had over French.

('A job created' consequently, he had to keep in with those concerned) all of which material was scrutinized by them in turn, additions made, and portions deleted, to meet their own particular case.

French saw little service in France or elsewhere, likewise Frape."

In a handwritten comment between the Author's Preface and the current Chapter 1, he notes: "The Blue pencil could be greatly brought into use. To write notes on this history is most difficult."

The personal tone and petty nature of Tamblyn's comments persist (see notes to later chapters). They rarely are substantive, or such as to suggest that French's book was unduly biased or unfair in interpretation or to individuals. They are in part untrue, since the manuscript was completed after Neill and Frape, and probably even Edgett, had left the scene; it is very unlikely that they scrutinized and edited it. His comments don't indicate that Tamblyn could have done better, and this is borne out by the superficiality of his own book. Duguid could have derived little help, had he hoped to use Tamblyn's comments to 'rehabilitate' French's manuscript for publication. *Tamblyn, c.1932; Tamblyn, Marginal comments, 1933.*

40. *French Papers, National Archives of Canada MG30, E 14.* This material is found in three volumes. Volume 1 contains working papers for the history of the C.A.V.C., and numerous illustrations, plans and maps. Volume 2 is in two folders, 5 and 6, which contain the manuscript in 17 chapters, with Tamblyn's comments on each. As well, nominal rolls of officers, and several other minor documents are included, so the volume totals 586 legal-size pages. Volume 3, in Folders 7 and 8, contains a slightly different version of the manuscript in 17 chapters, and ancillary documents similar to those in Volume 2. The manuscript in Volume 2 was used to produce this book.

Both versions of the manuscript as found have been heavily edited, with excision, insertion, and transposition of material in text, and paste-on and fold-out additions of pages or part pages. Who carried out these revisions, and when, presumably prior to 1933, is unknown. However, Duguid refers to the typescript as "prepared chiefly by Captain C. French". As discussed, their path to the National Archives is obscure; in 1962, Lieut.-Col. T.C. Evans understood that French's manuscript had been destroyed, having not been accepted in Ottawa *Evans, 1962.*

41. see Note 17, above.

42. *Evans & Barker, 1976*, on the first hundred years of the organized veterinary profession in Ontario; *Barker & Crowley, 1989*, on the history of the Canadian Veterinary Medical Association.

43. The original 17 chapters were numbered from what is now the Author's Preface. We begin numbering with the first chapter describing the C.A.V.C., so that what was manuscript Chapter 2 is Chapter 1, etc.; manuscript Chapter 17 is current Chapter 16. We have added a new Chapter 17, an Epilogue. All of the forepages, except the Author's Preface and Edgett's and Moore's letters, are the work of the editors; Moore's letter was part of the original manuscript material, Edgett's was not, though with the file. Appendices A, B and C were named as such with the original manuscript. Appendix D was found as a Nominal Roll of Other Ranks in the French Papers. Appendices E, F, G, H and I are based on other sources and were prepared by the editors.

The original text was typed on legal-size pages, with the numerous headings projecting into the left margin, delineating blocks of text as short as a single paragraph. Those familiar with the style of a military memorandum, which cites the 'marginally noted' subject, will recognize the model for this unusual format, which was maintained in modified form. During transcription of the original, which contained many areas of duplication due to literal 'cut and paste' editing, what was believed to be the original or intended form was followed. Other than Chapter 15, which was abridged, only a few minor changes were made to improve flow; French's style is intact. Notes on each chapter or appendix describe its origin and editing. Obvious spelling errors were corrected, but inconsistencies in spelling of names generally were not.

About the Author

1. *ffrench, Cecil, obit., The Times, Vancouver; French, C., obit., The Daily Colonist, Victoria.*
2. *Anon., Can. Vet. Rec. 3, p. 237, 1922; French, C., obit., The Daily Colonist, Victoria.*
3. *French, C., obit., The Daily Colonist, Victoria.*
4. *Anon., Can. Vet. Rec. 3, p. 237, 1922; Appendix A, Part 2.*
5. *Appendix A, part 2.*
6. *French, Florence S., obits., The Daily Colonist, Victoria; The Times, Vancouver.*
7. *French, Cecil Ernest, Service Record, CEF, NAC.*
8. *French, C., 1896.*
9. *Anon., Can. Vet. Rec. Vol. 3, p. 237, 1922; French, C., obit., The Daily Colonist, Victoria.*
10. French's book is well written and comprehensive, 408 pages long, with 91 photographs and drawings, and numerous references, the majority from the European literature. It seems progressive and up-to-date for the times, discussing the merits and necessity of aseptic surgery, and with an extensive section on general (chloroform vs. ether) and local (cocaine and replacements) anesthesia. *French, C., 1906.*
11. *French, C., obit., The Daily Colonist, Victoria.* The United States College of Veterinary Medicine, Washington, founded 1895, was a 2-term commercial veterinary school *Merillat & Campbell, 1935, p. 340; Teigen, 1998.*
12. Savage states "Has been all over the odd corners of the globe collecting wild animals for Zoos. Strange life!!". *Savage Diary, 23 Mar. 1918; French, C., obit., The Daily Colonist, Victoria.*
13. According to information which he entered in his service record, French's son, C. Ernest, was educated in public schools in Washington D.C. until 1912, and spent 1913-1915 in Switzerland learning languages. We assume that it was when Ernest returned from Switzerland at age 18 that French accompanied him to Canada, and unsuccessfully attempted to enlist himself. Ernest, while a bank clerk in Montreal, became a Lieutenant in the McGill C.O.T.C., from which he gained his commission in the infantry in 1916. He was seconded to the Royal Flying Corps, but his active flying career was brief. A P.O.W., he escaped twice, once by tunneling out of camp, secondly by jumping from a moving train while being transferred between camps. Both times he was recaptured, but at the time of the armistice he was engaged in another tunneling operation. *Anon., Can. Vet. Rec. Vol. 3, p. 237, 1922; French, C.E., Service Record, CEF, NAC.*
14. The desperate need for veterinarians in the C.A.V.C. as the war dragged on is described in Chapter 11. French's career in urban small animal practice, and his age, did not make him a prime candidate for a commission in the C.A.V.C. His initial posting at Shorncliffe would have been to bring him up to a minimum standard in equine medicine and surgery. His practice and lecturing experience may have resulted in his being made instructor at the Canadian Veterinary School there. Savage commented acerbically on many recently appointed veterinary officers who arrived at No. 1 Hospital in Le Havre. He thought French "...a most interesting person, but an awfully fussy one". Savage learned the subcuticular suture from French, a positive reflection on his surgical skill. In his canine surgery book French strongly advocated the use of this suture. His career as a veterinary officer seems uneventful, but for his injury, caused when his horse shied at the approach of a motor ambulance and fell on him. *French, C., 1906, pp. 6-7 ; Savage Diary, 19 Mar., 23 Mar., 13 Sept. 1918; Anon., Can. Vet. Rec. 3, p. 237, 1922; Appendix A, Part 2; French, C., Service Record, CEF, NAC.*
15. French was in Montreal in 1919, submitting documents to the military on his son's behalf. He may have lived in Montreal after he resigned his commission, since his wife had relatives there. *French, C., Service Record, CEF, NAC; French, C.E., Service Record, CEF, NAC; Jackson Diaries, D.H.H., D.N.D.*
16. *Voters' List, 1920; Voters' List, 1921; Henderson's Directory of Victoria, 1921; Certificate of Incorporation, The ffrench Remedy Company Limited.; French, C., 1938; French, C., 1948; Annual Report, The ffrench Remedy Co. Ltd., 1950; French, C., obit., The Daily Colonist, Victoria; Mattison, 1993.*
17. *Anon., Can. Vet. Rec. Vol. 3, p. 237, 1922; French, C., 1922, 1923a,b.*
18. French sought out, through an agent, a copy of Zimmerman's book in Switzerland. He bought it, and with Miss Michaelis, translated it, presenting the original volume to the British Columbia Archives, which, as it turned out, already had one. The British Columbia Archives and Records Service, Victoria, B.C., has copies of French's books, and his typescripts and notes on local history. *Anon., Zimmerman's travel story... The Daily Colonist, Victoria, Feb. 19, 1926; French & Michaelis, 1930; French, C., 1942; Mattison, 1993.*
19. *ffrench, Cecil, obit., The Times, Vancouver; French, C., obit., The Daily Colonist, Victoria; French, C., obit., The Sun, Vancouver.*
20. Ernest French took flight training with the nascent Canadian Air Force at Camp Borden in the summer of 1920, but he crashed once, and was unable to complete his long distance flight due to bad weather. Therefore he was unable to qualify for a commercial pilot's license. In 1920 he took up a position with the paper company owned by his uncle G. Howard Smith, and still was with it as a salesman when he died in 1961. His relationship with the air force seems to have lapsed, but in 1928 he became active in the army militia, in which he served during World War II. He did obtain a pilot's license,

and may have been a flying instructor. During his association with the Toronto Flying Club, it moved from Toronto Island to Malton Airport, and was involved in training pilots for allied air forces. *French, C.E., Service Record, CEF, NAC; French, C.E., death notice, 1961.*

21. The size of the French estate at Florence's death presumably reflects prosperity generated by the ffrench Remedy Company. Only small amounts were bequeathed to friends and relations (C. Ernest, who predeceased her, apparently was childless), but there was a connection still to a beneficiary in Germany. *Matheson, 1962; French, Florence S., obits., The Daily Colonist Victoria, The Times Vancouver.*

Author's Preface

1. This section is published as found, with the exception of transposition of two paragraphs to improve the flow.
2. Approximately $106 million in 1998 terms. *Statistics Canada, 1999.*
3. *Morton, 1993, p. 284, Note 62*, discusses use of the word 'imperial' related to W.W. I. His conclusion - "Confusing, eh?"
4. Among the French Papers is an undated document in French's handwriting entitled 'List of photographs wanted for Historical Review of Can. Army Vet. Corps.', subdivided into two parts 'At Havre' and 'At the Front'. At least Figs. 6.3, 6.11 and 6.15 are identifiable from those lists and probably were taken in 1918-19 for French's history, as well as some others among the large collection of relevant photographs in the French Papers and elsewhere in the National Archives (not all catalogued). Other photos, posed shots depicting the daily activity of Canadian Mobile Veterinary Section No. 2, appear, on the basis of the dates and battles cited, to have been taken in the late summer of 1917, before French was charged with producing the C.A.V.C. history, but French may have had access to them. The illustrations in this book are the editors' selections, drawn mainly from the National Archives, supplemented from other sources. Drawings made by David Tamblyn or by other C.A.V.C. personnel, as well as blueprints and maps, also are found in the French Papers, and the editors have selected from among these also. *The French Papers, NAC MG30, E14, C, Vol. 1.*

Chapter 1.

1. A veterinarian was first attached to a cavalry regiment in the British Army in 1795, and for the next hundred years, Veterinary Surgeons were dispersed among the regiments, with no overall coordination or organization. There was no provision for care of sick or injured horses that could not keep up with their unit on the move, and animal wastage was often high in colonial wars and in conflicts such as the Crimean War. During the 1870's, British Army Veterinary Surgeons were united in the Army Veterinary Department under a Principal Veterinary Surgeon. Although veterinary hospitals and depots were contemplated in regulations, at the outbreak of the Boer War, as a result of changes in the army establishment and conflict regarding the status and roles of the Remount Department and the Veterinary Service, there was little means of providing properly organized veterinary care in the field. *Smith, 1927; Leclainche, 1936; Clabby, 1963; Gray, 1985; Carter, 1996; Dunlop & Williams, 1996.*

   During the Boer War, well over 350,000 horses and mules were lost, mainly due to debility and contagious diseases such as glanders, epizootic lymphangitis and mange; actual battle casualties were few. As a result of the consequent public uproar over wastage of animal life, and a parliamentary commission, the Army Veterinary Corps was formed by Great Britain in 1903. Veterinary hospitals were established, and forward planning and inventory for active service were readied. Under the leadership of Major-General Henry Thomson (1902-1907), and particularly of Major-General Frederick Smith (1907-1910), by 1910 the Army Veterinary Corps had been re-organized, modernized and professionalized. *Smith, 1919; Smith, 1927; Curson, 1933a; Clabby, 1963.*

   An Army Veterinary Department had been organized to oversee the Regimental Veterinary Service in the Canadian Militia in 1905, but it was on the British model of a core permanent veterinary corps, supplemented by a ready reserve of veterinary officers, that the Canadian Army Veterinary Service was reorganized with the formation of the Canadian Permanent Army Veterinary Corps and the Canadian Army Veterinary Corps between 1910 and 1912. In 1913, Mobile Veterinary Sections were implemented in the British Army Veterinary Corps, as links in the care and movement of sick and wounded horses from the front lines to hospitals in the rear. In the C.A.V.C., Mobile Veterinary Sections were organized once the first contingent arrived at Salisbury Plain in fall 1914 (Ch. 4), probably under the guidance of General Fred. Smith; they were formally authorized under *G.O. 103-1915. Anon., 1912; Moore, 1921; Smith, 1927.*

   The German army also had a tiered arrangement for evacuation and care of horses in World War I. Moderately mobile Division horse hospitals relieved the front line troops of sick and unfit horses, and evacuated serious cases to Corps or Army hospitals in the rear. Unlike the British system, horses were identified in a manner such that they could be returned to the regiment and/or officer whence they originated. Corps or Army hospitals, which were more static, but not permanent, were equipped with ambulances to retrieve horses from the Division veterinary hospitals, and to transport horses to railheads for return to Germany. Corps and Army hospitals also had surgical facilities, post-mortem rooms, and bacteriology laboratories, especially to deal with glanders. Very severely ill or debilitated horses were sent to stationary horse hospitals in Germany, for prolonged therapy or recuperation, prior to being returned to duty via a series of depots for healthy remounts, or being sold on the civilian market. *Miessner, 1917.*

Similarly, at the onset of The Great War the French army had a large, well-educated, professionalized and well-organized veterinary officer corps extending from veterinary officers at the front, through evacuation stations to veterinary hospitals in the rear, under the command of a single Veterinary Inspector General. *Leclainche, 1936.*

In contrast, veterinary care in the United States Army was unprofessionalized (some non-graduates served into the early 20th century), up until 1917 the men were non-commissioned (Sergeants or Staff Sergeants), and there was no overall organization above the regiment. The organization and professional standards for appointment and promotion in the British and Canadian Army Veterinary Corps were held up as examples to emulate by American veterinarians urging change, and German approaches to management of wartime veterinary care were also viewed favourably. *Anon., 1912; Steele, 1914a,b; Miessner, 1917; Merillat & Campbell, 1935; Miller, 1961.*

Even after officer status for American Army veterinarians was secured, and they were placed under the Surgeon-General, they were unorganized; the Army Veterinary Corps was not functional when the U.S. entered W.W. I in 1917. There were then fewer than 60 veterinarians in the U.S. Army, and no effective veterinary reserve. In 1917, over 1,000 veterinarians were hurriedly inducted and trained; over 1500 eventually served. Capt. Alfred Savage, C.A.V.C., upon meeting a pair of American veterinary officers, fellow Cornell graduates and ΩΤΣ Β Chapter veterinary fraternity members newly arrived in France in 1917, noted that they "...do not know where they are bound for, who is the head of their corps, and NOTHING about soldiering. 'U.S.' A.V.C. a sort of nebulous thing it seems. Would like to be seconded to them in an advisory capacity!! Ha ha!" *Savage Diary, 12 Aug. 1917; Merillat & Campbell, 1935; Miller 1961.*

An American Veterinary Hospital did not arrive in France until April 1918, although divisions sent earlier had Mobile Veterinary Sections attached. However, the expectations of these units were unrealistic; they were to collect and evacuate horses over very large distances. American veterinary activity during operations in Europe was badly planned, organized and executed ("Ours was a service thrown into an action of extraordinary magnitude, not only unprepared for the task undertaken, but also without the guidance of competent regulations." *Merillat & Campbell, 1935, p. 786*; a French Army officer wrote "Votre service vétérinaire ne marche pas" *Merillat & Campbell, 1935, p. 873*). Animal wastage was marked in comparison with that in the British and French forces. The French feared outbreaks of disease in the domestic and military horse populations originating with sick animals abandoned by the Americans, and also accepted American horses into their veterinary hospitals simply to mitigate inhumane conditions. *Merillat & Campbell, 1935.*

Eventually, appointment of a chief veterinarian for the combatant units in the field and reorganization of delivery of veterinary services was forced upon the U.S. Army by the French. They simply refused remounts to the Americans, who they feared would entirely consume the supply of horses in France. Supplies and ammunition for the American forces ran short due to lack of horses, and they were reduced to using teams of men to haul guns. American veterinary officers visited No. 1 Canadian Veterinary Hospital several times during 1917-18, to obtain information on how to organize their veterinary service (see Chapter 6). *Savage Diary, 3 Nov. 1917, 21 Feb. 1918, 29 May 1918; Merillat & Campbell, 1935.*

2. From the left, the officers are: Surgeon-Major G.E. Fenwick, Lieut.-Col. C.E. Montizambert, Lieut.-Col. A.A. Stevenson, Major J.S. Hall, Lieut. Percy Girouard, Capt. G.R. Hooper and McEachran. *Nicholson, 1967, Fig. 23.* Note the busbies and cocked bicorn hats, with one spiked universal pattern cork helmet. Rank is denoted by the knotted braid on the cuffs of the tunic. McEachran's portrait and a photograph of his uniform are illustrated in *Pepin, 1986, p. 318.*
3. Veterinary Surgeons were attached to British regiments that served in Canada. J.J. Meyrick, Griffith Evans, and W.B. Walters served as Veterinary Surgeons with the 4th Brigade, Royal Artillery in Ontario, while William Varley was with the 13th Hussars *Smith, 1927, pp. ix, 174, 175, 193, 257; Dukes, 1993.* Meyrick was among the first lecturers at the Ontario Veterinary College in 1864 *Leclainche, 1936, p. 611; Gattinger, 1962, p. 26.*

The role and status of Canadian military veterinarians evolved with the roles of the citizen militia and permanent force after the withdrawal of British garrisons by about 1872. See *Harris, 1988* for an overview of the development of the army in Canada, and the relationship of the Non-Permanent Active Militia with the Permanent Force up until 1939. See Appendix H for a summary of veterinarians known to have served in a professional capacity in Canadian military units, or to have been commissioned in the C.P.A.V.C. or the C.A.V.C. and their successors, excepting those who only served overseas in World War I, who are found in Appendices A and B.

Between 1855 and 1868, 'Veterinary Surgeons' are found in Squadrons or Troops of Cavalry and Batteries of Field Artillery raised in Upper and Lower Canada under the Militia Act of 1855 (Appendix H). After James Mason departed Montréal in 1856, Félix Vodeli, who practiced there 1857-1859, probably was the only graduate veterinarian in Upper and Lower Canada until 1861, when Andrew Smith arrived in Toronto to stay *Pepin 1986, pp. 55-56; Evans, 1994.* Canadian colleges had no graduates until 1866-1869 (Appendix A, Note 1). Therefore, these men (A. Alloway, W.H. Carpenter, E. Howard, G. Swinburn and J. Tuthill) likely all were self-trained 'empirics' or 'quacks'. Edward Howard was a farmer on Amherst Island in the 1871 census. George Swinburn[e] Sr. was a farrier and smith in Montréal, who advertised himself as a 'Veterinary Surgeon' - "All diseases and lameness treated on the most improved principles...Cattle and dogs treated...Horses castrated at all ages" *Pepin 1986, pp. 56, 275* and this clearly was sufficient for an appointment as such in the Militia. His son, George Swinburne Jr., joined his business, so it is difficult to know which was active in the militia in the 1860's. But the George Swinburne who graduated from O.V.C. in 1875 almost certainly was the son.

Daniel M'Intosh, O.V.C. 1869, appointed in June 1870 to the Frontenac Squadron of Cavalry, was the first graduate Veterinary Surgeon in the Canadian Militia (Appendix H). Appointment of veterinary surgeons to cavalry units and batteries of field artillery became more common after 1872, and by the mid 1870's most were graduates of a veterinary college, as was required of veterinary surgeons in the British Army. From 1896, such men were accorded the compound rank 'Veterinary- Lieutenant', 'Veterinary-Captain' etc.; from 1903 they were referred to as 'Veterinary Officers', with compound military rank designated as before. Veterinary officers in the C.A.V.C. and the C.P.A.V.C., organized in 1910, were accorded non-compound rank, although those remaining in the Regimental Service retained compound rank.

We have no records of veterinary surgeons in the Canadian militia involved as such in the Fenian Raids of 1866 and1870, although their counterparts with the British garrison were *Dukes, 1993.* The first Canadian veterinarians known to have been associated professionally with Canadian military units that saw action served either in the force under Major-General Fred Middleton that subdued Louis Riel's Métis and their Cree allies during the North West Rebellion of spring 1885, or were with the North West Mounted Police in the region at the time: John A. Duncan (Medical Officer and Veterinary Surgeon [had both M.D. and D.V.S. degrees], attached 'A' Battery of Artillery *Wilson, 1975, p. 83*); John Gunion Rutherford (Veterinary Surgeon, Winnipeg Field Battery, 17 April 1885 *Boulton, 1886, p. 500; Wilson, 1975, p. 160*; later Veterinary Director General of Canada *Evans & Barker, 1976, pp. 80-81*); Robert Murray (Veterinarian, Boulton's Mounted Infantry [Boulton's Scouts, Manitoba], No. 1 Russell Troop *Boulton, 1886, p. 500; Wilson, 1975, p. 142)*; and Robert Riddell (N.W.M.P. 1881 *Boulton, 1886, p. 508; Record of War Service, Quarterly Militia List of Canada Oct. 1913; Loew & Wood, 1978*). Duncan received the North West Canada 1885 Medal, while Murray, Rutherford and Riddell received North West Canada 1885 Medals with a Clasp (see Fig. 12.2) in recognition of service on the Saskatchewan *German-Reed, 1936-37; Wilson, 1975.*

Membership in the Militia in the late 19th and early 20th century was socially desirable, slightly remunerative, fulfilled a sense of civic duty or patriotism, and satisfied physical or moral needs felt by some *Haycock, 1986 pp. 11-12.* Many veterinarians prominent in their communities and in the profession held commissions with a local regiment (see Appendix H). These included Joseph-Alphonse Couture, founder of l'Ecole vétérinaire du Québec in Québec City *Mitchell, 1938-40, pp. 42-43; Pépin, 1986, pp. 109-117*; Duncan McEachran, founder and Principal of the Montreal Veterinary College, later the Faculty of Comparative Medicine and Veterinary Science at McGill University, who during the Boer War was in charge of buying horses in the north-west for Lord Strathcona's Horse *Mitchell, 1938-40, pp. 30-33; Pépin, 1986, pp. 71-91, 318; Miller, 1993, pp. 296-297*; his half-brother Charles McEachran (Fig. 1.1), prominent in Montreal veterinary affairs and militia life *Pépin, 1986 p. 318*; Andrew Smith, founder and Principal of the Ontario Veterinary College in Toronto *Evans & Barker, 1976; Evans, 1994*; J.S. Caesar, Port Hope, Ont., active in Ontario professional associations *Evans & Barker, 1976, p. 39*; Mark Barker, active in professional affairs in Saskatchewan and nationally, eventually Veterinary Director General of Canada *Anon., Can. J. Comp. Med., Vol. 8, p. 24, 1944; Barker & Crowley, 1989, p. 177*; J.A. (Tiny) Campbell, active in professional affairs, on the faculty of the O.V.C. and later curator of the Toronto Riverdale Zoo *Evans & Barker, 1976, p. 133; Anon., Can Vet. Rec., Vol. 6, No. 1, p. 37, 1925*; A.O.F. Coleman, Ottawa, active in professional affairs provincially *Evans & Barker, 1976, p. 40*; Joseph Dufresne, later Principal of l'Ecole de Médecine vétérinaire de la Province du Québec *Can. Vet. J. Vol. 3, No. 8, p. xiii, 1962;* Charles Elliott, St. Catharines, active in the profession provincially and internationally *Evans & Barker, 1976, pp. 39-40*; A.A. Etienne, Montréal, prominent in Québec, Canadian and international professional affairs *Etienne, obit., 1941*; J.H. Frink, Saint John N.B., active in provincial and national professional affairs *Barker & Crowley, 1989, p. 197*; E.A.A. Grange, Guelph, faculty member, Ontario Agricultural College and later Principal of the Ontario Veterinary College *Evans & Barker, 1976, p. 46*; A.W. Harris, Ottawa, active in the Central Canada Veterinary Association *Evans & Barker, 1976 p. 39-48*; B.I. Love, Superintendent, Elk Island National Park, President Alberta Veterinary Association 1928, and active in national professional affairs *Love c.1965, About the Author*; C.S. Macdonald, President of the Ontario Veterinary Association during a difficult period *Evans & Barker, 1976, p. 111*; W.J. Morgan, Kingston, Ont., active in provincial veterinary affairs *Evans & Barker, 1976, pp. 120, 146*; John F. Quinn, Brampton, Ont., President of the Ontario Veterinary Association in 1889 *Evans & Barker, 1976, pp. 42-43*; W.B. Price, Calgary Alta., President of Alberta Veterinary Association 1919-1921 *Love, c. 1965, p. 113*; J. Hugo Reed, Professor of Veterinary Science at the Ontario Agricultural College in Guelph, Ont. and active in provincial veterinary affairs *Evans & Barker, 1976, p. 89*; John H. Wilson, London, active in provincial veterinary affairs *Evans & Barker, 1976, pp. 130, 146.*

The earliest veterinary appointees to the permanent military forces in Canada were W.B. Hall, M.V.C. '77 (Fig. 1.2), Veterinary Surgeon to 'B' Battery, Royal Canadian Artillery, Québec City (Jan. 29, 1887), and J.A. Massie, O.V.C. '79,

Veterinary Surgeon to 'A' Battery, Royal Canadian Artillery, Kingston, Ontario (May 9, 1887). The militia careers of Hall and Massie prior to joining the Permanent Force, and subsequent progress of Hall to Lieutenant-Colonel, C.P.A.V.C., with Massie following a few months his junior, are documented in Appendix H. Both retired in 1913. They were briefly joined in the Permanent Force by Joseph E. Couture, Veterinary-Lieutenant to the Royal Canadian Artillery in Québec City 1896-97, and by J.D. Duchêne, who followed as Veterinary-Lieutenant to the same unit, 1897-1902. T.J.deM. Taschereau (1907) and J.R.J. Duhault (1911) joined subsequently. Massie, and W.J. Morgan, a Dominion veterinary inspector and Veterinary-Captain to No. 5 Field Battery, R.C.A., N.P.A.M. in Kingston, Ontario, both served on the faculty of the short-lived (1895-1899) School of Veterinary Science at Queen's University, Kingston (Note 2, Appendix A). Their departure for the Boer War contributed to the demise of the school *Mitchell, 1938-40, p. 14.*

After the Boer War, with The Militia Act of 1904, the militia was expanded and reorganized, and equipment and training were upgraded. Military expenditure went from $1.16 million in 1898 to $3.9 million in 1904-05 to $9.1 million in 1912-13. As part of the reorganization, an Army Veterinary Department was recommended in 1904, with a Principal Veterinary Officer at a rank of Vet.-Lieut.-Colonel, and five Veterinary Staff Officers in each of the higher commands (Maritime Provinces, Quebec, Eastern Ontario, Western Ontario, and Manitoba, the Northwest Territories and British Columbia). The P.V.O. was to be paid a premium of $365.00 in addition to his usual annual military pay or allowance, and a Veterinary Staff Officer $75.00. No steps were taken in this direction until April 1905, when the first officers were appointed "as a nucleus of the establishment of a veterinary department". Rather than Veterinary Staff Officers, they were termed Principal Veterinary Officers: Veterinary-Majors W.B. Hall in Western Ontario, J. Massie in Eastern Ontario, and M.A. Piché in Quebec. At the same time, the former two were advanced a step in rank, and an increase in the rate of pay was authorized for a P.V.O. if he were Permanent Force rather than an officer of the N.P.A.M. Effective 1907, appointments to the Permanent Force were at the rank of Veterinary-Captain, and in 1908, the rate of advancement was established at 10 years to Veterinary-Major, and a further 10 years to Veterinary-Lieut.-Colonel, subject to passing examinations for promotion. Pay was $3.00/day on appointment, rising to $5.00/day as Vet.-Lieut.-Colonel *NAC RG24, Vol. 6532, File HQ 621-1-4, v. 1: G.O. (Special), File 621-1, 13 June 1904, signed 'Dundonald'; Memo, 17 April 1905, Q.M.G. to A.G., File 621-1; G.O. 172-1905; G.O. 177-1907; G.O. 144, 145-1908; Miller, 1993, pp. 438-439.*

From 1910, by *G.O. 151-1910*, the Army Veterinary Service was reorganized along the lines described in Chapter 1, with the Regimental Veterinary Service, to which appointments were no longer made, comprised of veterinary officers of mounted units who did not transfer to the C.A.V.C. However, the reorganization seems not to have been complete until 1912; memos from 1911 in *NAC RG24, Vol. 6532, File 621-1* of the Department of Militia and Defence are still sorting out confusion about the intent of the *Regulations*, which were not promulgated until 1912. The *Regulations for the Canadian Army Veterinary Service, 1916*, contained only minor modifications of the 1912 *Regulations.*

The Canadian Army Veterinary Service in the Canadian Expeditionary Force in W.W. I is introduced in Note 2.1, and described fully in French's text, while the Veterinary Service from 1919-1940 is discussed in Chapter 17.
Militia Lists (see Note 1, Appendix H), 1863-1939; Regulations, 1912, 1916; Steele, 1914b; Historical Section, D.N.D, 1929; Hamilton, 1930-31; Mitchell, 1938-40; Harris, 1988; Miller, 1993; Morton, 1969; Pépin, 1986, pp. 109-117, 318.

4. Canadians who served as veterinarians in the Boer War were summarized by Curson, who provided brief biographies and school of graduation. He recorded S. Hadwen, William B. Hall, A.D. Harrington, Alfred E. James, Roderick Macdonald, Adam McMillan, James Massie, William J. Morgan, William J. Neil [sic], John M. Parker, Robert Riddell, J.P. Spanton, George T. Stevenson, David S. Tamblyn, W.B. Wallis (see Appendix H for summary of their service). *The Quarterly Militia Lists, 1899-1919; Curson, 1933a, b.*

The Royal Canadian Regiment of Infantry, the Royal Canadian Dragoons (1st Battalion, Canadian Mounted Rifles until August 1900), the 2nd-6th Battalions, Canadian Mounted Rifles, and units of the Royal Canadian Field Artillery were the military formations raised by the Canadian government that served in the Boer War. Lord Strathcona's Horse, and units of the South African Constabulary, although raised in Canada, were British formations, as were postal, medical, nursing, artificer and other service elements raised in Canada. As reflected in the participation by Canadian veterinarians, many Canadians volunteered directly for or served in British, rather than Canadian units. Some veterinarians also served in a non-veterinary rôle. They include W.H. Blanchard and A.W. Tracy (Appendix H and Note 1.12), as well as Lieut. T.A. Wroughton, M.V.C. 1886, (2nd Battalion C.M.R.), A. Watson, O.V.C. 1887 [or may be E.A. Watson, below] (Tpr., 2nd Battalion C.M.R), and Lieut. M.-J. [M.G.] Blanchard, Royal Canadian Regiment, M.V.C.1884 of British Columbia, who died 15 June 1900 of wounds suffered in action a week before at Roodevaal. T.Z. Woods and E.A. Watson (Appendix H) attended O.V.C. after the war. *Ridpath et. al., 1889; Marquis, 1900; The Quarterly Militia List, 1 April 1913, pp. 407, 410; Pepin, 1986, p. 317; Roncetti & Denby, undated; Miller, 1993, pp. 164, 268, 296, 297, 304, 395, 434.*

Only Hall, Massie, Morgan and Spanton were veterinarians in the Canadian Permanent Force or N.P.A.M. prior to or during the Boer War, though James, McMillan, Neill, Riddell, Tamblyn, W.H. Blanchard, Tracy, Woods and A.E. Watson subsequently served in one or the other of those services (see Appendix H).

An obituary of William Patterson J.P., M.D., C.M, V.S., one of the first two graduates of the M.V.C., who died at 93 in Montreal in June, 1940, states that he was a veteran of the Fenian Raids and of the Boer War, where he served as Chief Veterinary Officer to the Canadian Forces. We can not corroborate this. *Patterson, obit., 1940; Pépin, 1986, p. 72.*

5. See Notes 1.3 and 1.4 above, and Appendix H, for information on Hall's career.
6. The officers are from left, front row: Maj. C.M. Nelles Adjutant., Maj. V.A.S. Williams, Col. F.L. Lessard C.B. A.D.C., Maj. Wm Forester; back row: Lieut. D.D. Young, Capt. J.H. Elmsley, Vet.-Maj. Wm. Hall, Capt. C.T. Van Straubenzee, Lieut. E.H. Bowen. The R.C.D.s had distinguished themselves in the Boer War under Lessard; Williams and Forester had been in charge of B and A Squadrons, respectively, and Van Straubenzee, Elmsley Young and Hall, at least, among this group also were veterans of the Boer War *Greenhous, 1983, pp. 74-137; Miller, 1993, pp. 161-163.* In this photo Hall is wearing the full dress uniform of the regiment to which he is attached. The pillbox hats and frock coats (blue-black with green braid and embroidery) worn by the R.C.D.s were replaced by the white cork helmet and red tunic with blue collars and cuffs in the Canadian Militia Dress Regulations, 1907; see *Ross & Chartrand, 1977.*
7. The Regimental Veterinary Service took over a decade to die. By 1912, when the C.P.A.V.C. and the C.A.V.C. were well-established, 26 of the 42 officers in the C.A.V.C. were transferees from the Regimental System, while 25 veterinary officers still held commissions under the Regimental System. Over the next 2 years, 8 of these retired and 5 joined the C.A.V.C.; in 1914, 12 Regimental V.O.s remained (Vet.-Lieut. A.H. Brother, Vet.-Capt. A.J. Cromwell, Vet.-Capt. L.S. Doyle, Vet.-Capt. J.G. Harvey, Vet.-Lieut. W.D. MacCormack, Vet.-Maj. W.J. Morgan, Vet.-Lieut. P.E. Pallister, Vet.-Maj. W.J.H. Patterson, Vet.-Capt. H.J. Pugsley, Vet.-Capt. W.H. Simon, Vet.-Lieut. W.G. Stedman and Vet.-Maj. E.C. Thurston). Ten held out until the reorganization of the Veterinary Service in 1921, when the Regimental Veterinary Service apparently was abolished. Between 1920 and 1924, Doyle, Harvey, Pallister, Pugsley, Stedman, Thurston and eventually Morgan were commissioned in the C.A.V.C. or R.C.A.V.C. (see Appendix H).
8. *G.O. 151-1910; G.O. 154-1911; G.O.s 39, 65, 66, 70, 83, 157-1912; Regulations, 1912.*
9. The official complement of the C.P.A.V.C. in January 1914 was two Lieutenant-Colonels, one Captain, two Lieutenants, and four Sergeants of different grades, in 5 Detachments. Lieut.-Col. Hall (Det. 1, Toronto Ont.) and Lieut.-Col. Massie (Det. 2, Kingston Ont.) had retired only in 1913, leaving 2 vacancies at that rank. The only C.P.A.V.C. officers listed on 1 January 1914 were Capt. T.J.deM. Taschereau (Det. 3, St. Jean Quebec), and Lieut. R. Duhault (Det. 5, Winnipeg Man.). Det. 4, Québec City, appears not to have been manned between 1910 and 1914. William J. Neill was appointed Major in the C.P.A.V.C. (Det. 2) in January 1914. Taschereau was promoted to Major in April 1914; C.S. Macdonald, formerly Captain in the C.A.V.C. with 9th Mississauga Horse, Toronto, was appointed Captain, C.P.A.V.C. (Det. 1), in April 1914, while Lieut. Joseph R.J. Duhault was still No. 5 Det. and V.O. to Lord Strathcona's Horse (Royal Canadians), Winnipeg. Neill was promoted Lieut.-Col. 11 August 1914, in the wake of the declaration of war, and on 10 August, Sergeant Arthur E. Frape was promoted Hon. Lieutenant and Quartermaster, C.P.A.V.C.; G.J. Simpkin was Warrant Officer C.A.V.C. Toronto in 1912; Alfred Newell was a Sergeant, C.P.A.V.C. 1913-1914. We are uncertain if Q.M.S. Farrier F.C. Rush (Fig. 17.9) was C.P.A.V.C. or LdS.H.(R.C.). Neill, Taschereau, Duhault, Frape and Newell are the only members of the C.P.A.V.C. known to have gone overseas in W.W. I. *Appendix A; The Quarterly Militia Lists, April 1912, April 1913, January, June, September 1914; Steele 1914a.*
10. Duhault's appointment as V.O. to Lord Strathcona's Horse (R.C.), which had just been established in 1909 in Winnipeg and Calgary as a regiment of the Permanent Force, reflected the obvious necessity of assigning veterinarians to specific horsed units, despite the demise of the Regimental Veterinary Service.
11. The pre-war establishment of the C.A.V.C. was to be 100 officers (Lieutenant-Colonels - 6, Majors - 12, Captains - 24, Lieutenants - 58); 35 Sergeants and Staff-Sergeants; and 115 Corporals and Privates, for a total of 250 men. However, in April 1912, the actual complement of officers was 3 Lieutenant-Colonels, 2 Majors, 6 Captains and 18 Lieutenants. In April 1913 it was 4 Lieutenant-Colonels, 1 Major, 10 Captains, and 47 Lieutenants. By 30 June 1914, just prior to the outbreak of war, it was 5 Lieutenant-Colonels, 3 Majors, 14 Captains, and 62 Lieutenants, 26 of whom were provisional trainees. Active recruiting clearly had gone on between 1912 and 1914, but it would have been impossible to fill quickly the prescribed complement of Captains and above, given the small beginning cadre of junior officers, and the period of service required prior to promotion. The 1912 Regulations dictated 5 years in rank for Lieutenants, and 10 years commissioned service in the C.A.V.C. for Captains, before promotion. In 1913, the term of service required before promotion was reduced to one year for the step from Lieutenant to Captain, presumably in recognition of the problem in filling the middle ranks reasonably quickly by natural progression of recruits. *Regulations, 1912; G.O. 56-1913; The Quarterly Militia List, 1912-1914.*
12. Tracy ('Tracey' in the original caption and in Militia Lists prior to March 1914, and 'Tracy' subsequently; signed 'Tracy' in correspondence, though typed 'Tracey' in some of the same), M.V.C. 1893, veteran of the Boer War, and former Veterinary Sergeant in the N.W.M.P., was Veterinary-Lieutenant to the C.A.S.C. company in Sherbrooke P.Q. in 1905 (Appendix H). He was the senior Captain in the C.A.V.C. following its organization in 1910, and senior Major prior to

its re-organization in 1921. He was O.C. No. 4 Section in 1914, but does not appear in Fig. 3.3, among the officers mobilizing that Section, and he did not proceed overseas himself. The remainder of his career is summarized in Appendix H. *Quarterly Militia Lists; NAC RG24, Vol. 4482, File 42-1-1: Tracy-Piché 1924.*

13. At the outbreak of war, Canada was divided for purposes of militia administration into 6 Divisional Areas in the east and 3 Military Districts in the west, corresponding with the nine Sections referred to by French. Inexplicably, Division 4, Western Quebec, H.Q. Montreal, and M.D. No. 11, British Columbia and Yukon, H.Q. Victoria, were omitted from French's list. *Duguid, Appendices and Maps, Appendix 9, p. 10, 1938; The Quarterly Militia List, 1912-1914.*
14. Under *G.O. 151-1910*, the Director of Transport and Supplies was the Officer Administering the C.A.V.C. Under *G.O. 39-1912*, command was transferred to the Senior Officer of the C.P.A.V.C., effective 1 Feb., 1912; Lieut.-Col. Hall presumably served in this capacity. However, *G.O. 157-1912*, perhaps anticipating the retirements of Hall and Massie, transferred command back to the Director of Supplies and Transport, effective 27 Aug. 1912; this remained the state until re-organization in 1920. According to French (Chapter 10), at the outbreak of hostilities, Major W.J. Neill, then in charge of Det. 2, C.P.A.V.C., was promoted to Lieutenant-Colonel and made Director of Veterinary Services, Canadian Militia by the Minister of Militia, Major-General Sir Sam Hughes. *The Quarterly Militia List, 1912-1914.*
15. On 30 June, 1914, just prior to the outbreak of war, P.V.O.s were: Division 1 - Maj. J.H. Wilson; Division 2 - Capt.C.S. MacDonald, No. 1 Det. C.P.A.V.C., with Capt. C.G. Saunders O.C. No. 2 Section; Division 3 - Major W.J. Neill from January, 1914; Division 4 - Lieut.-Col. M.A. Piché, with Capt. A.W. Tracy O.C. No. 4 Section; Division 5 - Lieut.-Col. J.D. Duchêne, with Capt. N.d'A. LaRoque O.C. No 5 Section; Division 6 - Capt. H.S. McFatridge; District 10 - Maj. H.D. Smith; District 11 - none named, but Capt. R. Riddell O.C. No. 11 Section; District 13 - none named. *The Quarterly Militia List, April, June, September 1914.*

    Tamblyn commented on this chapter that "Little interest was taken in the C.A.V.C. by N.D.H.Q. prior to 1910. Consequently, large numbers of senior officers were carried. This dead wood formed the advisory heads of the C.A.V.C. Good officers in their time, but by 1914 they were inert and had not the slightest idea of what was expected of them in war." *Tamblyn, Marginal comments, 1933.*
16. *G.O. 154-1911.*

Chapter 2.

1. Recruitment of officers and men for the C.A.V.C. in the Canadian Expeditionary Force in World War I was as idiosyncratic as it was for other units. This resulted from a decision on the eve of hostilities by Sir Sam Hughes, Minister of Militia, to abandon the established mobilization plan and to substitute a somewhat extemporaneous one of his own. As a result, although many of the officers and men had experience in the militia, militia formations were not translated into units in the C.E.F. Limitations on overseas service under the Militia Act and the mobilization procedures dictated that individuals, even if members of the militia, had to enlist anew in the C.E.F., with no necessary continuity in rank or unit. In effect, Canada had two armies during World War I, the Permanent and Non-Permanent Active Militia at home, and the Canadian Expeditionary Force. Hence, the Veterinary Service also had Permanent Force and Non-Permanent elements, the C.P.A.V.C. (P.F.), and the C.A.V.C. and Regimental Veterinary Service (N.P.A.M.), in Canada, with a distinct element overseas, the C.A.V.C. (C.E.F.), in which members of the home militia elements and civilian veterinarians enlisted. *Duguid, 1938; Nicholson, 1962; Morton, 1982; Harris, 1988.*

    Administratively, the C.A.V.C. (C.E.F.) was separate from the C.A.V.C. (N.P.A.M.) and C.P.A.V.C. in Canada, although the former presumably depended upon the units in Canada to some extent for ongoing recruiting. However, only 21/84 officers in the C.A.V.C. (N.P.A.M.) in June 1914 served overseas *The Quarterly Militia List*. The C.A.V.C. in England ultimately became a unit of the Ministry of Overseas Military Forces of Canada, headquartered in London England, which was established in fall 1916 to bring relative order out of the chaos of the first two years of wartime maladministration *Morton, 1982*. As French later describes, in turn, C.A.V.C. officers and organization were under only the most tenuous control of the H.Q. in London, reflecting the sometimes deliberate obfuscation of the lines of command and communication among H.Q. O.M.F.C. in London, H.Q. Canadian Corps in France, and the Imperial High Command.

    The usual practice regarding enlistment of veterinarians in Canada for service overseas, whether in the C.A.V.C. (C.E.F.) or in the Imperial A.V.C., was first to commission the man as a Provisional Lieutenant or Lieutenant in the C.A.V.C. (N.P.A.M.), then to commission him in the overseas corps. Overseas, officers might hold high rank, yet retain only nominal rank in the C.A.V.C. (N.P.A.M.) as recorded in the Militia Lists of the time. For instance, in the Militia List of 1 January 1919, A.B. Cutcliffe, D.S. Tamblyn and C.E. Edgett, with the overseas rank of Lieutenant-Colonel or, in Edgett's case, brevet Colonel, hold the rank of Lieutenant in the C.A.V.C. *Militia Lists 1914-1919.*
2. A total of 1178 names are listed in Appendix D as having served as Other Ranks in the C.A.V.C. at some time during the war. This is certainly an incomplete list, for reasons discussed in the Note to Appendix D.

Chapter 3.

1. This is reflected in the Quarterly Militia List of June 30, 1914, in which the actual complement of each Section was:
 Section 1: Lieut.-Col. - 0, Major - 1, Captain - 1, Lieutenant - 1, Provis. Lieutenant - 3, Total Officers - 6
 Section 2: Lieut.-Col. - 0, Major - 0, Captain - 2, Lieutenant - 5, Provis. Lieutenant - 2, Total Officers - 9
 Section 3: Lieut.-Col. - 3, Major - 0, Captain - 2, Lieutenant - 6, Provis. Lieutenant - 1, Total Officers - 12
 Section 4: Lieut.-Col. - 1, Major - 1, Captain - 1, Lieutenant - 10, Provis. Lieutenant - 3, Total Officers - 16
 Section 5: Lieut.-Col. - 1, Major - 0, Captain - 3, Lieutenant - 5, Provis. Lieutenant - 2, Total Officers - 11
 Section 6: Lieut.-Col. - 0, Major - 0, Captain - 1, Lieutenant - 1, Provis. Lieutenant - 4, Total Officers - 6
 Section 10: Lieut.-Col. - 0, Major - 1, Captain - 2, Lieutenant - 4, Provis. Lieutenant - 7, Total Officers - 14
 Section 11: Lieut.-Col. - 0, Major - 0, Captain - 1, Lieutenant - 2, Provis. Lieutenant - 0, Total Officers - 3
 Section 13: Lieut.-Col. - 0, Major - 0, Captain - 1, Lieutenant - 1, Provis. Lieutenant - 4, Total Officers - 6

 Military District 10, Winnipeg certainly was well-organized under P.V.O. Major H.D. Smith. Section 10 had a large turn-out at Camp Sewell in summer 1914 (22 N.C.O.s and Other Ranks). Smith sent a contingent to Valcartier within 6 days of the declaration of war, and a sheaf of correspondence in the NAC demonstrates that in early fall 1914, responding to the War Office request for Canadian veterinarians to serve in the Imperial Army Veterinary Corps, he was able to contact quickly numerous veterinarians throughout the west about their willingness to enlist. While some volunteered unconditionally for either the Canadian or Imperial Corps, others, such as David Tamblyn, were only prepared to enlist if their conditions with respect to rank or unit assignment were met. A.E. Cameron did not enlist immediately because he could not get leave from the Dominion Department of Agriculture to abandon his post as pathologist at the research laboratory in Lethbridge. *NAC RG24, Vol. 4593, File 20-2-29.*

 Lieut.-Col. Piché, P.V.O. in District 4 was equally well-organized, with 24 men at summer camp at Trois Rivières in 1914 and another 22 at Farnham. The men attending the camp at Trois Rivières are found in a photograph published in *Am. J. Vet. Med., Vol. 9, Nov. 1914*, accompanying an article on the effect of the outbreak of war on European veterinarians. In *Merillat & Campbell, 1935, p. 109* it is captioned 'Section 4, C.A.V.C., 1914'. The 24 who were at camp at Trois Rivières 23 June-4 July 1914 were: Sgt.-Maj. J. Blais; Sgts. - M.R. Hyatt, A.E. Armstrong, H.W. Berwick, J.F. De Garlais, F. Benoit; Corporals - G.W. Cloutt, J. McGee, Geo. Bernard, J. Bédard, J.E. Gosselin, W. J. Bédard, W. Morin; Privates - O. Dufresne, A. Wood, E. Lefebvre, W. Gendron, Luc Perrault, J. Vachon, J. Fortin, Arthur Boucher, J. Blouin, B. Mottram and C.A. Cheney. Only Hyatt went overseas with Section 4 C.E.F. (Appendix E). *NAC RG9, II, F6, Vol. 275, Pay List: Annual Drill Pay-List of No. 4 Section, C.A.V. Corps at Three Rivers, 1914-15* (see also Chapter 4). But other districts were relatively ill-prepared for mobilization. In 1914, Section 5, Québec, had only 10 Other Ranks at summer camp at Lévis; Section 6, Calgary only 7 men at Camp Sarcee; though Section 2, Toronto had 18 men at camp. *NAC RG9, II, F6, Vol. 275, Pay Lists - Annual Drill Pay-Lists, C.A.V. Corps, 1914-15.*
2. See *Duguid, 1938*, pp. 46-93 for details on the broader activity at Valcartier, and for a map of the camp. The C.A.V.C. is referred to on pp. 48 and 85-87, and its hospital, strategically located at the end of a secondary water main and adjacent to a main drain, is indicated on the map facing p. 93.
3. The men in this photo are unidentified, but probably include all those listed in Chapter 3; those named in the caption can be recognized from other photos. There were 26 men in the Winnipeg Contingent, including 3 officers, and there are 27 in this photo, with 4 officers. The unidentified officer in the cork helmet likely is supernumerary. This group illustrates pre-W.W. I khaki Service Dress, with three types of hat, the Navy style forage cap, the Stetson (of which Col. W.D. Otter disapproved: "...a useless commodity, and an article for abolition" *Ross & Chartrand, 1977, p. 96*), and the cork helmet covered with khaki cloth. Their casual appearance likely reflects their N.P.A.M. status and the prevailing hot weather. See note 3.5 below re the bear. As N10477 in the Colebourn Collection, Manitoba Provincial Archives, this photo is misidentified as Headquarters Staff, 2nd Canadian Infantry Brigade at Salisbury Plain, and it has been published as such *Weatherhead, 1989.*
4. Neill also was Officer-in-Charge, Remounts, for the First Contingent, C.E.F., and he was engaged in urgent correspondence with Principal Veterinary Officers in Military Districts in Eastern Canada, and with veterinary officers in rural districts, attempting desperately to purchase, within a space of about 4 weeks, sufficient horses for the Force at Valcartier. *NAC RG24, Vol. 4262, File 77-1-1: W.J. Neill, correspondence re remount purchases, August/September 1914.*
5. At the time that French wrote this, the bear's fame had not been established. That Winnie-the-Pooh was inspired by the mascot of a Canadian Army unit is now well-known, but that the formation was a Section of the C.A.V.C. is less well-recognized. Princess Patricia's Canadian Light Infantry, or, latterly, the Fort Garry Horse, to which Colebourn was attached, have taken the credit. Lieut. Harry Colebourn, Section 10, C.A.V.C., wrote in his diary: "On train all day Aug. 24. Bought (Winnie) Bear Cub at White River, Amt. Paid $20.00". The cub got its name for Winnipeg, where Colebourn lived, according to his son, Fed Colebourn. The bear was taken to Valcartier, and on to Salisbury Plain in England, staying in Colebourn's tent. But on 9 December 1914 Winnie was left at the London Zoo, when Colebourn was sent to

France. He intended to retrieve Winnie after the war, and visited her on leaves to England. But recognizing the bear's popularity with zoo visitors due to its tameness and love of human company, no doubt the result of having imprinted on Colebourn, he left her in England when he returned to Winnipeg at war's end. The young Christopher Robin Milne named his stuffed toy bear after his favourite zoo animal. A.A. Milne, Christopher Robin's father, wrote Winnie-the-Pooh (1926) and several sequels, based on his son's fantasies about his stuffed bear. These stories, in turn, stimulated several humorous contributions to the scientific literature on the diseases of the teddy bear '*Brunus edwardii*'. Winnie died in 1934. *Colebourn, undated; Blackmore et al., 1972; Scheer, 1980; Weatherhead, 1989.*

6. See *Duguid, 1938, pp. 94-109* for details of the Atlantic crossing. The conditions described by French were confirmed almost 50 years after the event by Colonel R.S. Timmis, who dropped out of the Ontario Veterinary College in 1911 to join the Royal Canadian Dragoons. As a Lieutenant he crossed on the S.S. Lakonia with 35 other officers and men of the R.C.D. and about 630 horses, attended by Major T.J.deM. Taschereau, V.O., who was sea-sick much of the voyage. The ship, a cattle carrier, was filthy, resulting in many cases of ringworm. It was unsuited to carrying horses; they could not lie down in the makeshift stalls, into which they were backed, after which the manger was replaced. Mucking out was difficult and flies became rampant. Heat was oppressive, and sails were rigged over ventilator openings to force air into the stable decks. Timmis, an animal advocate and in later life a prominent horseman, considered the conditions "criminal". The ship was provisioned only with oats, which Taschereau noted before departure and redressed by buying tons of hay, bran and salt himself at the last minute in Quebec. Vinegar was administered as a sea-sickness preventative to horses, which cannot vomit. The Lakonia was the first boat to load, and horses spent 7-10 days more than necessary on board, waiting at Gaspé for later ships to catch up. The men were busy day and night with sick horses, including over 100 cases of strangles, as well as colic, lymphangitis, fractures and pneumonia, though only 12 (2%) were lost. Animals judged unlikely to recover were shot; the front of the stall was removed and the carcass was dragged out with a windlass and slung into the sea. *Timmis, 1911; Timmis, 1961/62. Gattinger, 1962, pp. 74-76* published an account of Timmis' experience.

7. This photo was taken on or after October 20, 1914, the date that McCarrey and Daigneault enlisted in the C.E.F., and while Piché was organizing Sections 3 and 4 to go overseas in the wake of the main body of the First Contingent (Ch. 4). Evans commanded Section 3, assisted by McCarrey, while Daigneault commanded Section 4, with the recently-graduated Grignon (Appendix E). Piché did not proceed overseas until February 1919. Strathy, a Montreal stockbroker and Lieutenant in No. 15 Coy C.A.S.C., may be in the photo incidentally, as an officer who was on site at the time in support of the mobilization. He witnessed Daigneault's attestation papers on 20 October. He also appears in Fig. 4.1, though he did not enlist in the C.E.F. until July 1915, and did not serve with the C.A.V.C. *The Quarterly Militia List, Jan. 1915; Merillat & Campbell, 1935; Daigneault, F.A., Service Record, CEF, NAC; Piché, M.A, Service Record, CEF, NAC; Strathy, H.E.deB., Service Record, CEF, NAC.*

   Evans is wearing the blue 'undress' uniform with the 'patrol jacket universal', with upright collar. Daigneault and Grignon wear the drab khaki 'service dress', the jacket with lapels open at the neck. McCarrey and Strathy wear the same service dress jacket buttoned at the neck, with the collar folded down (see Chapter 17).

   John Joseph McCarrey, Food Inspector for the City of Montréal, had an unusual military career. In May 1915, he was struck off the strength of the C.E.F. for misconduct, apparently alcohol abuse; he resigned his C.A.V.C. commission and returned to Canada. In April 1918 he re-enlisted, in the Canadian Engineers, under the alias 'James McCarrey', denying previous military service, giving a Trenton Ontario address and his occupation as 'fitter's helper' on his attestation papers. However, in England, within the space of a few days in September1918, he was transferred from the Engineers, to the Army Service Corps, and then to the C.A.V.C., where he was made an Acting Sergeant. In July 1919, he regained a commission as a Temporary Lieutenant in the C.A.V.C., only to be invalided back to Canada in September with rheumatic fever. He ultimately was struck off strength of the C.A.V.C. in May 1920, as medically unfit. *McCarrey, J.J., Service Record, CEF, NAC; NAC RG9, III, B1, Vol. 3380, File 0-19-45: Neill, W.J., 19 May 1915, to Quartermaster-General, Ottawa re Officers C.A.V.C. Dismissed.*

   Grignon, born at Ste-Adèle P.Q., obtained a Bachelor of Science in Agriculture from l'Institut Agricole d'Oka, prior to graduating in veterinary medicine in 1914. After the war, he set up practice in Mont-Laurier, and also manufactured veterinary products. Prominent socially and politically locally, he became Registrar of Labelle County in 1939. He died in 1943. *Grignon, obit., 1944.*

Chapter 4.

1. The chaos of disembarkation at Devonport and transportation of men and materiel to Salisbury Plain is well-described by *Duguid, 1938, pp. 118-122.*
2. The location of the various Canadian formations, and of the C.A.V.C. units, on Salisbury Plain and in billets, can be visualized on the map opposite p. 171 in *Duguid, 1938.*

3. *Duguid, 1938, p. 143*, described how debilitation of exposed horses caused an order to be issued on 9 December, 1914, that "no artillery horses should go in draught, and that none should move faster than a walk."
4. The C.A.V.C. elements that sailed with the First Contingent were further reinforced, as the result of a belated request (dated 20 September) from the War Office for two Mobile Veterinary Sections and two Veterinary Sections, a total of 258 men, all ranks. The Mobile Veterinary Sections were organized from elements in the First Contingent, reinforced by men from the Remount Depot, which sailed independently on the 'Ansonia', 21 October, or the 'Iona', 2 November. The two Veterinary Sections organized by Piché, a total of 4 officers and 223 other ranks, departed Canada on 7 November, 1914, on board the 'Megantic'. See Appendix E. *Anon., The Call to Arms, 1914; Duguid, 1938, p. 70.*
5. Lieut.-Colonel Marcelin A. Piché was "one of the pioneers of veterinary medicine in the Province of Quebec" *Anon., Can. Vet. Rec. Vol. 3, p. 137, 1922.* Born 9 November 1866, Piché's educational career, based on the available information, is difficult to document and rationalize with college histories. He is reported to have received a Bachelor in Veterinary Medicine and Surgery in 1885, but we have been unable to confirm the school; he is not in the Calendar of the Montreal Veterinary College. He reportedly graduated from the 'Montreal Veterinary School' in fall 1886, and he received a diploma from the Dept. of Comparative Medicine, Laval University in 1887, as one of the first four graduates of Daubigny's Ecole vétérinaire de Montréal *Pepin, 1986, p. 100-101.* He may have moved with Daubigny from the M.V.C. to the E.M.v.M. and then to the E.v.f.M. *M. Pepin, pers. com., 1999* (see Note 2, Appendix A). He was a Charter Member of l'Association médicale vétérinaire française in Montréal in 1886.

   On 6 January, 1887 Piché was appointed veterinarian to the 1st Regiment of Cavalry (Regular), United States Army, which he joined at Fort Custer, Montana, only a few miles from the site of 'Custer's Last Stand' on the Little Bighorn River a decade earlier. His career choice may have been influenced by Daniel LeMay, an 1879 M.V.C. graduate, who in 1886 was veterinary officer to the U.S. 1st Cavalry, and had a long U.S. Army career. In 1892, while Piché was serving in the U.S. Army, the degree Doctor of Veterinary Science was conferred upon him by Laval University. He resigned from the U.S. Cavalry on 30 June, 1895 and returned to Montreal to enter practice. In 1903, he received a diploma from the Ontario Veterinary Dental College. A progressive practitioner, Piché established a partnership with Dr. A.A. Etienne that lasted from 1903-1915. Together, they "...raised the standard of veterinary science in the Dominion".

   He was commissioned as a Veterinary-Lieutenant in the Duke of York's Royal Canadian Hussars, Montreal, 30 August 1897. In April 1899 he received a First Class Certificate, Grade A at the Royal School of Cavalry in Toronto, and became a combatant officer in the 6th Duke of Connaught Hussars, Montreal, to which he had transferred in January. By 1905 he had risen to Major and Second in Command of the Regiment. That year he resigned from the Hussars to become the Principal Veterinary Officer in what was then Quebec Command of the re-organized militia. After the creation of the C.A.V.C. in 1910, Piché became Lieutenant-Colonel and Principal Veterinary Officer of Division 4, Non-Permanent Active Militia, Western Quebec. He organized Sections 3 and 4 to go overseas in 12 days, following receipt of an order to recruit them and have them ready to sail within 20 days, a feat which drew a letter of commendation from Ottawa.

   During the war, Piché remained P.V.O. M.D. No. 4, serving as Assistant Adjutant and Quartermaster General, and as acting General Officer Commanding Military District 4 during the absence of the Commanding Officer. He enlisted in the C.E.F. in 1917, but it wasn't until February 1919 that he went to England as Overseas Representative, Director of Records, Militia Headquarters, acting as Liaison Officer at the Headquarters of the Overseas Military Forces of Canada during demobilization. Piché returned to Canada in November, 1919. He remained in the C.A.V.C. as P.V.O. M.D. No. 4, receiving in 1919 the Colonial Auxiliary Forces Officers' Decoration for 20 years commissioned service.

   Piché was gazetted Lieut.-Col. in the R.C.A.V.C. on 1 April 1920. With the retirement of Lieut.-Col. T.J. deM. Taschereau in mid-1922, he assumed responsibility as Officer Administering Canadian Army Veterinary Service, a position that he held until June 1930. Piché retired as a Colonel and died in Montréal 19 March 1931. *NAC RG24, Vol. 6532, File HQ 621-1-4, v. 1: 7 March 1905, M.A. Piché, autobiography in own handwriting; Piché, M.A., Service Record, CEF, NAC; Anon., Can. Vet. Rec. Vol. 3, p. 137, 1922; List of Officers Defence Forces of the Dominion of Canada, July 1932, p. 490; Merillat & Campbell, 1938, pp. 225, 346, 979, 980; LeMay, obit., 1939; Etienne, obit., 1941; Irwin, 1971; Pepin, 1986, pp. 100-101.*
6. Major General Sir Frederick Smith K.C.M.G., C.B., F.R.C.V.S, H.A.R.C.V.S. 1857-1929, was considered by Clabby to have been "probably the greatest veterinarian produced by the Army of this or any other country." An 1876 graduate of the Royal Veterinary College, London, he served as a Veterinary Surgeon with the army in India, and was made Commandant of the Army Veterinary School in 1887 while a Captain. He published 49 papers during his 6 year career there. He participated in the Nile Campaign, and in the Boer War, serving as Principal Veterinary Officer South Africa for over 2 years. He was Director-General of the Army Veterinary Service 1907-1910. In that role, he brought the Army Veterinary Corps to a state of readiness to support a large mounted field force. Though he retired in 1910 in protest over the line of command above the Corps, Smith returned to duty in the Great War as Assistant Director of Veterinary Services, Southern Command, in which probable capacity he inspected the C.A.V.C. in January 1915. He subsequently

became Assistant Director-General of Veterinary Services, retiring again in 1919.

Smith authored '*A Manual of Veterinary Hygiene*', '*A Veterinary History of the War in South Africa 1899-1902*', '*A History of the Royal Army Veterinary Corps 1796-1919*', and a 4 volume work '*The Early History of Veterinary Literature and its British Development*', as well as numerous journal articles. He co-founded in 1882 the '*Quarterly Journal of Veterinary Science in India and Army Animal Management*', and he published his last paper in the first issue of the new '*Journal of the Royal Army Veterinary Corps*' just before he died in July 1929. His bibliography is in the preface to Volume IV of *The Early History of Veterinary Literature. Bullock, 1933; Curson, 1933a; Clabby, 1963.*

7. Tamblyn comments: "There is no doubt that Major-General Sir F. Smith (R.A.V.C.) came to the assistance of Neill none too soon, and that the former was responsible for the transferring of certain C.A.V.C. Veterinary Sections to France (Le Havre) to form No. 1 Canadian Veterinary Hospital so that such may become effective rather than ineffective by remaining in England and performing no actual role. The remarks of Sir F. Smith, re Neill is [sic] only an indication of the former's modesty". *Tamblyn, Marginal comments, 1933.*
8. The unit is not fully identified on the postcard, which was post-marked Montreal, 1915, but the officers, recognized as Daigneault and Grignon from Fig. 3.3, were with Section 4. The officer third from left, front row, is Lieut. E. Strathy of the C.A.S.C. (see Note 3.7). *Anon., The Call to Arms, 1914; Appendix E.*

Chapter 5.

1. Detection of horses infected subclinically with glanders, a highly-feared contagious disease (Appendix F), was extremely important, but interpretation of the diagnostic tests available was difficult. Mallein was an extract of a culture of the bacterium that causes glanders. Introduction of the intrapalpebral 'special mallein' test by the French during the early part of the war revolutionized detection and control of this disease. It was similar in basic principle to the intradermal tuberculin test. Glanders-infected horses developed a thickening of the eyelid into which a small amount of mallein had been injected, and conjunctivitis occurred in that eye. Though more reliable than other tests, it too was difficult for poorly-trained veterinarians to interpret, a major problem in the U.S. Army. Under-interpretation resulted in failure to detect subclinically-infected horses, which continued to transmit the disease. Over-interpretation resulted in needless destruction of horses required for the war effort. *Miessner, 1915, pp. 44-72; Merillat & Campbell, 1935, pp. 828-833.*

   Mallein testing was a common procedure for C.A.V.C. veterinarians, since glanders was very rigorously controlled. Within about 15 months of arrival in France, Savage calculated that he had applied the intrapalpebral test to over 1000 horses, and he pasted the "very familiar" label 'Institut Pasteur: Malléine dilueé au ¼ pour intra-derme réaction' from a mallein vial into his diary. He spent entire mornings malleining up to 400 horses at No. 1 C.V.H., and referred to his relief at finding no reactors. Only one reactor is mentioned among the 14 entries on mallein testing in his diary, a case with miliary lesions throughout the lung and liver "like TB in a fowl" *Savage Diary, 26/27 June, 12 July 1917.*
2. Wilson, a federal government meat inspector from London, Ontario, and P.V.O. District 1, C.A.V.C., was the most senior of the C.A.V.C. (N.P.A.M.) officers to go overseas. His father, James H. Wilson, had preceded him as Veterinary Surgeon to the 1st Hussars, London (see Appendix H). *The Quarterly Militia List, July, 1915; J. Mousseau & A. Neely, pers. com., 1999.*
3. With nervous exhaustion and incipient tuberculosis; see Note A.15.
4. French must have experienced this air raid first hand, since he was based at Shorncliffe on the day that it occurred. *C. French, Service Record, CEF, NAC.* Alfred Newell suffered shell-shock as a result (see Note A.7).
5. Prinn wears an officer's lapel tunic while a Warrant Officer, a practice that was subsequently forbidden by regulations. The issue pattern tunic for Other Ranks, with stand-up collar, was to be worn by W.O.s. *Law, c. 1998, p. 33.*
6. McLellan felt that as a training camp, Witley was "a grand location...the train service was really remarkable. We thought nothing of going in to London to have dinner and home the same evening." *McLellan-Barker, 1981.* The futility of the Canadian 5th Division as a superfluous training and home defence formation stranded in England until broken up in February 1918 is described by *Nicholson, 1962, 1967* and *Morton, 1982.*

Chapter 6.

1. On Montreal Island, with which French would have been well-familiar.
2. The unmistakable profile of the brick-yard, with its tall kiln chimney, looms in the background of two of Algernon Talmage's paintings in the collection of the Canadian War Museum, 'Mud Baths for Tender Feet', and 'Water Cure for Laminitis Cases', which portray horses with laminitis bathing their feet in the small ponds present on the site.
3. The site of No. 1 C.V.H. is now developed as a suburban area, with houses, schools etc. The Rue de l'Abbaye, upon which the hospital fronted, has been renamed Rue Pablo Neruda. The road that ran up the west side of the hospital approximates the current Rue de la Tour Robinson, and running east and south from it, back to Rue Pablo Neruda through what was the old mess and stables area of the hospital, is the only memento of its existence, Rue des Canadiens, a residential street.

David, 7 Oct. 1992, with maps and memo from Mme Barot, Ville du Havre Archives, 22 May 1992.

4. The blue-print from which this illustration was taken was included with a photo, possibly Fig. 6.3, attached to the original history of C.V.H. No. 1 sent to French over C.E. Edgett's signature. *NAC RG9, III, Vol. 3367, File C-27-45 (Vol. 1): Report on No. 1 Canadian Veterinary Hospital, Le Havre, France.*
5. Evans, born in England, immigrated to Canada in 1904, and soon entered O.V.C., from which he graduated V.S. in 1908. After a short period in practice in Winnipeg, he returned to demonstrate in Anatomy at O.V.C. in 1909, following its affiliation with the University of Toronto, and graduated B.V.Sc. in 1910. He joined the Biological Laboratory, Health of Animals Branch, Ottawa under Dr. C.H. Higgins, and in 1911 received the D.V.Sc. from the University of Toronto.

In 1910, he was commissioned a Lieutenant in the 8th Brigade, Canadian Artillery, and on 1 June 1911 he was gazetted Lieutenant in the C.A.V.C. Evans told D.J. McLellan that he took a course for army veterinary surgeons offered at Aldershot by the Army Veterinary Corps, during a trip to England that his family gave him. If true, this may have given him an advantage over his colleagues when the war began, and contributed to his rapid rise to Lieut.-Colonel. He trained No. 3 Section, raised under Piché in Fall 1914, and took it overseas to join the First Canadian Contingent at Salisbury Plain (Appendix E). His subsequent wartime career in the C.A.V.C. is covered by French in Chapters 6 and 7. Although he clearly contributed significantly to the establishment and quality of No. 1 C.V.H., Savage remarked, on the occasion of a visit much later in the war, that he was still "cordially hated" by the personnel there. *Savage Diary, 21 Feb. 1918.*

According to McLellan, Evans could be "a character". He recounted an episode with Evans, seeking a meal and a drink while on leave after the Armistice. Evans, upon being warned by the doorman of a private club not to enter, declared "Who won the war?", and barged past the doorman into the clubrooms. When approached by a waiter, Evans "...whipped off the old trench coat, handed it to the flunky...screwed the monocle to his eye, and...turned to the crowd...", staring them down and obtaining a cold roast beef sandwich and a beer. *McLellan, 1981.*

In July 1919, Evans returned briefly to his position as pathologist in Ottawa, but in 1920 he joined the Royal Canadian Army Veterinary Corps, and was posted to Stanley Barracks, Toronto as P.V.O. M.D. No.2. He was veterinary officer to 'B' Squadron, Royal Canadian Dragoons, and maintained an association with R.S. Timmis, a senior officer in that regiment, who had known Evans while a student at the O.V.C. prior to joining the cavalry. Evans was involved on the executive of the Ontario Veterinary Association, and he served as Editor of *The Canadian Veterinary Record* from 1921-1924. In 1938, after Tamblyn's retirement, he became Officer Administering, Canadian Army Veterinary Service, which he remained until the R.C.A.V.C. was disbanded in November, 1940. He then held a staff position as Liaison Officer in Military District 2 until he retired from the army in June, 1944. He moved to Victoria B.C., where he died on Easter Sunday 1962. *Anon., Can. Vet Rec., Vol. 1, No. 2, p. 55, 1920; Anon., Can. Vet Rec., Vol. 2, pp. 107-108, 1921; Anon., Can. J. Comp. Med., Vol. 8, p. 102, 1944; Timmis, 1961/62; Evans, obit., 1962; Evans & Barker, 1974, p. 141.*

6. Saunders was transferred from command of No. 1 Canadian Veterinary Hospital, in Savage's opinion, because he was considered a poor example of discipline for the men, by carrying on a flagrant extramarital affair. "As a man soweth, so shall he pay for the wild oats" *Savage Diary, 19, 27, 31 July 1917.* His promotion to D.A.D.V.S. 1st Division caused considerable consternation; consultations with the O.C. Canadian Corps had not been made, and there were no arrangements for a successor at C.V.H No. 1. *NAC RG9, III B1, Vol. 3382, File 154-45: corresp. in Q.M.G. file 1-1-37.*

Charles Greatly Saunders was born in Cuckfield, England on 6 November 1875, and was educated at Charterhouse and Trinity College, Cambridge before immigrating to Canada; he may have homesteaded near Fort Qu'Appelle Saskatchewan before entering the Ontario Veterinary College. Graduating as an excellent student with a V.S. diploma from the O.V.C. in March 1907, he returned to the college after graduation, probably demonstrating while completing the requirements for the B.V.Sc. degree, which he received from the University of Toronto in 1910. In 1908 he became Veterinary-Lieutenant with the 9th Field Battery of Artillery, Toronto, replacing Veterinary-Major Andrew Smith, Principal of the Ontario Veterinary College, who had served that battery since 1872 (Appendix H).

In 1910 he joined the faculty of the O.V.C., teaching Canine and Feline Diseases until 1914; according to C.A. Mitchell, O.V.C. '14, one of his students, he was known as 'Cats and Dogs' Saunders, and was a proficient surgeon. Although listed in the Calendar as teaching Anatomy, Surgery and Canine and Feline Diseases from 1915-1918, he was absent in the C.A.V.C. overseas from October 1914; his appointment is last found in the college Calendar in 1919. Saunders was a prominent small animal veterinarian. Editor of the Canine Department in the American Journal of Veterinary Medicine and of a column on 'Cynology' (literally 'knowledge of dogs', in this context canine medicine and surgery) during the pre-war period, he also was author of several texts, on *Canine Medicine and Surgery* (1915), and *Rabbit and Cat Diseases* (1920).

Saunders retired from the C.A.V.C. in England, where he qualified M.R.C.V.S. in 1919. He settled at Leigh Hill Farm, Cuckfield Sussex, and operated a private veterinary diagnostic laboratory service. He died in 1963. *Quarterly Militia Lists, 1908-1914; Saunders, C.G., 1915, 1920; Calendar, Ontario Veterinary College, 1916-1919; Mitchell, C.A. to C.A.V. Barker, personal communication c. 1960; Fox, 1994; Saunders, C.G., Service Record, CEF, NAC.*

7. Short of the information in his military record and French's brief allusion to his career with R.N.W.M.P., little is available on Richards. When he graduated from McGill in 1896, his address was Malden, Mass., U.S.A., but by 1900 he was in practice in Grand Forks B.C., where his brother was ranching. Richards was engaged in November 1902 as a Veterinary Staff Sergeant in the Royal North West Mounted Police. He served at Regina, North Portal and Estevan prior to leaving the force in June 1905. His army record indicates that he was Veterinary Inspector, 81 Section, probably a civilian inspector with the R.N.W.M.P. or with the Dominion Department of Agriculture after his discharge, based on French's remarks. Richards' address was Victoria, B.C. when in August 1914 he was commissioned as a Lieutenant in the C.A.V.C., though in 1916 his wife Florence lived in Winnipeg. His whereabouts and activities after demobilization in August 1919 are completely unknown to us. He may have returned to the U.S.A. *Gordon, Feb. 1992; Mattison, 1993; Richards, S.C., Service Record, CEF, NAC.*
8. French does not discuss the privileges of the officers. All C.A.V.C. officers had a batman or personal servant, and a charger with a groom to look after it. These were compensation for the fact that officers were few, often busy, and lack of motor transport necessitated a horse, which required considerable care. In addition to veterinary duties, resident officers at C.V.H. No. 1 were Orderly Officer every third day, responsible over 24 hours for hundreds of men and the routine activities of the base, from alertness of guards, to quality of food, to replenishment of fire buckets, to routine daily parades and inspections. However, when not on duty or writing reports, V.O.s at C.V.H. No. 1 occupied themselves in the officers' mess, played tennis at a court on the hospital grounds, engaged in tent-pegging, went riding, or to Le Havre for a social evening. Savage describes going to dinner and to a show with French on at least one occasion, and many times with others. Major Richards was a keen polo player, and matches were arranged with the officers from nearby bases. Minor graft was perpetrated from time-to-time to keep good polo ponies at the hospital. *Savage Diary, 1917-1918.*

   Capt. W.F.R. 'Buckie' Stubbs of Caledon, Ont., temporarily attached to C.V.H. No. 1 while awaiting a posting to the Artillery, wrote in a letter home: "Just think of it, it is now 6 p.m. I have just had 5 o'clock tea and am now waiting for 8 o'clock Dinner having played polo this afternoon, and there is a war on. There is too dam [sic] much swank here for me. Tomorrow night (Saturday) there is a dance here. American and French girls. They say it will be very nice, just a small affair, you know, about 12 officers and 12 girls. I dare say I will enjoy it for I sure would like to have a dance" *Stubbs Collection, 1 Nov. 1918.* Stubbs had spent the previous 17 months at rustic and isolated No. 5 District Canadian Forestry Corps camps in the Jura Mountains, broken only by short leaves to nearby towns and a 2 week leave to Nice, France in February 1918. About that same Saturday evening, Savage wrote: "Capt. Stubbs appears from C.F.C. Dance in Mess...Best show we've had yet - so they say. Our 3 Loots [Lieutenants] get tight." *Savage Diary, 19 Oct. 1918.*

   Social events involving local ladies were common. Among many, Savage described tea with a charming widow and her two spinster friends. "All very nice, last named reputed very wealthy and 'cherchant un officier anglais'. What hopes." Dr. Dumont, Le Havre City Veterinarian, worked hard to match his daughters up with Canadian veterinary officers. Numerous dinners with the family, movies in Le Havre, trips to the seaside, and tennis matches at the Hospital are recounted, involving Savage, Hunter, and other No. 1 C.V.H. officers. Savage related how with relief he put one daughter, René, his 'official wife-to-be', on the boat to England to wed an English officer, and he described Capt. Hunter's manipulation of the system to remain in contact with the other daughter, Irène, whom apparently he did marry. After the war Hunter became M.R.C.V.S., and in 1920 was living in Le Havre as the veterinary representative of a large meat exporting firm. In 1993, a Madame Le Roux of Le Havre recalled that a daughter of Dr. Dumont, Irène, "Madame Hunter", had married "a British veterinarian". They reportedly lived for an extended period in French Indo-China and retired to Monaco, where they died about 1970. *Anon., re A.H. Hunter, Can. Vet. Rec. 2, p. 40, 1921; Savage Diary, 26 June 1917- 20 Aug. 1918; David, 4 March 1993.*

   Savage, who was single, was dismayed to discover that the married C.O. and senior N.C.O.s had regular arrangements for 'sleeping out' in town, and he described removing a French paramour's letters from the personal effects of one of his men who had died of the flu, so that the wife at home would not be further upset. He spent self-described evenings 'tomcatting' in town with Capt. Harry Clapp, and he related in veiled terms apparent trysts involving himself. *Savage Diary, 27, 31 July 1917; 24 Sept. 1917; 5 June - Aug. 1918.*
9. Alcohol abuse was a problem for some of the Canadian V.O.s. Savage described episodes of heavy drinking in the Officers' Mess at C.V.H. No. 1, and binges by several officers, not all of whom were subject to official sanction. Capt. H.R. Sharp caused so much disruption while drunk on duty as Orderly Officer that he was suspended from duty for 29 days and court-martialed, resulting in a sentence of dismissal which was commuted to a severe reprimand by Sir Douglas Haig. However, within a few months he was returned to Canada as surplus to requirements. Also court-martialed for drunkenness, and dismissed, were Capt. W.H. Simon, Capt. P.A. Chambers, and Capt. C.C. Evely. Earlier in the war, Neill had dismissed J.J. McCarrey from the C.E.F. and sent him and Lieut. F.W. Gokey, attached Imperial Army Veterinary Corps, back to Canada, with the recommendation that their resignations from the C.A.V.C. be sought. In the letter covering their dismissals he asked that Headquarters "...impress veterinary officers coming over here, that

drunkeness will not be tolerated or misconduct of any kind...as they will be instantly dismissed and returned to Canada at their own expense." Given Savage's comments about Neill's drinking habits (see Note 10.4), his request of headquarters sounds somewhat hypocritical. In the circumstances, the number of officers severely disabled by alcohol abuse perhaps was what might have been expected in a group the size of the C.A.V.C. *NAC RG9, III, B1, Vol. 3380, File 0-19-45: Neill, W.J., 19 May 1915, to Q.M.G., Ottawa re Officers C.A.V.C. Dismissed. Records of Courts Martial, NAC, Files 2923-2 (Simon), 9568-3-11 (Chambers), 9568-5-1 (Evely), 9568-19-27 (Sharp). Savage Diary, 20 Mar., 3, 18, Apr., 27 May 1918.*

10. Care of the horses was very labour-intensive. Note that in Fig. 6.8, the ratio of stabled horses to men in the three hospital squadrons varied from about 2.5:1 to 3:1, as described on page 13. Note also that in the daily routine on page 39 horses were watered 3 times daily, at 0630, 1100 and 1400 hr, and fed 5 times, at 0630 (hay), 0700, 1200, 1630 and 1900 (hay). Feet were to be picked out at each 'stable' hour (0615, 0905, 1405), and whenever an animal returned from exercise, at which time it was to be groomed as well. *French Papers, NAC MG30, E14, Vol. 1: Canadian Veterinary Hospital Daily Routine for Winter Months from 1st October 1917 to 1st April 1918, S.C. Richards, Major C.A.V.C., Commanding Canadian Veterinary Hospital.*
11. The originals of Figs. 6.10, 6.12, 6.13 and 6.14 and several other unpublished drawings are to be found in the *French Papers, NAC MG30, E14.*
12. In addition, overhead irrigators supplied streams of warm saline solution to the wound, which was handled with sterile swabs (p. 181). This precluded touching the wound with fingers or instruments and helped prevent spread of infection.
13. Glover graduated from O.V.C. in 1920, and joined the faculty of the college as a lecturer in poultry pathology until 1959. Active in provincial professional veterinary affairs, he died in 1963. *Barker & Crowley, 1989, p. 189.*
14. See Appendix F for the plan and explanation of the operation of a similar dipping tank. The significance of the introduction of dips by Canadian officers was acknowledged by the Imperials. *Blenkinsop & Rainey, 1925, p. 67.*
15. This method of exercising horses was considered a most useful innovation by the Imperial Army Veterinary Corps. *Blenkinsop & Rainey, 1925, p. 67.*
16. Over 2.5 million admissions were made to the Imperial Veterinary Hospitals, of which 78%, or over 2 million horses, were returned to duty. Most of the remainder were humanely destroyed. *Blenkinsop & Rainey, 1925, p. 509.*

Moore discusses the disposal of "animals wasted by war", stating: "I regret exceedingly...that these creatures who in dumb obedience shared the dangers and hardships of campaign with human beings should suffer the indignity of classification under Salvage; still it must be remembered that they are also creatures of the mart...". In describing the disposal of 'cast' horses, and obviously sensitive to criticism leveled at the service over the treatment of wasted animals, he says: "Their actual disposal was a thing of itself, very carefully considered - and quite rightly so, and I am in a position to affirm that humane thought and fellow-feeling reigned supreme in their disposal, even though the best economic considerations were necessary." *Blenkinsop & Rainey* devote a detailed chapter to the matter of Disposal of Animals.

'Casting' was an official decision that a horse was unfit for further war service. It was made, not at the front, but in the Lines of Communication in the rear, to which such horses had been evacuated, by the Remount Department for aged horses or those with vices, and by delegates of the Director of Veterinary Services in the case of infirmity or disease. Moore emphasizes the importance of salvage, given the huge cost of war. The officer of the A.V.C. in charge of the Disposal of Animals Branch, Lieut., later Major, H.A. Crowe, had worked for an equine slaughtering firm in the U.K, and was both an expert on machinery for extraction of by-products, and a chartered accountant. His commission as an officer was controversial with the veterinarians in the R.A.V.C., and he was the object of considerable scorn and disquiet when he received an O.B.E., and at the end of the war was allowed to retain his rank, when V.O.s were forced to revert to Lieutenant on demobilization. *'One of Them', 1920.*

Although there was agitation by the public against the practice, horses were disposed of to bone fide farmers for work if considered fit enough for a domestic purpose. The alternative was destruction through being disposed of for food via the equine abattoirs, or, if, in the opinion of a veterinary officer, the animal was not fit for human consumption, disposal for by-products.

Many animals destined for human consumption were sold through the 'Abattoir Hippophagique' in Paris, where there was an established system of horse slaughter and inspection, with general oversight by a detachment from The Royal Army Veterinary Corps. *Blenkinsop & Rainey* report that 28,384 horses were sold to the Paris Abattoir prior to the Armistice, and 8,664 after the end of the war. Alternatively, horses could be disposed of through local abattoirs, as French describes here.

The Army Veterinary Corps also had 8 self-contained 'Horse Carcass Economizers', which were rendering plants, each manned by a staff of 14 and capable of handling 30 carcasses a day. Horses were destroyed, and the blood, skin, hair and hoofs were salvaged. If appropriate, the meat was dehydrated for use as meat meal in animal feed, while the fat was rendered for oil used in soap manufacture, bones were boiled, crushed, de-greased and sold for bone meal, while viscera and waste were rendered to fat and meat meal.

Animals that were killed or died at the front were skinned and buried, unless a serious contagious disease were involved, in which case they were buried without skinning.

Moore, 1921, pp. 161-176; Blenkinsop & Rainey, 1925, pp. 681-691.

17. Such visits reflect the necessity of the U.S. Army Veterinary Corps to learn how to manage veterinary work in the war zone. See also Note 1.1.
18. Savage described it as an "enormous day" when the delegation of "battleships and light cruisers" [V.I.P.s, possibly somewhat 'large'] from Le Societé Havraise de Protection des Animaux visited No. 1 C.V.H. to award the medals, which were presented on parade. He wondered if his were gold. *Savage Diary, 19 Aug. 1917.*
19. This medal is 4 cm. in diameter. Sgt. Dugmore was a dresser at C.V.H. No. 1.

Chapter 7.

1. Riding long distances for many hours, day in and day out, was an occupational necessity and hazard for Canadian veterinary officers at all levels. A number were injured in accidents when their horses either fell or rolled on them, or they were thrown. The author, Cecil French, was among these (see 'About the Author'), as were Capt. V.C. Best, Capt. W.G. Church, Capt. N. McCarthy, Capt. J. Harrington, and Capt. J.A. Roy and Capt. L.H. Durkin, the latter two being discharged as medically unfit due to the severity of their injuries. Capt. C.W. Baker died of such an event (see Ch. 12). Knee strain and synovitis associated with riding was also a problem (see Note 8.1 re Capt. J.H. Burnet). Capt. W.F.R. Stubbs wore his riding breeches to rags, and longed for shipments of ointment from his family to ease the pain in his "behind which was getting sore due to so much saddle work.... I can hardly sit down at times". Capt. C.A. Stevenson was discharged on medical grounds due to severe sciatica which may have been aggravated by riding. Savage was hospitalized for several weeks with hemorrhoids caused by months in the saddle while with the Field Artillery. He referred to others who were in the same circumstance having surgery, and the severity of this condition resulted in the discharge of Capt. R.C. Titus as medically unfit. *Baker, C.W., Service Record, CEF, NAC; Best, V.C., Service Record, CEF, NAC; Church, W.G., Service Record, CEF, NAC; Durkin, L.H., Service Record, CEF, NAC; French, C., Service Record, CEF, NAC; Harrington, J., Service Record, CEF, NAC; McCarthy, N., Service Record, CEF, NAC; Roy, J.A., Service Record, CEF, NAC; Savage Diary, 21 Feb. - 5 Mar. 1917, 12 Aug. 1918; Stevenson, C.A., Service Record, CEF, NAC; Stubbs Collection, 22 Jan. 1918, 19 Mar. 1918, 30 July 1918; Titus, R.C., Service Record, CEF, NAC.*
2. Tamblyn, in a marginal comment to current Chapter 4, says: "It was also known that the Senior Officers - C.A.V.C. [C.E.F.] sent to England and France were too old to really stand the strain and were sick most of the time. Thus they impeded the young and more modern officer." *Tamblyn, D.S. Marginal comments, 1933.* Incapacity caused by age or poor health was also a major handicap in the Imperial Army Veterinary Corps, rendering many veterinary officers unfit to perform executive duties in the field. *Blenkinsop & Rainey, 1925, p. 87.*
3. These officers and men display the variations in uniform style found in the C.E.F. and described in Chapter 17. Some wear stiff forage caps, others the softer cap, and three styles of cap badge are evident among the officers. Not all wear collar badges, and if worn, they do not necessarily match the cap badge. Some wear high lace-up boots, others ankle boots with leather leggings or puttees. The Sergeants wear 5 button British pattern tunics, some of which have been Canadianized, with a stand-up, rather than roll collar. A Warrant Officer (left rear) wears a Sam Browne belt. *Law, c.1998.*

   We have identified the officers from contemporary photographs in which they are named; some in this photo have been misidentified elsewhere, eg. *Gattinger, 1962.* Unfortunately, the N.C.O.s cannot be so identified. At the time of this photo, the following were the Sergeants C.A.V.C. still serving with the 2nd Canadian Division: J. Anderson, T. Anderson, C.C. Barteaux, A.M.I. Billie, W.R. Dewar, E. Duke, J.W. Edwards, U. Gauthier, E. Gill, R.P. Harland, J.C. Hornby, B.A. Insall, W.F. James, G. Johnson, F.B. Kendall, P.L. Kerridge, J. King, E.G. Langford, G.L. Marsh, G.A. McDonald, J. McKay, D. McPherson, J.A. Moison, G.C. Nattress, E.J. Olney, W.E. Perkins, O.M. Saunders, J.H. Stewart, J.B. Stobbart, R.A. Wallace *French papers, NAC MG30, E14, Vol. 1: Officers C.A.V.C. who have been with the 2nd Canadian Division since Formation, compiled by R.J. Vickers c. March 1919.*
4. A.E. Cameron, born at Broughty Ferry, near Dundee, Scotland in 1876, had a remarkable career in Canadian veterinary medicine. He served as a Trooper in the Rhodesian Mounted Police during the Boer War. After homesteading in Saskatchewan in 1904/5, he entered the O.V.C. in 1906, graduated in 1908, and joined the Dominion Department of Agriculture as a Meat Inspector at Winnipeg, then as a Veterinary Inspector, Contagious Diseases Division, Saskatchewan, 1911-1914. He was Pathologist at the Veterinary Research Station in Lethbridge, Alberta in 1914. He joined the C.A.V.C. as a Provisional Lieutenant on 1 June 1913, and was veterinary officer with the 27th Light Horse when the war broke out. He volunteered for overseas duty on 1 July, 1915, and served in several roles with units in the Canadian 2nd Division (Appendix A). After the war, he returned as Pathologist to the Health of Animals Laboratory, Lethbridge. Subsequently he became Chief Veterinary Inspector for Canada, 1925-1939, and ultimately Veterinary

Director-General from 1939-1943, when he retired.

He served as Lieut.-Col., R.C.A.V.C.(N.P.) prior to W.W. II, until disbandment in 1940, and in W.W. II as Lieut.-Col., Chemical Warfare and Smoke, commanding the men stationed at the War Disease Control Station, Grosse Isle, Quebec, supporting the research workers developing a rinderpest vaccine as a defence against biological attack, and producing anthrax spores for germ warfare. As a result of his military activity, he was awarded the Military Cross, the Long Service Medal, the Colonial Auxiliary Forces Officer's Decoration and the Coronation Medal.

He was active in veterinary professional associations on the regional, provincial and national levels, a strong proponent of a national Canadian veterinary association prior to the establishment of the Canadian Veterinary Medical Association, and received the International Veterinary Congress Award in 1948, for "...distinguished service to veterinary medicine and to mankind...". A member of the Gaelic and St. Andrew's Societies in Ottawa, he was an accomplished piper. He died in September 1964. *Anon., Can. J. Comp. Med., Vol. 3, p. 117, 1939; Anon., Veterinary Digest, Vol. 2, pp 22-23, 1940; Anon., Can. J. Comp. Med., Vol. 7, p. 97, 1943; Anon., 1948; Cameron, obit., 1964; Evans & Barker, 1976, p. 167; Bryden, 1989, p. 89; Barker & Crowley, 1989, p. 180.*

5. Walsh was hospitalized for 5 weeks in fall 1916 with a "contusion to the left knee", probably injured while riding. *Walsh, F., Service Record, CEF, NAC.*
6. Tamblyn, born in Cornwall, England on 28 January 1881, graduated with a D.V.S. from McGill University at the age of 20. He took a shipment of horses to South Africa, and volunteered as a Civilian Veterinary Surgeon in the Boer War. Subsequently he held veterinary appointments in several units of the British or colonial forces (Appendix H) *Curson 1933a,b.* Tamblyn had 2 horses shot out from under him as he distributed ammunition "along the bullet swept line" during the British defeat at Tweebosch, Western Transvaal in January 1902 *Smith 1919, p. 213.* In September 1904, Tamblyn petitioned the Minister of Militia for a commission as a veterinary officer in the Permanent Forces in Canada. His background was investigated, but in January 1905 he was turned down. Meanwhile, he married Kathleen Agnes Cherry in Montreal, 4 Oct. 1904. *Tamblyn File, D.H.H., D.N.D.: File 1-13-61, 8 Sept. 1904, Tamblyn to Sir F. Borden and reply 14 Sept, 1904; 11 Nov. 1904 Tamblyn to Col. Gordon; 12 Jan. 1905, Adjutant General to Col. Gordon.*

   In 1905 he joined the fledgling Health of Animals Branch of the Dominion Department of Agriculture as a Veterinary Inspector in Saskatchewan, a post that he returned to after the war, until in April 1920 he joined the R.C.A.V.C. While in Regina he was commissioned a Veterinary-Lieutenant and placed on the Reserve of Officers based on his record in the Boer War, under *G.O. 22-1908*; in 1913, he became V.O. to the artillery in Regina. He was member of Council, the Veterinary Association of Saskatchewan 1911-1914, and served as President in 1913.

   Tamblyn's career in the R.C.A.V.C. took him initially to Calgary, then in 1925 to Kingston, where he was stationed when he took over as Officer Administering the Canadian Army Veterinary Services in 1930. He published '*The Horse in War and Famous Canadian War Horses*' in 1932. Invalided by a near-fatal heart attack in April 1936, he was forced to retire in March 1937. He was appointed Honorary Lieut.-Col. of the R.C.A.V.C. in October 1937. Tamblyn petitioned unsuccessfully to be reappointed to the army after the outbreak of World War II. He resided in Kingston until he died of another myocardial infarction on 2 Jan.1943; he was buried in St. Mary's Cemetery, Kingston. *Tamblyn File, D.H.H., D.N.D.: Medical and Pension Records, April 1936-April 1937; Telegram 12 Sept., 1939, Adjutant-General to O.C. M.D. 3, re Tamblyn reappointment; Tamblyn, obit., 1943; Barker & Crowley, 1989, p. 210.*
7. Tamblyn said, in reference to this statement, which was applied by French both to himself and to Edgett in this chapter, "There were no great discoveries in the C.A.V.C. The success of any individual was due to the sterling qualities of the officers & men serving under them." *Tamblyn, Marginal comments, 1933.*
8. See Chapter 14.
9. Lapel tabs reflect staff officer status. Insignia on sleeve reflect years of service overseas (blue chevrons, lowest one red if departed Canada in 1914) and rank (crown over pip). He carries an officer's cane. *Overseas Military Forces of Canada, 1918, pp. 35-36; Law, c.1998, pp. 17, 40-42.*
10. Tamblyn described such a scene: "Once off the fascine road, horses became mired to such an extent that they were drowned, or shot from a humane point of view, as it was impossible to extricate them...The sight of a large number of carcasses of animals strewn all along the road from Spree Farm to the Guns was something never to be forgotten, so thick were they that one could use them as one would stepping stones over a stream...It was a wonderful sight yet terrible to witness, men and animals returning from the forward areas covered with mud, men asleep on horseback, some wearing bandages, others exposing ghastly wounds received between the First Aid posts and the M.V.S." *French Papers, NAC MG30, E14, Vol. 1: Tamblyn, D.S., The Canadian Army Veterinary Corps, Third Canadian Division, British Expeditionary Force 1915-1918.*
11. A line drawing of this shoe accompanied the original manuscript, but its quality did not permit reproduction.
12. See Chapter 14.
13. Tamblyn claimed to have been the first mounted Canadian officer to enter Mons, the day before it was taken. He crossed

the canal via a small bridge, but retreated when he encountered members of the Princess Patricia's Canadian Light Infantry confronting a German machine gun. *French Papers, NAC MG30, E14, Vol I: Tamblyn, D.S., The Canadian Army Veterinary Corps, Third Canadian Division, British Expeditionary Force 1915-1918.*

14. Tamblyn clearly was not enamoured of Edgett. He states in reference to this episode:

"The question of appointing an A.D.V.S., Canadian Corps, was a matter of great importance. Without any intimation, whatever, Lieut.-Col. Edgett arrived in the vicinity of the Corps H.Q. and assumed command of the C.A.V.C. Opening an office, he immediately called all officers of the Corps in conference. Upon this being made known General Sir Arthur Currie immediately proceeded to Lieut.-Col. Edgett's office to ascertain the authority of Edgett's presence.

Realizing that his authority was being impeached upon, General Currie immediately ordered Edgett to close his office and return to London, and recommended the appointment of Lieut.-Col. Cutcliffe as A.D.V.S. Canadian Corps, taking the attitude, and rightly so, that Col. Cutcliffe was the senior officer in of the C.A.V.C. in France, and that he had performed his duties in an entirely satisfactory manner and unstintingly.

General Currie was a man who stood for efficiency and loyalty, and gave those desiring to show their ability the opportunity of doing so, but not through the back door channel of political and semi-political methods.

Edgett returned to London, and feeling that he had been ill treated, obtained leave of absence to Canada. On his return to London he was, by some unexplained reason, appointed D.V.S. Canadians." *Tamblyn, Marginal comments, 1933.*

15. Ashton Bluett Cutcliffe was born in Swansea, Wales in 1867, and graduated from the Ontario Veterinary College in 1892. He became a Veterinary-Lieutenant with the 25th Brant Dragoons, Brantford Ontario in 1909, and continued with that regiment following organization of the C.A.V.C. He proceeded overseas with the First Contingent, as V.O. to the 1st Canadian Division Engineers. His subsequent war record is summarized in Chapter 7 and Appendix A. During the war his wife died, and he remarried, to a Belgian woman from Ypres. Following the war he returned to Brantford, where he became Lieutenant-Colonel in the C.A.V.C. as V.O. to the 10th Brant Dragoons, retiring in 1931. He was Inspector for Food of the City of Brantford, until he was disabled by a stroke in 1937. He died in January 1946, and is buried at Mount Pleasant Cemetery, Brantford, Ontario. *Anon., Can. Vet. Rec., Vol. 2, No. 3, pp. 36-36, 1921; Woodland, 1983.*
16. Decorations and medals, l-r: D.S.O., 1914-15 Star, British War Medal, Victory Medal 1914-1918, with leaf cluster (M.i.D.).
17. See *Nicholson, 1962, pp. 510-517* for a description of events in North Russia.
18. This citation accompanied the award of the Distinguished Conduct Medal *Anon., 1919.*
19. For an overview of the Siberian Expeditionary Force and a summary of the units involved (C.A.V.C. excepted, of course), see *Nicholson, 1962, pp. 517-523.*
20. An extract from the *Second Supplement to the London Gazette, No. 30648, of 24th April, 1918*, records the citation: "For most conspicuous bravery and dash when in command of a squadron... On reaching the first objective, Lt. Flowerdew saw two lines of the enemy, each about sixty strong, with machine guns in the centre and flanks...he led the remaining three troops to the charge. The squadron...passed over both lines, killing many of the enemy with the sword; and wheeling about galloped at them again. Although the squadron had then lost about 70 per cent of its numbers, killed and wounded, from rifle and machine gun fire directed on it from the front and both flanks, the enemy broke and retired...The survivors...then established themselves in a position where they were joined, after much hand-to-hand fighting, by Lt. Harvey's party. Lt. Flowerdew was dangerously wounded through both thighs during the operation, but continued to cheer on his men..." Machine gun bullets had shredded the flesh of Flowerdew's legs, and he died the next day.

Chapter 8

1. The realities of soldiering in The Great War are illuminated in Morton's *When Your Number's Up*: demeaning treatment and harsh discipline, class structure, bad food, filth, mud, infectious diseases, constant danger, terrible wounds, high risk of random death, and psychological trauma *Morton, 1993.*

Capt. J.G. Harvey described conditions with the 2nd Canadian Division at the Somme, in 1916: "...a sea of slimy mud the consistency of thick soup...from early September to December, no harder and more trying conditions for men and animals could be imagined. In addition to the terrible living conditions, the horse lines were periodically shelled during the day and night as well as subjected to machine gun fire and bombs from enemy aircraft at night." *French Papers, NAC MG30, E14, Vol. 1: Short Veterinary History of the 2nd Canadian Divisional Ammunition Column.*

The stress of war on C.A.V.C. personnel, even though non-combatants, was considerable. Capt. James H. Burnet, who spent 31 months with the 1st Division C.F.A. and the 2nd Canadian Reserve Park was hospitalized for several months and ultimately retired completely with 'nervous debility' (shell-shock) and arthritis of the knees from riding. Others, like Capt. Harry S. Clapp, were removed for up to a year at a time to duties away from the front on medical grounds, with 'nerves'. The 'chronic gastritis' which invalided Capt. E.M. Dixon (see Chapter 12) may have been an ulcer.

The stress of duty was felt in England as well. Hon. Lieut. A. Newell was invalided home with 'neurasthenia' or shell-shock following an air-raid on Shorncliffe. Overwork and worry of service contributed to the medical discharge of Capt.

V.C. Best, who also had incipient tuberculosis. Capt. J.F. Wood was discharged due to a severe duodenal ulcer that was exacerbated by service responsibilities. *Best, V.C., Service Record, CEF, NAC; Burnet, J.H., Service Record, CEF, NAC; Newell, A., Service Record, CEF, NAC; Savage Diary, 4 Oct. 1918; Wood, J.F., Service Record, CEF, NAC.*

2. William Fraser Rutledge 'Buckie' Stubbs, born in Caledon Ont., August 1891, had been a bugler in the 36th Peel Battalion of Infantry as a youth. His father William was an 1869 graduate of the Ontario Veterinary College, a militiaman, a strong Orangeman and an M.P. Buckie Stubbs graduated from the O.V.C. in 1913, and after several years in practice and as a meat inspector, he enlisted in the C.E.F. at the Exhibition Grounds Camp in Toronto in March 1917, although apparently blind in one eye. His letters home reflect the every-day existence of a veterinary officer under conditions of war which, though far from the front, could be trying psychologically and physically; Stubbs was initially with the Forestry Corps in an isolated posting. He marveled at the cities which he visited on leave; the European experience was broadening for a country boy from Ontario. He was briefly at No. 1 C.V.H., Le Havre (see Fig. 6.11 and Note 6.8), and finished the war with the 6th Brigade, C.F.A. (Fig. 7.3). He returned to the country practice established by his father in Caledon, where he died in 1975. *Stortz, 1982; Stubbs Collection; Stubbs, W.F.R., Service Record, CEF, NAC.*

   He wrote from his Forestry Corps camp "Men are damnable scarce. I have now got 4 Russians in the central hospital. They are darn good workers and talk a little French so that we get along very well. I also have 5 colored chaps. They are not bad, so you see we are a regular Coxes army but we get there all the same." *Stubbs Collection, 22 Jan. 1918.* These men are in this photo, with a Veterinary Sergeant (seated right), and a Farrier Sergeant (standing right).

   The black men were from the 2nd Construction Battalion, C.E.F., a segregated unit recruited mainly in Nova Scotia. Mobilized in Truro in March 1917, it arrived in France in May, when most of the men were assigned to the Canadian Forestry Corps at La Joux, Jura, where Stubbs was stationed *Ruck, 1986, pp. 26-27.* Not only were these men sent to an isolated posting, they were kept segregated except while working. Fortunately, the local commander of the Canadian Forestry Corps had the decency to reject a directive from the Imperial Army to reduce the rank, pay and privileges of members of the unit, to conform with the lower standards applied to Chinese, South African and Egyptian 'coloured labour' units in the British Army *Walker, 1989.* See also Note 11.8 on recruitment of blacks into the C.E.F.

Chapter 9.

1. It was estimated that 500,000 sick and injured horses were evacuated by mobile veterinary sections and veterinary evacuating stations of the B.E.F.; this probably includes the work of the C.A.V.C. *Blenkinsop & Rainey, 1925, p. 92.*
2. Pierre Souillard, born in Le Havre, France in 1887, was a merchant seaman and adventurer; he even tapped rubber in the Amazon. He studied at l'Ecole de médecine comparée et de science vétérinaire de Montréal, graduating in 1912. He pursued military interests at the College Militaire du Québec, becoming a Lieutenant before establishing a practice near Richmond, P.Q. He was devoted to his *alma mater*, and in August, 1916, he and eight other Montréal graduates at the front donated a gold medal to an outstanding graduating student, and a silver plaque to the school. After the war he traveled widely before settling in British Columbia, but ultimately he moved to Washington State. An actor, singer, violinist and painter, in 1962 he was Veterinarian of the Year for eastern Washington State *Pepin, 1986, pp. 319-321.*
3. The Passchendaele offensive.
4. O'Gogarty was "a real Irish horseman" according to his classmate Lieut.-Col. R.S. Timmis *Timmis, 1961/1962.*
5. Surprisingly, Daigneault was court martialed and reprimanded for commandeering 3 tarpaulins "which he knew at the time were not intended for his use". With the Dominion Department of Agriculture at Montréal and other areas in western Québec, 1912-1949, Daigneault died in January 1963, aged 76. *Daigneault, F.A., Service Record, CEF, NAC; NAC Records of Courts Martial, File 9568-4-3; Anon., Can. Vet. Rec. Vol. 2 No. 2, p. 41, 1921; Daigneault, obit., 1963.*
6. The aftermath of Moreuil Wood. See Notes 7.20 and 17.51.
7. Col. C.E. Edgett arranged that the proceeds from the sale of the motor horse ambulance ($1500) were used to endow the C.A.V.C. Scholarship at O.V.C. Awarded from 1923-24 to a returned soldier or to the offspring of a member of the armed forces for about 50 years, it continues as the Royal Canadian Army Veterinary Corps Prize of $250 to a student interested in the care and welfare of horses. *Calendar of the Ontario Veterinary College, Session 1923-1924, pp. 51-52.*

Chapter 10.

1. Neill is a man of mystery. He is W.J. 'Neil' in the *Annual Calendar Fac. Comp. Med. Vet. Sci., McGill, 1902-3* and Boer War records *Curson, 1933a; Roncetti & Denby, undated*, but the surname is 'Neill' elsewhere and on the family cemetery monument. As French notes, he was born in Omemee Ontario 23 May 1876. Little more can be gleaned about Neill's pre-war personal affairs in Canada or the USA from his Service Record, beyond that recorded by French. His militia unit, the 45th Regiment of Infantry, Lindsay, Ontario, was the home regiment of Sir Sam Hughes, Minister of Militia, and it seems highly likely that Neill's initial appointment and advancement were the result of personal friendship or political favouritism. Hughes was well-known for appointing "...favoured and unqualified militia officers to responsible positions

even in the permanent corps...on the whole, many of Hughes' appointees had no special qualifications, while others were political favourites who replaced professionals." *Haycock, 1976, pp. 155, 157.*

Hughes appointed Neill to the short-lived Acting Sub-Militia Council in London, in Fall 1916. Intended in theory to improve the efficiency of Canadian military operations in Britain and Europe, it actually was to act as a puppet instrument of the Minister of Militia. Hughes made the following gratuitously flattering statement about Neill: "...McRae and Neill have already earned everything that a government could confer upon men. Both are regarded as great men in business and economy..." *Morton, 1982, p. 81.* However, more probably, Neill was appointed to the Council as an officer indebted to Hughes, and in his thrall. It was apparent to Major-General John Carson, Hughes' representative in London, that Neill did not have a grip on his command. He was not alone in this regard; there were administrative and other problems with the Medical Corps, the Dental Corps, the Chaplain Service, the Pay Corps and the Forestry Corps *Morton, 1982, pp. 57, 70, 86, 87, 99, 103, 114, 115.* Misappropriation of a small sum from funds donated by an humane society (see Note 15.11, below) suggests that Neill suffered from lapses in ethical judgement as well.

Neill's capacity to command additionally may have been affected adversely by mental illness. In October 1917, shortly after returning to London from his tour of Canada investigating the remount situation (see this chapter and Chapter 13) he was diagnosed with 'neurasthenia', a vague term implying emotional disturbance that could encompass depression. At some point during the war, Neill separated from his wife, Erna Kate Neill, who he had married in South Africa following the Boer War. She remained in Ottawa during W.W. I, and the marriage breakdown may have been confirmed during his Canadian sojourn in 1917. He relinquished his appointment in mid March 1918, and on 1 May he was hospitalized for almost 2 months with 'gastritis'. He was returned home invalided in late June, 1918, and was posted to a Casualty Company in Kingston before being officially struck off strength of the C.E.F. on 19 January, 1919 as part of general demobilization. He was transferred from the C.P.A.V.C. to the Reserve of Officers effective 1 January 1919. Since he was released from the permanent force at his own request, he was disqualified from receiving a pension in later life. In mid-1919 Neill's wife claimed his War Service Gratuity under a provision that permitted payment to dependants who were not receiving maintenance; at that time, all efforts by his wife's lawyers to locate Neill had failed. Neill apparently abandoned veterinary activity, and ultimately he became involved in the investment business in Toronto, where he died on 6 August 1955 in his 79th year. He is buried in the family plot, Emily Cemetery, Omemee Ontario. His surviving sister was the only relative mentioned in his death notice. *Canada Gazette, 1 March 1919; Neill, W.J., death notice, 1955; Neill, W.J., Service Record, CEF, NAC & D.H.H., D.N.D.*

In many ways, Neill fits the pattern of Canadian Generals during World War I *Hyatt, 1979.* Though younger than average at age 38 when the war began, he was Canadian-born, from Ontario, English-speaking, Anglican, college-educated, an urban professional or businessman, married, apparently reasonably affluent, had a militia background, and served in the Boer War. Among 'administrative' rather than 'fighting' generals, he began the war at a relatively low rank, Major, being appointed Lieutenant-Colonel within days after the war began. Like most, he did not remain in the army after the war, and he seems to have changed careers at that point, as did about half the generals.

While Hyatt argues that the standard of leadership provided by Canadian Generals in W.W. I in most cases probably was good, Neill would seem to be an exception. Both his superiors and his subordinates were of the opinion that he was a poor administrator and leader (see Note 10.4 below). He appears to have isolated himself from his officers, and to have surrounded himself with administrative sycophants, who were loyal to him perhaps because he had appointed them beyond their rank, but were unable to solve problems, unfamiliar with the issues in the field, and as non-professionals and perceived toadies, despised by the veterinary officers. He clearly was confronted with a 'catch-22' administrative situation, and French does his best here to portray Neill's situation non-judgementally, probably even charitably. However, Col. Edgett, even though he too was a political animal, not universally liked by his colleagues, was able to put right within a few months most of the problems that Neill had failed to solve.

Neill must have been one of very few Canadian officers of his rank to relinquish his appointment. Recognition of his inadequacy and of the lack of respect of the officers of the C.A.V.C. may have contributed to any complicating mental problems, and to his resignation. However, one can only presume that Neill's departure, synchronized as it was with Capt. Frape's (see Note 10.7 below), may not have been entirely voluntary. More likely, it was planned and requested by a higher authority, at the least his direct superior, the Quartermaster-General, O.M.F.C., London; the *1918 Report, O.M.F.C.*, indicates "...it was decided to reorganize the Veterinary Services and an officer...was brought back from France and appointed Director..." Neill seems to have become a victim of his own political connections and good fortune. He lacked the administrative competence and leadership ability to meet the organizational challenges of the position, and to overcome the personal disrespect engendered among his subordinates by his being one of Sam Hughes' blatant political appointees. *Overseas Military Forces of Canada, 1918, p. 89.*

2. This photo is undated and none of the staff are positively identified. However, it was taken in late 1917 or early 1918, since Neill is a Brigadier-General. The Staff Sergeant on the right wearing the ribbon of the Meritorious Service Medal

probably is G.I. Brodie from Winnipeg, the only decorated N.C.O. at C.A.V.C. H.Q. (see later in Chapter 10). The two Staff Sergeants flanking Neill in the rear likely are D.H. Meers on the right, and J. Bailey on the left. The enlisted man on the left likely is Trooper H. Harrison, Neill's orderly. Fig. 10.2 may have been taken at the same time; it is in the same place - on the roof or outside stairs of the Headquarters on the third floor of Oxford Circus House in London.

3. Difficulties in communication between Canada, London, and France were by no means unique to the C.A.V.C. *Morton, 1982* and *Harris, 1988* describe the miscommunication and deliberate non-communication between Canadian Army commanders in England, and the commander of the Canadian Corps in France, related to their power struggle. Even at that level communications also were complicated by the question of what information passed directly to and from Canadian Corps, and what went via Imperial staff and command structures. Similar problems afflicted the Militia Department in Ottawa. At one point, Maj.-Gen. Willoughby Gwatkin, the Chief of General Staff in Ottawa, depended on newspaper reports to determine who commanded brigades and divisions in England and France *Harris, 1988, p. 107.*
4. There can be little doubt that Neill was not held in high regard by many of his officers in Europe.

T.C. Evans alluded to the internal politics of the C.A.V.C. when he explained to French his reasons for requesting a transfer from O.C. No. 1 C.V.H., Le Havre, to the Imperial Army Veterinary Corps at Abbeville, in April 1915, shortly after Neill became Director of Veterinary Services in London. "...disagreements with certain officers who were 'blessed' with strong political pull, intrigues, and other matters which would not make good reading for your work, but ...will eventually form a basis for a literary study that I shall publish later on, at my own expense, in Canada." [to our knowledge never published]. When he returned as O.C. No. 1 C.V.H. in September 1915, he "conducted a desultory correspondence with the Canadian D.V.S. in London in which I found it necessary to disagree with the present policy of administration as it affected No. 1 C.V.H....", and he requested a transfer to the field. *French Papers, MG30, E14, Vol. 1: 13 Feb. 1919, T.C. Evans to C. French.*

"Neill, who was quite content to remain in London, showing his ignorance and inability to administer the Service he commanded...the success of the C.A.V.C. was not due to any one officer stationed in England, but due to the combined co-operation of General Sir J. Moore, and Colonel A.E. Martin, R.A.V.C., and the senior and junior officers and men of the C.A.V.C., in France and Belgium.... Prior to 1917, chaos existed, due to inexperienced senior officers who were unable to impart any sound knowledge to their juniors, with the result that the latter did not hold them in respect... Neill was a politician, who flouted those in authority, for his own end". Elsewhere, "...selection of officers for senior appointments to the Corps, by political intervention, instead of by seniority and qualification, was no doubt responsible for the chaos..." *Tamblyn, Marginal comments, 1933.*

Savage made repeated derogatory references to Neill and the non-veterinarian N.C.O.s who he had commissioned as his staff officers. He commented [*27 Jan. 1918*] that "General Neill and his 2 staff captains [Frape and Denton?]...have been camping on us for some days. Know nothing, are anything but gentlemen and consume fabulous quantities of whiskey. How such blighters keep good jobs for so long is a question that a good Christian would not answer. Graft politics and inefficiency at the top!!" In his opinion, Neill was a "technical ignoramus" [*4 Feb. 1918*]. He refers to a colleague, who was apparently an alcoholic, as "...a technically helpless 'bum', drunken, dirty and conceited. Of course, considering who is running the C.A.V.C. he is not too bad" [*17 Mar. 1918*]. A year before Neill relinquished his command, Savage mentioned "Rumors of a big 'cleanup' in C.A.V.C. Would like to see Neill and Walsh go home: Frape and Primm [sic] lose their commissions!!" *Savage Diary, 22 Apr. 1917.*

However, Savage did not share Tamblyn's high regard for the upper echelons of the Imperial Service, for example, commenting that Moore "looks exactly like a butcher...and ignorant of clinical common sense. 'Keep your lines neat, stables painted and horses groomed, treatment follows in second place...Dipping vats no good or we would be using them.' No wonder the war is not over?**!! Mon Dieu!!" *Savage Diary, 1 Apr. 1917.*

5. Edgett and Tamblyn were trying to communicate, which makes the miscreant Wilson or Cutcliffe. Neill's correspondence was to the Administrative Veterinary Officer of the First Division (top p. 105), so Cutcliffe is implicated strongly.
6. The statistics indicate otherwise. We have no summary of the number of Other Ranks recognized, but of the 144 officers who served in the C.A.V.C., 14% (20) were Mentioned in Despatches, and 10% (15) were decorated (pp. 110-111). Based on French's Appendix C, which is probably incomplete, 10% (20) of the 208 Canadians who served in the Imperial Service are known to have been Mentioned in Despatches, and only a little over 4% (9) decorated. In contrast, across the Imperial Army Veterinary Corps as a whole, 33% (551) of the 1,668 officers were Mentioned in Despatches, and 23% (381) were decorated. Apparently, awards, honours and decorations were bestowed so freely on officers of the R.A.V.C. that it became known as the 'D.S.O. Corps' *'One of Them', 1920; Anon., Vet. Rec., 1921; Smith, 1927, p. 240.*

Officers of the Australian Army Veterinary Corps were also ill-rewarded. None received decorations until New Years 1917, and only 12% (15) of the 125 veterinary officers in that Corps had been decorated by war's end *Curson, 1933a; Whitfield, 1951.*

Does this lack of recognition of outstanding performance by other than British veterinary officers reflect the deprecating 'Imperial' attitude toward 'colonials' that officers of the C.A.V.C. perceived? Capt. E.M. Dixon, himself English, expressed his frustration at the lack of recognition when completing the form detailing the history of Canadian Mobile Veterinary Section No. 1 for the War Records Office. He filled in the space for 'List of Decorations...granted to Officers and Other Ranks...' with '**NIL?**' in black block letters over 2½ inches high and ¼ inch wide. *NAC RG9, III, D1, Vol. 4717, Folder 112, File 6.*

7. Captain A.E. Frape's military biography is described by French earlier in Chapter 10, and his C.E.F. record is summarized in Appendix A. In Canada, Frape resided in Kingston. His son, Tpr. Arthur Ernest Frape Jr., enlisted in the Royal Canadian Horse Artillery in October 1915, and subsequently was seconded to the C.A.V.C., where he served at No. 2 C.V.H. Shorncliffe, and No. 1 C.V.H. Le Havre, before it was discovered that he was a minor, in January 1917. He was transferred to C.A.V.C. Headquarters for about 6 months before being returned to Canada and discharged in July 1917.

   Capt. Frape relinquished his appointment as Assistant Director of Remounts and his functional, though not formal, role as Assistant Director Veterinary Services, on 12 March 1918, the same day that Neill resigned, and the same day that he was granted leave to Canada, where he was retained. Frape was discharged from the C.E.F. in Kingston, Ontario on 31 January 1919, and he retired on pension from the C.P.A.V.C. with the rank of Lieutenant on the same date. He was reported to have died in Toronto Ont. on 22 March 1956. *The Militia List 1 Jan. 1919; Canada Gazette, 22 March 1919; Frape, A.E., Service Record, CEF, NAC; Frape, A.E. Jr., Service Record, CEF, NAC.*

8. Edgett was a seaman prior to his engagement with the N.W.M.P. in April 1900 at the age of 22. He served as a teamster in Regina, Lethbridge and Macleod, and purchased his discharge from the force in November 1903. After graduating from O.V.C. he attempted to rejoin the R.N.W.M.P. in 1906 as a commissioned Veterinary Surgeon but was turned down. His military record is summarized in text and Appendices A and H. During 1916, he was placed on medical leave for over 4 months after a bout of influenza, and he was again hospitalized for a month in mid-1919, possibly again with influenza.

   Although Edgett apparently was allied with Neill in the minds of some officers, such as Tamblyn, this did not impair his ability to administer the C.A.V.C. in the long run. In civilian life he seems to have cultivated and exploited his Liberal Party connections to advance his career, and it is probable that he also was 'politically aware' as an ambitious army officer in a corps in which opportunities for promotion were scarce.

   Edgett seems to have worked his way up the ladder by a combination of competence and connections. There can be no question about his ultimate administrative ability. As French intimates, after he took charge in London following Neill's resignation, effective action was taken rapidly to mitigate or solve administrative problems and to remedy the lack of communication with and restore the confidence of veterinary officers in the C.A.V.C. at all levels in France. In several clear and well-thought-out memos and reports to the Quartermaster-General, O.M.F.C., he outlined the problems and proposed solutions. Among these was quarterly tours of the installations in France to learn about issues at the local level. This was quickly approved, and although only two such visits were made before the Armistice, they were clearly beneficial both to headquarters and the C.A.V.C. officers in France. They resulted in several succinct, constructive reports to the Q.M.G. O.M.F.C. suggesting steps that could be taken to improve matters at the Corps and individual level. These involved issues as small as having access to telephones and typewriters, as well as to motor transport and clerical help. Most of these were acted upon quickly. Savage, generally cynical about superiors, following Edgett's October 1918 visit thought that he was "full of enthusiasm for the corps. - wish he had had the job 3 years ago!!...really think he will do something. Hope so" *French Papers, NAC MG30, E14, Vol. 1: QMG.1b.21-2-69, Edgett, 3 June 1918, re Veterinary Officers and Canadian Forestry Corps; QMG.1b.31-1-17, Edgett, 13 June 1918, request for visit to France, with outcomes sought; V.6213, Edgett, 12 July 1918, to D.A. & Q.M.G. Canadian Corps re office staff etc.; QMG.1b 15 July 1918, Report of A.D.V.S. Headquarters O.M.F. of C. on Veterinary & Remount Matters in France; QMG.1b31-1-17, Edgett, 9 October 1918, Quarterly Progress Report, July, August, September, 1918; 29 October 1918, Col. Edgett's Report on Vet and Remount Matters in France. Savage Diary, 13 Oct. 1918.*

   Edgett returned to Canada in July, 1919 and separated from the C.A.V.C. In late 1919, he settled on a 'ranch' in Coldstream, B.C., near Vernon in the Okanagan Valley. Here he raised fruit, carried on veterinary practice, and later took on the Canadian Marconi Co. agency for the B.C. interior, selling radios. Edgett remained with the reorganized C.A.V.C. as a supernumerary Major, Section 11, British Columbia, or on the Reserve of Officers, until disbandment. He was active in local politics and community affairs, and twice ran for Parliament in the riding of Yale, in 1920 as an Independent soldier-farmer, against whom the Liberals did not field a candidate, and in 1925 as a Liberal; he was defeated in each attempt. In June, 1929, he was appointed Warden of the Federal Penitentiary in New Westminster, probably as a result of his political connections and experience in military command.

   In November 1931, after solicitations from the city, Edgett accepted the appointment of Chief of Police for the City of Vancouver, to revitalize the force. However, he seems to have interfered with the power that the mayor of the time had over internal police matters. After arbitrary reductions in his salary, derogatory public comments by the mayor, and a change in the membership in the Police Commission, Edgett, protesting rank injustice, was dismissed summarily upon the deciding vote of the mayor. He appears then to have turned his attention to business and community affairs up until his death at age 63, January 9, 1947, at which time he was manager of the Industrial Association of British Columbia. He was survived by his wife, two sons and two daughters; a third son, Flt. Lieut. George Edgett, was killed on a bombing raid in 1942. In his obituary, 'Charlie' Edgett was referred to as "a fair fruit grower and an average politician - but beyond compare" in recitation of the poems of William Henry Drummond. *Militia Lists, 1919-1939; Anon., Can. Vet. Rec., Vol. 1 No. 2, p. 74, 1920; Anon., 1929, 1932, 1933; Edgett, obit., Vancouver Province, Jan. 9, 1947; Edgett, obit., Can. J. Comp. Med., 1947; Edgett, C.E., Service Record, CEF, NAC; Gordon, Dec. 1992; Henderson, 1992.*

9. O.B.E. - Officer of Order of the British Empire, Capt. to Lieut.-Col., reward for conspicuous service, and for non-combatant military service, 259 issued to Canadian military in W.W. I; D.S.O. - Distinguished Service Order, reward to commissioned officers for meritorious and distinguished services in war, must previously have been Mentioned in Despatches, 710 issued to Canadians in W.W. I; M.C. - Military Cross, Warrant Officer to Capt., for gallant and distinguished service in action in time of war, 2,885 issued in W.W. I; M.M. - Military Medal, awarded to warrant officers, non-commissioned officers and men for individual acts of bravery, 12,345 to Canadians in W.W. I; D.C.M. - Distinguished Conduct Medal, awarded to non-commissioned officers and men for distinguished conduct in action in the field, 1,945 issued to Canadians in W.W. I; M.S.M. - Meritorious Service Medal, awarded to warrant and non-commissioned officers of the Canadian Permanent Force, discharged and pensioned after 21 years service, who possess the Long Service and Good Conduct Medal, 1,422 issued to Canadians for service in W.W. I; Mentioned in Despatches - 5,467 issued to Canadians in W.W. I. *Irwin, 1971.*

   Regrettably, no complete list is available of the C.A.V.C. Other Ranks who were recognized, though individuals are mentioned throughout the text. There is a list of honours and awards for the C.A.V.C. to about June 1918 which includes Other Ranks: O.B.E. [? not appropriate for man of this rank] - Tpr. A. Wetherell 11 Jun. 1918; Military Medal - S/Sgt. H.B. Kenner 13 Mar. 1918, Sgt. F.A. Scott 13 Mar. 1918; Meritorious Service Medal - C.S.M. A.J. Shirt 11 Nov. 1916, S/Sgt. G.L. Brodie 4 Jun. 1917, Sgt. G. Donaldson 17 Jun. 1918, S/Sgt. J.E. Gosselin 17 Jun. 1918, Sgt. W.F. James 17 Jun. 1918, Cpl. T.H. Southern 17 Jun. 1918; Mentioned in Despatches - Sgt. O.C. White 1 Jan. 1916, Sgt. Maj. A.J. Shirt 15 Jun. 1916, Sgt. F. Kendall 4 Jan. 1917, Sgt. E.G. Chudleigh 28 Dec. 1917, S/Sgt. H.H. Hatton 28 Dec. 1917, Cpl. C. Kelly 28 Dec. 1917, Vet. Sgt. F.G.C.C. Morgan 28 Dec. 1917, Pte. W. Taylor 28 Dec. 1917, Sgt. W.A. Walls 28 Dec. 1917, Sgt. J. Westbrook 28 Dec. 1917, S/Sgt. J.W. Johnstone 28 May 1918. *NAC, Unaccessioned, no locator: Canadian War Records Office - Historical Section, Summary of Historical Records of Units - Part IV - Honours and Awards C.A.V.C., 'A', 'B', 'D', 'E', 'G.'*

10. Robertson probably was the longest surviving member of the C.A.V.C. He practiced in Saskatchewan, retiring to British Columbia, where he died in 1985, at 96 years of age. *Barker & Crowley, 1989, p. 205.*

Chapter 11.

1. There is no estimate of the number of veterinarians in Canada 1914-1918. However, difficulty in recruiting veterinary officers suggests that the pool of suitable candidates was depleted by the absence of well over 200 men overseas; certainly it had a detrimental effect on availability of regulatory veterinarians *Cameron, 1942.* Note B.8 describes the dire effect of the war on veterinary manpower in the UK.
2. French himself fell into this category, having spent over 20 years in small animal practice before enlisting.
3. Appendix A lists 137 veterinarians and 7 non-veterinarians in the C.A.V.C. overseas. Appendix B lists 208 Canadians in the Imperial Army Veterinary Corps. A further 19 officers are indicated in Militia Lists as overseas in the C.A.V.C. or Imperial A.V.C. who are not found in these lists (see Appendix H). The reason for these discrepancies is not obvious.
4. This section sounds like 'the voice of experience' and presumably reflects French's personal impression, since he spent about 8 months at Shorncliffe as an inductee and then instructor.
5. Incredibly, at the beginning of the war, officers and men of the Imperial and the Canadian Army Veterinary Corps were armed only with swords. This resulted in several close calls with German troops for Imperial Mobile Veterinary Sections in forward areas in fall 1914. Consequently, officers and sergeants of both corps were armed with revolvers, and the men got rifles (note holstered carbine on horse in illustration on back cover). Since captive-bolt humane killers or other means of euthanasia were not part of a veterinary officer's kit at the beginning of the war, the Webley pistols, issued as 'instruments' to complete an officer's equipment, also provided a means of humane destruction of horses which could not be salvaged (see Appendix G). *NAC RG9, III, B1, Vol. 3382, File 1-52-45: Evans-Frape, 12 Oct./14 Oct, 1915; NAC RG9, III, Vol. 4717, Folder 112, File 10: 31 Mar. 1917, Saunders, C.G., C.W.R.O. Questionnaire, History of No. 1 C.V.H., Le Havre; Blenkinsop & Rainey, 1925, pp. 649-650.*
6. This was the second such draft, the first having occurred in March, 1915, though all but one of that group went to the Imperials (see Fig. 11.1). On 16 March, 1917, 14 men were gazetted as Lieutenants in the C.A.V.C. (H. Spearman, W.G.

Walks, A.C. Wagner, A.W. Hopkins, H.W. Simpson, D.J. McLellan, C.T. Beaven, W.F. Towill, J.B.A. Secord, J.D. Hogan, A.D. McAllister, R. Hanagan, E.L. Brown and W.T. Galbraith); none went to the Imperials. *NAC RG9, III, B1: Nominal Roll, Draft C.A.V.C., Military District 2, Toronto, Ont., 16 March 1917; Quarterly Militia List, July, 1917.*

Probably referring to two of these men, Savage said: "Two youths, graduates of this spring from Ontario Vety College, appear from Shorncliffe. One is posted to each half of hospital. I draw the boob; Doc [Richards] draws the good one....Young 'fella-me-lad' follows me round like a dog. Bit useless; says they had a rotten course at Toronto this year." *Savage Diary, 25, 26 July 1917.* On the other hand, he could be complimentary about a young graduate: "Lieut. Foreman is a capable chap...operating all day while I am officiating. He is a good little surgeon and has quite a few baddish cases too." *Savage Diary 17, 18 Oct. 1918.* Savage, only in his late '20s, seemed to have forgotten how professional competence is so much built on the opportunity to gain experience. He commented "2 new officers arrive from England. Youngsters of the usual sort - Toronto ?'14." He was Cornell '14 himself, and his army career was less than 2 years in duration at the time of the remark. *Savage Diary, 28 Dec. 1917.*

7. It is difficult to determine who were the French-Canadians to whom Neill refers. Sixty-seven men were gazetted as Lieutenants or Provisional Lieutenants during 1916; 11 joined the C.A.V.C., 37 joined the Imperial Army Veterinary Corps, and the remainder are not recorded as having proceeded overseas. Only four of the 67 were French-Canadian. Of the nine men who proceeded to England with the C.A.V.C. in the first 8 months of 1916, only one, Jean Biron, was French-Canadian, and he was a graduate of 1914, with several years' experience. Two of the other three French-Canadians gazetted in 1916 joined the Imperial Army Veterinary Corps; one is not recorded as having gone overseas. Although a number of French-Canadians served with distinction in the C.A.V.C. overseas, the remark may reveal anti-French-Canadian sentiment by Neill, whose upbringing in Protestant Orange Victoria County in rural Ontario likely would not have predisposed him to tolerance of francophones and Catholics. *The Militia List, July 1917.*

8. There were a few black students at the O.V.C. about the time of World War I, based on photographs in the O.V.C. Calendars of the era. A.L. Rooks, from Trinidad, one of two blacks in the 1916 graduation photo, may have been the 'coloured gentleman' who was rejected for service in the C.A.V.C. He is in the Militia List as a Provisional Lieutenant in the C.A.V.C., gazetted 22 July 1916, assigned to the Imperial Army Veterinary Corps. There is no record in the National Archives of Canada or in the British Public Records Office that he served in the C.E.F. or in the British Army, though he remained on the Militia List until 1921. These circumstances suggest that Rooks was accepted by the C.A.V.C. (N.P.A.M.) in Canada, and was intended to serve overseas. We have been unable to confirm the reasons for his failure to do so, or whether it was in fact he who was rejected by Neill for a commission in the C.A.V.C. (O.M.F.C.), after having been turned down also by the Imperial A.V.C. In 1921, Rooks was traced to the British West Indies in the course of reorganization of the C.A.V.C, and he then was placed on the Retired List, probably without ever seeing 'active' service. *Calendar, Ontario Veterinary College, 1916-1917; Graduates of Ontario Veterinary College, 1916, Composite Class Photograph, C.A.V. Barker Museum; Militia List, January 1917; NAC RG24, Vol. 6532, File HQ 621-1-4 v. 1: 2 Mar. 1921, Taschereau, Memo, Reorganization of C.A.V.C. M.D. No 2; M.J. Relf, pers. com., 1999.*

Selection of members of the C.E.F. was racist in effect, if not in official policy. Most battalion commanders simply refused to admit blacks who applied to enlist *Ruck, 1986, pp. 11-20.* Sir Sam Hughes, when challenged regarding the extreme difficulty blacks were experiencing in enlisting, in 1915 ordered that "coloured men are to be allowed to enlist in any battalion", but his order was ignored *Ruck, 1986, pp. 15-16, 109.* Major-General Willoughby Gwatkin, Chief of General Staff wrote an overtly racist 'Memorandum on the enlistment of negroes in the Canadian Expeditionary Force', dated 13 March 1916. In it he declared "...the civilized negroe is vain and imitative;...not likely to make a good fighter;...the average white man will not associate with him on terms of equality...in the firing line, there is no place for a black battalion", though he did recommend the formation of one or more segregated labour battalions. In another communication, he stated "...would Canadian Negroes make good fighting men? I do not think so." *see Ruck, 1986, pp. 14, 114.* Lieut.-Col. W.H. Allen, O.C. 106th Battalion from Nova Scotia, which did admit blacks, said of them "Neither my men nor myself, would care to sleep alongside them, or to eat with them, especially in warm weather..." *Ruck, 1986, p. 112.* East Indians and Japanese were also excluded initially from enlisting in British Columbia, where most lived, although some Japanese were later recruited *Walker, 1989.* Racial discrimination seems not to have extended so extensively to Amerindians, many of whom enlisted, with some gaining commissions; several served as enlisted men in the C.A.V.C. (see p. 39) *Morton, 1993, pp. 78, 99.* However, Amerindians also often were shunted to the Forestry Corps, or to other labour units, rather than into combat. And they, too, disliked associating with blacks *Walker, 1989.*

Neill's apparent refusal to admit a black to the C.A.V.C., when the need for veterinary officers was most desperate, was characteristic of the racism prevailing in the C.E.F, which only reflected attitudes and practices in Canadian society at large *Walker, 1989.* Appointment of a black officer would have been ground-breaking. Reportedly, only a single black was commissioned in the entire Imperial Forces, Capt. W.A. White, Chaplain of No. 2 Construction Battalion, C.E.F., the black labour battalion, all of the other officers of which were white *Ruck, 1986, pp. 8, 21-22; Walker, 1989.*

9. These letters were indeed vigorous. Evans was highly vexed by the fact that Major F.A. Daigneault strongly recommended for a commission Vet. Sgt. F.B. Kendall, No. 2 C.M.V.S., formerly of the firm Kendall Brothers Ltd., Teaming Contractors, Montreal. Daigneault stated that to his knowledge, Kendall had "...done a great deal of Veterinary practice in Montreal, and very successfully". Evans characterized this as "A stupid letter from a graduate veterinarian". Capt. Reginald Vickers, Kendall's O.C. at the time, endorsed his application with the notation "If this order results in giving an 'empiric' the same powers as a graduate veterinary surgeon possesses in the army, I recommend this man under protest - for this reason only". *French Papers, NAC MG30, E14, Vol. 1: T.C. Evans to A.B. Cutcliffe, 13 May 1918; F.A. Daigneault to O.C. No. 2 C.M.V.S., 15 May 1918; T.C. Evans to A.D.V.S. Canadian Corps, 17 May 1918, annotated by Cutcliffe 18 May 1918; Kendall Application for Commission, 17 May 1918; A.B. Cutcliffe to T.C. Evans, 18 May 1918; T.C. Evans to unknown, 18 June 1918.*

   At the same time, Major E.C. Thurston at Witley recommended the commissioning of Gnr. C.H. Snellson. A Veterinary Sergeant in the U.S. Army 1913-1916, he had taken a one-year course at the U.S. Army Veterinary Sergeants' School, Fort Raley, Kansas. Several other "qualified Veterinary Surgeons" serving in the Canadian Reserve Artillery, Witley, were also put forward as candidates for C.A.V.C. commissions. Gnr. W.W. Molthop, a graduate of Manhattan State Agricultural College [?Kansas] with "...10 years...Bar Zee Ranch, Texas"; S. Sgt. J. Moon, "passed the majority of examinations for M.R.C.V.S., Edinburgh"; Gnr. J.R. Everitt, "three years practice with veterinary, Brandon, Man."; and Gnr. J.R. Donahue, "Graduate of Ontario Veterinary College, holding certificate". A J.R. Donahue did graduate from O.V.C. in 1896, but none of these men appear in Appendices A or B. *NAC RG9, III, B1, Vol. 3380, file 0-17-45: A/D.A.A.G. Canadian Troops, Witley, to A.D.V.S., 27 Apr. 1918; Thurston, E.C. to A.D.V.S., 29 Apr. 1918.*

   See *Evans & Barker, 1976* for insight into the on-going conflict between graduate veterinarians and 'quacks' or 'empirics' as the profession matured and established its legitimacy.

10. Possibly the notorious London-based Ontario Veterinary Correspondence School *Evans & Barker, 1976, pp. 127-130.*
11. Lieut. Alexander Macintosh C.A.V.C. was court-martialed in 1918 for being absent without leave and for passing dishonoured cheques, and in 1919 he was court-martialed and dismissed from the service for falsely stating that he was M.R.C.V.S. and a graduate from the Royal (Dick) Veterinary College, Edinburgh. He is found in neither Appendix A nor D, but his Record of Court Martial is available. *NAC Records of Courts Martial, File 9568-13-49.*
12. Most C.A.V.C. veterinary officers who enlisted from 1913 on have the rank of Lieutenant in the Militia List, despite the rank accorded them overseas; see Note 2.1.
13. This policy explains reference to Lieutenants in Appendix A, at some points in the text and figures, and in Savage's diary, relating to individuals commissioned late in the war.
14. Actually 4 officers were sentenced to dismissal after courts martial related to drunkenness, but in one case the sentence was commuted. See Note 6.9.
15. Based on Savage's comments (see Note 10.4), this officer may have been Lieut.-Col. F.A. Walsh, who, like Neill, came from Militia Division 3. Gazetted in the Militia List as a Lieutenant in the C.A.V.C. only on 1 May, 1914, below officers such as Tamblyn, Edgett, Cutcliffe, Daigneault and Souillard who also went overseas early, he rose particularly rapidly to a staff position, then went into a decline in rank and responsibility that paralleled that of the Shorncliffe Area, where he spent the last half of the war, having been injured accidentally in France. Following review of his case, he relinquished his appointment and was returned to Canada as a surplus officer in October, 1918. There was a deliberate policy of weeding out surplus officers and political appointees during the last half of the war. By January 1918, 476 Canadian army officers had been persuaded to revert in rank, with adverse reports on some. *Appendix A; Chapter 5; Militia List, March, 1915; Morton, 1982, pp. 150-151; Savage Diary, 22 Apr. 1917; Walsh, F., Service Record, CEF, NAC.*
16. Of the 137 veterinarians in Appendix A, 67% were Canadian born (92 men, 18% of whom were French-Canadian, based on name and place of birth); 30% were born in the United Kingdom, its colonies and other Dominions; 4% were born in the USA. This almost exactly parallels the distribution by birth of officers in the First Canadian Contingent (2/3 Canadian-born, 29% British-born; *Duguid, 1938, p. 52*). The Ontario Veterinary College had graduated 64%; Laval University (l'Ecole vétérinaire française de Montréal, its successor, l'Ecole de Médecine comparée et de Science vétérinaire de Montréal, with one from the unrelated Ecole vétérinaire du Québec) 12%; McGill University 7%; and other universities in the USA, the UK and Australia 17%.
17. Recruitment of Canadians into the Army Veterinary Corps is described by *Duguid, 1938, pp. 164-165.* His count was 190 Canadians so commissioned over the four years of the war. See Note 11.3 and notes to Appendix B.

Chapter 12.

1. French seems not to have been aware of a second officer who died following being invalided back to Canada. Capt. J.B.A. Secord died on 4 August 1918 of leukemia diagnosed in mid 1917 while he was posted to C.V.H. No. 2, Shorncliffe. *Secord, J.B.A., Service Record, CEF, NAC.*

2. Places of interment recorded by the Commonwealth War Graves Commission are: C.W. Baker, Nunhead Cemetery, England; E.M. Dixon, Les Baraques Military Cemetery, France; F.D. Early, Brampton Cemetery, Brampton, Ontario; T.A. Girling, Belgrade Cemetery, Namur, Belgium; B.R. Poole, Faubourg d'Amiens Cemetery, France; T.Z. Woods, Lijssenhoek Military Cemetery, Belgium *Christie, 1988.*
3. The graduates of the O.V.C. among these men, along with others of the college who died in The Great War, were memorialized on a tablet that was unveiled in the Assembly Hall of the Ontario Veterinary College, Toronto, on 31 March 1920 *Anon., Can Vet Rec. Vol. 1, No. 1, p. 41, 1920.* The O.V.C. moved to Guelph in 1922, and after World War II, the following names of World War I casualties were inscribed inside the doorway of the MacNabb Memorial Library: Charles William Baker, John Leonard Clarke, Charles Cranston Corbett, Theodore Augustus Girling, William Huston, William John Kee, Gerald James O'Brien, Bernard Routh Poole, Thomas Zachary Woods, and Thomas Gregor Brodie M.D. (faculty). *Gattinger, 1962, p. 154.*
4. Based on his uniform, this photo is c.1907-1911, since Woods is a Veterinary-Lieutenant, in the 'undress' blue patrol jacket universal, with the white shoulder straps and wearing the cap and collar badges of the Canadian Army Service Corps *Ross & Chartrand 1977, pp. 17, 27, 44-45,* to which he was attached. The fact that he is wearing C.A.S.C. uniform and badges, rather than those of the Army Veterinary Department, introduced in 1907, suggests that the latter were not widely worn, and that previous custom persisted in the Regimental Veterinary Service (see pp. 187-189, and Note v-xiii.1). He is wearing his service medals, rather than ribbons, which is unusual for 'undress' uniform. They are, on the left, the North West Canada 1885 Medal with clasp, and on the right, the Queen's South Africa Medal with 4 clasps. Woods joined the C.A.V.C., formed in 1910, in 1911, at which time he would have adopted C.A.V.C. uniform and insignia.
5. Early wears the diamond distinguishing patch (upper half red, lower green) for Lord Strathcona's Horse (R.C.), of which he was V.O. Girling wears the blue patch of a 2nd Canadian Division Officer *Nicholson, 1962, Appendix G.*
6. The influenza pandemic, caused by a particularly virulent strain of the virus, struck worldwide in three waves between spring 1918 and 1920. More severe than typical influenza, the 'Spanish Flu' had a relatively high mortality rate, with unusual impact on the segment of the population 20-40 years of age *McGrew, 1985.* It struck unpredictably, and there was no effective treatment. Care-givers assumed a considerable risk of becoming infected; fear, and an air of fatalism with respect to contracting the disease, pervaded society. *Crosby, 1989* describes the pandemic from an American perspective, while *Pettigrew, 1983* documents its impact on Canada, where it caused monumental medical and social upheaval, leaving no family untouched.

   It "produced a disease that turned people the color of wet ashes and drowned them in the fluid of their own bodies, ...inspired names like the 'purple death'" *Crosby, 1989, p. 295* due to the profound cyanosis caused by the hypoxia resulting from viral pneumonia. *Kilbourne, 1987, p. 15* cites Grist, 1979 "...you can begin to see the cyanosis extending from the ears and spreading over the face... It is only a matter of a few hours then until death comes, and it is simply a struggle for air until they suffocate. It is horrible...", and Morton, 1973 "They all had pneumonia. We knew those whose feet turned black wouldn't live".

   While its impact varied considerably, figures of 20-40% of the population falling ill, and 1-2% of those dying, reflect the order of magnitude of its effect. Excess mortality in the U.S.A. during the ten months at the peak of the epidemic was over 500,000 people, while world-wide mortality likely was much greater than 20 million. Over 9 million man-days were lost to influenza by the American Army in 1918, and for every 100 American soldiers dying in battle that year, 80 more died of influenza *Crosby, 1989, pp. 203-207.* Between September 9 and December 12 1918, during the particularly severe second wave of the pandemic, over 10,000 of the 61,000 troops in Canada were stricken, and among the men in the C.E.F. overseas, there were almost 46,000 cases of flu *Pettigrew, 1983, p. 9.*

   Savage recorded the personal impact of influenza. It was rumored that so many civilians in Le Havre were dying that they were being buried in common graves at night, and he described the military funeral in October 1918 of one of his men from C.V.H. No. 1 who had died of "the flue". His mother died of pneumonia, likely due to influenza, in Montreal in October 1918. Savage learned of her death just before the Armistice, and he related his guilt at having left her to go overseas. *Savage Diary, 27, 30 Oct., 25 Nov. 1918.*
7. Girling died of influenza at age 43, after about 2weeks of illness, leaving a wife and family in Canada. Capt. D.J. McLellan, one of many with 'the flu' in the same hospital at the time, recalled making Girling's acquaintance only 2 or 3 days before he died *McLellan, 1981.* Born in Huddersfield England in 1876, he graduated with the Gold Medal from the O.V.C. in 1904, and entered practice in Saskatoon when it was the end of the rail line. From 1908-1911 Girling served as a Veterinary-Lieutenant with the 22nd Light Horse, but did not appear on the Militia List again until he was commissioned Lieutenant, gazetted 1 September, 1914. He became Veterinary Inspector for the Saskatoon Board of Health in 1912, and contributed significantly to elevating standards of community public health.

   A handwritten letter from Girling, dated 20th November, 1914, and directed to M.D. No.10, Winnipeg, confirmed his telegraphed affirmative response to an invitation to volunteer for overseas, and indicated that "indeed, I volunteered at the opening of the war". He stated "...I could easily recruit a few good men here for the A.V.C. if any are needed." *NAC RG24, Vol, 4593, File 20-2-29.* He left for Europe in November 1915; his service record is summarized in Appendices A and H. He was well-liked and respected; had he lived another few weeks, he would have appeared in Fig. 7.3.

Girling's poetic work "...remains in well-deserved oblivion, along with most other poetry of the period, of which it is a typical example", although his poems "...give us a flavour of the war seen though the eyes of a patriotic Canadian veterinary officer...serving close to the front, doing his bit for his country" *Dukes & Prescott, 1991.* Never-the-less, his book of poems saw two editions, the second, of 66 pages, being published in November, 1918 *Girling, 1918. Evans, 1921*, promoting sales of the book by Girling's widow, pointed out how evocative his poems were of the conditions under which the horses worked in war. 'Dumb Heroes', found here on the back cover, was included with Chapter 12 by French.

Chapter 13.

1. Lieut.-Col. W.J. Neill, O.i.C., Remounts, for the First Contingent, C.E.F., sought three types of horses, all 5-8 years old: riding horses, 15-16 hands, 1000-1150 lbs; artillery horses 15-16 hands, 1050-1250 lbs; and draft horses 15.2-16 hands, 1250-1400 lbs; bay, brown, black, chestnut, blue roan, red roan, "no greys"; "sound in wind and limb, and free from all blemishes". *NAC RG24, Vol. 4262, File 77-1-1: W.J. Neill, correspondence re remount purchases, 22 August 1914.*

   Remounts for World War I were predominantly light draft horses (~20:1, according to *Moore, 1921, p. 44*) and pack horses, with many mules employed, and many fewer horses of riding or cavalry type. Some heavy draft horses of Shire and Clydesdale type were used in hauling siege guns and other very heavy loads. But they proved troublesome and prone to breakdown on account of high feed requirements, predisposition to respiratory disease and debility under arduous conditions, and foot and leg problems associated with the effects of moisture and mud on the haired or 'feathered' lower limbs. Percherons, being clean-legged and smaller, were viewed more favourably as heavy draft animals. The light draft or gun horse was required to be capable of hauling 1200 lb. for 20 miles/day, walk at 3 mph, and trot at 6 mph. Examples were tram horses, at the time a disappearing type, due to the advent of motorized public transport. As a result of her large and varied horse population, and the heavy demand, which could not be met readily by other countries, the U.S.A. became the main source of remounts. *Moore, 1921, pp. 98-145.*

2. French glosses over a hugely important veterinary issue of World War I, although one in which the C.A.V.C. had minor involvement, other than in the First Contingent. That was preventative medicine related to procurement and transportation by rail and ship to England and Europe of hundreds of thousands of horses and mules from North and South America with minimal losses due to disease and debility. *Blenkinsop & Rainey, 1925* devote over 75 pages to discussion of veterinary issues related to procurement and transport of remounts, on many of which are described modifications to the physical facilities and management of horses at remount depots in Montreal and Toronto, as well as in the USA. Transportation-related 'shipping fever' is described, as are contagious diseases predisposed by mixing animals from various sources under crowded, stressful conditions with, in many cases, suboptimal feeding, housing and sanitation.

   Twenty-two Canadian and American practitioners were contracted, and Dr. David Warnock of Alberta was commissioned in the Imperial Army with the British Remount Commission as Chief Veterinary Officer and later O.C., Lachine Remount Depot, Montréal *Love, c. 1965, pp. 24-25.* However, the operation was overwhelmingly 'Imperial'; 40 British civilian veterinarians were imported to North America, and the administrative and executive military structure was comprised entirely of Army Veterinary Corps officers *Blenkinsop & Rainey, 1925, pp. 450-507, 723-742.* Although one finds reference to members of the C.A.V.C. or Regimental Veterinary Service, such as Vet.-Lieut.-Col. A.W. Harris and Vet.-Lieut. P.E. Pallister of Ottawa, procuring remounts, this must have been in a private capacity (see Note H.10). The C.A.V.C. seems not to have been involved in any official way in the operations of the British Remount Commission in Canada, other than Brig.-Gen. Neill's 1917 foray to promote the remount supply. It seems not to have occurred to the Imperials that 'colonial' veterinary officers might have something to contribute to the operation on their home turf.

3. This action was taken after Lieut.-Col. Edgett's first tour of C.A.V.C. facilities in France, in response to well-founded complaints that the class of horses assigned to Canadian cavalry officers was substandard. The partial resolution of this problem exemplifies Edgett's capacity to take effective action. *French Papers, MG30, E14: 15 July 1918, Report of A.D.V.S. Headquarters, O.M.F.C. on Veterinary and Remount Matters in France.*

4. Moore described the mule as the "hero of the late World War", and "as indispensable to War as a Commander of the Forces". Mules were acquired as heavy draft, light draft and pack transport types. *Moore, 1921, p. 135.*

5. L-r: Gnr. Tom Fieldhouse, Ptes. Gerry St. Soucy, Frank Barker, Jackson, Neill, Brown, Gnr. Weaver.

6. Tamblyn has an alternative, at best immodest, at worst self-serving, suggestion that this paragraph be replaced with material that reflects his personal rivalry with or dislike of Edgett. That this is his only editorial suggestion of substance speaks something for the general accuracy of French's manuscript. However, Tamblyn's arrogant self-assurance in making this substitution suggests that French was wrong to credit Edgett with the disposal of the Canadian horses to Belgium.

   "The greatest piece of work performed by Lieut.-Colonel Tamblyn was effected after his appointment as D.D.V.S.

(Can.) Canadian Section, G.H.Q. It was Tamblyn that finally settled with the Belgian Authorities (after a two week conference at Brussels) the question of the sale of all Canadian horses in France and Belgium. This officer also completed and carried out all arrangements for the disposal of these animals, which netted the Canadian Government close on $6,000,000...

It was certainly a great success, and a feather in Tamblyn's cap, as an Administrative Officer, for his action in this work speeded up the demobilization of the Canadian Corps...

An instance of Tamblyn's ability in administrative work was demonstrated in the care of the Can. Cavalry Brigade horses. He was instructed to take over the horses of the Cavalry Brigade at the earliest possible date; working all night on the matter...; action, without red tape, was the responsible factor in this piece of work.

Another instance of Tamblyn's sagacity was brought to notice, when Viscount Hendecourt requested that a certain pony be given the Crown Prince Leopold...Tamblyn was instructed on no account to hand the pony over...when approached later...he informed the Viscount that the Prince could have the pony and any other animal he took a fancy to...This little gift was responsible for the sale of the Canadian horses...for Viscount Hendecourt had the trump card in his hand to accept or reject our animals, so that a $15.00 pony netted the Canadian Government over $6,000,000. Sound judgement to say the least."*Tamblyn, Marginal comments, 1933.*

Although Panet concurred on the wisdom of the transaction, his letter gives no clue as to who consummated it *NAC MG30, E100, Vol. 38, File 173: 30 April, 1919, Minutes of the Council O.M.F.C.*

In *The Horse in War*, Tamblyn also referred to the sale of the Canadian horses to Belgium. He stated that their physical fitness and freedom from disease was "a feather in the caps of the Canadian troops who were responsible for their care". And he assuaged fears as to their fate (unstated, but undoubtedly related to the habit on the Continent of consuming horseflesh). "Many statements have been made as to their disposal, but I can assure readers that most of them found fitting homes. These were not rest homes entirely, for their labour was not over, and their task of assisting the re-establishment of Belgium was a very important one." *Tamblyn, c.1932, p. 32.*

Chapter 14.

1. Savage, with the 11th Brigade C.F.A., Canadian 3rd Division facing Vimy Ridge at the time, was battling rampant mange by clipping and washing with lime-sulphur under arduous winter conditions. New clipper blades could not be supplied by Ordnance, and equipment for sharpening, and quicklime, were difficult to obtain. All awaited an outbreak of pneumonia due to clipping and washing under in winter, with water troughs often frozen, contagious aphthous stomatitis breaking out, and German planes overhead frequently. On 23 January 1917, he recorded that he was ordered to continue clipping by Capt. Tamblyn, the A.D.V.S., in spite of conditions, and wrote "Hope we have a lot of pneumonia as a result". On the 29th of January, he reported a horse dead from eating a chunk of blanket, and another from the cold. "Old horses can't stand clipping in this weather without cover. However, 'Orders is orders'. Told both the C.R.A. and A.D.V.S. that we would kill a lot by clipping and scrubbing if they insisted on it, and here come the proofs". On the 30th, "Another horse dead!...More have died this week than in previous 6 months, proving the correctness of my assertions to the 'Brass Hats'...Capt. Tamblyn around in A.M. Stuck it into him." Friday Feb. 2, "...A.D.V.S....is now convinced of 'unwisdom' of clipping and scrubbing in this weather. Is going to give." *Savage Diary, 15 Dec. 1916-2 Feb. 1917.*
2. 'Mud fever' is a term that was applied to horses with dermatophilosis, greasy heal, or leptospirosis. In this instance, it probably refers to greasy heal, a painful seborrheic dermatitis on the back of the pastern of horses required to use wet standings. *Blood & Studdert, 1988, p. 596.*
3. 'Scratches' are the excoriations across the back of the pastern of a horse in the early stages of developing greasy heal; they are very painful, and cause severe lameness. *Blood & Studdert, 1988, p. 818.*
4. These figures, drawn by Tamblyn, appear also in his book, *The Horse in War*. *Tamblyn, c.1932, p. 20.*

Chapter 15.

1. This chapter as published has been abridged, omitting extensive lists of Canadian donors to the various animal aid societies, and a number of letters that were included in French's manuscript, to and from C.A.V.C. Headquarters and other units, regarding the disposition or otherwise of charitable donations. Those retained preserve the gist and tone of the correspondence.

   This chapter was published in a similar form in *The Canadian Veterinary Record* (in three parts: *French, C., 1922, 1923a*). The first part was republished in the *Can. Vet. J., Vol. 26, pp. 254-256, 1986.*

   Tamblyn comments: "Why wash dirty linen? Why not confine one's remarks to simple acknowledgment? e.g....", and he proceeds to suggest that the chapter be reduced to a single paragraph naming the charitable organizations, summarizing the purposes to which donations were put, and giving the approximate total amount of money collected. *Tamblyn, Marginal comments, 1933.*

2. At this point in the original, there is a list of over 100 individual and group donors to the Blue Cross Fund, many with mailing addresses. *NAC MG30, E14, Vol. 2, Folder 6, Ch. 16.*
3. Mrs. A.R. Benson, Secretary, wrote to Lieut.-Col. Tamblyn "Just to think that we have sent over $3000 to the Blue Cross and I would dearly have loved to see it go to our Canadian vets." *NAC MG30, E14, Vol. 2, Folder 6, Ch. 16.*
4. The original has an anonymous marginal note here, "Let it drop", possibly made by Tamblyn, suggesting that the tone of French's comments was considered vexatious.
5. The scope of R.S.P.C.A. interactions with the Imperial Army Veterinary Corps is summarized in *Blenkinsop & Rainey, 1925, pp. 56-58.* Those authors also allude briefly to the rivalry between the R.S.P.C.A. and the Blue Cross Fund of the Dumb Friend's League. They use a somewhat disparaging tone when referring to the latter, who "...were happy in their title of 'Blue Cross', which was erroneously considered by the public as bearing the same relationship to the Army Veterinary Services as the 'Red Cross' bore to the Army Medical Services".
6. A list of over 40 Canadian subscribers to the R.S.P.C.A. is included with the original at this point, along with the full text of a letter from the R.S.P.C.A. to French, dated 25 October, 1918, responding to his query for information on R.S.P.C.A. support for the C.A.V.C. There is a peevish allusion to the Blue Cross Fund: "Very possibly it may be that while they have got the support we have done the work". French, in the original, then goes on to comment further on the politics of C.A.V.C. support from the humane societies. *NAC MG30, E14, Vol. 2, Folder 6, Ch. 16.*
7. A letter of 24 April, 1917 from Neill to the R.S.P.C.A, thanking them for their efforts is found here in the original. *NAC MG30, E14, Vol. 2, Folder 6, Ch. 16.*
8. A list of officers of the Society, and a list of over 80 individuals and groups donating money are included here in the original. *NAC MG30, E14, Vol. 2, Folder 6, Ch. 16.*
9. Letters to and from Neill, dated late September and early October 1916, relating to this matter, are found here in the original. *NAC MG30, E14, Vol. 2, Folder 6, Ch. 16.*
10. The officers of the Fund, and a list of over 250 donors, are found here in the original. *NAC MG30, E14, Vol. 2, Folder 6, Ch. 16.*
11. Excerpts from over 20 letters to and from Lady Meredith, Montreal; Neill and Frape in London; the Quartermaster-General, O.M.F.C., London; the Bank of Montreal, London; the Adjutant-General, O.M.F.C., London; and to Cutcliffe in France, Walsh at Shorncliffe, and Stedman at Witley accompany the original at this point, along with some comments by French. It is not clear from the pagination whether or not these were intended to be part of the chapter.

    But they are revealing. In October 1917, Neill referred to the possible use of this money to offset the costs of preparation of the History of the C.A.V.C., which topic French stated Neill had broached with him about that time. Lady Meredith did not agree to this use of the money; it was for "comforts for the horses". Neill promised to apply it to that purpose, but the only disbursement he made against the account in the Bank of Montreal was for pocket cases, tooth rasps, magnifying glasses and protective boots and knee caps for a horse, purchased from Arnold and Sons, London. The pocket cases were sent by Neill in December 1917 as Christmas gifts to Cutcliffe (for the D.A.D.V.S.s in France), Walsh and Stedman; the rasps went to Cutcliffe, presumably for legitimate use. There is no record of what happened to the horse boots and knee caps, which, as a single set, may have been appropriated by Neill himself. French, in referring to this episode, commented that "...his disposal of the articles purchased...is open to criticism...The expenditure cannot be considered to have been altogether a judicious one.", and he noted that Neill did not credit the Purple Cross Fund, causing the articles to appear as personal gifts.

    French then revealed that he wrote to Lady Meredith after the Armistice, asking her to reconsider her refusal to have the Fund applied to the C.A.V.C. History, provided "...that all profits that might accrue should be turned over to ...Humane Society...". She acceded to this request, and French, at the time clearly anticipating publication, described an arrangement whereby "the sale of the book has been placed in the hands of the said Society (the Canadian Society for Prevention of Cruelty to Animals), into whose coffers all the money derived therefrom will go."

Chapter 16.

1. See *Blenkinsop & Rainey, 1925, pp. 509-546* for a full discussion of disease problems encountered by the Imperial forces. They were: debility brought on by overwork, malnutrition, exposure and bad management; pneumonia; glanders; mange; ringworm; ophthalmia; necrotic dermatitis; ulcerative lymphangitis; epizootic lymphangitis; contagious stomatitis; battle casualties; and accidental injuries. Battle casualties were, in comparison with other problems, quite low.

    It is surprising that laminitis, inflammation of the wall of the foot, where the hoof is joined to the underlying tissue, was not listed. Fig. 16.7 and Talmage's paintings of horses standing in foot-baths or pools (See Note v-xiii.2) suggest that the problem did occur, but it is not mentioned by French. *Blenkinsop & Rainey* do not cite laminitis as a problem on the western Front, though it did occur elsewhere.
2. 'Thrush', as it refers to the hoof of the horse, is a chronic disease of the horn on the sole, in which it softens, breaks down,

and gives off a foul odor. *Blood & Studdert, 1988, p. 915.*

3. Pustular stomatitis was probably horsepox; see contagious stomatitis, Appendix F.
4. Ulcerative cellulitis, also known as ulcerative lymphangitis, is caused by *Corynebacterium pseudotuberculosis*. Infection in the lymphatic vessels of the lower limbs causes skin ulcers which exude green pus. The etiology was in dispute for much of the war.

   It must be differentiated from epizootic lymphangitis, or pseudoglanders, also cited as a problem by *Blenkinsop & Rainey*. It is caused by the yeast *Histoplasma farciminosum*, and, while significant in its own right, was also important because of its resemblance to glanders. *Blood & Studdert, 1988, pp. 332, 546.*
5. Periodic ophthalmia is a recurrent, progressive inflammatory disease of the eyes, causing conjunctivitis and endophthalmitis, usually resulting in blindness. It probably is caused by infection with *Leptospira* bacteria, which are associated with damp ground and alkaline water, abundant on the Western Front. *Blood & Studdert, 1988, p. 645.*

   Iodine therapy would be destructive of tissue, not therapeutic, which Savage recognized. "By compulsory injection of Lugol's sol'n, it [Imperial Army Veterinary Corps] ruins hundreds of eyes daily." *Savage Diary, 23 June 1918.*
6. For a more extensive description of poison gases and their effects, see *Henry, 1935* and *Bryden, 1989.*
7. Alfred D. Savage was a Montreal native who went west as a young man, working on a ranch before returning to complete a B.S.A. in Animal Husbandry in 1911 at Macdonald College, McGill University, Montreal. He graduated D.V.M. from Cornell University in 1914, and was on the faculty at Macdonald College until going overseas in the C.A.V.C. in 1916.

   Following a stint with the artillery at the front, he became the senior practicing veterinary officer at No. 1 C.V.H. after Capt. S.C. Richards' promotion to O.C. in August 1917, and remained so until the hospital closed after the war. Most C.A.V.C. officers proceeding through Le Havre for training before going to the front during the last 20 months of the war fell under his critical gaze, if not his tutelage. His diary illuminates and provides penetrating insights into the life of a veterinary officer at the front and at No. 1 C.V.H.

   Savage was widely competent, and although later he was best known as a bacteriologist and pathologist, in the army, and for a time after, anesthesia and surgery were his forté. His contributions to this chapter reflect some of those skills, but in his diary he also recounts performing hundreds of other surgical procedures, including exploration of gunshot and shrapnel wounds; draining hematomas, and abscesses due to strangles and other causes; removal of tumors; and especially neurectomies. Neurectomy involves cutting the sensory nerves to portions of the foot in which pain is arising, causing lameness. It is symptomatic treatment, justifiable only to salvage an animal for use when the cause of the pain is untreatable, but will not progress to a state which could be considered inhumane. Savage designed a combined neurectomy hook and knife, to isolate and sever the sensory nerve. He had it manufactured by the firm of Arnold and Son, London, and in September 1918 published a paper on the design in *The Veterinary Journal Vol. 74, No. 9.*

   After the war Piché considered that "the efficiency of this officer is of the highest standard...well worth going to a great deal of trouble to secure", but Savage declined to serve in the C.A.V.C. except in the eventuality of hostilities. *NAC RG24, Vol. 4482, File 42-1-1 v. 1: 10 Nov. 1920, letter, Piché to Cape.*

   He returned to Macdonald College in 1919, then joined the Faculty of the Manitoba Agricultural College in 1921, as Director of the Bacteriology Department. In 1927-28 he attended the Royal (Dick) Veterinary College, Edinburgh, where he qualified M.R.C.V.S. He returned to Manitoba, marrying his wife Mary Norquay in 1929. He became Dean of Agriculture at the University of Manitoba in 1933, but resigned in 1938 to become Professor of Bacteriology and Animal Pathology, and the Provincial Veterinary Pathologist, a post which he retained until he retired in 1964. He served on the editorial boards of *The Canadian Veterinary Record* and the *Canadian Journal of Comparative Medicine*. Savage was the President of the Veterinary Association of Manitoba in 1924, and of the Canadian Veterinary Medical Association in 1951-52. He became F.R.C.V.S. in 1963 for meritorious contributions to learning, reflecting his numerous scientific publications. Savage died in 1970; he was inducted posthumously into the Canadian Agricultural Hall of Fame in 1978. *Savage Diary, 1916 - 1918; Anon., Vet. Digest. Vol. 2, pp. 118-119, 1940; Anon., Can. Vet. J., Vol. 4, No. 11, pp. xix-xx, 1963; Evans & Barker 1976, pp. 124, 212; Crowley and Barker, 1989, pp. 206-207.*
8. A collection of projectiles and shell fragments removed surgically from horses by Capt. A.E. Cameron is described and illustrated (though the plate is inverted) in *Tamblyn, c.1932, pp. 65-68.*
9. It was difficult to prevent or treat wound infections in the pre-antibiotic era. The therapeutic modalities listed translate as: use of simple antiseptics; cautery; use of locally inoculated antisera to neutralize bacteria, or autogenous bacterins to promote phagocytosis; neutralization of bacterial toxins and neutrophil lysosomal products by irrigation with Dakin's solution (sodium hypochlorite and sodium bicarbonate solution); stimulation of inflammation by injection or application of irritants; and debridement surgically or by irrigation with hypertonic saline solutions, which removed pus and stimulated local edema or tissue fluid production.
10. Quittor is necrosis and inflammation of the lateral cartilage of the 3rd phalanx or 'foot bone', resulting in lameness and a discharging sinus at the upper margin of the hoof. Therapy involves surgical removal of the dead cartilage, which can

be difficult. Savage described a technique developed mainly by Lieut.-Col. C.G. Saunders at No. 1 C.V.H., employing an instrument that facilitated complete removal of the dead cartilage. Savage recorded 64 operations for quittor in 34 surgical sessions over 19 months. He felt that he could return 80% of such animals to use if he had the first opportunity to operate. Re-operations on jobs botched by others were less successful. *Savage Diary, 21 Feb. 1918.*

11. E.A. Watson was an internationally-recognized veterinary microbiologist in the first part of the 20th century. Born in Devon England in 1879, he homesteaded at Eastend Saskatchewan prior to serving in the Boer War, where he became laboratory assistant for Sir Arnold Theiler, noted veterinary microbiologist and pathologist. Graduating from the Ontario Veterinary College in 1904, in 1905 Watson was employed in the Biological Laboratory by the Dominion Department of Agriculture in Ottawa as an assistant to C.H. Higgins, and in 1906 was placed in charge of the branch laboratory in Lethbridge, Alberta. He demonstrated *Trypanosoma equiperdum*, the cause of dourine, a venereal disease of horses, and he developed the complement-fixation test which facilitated the eradication of that disease from North America. Watson was at the peak of his scientific career during W.W. I, and his time as a veterinary officer at the front was a waste of his talent and expertise. Hence his secondment to head the Army Veterinary Corps Bacteriology Laboratory at Rouen made sense. In 1920 he became head of the Pathological Division of the Health of Animals Branch, and was responsible for development of the first Animal Diseases Research Institute at Hull, Quebec. Scientifically, he also was noted for work on the Preisz-Nocard bacillus, *Corynebacterium pseudotuberculosis*, the cause of ulcerative lymphangitis of horses among other diseases, and for work on glanders and tuberculosis. During W.W. II, he facilitated biological warfare research by members of his Division, especially Dr. C.A. Mitchell. In 1940, he was elected a Fellow of the Royal Society of Canada. Watson retired in 1943 due to ill-health, and died in Victoria B.C. on 12 March, 1945; his ashes were scattered over the hills at Eastend. *Anon., Can. J. Comp. Med., Vol. 4, p. 178, 1940; Anon., Can. J. Comp. Med., Vol. 7, pp. 98-99, 1943; Watson, obit., 1945; Evans & Barker, 1976, p: 117; Bryden, 1989, pp. 53, 87-89, 98.*

Chapter 17

1. The Epilogue is the work of the editors.
2. *Harris, 1988, pp. 146-153.*
3. *Harris, 1988, pp. 167-192.*
4. *Granatstein, 1993, p. 8.*
5. *Granatstein, 1993, p. 14.*
6. *Granatstein, 1993, p. 19.* About $53 million, $63 million and $71 million in 1998 terms. *Statistics Canada, 1999.*
7. *Tamblyn File, D.H.H., D.N.D.: HQ 7064-1 v.3, Computation of Pension, Late Lieut. Col. D.S. Tamblyn, 1 Feb. 1943*; equivalent to $56, 600 in 1998 terms *Statistics Canada, 1999.*
8. *Granatstein, 1993, p. 8.*
9. *Granatstein, 1993, p. 14.*
10. Maj.-Gen. C. Vokes cited in *Granatstein, 1993, p. 21.*
11. No concentrations of the entire permanent force were held from 1920-1926, and in 1927, all field exercises of any size were canceled. The permanent force camps in 1928 and 1929 were disasters technically. With the onset of the Great Depression in 1929, further permanent force field training at the regimental or combined arms level was canceled until summer 1938, with predictable results in terms of preparedness for operations. *Harris, 1988, pp. 196-198.*
12. *Granatstein, 1993, p. 9.*
13. *Service Records, CEF, NAC: C.E. Edgett, D.S. Tamblyn, A.B. Cutcliffe, T.C. Evans, C.G. Saunders.*
14. *G.O. 194-1920, Disbandment-Veterinary Units of the C.E.F.* The veterinary and remount units of the C.E.F. (Siberia) were disbanded officially by *Routine Order 2539, 30 Sept. 1920,* and by *G.O. 214-1920.*
15. *G.O. 27-1919.*
16. "In recognition of services rendered during the War, 1914-1918, His Majesty the King has graciously approved the grant of the title 'Royal' to the Canadian Permanent Army Service Corps, Canadian Permanent Army Medical Corps, Canadian Permanent Army Veterinary Corps and the Canadian Permanent Army Ordnance Corps." *G.O. 89-1919.*
17. Neill and Frape were demobilized from the C.E.F. in January 1919; Frape retired from the Permanent Force and Neill was transferred to the Reserve of Officers in the same month. *Frape, A.E., Service Record, CEF, NAC; Neill, W.J., Service Record, CEF, NAC; The Canada Gazette, No. 3 and No. 6, January, 1919; The Militia List of the Dominion of Canada, 1 Jan., 1 July 1919.*
18. *The Militia List of the Dominion of Canada, 1 July 1919.*
19. *Taschereau, T.J.deM., Service Record, CEF, NAC.* Taschereau was born 13 May 1869, the son of Sir Henri-Elzéar Taschereau, prominent Beauce and Québec politician, lawyer, and ultimately law professor and Chief Justice of the Supreme Court of Canada. His mother was Marie-Antoinette Harwood, daughter of the English seigneur of Vaudreuil *Howes, 1998; D. Howes, pers. com. 1999.* Mr. Montarville Taschereau's 1890 M.V. diploma from l'Ecole vétérinaire

du Québec is illustrated in *Pepin, 1986, p. 113.* He had an extensive and responsible background as a field officer and ultimately O.C. in several of the francophone infantry regiments in the N.P.A.M., and he also served in the Royal Canadian Regiment of Infantry Special Service Force, Halifax N.S. [Permanent Force garrison duty during Boer War] before joining the Army Veterinary Department; see Appendices A and H. *The Quarterly Militia List of the Dominion of Canada, April 1912, p. 79.*

20. *Duhault, J.R.J., Service Record, CEF, NAC; The Militia List of the Dominion of Canada April 1922.*
21. *Piché, M.A., Service Record, CEF, NAC; The Militia List of the Dominion of Canada April 1922.*
22. *Tamblyn, D.S., Service Record, Tamblyn File, D.H.H., D.N.D., Ottawa; The Militia List of the Dominion of Canada April 1922.*
23. *Anon., Can. Vet. Rec. Vol. 1, No. 2, p. 55, 1920; The Militia List of the Dominion of Canada April 1922.*
24. *The Militia List of the Dominion of Canada April 1922.*
25. *Anon., Can. Vet. Rec. Vol. 2, No. 1, p. 34, 1921; Anon., Can. Vet. Rec. Vol. 3, p. 108, 1922; The Militia List of the Dominion of Canada December 1922*
26. *G.O. 62-1920.*
27. Piché, born 1866, graduated in 1885; Taschereau, born 1869 graduated 1890; Evans, born 1874, graduated 1908; Walsh, born 1877, graduated 1894 [age 17!]; Macdonald born ?, graduated 1888; Tamblyn, born 1881, graduated 1901; Duhault, born 1888, graduated 1910. Macdonald was a former N.W.M.P. Veterinary Sergeant, and Walsh had not been a particularly effective officer overseas, having been returned 'surplus' from England. One wonders if they were motivated to accept a Captaincy in the R.C.A.V.C., with little prospect of advancement beyond Brevet Major, by the ease of service life. Were they classic 'P.F.ers', seeking a sinecure in the Permanent Force? *Note 11.15; Appendix A; Appendix H.*
28. Responsibility for administration of both the R.C.A.V.C. and the C.A.V.C. (N.P.A.M.) was transferred to a senior officer of the R.C.A.V.C., who carried out those duties in addition to his duties as Senior Veterinary Officer in his District. *Anon., Can. Vet. Rec. Vol. 2 No. 1, pp. 34, 40, 1921; G.O. 228-1920.*

    Command of the Canadian Army Veterinary Service was a sensitive political issue within the profession. On 20 January 1920, C.E. Edgett had sponsored a resolution to the Militia Council endorsed by the British Columbia Veterinary Association, that the Veterinary Service be directed by a qualified Veterinary Surgeon, "as it had not been so in the past". Major-General H. Burstall responded that such was the intention once the re-organization of the Canadian Army Veterinary Services then underway was complete. *Anon., Can. Vet. Rec., Vol. 1, No. 1, p. 34, 1920.*
29. *The Militia List of the Dominion of Canada December 1922; Anon., Can. Vet. Rec., Vol. 3, p. 137, 1922; The Canada Gazette, 31 Aug. 1922, Appointments, Promotions and Retirements.*

    French-Canadians were markedly under-represented in the Canadian Army at this time, as they were throughout the first century of Canadian Confederation *Morton, 1969; Pariseau and Bernier, 1988.* The proportion of French-Canadians in the Army Veterinary Service (including the R.V.S.) fluctuated greatly over time: 1887 - 1/20 (5%); 1892 - 1/23 (4%); 1897 - 2/27 (7%); 1902 - 3/31 (10%); 1907 - 3/47 (6%); 1912 (re-organized) - 13/71 (18%); 1914 - 23/99 (23%); 1919 (total in Militia List, including many, but not all, who served overseas) - 51/379 (13%); 1922 (re-organized) - 14/87 (16%); 1927 - 12/94 (13%); 1932 - 7/67 (10%); 1936 - 6/53 (11%); 1939 (re-organized) - 8/44 (18%). With the exception of a few mainly infantry regiments in Quebec, the N.P.A.M. as well as the Permanent Force used English as the language of command and communication, limiting the number of francophone officers in the army to 4 - 8% between 1870 and 1910 *Pariseau and Bernier, 1988, p. 48.* While the number of francophone veterinary officers in the N.P.A.M. should be evaluated in relation to the number of mounted units and Military District (eg. M.V.S.) openings in francophone regions, which was not high *Pariseau and Bernier, 1988, p. 52*, it is clear that until formation of the C.A.V.C. in 1910, representation was poor, and comparable to the militia as a whole. Not all francophones were in Quebec; L.G. Frédette, from Quebec, was with a largely French-Canadian unit in Edmonton until he left to pioneer veterinary practice in the Peace River district in 1912, and W. Lamaire was with units in Guelph Ont. and St. Boniface Man. Within the Permanent Force, the cadre of 2-3 veterinary officers during this period only intermittently included a francophone (J. E. Couture 1896-97; J.D. Duchene 1897-1902; Taschereau from 1907).

    After the C.A.V.C. was formed, a new pattern of francophone participation is evident: peaks within a few years after a reorganization, followed by a gradual decline. Reorganizations permitted pruning of deadwood and renewal of the organization. Given his effectiveness during mobilization of the C.A.V.C. in fall 1914, and the high degree of insight and activity evident in his correspondence of 1920-22, it is probable that Piché, who was P.V.O. for all or part of Québec from 1905-1930, was relatively successful in recruiting francophones during the re-organizations of 1910-12 and 1920-22. The impression gained from the data in the previous paragraph is that they then dropped out gradually. However, when service of officers commissioned between 1912 and 1936, excluding 1914-20, is compared (21 francophones and 50 randomly selected anglophones), the average years of service was similar (francophone 10.7 years, range 1-28; anglophone 8.9 years, range 1-20). But the length of service was distributed differently (francophone/anglophone, % of officers serving 1-3 yr - 5/20; 4-6 yr - 48/20; 7-9 yr - 9.5/20; 10-12 yr - 0/10; 13-15 yr - 9.5/18; 16-18 yr - 9.5/2; 19+ yr - 19/10). Although overall attrition within the first 9 years of service was comparable at 63% of francophones and 60% of anglophones, loss of anglophones was more uniform, while among francophones it peaked at 4-6 years. Among officers retained over 9 years, service by francophones was skewed, half of those retained serving 19 years or more, while only 25% of retained anglophones served that long. Francophones may have been retained longer because recruiting of new blood was more difficult. But 4/10 V.O.s recruited during 1938-39 were francophone.

Communication in the Veterinary Service was in English. All of the francophone veterinary officers in the P.F. must have worked effectively in an English milieu, including Couture and Duchene, who, although they were never posted beyond M.D. No. 5, eastern Québec, dealt with 'B' Battery, Royal Canadian Artillery, which was predominantly English-speaking. Taschereau at least may have come from a bilingual family background, though his education was in French.

Despite their small number, at the outbreak of W.W. I francophones were proportionately well represented in the C.P.A.V.C. (50% of the 4-officer cadre). Taschereau was one of 12 francophone Majors, and Duhault one of only 4 francophone Lieutenants in the entire Permanent Force, in which only 9% of officers were francophone *Pariseau and Bernier, 1988, pp. 64, 275.* The situation in the army as a whole did not improve between the wars; in1939, Duhault was one of only 4 francophone Lieutenant-Colonels *Pariseau and Bernier, 1988, pp. 101, 307.*

Francophone veterinary officers recruited into the C.E.F. and the Imperial Army were discriminated against if they had difficulty in English. This is explicit in some of Neill's remarks referred to by French in Chapter 11 (see Note 11.7), and is implicit in what appears to be rejection by the Imperial Army Veterinary Corps of a number of French-Canadian officers gazetted into the C.A.V.C. for duty in that Corps in 1918. Of 9 in the Militia List in January 1919, 7 do not appear in Appendix B (see Appendix H), although all 22 anglophone officers gazetted in 1918 do. Francophone officers acquitted themselves as well as anglophones, and appear to have been well-respected, though only Daigneault attained the rank of Major. But about the same proportion of francophones were promoted above Captain in the C.A.V.C. overseas as Canadian-born anglophones (5% vs. 7%), while 15% of British-born officers attained such rank.

Both Taschereau and Piché clearly had a strong military bent, indicated by their attainment of command in combatant roles, Taschereau in the infantry, and Piché in the hussars (Appendices A and H), as well as in support. They clearly were well-assimilated into army culture, and able to deal with the compromises that it dictated, as no doubt was Duhault, who spent many years in western Canada. They worked effectively in English, and Duhault, at least, was prepared to uproot himself from Québec to live in an unfamiliar society *Morton, 1969.*

30. *G.O. 90-1920.*

31. The distribution by rank was 10 Lieut.-Colonels, 20 Majors, 40 Captains, 70 Lieutenants, 49 Sergeants and Staff Sergeants, 54 Corporals, 9 Shoeing Smiths, and 148 Privates. Units were established in Military District 1-London (1st M.V.S); District 2-Toronto (No. 2 Sect., 2nd M.V.S.); 3-Kingston (3rd M.V.S.); 4-Montreal (4th M.V.S.); 5-Québec City (No. 5 Sect., 5th M.V.S.); 6-Halifax (No. 6 Sect.), Summerside P.E.I. (6th M.V.S.); 13-Calgary (No. 13 Section, 2nd Cavalry M.V.S.). It is not clear if establishments were authorized for Sections in Districts 1-Southwestern Ontario, 3-Eastern Ontario, 6-Nova Scotia; 7-New Brunswick, 10-Manitoba and Northwestern Ontario, 11-British Columbia, and 12-Saskatchewan, (there were no Districts 8, 9) and for the other two Mobile Veterinary Sections. Sections were to be manned according to Corps Orders. *G.O.s 12-1921, 20- 1921, 26-1921, 69-1921, 160-1921, 183-1921, 207-1921.*

32. For instance, Lieut. H.C. Hébert had been known on the Militia List as "Hibert"and in correspondence as "Hibbert"; however, Daigneault's name continued to be spelled "Daignault" to disbandment, though he signed with the 'e' in all documents that we have seen. The death of H.H. Lefebvre in Mesopotamia had not been confirmed. The effort required to reorganize the C.A.V.C. in the wake of the war is documented in letters by Piché; lists of former C.A.V.C. (N.P.A.M.), C.A.V.C. (C.E.F) and R.A.V.C. officers canvassed and their status (dead letter or letter not answered; interested in remaining active in the C.A.V.C., going on the Reserve or Retired List, or resigning) compiled by him and other S.V.O.s; draft establishments of the reorganized C.A.V.C.; correspondence with O.C.s of various units proposing candidate veterinary officers; and modifying letters and memos between Taschereau and the Directorate of Personal Service in Ottawa, dated late 1920-mid 1922. *NAC RG24, Vol. 6532, File HQ 621-1-4, v. 1, v. 2; Vol. 4482, File 42-1-1, v. 1.*

33. The C.A.V.C. officers serving as Senior Veterinary Officers were Lieut.-Col. J.H. Wilson, M.D. No. 1-London Ont.; Capt. L.A. Donovan, M.D. No. 7-Saint John N.B.; and Capt. V.C. Best, M.D. No.11, Victoria B.C.; considering the R.C.A.V.C. S.V.O.s, this left M.D. No. 6 Halifax, and M.D. No.12, Regina, without an S.V.O. *The Militia List of the Dominion of Canada, December1922.*

34. *G.O. 70-1922.*

35. In June 1922, prior to Taschereau's retirement, Piché was Lieut.-Col. (Brevet Colonel) and S.V.O. M.D. No. 4, at St. Jean Québec; Tamblyn S.V.O. M.D. No. 13, Calgary; Evans S.V.O. M.D. No. 2, Toronto; Duhault S.V.O. M.D. No. 10, Winnipeg; Macdonald a Brevet Major, S.V.O. M.D. No. 5, Québec City; and Walsh a Brevet Major, S.V.O. M.D. No. 3, Kingston. *Anon., Can. Vet Rec. Vol. 3, p. 108, 1922.*

36. *Report of the Dept. of Militia and Defence 1922, p. 42.*
37. The information here is taken from *Ross & Chartrand, 1977.*
38. We know little of the uniform and insignia worn by Veterinary Surgeons/Officers prior to 1907. See Figs. 1.1 and 1.2 for examples of Veterinary Surgeons in regimental Full Dress uniforms 1890-1903, and associated notes, and Fig. 12.2 and Note 12.4 for the period 1907-1910.
39. A donation to the C.A.V. Barker Museum, we know nothing of the artist who rendered this watercolour, nor its provenance. It appears to be accurate in all but one respect; the helmet worn by veterinary officers was not surmounted by a spike, but rather by a ball. The Canadian War Museum, Ottawa, has long displayed the full dress uniform of Lieut.-Col. A.E. Cameron R.C.A.V.C.(N.P.).
40. The Royal Cipher 'G.R.V.' replaced 'E.R.VII.' when King George V followed Edward VII to the throne in 1911. *Ross & Chartrand, 1977, p. 97.*
41. See Note 1, pp. v-xiii for a discussion of cap badges.
42. *G.O. 2-1912*; *Ross & Chartrand, 1977, pp. 95, 100.*
43. Information on service uniforms of officers and men in the C.E.F. is derived from *Law, c. 1998.* The C.A.V.C. is specifically dealt with on page 38 there, but relevant information is dispersed throughout.
44. See Note 1, pp. v-xiii, for a discussion of Veterinary Service cap and lapel badges.
45. *Burns, 1931-32.*
46. *Harris, 1988, figures on pp. xx, xxi.*
47. See Note 1, pp. v-xiii. Title 'Royal' accorded Non-Permanent Active Militia , including C.A.V.C., in *G.O. 75-1936.*
48. *G.O. 111-1923.*
49. Music by W.H. Weiss, words by Longfellow. *Stewart, 1982, pp. 24-25.*
50. *G.O. 38-1930.*
51. *Charrington, 1930-31a.* The relatively few glorious actions involving the Canadian Cavalry Brigade exemplified these facts; see Note 7.20, describing Flowerdew's Charge at Moreuil Wood. There, approximately 300 troopers and 800 horses of the Canadian Cavalry Brigade became casualties in an action that lasted about 90 minutes. Capt. Duhault of Cavalry M.V.S. 'A', with 8 men, collected "great numbers of wounded horses" at Moreuil Wood that day, and established a Casualty Clearing Station the next day so that they could be evacuated (see p. 96 and Note 9.6). *RG9, III, D, 3, Vol. 5043, Reel T-10, 935: War Diary, C.M.V.S. 'A', 30/31 March 1918.* The last Canadian Cavalry Brigade action, involving LdS.H. (R.C.), the R.C.D.s, the F.G.H. and the R.C.H.A. was the successful 8 mile sweep toward Le Cateau, 9 October 1918;168 troopers became casualties and 171 horses were killed in a few hours *Nicholson, 1962, pp. 462-465.*
52. *Greenhous, 1983, pp. 284-285, 288.*
53. *Harris, 1988, pp. 198-203; Greenhous, 1983, pp. 272.*
54. See *Granatstein, 1993, pp. 116-126.*
55. *Burns, 1923-24.*
56. Such as: *Burns, 1930-31, 1934-35, 1938-39; Goforth, 1932-33.*
57. See: *Timmis, 1925-26, 1931-32; Charrington, 1930-31a; Forneret, 1931-32.*
58. *Westmorland, 1931-32.*
59. *Can. Def. Quart., Vol. 8, p. 264, 1931-32*; *Greenhous, 1983, pp. 258-260.*
60. *Charrington, 1930-31b.*
61. *Nicholson, 1972, pp. 11-17.*
62. *Boulter, 1931-32; R.S.C., 1932-33.* The latter camp, 51 men in the field for 6 days, cost about $125, paid not from the public purse, but from 'Battery Funds'.
63. *Greenhous, 1983, pp. 285-288.*
64. *Harvey, 1934-35.*
65. *Mann, 1937-38, p. 43.*
66. Those in photo are: front, l-r, R.S.M. F. Wardell, Maj. M.H.A. Drury, Maj. G.F. Berteau, Duhault, Lieut.-Col. E.L. Caldwell, Maj. D.A. Grant, S.M. A.F. Madden, S.M.I. J. Maclean; rear, l-r, Galloway, R.Q.M.S. A. Hilton, S.M.I. J.M. Hallett, Sgt. P. Martin, Q.M.S.I. J. King, Sgt. J. Higgins, and F.Q.M.S. E.E. Taylor.
67. *Greenhous, 1983, pp. 288-296.*
68. *The Militia List of the Dominion of Canada, January 1924, p. 87; Appendix A.* Morgan and T.C. Evans were well-acquainted, working together with Lieut.-Col. J.H. Wilson on several Ontario Veterinary Association committees at the time. Likely, such connections helped his chances of employment. *Anon., Can. Vet. Rec., Vol. 2, No. 2, p. 107, 1921.*
69. *The Militia List of the Dominion of Canada, January 1924.*
70. *The Militia List of the Dominion of Canada, January 1925.*
71. *Department of National Defence List of Officers Defence Forces of the Dominion of Canada, February 1930.*

72. *Militia Order 437, 1 Oct. 1930.*
73. *Department of National Defence Defence Forces List Canada, November, 1935, p. 494.*
74. *Tamblyn File, D.H.H., D.N.D.: Memorandum, Quartermaster-General, 15 May 1936.*
75. *Department of National Defence Defence Forces List Canada, December 1936.*
76. *Department of National Defence Defence Forces List Canada, August 1938.*
77. *Canada Gazette, 8 Jan. 1938.*
78. *G.O. 104-1928.*
79. *Amended Regulations for the Canadian Army Veterinary Service (Peace) 1930, dated May 18, 1929.*
80. *Tamblyn, 1933.*
81. *Tamblyn File, D.H.H., D.N.D.: 28 June 1928, telegram re attendance at Barriefield, Petawawa; 20 Apr. 1929, memorandum, Quartermaster General to O.C. M.D. No. 3.*
82. *Bramley, 1983.*
83. Visible in the photo are bone and tooth forceps, firing irons, mortar and pestle and spatulas for powders, balance, and bottles containing medicaments described in veterinary *materia medica* courses and found in veterinary officer's Field Chests up to 1939, such as: carbolic acid; turpentine; linseed oil; tincture of iodine; tincture of opium; fluid extracts of *Cannabis indica*, *Belladona*, *Gentian*, nux vomica, *Digitalis*; spirits of ammonia; zinc sulphate; lead acetate; mercuric chloride tablets; quinine sulphate; potassium permanganate; silver nitrate; blistering liquid or ointment (*Cantharides* extract and silver iodide); purgative balls; arecoline hypodermic tablets; zinc oxide ointment; and vaseline. *Regulations, The Canadian Army Veterinary Service 1912, 1916, 1923 (and Drafts, 1930, 1939).*
84. S.H. Bramley, in the late 1920's and early 1930s one of a handful of N.C.O.s in the R.C.A.V.C., based first in Calgary and then in St. Jean as Veterinary Sergeant, stated that his "duties were far from arduous and consisted of some paper work and control of drugs and instruments in the barracks..." Ultimately he transferred to another Corps since he "...could see the writing on the wall due to mechanization, also I was frustrated due to lack of work". *Bramley, 1983.*
85. He assumed all of Piché's duties other than as P.V.O. M.D. No. 4; Piché was in veterinary charge of the R.C.D. horses at St. Jean. *Tamblyn File, Directorate of History, DND: 13 Oct. 1927, letter, Piché to Quartermaster-General*
86. *Harris, 1988, p. 158; Granatstein, 1993, p. 59;* Lieut.-Col. Tamblyn and Sgt.-Maj. A. Newell sought reimbursement for travel to and from Kingston related to the Unemployment Relief Scheme at the R.C.A.F. Station, Trenton. *Tamblyn File, D.H.H., D.N.D: 25 Jan. 1933, memo, D.O.C. M.D. 3 to Secretary, Militia Services, Ottawa.*
87. Referring to the veterinary hospital at the 1929 summer camp, M.D. No. 13, at Sarcee Camp, former R.C.A.V.C. Sergeant S.H. Bramley related "Major F. (Freddie) Walsh...was on extended sick leave at the time so that the unit was commanded by Dr. W.B. (Dick) Price who was a Capt. in the R.C.A.V.C. [sic], Non-Permanent Militia." *Bramley, 1983.*
88. *Tamblyn File, Directorate of History, DND: Undertaking signed by Tamblyn 9 Nov. 1929.*
89. *Tamblyn File, D.H.H., D.N.D.: 11 Dec. 1930-5 January 1931, Tamblyn correspondence to and fro with Q.M.G.*
90. *Tamblyn File, D.H.H., D.N.D.: 25, 26 Mar. 1930, letters from Paymaster Militia H.Q. Ottawa to Paymaster M.D. No. 3.*
91. *NAC RG24, Vol. 4482, File 42-1-1: Tracy-Piché correspondence 1924.*
92. *NAC RG24, Vol. 4462, File 42-1-1 v1: 22 August, 1928, letter, Major-General H.A. Panet to all District Officers Commanding; G.O.s 159-1928, 160-1928.*
93. Regulations stated that "...training of C.A.V.C. personnel will generally be limited to training in camp with other arms and services and the numbers trained will normally be confined to those required for veterinary duties with the animals in camp." *Memorandum on Training of the Canadian Militia, 1934, p. 193.*
94. *Amended Regulations for the Canadian Army Veterinary Service, 1930; Tamblyn, 1933.*
95. *The Militia List of the Dominion of Canada, 31 December 1922.*
96. *Department of National Defence Defence Forces List Canada, November 1935.*
97. *Tamblyn, 1933.*
98. *List of Officers Defence Forces of the Dominion of Canada, July, 1932.*
99. From 28 cavalry regiments, 119 infantry battalions, 10 machine gun battalions, 88 field and medium artillery batteries, plus auxilliary units, to: 9 cavalry regiments, 4 armoured car cavalry regiments, 61 artillery and anti-aircraft units, 16 rifle regiments, 26 machine gun regiments, and 6 tank regiments. *Anon., Can. Def. Quart., 1935-36; Anon., Can. Def. Quart. 1936-37.*
100. An establishment of 8 Lieut.-Colonels, 12 Majors and 30 Captains and Lieutenants. *G.O. 154-1936.*
101. No. 1 M.V.S.: London, Ont.; No. 2 M.V.S. - Kingston, Ont.; No. 3 M.V.S. - Monteeal, P.Q.; No. 4 M.V.S. - Quebec, P.Q.; No. 5 M.V.S. - Summerside, P.E.I.; No. 6. M.V.S. - Moncton, N.B.; No. 7 M.V.S. - Victoria, B.C.; No. 1 Cavalry M.V.S. - Regina, Sask.; No. 2 Cavalry M.V.S. - Calgary, Alta.; No. 1 Veterinary Evacuating Station - Winnipeg, Man.; No. 1 Veterinary Hospital - Toronto, Ont. *G.O.s 150-1936, 155-1936.*
102. A complement of 10 Lieut.-Colonels, 15 Majors, and 18 Captains and Lieutenants. *Department of National Defence*

Defence Forces List Canada, December 1936.

103. A complement of 7 Lieut.-Colonels, 10 Majors, and 27 Captains and Lieutenants. *Department of National Defence Defence Forces List Canada, November, 1939.*
104. *Regulations for the Canadian Army Veterinary Service, 1939.*
105. See *Wrightman, 1939*, for an overview of the program, and *Anon., Vet. Digest, p. 158, 1939* for its history at OVC.
106. *Anon., Vet. Digest p. 158, 1939*, and *Bigland, 1961* describe training under Kingscote and Cairns.
107. Based on *Anon., Vet. Digest p. 158, 1939*, L.G. Anderson, D.E. Faulkner and K.E. Brown completed in 1935; L. Turner and V.K.A. Alagaraju in 1936; D. Gerrick, R.G.H. Livermore and J.H. Wrightman in 1938. It is probable, based on information in *Vercoe, 1939; Anon., Vet. Digest p. 188, 1939* and *Bigland, 1961,* that at least E.F. Pallister, L.W.H. Vercoe, W.T. Carlyle, C.S. Bigland, C.C. Gardiner, D. Garrick and G.L. Brown also qualified in 1939 and 1940. Leon (Zlotnick) Saunders also completed C.O.T.C. training *L. Z. Saunders pers. com, 1999.* Only Wrightman appears on the complement of the R.C.A.V.C.(N.P.) in the Militia Lists accessible to us. *Department of National Defence Defence Forces List Canada, November, 1939.*
108. *Anon., Vet. Digest, Vol. 2, p. 192, 1940; Brown, 1940; Gattinger, 1962, p. 102.*
109. Names inscribed on the 'Memorial Doorway' to the O.V.C. Library as casualties of World War II are: H.L. Anderson '16, N.H.V. Brown undergrad., J.M. Curry '10, S.W. Elgie undergrad., J.M. McKague '39, E.G. Millidge undergrad., C.J. Mitchell '42, P.J. Pascoe '35, V.H. Reid '41, D.B. Robertson undergrad., D.K. Schroder undergrad., A.D. Traskus '38, R.W. Woolner '39 *Gattinger, p. 154, 1962.* Anderson, Curry and Traskus were Americans serving in the U.S.A.V.C.
110. *Anon., Can. Vet. Rec. Vol. 2, No. 2, p. 41, 1921.*
111. *Evans, Can. Vet. Rec. Vol. 3, pp. 51-52, 1922.*
112. *Anon., Can. Vet. Rec. Vol. 3, No. 2, p. 101, 1922.*
113. *Evans, Can. Vet. Rec Vol. 3, pp. 79-84, 1922.*
114. *Anon., Can. Vet. Rec. Vol. 3, p. 100, 1922*
115. *Anon., Can. Vet. Rec. Vol. 4, p. 275, 1923.*
116. *Timmis, 1923.*
117. *Taschereau, Can. Vet. Rec. Vol. 3, p. 37, pp. 99-100, 1922* (2 articles).
118. *Biscum, 1921*, see Note Foreword.16.
119. *Tamblyn, c. 1932.*
120. *Price, 1923.*
121. *Tamblyn, 1933.*
122. *Bramley, 1983.*
123. *NAC RG24, Vol. 54, File 621-3-28: 21 March, 1940, T.C. Evans, Letter to the Secretary, Dept. of National Defence.*
124. *Archives, Royal Canadian Dragoons: Veterinary Officer's Certificate and Descriptive Roll. Horses destroyed under N.D.H.Q. authority H.Q. S.8269 - H.Q. C.8037 - H.Q. C.8037 F.D. 284 dated 5th March, 1940.* Signed by 'J.R.J. Duhault, D.V.O., M.D. No. 4., St. Johns P.Que., 8-4-40'. None of the horses on this roll is a grey. See Appendix G, Destruction of Animals.
125. This account is derived from *Greenhous, 1983, pp. 295-296* and *MacAdams, undated, republ. 1992.* Greenhous had Teddy's death "in the spring of the year", but we do not know if it was April 8.
126. *Fraser, 1976, p. 138; Greenhous, 1983, pp. 294-295.*
127. *NAC RG2, 1, Vol. 1692, 17 October, 1940.*
128. *Memo, undated, in Tamblyn File, D.H.H., D.N.D..*
129. See Note 6.5 for a brief biography of Evans. *Anon., Can. J. Comp. Med., Vol. 8, 1944, p. 102; Bigland, 1961.*
130. *Dauth, obit., 1941.*
131. The Permanent Force N.C.O's in Toronto at the time of disbandment were Sgt.-Maj. Charles Lyne, a veteran of over 30 years, Sgt. Samuel Elby, who became a recruiting officer in Toronto, and Cpl. Norris Hope, who transferred to the Royal Canadian Engineers. At St. Jean were Sgt.-Maj. Al. Wheatly, and a Sgt. Roberts *Nichols, 1989.* We do not know the names of other Permanent N.C.O.s at the time of disbandment or of many earlier in the history of the Corps. Based on the *Militia Lists 1912-1939*, there were only 5 Warrant Officers in the history of the Veterinary Service from 1912-1940: G.J. Simpkin, Toronto, 1 Apr. 1912 - 1917; S.T. Nurse, Montréal, 15 May 1916 - 1932; A.M. Burn, Ottawa until 1927, then Montréal, 5 May 1917 - 1936; A. Newell, Kingston, 1 Sept. 1931-1938; C. Lyne, Toronto, 1 June 1937-disbandment. A.E. Frape was a Permanent Force Sergeant prior to W.W. I, as was Alfred Newell.
132. Maj. K.L. Douglas became a Quartermaster Lieutenant with his old regiment, The Princess Louise Dragoon Guards. R.V.L. Walker became a Captain in the Armoured Corps in 1939, but was recalled in 1942 to become Major, and Assistant Director, War Disease Control Station, Grosse Isle, working on development of a rinderpest vaccine. *Anon., Can. J. Comp. Med., Vol. 5., pp. 178-179, 1941; Barker & Crowley, 1989, pp. 212-213.*

133. *Anon., Can. J. Comp. Med., Vol. 5, p. 4, 1941; Anon., Can. J. Comp. Med., Vol. 5, p. 92, 1941; Anon., Can. J. Comp. Med., Vol. 5, p. 153, 1941; Anon., Can. J. Comp. Med., Vol. 5, p. 302, 1941; Anon., Can. J. Comp. Med., Vol. 6, p. 251, 1942; Anon., Can. J. Comp. Med., Vol. 7, p. 290, 1943.*
134. *Anon., Can. J. Comp. Med., Vol. 5, p. 302, 1941.*
135. See *Miller, 1961.* United States Army Veterinary Corps food inspection activities were described for Canadian veterinarians by *Kester, 1938.*
136. *Miller, 1961, pp. 226-227, 229-231.*
137. *Barker & Crowley, 1989, pp. 17, 28-31.*
138. Notes 17.138 and 17.144, no doubt incomplete, and limited to graduates of the O.V.C., were compiled from documentary sources and the collective recollections of *C.A.V. Barker, D.A. Barnum, G.C. Fisher, B.J. McSherry and J.D. Schroder, 1999.*

Among veterinarians who served in the navy were: A.W. Bett, who won the George Medal for leading a fire-fighting party on a burning tanker *Anon., Can. J. Comp. Med., Vol. 8, p. 23, 1944*; W.C. Stiles *Can. J. Comp. Med., Vol. 8, p. 327, 1944*; G.C. Fisher, J. Ballantyne (assigned duties as food inspector) *Can. J. Comp. Med., Vol. 8, p. 329, 1944.*

Enlisted men and officers in the army included G.H. Boyce; H.L. Bryson *Can. J. Comp. Med., Vol. 9, p. 86, 1945*; R. Clendinning; R.F. Colgate; H.J. Davis *Can. J. Comp. Med., Vol. 9, p. 143, 1945*; R.J. Devereux *Can. J. Comp. Med., Vol. 9, p. 144, 1945*; E.C. Eddy; R.T. Ingle *Can. J. Comp. Med., Vol. 8, p. 329, 1944*; J.B. Leatherdale *Can. J. Comp. Med., Vol. 8, p. 328, 1944*; R.J. Livermore; J.M. McKague (K.I.A.) *Can. J. Comp. Med., 8, p. 327, 1944*; A.J. MacKinnon; B.J. McSherry; F.C. Nelson *Can. J. Comp. Med., Vol. 10, p. 268, 1945*; V.H. Reid (K.I.A.) *Can. J. Comp. Med., Vol. 9, p. 260, 1945*; K.B. Rowe *Can. J. Comp. Med., Vol. 9, p. 86, 1945*; J. Schroder *Can. J. Comp. Med., Vol. 9, p. 143, 1945.* Major A.A. Kingscote's expertise as a parasitologist also was employed overseas *Can. J. Comp. Med., Vol. 8, p. 329, 1944.*

R.C.A.F. and R.A.F. pilots, flight and ground crew included W.C. Anderson; A.B. Armstrong *Can. J. Comp. Med., Vol. 9, p. 116, 1945*; J.T. Behan *Can. J. Comp. Med., Vol. 9, p. 143, 1945*; K.C. Campbell *Can. J. Comp. Med., Vol. 9, p. 115, 1945*; W.H. Cowan *Can. J. Comp. Med., Vol. 9, p. 60, 1945*; J.P.W. Gilman (P.O.W.) *Can. J. Comp. Med., Vol. 9, p. 60, 1945*; L.C. Hall *Can. J. Comp. Med., Vol. 9, p. 144, 1945;* L.F. Hill *Can. J. Comp. Med., Vol. 9, p. 232, 1945*; A. Kidd *Can. J. Comp. Med., Vol. 8, p. 328, 1944*; J.B. Leatherdale; C.J. Mitchell (K.I.A.) *Service Record, NAC*; H. Palmer *Can. J. Comp. Med., Vol. 9, p. 116, 1945*; P.J. Pascoe (K.I.A.) *Service Record, NAC*; W.A. Steep *Can. J. Comp. Med., Vol. 9, p. 115, 1945*; R.W. Woolner (K.I.A.) *Service Record, NAC.*

J.A. Henderson, sent overseas as an R.C.A.F. navigator, was seconded to Cambridge University School of Agriculture as an advisor on artificial insemination, then to the Milk Marketing Board to establish a national artificial insemination scheme for the British dairy herd. *Anon., Can. Vet. J., Vol. 4, No. 8, p. xiii, 1963; J.A. Henderson, pers. com., 1999.*
139. *Rumney, 1941; Anon., Can. J. Comp. Med., Vol. 6, pp. 61-62, 1942.*
140. *Rumney, 1943.*
141. *NAC RG24, Vol. 54, File 621-3-28: 19 November 1942, T.C. Evans, Letter to the Director General of Medical Services, National Defence Headquarters.*
142. *McGilvray, 1943.*
143. *NAC RG24, Vol. 54, File 621-3-28: 16 Mar., 1944, W.J. Rumney, Letter to Honorable J.L. Ralston, Minister of National Defence.*
144. *Currie, 1944.* Dr. A.L. McNabb was commissioned Lieut.-Col., R.C.A.M.C., as 'Consulting Bacteriologist to the Army Medical Corps' *Can. J. Comp. Med., Vol. 8, p. 328, 1944.* Among commissioned Non-Medical Bacteriologists were: D.L.T. Smith, D.A. Barnum *Can. J. Comp. Med., Vol. 8, p. 327, 1944*; D.J. McKercher, A.F. Bain *Can. J. Comp. Med., Vol. 8, p. 328, 1944*; J.G. O'Donoghue. Veterinarians commissioned as Assistant District Hygiene Officers included J.R. Wagner, M. Comfort *Can. J. Comp. Med., Vol. 9, p. 143, 1945*; G.P. Talbot *Can. J. Comp. Med., Vol. 9, p. 144, 1945*; L. (Zlotnick) Saunders *Can. J. Comp. Med., Vol. 9, p. 144, 1945.*
145. *Rumney, 1943.*
146. *Miller, 1961; Clabby, 1963; Hickman, 1983/84; Hickman, 1986; Carter, 1996.*
147. *Clabby, 1963, pp. 59-62.*
148. *Whitfield, 1951.*
149. *NAC RG24 Vol. 54, File 621-3-28: Currie, G.S. Draft letter to W.J. Rumney, March, 1944.* Sanderson, with a Diploma in Veterinary Public Health, became Major, O.i.C. Dept. of Preventative Medicine, Camp Borden, retiring in 1967 *Barker & Crowley, 1989, p. 206.* The role played by veterinarians in public health in Canada and the U.S.A. differs in the civilian sector to this day. In America, many public health veterinarians hold responsible positions. In Canada, although during the late 1940's and early 1950's many veterinarians gained post-graduate diplomas or degrees in veterinary public health, most who took up positions in provincial or municipal public health agencies left the field because they were

unable to gain positions in any way comparable in responsibility or remuneration to those of medical graduates.

150. W.J. Rumney and G. Cairns, ex R.C.A.V.C.(N.P.) accompanied shiploads of horses to the U.K. *Rumney, 1943.*

Eric F. Pallister, whose father Lieut.-Col. P.E. Pallister was for many years V.O. to the Princess Louise Dragoon Guards, Ottawa, had qualified via C.O.T.C. for a commission in the R.C.A.V.C.(N.P.), but was unable to take it up. At the outbreak of war the Royal Canadian Army Medical Corps would accept him only as an ambulance driver, so he enlisted in the Royal Canadian Army Service Corps, and was commissioned a 2nd Lieutenant. Between stints serving in secret biological warfare work (see Note 17.151, below), Pallister was seconded to the Royal Army Veterinary Corps, and accompanied a shipment of 421 mules from the U.S.A. to Karachi, in then British India *Pallister, 1992.*

Lieut. Leon (Zlotnick) Saunders, R.C.A.M.C. (Non-Medical) became an Assistant District Hygiene Officer (see Note 17.144) and also underwent training on gas warfare with Chemical Warfare and Smoke at Suffield Alta., after spells in the artillery and as an officer transporting trainloads of 'zombies' (conscripts) to army camps. When his veterinary credentials were recognized, he, too, found himself seconded to the British Remount Department/R.A.V.C., as veterinary officer, with an ex R.C.A.V.C. Sergeant and 45 Other Ranks, on Mule Convoy No. 3. They transported a shipload of mules destined for pack work with the British Army in Burma from New Jersey and Virginia, via the Suez Canal, to Karachi, just as the war in Europe ended. *Can. J. Comp. Med., Vol. 9, p. 231, 1945; Saunders, 1996, p. 541; L.Z. Saunders, pers. com., 1999.* We do not know if other Canadian veterinarians conveyed mules to India.

151. Eric Pallister recounted "...being summoned off the parade square and ordered to report to Chemical Warfare and Smoke in Ottawa. This ended up to be working on secret projects (chiefly anthrax) which was under the civilian direction of Dr. C.A. Mitchell at the A.D.R.I....The next move was to Queen's U. at Kingston to produce alum precipitated tetanus antitoxin under the late Dr. Reed and Christine Rice." After returning from India, Pallister ended the war working on rinderpest vaccine development and biological warfare research at Grosse Isle, Québec *Pallister, 1992.* Other army veterinarians involved in biological warfare work at Queen's University or Grosse Isle included A.E. Cameron, R.V.L. Walker, T.L. Jones, D.J. McKercher and D.L.T. Smith *Can. J. Comp. Med., Vol. 8, p. 327, 1944; Barker & Crowley, 1989, p. 193; Bryden, 1989; T.L. Jones, pers. com., 1999.*

152. E.g. C.A. Mitchell, E.A. Watson. See *Bryden, 1989* for a description of Canada's top secret chemical and biological warfare activity in W.W. II, in which these men played a significant rôle.

153. *Miller, 1961.* Among many were L. Durant *Can. J. Comp. Med., Vol. 8, p. 328, 1944* and H.R. Steadman *Can. J. Comp. Med., Vol. 9, p. 86, 1945.*

154. *Cameron, 1942.*

Appendix A

1. Other than minor re-organization, this roll is as found in the French Manuscript. An additional 5 officers were found in the Miltia Lists marked (E), signifying sent for duty in the C.A.V.C. C.E.F., but whose names are not found here; they are in Appendix H.

2. From: *Calendar of Ontario Veterinary College, 1909-1910, pp. 25-85; 1924, pp. 53-72; 1929-30, pp. 49-51; 1935-36, pp. 45-50; 1939-40, pp. 45-49; 1944-45, pp. 45-49. Annual calendar of the Faculty of Comparative Medicine and Veterinary Science, McGill University, late Montreal Veterinary College, 1902-1903, pp. 25-31. Diplômés de l'Ecole de Médecine vétérinaire depuis sa fondation par le Dr. V.-T. Daubigny, le 4 avril 1886, 12 pp. Dukes, 1997.*

The Ontario Veterinary College was initiated by Andrew Smith in Toronto in 1862 (first intake 1864/graduates 1866). Private institution with a 2 year course granting diploma as a 'Veterinary Surgeon' (V.S.) until 1908; then taken over by the Ontario Department of Agriculture, and affiliated with University of Toronto. In 1910, optional 3rd year introduced, leading to Bachelor of Veterinary Science (B.V.Sc.). The three year course became standard in 1916, and in 1920, it became 4 years. In 1922, the O.V.C. moved to Guelph, where it continues as a college of the University of Guelph.

The Montreal Veterinary College, established by Duncan McEachran in 1866 (first graduates 1869), was affiliated with McGill University and had a 3 year programme leading to the degree Doctor of Veterinary Science (D.V.S.). In 1889, it became the Faculty of Comparative Medicine and Veterinary Science of McGill University. Recognized internationally as a school of very high quality, it closed in 1902.

The French Section, Montreal Veterinary College (Orphir Bruneau and Joseph Alphonse Couture, later Victor Théodule Daubigny) operated from 1875-1885; same degree as English section.

L'Ecole de Médecine vétérinaire de Montréal (Orphir Bruneau [and Victor Théodule Daubigny until 1886]) operated from 1885-1894 (first graduates 1888), affiliated with Victoria University. It had a three year course.

L'Ecole vétérinaire du Québec (Joseph Alphonse Couture) operated in Québec City from 1885-1893 (first graduates 1887), affiliated with Laval University 1885-1889 and with the Seminary of Québec 1889-1893, offering a 2 year course leading to the diploma 'medecin vétérinaire' (M.V.).

L'Ecole vétérinaire française de Montréal 1886-1896 (Victor Théodule Daubigny) was affiliated with Laval University and had a 3 year course. In 1893-94, the other French language veterinary schools closed and consolidated with it. From 1896-1920 it operated as l'Ecole de Médecine comparée et de Science vétérinaire de Montréal, affiliated with Laval; a 4 year course was instituted in 1917. Through subsequent moves and changes of name and affiliation, it continues as the current Faculté de Médecine vétérinaire de l'Université de Montréal, St. Hyacinthe Québec.

The School of Veterinary Science, Queen's Univerity, Kingston, Ont. opened 1895, closed 1899 (~24 students total; ~12 graduates). Two year course for the diploma Veterinary Surgeon (V.S.); an optional 3rd year led to the degree Doctor of Veterinary Medicine and Surgery (D.V.M.S.).

Mitchell, 1938-1940; Evans & Barker, 1976; Pepin, 1986, 1988; Dukes, 1997.

3. Eckert had severe scars on his shins, resulting from scalds suffered as a child. Complications of these injuries caused his discharge as unfit for general service. *Eckert, H.A., Service Record, CEF, NAC.*
4. See Note 10.6.
5. See Notes 3.5, 6.9.
6. Suffered trauma to testicle with complications, as a sequel to a riding incident, and developed neurasthenia subsequent to experiencing an air raid in England. Returned to Canada for treatment and discharged as surplus to requirements. *McCarthy, N., Service Record, CEF, NAC.*
7. Discharged with shell-shock and nervous debility as a sequel to the explosion of a bomb during the May 1917 air raid on Shorncliffe (see Chapter 5). He returned to the C.P.A.V.C. in Canada. *Newell, A., Service Record, CEF, NAC.*
8. Surplus upon disbandment of the School of Farriery.
9. Spenomegaly due to leukemia diagnosed within about 4 months of arrival in England. Returned to Canada August 1917, discharged as medically unfit in March 1918, and died in August 1918. *Secord, J.B.A., Service Record, CEF, NAC.*
10. Shaver, a non-veterinarian, became surplus with the reduction in Canadian Remount activity in England.
11. Enlisted in the infantry, but after arrival in England was transferred to the C.A.V.C. and commissioned. Trained with the 5th Division for 7 months, but was returned to Canada as "surplus to requirements" when it was broken up in March 1918. Possibly a question of discipline or competence. *Williams, J.B., Service Record, CEF, NAC.*
12. Suicide, see Chapter 12.
13. Severe duodenal ulcer. *Wood, J.F., Service Record, CEF, NAC.*
14. Broken legs after horse accident, see Chapter 12.
15. Nervous debility due to overwork and worry of service; incipient tuberculosis. *Best, V.C., Service Record, CEF, NAC.*
16. Lues (syphilis). *Bishop, H.H., Service Record, CEF, NAC.*
17. Nervous debility related to time at the front. *Burnet, J.H., Service Record, CEF, NAC.*
18. Court martial, sentenced to dismissal, see Note 6.9.
19. Traumatic sciatica occurred after his horse fell on him. He subsequently suffered a fractured femur and shell-shock when a shell exploded in close proximity on the road to Ypres in July 1916. Concussion caused headaches, memory loss and insomnia, and he was left with a permanent limp from the fracture. *Church, W.G., Service Record, CEF, NAC.*
20. Cleveland suffered from severe phlebitis of the femoral veins in both legs, which may have been aggravated by riding. He was returned to Canada for medical care and invalided out. *Cleveland, H.R., Service Record, CEF, NAC.*
21. See Chapter 12.
22. After 3 months at the front, Duchêne was transferred to No. 1 C.V.H.; 7 months later he was ordered to report to the Adjutant-General, London, and returned to Canada for disposal by the Adjutant-General Canada. Suggests a discipline problem. *Duchêne, H.D.J., Service Record, CEF, NAC.*
23. Durkin injured his knee (variously referred to as synovitis, and as septic) when thrown from a horse due to a shell-burst nearby. He was invalided back to England, granted leave to Canada, where he was retained for further medical treatment. Ultimately struck off strength as surplus. *Durkin, H.L., Service Record, CEF, NAC*
24. Sarcoma, see Chapter 12
25. Went to Canada on leave for personal reasons; diagnosed with tubercular orchitis while home. *Edwards, C.L., Service Record, CEF, NAC.*
26. Court martial, sentenced to dismissal; see Note 6.9
27. Prior to being returned to Canada for disposal by the Adjutant-General, Gaudry had been transferred in May 1916 from the field in France back to minor duties in England, where he was for over a year. That he was "permitted to resign" his commission in July 1917 suggests a disciplinary matter. *Gaudry, M.T.A., Service Record, CEF, NAC.*
28. See Chapter 12.
29. Hanmore had been transferred in January1917 from the 3rd Divisional Train in France back to minor duties in England, and was returned to Canada in March for disposal by the Adjutant-General, ultimately to be struck off strength in June 1917 as "surplus to establishment". That this occurred when the force was desperate for veterinary officers suggests a question of competence or discipline. *Hanmore, G.S., Service Record, CEF, NAC.*

30. Harrington suffered from chronic abdominal pain and gastrointestinal disturbance, diagnosed as gastritis, after being thrown from a horse in France. He also was hospitalized with a severe bout of influenza in fall 1918. He was invalided back to Canada with general debility and discharged as medically unfit. *Harrington, J., Service Record, CEF, NAC.*
31. Hogan was with a Forestry Company in France for only 6 weeks before being returned to Shorncliffe "with a view to being granted leave to Canada", which he obtained "without expense to [the] public". Once in Canada, leave was extended "on compassionate grounds", and he was retained there. *Hogan, J.D, Service Record, CEF, NAC*
32. Severe varicose veins and phlebitis, and synovitis of the knee due to the kick of a horse, both preceding war service. *McGillivray, J.D., Service Record, CEF, NAC.*
33. See Chapter 10.
34. Service record cannot be found in NAC.
35. See Chapter 12.
36. Rogers developed neuritis and muscle wasting in his arm, then later complained of neuritis in his leg, with no objective symptoms; he was returned to Canada as permanently unfit. *Rogers, W.T., Service Record, CEF, NAC.*
37. April 27 1916 at Ypres sustained a dislocated thumb and fracture of left scapula when thrown from a horse. Roy returned to Canada to convalesce. Despite being judged "fit for service" by a Medical Board in December 1916, he was struck off strength in May 1917. He died in New Brunswick 17 February 1966. *Roy, John A., Service Record, CEF, NAC.*
38. Roy had a one month career at the front with 7th Infantry Brigade, before being ordered to report to the Adjutant-General, London. Within a few weeks he was returned to Canada for disposal by the Adjutant-General, Ottawa. This may have been a problem of competence or discipline. *Roy, M.A., Service Record, CEF, NAC.*
39. The reasons for Capt. Ruttan's leave, which seems to have been at public expense, and for his retention in Canada, are not apparent from his record. *Ruttan, C.W., Service Record, CEF, NAC.*
40. Court martial, sentenced to dismissal; commuted to severe reprimand; subsequently returned to Canada as surplus to requirements. See Note 6.9.
41. Court martial, sentenced to dismissal. See Note 6.9.
42. Smith, one of the older officers overseas, returned to Canada on leave in Sept. 1917 after serving for 5 months as Acting Director of Veterinary Services and Remounts during Neill's absence. There, he relinquished his commission in the C.E.F., and in Dec. 1917 returned to duty as A.D.V.S., M.D. No. 10, in Winnipeg, from which he did not retire until 1924; he left the C.A.V.C. in 1927. In 1922, he was operating an "up-to-date Canine Hospital" on Sherbrooke St. in Winnipeg. *Anon., Can. Vet. Rec. Vol. 3, p. 84, 1922; Appendix H; Smith, H.D., Service Record, CEF, NAC.*
43. Invalided out due to severe sciatica. *Stevenson, C.A., Service Record, CEF, NAC.*
44. Developed severe hemorrhoids while at front; given compassionate leave to England, then special leave to Canada in fall 1917. Retained in Canada on advice of Medical Board. *Titus, R.C., Service Record, CEF, NAC.*
45. Diagnosed with pulmonary tuberculosis, likely acquired in Belgium. Waddy died 26 June 1957, in his 71st year. *Waddy, R., Service Record, CEF, NAC.*
46. Walsh gave his date and place of birth as November 26, 1877, Accrington, Lancashire, England, at attestation *Walsh, Frederick, Service Record, CEF, NAC.* See Note 11.15 regarding the circumstances of his early return to Canada.
47. Welch may also have served in the Imperial Army Veterinary Corps, prior to joining the C.A.V.C. See J.W. Welsh, Appendix B. No J.W. Welsh graduated from O.V.C., and the periods of service are sequential.
48. Wilson, an older officer, returned to Canada on 3 months furlough leave in May 1917. There, he resigned his commission in the C.E.F. 15.8.17, and in Oct. 1917 returned to his duties as P.V.O. M.D. No. 1, London Ont. *Wilson, J.H., Service Record, CEF, NAC.*
49. See Chapter 12.

Appendix B

1. The numbers vary with the source. *Blenkinsop & Rainey, 1925, p. 23* have 169 regular veterinary officers; *Clabby, 1963, p. 16* has 164.
2. *Moore, 1921, pp. 6-7.*
3. *Moore, 1921, p. 7*, though *Clabby, 1963, p. 16*, has the strength of the A.V.C. at 1356 officers and 23,146 other ranks "by 1918". *Blenkinsop & Rainey, 1925, p. 26*, also cite 1356 officers in the A.V.C. "on November 11th, 1918", with 27, 950 other ranks "at its maximum" *p. 31.* The unit with which each of the 46 Mobile Veterinary Sections extant in France in spring 1917 was associated, and the number and location of the 18 British Veterinary Hospitals operation at the time is found in *Blenkinsop & Rainey, 1925, pp. 18-19.* There were, in addition, 11 Regular and Territorial A.V.C. and 5 or 6 A.A.V.C. Mobile Veterinary Sections in Egypt/Palestine, with 5 Veterinary Hospitals and one Camel Hospital; 6 Regular and Territorial A.V.C. Mobile Veterinary Sections and 3 Veterinary Hospitals in Salonika; and one A.V.C. and 4 Indian Mobile Veterinary Sections in Mesopotamia *Blenkinsop & Rainey, 1925, pp. 19-21; Curson, 1933a.*

4. *Moore, 1921, p. 7; Blenkinsop & Rainey, 1925, pp. 18-19.*
5. *Smith, 1927, p. 240.*
6. *Moore, 1921, p. 7.*
7. *Curson, 1933a; Henry 1929, 1931, 1932; Whitfield, 1951.*
8. About half the 2400 veterinarians under the age of 60 from Scotland, England and Wales were in the Army Veterinary Service by mid-1918; probably fewer than 120 of those still in practice were under age 40 *Blenkinsop & Rainey, 1926, pp. 23-26.* Recruitment of Canadians into the Army Veterinary Corps is described by *Duguid, 1938, pp. 164-165.* His count was 190 Canadians so commissioned over the course of the war, while *Blenkinsop & Rainey, 1925, p. 26* state that 182 officers from the Overseas Dominions, "...the majority of whom were Canadian graduates" were given temporary commissions in the A.V.C. This Appendix contains 208 names; an additional 14 officers in the Militia List were marked (*ia*), signifying sent to the Imperial Army Veterinary Corps, but do not appear here; they are found in Appendix H.
9. These totals are French's from Chapter 11. See Note 11.3 re deviations from these figures in Appendices A and B.
10. This list of names of Canadians who served in the Imperial Army Veterinary Service is as found in French's Manuscript, with the exception of minor additions by the editors, enclosed in square brackets.
11. Places of interment are: J.L. Clark, Cairo War Memorial Cemetery, Egypt; C.C. Corbett, Mendingham Military Cemetery, Belgium; F.J. Delaine, Toronto Prospect Cemetery, Toronto, Ontario; W. Huston, Bailleul Communal Cemetery, France; W.J. Kee, Fernhill Cemetery, St. John, New Brunswick; H.H. Lefebvre, Brookwood Military Cemetery, Woking, Surrey, U.K.; W.A. Morrin, St. Sever Cemetery, Rouen, France; W.S. Thompson, Deloraine Cemetery, Souris, Manitoba. *Commonwealth War Graves Commission, 1992, 1994.*
12. See note A.47 regarding possible identity of J.W. Welsh and J.W. Welch.

Appendix C

1. Lawrence A. Donovan, a native of Coldbrook N.B., practiced after the war in Saint John N.B. He was a leader in the Ayreshire Breeder's Association and on agricultural fair boards in the Maritime Provinces. He died March 3 1948. His son Lawrence A. of Saint John, and his grandson Paul, of Toronto, Ontario, also are graduates of the Ontario Veterinary College. *Donovan, obit., 1948.*
2. List as found in the French Manuscript; probably incomplete, since none of the awards are dated prior to 1917.
3. *Smith, 1927, p. 240*; see Note 10.5.

Appendix D

1. This nominal roll of the Warrant Officers, Non-Commissioned Officers and enlisted men in the C.A.V.C. overseas, without Rank and Regimental Numbers, was among The French Papers. An index of names and numbers of all men who served in the C.E.F., by the National Archives of Canada, is accessible via the Internet at http://www.archives.ca/db/cef/.

   The contents are as found, with two exceptions. A few duplicate names were eliminated, since it was impossible to identify, without regimental numbers, more than one individual with the same name. Deleted as well was reference to a C.A.V.C. unit which was associated with most names. Some surnames or initials were difficult to identify from the original typescript. There are several evident spelling errors based on what may be mistranscription of handwritten names at some point in early preparation of the list or of the French manuscript (e.g. H. Newett in list for A. Newell in text; R. Scheiding in list for R. Scheising in text; P.J. Tappin in list for P.J. Tappan in text), and there are further inconsistencies with names in the lists of Other Ranks in Appendix E, Part 2. *French Papers, MG30, E14, C - Roll, Other Ranks.*

   Several individuals, such as A.E. Frape and W.C.V. Prinn, were promoted from the ranks to officer status, and hence are in both Appendix A and Appendix D. But W. Denton, who also was promoted from Staff Sergeant to Honorary Lieutenant (Ch. 10), is found only in Appendix A.

   This list undoubtedly is very incomplete, since fewer than 30% of the over 90 N.C.O.s and men named in the text of Chapters 3 and 5-12 in French's manuscript, and only 53% of the 224 Other Ranks in Appendix E, Part 2, are found in Appendix D. The Royal Army Veterinary Corps, which had a total of 1,668 officers serve throughout the war, about 11 times the total of the C.A.V.C., had a total of 41,755 Other Ranks over the course of the conflict *Smith, 1927, p. 270.* If the C.A.V.C. were in proportion, about 3800 Other Ranks would have served, rather than the 1178 found here; such an estimate is consistent with the proportion of the Other Ranks found in both French's text and in this appendix, though a little higher than an estimate based on the names found in both Appendix D and Appendix E, Part 2.

   French (Ch. 10) notes that "At no time...was the London Office enabled to maintain an accurate record of the whereabouts in France of even the veterinary officers, not to speak of other ranks. It is to this fact that any shortcomings in the names of members of the veterinary corps in the pages of this work must be ascribed". This statement suggests that he was aware of deficiencies in this list, and perhaps of the names of Other Ranks mentioned in text, but the large discrepancy between names mentioned in text and in the list is amazing. In the French Papers is a document summarizing

Part 2 Orders at the War Records Office searched for details on other ranks, with notations that the unexamined records needed to be searched for names, numbers, units, distinctions and wounds. Movements of men out of and into the C.A.V.C. with 'comb-outs' related to the need for men of higher medical categories at the front clearly caused considerable flux in the roll of Other Ranks, complicating an accounting, and multiplying its size in relation to establishment (779 in 1918 - Ch. 2) due to high turnover. The same factors influenced the number of Other Ranks in the Imperial Army Veterinary Corps, and their training and efficiency *Blenkinsop & Rainey, 1925, pp. 30-31*; *French Papers NAC MG30, E14 C, Vol. 1*: *Part 2 Orders at records office - England and France.*

Appendix E

1. Part 1 of this Appendix is as found among The French Papers.
2. Called Section 3 in Chapter 4, p. 6, and in Part 2 of this Appendix.
3. Called Section 4 in Chapter 4, p. 6, and in Part 2 of this Appendix.
4. Part 2 has been transcribed from *Anon., The Call to Arms, 1914, pp. 67-68*. The lists of names have been alphabetized; spelling is as found in the source, even if inconsistent with other perhaps more reliable records. Lists of personnel of these units, plus No. 1 and No. 2 Mobile Veterinary Sections, the Veterinary Base Supply Depot, the Remount Depot, and veterinary officers attached to the horsed units of the First Contingent, can be found, with Regimental Numbers, in *Anon., List of Officers and Men Serving in the First Canadian Contingent of the British Expeditionary Force, 1914.* Since that list was presumably published, in England, later than 'A Call to Arms', the names do differ slightly, reflecting changes in personnel.

Appendix F

1. This appendix is the work of the Editors. The blueprint for the horse dip was with The French Papers.
2. *Miessner, 1917* summarizes well the information known on the cause and pathogenesis of mange during the Great War.
3. *Merillat & Campbell, 1935* describe, on pp. 898-902, the various means of treating mange in horses, and illustrate a sulphuration chamber on p. 900.
4. The epidemiology, signs, pathogenesis and control of glanders, including discussion of the correct reading of the intrapalpebral mallein test, may be found in *Miessner, 1917* and *Merillat & Campbell, 1935*. See also Fig. 5.3.

Appendix G

1. With the exception of the first paragraph, this material was with The French Papers.
2. *Moore, 1921*, p. 163.
3. *Merillat & Campbell, 1935* illustrate horses being destroyed in this manner on pp. 831 and 832.

Appendix H

1. Appendix H, compiled by the editors, records all individuals known to us who served in Canadian military units as Veterinary Surgeons or who were commissioned as Veterinary Officers prior to the outbreak of W.W. I.

   It also lists C.A.V.C. officers who enlisted for, but apparently did not proceed to, overseas service during the period 1 July 1914 - 1 January 1920. During W.W. I, most veterinarians who joined the C.A.V.C. (C.E.F./O.M.F.C.) (Appendix A) or the Imperial Army Veterinary Corps (Appendix B) were first commissioned in the C.A.V.C. with the rank of Provisional Lieutenant if they did not already hold a commission in the C.P.A.V.C. or C.A.V.C. This appendix contains name and date of gazetting in the C.A.V.C. of veterinarians who enlisted for service overseas from June 1914 to December 1918, but who are not found in Appendix A or B.

   This Appendix also records Canadian veterinarians commissioned in the R.C.A.V.C. or the C.A.V.C. (N.P.A.M.) and its successor, from 15 January 1921, when the wartime establishment had been fully demobilized and the C.A.V.C. reorganized, until November 1939, the last List of Officers published prior to disbandment in November 1940.

   Hence, the careers of individual officers may be followed from the Active Miltia to the C.E.F or Imperial Service in W.W. I, and back into the Militia, by consultation of this Appendix for the pre- and post-war periods, and Appendix A or B for the interval of the war. Veterinary officers who served only during W.W. I in either the C.A.V.C. (C.E.F./O.M.F.C.). or Imperial Veterinary Service will be found only in Appendix A or B.

   See Notes to Chapter 1 for organization of the Canadian N.P.A.M. and Permanent Force, and for ranks of veterinarians during various eras. The date of enrollment or promotion given is the date of seniority in rank given in the most up-to-date Militia List accessible to us. Since we could not gain access to a full run of the Militia Lists, some officers who had short careers may have been missed, and the last year of appointment may not be accurate; if in error it usually will be one year less than actual (eg. 1939 is listed as the last date for all officers prior to disbandment in 1940, since there was no list accessible for 1940). Militia Lists for 1920 and 1921 could not be found; they may not have been published.

NOTES - Appendices H & I

Revision, or disbandment and reorganization of the Army Veterinary Department or Veterinary Corps occurred in 1897, 1903, 1905, 1910-12, 1919-21, 1931 and 1936, with reappointment of most, but not all officers. Hence, many appointments and promotions date from, or careers end in, those years. Reappointments were sometimes at different rank, or in different units. Officers with a final date of 1919 in this Appendix likely were inactive, and were retired or placed on the Reserve List at disbandment and reorganization in January 1921; many such were found in the Reserve of Officers, 1925, and have a final date of 1921 here. A purge of over-age officers occurred in 1931. The 1936 reorganization of the N.P.A.M. reorganized and reduced the establishment of the Veterinary Service.

Sources: Lists of Officers published by the Militia Department and its successors; *Boulton, 1886* and *Wilson, 1975* (1885 Rebellion); and *Smith, 1919, Ridpath et al., 1899, Marquis, 1900, Curson, 1933a,b*, and *Roncetti & Denby, undated* (Boer War). Lists of Officers consulted were: *The Active or Volunteer Militia Force List of Canada - Apr. 1863; The Annual Volunteer and Service Militia List of Canada - Feb. 1865, Mar. 1866, Mar. 1867; The Annual Active Militia List of the Dominion of Canada - Apr. 1870; Dominion of Canada Militia - Aug. 1873, Mar. 1875; The Annual Militia List of the Dominion of Canada - Dec. 1876; The Militia List of the Dominion of Canada - Apr. and Dec. 1881, Jan. 1883, Jan. 1885, Jan. 1886, Jan. 1887, Jan. 1888, Jan. 1889, Jan. 1890, Jan. 1891, Jan. 1892, Jan. 1893, Jan. 1895, Jan. 1896, Jan. and Oct. 1897, Apr. and Oct. 1898; The Quarterly Militia List of the Dominion of Canada - Apr. and Oct. 1899, Jan. 1900, Jan. 1901, Apr. 1902, Jan. 1903, Jan. 1904, Jan. 1905, Jan. 1906, Jul. 1907, Jan. 1908, Jan. 1909, Oct. 1910, May and Oct. 1911, Apr. 1912, Apr. 1913, Jan. Mar. June. and Sept 1914, Jan. and Jul. 1915, Jan. 1916, Jan. and Jul. 1917; The Militia List of the Dominion of Canada - Sept. 1918, Jan. and Jul. 1919, Dec. 1922, Jan. 1924, Jan. 1925, Part II Sept. 1925; Department of National Defence, Canada List of Officers, Militia Service and Air Service - Apr. 1926, Apr. 1927, Jul. 1928; Department of National Defence, List of Officers, Defence Forces of the Dominion of Canada - Feb. 1930, Apr. 1931, Jul. 1932; Department of National Defence, Defence Forces List, Canada - Jul. 1934, Nov. 1935, Dec. 1936, Aug. 1938, Nov. 1939.*

Names are spelled as found, with alternative or correct spellings from other sources [bracketed].

2. See Appendices A and B for college of graduation of those in C.E.F. and Imperial Army Veterinary Corps respectively. See Note A.2 for college histories and sources of place/year of graduation. E.M.v.M. = Ecole de Médecine vétérinaire de Montréal; E.v.Q. = Ecole vétérinaire du Québec; Laval = Ecole vétérinaire française de Montréal and successors; M.V.C. = Montreal Veterinary College; McGill = Faculty of Comparative Medicine and Veterinary Science, McGill University; O.V.C. = Ontario Veterinary College; Qu = School of Veterinary Science, Queen's University.
3. See Note 1.3.
4. See Note 1.4.
5. See Chapter 12.
6. The entry in the Miltia List may have been in error. Bowlby is the 'Surgeon', not 'Veterinary Surgeon', in this unit for the rest of his career.
7. *Busselle, obit., 1942.*
8. Although Appendix A lists Church's date of graduation from OVC as 1914, borne out by the college calendar, he was a commissioned Veterinary-Lieutenant from 1908. He may have had a 2 year diploma (VS) and returned for a third year to graduate B.V.Sc. in 1914, a not uncommon practice, but if so, his initial diploma was not from OVC.
9. See Chapter 12.
10. Lieut.-Col. A.W. Harris was born in Ottawa, Ontario on 5 March 1861, and he died there 19 December 1924. His Militia career spanned over 40 years. He enlisted in The Princess Louise Dragoon Guards, Ottawa, in 1879 as a trooper. In 1884 he became Veterinary Surgeon to the Ottawa Field Battery, and he retained his association with its successors until he retired. He was a member of the Board of examiners of the Faculty of Comparative Medicine and Veterinary Science at McGill. During the Boer War, Harris secured remounts for the Canadian contingents. He served as P.V.O. for Camp Petawawa, and during W.W. I was Assistant Director of Veterinary Services on the home front, as well as purchasing remounts in a private capacity for the Canadian, British and French armies. *Harris, obit., 1922; Harris, obit., 1924-25.*
11. Macdonald lived in South Africa until at least 1911 *Smith, 1919, p. 227; Curson, 1933a,b.*
12. See Chapter 12.
13. See Note 17.18 and Appendix A for Taschereau's prior military record.
14. See Chapter 12.

Appendix I

1. These abbreviations are based in part on *Blenkinsop & Rainey, 1925, p. x; Duguid, 1938, Vol. I, Part 2, pp. 455-459;* and *Nicholson, 1962, pp. 557-559.*

SOURCES

Sources cited by author or title and date in the Notes are found here. Unattributed untitled articles, and most documents from the National Archives of Canada or Directorate of History and Heritage, D.N.D., are cited in full in the relevant note.

Amended Regulations for the Canadian Army Veterinary Service (Peace) 1930. Draft, May 18, 1929. NAC RG24, Vol. 6532, File HQ621-3-7 v2.

Annual Calendar of the Faculty of Comparative Medicine and Veterinary Science, McGill University, late Montreal Veterinary College, Montreal, 32 pp., 1902-1903.

Annual Report, The ffrench Remedy Co. Ltd., 1950. GR 1526, File No. 9717, Reel B-5349, frame 85. British Columbia Archives and Records Service, Victoria B.C.

Anon. Administration and Command in Canadian Army Veterinary Service. American Veterinary Review, Vol. 40, pp. 632, 685, 1912.

Anon. The Call to Arms. Montreal's Roll of Honour, European War, 1914. Southam, Montreal, pp. 67-68, 1914.

Anon. List of Officers and Men Serving in the First Canadian Contingent of the British Expeditionary Force, 1914. Sold for the benefit of the Queen's Canadian Military Hospital, Beachborough Park, Shorncliffe. 1914.

Anon. The New Badge R.A.V.C. The Veterinary Record, Vol. 32, p. 485, 1920.

Anon. Central Canada Veterinary Association. Canadian Veterinary Record, Vol. 1, No. 1, p. 34, 1920.

Anon. The Horse Still Thrives. Canadian Veterinary Record, Vol. 2, No. 2, p. 41, 1921.

Anon. Ontario Veterinary Association. Canadian Veterinary Record, Vol. 2, No. 2, pp. 107-108, 1921.

Anon. Recognition of the Work Done by the Royal Army Veterinary Corps During The Great War. The Veterinary Record, Vol. 33, p. 305, 1921.

Anon. The Australian Horse in the War. Canadian Veterinary Record, Vol. 3, p. 100, 1922.

Anon. Back to Horses in England. Canadian Veterinary Record, Vol. 3, p. 101, 1922.

Anon. Royal Canadian Army Veterinary Corps. Canadian Veterinary Record, Vol. 3, p. 108, 1922.

Anon. Reminiscences of the Great War. Canadian Veterinary Record, Vol. 3, p. 237, 1922.

Anon. A Famous Horse at Stanley Barracks. Canadian Veterinary Record, Vol. 4, p. 275, 1923.

Anon. Small Animal Section [re J.A. Campbell]. Canadian Veterinary Record, Vol. 6, No. 1, p. 37, 1925.

Anon. Zimmerman's Travel Story of Cook's Voyages Reaches Here. The Daily Colonist, Victoria B.C., 19 Feb., 1926.

Anon. Colonel Edgett is New Warden of B.C. Penitentiary. The Vernon News, 20 Jun., 1929.

Anon. Modernist in Police Work. Vancouver Province, 20 Mar., 1932.

Anon. Chief Edgett, Dismissed on Mayor's Casting Vote, Charges Rank Injustice. Vancouver Province, 7 Feb., 1933.

Anon. Reorganization of the Canadian Militia. Canadian Defence Quarterly, Vol. 13, pp. 468-469, 1935-36.

Anon. Reorganization of the Canadian Militia. Canadian Defence Quarterly, Vol. 14, pp. 218, 225-232, 1936-37.

Anon. The New Veterinary Director General. Canadian Journal of Comparative Medicine, Vol. 3, pp. 117-118, 1939.

Anon. The Canadian Officers Training Corps. Veterinary Digest, Vol. 1, p. 158, 1939.

Anon. Canadian Officers Training Corps. Veterinary Digest, Vol. 1, p. 188, 1939.

Anon. Alne Edward Cameron, M.C., V.D., V.S., Veterinary Director-General of Canada. Veterinary Digest Vol. 2, pp. 22-23, 1940.

Anon. Alfred Savage B.S.A., D.V.M., M.R.C.V.S. Veterinary Digest, Vol. 2, pp. 118-119, 1940.

Anon. C.O.T.C. Veterinary Digest, Vol. 2, pp. 192-193, 1940.

Anon. Dr. Watson Honoured. Canadian Journal of Comparative Medicine, Vol. 4, p. 178, 1940.

Anon. Canadian Army Veterinary Corps Disbanded. Canadian Journal of Comparative Medicine, Vol. 5, p. 4, 1941.

Anon. Royal Canadian Army Veterinary Corps. Canadian Journal of Comparative Medicine, Vol. 5, pp. 92-93, 1941.

Anon. A War Waste. Canadian Journal of Comparative Medicine, Vol. 5, p. 153, 1941.

Anon. Canadian Army Veterinary Corps. Canadian Journal of Comparative Medicine, Vol. 5, p. 302, 1941.

Anon. Ontario Veterinary Association - Presidential Address. Canadian Journal of Comparative Medicine, Vol. 6, pp. 61-62, 1942.

Anon. Veterinary Profession in Canada. Canadian Journal of Comparative Medicine, Vol. 6, p. 251, 1942.

Anon. Dr. A.E. Cameron V.D.G. Retires. Canadian Journal of Comparative Medicine, Vol. 7, pp. 97- 98, 1943.

Anon. Dr. E.A. Watson Retires. Canadian Journal of Comparative Medicine, Vol. 7, pp. 98-99, 1943.

Anon. Canadian Army Veterinary Corps. Canadian Journal of Comparative Medicine, Vol. 7, p. 290, 1943.

Anon. Appointment of Veterinary Director General [M. Barker]. Canadian Journal of Comparative Medicine, Vol. 8, p. 24, 1944.

Anon. Retirement of Lt. Col. T.C. Evans, M.C. Canadian Journal of Comparative Medicine, Vol. 8, p. 102, 1944.

Anon. Veterinary Congress Award. Canadian Journal of Comparative Medicine, Vol. 12, pp. 234-235, 1948.

Sources

Barker, C.A.V., and T.A. Crowley. One Voice - A History of the Canadian Veterinary Medical Association. Canadian Veterinary Medical Association, Ottawa, Ont., 260 pp., 1989.

Bigland, C.H. Letter to F.E. Gattinger, re C.O.T.C. and disbandment of R.C.A.V.C., 8 Dec., 1961, C.A.V. Barker Museum.

'Biscum'. Instructional value of the Canadian Army Veterinary Corps. Canadian Veterinary Record, Vol. 2, pp. 25-28, 1921.

Blackmore, D.K., D.G. Owen and C.M. Young. Some observations on the diseases of *Brunus edwardii* (*Species nova*). The Veterinary Record, Vol. 90, pp. 382-385, 1972.

Blenkinsop, L.J, and J.W. Rainey. History of the Great War Based on Official Documents - Veterinary Services. His Majesty's Stationery Office, London, 782 pp., 1925.

Blood, D.C. and V.P. Studdert. Baillière's Comprehensive Veterinary Dictionary, Baillière Tindall, London, 1124 pp., 1988.

Boulter, A.W. "Necessity is the Mother of..." (A Western Battery Goes to Camp). Canadian Defence Quarterly, Vol. 9, pp. 101-104, 1931-32.

Boulton, C.A. Reminiscences of the North-West Rebellions. Grip Printing and Publishing Co., Toronto, 531 pp., 1886.

Bramley, S.H. Letter to C.A.V. Barker, re R.C.A.V.C., 30 Jun. 1983. C.A.V. Barker Museum.

Brown, V.R. Auxiliary Military Training. Veterinary Digest, Vol. 2, pp. 193-194, 1940.

Bryden, J. Deadly Allies. McClelland & Stewart Ltd., Toronto, 314 pp., 1989.

Bullock, F. Memoir of the Author. In: The Early History of Veterinary Literature and its British Development, Vol. IV, F. Smith, edited by F. Bullock. Baillière Tindall & Cox, pp. xi-xvii, 1933.

Burns, E.L.M. The Mechanicalization of Cavalry. Canadian Defence Quarterly, Vol. 1, p. 6, 1923-24.

Burns, E.L.M. A Step Towards Mechanicalization. Canadian Defence Quarterly, Vol. 8, pp. 3-7, 1930-31.

Burns, E.L.M. Looks or Use? Canadian Defence Quarterly, Vol. 9, pp. 88-91, 1931-32.

Burns, E.L.M. A Step Towards Modernization. Canadian Defence Quarterly, Vol. 12, pp. 298-305, 1934-35.

Burns, E.L.M. Where Do Tanks Belong? Canadian Defence Quarterly, Vol. 16, pp. 28-31, 1938-39.

Busselle, A.W., obituary. Canadian Journal of Comparative Medicine, Vol. 6, p. 34, 1942.

Calendar, Ontario Veterinary College, 1864-1945. C.A.V. Barker Museum.

Cameron, A.E. War and the Health of Animals Division. Canadian Journal of Comparative Medicine, Vol. 6, pp. 46-49, 1942.

Cameron, A.E., obituary. Canadian Veterinary Journal, Vol. 5, No. 11, p. xx, 1964.

Canadian War Memorials Exhibition, Catalogue, The Royal Academy of Arts, Burlington House, Piccadilly, W., 1919.

Canadian War Memorials Exhibition, Catalogue, Anderson Galleries, New York, N.Y., 1919.

Canadian War Memorials Paintings Exhibition -1920- New Series the Last Phase, Catalogue, Toronto, 1920.

Carter, H.E. A Short History of the British Army Veterinary Services. Veterinary History, N.S. Vol. 9, pp. 38-45, 1996.

Case, J.N. An Introduction to the Veterinary Militaria of the British Empire. Veterinary History, N.S. Vol. 9, pp. 82-94, 1996.

Certificate of Incorporation, The ffrench Remedy Company Limited. GR 1526, File No. 9717, Reel B-5349, frame 1. British Columbia Archives and Records Service, Victoria B.C.

Charrington, H.V.S. The Employment of Cavalry, Canadian Defence Quarterly, Vol. 8, pp. 367-373, 1930-31a.

Charrington, H.V.S. Experiences of a Mechanized Cavalryman, Canadian Defence Quarterly, Vol. 8, pp. 498-503, 1930-31b.

Chisholm, A, and M. Davie. Beaverbrook - A Life. Hutchinson, London, 589 pp., 1992.

Christie, N.M. Officers of the Canadian Expeditionary Force Who Died Overseas 1914-1919. E.G. Ursual, Ottawa, 1988.

Clabby, J. The History of the Royal Army Veterinary Corps 1919-1961. J.A. Allen and Co., London, 244 pp., 1963.

Clement, C. Communication with I.K. Barker re Talmage Collection, National War Museum, February 1999. C.A.V. Barker Museum.

Colebourn, F. Biographical Sketch - Harry Colebourn V.S., B.V.Sc., M.R.C.V.S., F.Z.S., C.A.V.C. 3 pp., undated. C.A.V. Barker Museum.

Commonwealth War Graves Commission, Maidenhead, Berkshire, England. Letters to C.A.V. Barker, 5 Aug. 1992, 12 Apr. 1994. C.A.V. Barker Museum.

Crosby, A.W. America's Forgotten Pandemic - The Influenza of 1918. Cambridge University Press, Cambridge, 337 pp., 1989.

Cross, W.K. The Charlton Standard Catalogue of First World War Canadian Corps Cap Badges, 1st Edition. The Charlton Press, Toronto, 1995.

Curson, H.H. The Volunteer Veterinary Services of the Empire and the Second Anglo-Boer War (1899-1902). The Veterinary Record, Vol. 13, pp. 829-841, 1933a.

Curson, H.H. The Veterinary Profession in South Africa. 4.-Transvaal Volunteers (1902-1913). Journal of the South African Veterinary Medical Association, Vol. 4, pp. 36-45, 1933b.

Daigneault, F.A., obituary. Canadian Veterinary Journal, Vol. 4, No. 6, p. xviii, 1963.

Dauth, A., obituary. Hommage au Dr. Albert Dauth. Canadian Journal of Comparative Medicine, Vol. 5, p. 58, 1941.

David, Philippe. Letters to C.A.V. Barker re C.V.H. No. 1, Le Havre, 7 Oct. 1992, 4 Mar. 1993. C.A.V. Barker Museum.

Sources

Donnell, A. The Canadian Army Veterinary Corps. Appendix IV, In: Canada in the Great World War, Vol. V, The Triumph of the Allies. United Publishers of Canada Ltd., Toronto, pp. 327-340, 1920.

Donovan, L.A., obituary. Lawrence A. Donovan. Canadian Journal of Comparative Medicine, Vol. 12, p. 118, 1948.

Dress Regulations for Canadian Units Attached to General Officer Commanding Canadians, Canadian Overseas Military Forces, London, 10 Dec., 1916. RG9, III, B.1, Vol. 2765, D157-33.

Duguid, A. Fortescue. Official History of the Canadian Forces in the Great War 1914-1919. Minister of National Defence, the King's Printer, Ottawa, Volume I, 596 pp.; Vol. I, Appendices and Maps, 464 pp., 14 maps, 1938.

Dukes, T.W. A Glimpse at the Canadian Army Veterinary Corps. Veterinary History, N.S. Vol. 7, pp. 86-90, 1993.

Dukes, T.W. On the Middle Road: Queen's University's Foray into Veterinary and Comparative Medicine. Cognate Essay, M.A., Queen's University, Kingston, Ont., 83 pp., 1997.

Dukes, T., and J. Prescott. Theodore Augustus Girling (1876-1919): Canadian Veterinarian and Great War Poet. Canadian Veterinary Journal 32: 694-699, 1991.

Dunlop, R.H., and D.J. Williams. Veterinary Medicine, An Illustrated History. Moseby, St. Louis Missouri, 692 pp., 1996.

Edgett, C.E., obituary, Vancouver Province, 9 Jan., 1947.

Edgett, C.E., obituary, Canadian Journal of Comparative Medicine, Vol. 11, p. 10, 1947.

Etienne, A.A., obituary. A la Mémoire du Docteur Albert A. Etienne. Canadian Journal of Comparative Medicine, Vol. 5, p. 32, 1941.

Evans, A.M. Andrew Smith. In: Dictionary of Canadian Biography, Vol. XIII, 1901-1910, Ramsay Cook and Jean Hamelin, editors, University of Toronto Press, Toronto, pp. 961-963, 1994.

Evans, A.M., and C.A.V. Barker. Century One - A History of the Ontario Veterinary Association. A.M. Evans and C.A.V. Barker, 516 pp., 1976.

Evans. T.C. Girling's poems. Canadian Veterinary Record, Vol. 2, No. 3, p. 54, 1921.

Evans, T.C. Army Veterinary Service in War. Canadian Veterinary Record, Vol. 3, pp. 51-52, 1922.

Evans, T.C. A Study of Horse versus Tractor. Canadian Veterinary Record, Vol. 3, pp. 79-84, 1922.

Evans, T.C. Letter to F.E. Gattinger, re R.C.A.V.C. and French Manuscript, 7 Feb. 1962. The C.A.V. Barker Museum.

Evans, T.C., obituary. Canadian Veterinary Journal, Vol. 3, No. 10, p. xii, 1962.

ffrench, C., obituary. Cecil ffrench Dies Here; Credited with Saving the Fox. The Times, Vancouver, B.C., Sept. 7, 1951.

Forneret, R.G. Prepare to Mount. Canadian Defence Quarterly, Vol. 9, pp. 389-392, 1931-32.

Fox, E.M. Letter to C.A.V. Barker, re C.G. Saunders, 9 Aug.-30 Oct. 1994. C.A.V. Barker Museum.

Fraser, W.B. Always a Strathcona. Comprint Publishing, Calgary, 1976.

French, C. Some interesting canine cases. The Journal of Comparative Medicine and Veterinary Archives, Vol. 17, pp. 294-295, 1896.

French, C. Surgical Diseases and Surgery of the Dog. Washington D.C., 408 pp., 1906.

French, C. Reminiscences of the Great War. The Aid Extended by Humane and Kindred Societies to the Canadian Army Veterinary Corps. Canadian Veterinary Record, Vol. 3, pp. 149-158, 213-218 (Part II), 1922.

French, C. Reminiscences of the Great War. (Continued). Canadian Veterinary Record, Vol. 4, pp. 106-109, 1923a.

French, C. Reminiscences of the Great War. The Veterinary Officer. Canadian Veterinary Record, Vol. 4, pp. 160–164, 1923b.

French, C., and Elsa Michaelis, translators. Zimmerman's Captain Cook, An Account of the Third Voyage of Captain Cook Around the World, 1776-1780, by Henry Zimmerman, of Wissloch, in the Palatine. Ryerson Press, Toronto, 120 pp., 1930.

French, C. For Your Dog, 31st Edition. ffrench Remedy Company, Victoria, B.C., 64 pp., 1938.

French, C. Silkworm Rearing as a Pastime - First Canadian Edition. The Acme Press, Victoria B.C., 23 pp., 1942.

French, C. For Your Dog, 40th Edition. ffrench Remedy Company, Victoria, B.C., 55 pp., 1948.

French, C., obituary. Founder of Animal Medicine Firm, Cecil French, 80, Dies in Victoria. The Daily Colonist, Victoria, B.C., Friday 7 Sept., 1951.

French, C., obituary. Cecil French, Noted Animal Lover Dead. The Sun, Vancouver, B.C., 7 Sept., 1951.

French, C. Ernest, death notice. The Globe and Mail, Feb. 13, 1961.

French, Florence S., obituary. The Daily Colonist, Victoria, B.C., p. 16, 26 Sept., 1962.

French, Florence S., obituary. The Times, Vancouver, B.C., p. 21, 26 Sept., 1962.

French Papers, Inventory and Finding Aid, Volume 1 - Correspondence and Memoranda 1916-1919 re veterinary services; Volumes 2 & 3 - Manuscript, 1933, A history of the Canadian Army Veterinary Corps. MG30 E 14, National Archives of Canada, Ottawa, Ontario.

Gattinger, F.E. A Century of Challenge - A History of the Ontario Veterinary College. University of Toronto Press, Toronto, 224 pp., 1962.

Sources

General Orders. The Department of Militia and Defence, Dominion of Canada, Ottawa, and its successors, 1890-1939.

German-Reed, T. The North West Canada 1885 Medal, Together with Some Account of the Campaign for Which It was Awarded. Canadian Defence Quarterly, Vol. 14, pp. 86-100, 1936-37.

Girling, T.A. The Salient and other Poems, 2nd Edition with Four Additional Poems. Cecil Palmer and Hayward, London, 66 pp., 1918.

Goforth, W.W. The Influence of Mechanization and Motorization on the Organization and Training of the Non Permanent Active Militia. Canadian Defence Quarterly, Vol. 10, pp. 431-453, 1932-33.

Gordon, G. Letter to C.A.V. Barker, re Samuel Charles Richards, 13 Feb., 1992. C.A.V. Barker Museum.

Gordon, G. Letter to C.A.V. Barker, re Charles Edgar Edgett, 22 Dec., 1992. C.A.V. Barker Museum.

Granatstein, J.L. The Generals - The Canadian Army's Senior Commanders in the Second World War. Stoddart Publishing, Toronto, 370 pp., 1993.

Gray, E.A. The Trumpet of Glory - The Military Career of John Shipp, First Veterinary Surgeon to Join the British Army. Robert Hale, London, 127 pp., 1985.

Greenhous, B. Dragoon - The Centennial History of the Royal Canadian Dragoons, 1883-1983. The Guild of the Royal Canadian Dragoons, Belleville, Ont., 557 pp., 1983.

Grignon, L.M., obituary. Dr. Louis-Marie Grignon. Canadian Journal of Comparative Medicine, Vol. 8, p. 32, 1944.

Halliday, H.A. The Senate Paintings. The Beaver, Vol. 75, No. 5, pp. 4-8, 1995.

Hamilton, C.F. The Canadian Militia: The Change in Organization. Canadian Defence Quarterly, Volume 8, pp. 94-97, 1930-31.

Harper, J.H. Letter to C.A.V. Barker, re C.A.V.C. badges, 29 Mar., 1998. C.A.V. Barker Museum of Veterinary History.

Harper, J.H. Letter to I.K. Barker, re C.A.V.C. badges, 15 Feb., 1999a. C.A.V. Barker Museum of Veterinary History.

Harper, J.H. A Source of Pride - Regimental Badges and Titles in the Canadian Expeditionary Force 1914-1919. Service Publications, Ottawa, Ont., 160 pp., 1999b.

Harris, A.W., obituary. Canadian Veterinary Record, Vol. 3, p. 23, 1922.

Harris, A.W., obituary. Alexander Waddell Harris. Journal of the American Veterinary Medical Association, Vol. 19, p. 672, 1924-25.

Harris, S.J. Canadian Brass: The Making of a Professional Army, 1860-1939. University of Toronto Press, Toronto, 271 pp., 1988.

Harvey, F.M.W. Correspondence. Canadian Defence Quarterly, Vol. 12, pp. 118-121, 1934-35.

Haycock, R.G. Sir Sam Hughes: His Public Career, 1892-1916. PhD Thesis, The University of Western Ontario, London, 348 pp., 1976.

Haycock, R.G. Sam Hughes. The Public Career of a Controversial Canadian, 1885-1916. Wilfred Laurier University Press, Waterloo, Ontario, 355 pp., 1986.

Henderson, W. Letter to C.A.V. Barker, re S.C. Richards, C. French and C.E. Edgett, 10 Aug. 1992. C.A.V. Barker Museum.

Henderson's Directory of Victoria, 1921, cited in Mattison, 1993.

Henry, Max. Notes of a Veterinary Officer with the A.I.F. (1914-1919). The Australian Veterinary Journal, Vol. 5, pp. 149-153, 1929; Vol. 7, pp. 43-57, 1931; Vol. 8, pp. 12-20, 1932.

Henry, Max. The Transport of Horses by Sea and Land. The Australian Veterinary Journal, Vol. 9, pp. 208-212, 1933.

Henry, Max. The Activities of the A.V.C. The Australian Veterinary Journal, Vol. 11, pp. 11-16, 1935.

Henry, Max. Gas Warfare as Affecting Horses and Mules. The Australian Veterinary Journal, Vol. 11, pp. 143-148, 1935.

Hickman, J. The Veterinary Profession and the Horse. Veterinary History, N.S. Vol. 3, pp. 57-75, 1983/84.

Hickman, J. The Royal Army Veterinary Corps During the 1930's. Veterinary History, N.S. Vol. 4, pp. 107-117, 1986.

Higgins, C.H. Reminiscences of Events Before and After Formation of Health of Animals Branch. Canadian Journal of Comparative Medicine, Vol. 6, pp. 159-162, 1942; Vol. 7, pp. 3-6, 1943.

Historical Section, General Staff. Short History Canadian Army Veterinary Services. Department of National Defence, Ottawa, 2 pp., 30 Oct., 1929.

Howes, David. Sir Henri-Elzéar Taschereau. In: Dictionary of Canadian Biography, Volume XIV, 1911-1920, Ramsay Cook and Jean Hamelin, editors, University of Toronto Press, Toronto, pp. 961-963, 1998.

Hyatt, A.M.J. Canadian Generals of the First World War and the Popular View of Military Leadership. Histoire Sociale - Social History, Vol. 12, pp. 418-430, 1979.

Imperial Order Daughters of the Empire. "*A Mobile Veterinary Unit in France*" by Algernon Talmage, color lithograph, approx. 61 x 68.5 cm.; Fine Arts Publishing Company London; IODE impression seal and printed inscription on lithograph "*Presented by the Imperial Order Daughters of the Empire in memory of the Men and Women of the Empire who gave their lives in the Great War 1914-1918*"; imprinted on wooden frame "*Presented to the school by the Imperial Order Daughters of the Empire in cooperation with the Department of Education, 1926*". C.A.V. Barker

Sources

Museum of Canadian Veterinary History, Guelph, Ontario.
Irwin, R.W. A Guide to the War Medals and Decorations of Canada. Second Edition. R. Irwin, Guelph, Ontario, 92 pp., 1971.
Jackson, H.M., Lieut.-Col. Diaries, Volume XI, p. 3660. The Directorate of History and Heritage, Department of National Defence, Ottawa, Ont.
Johnson, J., and A. Greutzner, eds. The Dictionary of British Artists, 1880-1940. Antique Collectors' Club, England, 567 pp., 1976.
Kesten, S.H. Veterinary Corps Omitted. Canadian Journal of Comparative Medicine, Vol. 3, pp. 115-116, 1939.
Kester, W.O. Army Food Inspection. Canadian Journal of Comparative Medicine, Vol. 2, pp. 301-306, 1938.
Kilbourne, E.D. Influenza. Plenum Medical Book Company, New York, 359 pp., 1987.
Kipling, A.L. and H.L. King. Head-Dress Badges of the British Army, Frederick Muller Ltd., London. 468 pp., 1973.
Law, Clive M. Khaki Uniforms of the Canadian Expeditionary Force. "Upclose" No. 3., Service Publications, Ottawa, Ont. 48 pp., undated, c. 1998.
Leclainche, E. Histoire de la Médecine Vétérinaire. Office du Livre, Toulouse, 812 pp., 1936.
LeMay, D., obituary. Major Daniel LeMay. Canadian Journal of Comparative Medicine, Vol. 3, p. 29, 1939.
Loew, F.M., and E.H. Wood. Vet in the Saddle. Western Producer Prairie Books, Saskatoon, Saskatchewan, 128 pp., 1978.
Love, B.I. Veterinarians of the Northwest Territories and Alberta, Alberta Veterinary Medical Association, 126 pp., undated, c.1965.
MacAdams, A.L. Teddy The Grey, A Note From the RSM. Prob. orig. Springbok, publ.of Royal Canadian Dragoons, date unknown. Republished in Southwest Quebec Dialogue, Vol. 5, No. 9, p. 32, 1992.
Macphail, A. Official History of the Canadian Forces in the Great War 1914-1919. The Medical Services. Minister of National Defence, The King's Printer, Ottawa, 428 pp., 1925.
Mann, C.C. The March of "A" Sqn., Royal Canadian Dragoons from St. Johns, P.Q., to Petawawa Military Camp, Ont. July 13th-July 25th, 1937. Canadian Defence Quarterly, Vol. 15, pp. 42-51, 1937-38.
Marquis, T.G. Canada's Sons on Kopje and Veldt. Canada's Sons Publishing Co., Toronto, Guelph, Stratford, 490pp, 1900.
Matheson, D. Fortune for 'Army'. The Daily Colonist, Victoria, B.C., p. 13, 1 Dec., 1962.
Mattison, D. Letter to C.A.V. Barker, re C. French, 15 Jun., 1993. C.A.V. Barker Museum.
McGilvray, C.D. The Value and Usefulness of the Veterinary Profession. Canadian Journal of Comparative Medicine, Vol. 7, pp. 87-93, 1943.
McGrew, R.E. Influenza. In: Encyclopedia of Medical History, McGraw-Hill, New York, pp. 150-154, 1985.
McLellan, D.J. Interview with C.A.V. Barker, Lindsay, Ontario, 16 Jul., 1981. Transcript in C.A.V. Barker Museum.
Memorandum on Training of the Canadian Militia. J.O. Patenaude, Printer to the King's Most Excellent Majesty, Ottawa, 1934.
Merillat, L.A., and D.M. Campbell. Veterinary Military History of the United States, Volumes I and II. Haver-Glover Laboratories, St. Louis, Missouri, 1172 pp., 1935.
Miessner, H. Epizoötics and their control during war. A guide for army, government and practicing veterinarians. Translation by A.A. Leibold of *Kriegttierseuchen und ihre Bekämpfung* (1915). American Veterinary Publishing Company, Chicago, 215 pp., 1917.
Miller, Carman. Painting the Map Red - Canada and the South African War 1899-1902. Canadian War Museum/McGill-Queen's University Press, Montreal and Kingston, 541 pp, 1993.
Miller, E.B. United States Army Veterinary Service in World War II. Medical Department, United States Army, Washington, D.C., 779 pp., 1961.
Mitchell, C.A. A Note on the Early History of Veterinary Science in Canada. Reprinted from the Canadian Journal of Comparative Medicine, 48 pp., 1938-1940.
Moore, J. Army Veterinary Service in War. H. & W. Brown, London, 191 pp., 1921.
Morton, D. French Canada and the Canadian Militia, 1868-1914. Histoire Sociale-Social History, Vol. 3, pp. 32-50, 1969.
Morton, D. A Peculiar Kind of Politics: Canada's Overseas Ministry in the First World War. University of Toronto Press, Toronto, 267 pp., 1982.
Morton, D. When Your Number's Up - The Canadian Soldier in the First World War. Random House, Toronto, 354 pp., 1993.
Morton, D. and J.L. Granatstein, Marching to Armageddon - Canadians and the Great War 1914-1919. Lester and Orpen Dennys, Toronto, 288 pp., 1989.
Neill, W.J., death notice. The Globe and Mail, Toronto, 8 Aug. 1955.
Nichols, C. Letter to C.A.V. Barker, re R.C.A.V.C. N.C.O.s at disbandment, 29 Oct., 1989. C.A.V. Barker Museum.
Nicholson, G.W.L. Official History of the Canadian Army in the First World War - Canadian Expeditionary Force 1914-1919. Department of National Defence, The Queen's Printer, Ottawa, 621 pp., 1962.
Nicholson, G.W.L. The Gunners of Canada - The History of the Royal Regiment of Canadian Artillery, Volume I, 1534-1919.

McLelland and Stewart, Toronto, 478 pp., 1967.
Nicholson, G.W.L. The Gunners of Canada - The History of the Royal Regiment of Canadian Artillery, Volume II, 1919-1967. McLelland and Stewart, Toronto, 760 pp., 1972.
'One of Them'. Retention of Rank on Demobilization. The Veterinary Record, Vol. 32, pp. 438-439, 1920.
Overseas Military Forces of Canada. Report of the Ministry, 1918. London, 533 pp., 1918.
Pallister, E.F. Letter re war service, and father, P.E. Pallister to C.A.V. Barker. 1 Jan., 1992. C.A.V. Barker Museum.
Pariseau, J., and S. Bernier. French Canadians and Bilingualism in the Canadian Armed Forces. Volume I, 1763-1969: the Fear of a Parallel Army. Socio-Military Series No. 2. Directorate of History, Department of National Defence, Ottawa, 1988.
Patterson, William, obituary. Canadian Journal o f Comparative Medicine, Vol. 4, p. 209, 1940.
Pepin, M. Histoire et Petites Histoires des Vétérinaires du Québec. Editions François Lubrina, Montréal, 351 pp., 1986.
Pepin, M. A History of Veterinary Education in Quebec. Veterinary History, NS Vol. 5, pp. 111-115, 1988.
Pettigrew, E. The Silent Enemy. Canada and the Deadly Flu of 1918. Western Producer Prairie Books, Saskatoon, 156 pp., 1983.
Price, W.B. The Veterinary Association of Alberta. Canadian Veterinary Record, Vol. 4, pp. 53-54, 1923.
Regulations for the Canadian Army Veterinary Service, 1912. Published under the Authority of the Militia Council, Government Printing Bureau, Ottawa, 49 pp., 1912.
Regulations for the Canadian Army Veterinary Service, 1916. Published under the Authority of the Militia Council, Government Printing Bureau, Ottawa, 51 pp., 1916.
Regulations for The Canadian Army Veterinary Service, 1923. Published under the Authority of the Minister of National Defence, F.A. Acland, Printer to the King's Most Excellent Majesty, Ottawa, 60 pp., 1923.
Regulations for the Canadian Army Veterinary Service, 1939. Typescript, 61 pp. NAC RG24, Vol. 6532, File HQ 621-3-7, v.3.
Report of The Department of Militia and Defence Canada, Fiscal Year ending Mar. 31, 1922. F.A. Acland, Printer to the King's Most Excellent Majesty, 1922.
Ridpath, J.C., E.S. Ellis, J.A. Cooper and J.H. Aitken. The Story of South Africa. World Publishing Co., Guelph, Ont., 889 pp., 1899.
Riordan, J.J. Horses, Mule and Remounts - The Memoirs of a World War I Veterinary Officer. Privately published, Glendale, California, 115 pp., 1983.
Roncetti, G.A., and E.E. Denby. The Canadians - Those Who Served in South Africa, 1899-1902. E. Denby and Associates, 248 pp., undated.
Ross, D., and R. Chartrand (eds). Canadian Militia Dress Regulations, 1907. Illustrated with amendments to 1914. Reprint, The New Brunswick Museum, 124 pp., 1977.
'R.S.C.' Experiment and Experience, 1932. An Eastern Battery Goes to Camp. Canadian Defence Quarterly, Vol. 10, pp. 102-107, 1932-33.
Ruck, C.W. Canada's Black Battalion, No. 2 Construction, 1916-1920. Black Cultural Society of Nova Scotia, Halifax, Nova Scotia, 143 pp., 1986.
Rumney, W.J. Ontario Veterinary Association - 1941. Report of the Annual Meeting. Canadian Journal of Comparative Medicine, Vol. 5, pp. 58-60, 1941.
Rumney, W.J. Ontario Veterinary Association - 1943. Report of the Committee on the Employment of Veterinarians in the Canadian Army. Canadian Journal of Comparative Medicine, Vol. 7, pp. 92-93, 1943.
Saunders, C.G. Canine Medicine and Surgery. American Journal of Veterinary Medicine, Chicago, 249 pp., 1915.
Saunders, C.G. Rabbit and Cat Diseases. American Veterinary Publishing Co., Chicago, 121 pp., 1920.
Saunders, L.Z. A Biographical History of Veterinary Pathology. Allen Press, Lawrence, Kansas, 590 pp., 1996.
Savage, Alfred. Diary, 13 Dec. 1916 - 31 Dec. 1918. C.A.V. Barker Museum, and NAC MG30 E 472.
Scheer, B. Dental disease in *Brunus edwardii*. British Dental Journal 148, pp. 193-194, 1980.
Smith, F. A Manual of Veterinary Hygiene, 5th Edition. W.R. Jenkins, New York, 1035 pp., 1906.
Smith, F. A Veterinary History of the War in South Africa 1899-1902. H. & W. Brown, London, 1919.
Smith, F. A History of the Royal Army Veterinary Corps 1796-1919. Baillière, Tindall and Cox, London, 268 pp., 1927.
Smith, F. The Early History of Veterinary Literature and its British Development, Volumes 1-4. Baillière, Tindall and Cox, London, 1919-1933; in reprint, J.A. Allan, London, 1976.
Stacey, C.P. A Date With History, Memoirs of a Canadian Historian. Deneau , Ottawa Ont., 293 pp., undated, c. 1983.
Statistics Canada. Consumer Price Indexes for Canada, Annual, 1996 Classification, 1914-1998. Socio-Economic Information Management System P2000 9957, http://www.statcan.ca/english/CANSIM/, 10 Apr. 1999.
Steele, G. 1914a. What the Example of the Canadian Army Veterinary Service Can Teach Us. American Journal of

Veterinary Medicine, Vol. 9, pp. 16-19, 59-60, 1914.
Steele, G. 1914b. The Price of Neglected Veterinary Advice on Army Horse Conservation was Seventy-six Million Dollars. American Journal of Veterinary Medicine, Vol. 9, pp. 159-166, 1914.
Stewart, C.H. The Concise Lineages of the Canadian Army 1855-Date. Second Enlarged and Revised Edition. C.H. Stewart, Toronto, Ont., 1982.
Stortz, G.J. A Canadian Veterinarian Overseas in the First World War. Canadian Veterinary Journal, Vol. 23, pp. 183-186, 1982.
Stubbs Collection. W.F.R. Stubbs' letters home, March 1917-April 1919, and contemporary photographs. C.A.V. Barker Museum, courtesy Mrs. June Raeburn.
Tamblyn, D.S. The Canadian Army Veterinary Corps in France. Journal of the American Veterinary Medical Association, Vol. 57, pp. 4-27, 1920.
Tamblyn, D.S. The Horse in War, and Famous Canadian War Horses. The Jackson Press, Kingston, Ontario, 120 pp., undated, c. 1932.
Tamblyn, D.S. The Practicing Veterinarian and His Relationship to the Army. Journal of the American Veterinary Medical Association, N.S. Vol. 35, pp. 34-45, 1933.
Tamblyn, D.S., obituary. Lieut. Col. D.S. Tamblyn D.S.O., O.B.E. Canadian Journal of Comparative Medicine, Vol. 7, p. 22, 1943.
Taschereau, T.J. deM. Shoeing of Horses. Canadian Veterinary Record, Vol. 3, p. 37, 1922.
Taschereau, T.J. deM. Saddle and Carriage Horses in Canada. Canadian Veterinary Record, Vol. 3, pp. 99-100, 1922.
Taylor, Jessica. The Professionalism of Veterinary Science in Victoria. M.A. Thesis, University of Melbourne, 223 pp., 1990.
Taylor, Jessica. War and the Professional: The Australian Army Veterinary Corps. Journal of the Australian War Memorial, Vol. 24, pp. 26-33, 1994.
Teigen, Philip M. Viable Veterinary Schools in the United States, 1862-1995. Personal communication to C.A.V. Barker, 2 pp., 16 Jun. 1998. C.A.V. Barker Museum.
Timmis, R.S. Letter to The Principal, Ontario Veterinary College, 7 Feb. 1911. C.A.V. Barker Museum.
Timmis, R.S. Major R. Timmis, on Breeding Better Horses. Canadian Veterinary Record, Vol. 4, pp. 45-46, 1923.
Timmis, R.S. Some Lessons from a Four-days' Cavalry Trek. Canadian Defence Quarterly, Vol. 3, 1925-26.
Timmis, R.S. The Breeding of Light Horses. Canadian Defence Quarterly, Vol. 9, pp. 537-542, 1931-32.
Timmis, R.S. Letters to F.E. Gattinger, 23 Dec. 1961, 2 Feb. 1962. C.A.V. Barker Museum.
Tippett, M. Art at the Service of War: Canada, Art, and the Great War. University of Toronto Press, Toronto, Ontario, 136 pp., 1984.
Vercoe, L.W.H. C.O.T.C. Veterinary Digest, Vol. 1, p. 123, 1939.
Voters' List, Victoria City District, Polling Division No. 5, p. 22, 1920. Cited in Mattison, 1993.
Voters' List, Victoria City District, Polling Division No. 5, p. 23, 1921. Cited in Mattison, 1993.
Walker, J.W.St.G. Race and Recruitment in World War I: Enlistment of Visible Minorities in the Canadian Expeditionary Force. Canadian Historical Review Vol. 70, pp. 1-26, 1989.
Watson, E.A., obituary. Canadian Journal of Comparative Medicine Vol. 9, pp. 91-93, 1945.
Weatherhead, T. In which Pooh Joins the Army and Lands in the Zoo. The Beaver, Vol. 69 (Oct./Nov.), pp.35-38, 1989.
Westmorland, H. 1931-32. The Basket Hitch of the Rocky Mountain Pack Saddle. Canadian Defence Quarterly, Vol. 9, pp. 117-123, 1931-32.
Whitfield, L.C. The Veterinary Services in the Australian Military Forces. The Australian Veterinary Journal, Vol. 27, pp. 226-236, 1951.
Who Was Who, 1916-1928, Volume II, 4th Edition. Woodville, Richard Cation. Adam & Charles Black, London, pp. 1146-1157, 1967.
Who Was Who, 1929-1940, Volume III, 2nd Edition. Talmage, Algernon. Adam & Charles Black, London, p. 1324, 1967.
Wilson, Barbara. Index to the Medal Rolls, Military General Service 1793-1814, Egypt Medal 1882-1889, North West Canada 1885. Spink and Son, London, 1975.
Wodehouse, R.F. A Check List of the War Collections of World War I, 1914-1918 and World War II, 1939-1945. The National Gallery of Canada, Ottawa, 239 pp., 1968.
Woodland, R.B. Letter to C.A.V. Barker, re A.B. Cutcliffe, 27 May 1983. C.A.V. Barker Museum.
Wrightman, J. Canadian Officer Training Corps. Veterinary Digest Vol. 1, p. 77, 1939.

GENERAL INDEX

See Index of Persons (following) and Appendices A, B, C, D, E, H for names. An asterisk* indicates a photograph.

INDEX OF PERSONS

This index contains the names of individuals mentioned in text. See also Appendices A, B, C, D, E, H for names. An asterisk* indicates a photograph, an *italicized* page number some biographical information.

ABOUT THE EDITORS

Clifford A.V. Barker is a 1941 graduate of the University of Toronto (Ontario Veterinary College). He was awarded an M.Sc. by McGill University in 1945, and received a D.V.Sc. from the University of Toronto in 1948. He taught and carried out graduate work at Macdonald College, McGill University during the Second World War. A Professor Emeritus of the University of Guelph, he was a faculty member in the Department of Clinical Studies, Ontario Veterinary College from 1945-1984, where he established an international reputation in the field of theriogenology (animal reproduction). He was active provincially and nationally in veterinary professional affairs for over 30 years, serving in many executive capacities, including the Presidency, of the O.V.C. Alumni Association, the Ontario Veterinary Association and the Canadian Veterinary Medical Association. He is the author or coauthor of numerous scientific communications, and his former graduate students are scattered internationally. He served as Officer Commanding C.O.T.C. at Macdonald College during W.W. II, and subsequently was personnel selection officer with the 11th Field Regiment, R.C.A., Guelph, retiring as a Major, with the Canadian Forces Decoration. He has a long-standing interest in veterinary history, curating the collection that in 1990 was named by the University of Guelph in his honour, The C.A.V. Barker Museum of Canadian Veterinary History. He has mounted a number of museum exhibitions, and is the author of numerous articles on the subject. He is coauthor of two authoritative histories of the Canadian veterinary profession: with A. Margaret Evans *Century One: A History of the Ontario Veterinary Association 1874-1974*, and with T.A. Crowley *One Voice, A History of the Canadian Veterinary Medical Association.* He was inducted as a Member of the Order of Canada in 1986.

Ian K. Barker is a 1968 D.V.M. graduate of the University of Guelph, where he earned an M.Sc. in 1970. In 1974 he was awarded a Ph.D. by the University of Melbourne, Australia, where he briefly was Research Fellow, Wildlife Diseases in the Faculty of Veterinary Science. He is a Professor in the Department of Pathobiology at the Ontario Veterinary College, University of Guelph, where he has taught and carried out research and diagnostic work in the fields of veterinary pathology, parasitology and diseases of wildlife since 1975. He has a long-standing professional association with the Toronto Zoo, is Ontario Regional Coordinator for the Canadian Cooperative Wildlife Health Centre, and his former graduate students are active on three continents. He has published numerous scientific papers, contributed a number of book chapters, and coedited a book on wildlife diseases. He is active editorially and organizationally in several international scientific associations. His brief military career, as an Officer Cadet in the University Naval Training Division, Royal Canadian Navy, was truncated by one of the numerous cutbacks experienced by the armed forces of Canada.